# BRITISH WAR MEMORIALS

Mark Quinlan

**Visit us online at** www.authorsonline.co.uk

An Authors On Line Book

Copyright © Mark Quinlan 2005

Cover design by Richard Fitt ©

All rights reserved. No part of this publication may be reproduced, stored in a retrieval system, or transmitted in any form or by any means, electronic, mechanical, photocopy, recording or otherwise, without prior written permission of the copyright owner. Nor can it be circulated in any form of binding or cover other than that in which it is published and without similar condition including this condition being imposed on a subsequent purchaser.

The moral rights of the authors have been asserted.

ISBN 0 7552 0186 8

Authors OnLine Ltd
40 Castle Street
Hertford SG14 1HR
England

This book is also available in e-book format, details of which are available at
www.authorsonline.co.uk

# BRITISH WAR MEMORIALS

'And having each one given his body to the Commonwealth they receive in stead thereof a most remarkable sepulchre, not that wherein they are buried so much as that other wherein their glory is laid up on all occasions, both of word and deed, to be remembered for evermore.'

Pericles

# CONTENTS

| | |
|---|---|
| Foreword | IX |
| Prefatory Note | X |
| Abbreviations | XII |
| Remembrance | XIII |
| Introduction | XVI |

| | | |
|---|---|---|
| Chapter I | Early Memorials | 1 |
| Chapter II | The Great War | 41 |
| Chapter III | Overseas Memorials of the Great War | 107 |
| Chapter IV | The Second World War | 131 |
| Chapter V | Post-Second World War | 155 |
| Chapter VI | Royal Navy Memorials | 203 |
| Chapter VII | Royal Air Force Memorials | 261 |
| Chapter VIII | Victoria Cross and George Cross Memorials | 285 |
| Chapter IX | Biographies of Notable Figures | 301 |

## APPENDICES

| | |
|---|---|
| Bibliography | 358 |
| Plates Index | 360 |
| Great War Chronology | 364 |
| Second World War Chronology | 366 |
| The Western Front Association | 368 |
| The English Heritage Blue Plaque Scheme | 369 |
| Churchill's Memorandum | 370 |
| Report of Lord Midleton's Battlefield Memorials Committee | 373 |
| War Memorials Advisory Council 1944 | 380 |
| War Memorials Legislation | 388 |
| Index | 395 |

For each copy of this book sold, one pound is donated to the War Memorials Trust.

Front cover: The Royal Artillery War Memorial at Hyde Park Corner, London designed by Lionel Pearson and sculpted by Charles Sargeant Jagger. Photographed by Samuel J Brookes.

# FOREWORD

The memorialisation process strives for permanence of memory, to ensure that endeavours, hardship and sacrifice should be remembered and not forgotten. War memorials are the most common of all public monuments, found in every town and village across the country. Perhaps it is because they are so common that we have taken all too little notice of them in the past. Until recently, these memorials had been little studied or recorded. While I was Director General of the Imperial War Museum, I wrote a book on the subject, in the hope of arousing greater public interest in this aspect of our nation's heritage. It seemed to me then, as it does now, that these memorials were an important expression of our collective memory. They were often fine works of art in their own right, standing as a moving testimony to the sacrifice of those who had given their lives in war.

The most important thing to come out of my own research was the realisation that there was no proper record of existing memorials and, to remedy this, we established the National Inventory of War Memorials in the Museum. With the generous help of the National Heritage Memorial Fund, and the hard work of many volunteers, the Inventory has been able to build up a nationwide database. Although this is not, and perhaps never will be complete, the Inventory does record the majority of war memorials in the British Isles and provides a valuable resource for all who are interested in the subject.

At the same time, there was a growing interest in memorials and concern for their preservation. This led to the foundation of the Friends of War Memorials in 1997 (now the War Memorials Trust), whose members have done so much to ensure that the condition of these monuments is not allowed to deteriorate. There is now a much wider appreciation of the value of war memorials, but there is still a lot to do. For this reason it is a particular pleasure to welcome Mark Quinlan's second volume from his study on the subject of Remembrance. *British War Memorials* is a valuable addition to the literature on the subject. In these pages you will find details of both well-known and little-known memorials, including some of the most recent additions to the ever-expanding list - British forces are in action somewhere around the globe every year and each year lives are lost. We will have to go on building memorials, and one reason for looking at them, whatever their date, is to remind us of what we owe to those who are commemorated. I hope this book will encourage you to look at our rich heritage of war memorials more carefully - it is always worthwhile doing so.

Alan Borg

1 July 2004

# PREFATORY NOTE

As is customary with such a project, it is entirely appropriate here to thank those without whom it could not have been brought to press: Dr Alan Borg, former Director General of the Imperial War Museum for writing the Foreword; Lieutenant Colonel Richard Callander QOY, Clive Watson and Bill Floyd of AFMPT for their unfailing support; Professor Neville Brown of Mansfield College, Oxford for encouragement and advice; Colonel Tony Pinder for assistance with the Fovant Badges; John Reynolds for assistance with the National Liberal Club War Memorial; the Dean and Chapter of York Minster and Karen Sheridan for their assistance with the Astronomical Clock War Memorial; Ken McCallum for research and photography; John O'Keeffe for advice and research; Brian Watts for assistance with the battlefield of Waterloo; this study's indexer Alan Thatcher; Christos Tzanetis of Kall Kwik, Fleet Street for producing the proofs; Claire Balneaves of Naval Casualty Branch for assistance with naval memorials; Chris Oakford and Steve Lane of Army Casualty Branch for their extensive knowledge, support and advice; Angela Perry of the Falkland Islands Memorial Chapel Trust; Vince Duquemin of MOD for assistance with General Wolfe's statue in Greenwich Park; the Reverend Ray Jones of St George's Memorial Chapel, Ypres; David Houchin, Honorary Secretary of the Society of Portrait Sculptors and Dr Emmanuel Minne of the Royal Society of British Sculptors for their considerable assistance; Dr Pedro Gaspar, Conservation Officer of the War Memorials Trust for his support and advice; Margaret Richardson, Keeper of Sir John Soane's Museum and President of the Lutyens Trust for advice; Wendy Pitts of King Alfred's School, Wantage for permission to quote from *The Alfredian*; Lieutenant Colonel (Rtd) Peter Dick-Peter, SO1 PR at HQ London District for support and assistance; John Soanes, Chairman of the Ton Class Association for his assistance with the history of the Association and HMS FITTLETON; Laurie Chester of St George's Memorial Chapel at Biggin Hill; Christine Bradley of Colne Public Library for her assistance with the Colne War Memorial; Bill Ritchie for his help with the Bearsden War Memorial in Glasgow; Lieutenant Lig Hill RN PRO at Faslane and Leading Photographer Rob Harding FOSNNI for their help with the Battle of May Island Memorial at Anstruther Harbour; Ken Healy for considerable research; the Earl of Carlisle for considerable assistance with the details of British naval operations in the Baltic 1918-20; John Levitt of the Save London's Theatres Campaign for his assistance with the history of Westminster Theatre; Lieutenant Colonel (Rtd) Shaw-Brown of the RA Association and Major Les Carr of HQ Woolwich Garrison for assistance with RA Memorials; Mr Asbjørn Østdahl of the Royal Norwegian Embassy, London for assistance with Norwegian war memorials in UK; Tony Daley of HQ Household Division for his assistance with the Guards War Memorial; Sean Hayes of Transport for London for his assistance with the London Underground War Memorial; Josephine Grant of the London's Transport Museum Library for her assistance with London Transport's memorials; Jeff Ryan, and Ian Moss, respectively President and Secretary of the Stanier 8F Society, for their assistance with railway forms of memorialisation; Clive Blakeway of WMT for assistance with the history of Locomotive 48773; Brian Poag, the verger at St Clement Danes Church; Commander Jeff Tall RN (Rtd) Director of the Royal Navy Submarine Museum at Gosport, Hants; Sgt Peter Lavery RMP for assistance with the Rorke's Drift Memorial in South Africa; Dennis Durkin and Major (Rtd) Dick Gentry of the Inns of Court Regimental Museum for assistance with the history of the Regiment; the staff of MOD Library for their kind assistance; Matthew Little of the Royal Marines Museum, Eastney for assistance with the finer points of the history of the Royal Marines; Mrs Didy Grahame, Secretary of the Victoria Cross and George Cross Association for her kind advice and assistance; Terry Hissey for assistance with the George Cross; Bernard Hyde of the Battle of Britain Memorial Trust at Capel le Ferne; Mrs Prince for her help with the Far East Prisoner of War Memorial Church at Wymondham; Vince Webb for support, considerable photography and research; Peter Simpson of MOD for assistance with the Falklands Conflict;

Heather Birchall of the Tate for assistance with the sculpture of William Behnes; Isobel Hernandez of the Local Studies Department, Kensington and Chelsea Borough Council for assistance with the sculpture of John Bell; Mr and Mrs Basil Ashmead Gotto for assistance with the sculpture of Basil Gotto; Michael Regan of the Canadian High Commission, London and Dr Laura Brandon, Curator of War Art at the Canadian War Museum, Ottawa for assistance with the sculpture of Francis Derwent Wood; Rupert Harris of Rupert Harris Conservation for assistance with the sculpture of Charles Sargeant Jagger; Dr Peter Cannon-Brookes for his assistance with the sculpture of Ivor Roberts-Jones; Philip Jackson and Gill Trayner for assistance with the sculpture of Philip Jackson; Vivien Mallock for assistance with her sculpture; Faith Winter and Anne Lychlander for assistance with Faith Winter's sculpture; Carlo Dumontet of the National Art Library at the V&A for assistance; Captain Chris Page RN (Rtd), Head of Naval Historical Branch for his work on the Royal Naval Division Memorial and for the enthusiasm of his staff for this study; David McCarthy of the City of London Cemetery at Manor Park and Léon Lock of the Low Countries Sculpture Association in Brussels for assistance with the Vigiland Memorial; John Hampson of the British Defence Liaison Staff, Washington DC for his assistance with Captain James Cook; Susie Barson of English Heritage for assistance with Serverndroog Castle; Chris Cooke of English Heritage for assistance with the statuary of Whitehall; Reverend Tim and Mrs Partridge of St Michael and All Angels Church, Bugbrooke, Northants for their assistance with their Armistice Window; Commander John Prichard, RN for assistance with the history of The Naval Club, London; Ian Dougal of the Cabinet Office for his assistance with the Admiralty Civilians Memorial in the Office of the Deputy Prime Minister; Sidney Brookes, Clive Brookes and Samuel L Brookes for substantial research and photography; Michael Gaskin and Bill Hayter of the Art Bronze Foundry; Sharon Pink, Maurice Djanogly and Chris Boverhoff of Morris Singer Ltd for their support and assistance; Bob Whyte, Nick Bird and Colin Lathwell of MOD for substantial research; Richard Dunning for assistance with the Lochnagar Crater Memorial; Major Jeremy Lillies of the Royal British Legion for advice; James Grant of Tap O' Noth Community Council for assistance with the war memorials of Aberdeenshire; Nicola Graham of the Royal Society of Arts for her help with establishing the history of the War Memorials Advisory Council; the late Peter Roberts for assistance with the story of Jack Cornwell VC; Barbara Clarke for assistance with Britain's 'Thankful Villages'; Barry Atto of the Royal Mail Heritage Centre at Mount Pleasant, London for assistance with the history of the Post Office Rifles; Michelle Young, Steve Oram and Hilary Wheeler for their assistance with the history of the Western Front Association; Air Commodore Peter Dye RAF for assistance and advice on RAF memorials; Noel Cashford and John Philips for assistance with the Norfolk Landmines Clearance Memorial; John Montgomery of RUSI for support and advice; Rob Hill of DCSA MOD and Lieutenant Colonel (Rtd) David Murray for assistance with the history of piping in the British Army; Ian and Penny Nash for their assistance with the Commando Memorial at Spean Bridge in the Highlands; Steve de Agrela of the Department of Defence, Pretoria, South Africa for assistance with Epstein's statue of Smuts in Parliament Square, London; Jennifer Ullman of Battersea Park for assistance with Eric Kennington's 24th Division Memorial; Colonels Dolamore and Ingle of the Royal Logistics Corps for their assistance with the EOD Memorial at Marlborough Barracks, Kineton; Lieutenant Colonel A J Davies, Secretary of the Union Jack Club for assistance; David Miller for his help with the Binney Memorial Medal; Richard Kellaway, Keith Machin, John Worledge, Peter Francis, David Parker, Nigel Haines and all the staff of the CWGC for their assistance; Lieutenant Colonels Peter Willis and Alan Fairclough, Warrant Officers Tony Fernandez RN, Mick Robson PARA and Gary Gray RAF, Messrs Malcolm Lingwood, Mike Sands, Carl Crane, Paul Ingle, Martin Murphy and Guy Brewer of the MOD's Veterans Policy Unit for their substantial assistance. Lastly, many thanks are due to this study's editors Michael McAloon of MOD's Naval Historical Branch and Richard Graham, a volunteer with the UKNIWM at the Imperial War Museum for their faith, humour and unfailing erudition.

# ABBREVIATIONS

| | |
|---|---|
| ADS | Advanced Dressing Station |
| AIF | Australian Imperial Force |
| AFMPT | Armed Forces Memorial Project Team |
| ANZAC | Australia and New Zealand Army Corps |
| ASLEF | Associated Society of Locomotive Engineers and Firemen |
| BACSA | British Association of Cemeteries South Asia |
| BEF | British Expeditionary Force |
| BFBS | British Forces Broadcasting Service |
| BLESMA | British Limbless Ex-Servicemen's Association |
| CABE | Commission for Architecture and the Built Environment (previously RFAC) |
| CWGC | Commonwealth War Graves Commission (previously IWGC) |
| DNB | Dictionary of National Biography published by Oxford University Press |
| FOWM | Friends of War Memorials (now War Memorials Trust) |
| FRBS | Fellow, Royal Society of British Sculptors |
| GHQ | General Head Quarters |
| GOC | General Officer Commanding |
| HEIC | Honourable East India Company |
| IWGC | Imperial War Graves Commission (from March 1960 CWGC) |
| MOD | Ministry of Defence |
| MRA | Moral Rearmament |
| MRBS | Member, Royal Society of British Sculptors |
| NAAFI | Navy, Army and Air Force Institute |
| NATO | North Atlantic Treaty Organisation |
| NHMF | National Heritage Memorial Fund |
| NMA | National Memorial Arboretum |
| OTC | Officer Training Corps |
| PRA | President, Royal Academy |
| PRBS | President, Royal Society of British Sculptors |
| PRO | Public Records Office, (now the National Archive) |
| RA | Royal Academy of Arts, Royal Academician or Royal Artillery |
| RAF | Royal Air Force |
| RAFVR | Royal Air Force Volunteer Reserve |
| RAMC | Royal Army Medical Corps |
| RASC | Royal Army Service Corps |
| RBS | Royal Society of British Sculptors |
| RCHME | Royal Commission on the Historical Monuments of England |
| RFAC | Royal Fine Art Commission (now CABE) |
| RFC | Royal Flying Corps |
| RIBA | Royal Institute of British Architects |
| RLC | Royal Logistics Corps |
| RM | Royal Marines |
| RMA | Royal Military Academy |
| RN | Royal Navy |
| RNAS | Royal Naval Air Service |
| RSA | Royal Scottish Academy or Royal Society of Arts |
| SOE | Special Operations Executive |
| UKNIWM | United Kingdom National Inventory of War Memorials |
| USAAF | United States Army Air Force |
| WMAC | War Memorials Advisory Council |
| WMT | War Memorials Trust (previously Friends of War Memorials) |

# REMEMBRANCE

'In Britain we remember those no longer serving, including those who have died for their country; for we in this nation have a deep and abiding respect for our past'.[1] It is a fundamental characteristic of human nature to remember and commemorate the fallen, not merely for the sake of our own peace of mind, but also for the instruction of future generations that they might recognise the price of freedom. Of course what we choose to remember defines us both individually and collectively. Remembrance functions on a number of levels, some deeply personal. It will mean different things to the comrade, the spouse, family, friends, children and grandchildren, not forgetting the ordinary member of the wider society paying homage to the sacrifice of the fallen. Correspondingly, as the generations that fought our two World Wars pass, the oral tradition that connects us to these events fades by degrees and the duty of remembrance devolves to those of us who thankfully have not known war. All this can seem ancient history, but the name of Fusilier Stephen Satchell inscribed on the Old Town War Memorial at Rye, East Sussex ensures that it is not. He was killed in a 'friendly fire' incident in the Gulf War in 1991. Until the day comes when nations learn how to resolve their differences without the exercise of military force, remembrance will be a permanent feature of our existence. No longer does a quarter guard march down the hill from Howe Barracks to Canterbury Cathedral to turn a page of the Regimental Book of Remembrance and present arms. Those days are gone. Over the last half century British society has changed radically and with the continuous 'downsizing' of Britain's armed forces, the military no longer occupies so immediate or central a role in our society. However, the sacrifice of those who earned our freedoms is not forgotten and it is on Remembrance Sunday that the British Nation led by the Sovereign, honours its war dead at the Cenotaph.

Standing armed forces are a relatively modern development, Britain's small permanent army only being founded in the 17th century. Prior to the 20th century, the battles fought by the British engaged relatively small numbers and would be resolved within a day. The casualties sustained would be few enough to be interred in a mass grave. The bodies of officers would often be repatriated. 'As wars became larger in scale and were fought by conscripted soldiers rather than by small professional armies, so the popular concern for the fate of the individual soldier increased'.[2] In 1914 the nations of Europe went to war. By the close of that year, a line of unbroken opposing trenches had been established from the Belgian coast to Switzerland. The static nature of this new kind of warfare ensured that this would be a war of attrition, engaging men and materiel in numbers hitherto unimaginable. The Marne, Mons, Loos, Gallipoli, Ypres, The Somme, all became household names, as the life or death struggle between the Allies and the Central Powers dragged on for four long years. Britain and her Empire sustained 1,104,890 fallen in this war.[3] The immensity of these losses was of a magnitude inconceivable to the British People. The death of a loved one is hard enough to bear under any circumstances, to bear it without the normal rites of passage can only compound the trauma for those left behind and the outpouring of public grief that followed these momentous events seared the national consciousness and crystallised into the annual National Ceremony of Remembrance at the Cenotaph, the tomb of the Unknown Warrior, the two minutes' silence, Britain's war memorials and service museums. The creation of formalised modes of remembrance dates from this period.

Remembrance also serves another purpose, applicable to any nation in any age. In the words of one wise old warrior: 'The willingness with which our young people serve in any war, no matter how justified, will be directly proportional to how they perceive the veterans of earlier wars were treated and appreciated by their nation'.[4]

---

[1] The Queen's Jubilee Address to the Armed Services, broadcast on BFBS 26 June 2002.
[2] Gavin Stamp *Silent Cities*.
[3] Fabian Ware *The Immortal Heritage*.
[4] General George Washington.

The two minutes' silence to commemorate the first anniversary of the ceasefire of 11 o'clock on 11 November 1918 was almost as much of a surprise to the general public as the ceasefire itself had been. The decision to mark the first anniversary of the Armistice with a silent pause in the life of the nation was taken very close to the anniversary itself.'[5] The origins of the silence can be found in a minute dated 4 November 1919, submitted to the War Cabinet by Sir Percy Fitzpatrick, former High Commissioner to the Dominion of South Africa, His son had been killed in France in 1917. The War Cabinet discussed Fitzpatrick's proposal on 5 November and approved a 'Service of Silence' on Armistice Day. This was approved by the King and the first silence on 11 November 1919 was well observed the length and breadth of the UK. 'For two minutes after the hour of eleven had struck yesterday morning Plymouth stood inanimate with the nation… Two minutes before the hour the maroons boomed out their warning in one long drawn out note… As the hour struck a great silence swept over the town. People halted in their walks, chatter ceased as if by magic, traffic stopped and the rumbling note of industry stayed'.[6] From that day on, the silence became inseparable from Remembrancetide. It is a central feature of the national ceremony held on Remembrance Sunday at the Cenotaph. Recent years have seen the reintroduction of a two minutes' silence at 1100 on the 11 November itself, regardless of the day of the week. While not universally recognised, according to the Royal British Legion 73% of the population respected this gesture of remembrance in 2001. In the aftermath of the Great War, discontent amongst veterans led to the formation of a number of veterans organisations. These merged in 1921 to form The British Legion. Since its inception, this organisation has been dedicated to the care and welfare of those who have served in the Armed Forces and their dependants. It currently has more than 600,000 members and more than 4,500 branches in the UK and overseas. Some 13 million people in the UK are eligible to approach it for assistance. The poppy is the symbol of this organisation and is universally recognised in Britain as the symbol of remembrance. After four years of continuous bombardment on the Western Front, the poppy was the only thing that grew in the devastated moonscape. Lieutenant Colonel John McCrae, a doctor serving with the Canadian Expeditionary Force, wrote the poem *In Flanders' Fields* in response to his experiences on the Western Front. Moina Michael, an American war secretary with the YMCA and a writer, was touched by McCrae's work. She bought some red poppies, wore one herself and sold the remainder to her friends, giving the money raised to ex-Servicemen. And so a tradition was established.

Major George Howson, a decorated veteran was deeply moved by the plight of ex-Servicemen who had been disabled in the war and he founded the Disabled Society. The variety of wounds that had been inflicted by the technology of modern warfare was immense and had produced over 41,050 British major amputees. Howson thought that the making of artificial poppies might offer opportunities to the Disabled Society, approached the Legion with this suggestion and so the British Legion Poppy Factory was established. Initially located off the Old Kent Road in London, at first, it employed five disabled ex-Servicemen. Now based at Richmond in Surrey, it provides employment for many disabled making poppies, wreaths and other items associated with the Poppy Appeal. The funds raised from the sale of the 36 million poppies and 98,000 wreaths that are sold by its network of volunteers in the weeks before Remembrance Sunday go towards the charitable works of the Legion. In the year 2000 £20.1M was raised. In that year, the Legion spent a total of £43 million on its charitable works in the ex-Service community and in 2002 it assisted 1,000 people to visit war graves overseas, over 300,000 calls for help were answered, 54,000 people were assisted with war pensions claims and appeals, 100,000 visits were made to the housebound and those in hospital and 5,000 people were helped with a stay in the Legion's Rest and Recuperation homes. On the occasion of its 50th birthday in 1971, Britain's premier ex-Servicemen's organisation became the Royal British Legion.

---

[5] Adrian Gregory *The Silence of Memory*.
[6] *Western Morning News and Mercury* 12 November 1919.

The Commonwealth War Graves Commission is the authority responsible for all British and Commonwealth war dead from the period 4 August 1914 - 31 August 1921, and 3 September 1939 - 31 December 1947. It was founded by a remarkable man named Fabian Ware, who arrived in France in September 1914 to command a British Red Cross unit. The original role of his unit was to aid casualties behind the front line. They also took on the role of marking and caring for the graves of the fallen. As casualties increased, the unit expanded, dropped its Red Cross role and was eventually transferred to the British Army. In 1917 it was granted a Royal Charter as the Imperial War Graves Commission and once the Great War had finished, commenced the worldwide task of finding and commemorating the fallen of the British Empire. The Commission carried out the same role in the Second World War. Its title was amended from 'Imperial' to 'Commonwealth' in March 1960. The Commission has an archive of 1,694,883 commemorations, which has been available on the Internet since 1998. (www.cwgc.org). Their *Debt of Honour* website averages 250,000 hits a month. Its records are a powerful way of giving history a human face and of engaging the young in the importance of what was done by those who made the ultimate sacrifice. The Commission maintains all of the graves and memorials it cares for in perpetuity. Each member nation pays in direct proportion to the number of their war dead.[7] UK - 78.43%, Canada - 10.07%; Australia - 6.05%; India - 1.20%; New Zealand - 2.14% and South Africa - 2.11%. The Commission acts for its member Governments in all matters concerning their War graves of the two World Wars and is responsible for maintaining 1,147,192 war graves and 23,203 burial sites in 148 countries. It also maintains 170,000 War graves in over 12,000 burial grounds in the UK.[8] When David Lloyd George announced the Armistice to the House of Commons on the afternoon of Monday 11 November 1918, he hoped: 'that thus, this fateful morning, came the end to all wars'.[9] Given the enormity of their sacrifice, the British People truly believed that this *was* the war to end all wars. The Allied nations' failure at Versailles to address the underlying reasons for German aggression led again to warfare 20 years later. Thankfully, the tactically fluid yet more global nature of the Second World War and significant advances in medical care led to far fewer casualties for Britain and her Empire.

Over the last eighty years the practical aspects of remembrance have devolved to a number of complementary organisations, each with responsibility for a different aspect. Overseas the Commonwealth War Graves Commission is charged with maintaining the cemeteries of the two World Wars. In North Western Europe, the Western Front Association keeps an ever-wakeful eye on the honoured places of the fallen, and many of the ceremonies are organised by the Royal British Legion. Both the Legion and the Commission also have considerable responsibilities in the UK. Here their work is complemented by the War Memorials Trust and the United Kingdom National Inventory of War Memorials at the Imperial War Museum. In addition, the Service Casualty Branches of the three Services play an important role in recovering the war dead from both the World Wars and all other conflicts. Fortunately, Britain and her empire were on the winning side in both World Wars and despite enormous losses, this renders the issue coherent - unlike less happier nations.

In September 2000, Remembrance was introduced as an aspect of the citizenship modules of the National Curriculum, the teaching system used in the majority of UK schools. This led to a tremendous increase in pupils' awareness of the subject. The steady growth of websites on the internet devoted to all aspects of remembrance is another facet, as is the interest shown in recent years in the condition of war memorials in all parts of the British Isles. There is in no doubt that the ingenuity of future generations of Britons will establish means of honouring the fallen, undreamt of in our own time. The one aspect of remembrance we have not yet considered is the war memorial and having set our scene as it were, here it is:

---

[7] Resolution of Imperial War Conference, June 1918.
[8] Summary of evidence given by the CWGC in December 2000 to the Environment Transport and Regional Affairs Committee of the House of Commons. Volumes HC 91 - I and II.
[9] *Hansard* 11 November 1918. Column 2463.

# INTRODUCTION

The purpose of this study is to examine British war memorials both at home and abroad from a broad-brush perspective. Expert opinion holds that there are probably as many as 70,000 in the UK alone. It therefore seems sensible to look at representative and unusual examples, those of national importance, and also to share with the reader the benefits of some interesting research. The definition of a war memorial that will be used in this study is: any structure or object created, installed or adapted to commemorate those who served or were killed in time of war or conflict. The story encompasses the defeat of Napoleon in the long French Revolutionary Wars, the Crimean War, the Boer War, two World Wars and countless minor campaigns. As modern Britain becomes increasingly diverse, they can seem an anachronistic irrelevance, a throwback to an increasingly distant imperial past, but they act as a useful narrative to the issues exciting the pulse of the nation at the time they were erected and each one, however humble, has an intensely personal story to tell. As will be seen, the forms employed varied widely and were only limited by the imagination of the individual or the memorial committee concerned. They would range from the memorial at Eilean Donan Castle at Loch Duich, Scotland that commemorates all members of the MacRae Clan who were killed in two World Wars to the simple memorial plaque dedicated on 13 May 2003 in the Mediterranean Plot at the National Memorial Arboretum at Alrewas in Staffordshire which commemorates the 2,000 British and Commonwealth prisoners of war who died in the Mediterranean in the period 1941-42. They were aboard six vessels sunk by Allied Forces.

This is not a military history, although that subject is inevitably its frame. The story divides naturally into four distinct periods, these being; the 19th century, the Great War, the Second World War and the post-war period. Memorials proper to the Royal Navy and Royal Air Force are examined separately, as are the forms employed for recipients of the Victoria Cross and George Cross. Because memorialisation does not always occur contemporaneously, chronology can be tricky, but as a general rule of thumb the story is told in date order.

For as long as man has been able to work metal and hew stone, techniques have existed for the production of images, inevitably these would be of kings and military leaders. The Egyptians were casting statuary from bronze, an alloy of copper and tin as far back as 2000 BC. By 700 AD the Greeks were using the lost wax method, which is still in use today and this method was transmitted from them to the Romans who brought the technique with them to Britain and there are many surviving artefacts dating from the Roman occupation. The discovery of a bronze head of the Emperor Hadrian[10] dating from the second century in the River Thames, near London Bridge in 1834 and the discovery of a head of Mithras in 1954 on a bomb site at Walbrook in the City of London, are particularly good examples of their work.[11] As recently as August 2003, the discovery of a Roman bronze foot at an archaeological dig in a temple complex at Southwark, South London announced to a waiting world that the fashion-conscious Italians had always worn socks with sandals. By the close of the Dark Ages, Christianity had replaced the Roman Empire and the effigy tradition (usually in alabaster) continued with the commemoration of noblemen and saints in the nation's great churches and cathedrals. Despite the depredations inflicted on England's ecclesiastical heritage by the Reformation and the iconoclastic outlook of the Puritans, the tradition survived and it is in the tradition of commemorative statuary and the painted saints of the rood screen that we can discern the origin of the British war memorial. Britain's great churches and cathedrals were traditionally the sites where great commanders were commemorated and these buildings functioned as repositories for substantial quantities of statuary (often executed in white marble) and it would certainly not be untrue to state that the cafeteria situated in the crypt of St Paul's Cathedral, London is full of Bacon and Behnes.

---

[10] Hadrian, Roman Emperor AD 117-AD 138.

[11] The cult of Mithras originated in India and was first encountered by the Romans in Persia (modern day Iran) during the reign of the Emperor Nero. The Romans adopted him as the god of soldiers and traders.

One of the consequences of Britain's estrangement from mainstream European culture was the loss of bronze casting techniques and these had to be relearned from French craftsmen. Only a handful of bronze portrait busts of Britons survive from the 17th century and for these we can thank the renowned French bronze caster Hubert Le Sueur. He arrived on England's shores in the suite of the French Princess Henrietta Maria, who married King Charles I in 1625. Le Sueur was also responsible for casting in bronze the first equestrian statue of a British monarch. Concurrently, Classical themes persisted, occasionally crossed over into the ecclesiastical domain and as late as the 17th century one can observe statuary of European monarchs clad in togas (alluding to Roman virtue). Prior to the French Revolutionary Wars, British sculptors would need to travel to Europe to study first-hand the works of the Classical tradition. The commencement of the French Revolutionary Wars in 1792 rendered that avenue hazardous and the few examples available for study in Britain were primarily Roman, which were poor copies of the Greek. Providentially, Lord Elgin's single-handed mission to introduce the British public to Greek sculpture and ruin himself in the process served to reconnect the British with its original vitality. Given that the Greek nation *per se* no longer existed at that time, the British saw themselves as heirs to the Classical tradition and went crazy for all aspects of their civilisation. The Marbles removed by Lord Elgin (1766-1841) from the Parthenon were exhibited in London in 1816 and ignited an interest in sculpture that has never been rivalled. The British Museum was built by Sir Robert Smirke as a replica of the Parthenon to house them. Permanence began to feature as an issue and a humorous example as to why may be taken from the story of the seven-storey Chinese Pagoda designed by John Nash and erected for the Prince Regent's Gala in St James's Park in 1814. It commemorated (somewhat prematurely) Napoleon's defeat and celebrated 100 years of the Hanoverian dynasty. Generously furnished with rockets and gas lights, to the consternation of the assembled royal personages, it burst into flames and crashed into Charles I's canal on the night of its inauguration. Throughout the 19th century, churches and chapels would emerge as a distinct form of memorialisation in their own right. The church of St John the Evangelist (appropriately at Waterloo) in London was erected in 1824 as 'A Thanksgiving' for eventual victory over Napoleon in the French Wars and it was one of some 600 churches erected throughout the country specifically for that purpose. The Church Building Act was passed by Parliament in 1818 and it voted the enormous sum of one million pounds to fund the construction programme. In 1824 the work was given further impetus by the unexpected repayment of a two million pound war loan by the Austrian Government, which was added to the fund. The tradition of building memorial chapels would continue after the Great War, with public schools and infantry regiments leading the way. There are good examples of regimental memorials in cathedrals and churches dating from the mid-Victorian period, but of the community-funded war memorial as we would recognise it in the high street or at the village cross-roads, there was as yet no sign. The catalyst for a sea-change in the British public's feelings towards its Servicemen may be found in the reports filed during the Crimean War by *The Times* war correspondent Sir William Howard Russell (1821-1907). The Irishman missed little and he spared no reputations. As the British Army won victories, froze, starved and rotted, his reports telegraphed back to London unfolded to an incredulous readership a saga of incompetence and mismanagement beyond their wildest imaginings. The headlines written by his editor John Thadeus Delane confirmed the newspaper's nickname: 'The Thunderer', caused uproar in Parliament and brought down Lord Aberdeen's administration.

The cairn bears particular mention here and this form derives from the practice of Celtic warriors adding a stone to a pile before a battle and removing one if they survived, the stones left constituting a cairn and for this reason has inescapable Scots overtones. A recent example at High Wood on the Somme was constructed by the Scots historian Alex Aitken from 192 stones and it stands 5 feet 2 inches tall. The 9th Battalion of the Highland Light Infantry (Glasgow Highlanders) lost 192 men at High Wood on 15 July 1916 and 5 feet 2 inches was the minimum height requirement for recruitment to the battalion.

Another form that bears mention is the obelisk, and the earliest recorded example of this tapered square pillar capped by a pyramidion may be found in the reign of the female Pharaoh Hatshepsut of Ancient Egypt in 1500 BC. The vogue for acquiring such *objets d'art* can be traced to the certifiably insane Roman Emperor Caligula (AD 37-41), who shipped a 300 ton obelisk from Egypt and installed it as an ornamental feature on his private chariot racing track on the Vatican Hill, where it stands to this day in the middle of St Peter's Square in Rome. The obelisk first appears in England with Queen Elizabeth I being presented with an example for her palace at Nonsuch. By the 19th century the obelisk was widely employed for civil and military commemorative purposes in UK though not to universal approval, one journal commenting: 'Mr John Bell, who has been eagerly and rather unnaturally striving to erect an obelisk somewhere, is at length to be gratified. We are not sorry to say it will be placed far off, at Bermuda, to the memory of Sir William Reid.'[12] Other good examples may be found at Naseby commemorating the English Civil War, at Stowe commemorating General Wolfe and another at Carmarthen, commemorating General Sir Thomas Picton who was killed at the Battle of Waterloo.

Cleopatra's Needle on Victoria Embankment may be considered a memorial twice over. It was awarded to the British by the Egyptian Government for Nelson's victory over the French at the Battle of the Nile (1798) and Abercromby's victory at Alexandria (1801). Set in place in 1878, it sustained bomb damage in an air raid on 4 September 1917 and three passengers on a passing tram were killed. In accordance with the British custom of permitting honourable scars of war to remain unrepaired, the scars on the obelisk and the bronze sphinxes at its base remain. The obelisk would be widely employed both in UK and on the Western Front after the Great War with approximately a thousand examples dating from that period. Despite initial objections arising from its foreignness, the obelisk would eventually become widely accepted and in due course an unremarkable item of both street furniture and cemetery memorialisation. A good ornamental example cleverly disguising a ventilation shaft may be found at Circus Place in the City of London. Another good example may be found in the churchyard at Richmond in Surrey which has an obelisk carved with a springbok in honour of the South African soldiers who died in England during the Great War. Yet another good example may be found on the battlefield at Balaclava in the Crimea. The inscription reads: "IN MEMORY OF THOSE WHO FELL IN THE BATTLE OF BALACLAVA 25th OCTOBER 1854. ERECTED BY THE BRITISH ARMY 1856." During the Soviet era, the battlefields of the Crimea were a closed military zone and the only visitor known to have seen it was Prime Minister Winston Churchill, who was taken to see it by the Soviet dictator Josef Stalin during a break in the Yalta Conference in February 1945.

The Victorian era coincided with a period of radical social and far-reaching technological change in British society. These developments, combined with substantial reforms in the way the army was run led to the emergence of a very different kind of soldier, no longer would he be a drink-sodden illiterate, one step up society's rung from the workhouse. He would emerge from the Victorian age literate, skilled, relatively well-led and increasingly British rather than Irish. In consequence, by the dawn of the 20th century, the British public revised its hitherto hostile attitude towards him and increasingly deemed both him and his endeavours worthy of both individual and collective commemoration. The 19th century also marks the transition from public statuary of kings, warriors and great leaders to the commemoration of ordinary citizens in marble, granite or bronze, such works without exception being literal in execution. For the military, this development would lead to the arrival of an anonymous representative of the formation being commemorated. After a century of worldwide British military endeavour, space limitations in most of Britain's cathedrals resulted in new memorials having to be erected elsewhere. In consequence, the public spaces of 19th century London and other cities became littered with statuary of military figures and half-forgotten imperial administrators.

---

[12] The *Art Journal* 1861 p. 30.

The next major development would also have French connections. A number of French teachers would exercise a profound influence on the development of British figurative sculpture in the second half of the 19th century and at the forefront would be the multi-talented Alphonse Legros (1837-1911) and the sculptor Aimeé-Jules Dalou (1838-1902). Dalou was first Professor of Modelling at the Royal College, South Kensington and he would be succeeded by the even more influential Professor Édouard Lantéri. Thus an entire generation of British sculptors was trained by Frenchmen and nearly all espoused the naturalism of what the critic Edmund Gosse termed in 1894: 'The New Sculpture.' French influence would also be reinforced by the sculptor François-Auguste-René Rodin (1840-1917). This self-effacing combination of peasant and genius convulsed the world of the arts with his *The Kiss* and *The Thinker*. Another strong Continental influence would be the presence of numbers of skilled Italian foundrymen at work in England at the end of the 19th century and this fraternity guarded their trade secrets carefully. By the dawn of the 20th century, Britain had a number of war memorials relating to earlier conflicts, such the English Civil War, the Napoleonic Wars, the Crimean War, the African wars of the 19th century, the Sikh Wars and the Indian Mutiny. There were at least 1,000 memorials erected in the UK to commemorate the fallen of the Second Boer War (1899-1902) and they would often anticipate the forms employed after the Great War (1914-18). That conflict marks the point at which war memorials became a familiar part of the landscape of Britain's towns, villages and cities. So familiar are they, they seldom catch our eye or engage our attention, yet each one tells its own story. They marked the sorrow of those left behind for death of their loved ones and an enduring pride in their sacrifice. The individuals and committees that erected them connected with a popular feeling, the like of which the British had never experienced before. That generation of Britons experienced mass-bereavement on a scale hitherto unimaginable and the war memorial would be a significant aspect of their response. There is of course a wholly valid point of view that holds that the fallen did not give their lives willingly and that they were taken from them by the state in the most horrible manner. That having been said, such a point of view should not preclude an individual from commemoration. The forms employed after the Great War included: literal statuary usually cast in bronze, items of church furnishing, locomotives, memorial halls, hospital wards, hospital beds, murals, military musical instruments, the small plaque in a school, street, village church or bus garage, to the Cenotaphs erected in Britain's great cities. Such memorials were and still are the setting for annual ceremonies each November, these usually being conducted under municipal auspices. Memorials to the fallen of both World Wars are still being erected in the 21st century.

Another form employed on a significant scale after the Great War would be the stained glass window. 'Stained glass was in its heyday in the Middle Ages when such windows were used by the Church to educate the illiterate masses in the Scriptures. The windows were full of images of Christ, of angels and archangels, and scenes from the Bible; they were, in a sense, glazed parables. And it is only since the Great War that ordinary mortals and their works have been admitted to the company of angels; the first of these were the men who claimed the heavens as their element - the airmen.'[13] As will be seen in this study, this form offers some of the most interesting memorialisation stories, of which merely one example from the Second World War will suffice here. During the later stages of the war, Major George Fielding (1915-2005) of the Special Operations Executive was parachuted into northern Italy to assist Italian partisans in carrying out offensive operations against the Nazis in southern Austria. Disguised as a peasant he reconnoitred the Upper Gail Valley. After a hair-raisingly unsuccessful mission, many failed air drops, with a bounty on his head and with 6,000 crack troops on his tail, Fielding was extracted from Slovenia by SOE in December 1944. Later, in his debriefing in Italy he was asked to account for the monies that had been issued to him and somewhat surprisingly responded that he had given it to a priest to pay for a stained glass window to be erected in memory of the partisans who had died fighting for him.

---

[13] David Beaty *Light Perpetual*.

The Second World War produced no new architectural vocabulary and essentially the same forms of memorialisation were employed as for the Great War. In the vast majority of cases in the United Kingdom existing war memorials were utilised or extended. That same war also marked the debut of that curious phenomenon, the war memorial bus shelter. Another significant form increasingly employed in the 20th century was the boulder and a good example can be found outside the Street Lane Gardens Synagogue in Leeds. The boulder was set in place in 1970 to commemorate the Jewish dead of two World Wars and the 6,000,000 Jews killed by the Nazis. Another placed in Princes Gardens in Edinburgh in 1978 marked the gratitude of the Norwegian Government to the Scots for their friendship to the Norwegian Army stationed there in the Second World War. As will be seen in this study, that war also marked the erection of a number of memorials to non-British figures. For historical reasons there are also examples of commemoration in UK of both foreign military leaders and foreign national formations. The exertions of the Dominions and Indian Empire in the two World Wars were indivisible from those of Britain and their memorials are included in this study too.

Ordinarily, memorialisation of individuals does not occur in their lifetime and inevitably there were cases after the Second World War, of Servicemen (usually former prisoners of war) arriving home, to find their name engraved on their local war memorial. Conversely, memorialisation does not always take place contemporaneously and the reasons for this can be varied. The highly original Battle of Lewes Memorial in Sussex sculpted by Enzo Plazzotta (1921-81) was inaugurated on 14 May 1966 and it belatedly commemorated the battle fought there on 14 May 1264 [14] and clearly its significance was of a very different order to that of the Norfolk Landmines Disposal Memorial at Mundesley in Norfolk - which, while only inaugurated in 2004, had a direct link with the next of kin and the 26 men who died engaged on the unglamorous and highly dangerous task of clearing mines from Norfolk's coastline. Another good example may be taken from the inauguration in 1999 of the Walter Tull Memorial and Garden of Rest at Sixfields Stadium, Northampton to the former Tottenham Hotspur and Northampton Town footballer W D J Tull by Northampton's mayor. Second Lieutenant Tull had been killed on the Somme in March 1918. Apart from being a famous footballer, he was the first Black Briton to be commissioned into the British Army.

After both World Wars, a considerable number of war memorials were erected overseas at the scene of battles and exploits, and with tragic inevitability they stand at locations with particular meaning to the nations, formations or regiments that raised them. The generations that erected the vast majority of Britain's war memorials have all but passed and the care of these memorials devolves to this and to future generations. In recent years, experts in this field have increasingly encountered memorials where the names commemorated have either worn off, or where elements have been lost. In response to these concerns, the organisation Friends of War Memorials[15] was founded by Ian Davidson in 1997. This organisation concerns itself with the care and conservation of war memorials, so that they might be appreciated and understood by future generations. Another welcome development was the establishment of the UK National Inventory of War Memorials in 1989 by Dr Alan Borg. It is managed and held by the Imperial War Museum and it is ultimately intended that its database will hold comprehensive details of every war memorial in the UK and be available on the Internet. It is hoped that the representative examples included in this study will give the reader a guide to the memorialisation process, the difficulties encountered, the forms employed, the personalities involved, the materials used - and afford the reader a glimpse of the sentiments these memorials gave voice to when they were raised.[16]

---

[14] The high point of the career of Simon de Montfort, 6th Earl of Leicester, who defeated the army of King Henry III at Lewes. The Royal Army was commanded by his son the Prince of Wales (later King Edward I). De Montfort's victory delivered the King, his heir and England into the hands of the barons. De Montfort briefly became uncrowned King of England, but was killed at the Battle of Evesham in August 1265.

[15] From 1 January 2005 The War Memorials Trust.

[16] Website for *Remembrance* and *British War Memorials* at www.web-mouse.co.uk/remembrance/

# CHAPTER I

# THE EARLY YEARS

# EVENTS IN THE MIDDLE AGES

One of the earliest examples of individual memorialisation is not to be found in Great Britain at all but in the Cathedral of Santa Maria del Fiore, or Duomo at Florence in Italy. Here, a fresco of John Hawkwood's equestrian monument by the Florentine master Paolo Uccello may be found with a Latin inscription which translates: 'This is John Hawkwood, British knight, esteemed the most cautious and expert general of his time' and thereby hangs a tale: Hawkwood was an English soldier believed to have been born in Essex in 1320. A career freebooter who had fought in the French wars, he is recorded in 1360 as besieging Pope Innocent VI at Avignon in Provence. His Holiness purchased his freedom with 100,000 florins and persuaded Hawkwood to join the Marquis of Monteferrat in a church-sponsored war against the Visconti of Milan. Hawkwood's Essex yeomen then raped, pillaged and burned their way across Italy and against a background of warring city-states, embarked on a programme of systematic wealth extraction through terror. Riven by religious, political and dynastic feuds, these self-same states cursed Hawkwood (Giovanni Acuto) as: 'The Son of Belial' whilst secretly vying for his services as *condottiere*. He extracted enormous sums from all of them and died of old age in Italy an exceedingly rich man indeed.

After the French reconquest of Normandy in 1450, King Charles VII of France sent the Comte de Dunois, with a large French army to reconquer Guyenne in 1451. The English had relied considerably on the loyalty of the Gascons in their long association with England for regional defence against incursions by the French. The English deployed few troops in the region and the pro-English Gascons (whose numbers were rapidly diminishing as French fortunes were changing in the north), were unable to resist the onslaught of the French royal army and Guyenne was regained in a remarkably short time. The successful campaign of reconquest ended with the French entrance into the regional capital, Bordeaux on 30 June 1451. Unhappy with constraints placed on their lucrative trade with England, the merchant leaders of Bordeaux sent a delegation to London and persuaded King Henry VI to send an army over the France. The veteran John Talbot, 1st Earl of Shrewsbury, by now in his seventies, was appointed to lead an expedition of 3,000 men which landed at Guyenne on 17 October 1452. The citizens of Bordeaux opened their gates and ejected the French garrison. Many towns quickly reasserted their loyalty to the English crown and Charles VII's reconquest was undone. It was not until mid-summer of 1453, that Charles VII assembled an invasion force. Three French armies marched on Guyenne, one from the northeast, one from the east, and one from southeast. Charles VII followed with a reserve army. Talbot's son, Lord de Lisle, arrived in Bordeaux with additional troops, bringing the English total to nearly 6,000. The English counted on reinforcing their army with loyal Gascons and potentially could have assembled more men than any French royal army. In mid-July, the French army from the east besieged the town of Castillon, on the Dordogne River. The French camp reportedly contained 300 guns and was essentially an artillery park. It contained 6,000 men and 1,000 Breton men-at-arms were located a mile to the north of the camp on a rise. Critically, the French camp was beyond artillery range of the town of Castillon. The English had by now reoccupied part of Gascony and Shrewsbury decided to relieve the siege of Castillon by attacking the French encampment. The French used their artillery against the English, repelled the attack and killed Shrewsbury, after which the English army quickly fell apart under the barrage. After the battle, the French reoccupied Gascony, thus ending an intimate association with England that had commenced with the marriage of Eleanor of Aquitaine to King Henry II in 1152. The English defeat at Castillon would bring the Hundred Years War to a conclusion and result in the emergence of the French nation state. Talbot was reputedly slain because of the conspicuousness of the bright clothes he wore to Mass that morning. On 17 July 1953 in a ceremony marking the 500th anniversary of the momentous events at Castillon, the *Monument à Talbot* was unveiled on the banks of the Dordogne and interestingly it does not depict Talbot himself, but the Virgin and Child on a pillar.

# KING CHARLES I

Queen Eleanor of Castile (1244-90) died of a fever at Lincoln on 24 November 1290and her body was brought back to London for burial at Westminster Abbey. Her heart was buried in Blackfriars Church. She was the beloved wife of King Edward I (1239-1307) and he decreed that at each location at which her cortege halted a cross be erected. The twelfth and last stopping place was the hamlet of Charing near Westminster. The Charing Cross was erected by the master masons Roger of Crundale and Richard of Crundale in the years 1291-94. In 1647 the Puritans demolished the monument. A replica was made after the Restoration, but not put back in its original place. In 1865 the owners of the Charing Cross Hotel paid for the replica to be set up on the forecourt of Charing Cross Station, which is where it may be seen.

Trafalgar Square stands on the site of the King's Mews, which was adjacent to the Palace of Whitehall and from the time of King Henry VIII, it housed the royal hawks and stables. During the English Civil War (1642-51) it was used as a barracks by the Parliamentary Army and after the Battle of Battle of Naseby in 1645 it was used to imprison 4,500 Cavaliers. Due to the negligence of a Flemish laundrywoman, the Palace burned down in 1698, the only surviving structure, being that monument to Stuart megalomania the Banqueting Hall designed by the eminent English architect Inigo Jones (1573-1652).

Having lost the English Civil War, run out of parties to double-cross and been sentenced to death for treason by Parliament at the behest of Oliver Cromwell, on the bitterly cold afternoon of 30 January 1649, King Charles I stepped out of the window of the Banqueting Hall onto the scaffold for his appointment with the executioner. He wore two shirts, lest the crowd assume he shivered from fear. 'Suddenly he stretched out his hands and with one blow the grey-bearded man severed his head from his body. It was now, noted another spectator, precisely four minutes past two'.[1] The crowd did not cheer, but merely stood in silence, awed by the enormity of what had been committed in their name.

In 1633 Hubert Le Sueur (1580-1658) had sculpted an equestrian statue of King Charles I for the Earl of Portland. It depicted the King in contemporary armour and carrying the baton of a general. (The suit of armour may be seen in the collection of HM Tower of London). The sculptor's name may be seen inscribed on one of the horse's hooves. Richard Weston, 1st Earl of Portland (1577-1635) erected the statue in the garden of his house at Roehampton, where it remained until the estate, by then the property of Sir Thomas Dawes was sequestered by Parliament. The statue was sold for £150 to St Paul's Church, Covent Garden and placed in their churchyard. In 1650 during the anti-monarchist hysteria caused by the Scottish invasion and King Charles II's Worcester Campaign, the Puritan authorities ordered the statue be destroyed and it was delivered to John Rivett, a Holborn brazier who supposedly melted it down to produce souvenirs, which were eagerly purchased by Royalists as mementoes and prized as trophies by Puritans. However, Rivett had hidden the statue in his garden. After the collapse of the Commonwealth in 1660, he produced the statue and was rewarded by being appointed the King's Brazier. The statue was returned to Jerome Weston, 2nd Earl of Portland (1605-63). King Charles II subsequently purchased it from him and in 1675 had it erected on what is now the south side of Trafalgar Square. In defiant self-justification, it looks accusingly down Whitehall to the scene of the King's execution. In placing it on the site of a medieval royal monument destroyed by the Puritans, King Charles II left Londoners in no doubt of their return to royal authority. During the Second World War the statue was removed for safety to Mentmore Towers. In 1947 it was set up again with a new sword in the king's hand, the original having disappeared in 1867 when a newspaper reporter climbed on the statue for a better view of a procession and grabbed the sword to steady himself. It fell amongst the crowd and was never seen again. On 30 January each year the Royal Stuart Society holds a wreath-laying ceremony at the statue which commences at 1100. The King's statue is the location from which all distances to London are measured.

---

[1] Charles Firth *Oliver Cromwell* G P Puttnam's Sons 1901.

# GENERAL SIR JOHN MOORE

John Moore was born in Glasgow in 1761. He was the son of a doctor and was educated at Glasgow High School. He travelled widely in Europe with his father as a child. In 1776 he joined the British Army as an ensign. He served with distinction in America (1779-1783), Corsica (1794), the West Indies (1796), Ireland (1797-1799), Holland (1799), Egypt (1801), Sicily and Sweden (1802). He served as a Member of Parliament from 1784 to 1790.

Moore was a revolutionary military thinker, apart from the tactical innovations he introduced to the British Army which led to the formation of the Light Brigade in 1803 (later the Light Division), he held that true discipline proceeds from trust and that the King's Commission was an honour and not a social privilege. He commanded the universal respect of all who served under him - in whatever capacity. William Napier of the 43rd Regiment of Foot would write: 'His was the fire that warmed the coldest nature and urged all who came into contact with him onward in the path of glory along which he rode so mightily himself.'

In 1808 Moore commanded a force sent to bolster the resistance of the Spanish against Napoleon on the Iberian Peninsula. That October he advanced from Lisbon towards Valladolid. As he approached Madrid, he learned that Spanish resistance had collapsed and, faced by 70,000 troops under Maréchal Soult, he was forced to retreat. The withdrawal started at Sahagun on 24 December 1808 and Moore's army of 25,000 marched over 200 miles through mountains snow and rain before being evacuated at the port of Corunna. 5,000 British soldiers died during the retreat, often in the most pitiful of circumstances. The French attacked Moore's army at the village of Elviña on 16 January 1809 and were repelled, losing more than 2,000 men. Moore was mortally wounded at the moment of victory by a cannon ball which struck his left side and he was carried to the rear by his devoted Highlanders. That night, after dealing with promotions and administrative issues, he died and was buried in what is now known as San Carlos Gardens. A German commissary noted: 'At ten o'clock in the evening the victorious English troops gradually marched into the town in the finest order to embark. They were all in tatters, hollow eyed, and covered in blood and filth. They looked so terrible that the people made the sign of the cross as they passed.'[2] Moore's army embarked at Corunna unmolested by the French and set sail for England. No preparations had been made by the military authorities to receive them or relieve their wretched condition and this duty was undertaken by Portsmouth's shocked citizenry. Three months later another British army under the command of Sir Arthur Wellesley (later the Duke of Wellington) would return, challenge and eventually expel the French from Spain. Some years after the Napoleonic Wars had ended, the Iron Duke was recorded as saying to his Military Secretary at Horse Guards: 'You know, Fitzroy, we'd not have won, I think, without him.'[3]

Paid for by public subscription, in 1815 John Bacon the Younger sculpted the dramatic depiction in white marble of Moore's burial attended by allegorical figures that stands in St Paul's Cathedral in London. San Carlos Gardens now contains the tombs of both Moore and his widow, both of which are reverentially maintained by the Spanish authorities. In January 2004 a memorial bust of Moore was unveiled in San Carlos Gardens by Stephen Wright, British Ambassador to Spain, at the invitation of Francisco Vásquez, Mayor of La Coruña. Mañuel Arenas, President of the city's Royal Green Jackets Historical Association said: 'It's important that we remember our history and Moore especially. He's practically a Corunnan, he's been with us 195 years now.' In the 20th century a Britannia class locomotive No. 70041 was named *Sir John Moore* and shedded at both March in Cambridgeshire and Ipswich in Suffolk. The nameplate may be seen in the National Railway Museum at York. The British Army has not forgotten Sir John Moore and sculpted by James Butler, a statue of him stands outside Sir John Moore Barracks at Winchester in Hampshire. Another Sir John Moore Barracks may be found at Shorncliffe, Folkestone in Kent.

---

[2] A L F Schaumann *On the Road with Wellington*.
[3] Lord Fitzroy Somerset (1788-1855) Military Secretary to the Duke, later Lord Raglan, C-in-C in Crimea.

## THE BURIAL OF SIR JOHN MOORE AFTER CORUNNA

Not a drum was heard, nor a funeral note,
As his corse to the rampart we hurried;
Not a soldier discharged his farewell shot
O'er the grave where our hero we buried.

We buried him darkly at dead of night,
The sods with our bayonets turning;
By the struggling moonbeam's misty light
And the lanthorn dimly burning.

No useless coffin enclosed his breast,
Nor in sheet nor in shroud we wound him;
But he lay like warrior taking his rest
With his martial cloak around him.

Few and short were the prayers we said,
And we spoke not a word of sorrow;
But we steadfastly gazed on the face that was dead,
And we bitterly thought of the morrow.

We thought, as we hollowed his narrow bed
And smoothed down his lonely pillow,
That the foe and the stranger would tread o'er his head,
And we far away on the billow!

Lightly they'll talk of the spirit that's gone
And o'er his cold ashes upbraid him -
But little he'll reck, if they let him sleep on
In the grave where a Briton has laid him.

But half of our heavy task was done
When the clock struck the hour for retiring;
And we heard the distant and random gun
That the foe was sullenly firing.

Slowly and sadly we laid him down,
From the field of his fame fresh and gory;
We carved not a line, and we raised not a stone,
But left him alone with his glory.

It is of course possible that Sir John Moore's heroic death at the Battle of Corunna might have been forgotten with the passage of time, but for the Reverend Charles Wolfe (1791-1823), a young curate from Castlecaulfield in County Tyrone, Ireland, who wrote a poem about Moore's death and sent it to the *Newry Telegraph*. The newspaper printed it anonymously as a 'space filler'. Unexpectedly, it became a word-of-mouth hit and in 1822, no less an authority than Lord Byron declared it the finest ode in the English language. Either side of a glazed balcony in San Carlos Gardens may be seen marble tablets which contain both Wolfe's poem and a tribute in Galician by Rosalia de Castro, Galicia's most famous poet.

# BADAJOZ

After three attempts to take the town, the Duke of Wellington secured a hard-won victory over the French at Badajoz, Spain on the night of 6 April 1812. It is recorded that as the Duke wept over the size of the 'butcher's bill', General Sir Thomas Picton famously said to him: 'Good God man, what on earth's the matter'. The next morning, in one of the most inglorious episodes in the history of the British Army, 10,000 British troops, maddened by drink, went berserk in an orgy of rape, looting and murder. Of the town's 21,000 population, only 5,000 remained during the siege and they were slaughtered. Robert Blakeney, an officer who was present, wrote: 'Every house presented a scene of plunder, debauchery and bloodshed committed with wanton cruelty... the infuriated soldiery resembled rather a pack of hell-hounds vomited up from the infernal regions for the extirpation of humanity.' The situation was eventually brought under control with a number of soldiers being hanged. The scenes of violent disorder and the mass rape of a convent of nuns led the Iron Duke to conclude that the troops under his command were: 'the scum of the earth'. Controversy over events that night rankles still with the local population and their reaction to the proposal in 2003 to erect a memorial at Badajoz indicated that wounds were still raw. One local commented: 'It does not seem such a good idea to erect a memorial for a horde of devils and savages that raped women and profaned our churches.'[4] It should be noted that such behaviour by British soldiery was highly uncharacteristic - and also that atrocities were regularly committed by both the Spaniards and French during the Peninsular War. Over the border in Portugal is Elvas, where the English cemetery contains the tomb of Lieutenant Colonel James Oliver, the only marked grave from the battle. Here too is the plaque commemorating the 5,000 British troops who died taking Badajoz. Mindful of economy, the men's bodies were stripped and they were interred in unmarked graves at the foot of the town's walls. The only saving grace in this otherwise repulsive story is the tale of a 14 year old Spanish girl named Juana Maria de los Dolores de Leon who had sought the protection of Major Harry Smith, one of Wellington's officers. They would fall in love and marry. He would become Lieutenant General Sir Harry Smith, Governor of Cape Province in South Africa. 87 years later, the town named after his wife would be unsuccessfully besieged during the Boer War. The Duke of Wellington's victory over Maréchal Jourdan at the Battle of Vittoria on 21 June 1813 effectively spelled the end for Napoleonic ambitions on the Iberian Peninsula and precipitated the withdrawal of the demoralised French Army over the Pyrenees. Napoleon abdicated on 5 April 1814 and the Duke defeated Maréchal Soult at the Battle of Toulouse on 10 April. In the middle of the night of 14 April, whilst bivouacked at Bayonne, Wellington's army was attacked by French troops commanded by General Pierre Thouvenot. The Guards Brigade bore the brunt of the assault and by dawn it had been repulsed. The Allied Army had lost 826 dead and 231 captured and General Lord Andrew Hay was mortally mounded. 'The dead from the Guards Brigade were buried by their comrades in military cemeteries on the outskirts of Bayonne, one for the Coldstream Guards and one for the Third Guards. These are on the site of their battalion camps in 1814. The Coldstream Guards cemetery is located in the Rue de Laharie, just east of the village of St Bernard and is marked on maps as Cimetière des Anglais'.[5] Responsibility for the cemeteries passed to the French authorities in 1989. Both the Coldstream and Scots Guards wrote to renounce all claim to the plots, the keys to them being handed over to the Mayor of Bayonne in a ceremony. Prior to that date, the cemeteries were maintained with monies from a Trust set up by Mary Ann Barbara Holbourne sister of one of the casualties in 1876. The Trust expired in 1956 when Princess Mary Louise, the last grandchild of Queen Victoria died - one of its terms. The cemeteries are well cared for by the French and host an important local commemoration of the battle each April.

---

[4] *Daily Telegraph* 28 November 2003 p. 19.
[5] Sir Julian Paget *Second To None: The Coldstream Guards 1650–2000*.

# WATERLOO

'One long June day, memorable in human annals, decided the outcome between the revolution and the dynasts which had opened with the cannonade of Valmy twenty-three years before. Wellington's thin line, part British, part German, Belgian and Dutch, and powerfully aided as the shades of evening drew on by Blücher's Prussians, shattered the last army of Napoleon'.[6] The Duke of Wellington's army at Waterloo consisted of 23,900 British, 17,000 Dutch and Belgians, 11,000 Hanoverians, 5,900 Brunswickers and 2,800 Naussauers.

In recognition of Wellington's victory on 18 June 1815 and its world-changing consequences, a number of memorials were erected on the battlefield of Waterloo. In 1820 King Willem I of the Netherlands ordered the erection of a monument to his son the Prince of Orange, who had been wounded in the battle. Quite what he would have done had his son been killed bears some consideration. Given the ambivalent manner in which the Dutch and Belgian troops participated in the battle, such ardour on the King's part can be considered surprising. A number of chroniclers record that at least one British infantry square fired on the Belgian cavalry as they fled the field during the course of the battle. The Prince of Orange's Monument takes the form of an enormous hill surmounted by a bronze lion. Work commenced in 1824 and was completed by November 1826. The hill was constructed from 300,000 square metres of earth. It is 43 metres high and has 226 steps. From the top, the exhausted visitor can view the entire battlefield. The lion weighs 28 tons and stands 4.45 metres tall. It was cast by the Cockerill Company of Liège. Legend has it that the lion was cast from French cannon left abandoned on the field of Waterloo.

The Gordon Monument was erected on the battlefield in 1817 by the Gordon family to commemorate Lieutenant Colonel Gordon, who had been killed by having his leg blown off by a cannon ball whilst working in Wellington's headquarters. The monument consists of a square pedestal and fluted column.

The photograph above is of the curious beehive design of the Hanoverian Memorial erected by the King's German Legion to commemorate their fellow Germans who had fallen on the field of battle.[7] This form of memorial was fairly common in the 19th century and copies and variations of the design can be seen in many English cemeteries.

---

[6] H A L Fisher *A History of Europe* Volume II. Fontana 1960.
[7] From the accession of George, Elector of Hanover to the British throne as King George I in 1714, all British monarchs were also Kings of Hanover. Under Salic Law females were barred from Hanover's throne. With the accession of Queen Victoria in 1837, the throne of Hanover went to Ernest Augustus, son of King George III.

# WELLINGTON ARCH

Decimus Burton's arch was originally erected in 1826 as a grand entrance to Buckingham Palace. It was topped off by a massive statue of the Duke of Wellington (1769-1852) on his horse 'Copenhagen' at the Battle of Waterloo by Matthew Cotes Wyatt (1777-1862) and his son James. The sculpture weighed 40 tons and was 27 foot tall.[8] It was placed on the arch in 1846. In 1882 the arch was shifted to the top of Constitution Hill and, to the delight of the critics, Cotes Wyatt's sculpture was removed to Round Hill, Aldershot and handed over to the Aldershot Division of the British Army in August 1885. In 1891 the sculptor Adrian Jones exhibited the group *Triumph* at the Royal Academy, the Prince of Wales saw it, sent for him and spoke of the need for Burton's arch to be crowned by a suitable sculpture. Jones produced a design, which for the want of money and direction lay gathering dust for many years in the Office of Works. Eventually the project was initiated by Lord Farquhar and later sponsored by Lord Michelham - whose name appears on the dedicatory plaque as patron. Jones' design consisted of *Peace Triumphant Descending on the Chariot of War* drawn by four horses. A child may be seen leaning forward on the central shaft between the horses. There exists a photograph of a dinner party thrown by Jones in the belly of one of the horses. The work was cast by the Thames Ditton Statue Foundry in 1911. The precursor for Jones' design can be found in Gottfried Schadow's Quadriga (1794) on top of the Brandenburg Gate in Berlin. 'Of the purely decorative or allegorical statues or groups, the Quadriga has no equal and is undoubtedly a very fine achievement. Sculpture needs space if it is to be seen at its best. In London many statues suffer from their site. The Quadriga, however, is fortunate in having a perfect location by the Park, and looks especially impressive when viewed from the North side of Piccadilly'.[9] There was no formal inauguration ceremony and the plaque added in 1913 surprisingly makes no mention of Jones. The arch was recently re-opened to the public. Between 1840 and 1962 it was London's smallest police station, with accommodation for ten constables, a sergeant and a cat.

---

[8] The remark 'dat a donkey up dere' attributed to two-year old Alfred Watkin (later the 2nd Baronet) in September 1848 seems appropriate. *The Diaries of Absolom Watkin* edited by Magdalen Goffin,1993.
[9] Selwyn Hodson-Presinger *Adrian Jones (British Sculptor)* 1996 pp 40-41.

# MARBLE ARCH

Marble Arch stands on the site of what was Tyburn Field and from 1196 to 1783 it was the site of the 'King's Gallows'. An estimated 50,000 public executions took place there. The nearby Tyburn Convent houses the relics of 105 Roman Catholics martyred at Tyburn between the years of 1535 and 1681. The 45 foot tall Marble Arch was commissioned by King George IV to commemorate Britain's victories at Trafalgar and Waterloo and appropriately it was modelled on both the Arch of Constantine in Rome and Napoleon's own victory monument in Paris, the Arc de Triomphe. It was designed in 1828 by John Nash as the main entrance to Buckingham Palace and was constructed of Carrara marble at a cost of some £80,000. The reliefs on the Arch were executed by Flaxman, Westmacott and Baily, the three most distinguished English sculptors of the age. 'The reliefs in the monument's square panels show three female figures representing England, Scotland and Ireland, and another group depicting Peace and Plenty. The ones on the south side show a naval warrior with a figure of Justice and another group depicting Peace and Plenty, while the bronze gates - the largest in Europe, when they were made by Samuel Parker - show the Lion of England, the cypher of George IV and the figure of St George and the Dragon.'[10] After the death of King George IV, Nash was fired from the Buckingham Palace project, (all that survives of his work there is the west wing). It was then discovered that the Royal State Coach could not fit through the arch he had designed. In 1851 his replacement Edward Blore removed the arch from Buckingham Palace to its present site at the northern entrance to Hyde Park. It was originally intended that Sir Francis Chantrey's equestrian statue of King George IV would be placed on top of the arch but, due to the intercession of Sir Robert Peel, the statue ended up in Trafalgar Square, where it may be seen today. The arch is used for royal processions and by the King's Troop of the Royal Horse Artillery on their ceremonial route to Hyde Park.

In 2004 the arch was restored at a cost of some £75,000. Chris Cooke of English Heritage stated: 'The biggest problem was the filth - a combination of road pollution and pigeon guano. It was not really damaged - it just needed that extra bit of loving care to bring it back to its former glory'. In March 2005 active consideration was being given to moving the Arch from its current isolated location to Speakers' Corner in Hyde Park.

---

[10] London *Evening Standard* 23 June 2004.

# ACHILLES

'Precisely when the monument - the earliest raised to Wellington in England - was commissioned is not known. What appears to be the first reference to it dates from 8 July 1814, slightly less than a year before the Battle of Waterloo. On that day Joseph Farington noted in his diary that Lavinia, Lady Spencer (1762-1831) wife of George John, second Earl Spencer, had initiated a public subscription for the ladies of Great Britain to erect a monument to Wellington that would take the form of one of the *Horse tamer* groups on the so-called Monte Cavallo in Rome'.[11] Sculpted by Sir Richard Westmacott, this statue was erected 'by the women of England to Arthur, Duke of Wellington and his brave companions in arms'. It stands in Achilles Way in Hyde Park and was cast in bronze from a dozen 24-pounder French cannon captured by the Iron Duke in his campaigns. Weighing some 33 tons and standing 18 feet tall, it was the largest statue cast in the West since antiquity.

The unveiling on 18 June 1822[12] caused a sensation. To gasps from the crowd, a colossal nude holding a circular shield, with the head being modelled on the Iron Duke himself, was revealed - the statue's modesty was covered by a fig leaf, which has since been chipped off in both 1870 and 1961.[13] The women of England who had subscribed £10,000 to pay for it were scandalised, the public who were unable to grasp its classical antecedents were astonished and the press inevitably delighted. The controversy raged on for years. It should be noted that the conception was not Westmacott's, but that of the organising committee chaired by the Duchess of York.

The statue, when originally unveiled, had no sword in its right fist, although Westmacott had provided the groove for it to be inserted. The statue subsequently acquired a broom thoughtfully provided by a wag. The plinth, which has a considerable number of holes drilled symmetrically into the front of it, proclaims the statue to have been erected on the order of George IIII.

---

[11] *The Burlington Magazine* Vol 130 (1988).
[12] Seventh anniversary of the Battle of Waterloo.
[13] London *Evening Standard* 17 February 2000.

## THE IRON DUKE

Given his enduring fame as Britain's greatest soldier, it is unsurprising to find there are a substantial number of memorials to the Duke of Wellington, with notable examples being John Bell's equestrian statue of the Duke *sans* stirrups outside the Guildhall, London and the Wellington Testimonial in Dublin (1861), which takes the form of an obelisk. At the last count, worldwide there were also 23 towns named after him including the capital of New Zealand. Whilst not an exhaustive list, the Duke's memory would also give posterity: Wellington Barracks in London, the dish 'Boeuf Wellington', the Wellington Bridge over the River Dee in Aberdeen, Wellington Road alongside Regent's Park in London, the Wellington Bomber, Wellington Boots, Wellington Square, Oxford, Wellington Hall at the Royal Hospital, Chelsea and the Duke of Wellington Hall at the Royal United Services Institute for Defence Studies. Wellington College in Berkshire was established in 1853 as a memorial to the Iron Duke and was paid for by the levy of a day's pay from the Army. The third Royal Navy warship to bear the name HMS IRON DUKE, a type 23 frigate, was commissioned on 30 May 1991. Another form of memorialisation may be taken from the fact that the Duke's office over the archway at Horse Guards remains preserved exactly as it was on the last day he rode out and is in the care of English Heritage who steadfastly refuse to allow any alteration, their only concession to modernity being a discreet telephone on the desk of the present General Officer Commanding the Household Division. Likewise, the Duke's bedroom at Walmer Castle, Kent, dating from his tenure as Lord Warden of the Cinque Ports (1829-1852), remains preserved exactly as he left it. In 1826 he was appointed Constable of HM Tower of London. He instituted radical reforms in its running and ended abuses and the tradition of staff selling on their appointments. He retained the post until his death in 1852 and his death mask is in the Tower's collection.

The sculpture at Hyde Park (pictured above) was executed by Sir Joseph Boehm in 1888. Four figures stand on small projecting buttresses at each corner of the plinth. They are representations of soldiers from 6th Inniskilling Dragoons, 23rd Royal Welch Fusiliers, 42nd Royal Highlanders and 1st Guards. Informed opinion in sculptural circles holds that at least two of the four bronze soldiers at the base of the Duke of Wellington's Memorial were sculpted by Boehm's French chief assistant Édouard Lantéri (later to find fame as the teacher of an entire generation of British sculptors).

# THE WELLINGTON MONUMENT

Wellington is a small country town standing between the River Tone and the Blackdown Hills in Somerset. The earliest reference to it may be found in a grant made between 899 and 909 in which it was called 'Weolingtun'. The town was mentioned in the Domesday Book, which recorded: that land at 'Walintone' and West Buckland was being worked by 61 farmers, 65 smallholders and 32 serfs. Although General Arthur Wellesley took the title of 'Viscount Wellington of Wellington and Talavera' in 1809, and later became Duke of Wellington, he is reputed to have visited the town only once (in 1819), even though he had an estate in the area.

    The Wellington Monument stands prominently on the skyline of the scarp of the Blackdown Hills within 4.8 hectares of National Trust land, with spectacular views across to Exmoor, the Quantocks, the Bristol Channel and, on a clear day, Wales. It is 175 feet tall and 80 feet wide at the base. A counterweight hangs inside to help balance it in a high wind. An internal staircase leads to a viewing platform. To gain access to the stairs, a key and a torch may be obtained for a small charge and deposit from the adjacent Monument Farm.

    The monument stands on what was the Duke's own land and was erected to celebrate his famous victory at Waterloo in 1815. The foundation stone was laid in 1817, but it was not until 1854 that the Monument was completed. The inspiration for its design derives from the Egyptian obelisk, the Egyptian influence being particularly noticeable in the large stone scarab over the entrance door. The Monument is floodlit at night, courtesy of Taunton Deane Borough Council. Originally four cannons surrounded it. However, during the Second World War they were removed for scrap to help the war effort. The Wellington Rotary Club donated the cannon currently standing at the base of the Monument in 1985.

# THE GRAND OLD DUKE OF YORK

The Duke of York's Column stands at the top of Duke of York's Steps, which break the front of John Nash's Carlton Terrace in London and he looks out from his lofty perch over the Horse Guards Parade Ground. The column on which he stands was designed by Benjamin Wyatt and erected in 1831-34 at a cost of some £25,000. 'It is of the Tuscan order after Trajan's column in Rome, and carries above its capital a square balcony and then a drum and dome (on the pattern of Wren's Monument in the City). The stones are grey Aberdeenshire and red Peterhead granite, the foundation a concealed pyramid'.[14] The 13 foot tall bronze sculpture of the Duke in his Garter Robes at its summit was executed by Sir Richard Westmacott in 1834. According to the wits of the time, the Duke was placed on a 124-foot high column so that he would be well out of reach of his creditors. (He owed the staggering sum of £2,000,000 at his death). Most unusually, the Duke of York's Column was paid for by the deduction of a day's pay from every soldier in the British Army, and whilst this may appear a supreme example of high-handedness on the part of officialdom, in this case not so.

Frederick Augustus, Duke of York was born on 16 August 1763 at St James's Palace, second son of King George III. His royal career got underway six months later with his election as Prince Bishop of Osnabrück. In 1771 he was invested a Knight of the Garter and in 1780 gazetted a Colonel in the Army. In 1782 he was appointed Colonel of the 2nd Horse Grenadier Guards and in 1784 was created Duke of York and Albany. He took his seat in the Lords in 1787. At the outbreak of war against the French in 1793, at the insistence of the King he was placed in command of the British army despatched to Flanders. The Duke's experiences in the Flemish and Dutch campaigns of 1793, 1794, 1795 and 1799 taught him that soldiering was best left to professionals. In 1795 he was appointed Commander-in-Chief of the British Army and it fell to him to bring order out of the chaotic manner in which it was organised and he would prove himself an outstanding administrator. As the politicians intended, the 'divide and rule' manner in which the army was run obstructed and prevented army business at every turn and he would deal indefatigably with its hydra-headed monster of independent departments. The Duke's independence from political faction and his dynamism kept Wellington's armies in the field during the long years of the Napoleonic wars and he ended many of the abuses associated with political jobbery. Wellington's phenomenal success on the battlefield earned him the status necessary to introduce root and branch reform to the army and, although he was the greatest soldier these islands have ever produced, he had no stomach for that fight - not even when he became Commander-in-Chief himself. 'So the Duke of York was left to march alone to the top of the hill. He marched to some purpose. First he succeeded in securing control of almost all the military forces within the United Kingdom (although not of commanders abroad, who reported directly to the Secretary of State). All promotions except those to the highest ranks, passed into his hands. He took responsibility for discipline, training, man-management, and tactical innovation. He even won the first pay increase for private soldiers since 1702. Single-handed, he resisted the attempts of successive Secretaries-at-War to clip his wings. In the end he was submerged by weight of numbers. But arguably he was the greatest Commander-in-Chief and the best friend the British Army has ever had.'[15] The Duke of York resigned his post on 18 March 1809 after questions were raised in the House of Commons by Colonel Gwyllym Lloyd Wardle about the patronage being dispensed by the Duke's mistress, Mrs Mary Clarke (1776-1852), who had been selling military appointments. The scandal which subsequently unfolded in the law courts brought no credit to any of the parties involved, but the Duke was found innocent of any wrong-doing. After a decent interval he was reappointed in 1811 by his brother the Prince Regent and continued to hold the post with distinction until his death from dropsy in 1827. The Duke was wholly uninterested in politics, excepting his resolute opposition to Catholic Emancipation.

---

[14] S Bradley and N Pevsner *Buildings of England Series: London and Westminster.*

[15] David Ascoli *A Companion to the British Army* p. 306.

# THE CHILLIANWALLAH MEMORIAL

The Second Sikh War commenced in April 1848 with the revolt of Mulraj, Governor of Multan. Matters got seriously out of hand when the Sikh Army joined the revolt in September. At the Battle of Ramnagar (22 November), General Lord Gough's army was defeated by the Sikhs under Shere Singh. This was followed by the indecisive battle of Chillianwallah on 13 Jan 1849, which further fanned the flames and led to Gough's (delayed) dismissal. The decisive battle of the campaign was fought at Gujrat on 21 February and this led to the eventual surrender of the Sikh Army on 12 March. The British then annexed the Punjab. Tradition has it that the surgeon's table from Chillianwallah originally owned by the Honourable East India Company is the top table in the Officers Mess at the Royal Artillery Barracks in Woolwich. The role of the 14th and 20th Hussars at Ramnagar is commemorated by the Ramnugger Memorial in All Saint's Church, Maidstone, Kent by Richard Westmacott the Younger. Standing in the South Grounds of the Royal Hospital, Chelsea, the Chillianwallah Memorial designed by the celebrated architect Christopher Cockerell, is a fifty foot tall obelisk. 255 men of the 24th Regiment of Foot died at Chillianwallah. The manner in which their names are carried on the memorial is noteworthy: The names of the 14 officers who died in the battle are carried on one side of the plinth and 14 non-commissioned officers on the other. The names of 227 private soldiers are carried in alphabetical order on each face of the needle of the obelisk itself. The memorial is topped off by a gilded crowned orb. The general inscription on the plinth reads:

"TO THE MEMORY OF
TWO HUNDRED AND FIFTY FIVE
OFFICERS, NONCOMMISSIONED OFFICERS
AND PRIVATES
OF THE XXIV REGT
WHO FELL
AT CHILLIANWALLAH 13 JANUARY 1849
THIS MONUMENT HAS BEEN ERECTED
BY THEIR SURVIVING COMRADES
A.D. 1853."

# THE GUARDS CRIMEA MEMORIAL

Erected in 1860, this 38 ft tall monolithic memorial by John Bell stands confusingly in Waterloo Place just off Pall Mall in London. It takes the form of a large granite pedestal, in front of which stand, backed by the colours of their regiments, three bronze figures representing respectively men of the Grenadier, Coldstream and Scots Fusilier Guards. At that time these three regiments comprised the Brigade of Guards. The men are in short-caped greatcoats, exactly the order they fought in at the Battle of Inkerman on 5 November 1854. Above them stands the figure of Honour, arms extended distributing coronals (unkindly described by one critic as quoits). The pile of Russian guns at the rear of the memorial were recovered from Sevastopol. The memorial was shifted 36 ft in 1914 to make way for A G Walker's statue of Florence Nightingale and John Henry Foley's statue of Sidney Herbert which stand immediately before it. Inscribed either side of the memorial are the words:

"ALMA
INKERMAN
SEBASTOPOL
CRIMEA"

Inscribed on a bronze plaque at the north end are the words:

"TO THE MEMORY OF
2162
OFFICERS NON-COMd OFFICERS AND
PRIVATES OF THE BRIGADE
OF GUARDS WHO FELL DURING
THE WAR IN RUSSIA 1854-5-6"

# THE ROYAL ARTILLERY CRIMEAN WAR MEMORIAL

Also sculpted by John Bell, the Royal Artillery Crimean War Memorial was erected to commemorate the gunners who died in that most pointless of conflicts. Bell's memorial, modelled on Victory, stands on the parade ground at Woolwich and she faces the elegant Grade I listed Georgian façade of the Royal Artillery Barracks. The plinth is ornamented on both its left and right side by the Ordnance Board coat of arms with its trademark cannon and (outsized) three balls. The memorial itself is flanked by two mortars. They were originally the two Chinese mortars removed from Sevastopol, from which the cascabels were sawn off to cast the Victoria Cross, and they may now be seen in the Royal Artillery's Museum *Firepower* on the site of the old Royal Arsenal. The inscription on the bronze shield on the front of the memorial reads:

"HONOR
TO THE DUTIFUL
AND
BRAVE"

The inscription on the bewreathed shield at the rear of the memorial reads:

"TO THE MEMORY
OF THE OFFICERS
NON COMMISSIONED OFFICERS
AND MEN OF THE
ROYAL ARTILLERY
WHO FELL DURING
THE WAR WITH RUSSIA
1854, 1855, 1856"

# ARMED SCIENCE

John Bell exhibited *Armed Science* in 1855 and completed it in marble a year later. The version above was commissioned by Robert Adair, Lord Waveney who was Colonel of the Suffolk Militia Artillery. It stands in the Officers Mess of the Royal Artillery Barracks at Woolwich in South East London. '*Armed Science* is a female figure of heroic size. Standing on an inscribed plinth, clad in demi-armour and an unusual antique spiked helmet, she wears a short sword at her side. Thoughtful, her chin resting on her hand, she holds a short staff, presumably a sponge or rammer for cannonry, above folded robing. Adair's gift to Woolwich was a successful and elegant statue in marble, much admired in the Officers' mess hall, where during evening balls, it was surrounded by the Artillery band.'[16] Bell's cordial relations with the Royal Regiment of Artillery led to his commission for their Crimean War Memorial, which stands immediately outside on the Parade Ground at Woolwich.

Bell produced three copies of *Armed Science* in terra cotta. One was erected at Flixton Hall near Bungay in Suffolk and is presumed lost when that building was demolished in 1953. Another stood in Lord Waveney's castle at Ballymena, County Antrim in Ireland and was also presumed lost when that building went up in flames, but it did in fact survive the fire seriously damaged. (In 2005 the local authority concerned was liaising with the Royal Artillery to commission a copy). Another copy was produced for Lord Armstrong. Yet another copy was produced by Doulton and erected as the Soldiers Memorial in Norwich and it stands in Norwich Cemetery. A miniature version 24 inches tall was produced by the Coalbrookdale Company for retail sale.

---

[16] Richard Barnes *John Bell: The Sculptor's Life and Works.*

# THE SCUTARI MONUMENT

Haidar Pasha Cemetery's origins can be found in the Crimean War (1853-1856). It is located in Asian Turkey, opposite Istanbul. Turkey, 'the Sick Man of Europe' was an active ally of the British and the French in that war against the Russians. 6,000 British soldiers who fought and died were interred there in a mass grave. The wounded who expired during the crossing from the Crimea (74 per 1,000) were committed to the Deep. The Scutari Monument (pictured above) was designed by Baron Carlo Marochetti and a facsimile in imitation granite was inaugurated by Queen Victoria in the south nave of Sir Joseph Paxton's Crystal Palace at Sydenham on 9 May 1856. The occasion was recorded by Sir John Tenniel and the original of his drawing is in the Royal Collection at Windsor. Never popular with the British public because of his Franco-Italian origins, Marochetti was a favourite of Queen Victoria. He was paid the sum of £15,000 for his controversial sculpture, which earned him the scorn of the critics and accusations of profiteering. 'The Queen was not impressed with the occasion, complaining in her diary about the music, coarse decoration and the 'blundering' in the management and timing of the ceremony. Five or six hundred men who had fought in the war paraded inside the Palace and were cheered; the bands played pieces from *Il Trovatore*, *Semiramide* and *The Magic Flute*, Verdi's *Miserere* and the slow movement of Beethoven's *Eroica* Symphony. A pattern was being set for 'ceremonial of a national character.'[17]

The memorial at Haidar Pasha was erected in 1857 and constructed from Aberdeen granite. To give the reader some idea of scale, the angels on the corners are 11 ft tall. On Empire Day 1954 a plaque was added to the plinth commemorating the pioneering work in the nearby Scutari Barracks of Florence Nightingale. A memorial also stands in the cemetery to the German Jäger officers who fell in the Crimea serving with the British Army.

---

[17] J R Piggott *Palace of the People: The Crystal Palace at Sydenham 1854–1936* Hurst & Company London 2004.

# MARY SEACOLE

Mary Jane Grant was born in 1805, the daughter of a Jamaican lady doctor and a Scottish army officer. She was raised in Kingston, Jamaica where her mother ran a nursing home. Having acquired the arts of Creole medicine from her mother and surgical principles from British Army surgeons, she travelled widely. During her travels to Nassau, Panama, Haiti and Cuba she learned to care for patients with many tropical diseases and developed her own remedies using herbs and local plants. It was these skills she would employ to such effect on the battlefields of the Crimea. A widow at 50, she learned of the shortage of nurses in the Crimea and travelled to London to offer her services, which were declined due to her ethnicity. Nonplussed but not deterred, she raised the necessary funds to travel to the Crimea and set up the British Hotel at Balaclava, providing accommodation, food and nursing care for wounded British troops. Her British Hotel stood on Spring Hill at Sevastopol. She tended the wounded of both sides on the battlefield and the British troops swore by her skills. At the end of the war she returned to London, ill, penniless and facing bankruptcy proceedings. She was not without friends and supporters, as her work had been publicised by both *The Times* and *Punch* magazine. A fund chaired by Colonel Henry Daniel of the Coldstream Guards was established to assist her, with patronage from the Prince of Wales, the Duke of Edinburgh and the Duke of Cambridge. Queen Victoria signalled her approbation. Organised by Lord Rokeby, Lord George Paget and *Punch* in 1857 a four-day military gala was held in her honour at the Royal Surrey Gardens, Kennington, which was attended by more than 80,000 people. Unusually for a non-combatant, she was also awarded the Crimean Medal and the *Légion d'Honneur*. That same year her autobiography *Wonderful Adventures of Mrs Seacole in Many Lands* was published with a foreword by *The Times* war correspondent Sir William Howard Russell (1820-1907), who wrote: 'I have witnessed her devotion and her courage... and I trust that England will never forget one who has nursed her sick, who sought out her wounded to aid and succour them and who performed the last offices for some of her illustrious dead'. She worked as a masseuse to the Princess of Wales until her death after a short illness in May 1881. She left £3,000 in her will and was buried in St Mary's Roman Catholic Cemetery, Kensal Green, London. Whilst not as well known as Florence Nightingale, she is far from forgotten. In February 2004 she was voted No 1 in the 100 Greatest Black Britons Poll and her memory is commemorated in a variety of ways, including an annual wreath-laying ceremony at her grave each May. There is a Mary Seacole Association and a Mary Seacole Foundation. The Mary Seacole Research Centre is located at De Montfort University, Leicester and was set up as a collaborative initiative between the University and The Royal College of Nursing. The Centre works closely with staff in all departments of the Faculty of Health and Life Sciences and others across the University with an interest in issues of race and ethnicity in health. There is also a Mary Seacole Centre for Nursing Practice located on the Thames Valley University campus in Ealing, West London, which is an academic centre within the faculty of Health and Human Sciences. The University also has a Mary Seacole School of Nursing on the campus at Slough. She is also recognised by the annual Mary Seacole Nursing Leadership Award of £25,000 established in 1994 by the Department of Health. A number of books about her life have also been written in recent years and several academic papers have also been published. There little doubt of the impact she had on nursing generally and the inspiration she provided to people from all backgrounds. There is no English Heritage Blue Plaque on the wall of her house at St Martin's Lane in London, but at the time of writing there was a well supported campaign underway to erect a memorial to her in London. In 2004 a nine by seven inch print was sold in a car boot sale in Oxfordshire and the purchaser subsequently discovered that there was a portrait in oils underneath the print. The portrait was purchased by the historian Helen Rappaport and identified as a portrait of Mary Seacole painted by Albert Charles Challen in 1869. In January 2005 the painting went on permanent display at the National Portrait Gallery in London.

# THE INDIAN MUTINY

A bronze statue of Brigadier General John Nicholson (1821-1857) in Delhi was erected by public subscription and sculpted by Sir Thomas Brock. In 1956 the Indian Government removed it from the Kashmir Gate and shipped it to the Royal School at Dungannon in Northern Ireland. John Nicholson was an Ulsterman who had arrived in India in 1839 and served in the Afghan War and subsequently held civil appointments in the newly annexed Punjab and modernised it ruthlessly. A deeply religious man, he imposed discipline on those he ruled with a rod of iron. He would personally pursue criminals, bring them to justice and display their severed heads on his desk. Unsurprisingly, his actions and personality had a profound effect upon those he ruled. To his disgust, this led to a brotherhood of Hazara fakirs founding 'the cult of the Nicolsenites' and they worshipped him as a deity. His efficiency, imperious manner and notoriously short fuse ensured that the British officers who served under him (but did not know him, due to his shyness) loathed and feared him. In 1857 mutiny broke out. After taking measures to pacify the Punjab, Nicholson arrived with his Sikhs on 14 August 1857 on The Ridge before Delhi. His arrival transformed the mood of the force assembled for the assault on that city and he was killed in its retaking. Fifty years later, Field Marshal Earl Roberts (who won a Victoria Cross in the Mutiny) recalled that Nicholson had impressed him more profoundly than any man he had ever met. The Cawnpore Memorial Church of All Souls was built in 1875, in honour of the British who lost their lives in the Mutiny. It was designed by Walter Granville, architect of the East Bengal Railway Company, in the Lombard Gothic style. Its interior contains monuments and memorial tablets to those killed. To the east of the church was a memorial garden with a carved gothic screen designed by Henry Yule. At its centre stood a carved figure of an angel with crossed arms, holding palons, the symbol of peace by Baron Carlo Marochetti. Originally the statue and the screen stood in the Municipal Gardens in the centre of the city, over the site of the Bibighar Well down which the bodies of massacred British women and children were thrown by mutineers. The memorials were relocated by the Indian Government after independence in 1948. Another form of memorialisation may be taken from the neighbourhood of Addiscombe near Croydon in Surrey. From 1809 Addiscombe was the site of the Honourable East India Company's military academy and it educated officer cadets for service with the armies of the various presidencies in India. On 1 November 1858 the British Government abolished the HEIC and from that date India was ruled directly from London. In 1863 Addiscombe was sold for redevelopment and the academy demolished. Shortly thereafter, the developer named a number of new roads in the area after significant figures from the Mutiny. CANNING ROAD was named for Earl Canning (1812-1862) Governor General of India 1855-1858, first Viceroy of India 1858-1862; OUTRAM ROAD was named for Lieutenant General Sir James Outram Bt (1803-63), the Defender of Lucknow; CLYDE ROAD was named for Field Marshal Sir Colin Campbell, Baron Clyde (1792-1863) C-in-C India 1857-60; GRANT ROAD and GRANT PLACE could conceivably have been named for any one of three individuals, these being Sir John Grant (1807-1893) Lieutenant Governor of Bengal 1859-62, General Sir James Grant (1808-75) C-in-C Madras 1862-3 and Field Marshal Sir Patrick Grant (1804-95) C-in-C Madras 1856-61; INGLIS ROAD was named for Major General Sir John Inglis (1814-62); NICHOLSON ROAD was named for John Nicholson; HAVELOCK ROAD was named for Major General Sir Henry Havelock Bt (1795-1857) who died of dysentery during the Mutiny; WARREN ROAD and HASTINGS ROAD were named for Warren Hastings (1732-1818), first Governor General of India 1773-85. Despite his brilliance and all the good he did in India, at the instigation of enemies in Parliament, he was impeached in 1788 eventually being acquitted in 1795. On 22 May 2002 *BBC News* reported that the Sikh Community in West London were actively campaigning to get the name of Havelock Road in Southall changed because of General Havelock's role in the suppression of the Mutiny, (an interesting example of historical revisionism, given the prominent role of the Sikhs on the British side).

# THE WESTMINSTER SCHOOL CRIMEAN AND INDIAN MUTINY MEMORIAL

This Westminster School Crimean and Indian Mutiny War Memorial stands in Dean's Yard by Westminster Abbey in London on the site of the old Gatehouse Prison (demolished 1776). It commemorates all the former pupils of Westminster School who died serving in the navy and army in the period 1854-59. The plinth is of Portland stone and the column of Peterhead granite. The column is surmounted by sculpted representations of King Edward the Confessor, King Henry II, Queen Elizabeth I and Queen Victoria. These are in turn surmounted by a representation of King George and the Dragon. The sculptor was John Birnie Philip and the designer Sir Gilbert Scott, RA. The four lions at the base of the column were modelled by Sir Edwin Landseer. The inscriptions were composed by the Reverend T Weare an Under Master at the School. It was unveiled in 1861. 'The Monument was not erected without criticism. On April 17th 1861, the Chief Commissioner of Works was asked in the House of Commons if his attention had been directed to the Monument then in process of erection at the entrance to Westminster School, and if he had any power to prevent its erection. The Chief Commissioner thereupon made the following reply: "Sir, the answer to the question of my hon. and gallant friend depends upon the construction of an Act of Parliament. It appears that it was assumed that this work of art, being called a monument, did not come within the provision of the Act which declares that no public statue shall be erected in a public place without the written assent of the First Commissioner of His Majesty's Works. I presume the subscribers to this monument had grounds for that assumption, though it might be urged on the other side that, as the monument consists of the statues of public personages, namely four sovereigns who especially favoured the School of Westminster, and St. George and the Dragon, it is not exempted from the operation of the Act. But, however that may be, supposing the promoters were incorrect in their construction of the Act, I think it would be a harsh step on the part of the Commissioner of Works to remove the monument on that account. At the same time, I must say that if my assent had been asked to this monument, I should have hesitated to sanction the extraordinary incongruity of placing statues in the medieval style on a classical column. The incongruity has arisen from the struggle which prevails in this House and elsewhere between the advocates of the Gothic and the advocates of the Classical style, and I presume they came to a compromise, which like other compromises, has been less successful than a frank adoption of either alternative.'[18]

---

[18] E Tanner *Westminster School: Its Buildings and their Associations.* Philip Allen 1923.

# ISANDHLWANA

The Battle of Isandhlwana in the Anglo-Zulu war has gone down in African history as a victory over British imperial aggression and in British history as the most serious defeat in colonial warfare against an indigenous army. The Anglo-Zulu war was part of a British attempt to amalgamate the British colonies and Boer republics of South Africa into a single British imperial confederation. The security of white settlement in such a confederation could only be ensured by the defeat of the remaining independent African kingdoms of the region. The most powerful of these was the Zulu kingdom which lay to the north of the British colony of Natal. Sir Henry Bartle Frere, Governor of the Cape Colony and High Commissioner for Natal manoeuvred the Zulu King Cetswayo into a situation from which he could not escape and ordered an invasion, commanded by General Lord Chelmsford. King Cetswayo had done all he could to avoid war, but once the invasion began he mobilised to meet the threat. On 11 January 1879 Chelmsford's forces crossed the Tugela River in three columns intending to converge on the Royal Kraal at Ulundi. Taking command of the central column, Chelmsford encamped on open ground at the foot of Isandhlwana Hill while he led forward a small scouting force. On the afternoon of 22 January the Zulu army, moving unseen through hidden valleys, came upon the British encampment at Isandhlwana. Using traditional strategy, the Zulu commanders sent out two encircling 'horns' to cut off any retreat while the bulk of the force made a frontal attack. At first creeping low to get below the British muzzle-loading guns, on a single order, the Zulu regiments rose as one and charged the British with their assegais. The British defenders were overwhelmed by the ferocity and speed of the assault. Several thousand Zulus died in the battle and only a handful of the British force escaped. Chelmsford returned from his reconnaissance at dusk to find 1,700 of his men dead, half of them native recruits and most of a British regiment wiped out. Over the years there has been much debate about the speed of events at Isandhlwana, the difficulty in opening ammunition boxes during the battle and other commissariat problems. However, military opinion has in recent years has concluded that defeat was due to failure at the operational and tactical levels of command. Brigadier Frank Steer in the *Daily Telegraph* on 27 January 2004 pointed out that events at Rorke's Drift later that same day rather support this contention, noting that the troops there: 'had the same equipment, same weapons, same ammunition, same everything; but they barricaded and concentrated, and prevailed'.[19] The verdict of history lays the responsibility for the disaster on the 'day of the dead moon' (there was a partial eclipse that day) squarely at the door of Lord Chelmsford and his underestimation of a well-trained, well-led foe was certainly a decisive factor in its outcome. By 1 September Cetswayo was taken and Ulundi captured. The Zulu victory would postpone British plans for the confederation of South Africa for a generation. Upon returning to England, Chelmsford persuaded Queen Victoria he was not responsible for the disaster and that the fault lay with Colonels Durnford and Pulleine, (who both died in the battle). Prime Minister Disraeli refused to receive him and had good reason to feel aggrieved, as he was lumbered with the political consequences of a campaign he had not authorised and it presaged the fall of his government. Lord Chelmsford enjoyed a long retirement and continued royal favour. He died at his club in 1905 while playing billiards. One of the soldiers who died at Isandhlwana was 24 year old Private Ashley Goatham of the 24th Regiment of Foot. The son of a carpenter, his family home was at Bredgar near Sittingbourne, Kent. He married in Durban whilst serving in South Africa and had a son, also named Ashley. He was a crack shot and a proud soldier, but his letters home to his family before the campaign show that he was fully aware that Cetswayo would give the British a run for their money. Unusually for the time, given his military status, after his death his family paid for the erection of an 8 foot tall marble obelisk to his memory in the churchyard of the Church of St John the Baptist, Bredgar. The memorial was refurbished and rededicated in a well-attended ceremony in the churchyard on 20 June 2004.

---

[19] *Daily Telegraph* 27 January 2004 p. 24.

## RORKE'S DRIFT,

'You will be in charge, although of course, nothing will happen, and I shall be back again this evening early' - Major Henry Spalding to Lieutenant John Chard, 22 January 1879.

'It was at 3.30 on the afternoon of 22 January 1879 that Private Fred Hitch saw the whites of the enemy's eyes. He had been making tea outside Rorke's Drift, a small Swedish mission station in Natal, South Africa, when two riders came galloping furiously over a rise. They brought bad news. Zulu warriors had slaughtered 1,700 troops at Isandhlwana and they were now headed towards the mission. Fred grabbed his rifle and four kettles of tea and hurried to the fort that B Company, 2nd Battalion, the 24th Regiment (later the South Wales Borderers) had been left to guard. His company commander, Lieutenant Gonville Bromhead, ordered him to shin up on to a roof as a lookout. What he saw was enough to make Fred gasp. The Zulus had already crept up to the perimeter and were preparing to attack.'[20] What Fred Hitch observed was the Zulu Reserve consisting of the senior regiments of King Cetswayo's homestead at oNdini, which had missed much of the fighting and who were keen to take advantage of Lord Chelmsford's defeat by raiding into Natal. These 4,000 warriors were led by Prince Dabulamanzi kaMpande. Lieutenants Chard of the Royal Engineers and Bromhead of the 24th decided that retreat was hopeless, fortified the mission's two buildings and prepared their 140 men for the onslaught. The brunt of the attack fell on the dwelling-house which the British were using as a hospital. Early on its roof was fired and the defenders fought their attackers from room to room whilst evacuating the patients by hacking out its walls. The British fought for more than 10 hours from behind barricades of mealie bags, upturned wagons and boxes of biscuit. Much of the combat was hand-to-hand, with the assegai and bayonet much in evidence. In the early hours the ferocity of the assault declined and gradually petered out. There were 17 British dead, who are commemorated by name on the above memorial sited at Rorke's Drift. To the consternation of the Duke of Cambridge, the garrison was awarded a total of 11 Victoria Crosses - a record number for a single action.

---

[20] *Sunday Express* 1 February 2004 p. 52.

## ST MICHAEL'S ABBEY, FARNBOROUGH

Napoleon Eugène Louis John Joseph Bonaparte, only son of the Emperor Napoleon III, was born at the Tuileries Palace on 16 March 1856. He was 14 years old when the Franco-Prussian War broke out and witnessed the French defeat at the Battle of Sedan on 1 September 1870, which simultaneously ended the French Second Empire and the political career of the Bonaparte dynasty. The Imperial Family fled to England and when he was released from captivity, Emperor Napoleon III joined them at Camden Place, Chislehurst, Kent. He died there and was buried in St Mary's Roman Catholic Church, Chislehurst in January 1873. The Prince Imperial renounced French citizenship and applied for permission to join the British Army. He studied at the Royal Military Academy, Woolwich (the Workshop) and was commissioned into the Royal Artillery. Anxious to win his spurs, he persuaded both his mother the Empress Eugênie and Queen Victoria to permit him to join the expedition to Zululand and departed England on 27 February 1879. Upon arrival in Durban he was placed on Lord Chelmsford's staff. On 1 June he was a member of a reconnaissance patrol commanded by a Lieutenant Carey. Near the Ityotyozi River it was ambushed by 40 Zulus. The Prince was unable to mount his horse which shied and bolted. The rest of the patrol turned tail and escaped. 'After the fugitives had ridden some hundreds of yards they drew up for a moment on rising ground, and Lieutenant Carey had his attention drawn to the Prince's horse, which was seen galloping away by one of the men, who said that he feared the Prince was killed'.[21] The Prince's naked body was recovered from the same area by a cavalry patrol the next day. His body had 17 wounds, all in front. Lieutenant Carey was court-martialled and found not guilty, but cashiered nevertheless. Obsequies were conducted by the Roman Catholic hierarchy at Pietermaritzburg, Durban and Simon's Bay, with civic dignitaries, garrisons and the fleet turned out en masse.[22] The Prince's body was brought back to England in HMS ORONTES, landed at Woolwich on 10 July and conveyed to Camden Place by a troop of Artillery. On 12 July a full military funeral was held at St Mary's attended by Queen Victoria, the Ambassadors to the Court and the principal dignitaries of the realm. The pall bearers were the Prince of Wales, the Duke of Edinburgh, the Duke of Connaught, Prince Leopold of Belgium, the Crown Prince of Norway and Sweden, the Duke of Cambridge, the Duke of Bassano and M. Rouher. Lieutenant Colonel George Villiers of the Grenadier Guards subsequently recovered the Prince's uniform and personal effects. He brought them back to England in January 1880 and on Queen Victoria's orders handed them over to Empress Eugênie. Funded by subscription in both France and England, a white marble recumbent effigy on a sarcophagus was erected in St George's Chapel, Windsor. Inscribed on it is a prayer that was found written in the Prince's notebook. Prince Imperial Road in Woolwich was named after him and a statue was also erected at RMA Woolwich and removed to RMA Sandhurst when the 'Workshop' closed in 1947.

Empress Eugênie was unable to obtain permission to build a mausoleum at Chislehurst and in 1883 commissioned Gabriel Destailleur to build St Michael's Abbey in Hampshire. The bodies of the Emperor and the Prince Imperial were interred there in 1888. 'The church of St Michael's Abbey, Farnborough, is designed in soaring, spiky French flamboyant Gothic, surmounted by a dome that pays homage to that of the Invalides in Paris beneath which Napoleon I is buried with the full honours of the French state'.[23] In accordance with French medieval tradition, a colony of monks was established to pray for the souls of the departed and care for the Abbey. Originally they were from France, but since the end of the Second World War they have been provided by Prinknash Abbey in Gloucestershire. The Spanish-born Empress died whilst visiting her family in Madrid on 11 July 1920 and her body was interred in the Abbey alongside her husband and son. Website at www.farnboroughabbey.org

---

[21] J P Mackinnon and S H Shadbolt *The South African Campaign of 1879* published by Greenhill Books.
[22] *The Times* 5 and 7 July 1879.
[23] *The Times* 30 March 2002.

# THE ROYAL ARTILLERY AFGHAN/ZULU WAR MEMORIAL

On 21 July 1871 a letter appeared in *The Times* newspaper which stated that it had been decided that a memorial would be erected to commemorate all ranks of the Royal Regiment of Artillery who had fallen in the campaigns in Afghanistan and South Africa. It further announced that the Royal Artillery Memorial Committee had selected His Serene Highness Count Gleichen as sculptor. The Count's successful design was selected by the Royal Artillery Memorial Committee from a number submitted.

As a nod to convention Gleichen ornamented it on the left side with copper coloured Zulu shields, spears, knobkerries and on the right with Afghan shields, powder flasks and flintlock pistols. The central tablet commemorates by name all 379 gunners who fell in both Afghanistan and Africa. Gleichen's design is particularly noteworthy, as it represented a significant departure from what had gone before on a number of levels. Firstly, it collectively commemorated a body of men specifically by name and the names were legible and could be read by those who had served with these men, or their kin. Secondly, it did not employ figurative sculpture. Thirdly, the form chosen in the age before the advent motor transport presented considerable handling and transportation problems and these were overcome ingeniously by cutting the boulder into five sections where it was quarried and transporting them to Woolwich by railway and then carting them up the hill to the Barracks. The granite monolith was skilfully reassembled on site and one needs to look hard to see the join. The memorial was for many years tucked away in a square in the Royal Artillery Barracks, but it may now be seen by the public outside Napier Lines in Repository Road, Woolwich in South East London.

# COLONEL FRED BURNABY

Frederick Gustavus Burnaby was born at Bedford, son of the Reverend Gustavus Burnaby of Somerby Hall, Leicestershire on 3 March 1842 and educated initially at Harrow, from where he was rusticated to Oswestry School in 1857 after objecting to the practice of 'fagging'. Aged 16 he passed the officer entry examination for the army and was gazetted cornet in the 3rd Regiment of Cavalry of the Household Brigade in 1859. Standing 6 feet 4 inches tall and with a 47 inch chest, he boxed and performed feats of strength. He once bent a poker round the Prince of Wales' neck after dinner. He stood unsuccessfully for parliament in 1878 as Tory candidate for Birmingham against the (then) Liberal Joseph Chamberlain and his method of dealing with hecklers at public meetings was spectacular. He is recorded as plunging into audiences to thump opponents, or physically lifting hecklers out of the crowd with one hand and depositing them on the platform to explain themselves. He was a skilled balloonist and flew solo from England to France in the balloon *Eclipse* on 23 March 1882.

General Charles Gordon was appointed Governor General of the Sudan by the Khedive of Egypt on 3 May 1877. He introduced wholesale reform to that country's administration and abolished slavery. His departure in 1880 created a dangerous vacuum which was filled in May 1881 by the Mahdi, who proclaimed himself twelfth Imam. His army annihilated Colonel Williams Hicks' force at El Obeid on 2 November 1883. Burnaby was present at the first and second Battles of El Teb. In the first, the Egyptian soldiery fled the field. In the second, on 21 February 1884, the presence of British troops ensured a bloodier outcome. In that engagement Burnaby is recorded as being the first man to have mounted the parapet and his lethal presence with a double-barrelled shotgun led to questions in the House of Commons. Prime Minister Gladstone misread the situation in the Sudan and sent Gordon back on a mission to pacify the Mahdi. 'The Mahdi's success and influence had grown since the battles of El Teb: he refused all Gordon's approaches and in a short time was investing him in Khartoum. Reluctantly Gladstone sanctioned a relief force commanded by General Sir Garnet Wolseley. Burnaby was anxious to be in at this, but knew that he would not be allowed to go by the Commander-in-Chief of the Army, the great Duke of Cambridge, nevertheless he set off for Cairo in a private capacity. Wolseley writing home to his wife says: "I have had a telegram from Burnaby, saying he will be in Cairo on the 20th inst. There will be the devil's own row if I give him anything to do, and yet I would like to do so, as he is clever and as brave as a lion. I shall let him come to the front at any rate, and if there is fighting he shall have a place on the forefront of the battle which will please him and confound his enemies," He was, in fact, given a sector of the Nile to supervise the hauling and passage of boats through the cataracts, but when urgent news came of the imminent danger to Khartoum and the garrison, Burnaby was allowed to join the desert force under General Sir Herbert Stewart, to whose staff he was appointed. This force was to cut off the bend in the Nile from Korti to Metemmeh, where transports from Khartoum were awaiting them.'[24] Burnaby was killed on 17 January 1885 at the Battle of Abu Klea whilst rescuing skirmishers outside the British infantry square. He was buried where he fell. Lieutenant Lord Binning of The Blues later said: 'In our little force, his death caused a feeling akin to consternation. In my own detachment many of the men sat down and cried.' The forms of memorialisation to Colonel Burnaby's memory included an organ at Oswestry School, a stained glass window in St Peter's Church Bedford (1885), the David and Jonathan Window in Somerby Church, a red marble plaque in Harrow School Chapel, two stone tablets in Holy Trinity Church, Windsor (1886) and a 50 ft tall Portland stone obelisk with a medallion portrait erected in the grounds of St Philip's Cathedral, Birmingham (1885). After the Second World War the organ at Oswestry needed refurbishment and the greater part of the expense was borne by Mrs Margaret Buchanan in memory of her son who had died whilst serving in the RAF. Ian Buchanan had served as the Chapel's organist whilst a pupil at the School.

---

[24] R R Oakley *A History of Oswestry School* London 1964.

## MAJOR GENERAL CHARLES GORDON

In 1863 Charles George Gordon was nominated by the British Government to succeed the remarkable American adventurer Frederick Townsend Ward as commander of the 'Ever Victorious Army' in the service of the Imperial Chinese Government. The Taiping Rebellion (1850-1864) was the bloodiest conflict of the 19th century, with over twenty million dead. Gordon resigned his commission after the Chinese Government executed rebel leaders to whom he had granted safe conduct. His service in China earned him the nickname 'Chinese Gordon'. The grateful Chinese Government awarded him the honours of mandarin. By the end of the campaign Gordon was a Field Marshal in the Imperial Chinese Army, a Lieutenant Colonel in the British Army and a Captain in the Royal Engineers. In 1884 he was sent back to Khartoum to supervise the evacuation of the Sudan by Egyptian forces. He was besieged there for over a year and killed when it fell to the forces of the Mahdi on 26 January 1885. General Sir Charles Wilson reached Khartoum two days later. Prime Minister Gladstone's vacillation in mounting an expedition to rescue Gordon caused public outrage and political uproar. It was said that had Colonel Fred Burnaby survived, Gordon would have been saved.

    The brooding depiction of a hatless Gordon carrying a bible and a cane, with his left foot resting on a shattered cannon barrel, was sculpted by Hamo Thornycroft and originally erected in Trafalgar Square. It was inaugurated on 16 October 1888 by David Plunket, First Commissioner of Works. Commencing with the Crimea, every campaign in which Gordon served was carved on the plinth. It cost £3,000, which was paid out of the £20,000 voted his family by Parliament. The statue was removed from the Square in 1943 and spent the rest of the war at Mentmore Towers. It was re-erected in 1953 on Victoria Embankment. Each January yellow wreaths are laid at the statue by the Gordon family, the Old Gordonians, the Gordon Foundation and the Governors, staff and pupils of Gordon's School at Woking in Surrey. The ceremony is followed by a memorial service attended by the entire school at Guildford Cathedral. The school was founded in 1885 at the express wish of Queen Victoria as the National Memorial to General Gordon. A bronze statue of him by T S Burnett also stands in front of Gordon's College in Aberdeen (1888). Gordon's full-length portrait in the yellow court dress of a mandarin hangs in the Royal Engineers Officers Mess at Chatham.

# THE WATERLOO MEMORIAL

In 1887 the Municipality of Brussels decided to close a number of old cemeteries and transfer the bodily remains to a new cemetery at Everè, a suburb in the north-east of the city between the Dieghem and Louvain Roads. The site was donated by the Municipality of Brussels. It was felt by many that the opportunity should be taken to secure permanent commemoration in the cemetery of the British dead from the Battle of Waterloo. In due course committees were formed in Brussels, London and Antwerp for the collection of subscriptions to a 'Fund for erecting a monument over the remains of British Officers and Men who fell during the Waterloo Campaign'. Unusually, a contribution of £500, about one fifth of the total cost, was donated by the British Government.

The memorial took the form of a Britannia, holding a trident in her right hand, her helmet in her left. Standing on a separate base, she overlooks a draped coffin further adorned with two panoplias and three lions. It was designed and executed by the anglophile Belgian sculptor Comte Jacques de Lalaing assisted by the architect Geerling. The memorial is highly unusual because it incorporates a vault containing the remains of 15 officers and one warrant officer. Their remains were transferred from the cemeteries of Brussels, Quatre Bras, Quartier Leopold, St Gilles, Waterloo and Hougoumont Farm. They are buried in the vault in separate graves, each covered by an inscribed stone slab. These, the only remains traced in 1887, in effect symbolise the 12,000 British dead of the battle. On both sides of the entrance to the vault are shields bearing the names of the regiments which took part. The memorial was inaugurated by the Duke of Cambridge on 26 August 1890. It is maintained on behalf of the UK Ministry of Defence by the Commonwealth War Graves Commission. Interestingly, given the critically important role played by the Prussians at the Battle of Waterloo, Everè was one of the locations from which German zeppelins flew to bomb mainland Britain during the Great War. In 2002 it became apparent that the provision of a new trident for the memorial in the early 1960s had created a number of problems, because it was too heavy for the structure, resulting in movement and fissures in Britannia's right hand and shoulder. In 2004 rectification works were being undertaken by the Janet and Andrew Naylor Sculpture and Conservancy Consultancy in concert with the Low Countries Sculpture Association.

# THE DUKE OF WELLINGTON MEMORIAL, ST PAUL'S CATHEDRAL

Although it would have horrified him had he known it, the Iron Duke enjoyed the unusual distinction of being late for his own funeral on 18 November 1852. His hearse, a carriage decorated with war trophies and weighing some 18 tons, was so heavy the horses pulling it were unable to ascend the hill from Ludgate Circus to St Paul's Cathedral. Sailors were sent for post-haste from the Pool of London and 13,000 of the assembled great and good waited until the sailors hauled the hearse up the hill with ropes. Thus was established the tradition of Royal Navy sailors hauling the hearse at state funerals. 83 Chelsea pensioners attended the funeral in their distinctive red coats, their number being the age of the Duke at his death.

Dr Alan Borg wrote: 'The official memorial to Wellington is in St Paul's Cathedral, consisting of a tall canopied tomb by Alfred Stephens and crowned incongruously with an equestrian figure by John Tweed'.[25] Standing on the north side of the nave, it is the most remarkable and certainly the grandest memorial in St Paul's. It was designed in approximately 1856 by Alfred Stevens and he spent most of the last 20 years of his life working on it. His pupil Hugh Stannus completed the main structure in 1878, three years after Stevens' death. In 1901 the sculptor John Tweed commenced work on the memorial's crowning feature, Wellington on his charger Copenhagen. After a long-running controversy and a great deal of debate in the press, it was finally completed in 1912.

Whilst the design (above) included a tomb, the Duke's immense Cornish granite casket designed by Francis Cranmer Penrose is actually situated in below in the crypt, nearby to that of Admiral Viscount Nelson. The Iron Duke's casket was so large it had to be lowered into the crypt through a hole cut in the Cathedral's floor. The banners hung about the Duke's tomb were made specifically for his funeral procession. Originally, there was one for the Kingdom of Prussia. It was removed from the crypt during the Great War and has never been reinstated.

---

[25] Alan Borg *War Memorials* p. 43.

# FIELD MARSHAL LORD NAPIER OF MAGDALA

Field Marshal Lord Napier's five metre tall equestrian statue stands in Kensington Gore near the Albert Hall in London. It is a replica of that originally sculpted by Sir Joseph Boehm and erected by public subscription in Calcutta in 1883, (removed to Barrackpore in the 1970s). After Boehm's death in 1890, the above replica was supervised by Alfred Gilbert and cast by Singer & Co of Frome and erected in Waterloo Place. It was inaugurated by the Prince of Wales on 8 July 1891. On 4 June 2004 the London *Evening Standard* reported that an Italian artist named Eleonora Aguiari had obtained permission from the present Lord Napier to cover the entire statue in red gaffer tape. The 'enwrapment' apparently forming part of her graduation show from the Royal Academy of Art. On 9 June 2004 the *Standard* published a letter from Major H G N Gore who wrote: 'I was intrigued to see the picture of my grandfather's statue in Queen Anne's Gate (4 June) wrapped up in red tape by Ms Aguiari. My mother was Lord Napier's youngest daughter and I suspect might not have approved. The statue shows Lord Napier glancing up and to the right. In its original position in Waterloo Place, he would seem to be looking at the window of the room he normally stayed in at his club, The Senior (now the Institute of Directors). The statue was moved in 1921 at the request of Queen Alexandra to make way for one of King Edward VII. My grandmother could only agree to a royal request.' The front of the plinth bears the inscription:

"LORD NAPIER OF MAGDALA G.C.B. G.C.S.I.
FIELD MARSHAL
AND
CONSTABLE OF THE TOWER OF LONDON
BORN 6 DEC 1810 DIED 14 JAN 1890"

The rear bears the inscription:

"ERECTED BY HIS COUNTRYMEN
MDCCCXCI
HE RESTS IN ST PAUL'S CATHEDRAL"

# FIELD MARSHAL FREDERICK SLEIGH, EARL ROBERTS OF KANDAHAR, PRETORIA AND WATERFORD VC OM

Frederick Sleigh Roberts was born at Cawnpore in India on 30 September 1832 and educated at Eton, Sandhurst and Addiscombe and was commissioned a second lieutenant in the Bengal Artillery. By 1878 he had advanced to the rank of Major General. He commanded one of the three divisions that invaded Afghanistan from India that year. He seized Kabul in 1879 and the following year led the relief of the British troops besieged in Kandahar, where he defeated the Afghans and ended the war. He was promoted Field Marshal in 1895. In 1899 his only son Lieutenant Frederick Roberts VC died needlessly in General Buller's fiasco at Colenso. In response to Buller's disastrous leadership, Roberts was appointed commander of the British forces in South Africa and by December 1900 had relieved Kimberley, taken Pretoria and handed over to Kitchener. In 1901 Roberts was created earl and appointed Commander-in-Chief of the British Army. He became the most distinguished and efficient British army commander of the Victorian era, earned the grateful thanks of Parliament several times and was duly loaded with honours by a grateful nation. He retired in 1904 and died from pneumonia on 14 November 1914 at St Omer in France whilst visiting his beloved Indian troops. He was buried in St Paul's Cathedral.

In 1894 a fund was established in Calcutta which intended to commission his portrait in oils, but the appeal raised so much money that its committee discovered that they could afford a bronze equestrian monument instead and commissioned the eminent Victorian sculptor Harry Bates RA (1850-99) to undertake the work. The statue was inaugurated by the Viceroy on the Maidan in Calcutta in March 1898. It was shifted by the Indian authorities to Nasik Road Camp, Deolali in the 1970s. A full-sized copy was erected at Park Terrace, Glasgow in 1916 and another on Horse Guards Parade Ground in 1924 (pictured above). Harry Bates' maquette was exhibited at the RA in 1898 and to the surprise of the Royal United Services Institute for Defence and Security Studies was identified by the author as residing on the mantelpiece of their library in July 2004.

# OLIVER CROMWELL

Having defeated the Royalists in England's civil war, Oliver Cromwell closed that chapter of England's history by stage-managing the execution of King Charles I in Whitehall on 30 January 1649. He then turned his attention to Ireland, where both the Protestant and Catholic populations were unreconciled to the notion of being governed by an English republic. Cromwell perceived their continuing support for the House of Stuart as a direct threat to the new order and landed at Dublin with an army of 12,000 men on 13 August. His campaign that autumn was a resounding military success and he gave no quarter. There followed deportations, the confiscation of estates, plague, famine and the death of a third of Ireland's population. All of which ensured that the real losers in England's civil war would be the Irish. Cromwell's mercilessness earned him their undying hatred. His campaign, its horrific aftermath and bitter legacy would poison Anglo-Irish relations for three centuries.

In 1894 a proposal was mooted to erect a statue of Oliver Cromwell in the Palace of Westminster to mark the tercentenary of his birth. The prime mover behind the proposal was Prime Minister, Lord Rosebery, who was 'sent to Coventry' for his presumption by an unamused Queen Victoria. He would learn that the crime of regicide knows no forgiveness, apparently a lesson not learned by others. In 1912 Winston Churchill, as First Lord of the Admiralty, attempted to name a Royal Navy warship after the Lord Protector and earned himself the anger of King George V for his pains. In 1894 Ireland's MPs sat in the House of Commons and they took the proposal as a deliberate insult. There followed a first class hoo-ha with deputations being sent over from Ireland, hundreds of petitions being sent to Parliament, a debate and a vote in the House that the Government embarrassingly lost by 137 votes, followed by a retaliatory Motion from the Irish Members to reduce the salary of the First Commissioner of Works. Every development in the long-running controversy was gleefully and often entertainingly chronicled by the press. Cromwell eventually got his statue. Sculpted in bronze by Hamo Thornycroft, it stands outside Parliament in Palace Yard. There was no inauguration ceremony and workmen removed its coverings in the early hours of 14 November 1899.[26] Rosebery was rumoured to have contributed £3,000 towards its cost and he gave a speech on Cromwell's merits that night to a packed Queen's Hall. Unsurprisingly, Her Majesty's Government took no action on Viscount Sidmouth's amusing proposal for the erection of a statue to Guy Fawkes,[27] regarded by some as: 'The last man to have entered Parliament with honest intentions'.

---

[26] *The Times* 15 November 1899.
[27] *The Times* 4 November 1899.

# THE SOUTH AFRICAN WAR

The South African War 1899-1902 was significant in that, after initial resistance by the War Office, for the first time British volunteer formations served overseas and this is reflected in the memorials that commemorated those who died whilst serving. Utilitarian modes of commemoration were often employed, a good example being the erection of 18 memorial cottages all over the UK in memory of HSH Prince Christian Victor of Schleswig-Holstein (grandson of Queen Victoria), who died in 1900 from enteric fever at Pretoria whilst serving as a major in the King's Royal Rifle Corps. He, along with three other alumni, were commemorated on the east wall of the Chapel at Magdalen College, Oxford. Another good example may be taken from the installation of gas standards (subsequently converted to electricity) in the choir of St Lawrence Church, Alton, Hants to commemorate those Altonians who fell. The Midland Railway Memorial at Derby, the first recorded railway memorial, dates from this war, as do the first war memorials commemorating women. The Officers Mess of the Inns of Court & City Yeomanry in London possesses a silver mounted horse's hoof snuff box which commemorates the men of the City of London Yeomanry who died. The names of the 114 Jews who fell may be found inscribed on a tablet in the Chapel of Willesden Cemetery. The memorial pictured above is the Worcester Boer War Memorial in the grounds of Worcester Cathedral. It was sculpted by Robert Colton and inaugurated by Lieutenant General N G Lyttleton on 23 September 1908. Tablets were also erected at St Mary's Hospital, Paddington to their staff and also at St Botolph's Church, Bishopgate, London to the members of the Honourable Artillery Company who died. St Paul's Cathedral, London contains a plaque with 13 names on, erected: 'TO THE MEMORY OF THE JOURNALISTS WHO LOST THEIR LIVES WHILE SERVING AS SPECIAL CORRESPONDENTS IN THE SOUTH AFRICAN WAR 1899 - 1902'. What is especially noticeable in statuary of the period is the presence of the pith helmet. The Army Ordnance Corps Memorial was originally erected at Artillery Place, Woolwich, but moved in 1950 to Princess Royal Barracks at Camberley, Surrey. In this example, the figure is kitted out rather in the manner of Lionel Jeffries playing the part of 'Grandad' in the film *Chitty Chitty Bang Bang*. The steel helmet or 'tin lid' would only arrive with the Great War and the difference between Boer War and Great War statuary can often be deduced from this tell-tale detail.

## THE UNION JACK CLUB

The notion of a club for Servicemen in transit through London was conceived by Ethel McCaul, RRC who had nursed in South Africa during the Boer War. She was appalled by the conditions endured by soldiers and their families whilst awaiting rail transportation from Waterloo Station, the principal railhead leading to the ports and garrisons of the British Empire. With no accommodation to be had in the area, they were in effect living rough on the streets. Her vision and energy ensured that this situation would change. An appeal for funds was launched at the Mansion House by the Lord Mayor of London in February 1903. All manner of entertainments and concerts were held to raise funds. On one occasion an 'Ice Carnival' was held during which King Edward VII persuaded John Philip Sousa[28] to donate the proceeds of the *Jack Tar March* which he had written overnight. A copy is displayed in the Club. The foundation stone was laid by the Prince of Wales (later King George V) on 21 July 1904.[29] King Edward VII officially opened the establishment on 1 July 1907 as 'A national memorial to the men who died in the South African War and a continual benefit to soldiers and sailors'.[30] When construction was completed at No 91 Waterloo Road at the end of 1904, the establishment had 208 bedrooms and extensive public rooms. Membership was restricted to servicemen below the rank of commissioned officer. No officer was permitted to be a member of the Club. (Serving Service personnel are automatically members of the Club without fee). One of the Club's rooms is named the Lawrence Room after Lawrence of Arabia (1888-1935) who used the establishment whilst serving in the ranks of the RAF after the Great War under the *nom de guerre* Aircraftsman Shaw. Many of the rooms were originally sponsored by regiments or companies and their brass plates, which were originally affixed to the doors of the bedrooms, are displayed on the walls of the Club's common areas. The Club's Library was furnished and decorated in memory of those 114 members of the Jewish faith who lost their lives in the Boer War.

For many years after the Great War an annual donation was sent to the Club anonymously. Each payment came with the words: 'In gratitude for a scrap of comfort' and these words sum up the ethos of the Club. They appear on a marble plaque in the Club's reception area. Further additions, including the establishment of a separate Families Club, were made before and after the Great War so that by 1939 the Club contained a total of some 800 bedrooms. During the Second World War, Waterloo was heavily bombed in the Blitz and the Club sustained damage, but survived. By the late sixties the Club required a considerable amount of refurbishment to bring it up to modern standards and in 1970 it was decided to pull it down and re-erect it on the same site. The Club concluded a deal with the Industrial and Commercial Finance Corporation (now Investment In Industry - 3i), whereby they would build three tower blocks on condition that they could lease one of them for a period of 125 years for a peppercorn rent; the remaining two tower blocks would constitute the new Club, thus combining under one roof the functions of the original Club and the Families Club. The new Club was officially opened by the Queen on 12 February 1976. The radical downsizing of Britain's armed forces in the post-Imperial era and again in the post-Cold War era has in recent years led to the Club widening its membership criteria. The doors were therefore opened to such bodies as the Police, the Fire and Ambulance Services, the Merchant Navy, HM Coastguard, the Prison Service, the Civil Service and other groups sponsored by reputable organisations. The Club has probably the finest display of Victoria Cross holders in the country and is the location of the biannual reunion of the members of Victoria Cross and George Cross Association. Whilst Waterloo has changed radically in recent years, after 100 years the Club continues to carry out the task for which it was originally conceived by the remarkable lady who founded it and her portrait in oils hangs in the Club's reception area.

---

[28] Director of the United States of America Marine Corps Band - 'The March King'.
[29] *The Times* 22 July 1904.
[30] *The Times* 2 July 1907.

# THE UNION JACK CLUB

The Club in 2003.

The Memorial Wall in the basement of the Club.

# THE ROYAL ARTILLERY BOER WAR MEMORIAL

The Royal Regiment of Artillery has fought in all sizeable battlefield engagements involving the British Army since its formal establishment in 1716. Traditionally, the British monarch is Captain-General of the Regiment. Batteries are often named after engagements where the regiment has distinguished itself, or rendered signal service, and in some cases after individuals too. Unlike other regiments of the British Army, units of the Royal Artillery do not carry regimental colours; therefore battle honours are not awarded them. When the Regiment parades with its guns these are saluted, or paid honours in place of a colour. The Royal Horse Artillery on parade with its guns takes precedence over all other regiments of the British Army.[31] The regiment's motto is: "UBIQUE, QUO FAS ET GLORIA DUCUNT"[32] - Translated: "EVERYWHERE, WHITHER RIGHT AND GLORY LEAD".

In the Victorian era the loss of British guns on a battlefield would be considered a national disaster. The Iron Duke never lost a gun in all his battles and this well-known fact would in moments of crisis have an irrational influence on the thought processes of a number of British commanders, the actions of General Raglan at Balaclava and General Buller at Colenso being good illustrations of this point. In 1905 the Royal Artillery Memorial Committee convened to erect a memorial to commemorate the 1,000 gunners who had died in the campaign in South Africa and the memorial they commissioned stands on the corner of The Mall and the Horse Guards Approach Road, St James's Park in London. It was designed by Sir Aston Webb, sculpted by Professor Robert Colton[33] and inaugurated in 1910. The central feature is a curved plinth on which stands a bronze winged figure of Peace subduing a horse representing War. On the Portland stone posts either side of the memorial are bronze panels, which list the name, rank and battery of every officer and gunner who fell in South Africa during the Boer War. The bronze band on the rear of the memorial carries the inscription:

"ERECTED BY THE OFFICERS AND MEN OF THE
ROYAL ARTILLERY IN MEMORY OF THEIR HONOURED DEAD
SOUTH AFRICA 1899 – 1902"

---

[31] Queen's Regulations 1873.
[32] Motto granted in *London Gazette* 10 July 1832.
[33] William Robert Colton (1867-1921). Born Paris, France. Studied at Lambeth Art School and South Kensington School of Art. Trained under William Silver Frith. Elected ARA 1903, Professor of Sculpture at the RA 1907-10, PRBS 1919, RA 1919.

# THE GUY'S HOSPITAL BOER WAR MEMORIAL

After the Boer War, friends, former students and staff of Guy's decided to erect a memorial to commemorate the Hospital's staff who had died in South Africa. It cost £260 and took the form of a 7 ft 6 inch tall and 6 ft 6 inch wide marble drinking fountain. It is situated below a fanlight on the corner of a building abutting the Hospital's colonnade. It was designed by Frederick Wheeler, FRIBA (1853-1931) and built by the Coalbrookdale Company.[34] The base is of Sienna marble, the columns are of verte-antico, the entablature is of pavanazza and the ionic capitals are of gunmetal, as is the lettering. The memorial was inaugurated by General Sir Richard Harrison,[35] one of the Hospital's governors on 3 July 1903. It carries the names of 11 men in the order of their joining Guy's Hospital:

THOMAS JONES - Superintendent of the Welsh Army Hospital, Springfontein. Died there.
QUINTEN REID VETCH - Major, Cape Medical Staff Corps, died Cape Town.
CHARLES POPE WALKER - Major, RAMC, died during the Siege of Ladysmith.
FREDERICK MURRAY RUSSELL - Captain, New Zealand Contingent, killed in action at Rhenoster Kop.
HUGH ARNOLD BRYANT - Civil Surgeon. Died at Bloemfontein.
FRANCIS WELLFORD - Surgeon-Captain, 7th Imperial Yeomanry. Died of wounds received at the Battle of Vlakfontein.
STANLEY WHICHER - Civil Surgeon, Natal Field Force. Died at Mooi River.
RICHARD TRUMAN FITZ-HUGH - Civil Surgeon attached to Imperial Yeomanry Hospital, Dielfontein. Died there.
HUGH BERNARD ONRAET - Lieutenant, RAMC. Killed in the Battle of Pieter's Hill.
CHARLES BERNARD SELLS - Surgical Assistant at Imperial Yeomanry Hospital, Dielfontein where he died.
LAWSON JERVIS HUGHES - Mounted Medical Orderly, Imperial Yeomanry. Killed in action at Kroonstad after refusing to surrender.

---

[34] *The Times* 4 July 1903, p. 14.
[35] General Sir Richard Harrison (1837-1931). Educated at Harrow and RMA Woolwich. Commissioned Royal Engineers. Served as Assistant Quartermaster-General to Lord Chelmsford in South Africa and was censured by Field Marshal HRH the Duke of Cambridge, Commander-in-Chief of the British Army over the instructions he gave to Lieutenant Carey, which resulted in the death of the Prince Imperial. Harrison's son-in-law, Lieutenant Richard John Jelf, RE died on board the troopship DILWARA on 2 June 1900 aged 28.

## THE NORWICH BOER WAR MEMORIAL

The Norfolk Boer War Memorial stands at a busy traffic junction in Castle Meadow, Norwich. Replete with symbolism, it takes the form of a graceful 9 foot tall bronze winged figure of Peace alighting on the globe, whilst sheathing a sword in a scabbard. Funded by public subscription, it was inaugurated by Lieutenant-General Sir A S Wynne on 17 November 1904.[36] The memorial was sculpted by George Wade and the architect was Fairfax Wade. This remarkable memorial records by name on bronze panels 294 officers and men from Norfolk who died in the South African War. The general inscription reads:

"ERECTED BY THE COUNTY OF NORFOLK AND CITY
OF NORWICH AS A TRIBUTE TO THE MEMORY
OF THE GALLANT NORFOLK MEN WHO DIED FOR
THEIR COUNTRY DURING THE WAR, 1899-1902"

---

[36] *The Times* 18 November 1904 p.6.

## THE SCULPTURE OF CAPTAIN ADRIAN JONES

Detail of the Royal Marines Memorial in The Mall.

The Carabiniers (6th Dragoons) Boer War Memorial, Chelsea Embankment, London.

# THE TIRAH MEMORIAL

The Tirah Campaign was fought by the British Army against Afridi tribesmen on the North Western Frontier of India in the period 1897-98 and the Oxford Light Infantry were present. 'In 1897 the 52nd was once more in the Punjab at Ferozepore where orders arrived for the regiment to join the Tirah Expedition on the North West Frontier. The tribal territory between India and Afghanistan was a mountainous strip inhabited by tribes often at war amongst themselves and sometimes in temporary unity against the British. Incredibly tough and agile, fine marksmen, and as elusive as morning mist, they could also show Oriental patience in watching the ways of each regiment before pouncing on any weakness. The 52nd first appeared on the scene in September operating against the Mohmands north of the River Kabul.'[37] The memorial to Oxford's fallen in that campaign was erected in 1900 and it stands in Bonn Square, Oxford.[38] The 25 foot tall obelisk was made of stone from Monk's Park Quarry, Bath. It stands on a base of Doulting stone consisting of three plinths topped by a truncated obelisk. The overall effect is untidy. The obelisk bears a sculpted representation of the strung bugle horn badge of the 52nd (Oxfordshire Light Infantry) Regiment. In March 2004 the memorial was found to be in poor condition. The stonework had at some time in the past been repointed, but a number of lead letters carrying both the names and general inscription were missing. The fatalities commemorated on the memorial are listed by category. These included: 'Died of disease on active service', 'Died of wounds', 'Killed in action' and 'Died of disease'. The memorial is an interesting example of poor alphabeticisation, with the names WILTSHIRE and WIGGINS listed in the wrong order.

The Memorial also includes the name of Major A B THRUSTON who was killed at Fort Lubwas in Uganda on 19 October 1897. He is also commemorated by a monument in the crypt of St Paul's Cathedral, London. (A fluent Arabic speaker, he was in charge of a garrison who were part of General Sir Hector MacDonald's expedition in 1897. Thruston was killed by 'mutinous native officers' who shot him in cold blood with two other officers). The names of the Oxford Light Infantry casualties of the period from were listed on three sides of the plinth of the Tirah Memorial with the general inscription on the fourth side. It reads:

> "THIS MONUMENT WAS ERECTED
> BY THE OFFICERS NON COM-
> MISSIONED OFFICERS & MEN
> OF THE SECOND BATTALION
> OXFORDSHIRE LIGHT INFANTRY
> IN MEMORY OF THEIR COM-
> RADES WHO DIED BETWEEN
> THE 15 AUGUST 1897 AND
> THE 4 OF NOVEMBER 1898"

Under the changes instituted by the Haldane Reforms[39] the Oxfordshire Light Infantry was redesignated the Oxfordshire and Buckinghamshire Light Infantry in 1908.

The memorial to the Oxfordshire Light Infantry's fallen of the South African War is at Magdalen College, Oxford and their Memorial Chapel is in Christ Church Cathedral, Oxford. Here the names of the fallen of the regiment are inscribed on a Roll of Honour preserved in a glass case. Memorial tablets to the men of the Imperial Yeomanry who fell in the South African War are also to be found in the Cathedral's south aisle.

---

[37] Philip Booth *The Oxfordshire & Buckinghamshire Light Infantry* Leo Cooper 1971.
[38] Previously New Road, Oxford. Renamed Bonn Square on 5 October 1974.
[39] Viscount Haldane (1856-1928) as Secretary of State for War 1905-12 was responsible for substantial army reform. Excluded from high office during the Great War because of his well-known pro-German sympathies.

# CHAPTER II

# THE GREAT WAR

# THE GREAT WAR

The Rhynie and Kearn War Memorial, Aberdeenshire.

The United Kingdom lost 723,000 men killed in the Great War; 63 per 1,000 males in the 15 - 49 age group, of whom 37,452 were officers. By contrast Germany lost 2,037,000 men; 125 per 1,000 males in the age group 15 - 49.[1]

Following long established tradition and even more understandably in view of the sheer number of casualties, neither the British Government, nor the newly-founded Imperial War Graves Commission, permitted repatriation of the war dead. As a result, millions of the bereaved at home were left without a tangible focus for their grief. The spontaneous erection of street shrines in urban areas provided food for thought for many communities and led to campaigns for the erection of permanent memorials to those who had died. Such was the scale of the British losses in the Great War, most communities have a war memorial and often more than one. Firms and municipal bodies had made lists of local men and women who were serving in the forces. As news of casualties reached home, these were amended and became revered objects, published or posted in a prominent place as testament to the loss of individual families and whole communities. Ordinarily, war memorials were raised by entire communities to commemorate their fallen, but they were also erected by schools, universities, businesses, clubs, municipal authorities, regiments and formations of the armed forces, or in some exceptional cases by the entire nation to commemorate a particular individual.

---

[1] J M Winter *World War I and the British People* London MacMillan 1986.

# WAR MEMORIAL COMMITTEES

There would also be memorials to commemorate battle exploits and feats of arms, the Western Front would also be heavily populated with memorials to the divisions, regiments and formations of the Allied armies that fought there. Both the Scots and the Welsh erected national memorials at home. Some memorials recorded the names of the fallen in full, with rank and unit and even the theatre of war, others just the names and initials. Many list no names whatsoever, in which case, the roll of honour would usually be held in the local church.

Memorialisation took a wide variety of forms, there would be cottage hospitals, cenotaphs, the Great War Cross, Celtic crosses, arches, clock towers, brasses, murals, locomotives, screen walls, ornamental fountains, columns, cottages for retired servicemen, artillery pieces, obelisks, memorial plaques, halls of remembrance, murals and books of remembrance. Statuary of all kinds with literal, religious, symbolic and allegorical figures would also appear. The commonest type of memorial would consist of a bronze soldier on a stone plinth situated in the high street, local churchyard, or dedicated garden of remembrance. The local community usually formed a war memorial committee and it would be composed of local worthies with civic leadership well to the fore, the mayor usually being invited to become *ex officio* chairman, the town clerk being appointed secretary and the local bank manager appointed treasurer. Many committees held public meetings where there would be discussion about who was to be commemorated, the form the monument would take, land acquisition, funding, sight lines etc. The key to obtaining consensus lay in the construction of a broad-based committee. 'Memorial committees normally had a structure which was intended to make them representative of the local community as a whole. The purpose of this arrangement was to encourage all sections of the community to contribute to the memorial and feel that their views were taken into account in deciding what sort of memorial to erect'.[2] The usual criteria for inclusion of names on the memorial were birth in the locality or a specific period of residence. When one includes regimental or formation memorials, an individual could easily appear on as many as four memorials. (Field Marshal Earl Kitchener appears on far more than that). If a committee encountered problems the process could drag on for years. The last unveiling of a memorial recorded by *The Times* newspaper before the outbreak of the Second World War was at The Mumbles, a resort near Swansea in July 1939. Regrettably, there are recorded instances of memorial committees dividing into factions and erecting rival memorials. Composition varied a great deal and a good example may be taken from the committee for Sleaford, Lincs. It was composed of 12 councillors, 12 clergy, 15 ratepayers, 18 ladies and 15 ex-Servicemen. In London, the Bethnal Green committee was composed of the local council, Christian clergy, the synagogue, two benevolent funds, the friendly societies, two hospital aid funds, the Union of Boot and Shoe Operatives, the rifle club and the special constables. In the case of regimental, divisional or corps memorials, the committee would be overwhelmingly composed of serving and retired senior officers. The War Office and Admiralty were not involved in the erection of community war memorials, other than answering specific enquiries from memorial committees concerning the details of Service personnel. The names of those to be commemorated were usually taken from the rolls of honour which were compiled by the War Office after the Armistice. Both the *Soldiers Roll of Honour* and the *Officers Roll of Honour* became available in March 1922. The *Soldiers Roll* was produced in eighty parts, the *Officers Roll* in two parts, Regular and Territorial. The rolls cost between one shilling and seven shillings and sixpence. The cost to the War Office had been over £10,000 and sales fell far short of expectations.

---

[2] Alex King *Memorials of the Great War in Britain*.

## FINANCE

The financing of war memorials is another interesting aspect of the memorialisation process, as funding was, then as now, raised by public subscription and private donation. One carrot and stick method used to encourage the tardy would be to advertise the intention to publish the names of all subscribers in the local press, in the hope that the odium of not seeing one's name there would compel individuals to subscribe. Professional fundraisers were frequently employed. If the committee took decisions that were not supported by the community, then it exercised the one power available to it and funding dried up until such time as consensus was re-established. The sum raised did of course determine the type of memorial that was erected. Most memorials cost between £1,000-£2,000 although some did come in under £1,000. The larger memorials in the cities, depending on how ambitious the committee was could cost many times this sum. Many of the fund raising schemes were ingenious. Charity balls, 'leave your change' boxes in shops, brass band concerts in the park and collections in cinemas would all feature. In both rural and urban areas there are well documented examples of great landowners and aristocrats erecting war memorials to the fallen of the community entirely at their own expense. In the case of the Metropolitan Railway, the company donated half the cost of the memorial, the men paid the other half by each donating a day's pay. Where the community was of modest means, such as the Dockland communities in the East End of London, this would inevitably be reflected in the nature and scale of their memorial. The records of Deptford Borough Council in South East London show that the Mayor was fined by the magistrates in June 1920 for running an illegal 'Derby Draw' in support of the memorial fund. (He was reported to the authorities by the local Council of Christian Churches). The Borough Council reaffirmed its 'unabated confidence' in its Mayor after his conviction. After widespread unrest in the army at the end of 1918, Winston Churchill, Secretary of State for War and Air, moved swiftly to speed up demobilisation. The veterans, unsurprisingly, had some strong views on the commemoration of their comrades and were usually consulted by memorial committees. There are examples of unilateral action by veterans when conventional avenues did not produce the results they desired. The most interesting manifestation of this was the erection of snow memorials. One inscribed "LEST WE FORGET" was built on Newtownards Green, Northern Ireland in the 1920's by veterans of the 36th (Ulster) Division to shame their local council into building a memorial to the fallen. This famous Division had served with distinction on the Western Front. Irony of ironies, the Somme Heritage Centre in Northern Ireland, located between Newtownards and Bangor, opened its doors for business in April 1994. There is also photographic evidence that a snow memorial was built in a coal yard at Pateley Bridge, North Yorkshire in 1921, which was inscribed "PB WAR MEMORIAL RIP". Another aspect of the veterans' involvement may be taken from following story relating to the decision to erect an ex-Serviceman's club: 'In North Wales, the Prestatyn branch of the Comrades of the Great War Association decided to have drinking facilities at their new club. A meeting of the Prestatyn Temperance Women's Group learnt of this: 'with deepest regret... The Prime Minister stated during the War that we had three great enemies to fight - Germany, Austria and drink. Our boys have defeated Germany and Austria, and we must help them to defeat Drink'.[3] Discontent among unemployed veterans would also lend colour to ceremonies. In the early 1920s there were reports of the silence at remembrance ceremonies being interrupted by shouts of 'Anyone want a medal?' The unscheduled singing of *The Red Flag* during the silence at the remembrance ceremony at Dundee[4] in 1921 caused a full scale riot and the ceremony ended with the veterans being dispersed by police with drawn truncheons.

---

[3] Angela Gaffney *Aftermath: Remembering the Great War in Wales.* University of Wales Press 1998.

[4] Winston Churchill's constituency. He lost the seat in the 1922 General Election.

# INAUGURATIONS AND CEREMONIES

Where the inauguration of a memorial was of such importance as that of the Royal Artillery Memorial at Hyde Park Corner, these occasions would involve royalty, senior church figures, generals, a constellation of VIPs, choirs, bands, widows, veterans and a cast of thousands. More usually inaugurations would be superintended by the local Bishop, Lord Lieutenant, Mayor and corporation, or by a military figure with local connections. There are also many recorded instances of parents of the fallen also carrying out this role. Penarth War Memorial in Wales was inaugurated by two mothers who had both lost three sons and the Greenwich War Memorial in south east London, was dedicated by Dr William Woodcock Hough, Bishop of Woolwich and inaugurated on 11 November 1922 by Mr Harry Bolton Sewell, who had also lost three sons, (one a VC). He was assisted by Charlotte Saunders, a girl whose father, a former postman, had also been killed. Committees paid careful attention to the date on which their memorial would be inaugurated. Examination of dates reveals that a considerable number were inaugurated on Remembrance Sunday or Armistice Day. However, other dates also had symbolic significance: The Bradford War Memorial was unveiled on 1 July 1922, the sixth anniversary of the first day of the Battle of the Somme (the Bradford Pals fought in that battle) and the Bury War Memorial in Lancashire, designed free of charge by Sir Edwin Lutyens,[5] was unveiled on 25 April 1925, the significance of this date being the tenth anniversary of the landings at Gallipoli, in which the Lancashire Fusiliers displaying incredible bravery earned immortal fame and 'six VCs before breakfast'. The Royal Naval Division Memorial on the Horse Guards Parade Ground was inaugurated the same day. The closest Sunday to 1 July is still the date for annual ceremonies for those (surviving) regiments and regimental associations with links to the Battle of the Somme.

Having established a focus for remembrance by erecting and inaugurating a war memorial, communities needed to organise appropriate ceremonies. This would involve the establishment of ritual and the consolations of organised religion. In consequence, religious leaders were heavily involved in giving a lead in deciding the form in which remembrance would be handled. Central government was not involved and local authorities were given a free hand to arrange ceremonies as they saw fit and there was considerable variation in their form.

Despite having opened negotiations with the Home Office as early as 1923, the first BBC radio broadcast of the National Ceremony at the Cenotaph would not take place until 1928 and this would give a significant lead to communities as to the form their own ceremonies would take from then on. As the years went by, the silence established itself as the focus of both the national ceremony and those conducted at local levels. Where ceremonies were conducted on a regimental or corps basis, the practice of amending prayers and hymns to incorporate the name of the formation concerned was often adopted, a practice that can be observed to the present day. The hymn *O Valiant Hearts* was composed by Sir John Stanhope Arkwright in 1919 and it remains one of the most moving of all pieces of music used at remembrancetide ceremonies.

The establishment of remembrance traditions also dates from the post-war period. A good example may be taken from St Andrew's Church, Cuffley, Herts. Each Remembrance Sunday, the vicar reads out the names of Cuffley's fallen followed by those of the 16 crew members of a German Navy Schutte-Lanz airship who were killed when it was shot down in the early hours of Sunday 3 September 1916 by the pilot Captain Leefe Robinson, VC RFC.

With the passage of time new traditions appear. On 11 November 2003 the Mayor of the Borough of Newham in London's East End observed the two minute silence at 11 o'clock on the steps of Newham Town Hall accompanied by the Borough's 'Civic Ambassador'.[6]

---

[5] The Lancashire Fusiliers had been Lutyens' father's regiment.
[6] *Stratford and Newham Express* 8 November 2003, p. 3.

# THE ARCHITECTS

There was another viewpoint to be considered, that of the architects who would design the memorials. The eminent architect Sir Herbert Baker set down his thoughts on the matter in his book *Architecture and Personalities* and he was well qualified to comment, as he was one of the Principal Architects of the Imperial War Graves Commission. This excerpt amply illustrates his feelings on the issue: 'My inclination for war memorials at home was the same as for the War Graves Cemetery, that generally they should express the sense of reverence and peace, "uniting the living with the dead in manifold memories." I must admit, however, that there is something to be said for the opposite point of view; for the public place "hard by the hurrying feet of men," the sentiment that has made the popular appeal of the Cenotaph. Yet my own thoughts always turned to the beauty associated with the churchyard and the cloister, a sacred *place*, a *temenos*. It was also my belief that war or other memorials lose much of their spiritual value and appeal if they are not placed in sites already hallowed by past associations or where these associations can grow in the course of the years, in peaceful places where attention is arrested and emotions heightened by their surroundings. Such sacred places, if they could not be found, must, I thought, be created. So when I was asked by the War Memorial Committee of the Royal Artillery to select a site and suggest designs for their memorial in London, I sought for some place where this "aura" might be found or created. The Committee had considered a site on the pavement at Hyde Park Corner, where the memorial now is. My first suggestion was to build a semicircular colonnade on the angle of the garden of Buckingham Palace where it fronts on Hyde Park Corner. There was to be a paved court in front and, in the centre of that or in a niche in the back wall of the colonnade, a group of statuary; bas-reliefs and inscriptions on the back wall could be added from time to time at the death of distinguished survivors of the war - and, alas! of another war! The whole might have become an enclosure sacred and dedicated to the Corps. But a proposal for a National War Memorial (to a design emanating from an official in the Board of Works), of a monstrous pylon in Hyde Park, so revolted public opinion that in answer to protests in Parliament the Government issued an edict that no land in the Parks would be given for any memorial. So this project for the Artillery had to be abandoned.' By coincidence, one of the most successful collaborations between an architect and a sculptor after the Great War was the Royal Artillery War Memorial in Hyde Park. The critic Gavin Stamp would write of it: 'Among regimental memorials, that to the Royal Artillery at Hyde Park is worthy of comparison with the War Graves Commission's work as it was designed by Holden and the sculptor Charles Jagger; the sculpture, the lettering and the general architectural form - together with the literal and brutal replica of a gun in stone - are all superbly integrated'.[7] On 16 January 2004 the sometimes controversial, but always erudite award-winning art critic Brian Sewell of the London *Evening Standard*, after years of hinting at such a judgement, finally got it off his chest and pronounced the Royal Artillery War Memorial: 'the greatest sculpture of the 20th century'.[8]

There appears to have been plenty of recycling of designs by both architects and sculptors alike and, whilst one obelisk or cenotaph looks pretty much like another, there are instances of duplication worthy of comment. A good example may be taken from ANZAC Square, Brisbane, Australia. Here the war memorial took the form of a circular classical colonnade and it looks uncannily like the American Memorial on the Butte de Mont Sec in France. It should be noted that in the period 1919-26, when the vast majority of memorials to the fallen of the Great War were erected, there were many recorded instances of generosity, with architects, masons and sculptors often donating services and materials for free.

---

[7] Gavin Stamp *Silent Cities*.
[8] Although often credited to Holden, the memorial was designed by his business partner Lionel Pearson (1879-1953).

# THE AIR WAR OVER BRITAIN

Britain's civilians got one hell of a rude awakening on 16 December 1914 when the German navy bombarded the towns of Hartlepool, Whitby and Scarborough. At this point they learned that civilians many miles from the battlefield would be legitimate military targets in the war. The most interesting manifestation of this development would be air warfare initially conducted by airships and later also by aircraft. Disturbingly, the invariable reaction of the civilian population would be to rush outdoors to observe a zeppelin raid in progress and the official total of civilian dead is 1,415 killed, but the real figure is higher, due to casualties succumbing to injuries. Death from shock was common and usually affected the very young and the elderly. This created a new dimension to the issue of commemoration and was in some instances addressed by placing the names of the civilians killed in raids alongside the names of the fallen on the local war memorial and this was certainly the case with the war memorials at Sheerness and Margate in Kent and also that which stands in the churchyard of St Stephen and St Wulfstan, Selly Park, Birmingham.

In the early hours of the morning of 1 April 1916 during an attack on the coast of Lincolnshire, a bomb was dropped by zeppelin L22 on the Baptist Chapel in Cleethorpes, which killed 27 men of the 3rd Battalion of the Manchester Regiment billeted there. 53 were wounded, with five dying later. A memorial was raised by public subscription and erected over a mass grave in Cleethorpes Cemetery. This was the biggest single loss of life in any air raid in the Great War. The Manchester Chapel at Cleethorpes Baptist Chapel was dedicated on 1 April 2001.[9]

A bomb dropped from a German airplane on the London County Council Upper North Street School, Poplar, London on 13 June 1917 killed 18 five-year old children. They were commemorated by the Air Raid Memorial, which takes the form of an angel standing on a pillar in Poplar Recreation Ground. Dr Alan Borg in his book *War Memorials* observed: 'This is by A R Adams of Poplar, who was clearly the local purveyor of tomb monuments and the result fails to match the tragedy.'

A plaque affixed to the outside of the Bedford Hotel, Bloomsbury, London underlines the disproportionate amount of attention the Holborn and Bloomsbury area received from the Germans in the Great War, probably due to direction finding reasons. The plaque records the events of the night of 24 September 1917 when 13 people were killed and 22 injured by a 112 pound bomb dropped from a Gotha bomber on to the steps of the old Bedford Hotel.

On the night of 19 October 1917 zeppelin L41 attacked the West Midlands. During the course of this raid, a bomb was dropped on the Austin Motor Works at Longbridge, Birmingham and two people were injured. A mile away at Northfield, the home of Dame Elizabeth Cadbury, her pet monkey Jacko died from fright at the sound of the explosion. (Interestingly, Dame Elizabeth's son, the pilot Major Egbert Cadbury, RFC, would be directly involved in the shooting down of zeppelins L21 and L70). Jacko was buried with due ceremony in Dame Elizabeth's pet cemetery. A triangular carved wooden headboard marks his grave. The memorial is still in existence and its inscription reads:

"JACKO
A MONKEY KILLED
WITH FRIGHT
CAUSED BY A ZEP
THAT CAME OVER
ONE NIGHT
1917"

---

[9] Thomas Fegan *The 'Baby Killers': German Air Raids on Britain in the First World War.*

# UTILITARIANISM

Utilitarian forms of commemoration were not unknown after the Great War but, as will be seen in this study, did not always produce satisfactory outcomes. This form was deliberately disregarded by the Imperial War Graves Commission. 'The Commission had always tried to avoid the possibility of any ambiguity in its memorials to the missing. It had set its face against buildings of practical utility, knowing that ultimately they must invite association with their function rather than with the sacrifices the dead had made'.[10] Interestingly, most French war memorials took a literal form, with utilitarian examples being only rarely found and these usually in the area that had known either occupation or the devastation of war.

Good examples of the utilitarian impulse in the UK were: the MacNaghten Library at Eton College, (1,160 Old Etonians were killed in the Great War), the Star and Garter Home at Richmond, as well as a substantial number of war memorial halls, chapels, clubs, sports fields and pavilions, hospitals, hospital wards and beds.

The Royal Scots Club in Edinburgh was founded in 1919 as a memorial to the 12,000 members of The Royal Scots (The Royal Regiment) who fell in the Great War. For many years membership was restricted to those who had served in the regiment, but in recent years this rule has been relaxed. The Scottish Veterans Garden City Association maintains cottages dating from the Great War for disabled ex-Service Personnel at Penicuik at the foot of the Pentland Hills.

Westfield Memorial Village was founded and built on land donated by the Lancaster industrialist Herbert Storey. Thomas Mawson the landscape architect designed the village in 1918. The War Memorial Village Council was formed and registered as a charity in 1919 with the primary aim of providing residential accommodation for Disabled and Necessitous Members and Ex-Members of His Majesty's Forces and their relatives and dependants who came from Lancashire and the North West of England. Finance was raised locally by public subscription and the first stage of the village was completed and opened on 27 November 1924 by Field Marshal Earl Haig. The War Memorial Village is a private estate of tree-lined streets with plentiful grassed areas. There are residents and community room committees who organise a variety of social functions and events, a bowling green a resident caretaker and gardener. In 1980 the tenants proposed that the running of the village was handed over to Northern Counties Housing Association and 23 cottages were sold.

In our own age the utilitarian forms employed in both World Wars continue to fall prey to property developers, cash-strapped NHS Trusts and sometimes local authorities. The weakness of the poorly-drafted legislation in this area has often permitted councils to wriggle out of their responsibilities, or else act in a perverse manner. Recent history is replete with interesting decisions made by local authorities and a particularly good example may be taken from the actions of Rhondda Cynon Taff Borough Council in Wales. In 2003 this council gave approval to a scheme for the redevelopment of Pontypridd town centre. These plans included the construction of a multi-storey car park for Sainsbury's Supermarket inside the grounds of the town's war memorial park. The grounds of Ynysangharad House had been purchased by public subscription in the period 1922-24 and they formed Pontypridd's war memorial to its fallen of the Great War and ownership was governed by a charitable trust deed. The grounds of the Park contained a cricket pitch, pavilions, tennis courts, a rugby pitch and a swimming pool. In short, a truly utilitarian war memorial available to all. The quality of the park's landscape was recognised by Cadw, the Welsh equivalent of English Heritage, which designated it as Grade II in their Historic Parks and Gardens Register.

---

[10] Philip Longworth *The Unending Vigil.*
[11] *Underground News*, November 2000, No 467, pp 431 - 432.

# MEMORIALISATION OF NOTABLE INDIVIDUALS

The poet Rupert Chawner Brooke was born in 1887 at Rugby, Warwickshire. 'He was educated at Rugby and Cambridge and his all-round talents, charm and looks soon made him a charismatic figure in literary and social circles, a Cambridge Apostle and Fellow of King's and a poet whose verse reached a wide audience through the first two volumes of Edward Marsh's Georgian Poetry.'[12] Upon the outbreak of war, he joined the Royal Naval Division and was appointed sub-lieutenant. Just before the Gallipoli Landings he died of septicaemia on a French hospital ship off the Greek island of Skyros on 23 April 1915. He was buried on Skyros. 'Freyberg, Browne, Lister and others of his friends had carried him up to an olive grove on the heights of the island, and had buried him there with a rough pile of marble on the grave'.[13] Brooke is commemorated by a marble relief of him in Rugby School Chapel (1919) by James Havard Thomas. The design of the relief was taken from a photograph of Brooke by the American photographer Sherril Schell in London in 1913. The memorial's text is Brooke's poem *The Soldier* 'If I should die. Think only this of me; that there's some corner of a foreign field…..'

Castle Drogo in Devon was designed by Sir Edwin Lutyens and built by Julius Drew. His son Adrian was educated at Eton, Cambridge and studied medicine at Barts. He was killed at Vlamertinghe, Belgium on 12 July 1917. His room at the Castle is preserved as the Adrian Drew Memorial Room. It contains his school and college memorabilia and his full length portrait.

The Honourable Captain Thomas Charles Reginald Agar-Robartes was a Liberal MP. 'Tommy's family home was at 'Lanhydrock' near Bodmin, Cornwall. He joined the Royal Buckinghamshire Hussars upon the outbreak of war, but keen for active service, he transferred to the Coldstream Guards. He was killed trying to rescue a comrade during the Battle of Loos on 30 September 1915 at the age of 34. 'The heartbroken family packed many of Tommy's possessions into his trunk, adding their favourite picture and a copy of his obituary from the local paper, before locking them in the attic at Lanhydrock. This time capsule was opened 84 years later by the National Trust's Property Manager and can be seen at the house which is open to the public - itself something of a time capsule giving a glimpse of Victorian life.'[14]

In the main hall of the Caledonian Club in London can be found a (real) ram's head snuff box which was presented to the Club by J A Milne in memory of his son Captain John Theobald Milne, MC RFC who was killed in Flanders on 24 October 1917.

'At the National Eisteddfod of Wales in 1917 a tense and dramatic silence followed the summons of the Archdruid to Hedd Wyn to reveal his identity and take his victor's place on the Bard's Chair. The vast audience was stunned when at last it became known that Ellis Humphrey Evans - Hedd Wyn, the shepherd and poet from Trawsfynydd, the Royal Welch Fusilier had been killed on Pilckem Ridge in Flanders'.[15] He won the Bardic Chair for his poem *Yr Arwr* (*The Hero*) and it was draped in black in remembrance of him. Born in Monmouthshire in 1887, he served in the 15th Battalion of the Royal Welch Fusiliers and was killed on Pilckem Ridge on 31 July 1917, aged 30, on the first day of the 3rd Battle of Ypres. He was buried in the Imperial War Grave Commission's Artillery Wood Cemetery, Thourout, Belgium. The memorial erected outside the Moriah Chapel at Trawsfynydd in his honour took the form of a life sized bronze figure of a shepherd with a crook on a granite plinth. It was unveiled by Mrs Mary Evans on 11 August 1923. Evans' bardic name 'Hedd Wynn' translates from Welsh as 'White Peace'. Part of the memorial in his name is the annual prize for best essay on Welsh history presented each year. His story was the subject of the Oscar-nominated Welsh language film *Hedd Wyn* in 1993.

---

[12] Alan Judd and David Crane *First World War Poets*. National Portrait Gallery 1997.
[13] Alan Moorehead *Gallipoli*.
[14] *National Liberal Club News* No.46 (April 2004).
[15] *The Royal Welch Fusiliers* Pitkin Pictorials 1969.

# COMMERCE AND BUSINESS

Given the uncertainty of its outcome, the vast majority of war memorials were erected after, not during, the Great War and a curious exception is the Plaistow War Memorial which stands in East London Cemetery. The inauguration of this granite monolith on 22 February 1917 would appear to indicate a degree of prescience on the part of the directors of the East London Cemetery Company, not normally associated with mere mortals.

A good example of a satisfactory outcome for a memorial when a commercial enterprise ceases to exist may be taken from the story of Sir George Frampton's bronze sculpture of St George and the Dragon in Holborn, London (inaugurated 4 July 1921), which commemorated the 444 men of Pearl Assurance who fell in the Great War and subsequently the 215 men of that insurance company who fell in the Second World War. The memorial was removed from Holborn in 1992 after Pearl was acquired by AMP (Australian Mutual Provident) and relocated to their UK headquarters at Lynchwood, Peterborough. There it became the focus of their annual Remembrance Day Service.

In Liverpool there stands a war memorial in the courtyard of the City's Cotton Exchange Buildings, facing Old Hall Street. The statue is a life-sized representation in bronze of a British soldier advancing with his rifle at the port. It was sculpted by Professor Francis Derwent Wood and inaugurated by Field Marshal Earl Haig in 1922. In its original position 'Tommy' as he was named by the staff, was flanked by stone tablets bearing the names of 358 men from the Cotton Exchange who fell in the Great War. After the Second World War tablets bearing a further 65 names were added and these were unveiled by the Earl of Derby in 1949. In 1966 the frontage of the Cotton Exchange was reconstructed and it was found impossible to incorporate the tablets into the new design. The names of the fallen are now to be found on a Roll of Honour in the Liverpool Cotton Association Members Room. The LCA also has in its possession an 18 inch tall bronze statuette commemorating the soldiers of the 17th, 18th, 19th and 20th 'Pals' battalions of the King's Liverpool Regiment, in which many of the Cotton Exchange volunteers served.

'On 8 September 1915, after bombing Queen Square and en route to bombing Farringdon Road and Bartholomew Close, L13 commanded by Kapitänleutnant Mathy dropped a high explosive outside the Dolphin Tavern. Henry Coombs who was watching the raid was killed instantly by the blast and the front of the pub was torn out. In Lamb's Conduit Passage, house fires were started at numbers 7 and 10, and Fireman Green suffered fatal burns while helping to put them out. He was posthumously awarded the Silver Medal of the London County Council for his brave conduct'.[16] To this day, high on the rear wall of the bar in the Dolphin, may be seen the smoke blackened clock stopped at 1039, the exact time the bomb ripped out the front of the pub. The clock is something of a tourist attraction, with successive publicans having to bone up on their Great War history, as a stream of visitors call in to photograph and ask questions about it.

Within 48 hours of the outbreak of war, drivers of the London General Omnibus Company had crossed over to France to ferry troops to the Front. Their contribution was recognised by King George V. At his instigation, they became the first civilian contingent to be permitted to march past the Cenotaph on Remembrance Sunday - an honour that is exercised to this day by the London Transport Veterans Association. 10,112 employees drawn from the company's 30 garages served with the colours. Of that number, 803 did not return. Each garage commissioned a memorial tablet to their fallen. A good example may be taken from Middle Row Garage at Kensington which had 400 male staff. Of that number, 241 enlisted, 19 were killed, 20 wounded and two taken prisoner of war.

---

[16] Thomas Fegan *The 'Baby Killers': German Air Raids on Britain in the First World War.*

# THE COMMUNITY

The practice of 'twinning' of British and French communities also dates from the post-war period. This impulse was brought to life by the fact that the men of British regiments were usually recruited from the same town or city – and, where they lost a substantial number of men, a sympathetic bond was often established with the French communities where this had taken place. Serre was twinned with Sheffield, Albert with Birmingham, Fricourt with Ipswich, Gommecourt with Wolverhampton, Foncquevillers (known to the British troops as: 'Funky Villas') with Derby. These links were of immense practical value to the French communities in the long years of reconstruction that would follow the Great War.

In common with most towns and villages across Britain, the village of Pershore in Worcestershire resolved to remember its sons that had fallen in the war. Pershore sent a fifth of its adult male population to war. Of the 460 men who joined up, 101 did not return. A committee was formed at a Town Meeting held in 1919 to plan and raise funds to commemorate their sacrifice. It was decided that there would be two memorials, one to the fallen and one to those who served. There was agreement that the memorial to the fallen should be placed in Pershore Abbey. The site decided on was the south transept. The committee sought the assistance of Sir Aston Webb who had local connections. He recommended Alfred Drury as designer and sculptor. In Drury's design, the allegorical figure of Immortality is represented as having just alighted on the terrestrial sphere, holding in her left hand the Olive Branch of Peace, while with her right hand she is bestowing the Crown of Everlasting Life that Fadeth Not Away. She stands on a pedestal of Portland stone. The Memorial was dedicated on 1 November 1921 and the Earl of Coventry, Lord Lieutenant of Worcestershire, unveiled it. The address was given by General Sir Francis Davies, GOC Scottish Command.

In the case of the town of Sittingbourne in Kent, their war memorial took the form of an avenue of remembrance, with each tree being planted in remembrance of one of the fallen of their community. The text of the dedicatory plaque on the corner of the town's Avenue of Remembrance was refurbished by Swale Council in 2003. The cost of the project was shared with the private company on whose wall the plaque is fixed. The text reads:

---

## AVENUE OF REMEMBRANCE

## 1914 ~ 1918.

**THE TREES IN THIS AVENUE WERE PLANTED AND NAMED IN REMEMBRANCE OF SITTINGBOURNE MEN WHO FELL IN THE GREAT WAR**

---

In heavily populated urban areas the men would have served in different arms of the forces and a good idea of how this was addressed may be understood from Thomas Rudge's Finsbury War Memorial in London. Here the sides of the plinth were allocated to 11th Battalion of the London Regiment (the Finsbury Rifles), the Royal Navy and the Royal Flying Corps. Each engraved names, badges and theatres of war as appropriate. The fourth side carried the general inscription.

Upon occasion authorities misjudged the mood of the community and attempted to add the names of councillors or architects to the memorial and were in turn rebuffed by the relatives of the fallen. In 1919 the vicar of Hayton in Cumberland asked the parish council if they intended to erect a war memorial to Hayton's fallen. Upon being informed that they did not intend to do so, he called a public meeting and with the community behind him immediately commenced the erection of the Hayton War Memorial without any further ado.

# THE RELIGIOUS CONNECTION

Church furnishing for memorialisation purposes is a subject that probably merits an in-depth study in its own right and, whilst it has featured as a mode of commemoration principally since the Great War, the origins of the tradition can be found much further back in British history. After the Great War there would be memorial chapels constructed to commemorate particular individuals and the war dead of regiments and educational foundations. The United Kingdom National Inventory of War Memorials at the Imperial War Museum records that at least 170 were constructed after the Great War. Particularly good examples are the regimental chapels of the King's Own Yorkshire Light Infantry and the Duke of Wellington's Regiment in York Minster, the Antechapel at King's College Chapel at Aberdeen University and the Kitchener Memorial Chapel in St Paul's Cathedral, London (1925). The chapel's silver-plated candlesticks were made from melted down trophies won by the London Rifle Brigade.

Almost any item of church furnishing could function as a war memorial. There would be lecterns, calvaries, crucifixes, pews, choir stalls, organs, or components of organs, commemorative plaques, altars, stained glass windows, decorative schemes, reading desks, lychgates, pulpits, credence tables, fonts, chancel screens, altar rails, church wardens' staves, clock mechanisms, nativity sets, framed paintings or photographs, hassocks, wooden crosses that originally marked the graves of the fallen, trench art, incendiary bombs dropped by zeppelins and other memorabilia.

St Nicholas Church at Little Wigborough in Essex contains spars from the superstructure of zeppelin L33, downed by anti-aircraft fire on 24 September 1916 after raiding London.[17] The lectern in St John the Baptist Church at Knutsford in Cheshire was fashioned from brass shell cases brought back from the Western Front by the Reverend 'Tubby' Clayton.[18] He found fame as the chaplain who ran Talbot House, a church club for soldiers in an abandoned house in Poperinghe, Belgium during the war. Thousands of troops in the Ypres Salient worshipped there. In the alphabet used at that time by British Army signallers, the letters T and H were rendered Toc H and the club became known by this abbreviation. 'In 1919 the Christian movement Toc H was founded to help men and women who in the harsh days of peace searched vainly for employment and the 'brotherhood of the trenches'. Thus the name was perpetuated and the organisation grew worldwide.... Each branch on formation was presented with a lamp, similar to those used in the time of Christ, to recall that which burned in the Upper Room at Pop'.[19]

The congregation of St Mary's Church in the village of Rothley, Leicestershire decided to raise funds to install an organ in memory of its fallen. This was built by Norman & Beard Limited and William Hill and Son of London. The village having no electricity at that time, the organ was powered by water. At a Parochial Church Council meeting the issue of how to dispose of the water being generated was discussed and Colonel Abbot Robinson of Rothley Grange undertook to take in hand the laying of pipes and disposal of the water. It subsequently transpired that the Colonel's wife was a keen gardener. Each summer Mrs Abbot Robinson, resplendent in her golden wig (with something red always worn), would waylay the organist on his way to divine service on Sunday, beseeching him to play a long voluntary and all the hymns at full blast, as the goldfish and trout in her ponds were gasping for fresh water.

---

[17] Thomas Fegan *The 'Baby Killers' German Air Raids on Britain in the First World War* p.120.
[18] The Reverend Philip Thomas Byard Clayton CH MC DD (1885-1972). A memorial plaque to 'Tubby' Clayton in St John the Baptist Church, Knutsford mentions both Toc H and the School for Ordinands he ran in the disused prison there in the period 1919-1922. 435 men who trained at Knutsford went on to be ordained. Tubby Clayton is also commemorated on Tower Hill where he preached the good news for fifty years. He was incumbent of All Hallows by the Tower.
[19] Rose E B Coombs *Before Endeavours Fade*.

# THE BACKGROUND

Another interesting aspect of the memorialisation issue may be taken from the donation of the bronze statue of St George in full armour on horseback slaying the Dragon which stands at the junction of Prince Albert Road and Park Road in the centre of a traffic roundabout at St Mary-Le-Bone, London. This sculpture was originally sculpted by Charles Leonard Hartwell, RA in 1907, but only donated by Mr Sigismund Goetze, its owner, for memorialisation purposes in 1936 to commemorate the fallen of the Borough of St Mary-Le-Bone and the donor insisted on no ceremony of inauguration. A considerable number of memorials such as the Cenotaph in Whitehall, the Clatt War Memorial in Aberdeenshire and the Hobart War Memorial in Tasmania, Australia carry the dates 1914-1919. The reason being that the Armistice of 11 November 1918 was a truce. The Treaty of Versailles formally ending the war between the Allies and the Central Powers not being signed until 28 June 1919 in the Hall of Mirrors, Versailles, France, the symbolic significance of this date being that it was five years since the day the Serbian student Gavrillo Princip assassinated the Austro-Hungarian Archduke Franz Ferdinand and his wife Lady Sophie Chotek on the Apfel Quay in Sarajevo. In 1918 both the British Army and RAF were engaged in the Russian Civil War and the Royal Navy's Baltic Battle Squadron was in action until withdrawn in January 1920. The IWGC wrote to the Admiralty in 1922, asking what dates they thought should appear on the three memorials they were erecting for the Royal Navy. That they had to so, is a fair indication as to how much confusion surrounded the issue at that time.[20] Another good example may taken from the Commission's Basra War Memorial in Iraq, which was dismantled by Presidential decree in 1997. It was removed from Basra's port area and reassembled 30 miles north-west in the town of Nasiriyah. Interestingly, it bears the dates 1914-21. There are a number of villages that have no war memorial because their men did not go to war and these were often pit villages. Mining being a 'reserved' occupation, miners were officially not permitted to enlist - although the ranks of the 63rd (Royal Naval Division) were full of them. Conversely, Britain had 43 'Thankful Villages' that erected no memorial because all their men returned safe from the war. These villages (with the numbers of men returned) were: Stanbridge, Bedfordshire (43), Knapwell, Cambridgeshire (23), Bradbourne, Derbyshire (18), Brierley, Gloucestershire (14), Coln Rogers, Gloucestershire (25), Little Sodbury, Gloucestershire (6), Upper Slaughter, Gloucestershire (44), Puttenham, Hertfordshire (15), Knowlton, Kent (12), Arkholme, Lancashire (59), Willesley, Leicestershire (3), Bigby, Lincolnshire (10), High Toynton, Lincolnshire (14), Ovington, Norfolk (14), Woodend, Northamptonshire (19), Maplebeck, Northamptonshire (2), Wigsley, Northamptonshire (7), Wysall, Northamptonshire (17), Teigh, Rutlandshire (11), Swanbourne, Buckinghamshire (67), Colwinston, Glamorgan (23), Cowbridge, Glamorgan (11), Aisholt, Somerset (8), Chelwood, Somerset (4), Rodney Stoke, Somerset (17), Stanton Prior, Somerset (4), Stocklinch, Somerset (19), Tellisford, Somerset (3), Woolley, Somerset (13),[21] South Elmsham, Suffolk (11), Littleton Drew, Wiltshire (20), Catwick, Yorkshire (30), Cayton, Yorkshire (43), Cundall, Yorkshire (12) and Norton Le Clay, Yorkshire (16). Villages where all the men were known to have returned, but for which no figures are available were: Saxby, Leicestershire, Cromwell, Nottinghamshire, Chantry, Somerset, Ilketshall, Suffolk, Priddy, Somerset, Culpho, Suffolk, Gisleham, Suffolk and Rushmere, Suffolk.[22] Fulstow, near Louth, Lincolnshire erected no memorial to its seven war dead, because Private Charles Kirman of the 7th Battalion, the Lincolnshire Regiment was shot for desertion and the villagers were refused permission to include his name on it.

---

[20] Major H H Chettle, Director of Records IWGC, to Secretary of the Admiralty 8 May 1922.
[21] This figure gave rise to the local tradition of 13 being a lucky number. Woolley counted itself 'Twice Thankful' - as it lost no men in the Second World War either.
[22] *Daily Mail* 14 January 2004. (With thanks to Ann Diver of Sheffield).

Canterbury in Kent has a number of war memorials dating from the Great War, but the one that invariably catches the eye of the visitor is a horse trough dedicated: "TO OUR PATIENT COMRADES IN THE HORSE LINES".

After considerable controversy and at the insistence of Dr William Spooner (yes, that Dr Spooner),[23] Warden of New College, Oxford, a rectangular stone tablet with the names of three German alumni who fell fighting for the Kaiser inscribed on it was erected. A number of Oxford Colleges utilised archways connecting quads for memorialisation purposes and this was a relatively inexpensive and highly successful form of memorialisation. Often the left hand wall of the archway will have the names of the College's alumni from the Great War carved with an appropriate inscription and the right wall the names from the Second. Of the undergraduates who matriculated from Oxford University in 1913, 31% were killed in the Great War. The names listed on the four stone panels to the left of the entrance to Christ Church Cathedral, Oxford are a veritable roll-call of the sons of the greatest families in the land. A recent addition can be found on the Great War Memorial Arch at Merton College, Oxford which has the name of C F L von Wurm, who was killed fighting for the Germans in their 75th Infantry Regiment. Manchester Grammar School Roll of Honour has as its last entry for the Great War the name of its German Master, Dr Bernhard Neuendorff who also fell fighting for the Germans.[24]

The public war memorial as the British would recognise it is not common in Germany, memorials more usually being found in church or cemetery settings and for obvious reasons Germany was not permitted to erect monuments to its dead on the battlefields of the nations she had despoiled. It has certainly been the case since the Second World War that where they did erect memorials on the Western Front, these have been destroyed or defaced by the local population - and it would be easy to rush to judgement, but it should be noted that mainland Great Britain was not occupied by the Germans in either World War. The only significant German memorials on the Western Front are the Kollwitz sculptures in Vladslo German Cemetery near Diksmude, Belgium and they take the form of two larger than life-size, kneeling granite figures on plinths, representing grieving parents. They were sculpted in 1932 by Käthe Kollwitz (1867-1945) in memory of her son Peter, who was killed in action on 23 October 1914.

The Coulport and Jackfield War Memorial takes the form of a footbridge which spans the River Severn between the two villages near Ironbridge in Shropshire. It was constructed by the Cleveland Bridge Company of Darlington in 1922. The inscription reads: "THIS BRIDGE IS FREE/ O TREAD IT REVERENTLY/ IN MEMORY OF THOSE/ WHO DIED FOR THEE".

Another aspect of the memorialisation issue may be taken from the odyssey of the Great War Memorial Arch that was originally erected at Guy's Hospital in London to commemorate their staff who died in the Great War. The Hospital discovered in the 1970s that the Arch was too narrow for the latest generation of modern ambulances to pass through safely and it was dismantled. The Arch was initially stored broken down into its ten constituent blocks, in the grounds of St Olave's Hospital, Lower Road, Rotherhithe and, when that hospital was closed in the late 1980s, the blocks were shifted to Grove Park Hospital. The Arch was eventually re-erected outside Nuffield House in the grounds of Guy's and rededicated in November 1994.

The South African High Commission at Trafalgar Square, London has a lobby dedicated to Delville Wood, with a Roll of Honour in a lectern and a picture of the Wood painted by the artist Mrs Bertha Everard. The names of the High Commission's staff who died in the Great War are also recorded there on a brass tablet.

---

[23] William Archibald Spooner (1844-1930) Warden of New College, Oxford 1903-24. 'Suffered from .... lapse of speech known as Spoonerism' - Concise Dictionary of National Biography.
[24] James Bentley *Dare To Be Wise: A History of The Manchester Grammar School*. London 1990.

# THE BOARD OF TRADE WAR MEMORIAL

The Board of Trade Roll of Honour 1914-1919 listed that government department's civilian members of staff killed in the Great War and its chequered career is an instructive example of the difficulties that can be encountered in commissioning and maintaining a war memorial.

In 1914 the Board of Trade had some 7,500 staff, of whom 4,800 were engaged on labour issues, chiefly staffing labour exchanges. During the Great War more than 2,000 staff left to 'join up' and 305 were killed. The Board appointed a War Memorial Committee in December 1921 and in all, it met a total of 15 times. It ran a design competition which attracted 15 entries and that chosen was submitted by the Board's senior draughtsman, Mr H Slicer. It depicted a bronze plaque and frame, surmounted by a broken pediment with a representation of a galleon's hull, inspired by the crest of the Board of Trade. The Committee determined that the criteria for inclusion on the Roll would be restricted to staff who, at the time of their enlistment, had been employed by the Board. The details of all staff known to have died were verified with their naval, army or air force unit and efforts were made through circulars to staff and by advertisements placed in national newspapers to identify any permanent or temporary Board staff who had died. The Committee's work was hampered by lack of funds, as the initial subscriptions had been deposited with a bank which subsequently failed. Several further requests for subscriptions were made, the last two being confined to headquarters and to heads of departments respectively. Eventually, sufficient funds were raised to commission an adaptation of Mr Slicer's original design and a bronze plaque in an oak frame, rather than a memorial fashioned entirely from bronze, was produced. The work was carried out by William Morris & Co (Westminster) Ltd for £158. The Roll of Honour was unveiled on 19 December 1923 at the Park, or West, Entrance of the Board's headquarters at Great George Street, London by Prime Minister Stanley Baldwin, a former President of the Board of Trade. About 120 photographs of the Roll of Honour were produced and sent to all the outlying offices of the Board, with the recommendation that they be framed and displayed prominently in each office. No fewer than 37 men of the Board's war dead served in the 15th Battalion of the London Regiment, the Civil Service Rifles. (The Civil Service Rifles War Memorial designed by Lutyens may be found on the West Terrace at Somerset House in London. Its Roll of Honour was embedded within it upon inauguration). It subsequently became apparent that 170 of the names were duplicated on the Roll of Honour to fallen staff of the newly created Ministry of Labour, which had by that time taken over the responsibilities of the Board's labour exchanges and Unemployment Insurance Department. This memorial can be seen in the headquarters of the Department for Education and Skills at Caxton House in Tothill Street, London. In 1925 William Morris were engaged to supply an additional oak panel to match the memorial with three ornate oak pegs for the hanging of wreaths. This was funded by an unexpected late dividend from the failed bank. In 1936 Morris Singer carried out further works to substitute bronze letters for the wooden letters, which had begun to break away from the oak frame at the foot of the memorial. According to the illustrated history of the Board of Trade[25] the Board's headquarters were moved in 1940 to Imperial Chemical House at Millbank in 1940 and to Horse Guards Avenue in 1952 and thence to 1 Victoria Street in 1963, which it inhabits today. During the Second World War the memorial went missing and one theory holds that it was removed and stored for safe-keeping during the Blitz and mislaid during the various changes of location. It has never been found, despite diligent enquiries and repeated searches during the 1980s and 1990s and advertisements placed in the specialist press. A replica Roll of Honour was unveiled by Secretary of State Patricia Hewitt in a ceremony on 11 November 2002 at the headquarters of DTI at Victoria Street. Website at www.dti.gov.uk/warmemorial

---

[25] Susan Foreman *Shoes, Ships and Sealing Wax* HMSO 1986.

# THE CENOTAPH, WHITEHALL

At the end of the Great War, the War Cabinet determined that a day of celebration would be held to mark the signing of the peace treaty on 28 June 1919. A Peace Celebrations Committee was appointed chaired by Lord Curzon, Lord President of the Council. It first met on 9 May and began to organise a programme of festivities, the high point of which would be a victory parade. At the beginning of July Sir Edwin Lutyens was invited to Downing Street and asked to design a non-denominational structure for the parade, to be designed and built in two weeks. The temporary wood and plaster structure was unveiled on the morning of 19 July 1919.[26] Later that day, the troops of the 14 victorious nations (including Japan and Portugal) marched past the Cenotaph in solemn silence led by the Allied commanders Field Marshal Earl Haig, Maréchal Foch and General 'Black Jack' Pershing. It was saluted by the commanders and the marching detachments (a tradition that continues to this day). 'The temporary Cenotaph was such a minor detail in the planning of the Peace Day Celebration and the winding down of the war effort that no one involved could have possibly imagined its becoming the official memorial. But it was the Cenotaph which had caught hold of the public's imagination. From then on, this understated and abstract monument became the symbol of England's grief'.[27] The parade was barely over before a campaign led by Members of Parliament was mounted to make the Cenotaph a permanent structure. Clearly the Cabinet had not set out to erect a national war memorial, but the spontaneous reaction of the British People ensured that was exactly what they had done. It remained only for them to recognise the fact. After strong advocacy by Sir Alfred Mond, on 30 July the Cabinet took the decision to re-erect it in a permanent form on the same site.

---

[26] PRO file Works 20/1/4.
[27] Allan Greenburg *Journal of the Society of Architectural Historians* (USA) 1989 Vol 48.

The Cenotaph's design deliberately omitted any religious symbol, because those it commemorated were of all creeds and none. It is overlooked by an enthroned statue of Queen Victoria, sceptre in hand, on top of the Old Home Office building (now the Foreign and Commonwealth Office), immediately opposite. Its overall height is 35 feet, the base is 15' x 8'6", the top is 11'6 x 6'6". The laurel wreaths at the ends are 5 feet in diameter, the one at the top 3'6". All letters and Roman numerals are approximately 5" square. It was constructed from 120 tons of Portland stone. Lutyens utilised the Greek technique of entasis, in which curved surfaces create the illusion of linearity. All of the horizontal surfaces and planes are spherical. The 'verticals', if extended, would converge at a point over 1,000 feet above the ground. The 'horizontals' are radials of a circle whose centre is 900 feet below ground. The accurate rendition in stone of the design specification called for masonry skills of the highest order. Messrs Holland, Hannen and Cubitts Ltd erected it at a cost of £7,325.[28] Unusually, the cost of its erection was met by funds voted by Parliament. Lutyens declined his fee. The unveiling of the permanent structure by King George V on 11 November 1920 was combined with a ceremony to mark the passing of the body of the Unknown Warrior for re-burial at Westminster Abbey. The first National Ceremony took place there on the same date the following year. Since that time, the Cenotaph and the ceremony held there on Remembrance Sunday has been the national focus for commemorating the British People's war dead.[29] When originally designed, the only inscriptions were "THE GLORIOUS DEAD" on the western face and the dates MCMXIV (1914) and MCMXIX (1919) above the wreaths on the north and south faces. At the commencement of the National Ceremony on 10 November 1946, King George VI unveiled the dates MCMXXXIX (1939) and MCMXLV (1945), which had been inscribed on the upper portions of the east and west faces. So remarkable were the origins of the Cenotaph that Lutyens was called in by the Office of Works and asked to explain the story of its creation for the official record. This record is called *The Journal of Remembrance*.[30] In his words: 'This, so far as my work goes, completes the story of the Cenotaph. The majestic unveiling ceremony by the King on Armistice Day, 1920, is part of our national history. My task was done when the masons left. My hope is that, as the years pass into centuries, the Cenotaph will endure as a sacred symbol of remembrance'.[31] When Lutyens died on New Year's Day in 1944, he left word that should the Cenotaph be adopted as a national memorial also for the dead of the Second World War, it was his wish that nothing further should be added to the structure, other than the inscribing on it of the appropriate dates. At the end of the Second World War, the War Memorials Advisory Council, headed by Admiral of the Fleet Lord Chatfield, mounted a campaign for a national memorial to the fallen of that war and sent out a questionnaire to its member organisations canvassing their opinion. Major General Sir Fabian Ware, who had founded the Imperial War Graves Commission and led it through two World Wars, replied: 'My personal view is that new dates only should be added to the Cenotaph, and I should deprecate any competing monument or any structural addition to the Cenotaph (which would be aesthetically unpardonable). At the same time, it seems to me almost impossible to pick out a beneficient object which would command universal assent.'[32] This reply from 'The Great Commemorator' was sufficient to end the campaign to erect another national war memorial in this form. Thus the Cenotaph became the symbol of the nation's loss for both World Wars. Apart from the national ceremony held there each November, most weekends a ceremony of some kind will be taking place there and as the passer-by will observe, it is bedecked with wreaths all year round. It is cleaned every fortnight and wreaths removed after the same period.

---

[28] PRO file Works/20 8/5.
[29] PRO file Works/20 1/4.
[30] *Journal of Remembrance* loose enclosure in leather wallet to PRO file Works/20/139.
[31] Sir Edwin Lutyens *Journal of Remembrance*.
[32] Royal Society of Arts archive Ref PR.GE/117/10/14.

# THE SCOTTISH NATIONAL WAR MEMORIAL

In 1917 the Scottish People determined that their contribution in the cause of freedom would be commemorated by a National War Memorial as an official and historic record of Scotland's War Service in The Great War. It would be an expression of Scotland's sorrow for her dead, pride in their achievement, and her profound faith in the ultimate good of their sacrifice. The Prince of Wales was appointed President of the Appeal Committee and the Duke of Atholl its Chairman. Sir Robert Lorimer was appointed architect. It was decided that the memorial would be situated inside Edinburgh Castle atop Castle Rock. The location chosen breathes Scotland's history, from long before the birth of Britain's first Stuart King there to the attempted bombing of the Castle by a Zeppelin in 1916, and much in between. Seasoned stone was used in its construction from the Billings Building, a redundant barracks on the Rock. In the Hall of Honour there are the memorials and laid up colours of all of Scotland's infantry and cavalry regiments. There are bronze friezes by Morris and Alice Meredith Williams depicting all manner of soldiery and memorials to the Royal Navy, the Merchant Navy and Air Forces. The stained glass windows were produced by Douglas Strachan and the floor is of granite from Ailsa Craig. The names of all the Scots fallen are recorded in Books of Remembrance. On the exterior walls are carved the divisional symbols of the uniquely Scottish formations that served. There is even a memorial to the beasts of burden and the canaries and mice, which served the sappers and miners. The ruling principle had been that no service, however slight or humble, should be overlooked. The memorial was inaugurated by the Prince of Wales on 14 July 1927. Cut deep above the keystone of the central arch of the doorway is the simple inscription:

"TO THE GLORY OF GOD,
AND IN MEMORY OF SCOTS WHO FELL, 1914 – 1918"

# THE WELSH NATIONAL WAR MEMORIAL

The Welsh National War Memorial stands in Cathays Park, Cardiff. It was erected to commemorate the Welsh fallen of the Great War. The process by which it was funded is of particular interest. The authorities in Cardiff corresponded with local Welsh councils to elicit contributions, but were refused, the councils reasoning that they would not fund the beautification of Cardiff. The deadlock was broken by the *Western Mail* newspaper which raised the necessary £25,000 by subscriptions from its readers. It was designed by Sir Ninian Comper, the outstanding church architect and ecclesiastical designer. The statues were sculpted by Henry Alfred Pegram, RA and cast by the Burton Foundry at Thames Ditton. William D Gough and Messrs E Turner and Sons carried out the masonry work. The design took the form of a sunken court with a central fountain surrounded by a circular classical colonnade. Bronze figures of a sailor, soldier and airman raise wreaths to a central winged bronze figure on a plinth in the centre representing Victory, sword held aloft. The Prince of Wales inaugurated the memorial on 12 June 1928. Beneath the central figure is the inscription:

"REMEMBER HERE IN PEACE THOSE WHO IN TUMULT OF
WAR BY SEA, ON LAND, IN AIR, FOR US AND FOR THE
VICTORY ENDURETH UNTO DEATH"

The inscription outside the frieze is in Welsh:

"I FEIBION CYMRU A RODDES EU BYWYD DROS EI
GWLAD YN RHYFEL MCMXIV – MCMXVIII"[33]

---

[33] 'To the Sons of Wales who gave their lives for their Country in the War 1914 - 1918'.

# THE GUARDS MEMORIAL

The Guards Memorial stands in the Horse Guards Approach Road and faces Horse Guards across the Parade Ground. It takes the form of a cenotaph adorned by five large bronze figures. Immediately below are the badges (from left) of the Grenadier, Scots, Welsh, Irish and Coldstream Guards. The wreaths in the photograph are placed in exactly the same order, and are permanently present. Household Division casualties for the Great War were 14,653 men killed and 28,398 wounded. The statues and the three bronze relief panels were cast from German guns by the Morris Art Bronze Foundry at Dorset Rd, Lambeth. Above the figures are engraved the titles of all the formations of divisional troops which served with the Division in the Great War. A bronze panel on the rear of the monument shows a battery of 13 pounder field guns in action. Inscribed above this are the names of every battle the Household Division fought in during the Great War. The judges of the competition for the most successful design were Sir Reginald Blomfield and Sir Thomas Brock. They awarded the commission to H Chalton Bradshaw. Professor Gilbert Ledward executed the sculpture. The dedicatory inscription was composed by Rudyard Kipling. His only son John was an officer in the Irish Guards killed at Loos in 1915. The Duke of Connaught inaugurated the memorial on 16 October 1926. It bears scars from the Blitz, but it remains unrepaired in accordance with government policy on 'honourable scars of war'. After the Second World War the following inscription was added:

"THIS MEMORIAL ALSO COMMEMORATES ALL THOSE MEMBERS
OF THE HOUSEHOLD DIVISION WHO DIED IN THE SECOND WORLD WAR
AND IN THE SERVICE OF THEIR COUNTRY SINCE 1918"

The inscription on the base reads:
"THIS MONUMENT
WAS ERECTED BY THEIR FRIENDS AND COMRADES"

# THE ROYAL ARTILLERY MEMORIAL

This memorial stands at Hyde Park Corner in London. It commemorates those members of the Royal Regiment of Artillery who fell in the Great War. The Duke of Connaught inaugurated it on 18 October 1925 and it takes the form of a platform and a pedestal surmounted by a sculptured representation of a 9.2 inch howitzer sculpted in Portland stone. Cast in bronze by the A B Burton foundry, on a scale one third larger than life-size are four figures. At the south end stands a subaltern in field kit, at the north end lies the recumbent figure of a dead gunner, covered with his greatcoat and steel helmet. Above this figure is the inscription: "BENEATH THIS STONE LIES BURIED THE ROLL OF HONOUR OF THOSE WHOSE MEMORY IS PERPETUATED BY THIS MEMORIAL. THEY WILL RETURN NEVER MORE, BUT THEIR GLORY WILL ABIDE FOR EVER" and beneath it the inscription: "HERE WAS A ROYAL FELLOWSHIP OF DEATH". At the east end stands a Gunner in shirt-sleeves carrying 4 rounds of 18 pounder ammunition in carriers and at the west end, a driver clad in a waterproof with arms outstretched, holding in his hands a whip and a horse's bridle. At the south end there are three bronze panels listing every theatre in which this most ubiquitous of regiments fought in both World Wars. At the base of the howitzer on the east and the west sides is the inscription:

> "IN PROUD REMEMBRANCE OF THE
> FORTY-NINE THOUSAND AND SEVENTY SIX
> OF ALL RANKS OF THE
> ROYAL REGIMENT OF ARTILLERY
> WHO GAVE THEIR LIVES FOR KING
> AND COUNTRY IN THE GREAT WAR
> 1914 - 1919"

# THE RIFLE BRIGADE MEMORIAL

The Rifle Brigade was formed as an experimental 'Corps of Riflemen' in 1800 and the Regiment was numbered as the 95th Foot in 1802. It served with distinction in the Peninsula War in Portugal and Spain and at the Battle of Waterloo on 18 June 1815. In 1816, on the recommendation of the Duke of Wellington, the regiment was removed from the numbered infantry regiments of the Line and designated 'The Rifle Brigade'.

Standing on the corner of Grosvenor Gardens and Hobart Place, opposite the Royal Mews at Buckingham Palace in London, is the Rifle Brigade Memorial. It consists of a plinth and three bronze life size figures sculpted by John Tweed in 1925. On the left is a bronze sculpture of a rifleman and to the right one of an officer, both in the uniform worn by the Brigade in the Napoleonic Wars. The central figure is a Rifleman in Great War marching order with his rifle slung and he is best viewed from the gardens immediately behind the memorial. The perfectly captured movement of the life-like figure is pretty much Tweed at the top of his game. The inscription on the memorial reads:

"IN MEMORY OF
11575 OFFICERS
WARRANT OFFICERS
NON-COMMISSIONED
OFFICERS AND
RIFLEMEN OF
THE RIFLE BRIGADE
WHO FELL IN
THE GREAT WAR
1914 – 1918"

# THE ROYAL FUSILIERS MEMORIAL

195,000 men served in the Royal Fusiliers in the Great War. 80 battle honours were awarded and they won 12 Victoria Crosses. 46 battalions in all were raised and these served in France, Gallipoli, Salonika, East Africa and Russia. The Royal Fusiliers City of London Regiment Memorial stands in the middle of the road in High Holborn, London. It was sculpted by Albert Toft and his design consists of a bronze statue of a Royal Fusilier in battle dress mounted on a tall Portland stone tapered pedestal plinth with a stepped base. The pedestal is mounted on the west face with the Fusilier's badge in bronze and carved dedications with black letter infill. On the east face is a large bronze plaque with raised lettering listing the Fusiliers' battle honours. Around the lower stepped base are placed small stainless steel hooks for wreaths. It was inaugurated by Dr A F Winnington-Ingram, Bishop of London and Sir John Baddeley, Lord Mayor of London on 4 November 1922. It stands on the very boundary of the City of London and each Remembrance Sunday one can observe the ceremony, which proceeds without music, until the boundary is crossed and the Fusiliers exercise their Freedom of the City. The memorial was for many years looked after by the female staff of the Prudential Insurance Company, whose premises can be seen on the left of the photograph above. The inscription on the plinth reads:

"THE ROYAL FUSILIERS
(CITY OF LONDON REGIMENT)

TO THE GLORIOUS MEMORY
OF THE
22000 ROYAL FUSILIERS
WHO FELL IN THE GREAT WAR
1914 –1919"

# THE MACHINE GUN CORPS MEMORIAL

The Machine Gun Corps existed for only seven years; it was established by a Royal Warrant on 14 October 1915. The last element to be disbanded was the Depot at Shorncliffe on 15 July 1922, by which time 11,500 officers and 159,000 other ranks had served in the Corps. In all 1,120 officers and 12,671 other ranks of the Corps were killed. It served in Flanders, Mesopotamia, Russia, East Africa, Italy, Egypt, Palestine, France, Salonika, India and Afghanistan. The Corps banner was laid up at St Wulfram's Church, Grantham, Lincs in 1967 and its Book of Remembrance was presented to the Imperial War Museum on 7 April 1972. Standing in the shadow of nearby Apsley House, its memorial at Hyde Park Corner in London takes the form of a figure of a 9-foot tall bronze figure of a naked David leaning on Goliath's sword (he originally possessed genitalia). It is flanked by laurel wreathed machine guns and a soldier's helmet and pack, set on lower pedestals of Mezzano marble. The memorial was designed and sculpted by Professor Francis Derwent Wood. It was unveiled on 10 May 1925 by the Duke of Connaught and dedicated by the Chaplain-General to the Forces. The inscription led to questions in Parliament, but remained unchanged. It reads:

"ERECTED TO
COMMEMORATE
THE GLORIOUS
HEROES
OF THE
MACHINE GUN
CORPS
WHO FELL IN
THE GREAT
MCMXIV        WAR        MCMXIX"

Beneath the general inscription are the words from I Samuel 18.7 that caused the controversy:

"Saul hath slain his thousands
but David his tens of thousands"

# THE IMPERIAL CAMEL CORPS MEMORIAL

The Imperial Camel Corps was yet another fighting formation raised for a specific purpose that would not survive the end of the war. The Corps was organised in the manner of a cavalry brigade, with its 1st and 3rd battalions being raised by the Australian Light Horse, the 2nd battalion raised from the British Yeomanry and the 4th being raised from a mixture of both Australian and New Zealand Light Horse. The artillery element was provided by a mountain battery of Hong Kong and Singapore Royal Garrison Artillery manned by Sikh gunners. The 'Cameliers' did sterling work against the Turks in the Middle East and earned the approbation of Lawrence of Arabia who would write of them: 'Each march saw them more workmanlike, more at home on the animals, tougher, leaner, faster. They behaved like boys on holiday, and the easy mixing of officers and men made their atmosphere delightful'.[34]

Refurbished by Westminster City Council in 1998 and standing in Victoria Embankment Gardens, this charming memorial was sculpted by Major Cecil Brown, RASC and cast by A B Burton's foundry at Thames Ditton. It takes the form of a trooper mounted on a camel and it commemorates all the fallen of the Corps in the Great War. The names of those who died are listed by national contingent. The general inscription reads:

"TO THE GLORIOUS AND IMMORTAL
MEMORY OF THE OFFICERS NCOs AND MEN
OF THE IMPERIAL CAMEL CORPS· BRITISH
AUSTRALIAN NEW ZEALAND INDIAN
WHO FELL IN ACTION OR DIED OF WOUNDS
AND DISEASE IN EGYPT SINAI AND PALESTINE
1916-1917-1918"

---

[34] T.E. Lawrence *Seven Pillars of Wisdom* p. 586.

# THE 24th INFANTRY DIVISION MEMORIAL

In the period November 1917 - January 1918 Eric Kennington was attached to the 24th Infantry Division in France, as an official war artist for the Department of Information and, whilst undertaking this role, he befriended Lieutenant Colonel M V D Hill, DSO MC of the 9th Battalion of the Royal Sussex Regiment. In 1921 Colonel Hill approached Kennington and asked him if he could recommend a sculptor to produce a war memorial to commemorate the 24th Infantry Division's 10,865 war dead. Kennington volunteered himself for the task, suggested that it be sculpted from Portland stone and asked only for money for materials, the mason's fee and the cost of transporting the finished work from his workshop at Chiswick Mall, Hammersmith to Battersea Park, London. In May 1922 he presented his maquette for inspection by the Division's Memorial Committee and gained their approval. Despite one expert's theory that the origin of Kennington's design was probably Kipling's *Soldiers Three*, the author believes the design was based on the three figures on the 37th Division Memorial at Monchy-le-Preux (1921) by Lady Feodora Gleichen.[35] The only difference being, Kennington rendered the figures in his trademark totemic style, rather than in the literal manner. According to Colonel Hill, the left-hand figure was based on Trooper Morris Clifford Thomas of the Machine Gun Corps, the central figure on Sergeant J Woods of the 9th Battalion of the Royal Sussex Regiment and the right-hand figure on Robert Graves of the 2nd Battalion of the Royal Welch Fusiliers. Kennington believed: 'all three men have boundless strength, courage and resolve and their progress is unimpeded by the common danger at their feet. They are British soldiers in uniform and also men journeying through life - the enemies which they overcome are not so much German soldiers as the internal, inner, enemies of all of us'. 'It took Kennington from November 1922 to July 1924 to carve the three six-feet nine-inch figures, with the 14-inch high preparatory maquette as his sole guide. The figures were then placed on a circular base, which the artist had designed, measuring just over five feet high.'[36] Kennington accepted an engraved silver cigarette case in payment. The memorial was inaugurated by Field Marshal Sir Herbert Plumer on 4 October 1924. It moved Major General Lord Edward Gleichen[37] (Lady Feodora's brother, who had commanded the 37th Division) to fulminate: 'That limited group of people who admire 'futuristic' art will doubtless highly approve of this monument. It represents in stone three tin-hatted figures - a sergeant, corporal, and lance corporal - crunched together and looking straight to their front, while a serpent disports itself among their legs - which by the way, are held together with stone billets. The fore-end of one man's rifle has had to be cut away in order to get it under his hat; and there are no folds in their clothes anywhere.' There exists a photograph of Robert Graves in his old age standing beside it.[38] The discolouration and erosion on the memorial after 80 years in the park is a good indicator of the unsuitability of porous stone for outdoor memorialisation purposes.

Further echoes of Lady Feodora's design can be found in the Memorial to Other Ranks at the Royal Military Academy, Sandhurst (1927) and the Commando Memorial at Spean Bridge in the Highlands (1952). At which point one could say, her design had become a convention. Major General Lord Gleichen must have had Eric Kennington in his mind's eye when he condemned the modernists as: 'the Easter Island school of sculpture' and he was spot on. In a 1929 lecture, Kennington cited an Easter Island divinity as an important influence on his work.

---

[35] Lady Feodora Gleichen (1861-1921). Daughter of Admiral HSH Prince Victor of Hohenloe-Langenburg. Trained at the Slade School of Art under Alphonse Legros. An award is made in her name each year by the RBS.
[36] *Friends of War Memorials Newsletter Number 17 Spring 2003*, essay by Jonathan Black.
[37] Major General Lord Albert Edward Gleichen (1863-1937). Formerly Count Gleichen, son of Admiral HSH Prince Victor of Hohenloe-Langenburg. British Military Attaché to Washington D C 1906-7, Commander 15th Brigade 1911-15, Commander 37th Division 1915-16. Author: *A Guardsman's Memories* and *London's Open Air Statuary*.
[38] Robert Graves' best-selling autobiography *Goodbye to All That* was published in 1929.

# BATTERSEA PARK

Eric Kennington's 24th Infantry Division Memorial in Battersea Park.

# THE FOVANT BADGES

During the Great War thousands of soldiers were housed in an enormous encampment that straddled the Wiltshire villages of Fovant, Compton, Chamberlayne and Sutton Mandeville. At Fovant may be found a group of badges carved into the chalkland of Fovant Down by soldiers from all over the Empire who were stationed at Fovant Camp nearby. The turf was first removed, some of the chalky earth dug out and proper chalk, which had been dug out of deep pits on the Down, packed into the outline. The first badge was cut in 1916 by soldiers from the London Rifle Brigade and it was soon followed by others. By the end of the Great War there were some 20 badges on the Compton, Fovant and Sutton Downs and by the end of the Second World War only nine remained. The panoramic photo above was taken in 2001 (and it includes the old Saxon fort of Chiselbury Ring). In it can be seen the badges of the Royal Wiltshire Yeomanry, the Wiltshire Regiment (added in the early 1950s), the Devonshire Regiment, the London Rifle Brigade, 6th Battalion, the City of London Regiment, the Post Office Rifles (second from the right) and the 'Rising Sun' of the Australian Commonwealth Military Forces badge. The last to be cut was that of the Royal Corps of Signals in 1970 (the figure of Mercury centre left of the picture). The badges are the largest group of hillside chalk figures in the UK and they follow in the ancient Wessex tradition of carving significant symbols on hillsides. The largest badge is the Australian Commonwealth Military Forces with a height of 32.08 metres and a width of 51.26 metres. Many of the badges have been reclaimed by the hillside over the years and nine remain. In June 2001 English Heritage scheduled all 12 badges spread over the three Downs as Ancient Monuments. However, on sheer practical and financial grounds, the Fovant Badges Society decided in November 2000 to maintain only eight badges on Fovant Down - the ones best seen and enjoyed by the public. The YMCA badge on Fovant Down, together with the Map of Australia on Compton Down and two badges on Sutton Down are being allowed to fade away, but for some years to come their outlines will remain visible, particularly from the air. Website at www.fovantbadges.com

Other good examples of this form can be found in the Kiwi carved during the Great War by New Zealand troops stationed at Bulford Camp in Wiltshire and also in the badges of British and Indian Army regiments carved in to the slopes of the Pakistani 26 miles of the Khyber Pass.

# THE POST OFFICE RIFLES

The origin of the Post Office Rifles can be found as far back as 1867 when, in response to public alarm at Fenian explosions in both London and Manchester, thousands of special constables were recruited. 1,600 post office volunteers were enrolled under Major J L Du Plat Taylor, Private Secretary to the Postmaster General, and they were formed into the 21st Middlesex Civil Service Volunteers (Post Office Company). In answer to a subsequent suggestion that these men should form themselves into a permanent Volunteer Regiment, the War Office sanctioned the proposal and promoted Du Plat Taylor to Lieutenant-Colonel. The unit was titled the 49th Middlesex Rifle Volunteers (Post Office Rifles). In 1877 Du Plat Taylor suggested to the War Office that an Army Postal Corps be formed for the Regular Army. They chose not to pursue his suggestion. In 1882 hostilities broke out in Egypt. The War Office contacted Du Plat Taylor who quickly embodied 100 men for service in Egypt and the Army Postal Corps was born. They became the first British Volunteers to come under fire at the Battle of Kassassin and were complemented on their efficiency by the campaign commander Sir Garnet Wolseley. In October 1899 the Army Post Office Corps was called up to serve in the South African War and quickly established an efficient postal service in theatre. However, the standard of service provided by the 'Posties' was strongly criticised in print by a young *Morning Post* journalist named Winston Churchill. Haldane's Territorial and Reserve Forces Act of 1908 led to the formation of a single Territorial Army and the 24th Middlesex were redesignated 8th Battalion, City of London Regiment (Post Office Rifles). In the Great War the Post Office Rifles arrived in France on 18 March 1915. By the Armistice 1,800 men had died and 4,500 had been wounded. Such was the British public's enthusiasm for service at the outset of the war, that a second Post Office Rifles Battalion - the 2nd/8th Londons was formed in September 1914. Between them, these two battalions would earn the London Regiment a total of 27 battle honours. At the Battle of Wurst Farm Ridge in September 1917 the 2nd/8th lost over half its fighting strength, dead or wounded, and its men were awarded a total of 40 gallantry medals. These included a Victoria Cross to Sergeant A J Knight - the only one awarded a Post Office Rifleman.

The post war years were not kind to the Posties and the 8th Battalion of the London Regiment was merged with the (non-Post Office) 7th Battalion in 1921. In 1935 the battalion underwent conversion from infantry to ack ack and was given the unwieldy title the 32nd (7th City of London) Anti-Aircraft Battalion, Royal Engineers. In 1940 the unit was rebadged again and it became 32nd Searchlight Regiment, Royal Artillery. The memorials to the Post Office Rifles can be found at St Lawrence Parish Church, Abbots Langley, at the Paignton War Memorial and on a plaque outside Uckfield village church. The General Post Office Memorial at the National Memorial Arboretum at Alrewas in Staffordshire was dedicated in 2001. The Post Office Rifles Book of Remembrance may be found in St Botolph's Church, Aldersgate, London EC1. Cared for by the CWGC, Post Office Rifles Cemetery may be found at Festubert in France.

## THE UNVEILING OF THE WAR MEMORIAL

'At two o'clock, on Saturday, July 8th, an impressive ceremony that will long linger in the memory, began. The roads were flanked with crowds of people, eagerly waiting the event that will surely play an important part in the history of the school - the unveiling of the War Memorial. First the attention of the audience was claimed by the band, who took up their position in the field, and then by the Guard of Honour, composed of members of the OTC who are in every way to be congratulated on their smartness and general efficiency. A profound silence reigned when Colonel Earle made his appearance, accompanied by the Headmaster, the Vice-Chairman of the Governors and the School Chaplain, and inspected the Guard. The *Last Post* was sounded after the reading of the names of those who fell in the Great War.

After the last strains of the bugles had died away, Colonel Earle gave a speech in every way impressive and interesting, from which the following is quoted. "It is a great privilege to me to assist at this ceremony in this ancient school. In the course of my work, I visit a great number of Officer Training Corps Schools and in each I find a memorial to those who fell in the war. When I ask a senior master to tell me about those whose names are recorded, he invariably says (and I know King Alfred's School is no exception), 'It is terribly sad, the cream of the old boys seems to have been taken'. It is terribly sad, but this memorial has not been erected to make us sad. On the contrary it is to make us glad and proud to remember the gallant hearts which once beat within these precincts. The memorial has, I hold, two other objects. First, to make us hope and wish that never again may the Empire be struck, as she was struck at the beginning of the summer holidays eight years ago, by the sudden tornado of war. Whether that hope and wish are fulfilled or not depends on you young people. Now is not the moment to discuss the way you should adopt, but it is certain that you can gain your wish only by action and never by inaction. I am sanguine as to the future - I believe that History teaches us that in a Democracy such as ours the parents of war are Ignorance and Indifference on the part of the Sovereign People. This school exists for the purpose of dispelling ignorance and indifference, for are not knowledge and keenness your watchwords? Long may the school continue its work. The other object of the memorial is to teach us Duty towards our King and fellow citizens - generous wholehearted Duty as was given by those whose names we honour today in order that we might live and preserve all that we hold most dear. May we prove worthy of their sacrifice".

So saying, he drew aside the flag which concealed the entrance to the War Memorial Gateway. The Vice-Chairman of the Governors then said prayers, which were followed by a hymn. After that, a short pause unbroken any sound until the eerie *Reveille* was sounded. Then the pronouncing of the blessing and finally the National Anthem. The ceremony is over; brief, perhaps, but in the short twenty minutes it lasted, was far more real feeling and reverence than might have been inspired by a lengthy one. The Memorial itself is amazingly effective in its simplicity. There is no extravagance in decoration - no flamboyance of design. The architect, Mr J. Stanley Beard FSA, himself an old boy, has thought it out admirably and Messrs. Barrett and Sons of Hanney have carried it out with the utmost celerity and competence. In every way, the ceremony has been satisfactory. Everything has been quiet and without pomp. So we, in the school, have given the greatest offering in our power - paltry, indeed, in comparison to their sacrifice, but nevertheless our best - to the Glorious Dead'.[39]

---

[39] *The Alfredian* July 1922.

# THE LYCH GATE AT KING ALFRED'S SCHOOL, WANTAGE, OXFORDSHIRE

The Lych Gate.

The inscription on the Lych Gate.

# THE SANDHAM MEMORIAL CHAPEL

Given Stanley Spencer's deeply religious upbringing, it is unsurprising that a friend had noted him saying before the Great War: '....we are going to build a church, and the walls will have on them all about Christ. If I do not do this on earth, I will do it in heaven.' His aspiration would be realised on earth - but first he would have to endure the horrors of war. Lieutenant Henry Willoughby Sandham, RASC had died in 1919 from an enlarged spleen, the consequence of malaria. Like Spencer, he too had served in the Army of the Orient in Macedonia. He was the brother of Mary Behrend. She and her husband Louis decided that they would erect a memorial chapel to him at Burghclere. The architect chosen was Lionel Pearson and the chapel stands in lawns and orchards overlooking Watership Down. Spencer, who had already sketched a number of pictures on the theme of his war service for an abortive project, was commissioned in 1923 to undertake the paintings in the chapel. His response to the news that the Behrends had agreed to sponsor the work was recorded as: 'What Ho Giotto!' and this exclamation was not without significance. 'Spencer's plans for the chapel were reminiscent of Giottos's frescoes in the fourteenth century Arena Chapel in Padua. The side walls of the building were to be divided into two registers, with an unbroken east wall behind the altar, for which he originally envisaged an arched design which was later eliminated.'[40] 'The dedication of the building as an Oratory of All Souls took place in March 1927. The ceremony was performed by the Suffragan Bishop of Guildford and it was deemed tactful that no hint of the proposed paintings be revealed lest he be disquieted.'[41] This artistic licence gave Spencer a free run at exorcising his demons and the outcome would be the Great War's most astonishing war memorial. Throughout the project Spencer was visited by the Bloomsbury Set and they carried the news far and wide of the great work there. Had Spencer never lifted a paintbrush again his fame would have been assured. Despite the concerns of the Behrends over the time he was taking, he finally completed the project in the summer of 1932. Dr Alan Borg wrote: 'There is clearly a form of narrative sequence in the Burghclere paintings, even though they do not present a coherent or continuous story. Spencer's cycle is the supreme example of what may be termed the anonymous highlight technique. The scenes themselves are ordinary and certainly do not depict heroes in the accepted sense. Yet the result is perhaps the most memorable narrative sequence to be inspired by the First World War'.[42] Each of the panels dealt with a specific aspect of Spencer's war service at either Beaufort War Hospital in Bristol, the Royal Army Medical Corps Depot at Tweseldown, or his service in the Army of the Orient. They bear titles such as: *The Camp at Todorova, The Camp at Kalinova, Making a Firebreak, Reveille, Kit Inspection, Sorting Laundry, Scrubbing the Floor, Ablutions, Washing Lockers* and *Map Reading*. The murals were painted in oils on framed canvas. There being no looms large enough in UK to produce the frames in the size required, they were manufactured in Belgium. There is only one officer depicted in the entire scheme - and he with a map. As any old soldier will tell you, a fairly lethal combination, Stanley's little joke perhaps. The east end of the chapel required a different treatment. Here, Spencer painted the entire wall behind the altar with the most remarkable depiction of all. Set in Macedonia, *The Resurrection of the Soldiers* depicts a scene littered with white crosses. Here, the resurrected soldiers hand over the crosses that had marked their graves to Jesus Christ. In 1947 the Behrends handed the chapel over to the National Trust and in recent years the paintwork has suffered from a white bloom, which was probably the consequence of pollution, but this has been successfully treated by art conservators engaged by the Trust. Website at www.nationaltrust.org.uk/sandham

---

[40] Royal Academy of Arts *Stanley Spencer RA* 1980.
[41] Kenneth Pople *Stanley Spencer: A Biography* Collins 1991.
[42] Alan Borg *War Memorials* Leo Cooper 1991.

# BURGHCLERE

MAP READING by Stanley Spencer
1932 Oil on canvass 213.5 x 185.5 cm, Sandham Memorial Chapel, Burghclere.

'This scene is just part of Spencer's great scheme of decoration for the Sandham Memorial Chapel, built in memory of Lieutenant Henry Willoughby Sandham, who had died from war wounds in 1919. Behind the altar, the Resurrection of the Soldiers shows the men rising from their graves, but on the side walls Spencer painted scenes inspired by his own active service in Macedonia and the time he had spent in military hospital in Bristol. In all the scenes soldiers perform simple domestic tasks, often acts of charity - such as bed making and the berry-picking seen here. The map-reading scene is particularly idyllic, Spencer commenting that he loved it for the obvious reason of resting and contemplating'.

- Neil MacGregor, Director National Gallery

# MARÉCHAL FERDINAND FOCH

Ferdinand Foch was born at Tarbes, France on 10 February 1851. He trained at Saint-Cyr and was commissioned into the artillery in 1873. He became Professor of Strategy at the École Supérieure de Guerre in 1894 and by the outbreak of the Great War was France's leading military theoretician. In 1917 he was appointed Chief of the General Staff of the French Army. It became apparent during the course of the German Spring Offensive in 1918 that the Allies needed, as a matter of some urgency, to appoint a Generalissimo to command all the Allied armies on the Western Front and Foch was appointed to this role. He was created Maréchal de France in August 1918 and elected to the Académie Française. He prophetically observed of the Treaty of Versailles: 'This is not a peace treaty, it is an armistice for 20 years'. As a mark of the high regard in which he was held by the British, in 1919 he was accorded the honour of being appointed Field Marshal of the British Army. He died in Paris on 20 March 1929 and was buried with great ceremony in Les Invalides. His remarkable bronze tomb there by Paul Landowski (1875-1961) is ornamented by a life-sized sculpture of eight poilus carrying a depiction of the Maréchal on a funeral bier. Almost every city, town and village in France has an Avenue or Rue Foch. The Maréchal had the unusual distinction of having a memorial erected to him in London. One of the last equine sculptures erected in London, it is a copy of that at Cassel in France. Sculpted by François Georges Malissard (1877-1942), it stands in Lower Grosvenor Gardens facing the entrance of Victoria Station in London. It was inaugurated by the Prince of Wales on 5 June 1930. Apart from the misspelling of the sculptor's name on the stepped Portland stone plinth, the memorial bears the interesting inscription:

> "I AM CONSCIOUS
> OF HAVING SERVED ENGLAND
> AS I SERVED
> MY OWN COUNTRY"

# FIELD MARSHAL EARL HAIG

The wars of the 20th century ushered in the age of modern warfare and since that time military commanders have not gone to war on horseback. The 20s and 30s witnessed the erection of the last military equestrian sculpture, with notable examples being Harry Bates' Field Marshal Earl Roberts, VC on Horse Guards Parade (1923), Francois Georges Malissard's Maréchal Foch (1930) and Earl Haig by Alfred F Hardiman and cast by Morris Singer in 1936.[43] Haig's statue stands on a traffic island in the middle of Whitehall. It was damaged by paint in the 2000 May Day Riots, but has since been restored by English Heritage. Hardiman's design earned a scathing review from the cartoonist Osbert Lancaster who wrote with some humour: 'Is this curious charger of doubtful breeding, walking forward, standing still or preparing to indulge in a capriole or one of the other decorative feats which have earned the Lipizaner horses in Vienna such deserved commendation? Is the fact that its hind quarters appear to be stationary while its forelegs advance a subtle indication of the dual nature of the late Field-Marshal's command, or an unkind sculptural suggestion that his strategy suffered from divided counsels? These are questions which each man must decide for himself, but personally we can never feel that an equestrian statue is really equestrian if the steed is not rearing up in a dramatic manner with its stomach supported by a small iron rod and its rider's hand waving a baton'.[44] However, Hardiman's design earned the approval of the Viscount Esher, who in a debate in the House of Lords some years later stated: 'Lord Haig's memorial is compact in power and imagination. The horse's head is compressed and strong, the cloak more rigid than any cloak should be in real life, and the whole conception alive with the grave integrity of the man himself and the indomitable tenacity of the people who held the Western Front. Here is an undoubted work of art, an undoubted work of artistic merit, impossible to pass by without receiving an aesthetic emotion - at any rate for those who know what an aesthetic emotion is and are capable of experiencing it'.[45]

---

[43] Alfred F Hardiman (1891-1949). MRBS 1918, ARBS 1923, ARA 1936, FRBS 1938-49, RA 1944.
[44] Richard Boston *Osbert: A portrait of Osbert Lancaster* London: Collins 1989.
[45] House of Lords *Hansard* 23 May 1946 column 476.

# EDITH CAVELL

Edith Louisa Cavell was born 4 December 1865 to Louisa and the Reverend Frederick Cavell at Cavell House (the vicarage), Swardeston, Norfolk. Whilst caring for her sick father, Edith realised that nursing would be her life and she trained as a nurse at the London Hospital, Whitechapel. In 1901 she went to St Pancras Infirmary and two years later became Assistant Matron at Shoreditch Infirmary. In 1907 she was invited by Dr Antoine Depage to become matron of the Institut Medical de Birkendael, Brussels. She was on holiday with her mother in Norfolk when war was declared in 1914 and immediately returned to Brussels. After the fall of that city to the Germans, she ran an escape line for Allied soldiers trapped behind the lines. On 5 August 1915 she was arrested by the Germans and interrogated at St Gilles Prison. She was given the names of her 34 fellow conspirators and assured that they had all confessed. She confessed in the hope that she might reduce their penalty. With the others, she faced a military tribunal on 7 October 1915 charged with 'conducting soldiers to the enemy'. Not with spying as has often been claimed. She admitted having helped 60 British and French soldiers and about 100 French and Belgian men of military age escape to Holland. She was sentenced to death on Monday 11 October under paragraph 58 of the German Military Code. Despite the desperate intercession of the Spanish, American and Vatican diplomatic representatives, General von Sauberzweig, the Military Governor of Brussels resolved that Edith Cavell would pay the ultimate price for her actions. That night she was visited in her cell by the Reverend Stirling Gahan and uttered the words that would echo round the world: 'This I would say, standing as I do in view of God and eternity, I realise that patriotism is not enough. I must have no hatred or bitterness for anyone'.

At 0700 on 12 October 1915, at the Tir National shooting range in the Place des Carabiniers, Brussels she was led to her spot and stood with her skirts pinned for modesty's sake. Her fellow Resistance member, the architect Philippe Baucq, stood alongside her. The firing squad, commanded by Colonel Bulke fired from a range of 20 feet, killing both immediately.

Edith Cavell was buried in St Gilles prison cemetery. The shaft of the cross that marked her grave can be seen in Swardeston parish church. The Dutch *De Telegraaf* newspaper subsequently reported that her calm courage had made such an impression on the firing squad, that, to a man, they fired wide; she fainted and was executed with a single shot from the pistol of the officer in charge. This version of events was picked up by American newspapers and retold around the world. It was also taken up by Allied propagandists. Her execution galvanised American public opinion against Germany. On Saturday 12 October 1918 Queen Alexandra inaugurated her memorial in Norwich. The memorial consisted of two parts. The greater of these was considered to be the purchase of a property in Norwich to provide a permanent home for the Queen's Institute Nurses and their training as District Nurses to tend to the poor of the community. This was to be known as the Cavell Memorial Home. The Lord Mayor's City Appeal raised £1,000 for a wing to be added. Likewise, the Earl of Leicester, Lord Lieutenant of Norfolk, raised substantial funds from the county. The second part of the memorial was a monument designed by Henry Pegram. It was 14 feet tall and featured a bronze bust of Edith Cavell atop a Portland stone pedestal. A life-size full relief figure of a soldier is to the front. He holds a rifle in his left hand and reaches up with his right, to place a second wreath of immortelles under the bust. After the war the Belgian Government determined that those members of the Resistance who had been executed by the Germans would be exhumed from St Gilles and returned to their home communities for honoured burial. Edith Cavell's body was exhumed on 7 May 1919 and, according to doctors and religious observers, the double coffin (zinc lined in oak) revealed a barely corrupted unembalmed body. However, the four bullet holes to the upper body, one of which had passed through the heart, clearly proved that the firing squad had performed its task.

A gun carriage bore the coffin through the packed streets of Brussels. It was escorted by representative detachments of the Red Cross and the Allied armies. A religious ceremony was held at the Gare du Nord conducted by Mr Gahan. The coffin was placed on a train for Ostend and conveyed to England by the destroyer HMS ROWENA. It was placed under the amidships gun draped in the Union Flag. On 14 May 1919 the coffin was transferred to HM Tug ADDER and landed at Dover. It arrived ashore to the strains of Chopin's *Funeral March* played by a Royal Marine band. It was guarded overnight by The Buffs (the Royal West Kent Regiment) at Dover Marine Station. 'Early in the morning of Thursday 15 May 1919, a coach containing the coffin and a coach for mourners were attached to the train which left Dover Marine at 7.30 a.m. for Victoria. It passed through Sittingbourne and the two coaches were slipped at Herne Hill, to be brought on later to Victoria, arriving shortly after 11.30.'[46] The coffin was conveyed from Victoria to Westminster Abbey for the funeral service and the opportunity for national mourning in the presence of Queen Alexandra and the memorial service was conducted by Herbert Ryle, Dean of Westminster Abbey. Immense crowds thronged the route from Victoria to Westminster to see the coffin pass, as Guards bands played sombre melodies. The bearer party was found by the Coldstream Guards. The Abbey was packed to the rafters with the great and the good, soldiers, sailors and particularly representatives of the nursing services and the armed forces of the Allies and the Empire. After the service the coffin was conveyed on a gun carriage draped with the Union Flag through vast crowds to Liverpool Street Station. There it was placed in a carriage (specially built by Great Eastern's Stratford Works) for the continuation of the journey. On arrival at Norwich Thorpe, a bearer party was found from 100 men of the Norfolk Regiment under the command of Captain Paget. Red Cross nurses walked in front of the gun carriage and its six black horses were provided by the 67th Divisional Train of the RASC at Colchester. After a service in Norwich Cathedral, the coffin was carried outside to Life's Green by six Sergeant Majors: Cocksedge, Goulder, MC, Fisher, MC, Mornument and Woodward. The sixth was Jesse Tunmore, who had been nursed and returned to safety by Edith Cavell and her nurses. (He had been suspected by Edith Cavell of being a German spy, but cleared himself by identifying (unbidden) a print of Norwich Cathedral on the wall of her office). Dr Bertram Pollock, Bishop of Norwich conducted the graveside ceremony, with the Cavell family in attendance. On top of the coffin was a wreath of red and white carnations which bore a card with the inscription:

> "IN MEMORY OF OUR BRAVE HEROINE AND NEVER TO BE FORGOTTEN MISS CAVELL
> LIFE'S RACE WELL RUN,
> LIFE'S WORK WELL DONE,
> LIFE'S CROWN WELL WORN,
> NOW COMES REST,
> FROM ALEXANDRA"

Her statue outside the hospital at Belfort was removed by the Germans during the Second World War and reinstated afterwards by the Belgian Government. In 1992 her memorial in Norwich was moved from its position in the middle of a busy junction, to be placed outside Norwich Cathedral's Erpingham Gate and rededicated on 4 December. On the wall behind it is a bronze plaque, with the images in relief of both Edith Cavell and Dr Depage. In March 2003 the small garden surrounding the memorial was planted with Edith Cavell red roses. Edith Cavell is not forgotten in Norfolk; this year as every year, Swardeston Church holds its fete on the Sunday nearest the anniversary of her death. There are hospitals named for her at Peterborough, Northamptonshire and Brussels. She is also commemorated by Mount Edith Cavell in the Athabaska Valley, Jasper National Park, Alberta, Canada. Website at www.edithcavell.org.uk

---

[46] *The Times* 16 May 1919, page 13f.

# LONDON

This memorial stands at the junction of St Martin's Lane and Charing Cross Road on the north side of Trafalgar Square in London and was designed by Sir George Frampton. A British Lion is carved in relief on the rear of the memorial. Frampton's uncharacteristic design was heavily criticised, this controversy being encapsulated by the apocryphal tale of the bystander at the unveiling by Queen Alexandra on 17 March 1920, who reportedly exclaimed: 'Good God, they shot the wrong woman'. The memorial was restored by David Bell Restoration Ltd in 2003 and an exhibition was mounted at the adjacent National Portrait Gallery detailing its history.

Although there is a school of thought that regards war memorials as being an anachronistic throwback to an increasingly distant imperial past, throughout 2003 the memorial was the venue for a series of demonstrations by a campaigning group calling itself: 'The Women in Black' - 'Jews for Justice for Palestinians'.

The following inscriptions are carved on the plinth of the statue:

"EDITH CAVELL. BRUSSELS. DAWN OCTOBER 12th 1915.

HUMANITY, SACRIFICE, FORTITUDE and DEVOTION".

Some years after the memorial's inauguration Edith Cavell's own words were added:

"PATRIOTISM IS NOT ENOUGH.
I MUST HAVE NO HATRED OR BITTERNESS FOR ANYONE".

# NORWICH

Edith Cavell's grave on Life's Green.

Henry Alfred Pegram's memorial to Edith Cavell at Norwich consisting of a bronze bust atop a stone pillar was inaugurated by Queen Alexandra on 12 October 1918, the third anniversary of her execution. The inscription reads: "EDITH CAVELL. NURSE, PATRIOT AND MARTYR".

# THE ROYAL STAR AND GARTER HOME, RICHMOND

The Royal Star and Garter Home for ex-Servicemen stands at the summit of Richmond Hill with a sweeping vista of the Surrey Hills, Hampton Court and Eel Pie Island. It stands on the site of what was the Star and Garter Inn and then the Star and Garter Hotel, which, in the Victorian era had something of a racy reputation. The *Richmond Times* hinted in 1915 that: 'fashionable London society in the later seventies was vivacious, and the Star and Garter figured considerably in its doings'. Such was the hotel's reputation in the late 19th century that local parents forbade their daughters to attend dances there - even if chaperoned. By the turn of the century, the five storey semi-derelict pile was abandoned. The Auctioneers' and Estate Agents' Institute purchased it in 1915 and presented it to Queen Mary for the purpose of establishing a home for the long term care of disabled ex-Servicemen after discharge from hospital. Queen Alexandra inspected the site with the Surgeon-General, who declared it 'first-rate for the purpose'. A prestigious governing body composed of the great and the good was established and an appeal for funds launched. It caught the public mood and funds were raised by women's patriotic groups in Britain and every corner of the Empire. Fund-raising was the war service of society ladies and by the end of 1916 the endowment fund totalled £217,957, the capital fund for building and equipment had raised £110,000 and the British Red Cross contributed £100,000. The Home's first 65 residents were admitted on 14 January 1916 and accommodated in the ballroom and banqueting hall. Work was provided with needlework, salmon fly dressing, basketwork, painting, horology, pigeon keeping and a banjo band was established for the musically inclined. The Home's records show that of 112 patients admitted that first year, 20 died, 18 left 'improved', five were 'immeasurably improved', 12 were 'in almost a dying condition on admission' and 'two who showed suicidal tendencies were transferred to Brookwood Asylum'. Quickly it became apparent that the hotel was unsuitable for its new purpose and it was decided to erect a new purpose-built home on the same site. The British Women's Hospital Committee launched a worldwide appeal for funds to build it. They raised the equivalent of £9 million in today's terms. The new Home was designed without fee by the architect Sir Edwin Cooper. It was formally opened by King George V and Queen Mary on 10 July 1924 and dedicated as the 'Women of the Empire's Memorial of the Great War'. In 1916 a Board of Governors was established and they run it to this day. (A representative of the British Red Cross is a member). Upon Queen Mary's death in 1953, Queen Elizabeth II became Patron and Princess Alexandra was appointed President in 1964. Today the home caters for up to 172 residents. Anyone who has served in Her Majesty's Forces regardless of rank is eligible for a place. No distinction is made between those injured on active service or those disabled through accident or illness in civilian life. The Home cares for up to 185 disabled ex-Service men and women. Residents have the best medical and nursing care available, provided by a staff of 40 nurses and 70 care assistants. Many have suffered injury on the field of battle and others were accidentally injured, or fell victim to chronic illness. For most of them the Home is their permanent residence. Others come for short term visits for rehabilitation or respite care. The Home has one of the best rehabilitation units in the country, which helps residents through therapy and training to come to terms with disability. Additional services provided by the Home include a Pharmacy, where residents can purchase non-prescription medicines, toiletries and have their films developed, a dental surgery, hairdressing salon, a counselling service, and regular visits by an aromatherapist and chiropodist. Many ex-Service organisations arrange outings or parties at the Home and the residents have their own bar, music club, bridge club, chess club, jazz club and library. For more than eight decades the Home has provided the very best care for the disabled ex-Service community and this has been made possible thanks to voluntary support in the form of legacies, donations, and fundraising activities. Events in recent years demonstrate the continuing need for the Royal Star and Garter Home on Richmond Hill.

# THE BELGIAN WAR MEMORIAL

On 3 August 1914 Germany invaded Belgium and on the morning of 4 August the British Cabinet voted to go to war to defend her territorial integrity, which was guaranteed by the Treaty of London (1831). Brussels fell without a fight on 20 August. The Belgians flooded the Yser Estuary that day and their Army sat behind the resulting mile wide barrier for the rest of the war. Further south, the British Expeditionary Force recaptured Ypres from the Germans on 13 October and bled itself white over the next four years holding it. The myth of 'plucky little Belgium' has its roots firmly in the German invasion of Belgium and the British press lionised King Albert I throughout the entire war. However, behind the backs of the Allies, he entered into negotiations with the Germans through his brother-in-law, the diplomat Count Hans von Törring zu Jettenbach. The unwillingness of the Germans to guarantee a Belgian future for the Congo proved an intractable obstacle to Belgium changing sides and Maréchal Foch's successful offensive, which commenced on 18 July 1918, permanently derailed the King's plans. The German Army then collapsed in the most dramatic manner. Recognising the end was in sight on 26 September 1918 King Albert finally placed the Belgian Army under Allied command.

In the autumn of 1918 a committee met in London under the chairmanship of two Belgian princesses to erect a memorial commemorating Britain's effort in defence of Belgium. The architect chosen was Sir Reginald Blomfield, the sculpture was executed by the distinguished Belgian sculptor Victor Rousseau (1871-1958) and the statuary was cast by the A B Burton foundry at Thames Ditton. Situated on Victoria Embankment, Blomfield's design took the form of an elliptical Portland stone wall with Rousseau's bronze sculpture forming the central feature. Above it are carved shields depicting the provinces of Belgium. The inscription reads:

"TO
THE BRITISH NATION
FROM THE GRATEFUL
PEOPLE OF BELGIUM
1914 - 1918"

# THE WAGONERS MEMORIAL

In 1911, in that golden age of amateur soldiering, Sir Mark Sykes[47] founded the Wagoners Reserve. He raised this corps of 1,000 men from his estates in the Yorkshire Dales. He trained, drilled and paid each reservist a guinea a year retainer. In 1914, with the outbreak of war, the corps duly embarked for France and served on the Western Front. After the war a memorial to the fallen was erected at Sledmere. 'The sculptor was Carlo Magnoni, who is not otherwise recorded but who reveals an unsophisticated and amusing style which is (either intentionally or unintentionally) an excellent medieval pastiche'.[48] This extraordinary memorial consists of three rings of frieze. The narrative commences with the wagoner working in the fields, the postman arriving with a letter, the wagoner presenting himself to Sir Mark etc. It is perhaps, the most unusual, successful and entertaining use of an extended narrative on a memorial.

In 1938 Sir Richard Sykes, Sir Mark's son, received a letter from the German Embassy asking him to remove the war memorial from public display. The German Consul had taken considerable exception to the relief of a German soldier setting fire to a church and another of a German soldier standing with a sword upraised over a kneeling girl whilst holding her by the hair. Mlle Ludovicy, Sir Richard's secretary helpfully informed the press: 'It was Sir Mark's wish that the memorial should be in crude Old Saxon style. I am afraid the finished article is rather more refined than he would have wished. I do not know who told the Consul. Probably someone bought a picture postcard of the memorial and sent it to the German Embassy. There has been an exchange of very friendly letters and I think that after Sir Richard's explanation that the figures were intended to be crude old Saxons, the whole controversy will finish'.

---

[47] Sir Mark Sykes, 6th Baronet, born 1879. Educated privately. Served in Boer War. MP for Hull 1911-19. In 1914 mobilised his territorial battalion (5th Yorkshire Regiment) and took it to France. In 1915 seconded to General Staff. Negotiated the secret Sykes-Picot Agreement which determined British and French spheres of influence in the post-Ottoman Near East. Attended the Peace Conference in Paris, succumbed to 'Spanish Flu' and died February 1919.
[48] Alan Borg *War Memorials*.

# CRICH STAND

The summit of Crich Hill in the Amber Valley, 15 miles north of Derby, is reputed to have been the site of one of the beacon fires that signalled the arrival of the Spanish Armada in 1588. Over the centuries a number of towers were erected on the site, the last falling into disuse at the start of the 20th century. In 1914 the men of Derbyshire and Nottinghamshire went to war. During the course of the Great War 33 battalions of the Sherwood Foresters were raised and some 140,000 men served with the regiment, 11,409 being killed. In 1921 the Regiment decided that a memorial would be required to commemorate their fallen and the tower was erected in 1923 with money being raised through public subscription. Mr Joseph Payne, a local builder, was commissioned to undertake the work. It was inaugurated on 6 August 1923 and this Grade II listed building is highly unusual, in that it takes the form of an inland lighthouse nearly 1000 feet above sea level. Set in the top of the tower is a 28 inch searchlight with a luminous range of 38 miles. It rotates 8 times a minute and can be seen in several counties. It shines each night in memory of the men of the Regiment who gave their lives in all conflicts. In the Second World War the Regiment raised 17 battalions, 11 of which saw service overseas. 1,520 men died in that war. Although it cannot be seen in the photograph above, at the front of the tower is a Garden of Remembrance. Each Remembrancetide it is planted with crosses. The regiment still holds an annual pilgrimage to Crich Stand on the first Sunday in July, with civic dignitaries and religious in attendance. The Sherwood Foresters were amalgamated with the Worcestershire Regiment in February 1970, to form the Worcestershire and Sherwood Foresters Regiment. Website at www.crich-memorial.org

# THE CAVALRY MEMORIAL, HYDE PARK, LONDON

During the 19th century the cavalry regiments would add many a distinguished chapter to the annals of the British Army and these episodes would include: the charge of Captain Norman Ramsay's troop of Royal Horse Artillery complete with bounding limbers and cannons in 1811 at the Battle of Fuentes de Oñoro; the charge of the Scots Greys at Waterloo; the spectacular but bizarre charge of the Light Brigade in the Crimea and the charge at the Battle of Omdurman. Sadly, the days of 'lending tone to what otherwise might degenerate into a vulgar brawl' ended with the invention of the machine gun and despite a strenuous rearguard action fought by senior army commanders, commonsense eventually prevailed, and, by the commencement of the Second World War, the cavalry had been converted from horses to armoured cars and tanks. 'During a Commons debate in 1934 the Labour MP for Leigh, Mr Tinker had the temerity to question the value of horsed cavalry. Hardly had he finished speaking than a Conservative MP, Brigadier Making, spurred to the attack. Having cut down the unfortunate Mr Tinker, the brigadier concluded with the immortal words; 'There must be no tinkering with the cavalry!' From all accounts it seems unlikely that his wit was even deliberate.'[49] A fire at the MOD ordnance depot at Donnington in the 1980s revealed the existence of 14,000,000 horse shoes, which were destroyed in the blaze. This would seem somewhat excessive given that the army's only remaining horsed formations at that time were the Household Cavalry Mounted Regiment at Hyde Park, King's Troop of the Royal Horse Artillery at St John's Wood and a detachment of mounted Royal Military Police at Aldershot. The Cavalry Memorial in Hyde Park was executed by that most accomplished of British equine sculptors, Captain Adrian Jones and cast by the A B Burton foundry. The heroic figure of St George is depicted as having just slain the Dragon, and interestingly, the Dragon has two outsized 'handlebar' moustaches rather in the manner of those sported by Kaiser Wilhelm II. The architect was Sir John Burnet and the memorial was inaugurated on 21 May 1924. Originally sited at Stanhope Gate, it was shifted to Serpentine Road in 1961 to accommodate the road widening scheme for Park Lane. This finely executed memorial is the venue for 'Cavalry Sunday' the annual memorial service for cavalrymen held each May.

---

[49] Norman Dixon *On the Psychology of Military Incompetence* p. 116.

# DR BRIGHTON'S INDIAN PATIENTS

In consequence of Germany's invasion of Belgium, Britain declared war on Germany on 4 August 1914. The Dominions immediately recognised the urgency of the situation. However, only India - not a Dominion - had standing regular forces immediately available and the War Office was inundated with offers from Princes and Maharajahs. The first Indian troops duly arrived at Lyons, France on 26 September. Given the heavy fighting in France, provision had to be made for the care of their wounded. In November the King inspected the adapted hospital for the Indian soldiers at Southampton, which at that time was seriously overcrowded due to a fire on one of the hospital ships on Southampton Water. He was most displeased by what he found there and made his feelings clear to the authorities responsible. Urgent action was undertaken by the War Office to rectify matters. Brighton, long recognised for its recuperative effects, was quickly identified. Swiftly the town prepared the Pavilion, Dome and Corn Exchange to receive the Indian patients. The chances of survival at Brighton were good - if the patient survived the journey by hospital train and then hospital ship. Hindus and Sikhs who died at Brighton were cremated after the customary religious rites at a burning ghat constructed at a specially chosen site high up on the Downs. Muslims were buried with appropriate rites in the grounds of the mosque which was established at Slough in 1899. There are no Indian graves from the Great War in Brighton.

After the war on the site of the ghat a white marble memorial approximately 2.8 metres wide and some 8.8 metres tall with eight pillars rising from the octagonal base supporting a hollow dome. It was designed by E C Henriques of Bombay and was inaugurated by the Prince of Wales on 1 February 1921. Its construction was jointly funded by the India Office and Brighton Corporation. The Chattri bears the inscription in Urdu, Hindi and English:

"TO THE MEMORY OF ALL INDIAN SOLDIERS WHO GAVE THEIR LIVES FOR THE KING – EMPEROR IN THE GREAT WAR, THIS MONUMENT, ERECTED ON THE SITE OF THE FUNERAL PYRE WHERE THE HINDUS AND SIKHS WHO DIED IN HOSPITAL IN BRIGHTON PASSED THROUGH THE FIRE, IS IN GRATEFUL ADMIRATION AND BROTHERLY AFFECTION DEDICATED".

# THE GALLIPOLI MEMORIAL

This memorial in Westminster Abbey commemorates all those who died in the Gallipoli Campaign which lasted nine months. 'With the possible exception of the Crimean War, the Gallipoli expedition was the most poorly mounted and ineptly controlled operation in modern British military history'.[50] After the failure on 18 March 1915 of an Anglo-French fleet to force the Straits, Winston Churchill, (initially) supported by Field Marshal Earl Kitchener, determined that troops would be used to succour Russia and eliminate Turkey as an ally of Germany. The landings at Gallipoli took place on 25 April and had the generals in charge executed their duties in anything like a competent manner, the outcome would have altered the entire course of the war. Their failure would seal Russia's fate, do considerable damage to Churchill's reputation, expose Kitchener as a vacillator and serve as an object lesson to the War Office on the folly of employing retired, inexperienced generals. Churchill would be dogged for years afterwards at public meetings by the anonymously shouted jibe: 'What about Gallipoli then?' British Empire forces during the campaign comprised some 420,000 British, 50,000 Australians, 9,000 New Zealanders aided by some 80,000 French. British casualties were 20,000 killed, those of Australia and New Zealand - 11,200 killed and the French sustained over 10,000 killed and wounded. A total of 39 Victoria Crosses were awarded to British and Empire troops in the campaign.

Despite the consternation caused at the War Office by Lord Milner and his friends openly discussing the highly secret operation in the House of Lords, the British completed the evacuation of the last of their troops from the Peninsula, under cover of darkness on the night of 8-9 January 1916 without the loss of a single man.[51] It has in recent years become apparent that German military intelligence had concluded that Milner's thoughtless indiscretion was a typically clever example of English bluff.

---

[50] R Ernest Dupuy and Trevor N Dupuy *The Collins Encyclopedia of Military History (Fourth Edition)*.
[51] Alan Moorehead *Gallipoli* p. 341.

# THE RESPONSE

This highly original memorial stands close to St Thomas the Martyr Church, Barras Bridge, Newcastle upon Tyne. It was designed by the outstanding sculptor Sir William Goscombe John and was inaugurated by the Prince of Wales in 1923. It was the gift of Sir George and Lady Renwick. The life-size figures are of bronze, the plinth and monument are of granite. The memorial portrays the men of Tyneside answering 'the call to the colours'. They are led by two drummer boys in uniform. The work comprises men, some in uniform, others dressed in work clothes carrying tools. There are also children and sweethearts in the group bidding farewell to their loved ones. At the front, two flags fly and a winged Victory blows a trumpet. The plinth bears the inscription:

"NON SIBI SED PATRIAE[52]

THE RESPONSE 1914"

On the reverse of the memorial are the figures of St George flanked by a Northumberland Fusilier in the uniform of the Great War and another in the uniform of 1674, the date the Regiment was formed. (A typical Goscombe John device, which he used on a number of his memorials). The memorial bears the inscription:

"TO COMMEMORATE THE RAISING OF B COMPANY
9TH BATTALION AND THE 16TH, 18TH AND 19TH SERVICE
BATTALIONS, NORTHUMBERLAND FUSILIERS, BY THE
NEWCASTLE AND GATESHEAD CHAMBER OF COMMERCE
AUGUST - OCTOBER 1914"

---

[52] Not for themselves, but for their country.

# THE COLNE WAR MEMORIAL

This memorial commemorates the Great War dead of Colne in Lancashire. It was constructed from both Shepley and Portland stone. It takes the form of a colonnade, measuring 13 feet 6 inches in height, 30 feet 9 inches in length and fifteen feet 1 inch in width. The outer curb of the base measures 32 feet by 16 feet 4 inches. The marble tablets which are let into panels on the inside of the two end walls are of white Sicilian marble and contain the 650 names of the fallen in inlaid lead letters. The Arms of the County and the borough are carved on the outside walls. The memorial was designed by Mr T H Hartley, the Borough Engineer, and erected under his supervision by Messrs Wm. Kirkpatrick of Trafford Park, Manchester. The memorial cost £2,000, which was raised by public subscription. The grounds around the memorial were laid out by the Corporation as an Unemployment Scheme under the supervision of the Borough Engineer.

The memorial was inaugurated on 11 November 1930. The ceremony commenced with a hymn followed by the Blessing. The buglers of the Colne Corps of the St John Ambulance Brigade sounded the *Last Post*, followed by a one-minute's silence. Then *Reveille* was sounded followed by the national anthem. The Mayor, Councillor Mr J King, JP, and the Deputy Mayor Mr J E Keighley, JP laid wreaths upon behalf of the Corporation and the War Memorial Committee respectively. Relatives and friends of the fallen then laid wreaths and floral tributes. The lintels on the four sides of the memorial bear the following inscriptions:

North:     "AT THE GOING DOWN OF THE SUN AND IN THE MORNING WE WILL REMEMBER THEM"

South:     "ERECTED TO THE MEMORY OF THOSE WHO MADE THE SUPREME SACRIFICE"

East:     "GREAT WAR 1914 - 1918"

West:     "LEST WE FORGET"

# THE ABERDEEN WAR MEMORIAL

In 1919 the city fathers of Aberdeen announced a scheme to commemorate the city's war dead. Their plan consisted of a Memorial Hall or Hall of Remembrance, an extension to the city's art gallery, a large hall and an art museum. Despite the scope and complexity of the scheme, once the details were published in the *Aberdeen Daily Journal* in August 1919, little change was ever made to the initial plans. The architects chosen for the task were Dr A Marshall Mackenzie (the architect of the original building) and A G R Mackenzie. The cost of the works was £70,000. Facing Union Terrace Gardens, the exterior of the Memorial Court was of concave shape, with six Corinthian pillars on a raised platform, in front of a wall on which were carved a wreath of laurels, the arms of the city and county, the dates 1914-1919 in Roman numerals and the words:

"TO OUR GLORIOUS DEAD"

The figure of a lion in the courtyard was sculpted by the distinguished Aberdeen-born sculptor William McMillan. The memorial was inaugurated by King George V on 29 September 1925 and dedicated by the Moderators of the Church of Scotland and the United Free Church of Scotland. The Gordon Highlanders provided the King's Guard of Honour.

The Roll of Honour contained the names of 535 officers, 4,505 other ranks and two women, these being a nurse and a medical missionary. Four Aberdonian Victoria Crosses were listed on it, these being: Captain James A O Brooke of the Gordon Highlanders, Lieutenant Robert Grierson Combe of the 27th Battalion of the Manitoba Regiment CEF, Captain Archibald Smith of the Royal Naval Reserve and Brigadier-General Frederick W Lumsden of the Royal Marine Artillery. The Roll was placed within the Shrine by Mr Peter Tocher, who had served during the war in the Gordon Highlanders. Inscribed on the Roll were the names of his five sons who had died serving in the same Regiment.

# THE LEWIS WAR MEMORIAL

In the Great War the island of Lewis in the Western Isles of Scotland, with a population of 29,603 sent 6,172 men to serve with the colours and of that number, 1,151 did not return. 376 Lewis men and women also gave their lives in the Second World War.

In January 1920 a public meeting was held at Stornoway to discuss the form of commemoration for the fallen of the island. Viscount Leverhulme, the owner of Lewis, was elected Chairman of the Appeal Committee. Advertisements placed in the *Stornoway Gazette* were used to canvass for subscribers to the memorial. Leverhulme match-funded the community's subscription and donated half the £4,000 cost. On 1 August 1920 the Committee selected the design from four submitted. The memorial took the form of a Scottish baronial tower 85 ft tall. It was designed by the architect Mr J H Gall of Inverness. It stands on a 300 foot tall hill overlooking Stornoway and is a conspicuous landmark. Internally the tower was divided into an arched entrance chamber 20 ft high and four upper chambers reached by square and circular steel stairs until the granite turnpike stairs are reached in the turret. In the chambers bronze panels containing inscriptions and the names of the fallen of the four parishes of Lewis were affixed, a separate chamber being allocated to each parish. The entrance to the tower on the south face has a richly moulded arched doorway which originally contained a massive door of Scottish oak, above which were two moulded panels on which the dedicatory inscriptions were cut. All the dressed stonework was of either Aberdeenshire granite or gneiss (a local metamorphic rock). The Memorial was inaugurated by Viscount Leverhulme on 5 September 1924.

# THE BEARSDEN WAR MEMORIAL

This war memorial commemorating the sons of Bearsden, Glasgow who fell in the Great War was designed by Alexander Proudfoot, ARSA and stands at the junction of Drymen and Roman Roads. Laden with symbolism, it takes the form of a nine feet tall bronze figure of Victory holding in her arms Sacrifice. The figures stand on a Portland stone pedestal fifteen feet high. Carried round the top of the pedestal is a laurel bronze band.

The well-attended inauguration ceremony was conducted on 10 May 1924. The band and Guard of Honour were provided by the 1st Battalion of the Royal Scots Fusiliers. 'The impressive service was opened with a voluntary by the band followed by the singing of Kipling's recessional hymn *God of our fathers, known of old.* The Rev. Mr Paterson then read a passage from the Scriptures and the dedicatory prayer was offered by the Rev. Mr Purves.'[53] The Reverend Mr Dickie then introduced Sir Iain Colquhoun of Luss, Lord Lieutenant of Dumbartonshire, who made a speech that had much to say about the country's 'unexampled economic distress' and the 'unemployment of ex-Servicemen.' He then pulled the cord and the coverings fell away. The Rev. Mr Dickie then dedicated the memorial in the following terms: 'In the name of the Father, and the Son, and the Holy Ghost, I dedicate this memorial to the glory of God and in everlasting remembrance of the men of Bearsden who gave their lives for us in the Great War. Greater love hath no man than this, that a man lay down his life for his friends. Amen.' The New Kilpatrick Pipe Band then played *The Flowers of the Forest* and wreaths were laid. A young member of the Boy's Brigade fainted as the *Last Post* was sounded.

At the unveiling there were seventy names engraved on bronze plaques affixed to the pedestal of the memorial. In common with many other community war memorials, after the Second World War the names of the fallen of the parish in that war were added.

---

[53] *The Herald* 16 May 1924.

# THE LONDON ZOO WAR MEMORIAL

Founded by Sir Thomas Stamford Raffles, London Zoo stands in Regents Park, London and is run by the Zoological Society of London. Upon the outbreak of war in 1914 the Society encouraged those of its employees who were physically able to answer 'the call to the colours'. 'The Society's normal staff consisted of about 150 males, including those unfitted for active service. Of these, 92 volunteered or were called up and 14 were subsequently rejected on medical grounds. The following 12 were killed:- H D Monro, W Bodman, A G Whybrow, G Patterson, William Dexter, William Perkins, Alfred L Day, and Charles W Dare, *Menagerie Staff;* A A Dermott, *Office Messenger;* H G J Peavot, *Librarian;* R Jones and Albert Staniford, *Gardeners.*'[54] Examination of the men's service records reveals that they served in different regiments rather than together, as one would expect. If any regiment does predominate, it is the Rifle Brigade in which three of the men served. Unusually, the Zoo held the men's posts open for them to return to after the war. The Society 'did its bit' for the war effort and removed from its Roll of Members the names of all those Corresponding Members who were subjects of the Central Powers. In 1919 the Society decided to erect a permanent war memorial in the Gardens to commemorate those who had gone to war and did not return. A number of designs were considered, but that chosen was a mediaeval French 'Lantern of the Dead' such as that found at La Souterraine in the Valley of the Creuse; the inspiration for this form was most likely the 12th century ecclesiastic Peter of Cluny, who is recorded as stating: 'the light shining by night was a homage paid by the faithful to dead Christians' The memorial was constructed from Portland stone to a design prepared by the Society's architect, Mr J J Joass. It took the form of a hexagonal column placed on steps with a tapered conical roof surmounted by a cross. A bronze plaque was affixed to a tablet at the foot of the memorial listing each of the men by name. It was unveiled in 1919. Three further names of staff were added after World War II and the names of five staff from Whipsnade Zoo added later. The memorial was moved from its original site near the Monkey House in 1952 and it now stands opposite Three Island Ponds, home of the pelicans.

---

[54] *Zoological Society Annual Report 1919.*

# THE NATIONAL LIBERAL CLUB WAR MEMORIAL

This bronze memorial panel commemorates by name all 15 members of the permanent staff of the National Liberal Club in London who fell in the Great War. (There is no equivalent memorial to the Club's members). It was unveiled by the then President of the Club, the Marquess of Lincolnshire, on 14 May 1924. The names are given in full, in alphabetical order. The inscription reads:

"THE NATIONAL LIBERAL CLUB

IN MEMORY OF THE MEMBERS
OF THE STAFF OF THE
CLUB WHO FELL IN THE
GREAT WAR 1914 - 1918

BALLARD, GEORGE BERNARD
BRADFORD, SAMUEL
BURNETT, WILLIAM ALEX
BUTLER, HENRY EDMUND
CLARK, HENRY WILLIAM
CROCKFORD, CHARLES
DANCE, NATHANIEL WILLIAM
ELLIOT, JOHN FREDERICK
FAHEY, ALBERT
HAINES, HENRY
JUSTICE, WILLIAM JOHN
MOAKES, WILLIAM ALFRED
PHEBY, GEORGE HENRY
WATTS, HUBERT WILLIAM
WRIGHT, WILLIAM

FAITHFUL UNTO DEATH"

# THE LONDON HOP TRADE WAR MEMORIAL

The Hop is the English name given to the climbing plant *humulus lupulus,* which was grown in England from the 17th century onwards to give beer its bitter flavour and prior to the invention of the chemically produced beers of the 20th century, was intensely cultivated in Kent, 'the Garden of England'. 'Hopping' was an annual activity, with many thousands of Londoners travelling by train down to Kent each summer to pick the harvest. During the Second World War, so great was the shortage of 'Hoppers' that the government drafted the army in to gather the harvest.

The London Hop Trade War Memorial is affixed to the corner of a building in Borough High Street in London. The building was previously the Town Hall Chambers, but is now appropriately enough the Slug and Lettuce Public House. The London Hop Exchange is located just around the corner in Southwark Street. Overshadowed by the dramatic urgency of Philip Lindsey Clarke's St Saviour's War Memorial, the London Hop Trade War Memorial takes the form of a simple bronze tablet ornamented by sculpted hops. Most surprisingly, it was designed by the celebrated English silversmith Omar Ramsden (1873-1939) and cast by his founder M Manenti. It commemorates by name the 34 hop trade workers who died in the Great War. Their names are carried on the memorial in alphabetical order and include their regiments or arms of service. The memorial was inaugurated by Brigadier-General J T Wigan in a ceremony held on 12 January 1922.[55]

---

[55] Brigadier-General J T Wigan, CB CMG DSO TD (1877-1952). Educated Rugby, fought in Boer War. Left 13th Hussars in 1909 to join the family hop business. Served as adjutant of the Berkshire Yeomanry and saw action in the Great War. He was Coalition Unionist MP 1918-21. He worked in the family business for 43 years and was great grandson of the founder. He was partner of Wigan, Richardson and Co, Hop Merchants and director of G Nott & Co Ltd Hop Growers. Honorary Colonel 4th Battalion the Essex Regiment 1922-45.

# THE VICTORIA COLLEGE WAR MEMORIAL, JERSEY

The names of the 127 Old Victorians who gave their lives in defence of their country in the Great War may be found on the reverse and sides of the statue of Sir Galahad, which has dominated the College quadrangle since its unveiling by the Lieutenant Governor in a ceremony on 25 September 1924 to the strains of Sir John Stanhope Arkwright's *O Valiant Hearts* sung by the College Choir. In his address, the Lieutenant Governor, Major-General the Honourable Sir Francis Bingham, pointed out that: '636 Old Victorians took part in the Great War, and studying these figures I see that 25 per cent, or one in four, of the Old Victorians who actually took the field lost their lives. Surely a wonderful proportion and perhaps unequalled by any school or college in the British Empire.' In commenting on the posthumous awards of the Victoria Cross to Captain Bruce and Captain McReady-Diarmid, he also included Lieutenant Richard Meade, saying that the: 'young officer of 23, who lost his life at Gallipoli, was twice recommended for this coveted honour'. The sculptor of the life-size bronze figure, which stands on a granite pedestal eight feet in height, was Alfred Turner. The inscription on the face of the pedestal is: 'This figure of Sir Galahad commemorates the Victorians who gave their lives in the Great War, 1914-1918'. This is followed by a brief quotation from Alfred Lord Tennyson's Holy Grail, suggesting the symbolic character of the figure:

> "AND COME THOU TOO
> FOR THOU SHALT SEE THE
> VISION WHEN I GO"

The emblem above the inscription is a symbol taken from Celtic art of the early Christian period. It signifies the manifestation of God through the Holy Ghost and it was used to represent the voice saying: 'This is my beloved Son, in Whom I am well pleased.' Sir Galahad was chosen because he was predestined to achieve the quest of the Holy Grail and foredoomed, the quest achieved, to vanish. On the reverse and side faces of the pedestal are carved the 127 surnames, with initials only, or Christian names, not distinguished by rank, regiment or honour, as: 'in their sacrifice all men are equal'. Turner exhibited the sculpture at the RA, where Old Victorians within reach of London were able to view it before its journey to Jersey. The position originally proposed for the statue in front of the main door of the College was abandoned on Turner's recommendation. He was of the opinion that that position would spoil the façade and dwarf the statue. The contractor was C J Le Quesne and the lettering was carried out by Mr F Huaut. The statue cost £850; the pedestal, foundation and lettering, £200; a scholarship scheme £272; and the £70 left over from the subscriptions raised by the Old Victorians Association was put aside as a contingency fund. As part of the memorial to the fallen, a Book of Remembrance was prepared and on a practical note, scholarships were offered for the sons of Old Victorians who fell in the war. In his speech before the unveiling of the statue by the Lieutenant Governor, Mr E T Nicolle, President of the Memorial Committee, said: 'This memorial will endure to remind present and future generations of Victorians of the splendid services rendered to their country by those who passed out of this school, may Victorians past, present and future, when passing this monument, bare their heads in memory and in reverence for those of their school who fell in the Great War.' And, until the demise of the hat, school cap and boater, all College boys from the grandest school prefect to the smallest prep boy and every Old Victorian doffed their headgear on passing the statue. Such was the impact of the deaths of their menfolk sustained by the small communities of the Channel Islands in the Great War, that in the Second World War, the men were never drafted together into one unit, instead being posted into different branches and regiments of all three Services to avoid a repetition of such heavy losses.

# THE RAILWAYS

Although engine-driving and signalling were 'reserved occupations' and, as such, exempt from military call-up, 18,957 British railwaymen died in the Great War. They worked for a total of 66 railway companies and are commemorated at more than 60 stations throughout Britain and a wide range of forms were employed to commemorate their sacrifice. 'These memorials are interesting not just as memorials to the dead of that terrible conflict but for their excellent design. They are also of considerable interest to railway historians, as they are constant reminders of the corporate origins of British railways and for the smaller companies often its only publicly-visible evidence. For most companies their war memorial was also their swan-song, for the memorial often seems to have been hurried into existence before grouping. The memorials also reflect the social history of the time, the 'paternalism' of the management and the allegiance of the workers to their company. They are evidence too, of the way railways at that time were an integral part of people's lives not just as a means of transport'[56]

Of the travellers arriving daily at London's Waterloo Station, many will be unaware that the Victory Arch forming the station's main entrance is the Great War Memorial to the fallen of the South Western Railway Company. It was inaugurated by Queen Alexandra on 21 March 1922. 'The Victory Arch at Waterloo is Britain's largest railway war memorial. It was also the most prestigious, uniquely unveiled by the Queen. Designed by James Robb Scott, it forms the architectural focus of the station. The whole composition is highly symbolic. Around the Arch, shields bear the names of the theatres of conflict: Belgium; Dardanelles; France; Mesopotamia; Egypt; North Sea and Italy. Statuary groups sculpted by Charles Whiffen flank the entrance.'[57] On the left, 1914 is symbolised by Bellona, goddess of war, a grieving woman and a dead man. In 1918, on the right, a figure representing peace brings contentment, abundance and enlightenment to the world (!) The names of the men are inscribed on tablets within the Arch, while Britannia tops the whole thing off. Usefully the Arch also houses a fine clock.'[58] The memorial lamps that ornament the Arch were added later.

The Metropolitan Railway (now part of London Underground) decided that its tribute to their 137 war dead would take the form of a memorial at both Baker Street Station, which was inaugurated by the company's chairman Lord Aberconway on 11 November 1920, and a recreational facility at Forty Lane, Wembley Park. This Remembrance Hall burned down in a mysterious blaze on 4 September 1929.

In the early hours of 22 May 1915 a troop train was carrying A and D companies and battalion HQ of the 1/7th (Leith Territorial) Battalion of the Royal Scots from Larbert, Stirlingshire to Liverpool, where they were to embark for Gallipoli. At Quintinshill, just north of Gretna Green, the train was routed onto a line on which stood a stationary empty coal train, the signalman on duty having forgotten it was there. There followed a collision. Less than a minute later, a north-bound London express crashed into the wreckage of the two trains, the debris then caught fire. Fire engines from Carlisle took three hours to arrive at the scene. 485 soldiers were on board the train and of this number, three officers, 29 NCOs and 182 men were killed, as well as 12 railwaymen and civilians. The mass grave, the memorial carrying the names of those who died that day and a 20 foot tall massive Ionian Cross all stand in Rosebank Cemetery, Leith. The reader may consider the negligent signalman fortunate to get only three years penal servitude.[59] The remnants of 1/7th Battalion of the Royal Scots eventually made it to Gallipoli where they fought at Achi Baba and Gully Ravine.

---

[56] *Backtrack* Vol. 10 (1996) pp 689-691.
[57] Charles E Whiffen MRBS 1920, ARBS 1923-27.
[58] *The London Railway Record* July 1998.
[59] J A B Hamilton *Britain's Greatest Rail Disaster: The Quintinshill Blaze of 1915*. Allen & Unwin 1969.

# LOCOMOTIVE NAMING

Britain's railway companies have a long history of naming passenger locomotives. Themes have long included railway personalities, locations served by the railways and classical heroes. Unsurprisingly, the use of military names increased after the Great War and included warships and regimental names. Some companies also had a memorial locomotive honouring their fallen. Lawson Billinton's Class L express 4-6-4T, No. 333 *Remembrance* was named in memory of the 532 London, Brighton and South Coast Railway Company men who fell in the Great War. This was the last engine ever constructed for LBSCR (April 1922). One of the engine plates is on display in the National Railway Museum in York. No. 1165 named *Valour* was the Great Central Railway's war memorial locomotive; she was built at Gorton as the third of six class 9P 4 cylinder 4-6-0's in July 1920. She was withdrawn from Lincoln Shed as LNER No. 146 in December 1947. The post-war West Coast 'Corridor' express was often hauled by the Claughton class 4-6-0, No. 1914, *Patriot*. This engine built at Crewe was the war memorial of the London and North Western Railway Company. One of the engine plates is on display in the National Railway Museum in York. Other locomotives were also named *Zeebrugge, Marne, Ypres, Mons, Edith Cavell, Somme, Jutland, Earl Haig* and *Lloyd George* (the nameplate of which was removed in 1922 for reasons that remain the source of hot debate in railway circles to the present day). New Zealand Railways adopted the same form of memorialisation to their fallen railwaymen. The Pacific 4-6-2 'Ab' No. 608, built in 1915 was named *Passchendaele* and inaugurated as a war memorial by General Sir Charles Fergusson, the Governor General on 17 November 1925. Contrary to the convention that 'goods' locomotives have numbers not names, a number were named after British generals such as Plumer and Haig and were working in the collieries of Fife in Scotland until at least the late 1930s. In 1931 the London Midland and Scottish Railway Royal Scot 4-6-0 express locomotive No. 6159 became the first locomotive to carry a name associated with military aeronautics. It was named *The Royal Air Force* and it ran until November 1962. During the Second World War, the Great Western Railway renamed twelve of its 'Castle' class locomotives after British aircraft. Numbers 5071 to 5082 commemorated such aircraft as the Spitfire, Hurricane and Wellington and were withdrawn from service by British Rail by September 1964. The sole survivor, No. 5080 *Defiant* is owned by the Birmingham Railway Museum, Tyseley and is currently on loan to the Buckinghamshire Railway Centre at Quainton Road, pending overhaul. At auction in December 2003, the nameplate of No. 5081 *Lockheed Hudson* was sold for £35,000. In May 1997 Virgin Trains named their High Speed Train power car No. 43155 *The Red Arrows* in a ceremony at York Station attended by members of the Red Arrows Display Team. Virgin Trains also has an electrically hauled control trailer No. 821010 named *101 Squadron* (RAF). The tradition continues still. On 30 August 1992 a class 31 locomotive No. 31107 was named *John H Carless VC*.[60] At Sheffield, on Armistice Day 2003, a class 66 locomotive No. 66715 was named *Valour* by Great Central Railway Society Chairman Mike Hartley and GB Railfreight Chairman Ward Simpson. It was then dedicated as a war memorial by the Very Reverend Peter Bradley, Dean of Sheffield. The ceremony was attended by both the Lord Mayor of Sheffield and the Mayor of Grimsby and Cleethorpes.

On 27 April 2004, in ceremonies at both the Gare du Nord Station in Paris and at Waterloo Station, a Eurostar train was named *Michel Hollard* after the French Resistance hero. During the Second World War, he saved thousands of British lives by repeatedly crossing the heavily-guarded Franco-Swiss border to provide intelligence officers at the British Legation in Berne with sketches and information on the location of 102 V1 rocket launch sites in Northern France, thus enabling them to be targeted and repeatedly bombed by both the RAF and USAAF.

---

[60] Able Seaman John Henry Carless VC, killed in action aged 21 at the Battle of Heligoland on 17 November 1917.

## THE GREAT CENTRAL RAILWAY MEMORIAL, SHEFFIELD

'On a wet and dismal August 9th, 1922, trains converged on Sheffield Victoria from Manchester, Cleethorpes and Marylebone, their sombre passengers coming to swell the ranks of the 8,000 friends and relatives standing in the rain to see the unveiling of the Great Central's memorial to its Great War dead. Over 10,000 men of the Great Central had answered the call to the Colours, so very many to return maimed or disabled, but 1,304 never to return at all. From Charles Abey, one-time Platelayer at Mexborough but latterly Lance Corporal 15329 of the 10th Yorks and Lancs, through to Thomas George Young, formerly an Ardwick Brakesman but latterly Sergeant 3/10910 of 'B' Company 7th Northants, all were listed on the memorial's bronze tablets. Ironically these first and last named on the memorial fell on successive days in September, 1915, at Loos'.[61] Field Marshal Earl Haig travelled up from Marylebone in the 'Directors' Saloon pulled by the locomotive *Earl Haig*. He inaugurated the memorial accompanied by Sir Sam Fay, the Great Central Railway's General Manager and the directors and officers of the Company.

Alterations to the station and forecourt area in 1938 saw the colonnaded memorial moved inside the station's booking hall. Prior to the demolition of Sheffield Victoria Station in 1971, due to the intervention of the late Sid Rimmington, Sheffield's ASLEF Branch Secretary, the memorial plaques were saved. They were dismantled and shifted to the Wicker Arches and rededicated in a ceremony on 10 November 1971 by the Very Reverend Ivan Neill, Provost of Sheffield Cathedral. The Great Central Railway Society (GCRS) was founded in 1974. The location of the memorial at Wicker Arches subsequently proved unsuitable and the tablets were subjected to graffiti and worse. 'But to some at least the memorial was never forgotten and over the years a number of proposals had been floated for more fitting locations. All had received a degree of support, just about anything seemed better than 'the Wicker', but none of the proposals represented an ideal solution. Then Hermann Beck, co-owner and General Manager of the Royal Victoria Holiday Inn enthusiastically gave his backing to the February 2000 scheme for the GCRS to restore the memorial to its original position at the head of the Victoria Station Approach.'[62] The GCRS threw its weight behind this proposal, formed a war memorial sub-committee and set about the issues of planning permission and listed building consent. By Spring 2003 a wide range of bodies had contributed £24,000 and a Heritage Lottery support application was successfully submitted and Network Rail had transferred ownership of the memorial to the Society. At which point it was discovered that the tablets were not bronze at all, but copper treated to look like it.

Immediately after the City of Sheffield's Remembrance Ceremony on 11 November 2003, and just before noon, Sheffield's veterans and railwaymen led by the Waterloo Band of the King's Regiment playing *The Boys of the Old Brigade* marched down Station Approach to the memorial. The Guard of Honour was furnished by the Duke of Wellington's Regiment. John Fay, grandson of Sir Sam, then unveiled the plaque commemorating the restoration of the memorial. Elgar's *Nimrod* was played during the laying of wreaths by the President of the GCRS, Sheffield's Lord Mayor, the Railway Heritage Trust, Network Rail, the Royal British Legion and the relatives of the fallen. Once the wreaths had been laid, a bugler sounded *Last Post* followed by a two minutes' silence. *Rouse* was then sounded, followed by the Act of Remembrance which was intoned by the Reverend Howard Such, Canon of Sheffield Cathedral. The gathering then sang *O God our help in ages past* and the memorial was rededicated by the Very Reverend Peter Bradley, Dean of Sheffield. The Legion's Standards were dipped for the *National Anthem*, which was followed by The Blessing. Website at www.gcrs.org.uk

---

[61] *Forward: Journal of the Great Central Railway Society* No. 135 Spring 2003.
[62] *Forward: Journal of the Great Central Railway Society* No. 139 Spring 2004.

# LIVERPOOL STREET STATION

The Great Eastern Railway Staff War Memorial stands just inside the main entrance at Liverpool Street Station in London. The issue of a memorial to the Company's fallen was first raised by Lord Claud Hamilton, the company chairman at a board meeting on 2 December 1920. Employees were invited to submit designs and that selected by the board was submitted by Mr Tankard, a porter at Chigwell Station. It stands 20 feet high, twenty-five feet wide and is surmounted by the company coat of arms. It was made of white marble by Farmer & Brindley of Westminster Bridge Road. The cost (including £500 for lettering) was £3,326 which was paid for by the company. The names of 1,220 men of the Company who died in the Great War are carried in alphabetical order on the memorial's 11 panels. (9,743 men of the company served in the Great War). Inspection of the memorial in February 2004 revealed that the lower far left panel now housed a disabled person's lift, thus unexpectedly rendering it a utilitarian memorial.

On the morning of 22 June 1922 Field Marshal Sir Henry Wilson, MP, former Chief of the Imperial General Staff, arrived to inaugurate it. He inspected a hundred members of the GER Old Comrades Association on Platform 9 and at 1315 the Bishop of Norwich commenced the service. The choir, provided by nearby Church of St Botolph's Without Bishopsgate, sang *O God Our Help in Ages Past* followed by *The National Anthem*. The Field Marshal arrived home at Eaton Place at 1430 that afternoon and was shot dead on his front doorstep by two Irishmen named Reginald Dunn and Joseph O'Sullivan. Wilson's implacable opposition in the House of Commons to Irish nationalist aspirations had made him a marked man. The assassins were hanged in Wandsworth Prison on 10 August 1922. Sir Henry Wilson was buried in the crypt of St Paul's Cathedral and was later commemorated by the bronze portrait relief sculpted by C L Hartwell, ARA in 1922 which appears on the far bottom right of the memorial.

The bronze portrait relief at the bottom centre of the memorial commemorates Captain Charles Algernon Fryatt, a merchant master who captained the GER steamer SS BRUSSELS and despite the dangers of wartime, the company maintained its continental services throughout the war. On 28 March 1916 Fryatt attempted to ram German U-Boat U33 in the English Channel. On 22 June 1916 his ship was ambushed and captured by a force of German destroyers. He was tried on charges of piracy in Bruges and executed by firing squad on 27 July 1916. Fryatt's execution caused an international outcry and Prime Minister Herbert Asquith condemned his 'murder' in the House of Commons. Fryatt was subsequently exhumed and reburied at Dovercourt, near Harwich on 8 July 1919. His memorial plaque was sculpted by J H van Golberdinge and presented by the People of Holland. It was unveiled in a ceremony on 2 August 1923.

## ST MARTIN'S CHURCH, LECONFIELD

In 1935 Brigadier Langley, commanding 8th Railway Company, Royal Engineers at Longmoor Camp, Hants received a letter from the bank manager who held the regimental funds, accompanied by an uncollected parcel that had lain in the bank's vault for 17 years. When opened it was found to contain hundreds of War Savings Certificates, which was the balance of the Garden Depot Fund raised by the cultivation of allotments on the camp by railwaymen during the Great War. After consultation it was decided that this bounty would be donated towards a memorial for the fallen railwaymen of the Great War. The memorial produced for St Martin's Church on the camp took the form of a large triptych, the centre panel of which featured a life-size Risen Christ, His right hand raised in benediction, depicted against a red background surrounded by golden rays. The foot of the panel bears the dates "1914" and "1919". The figure of Christ is encircled by the inscription:

"GREATER LOVE HATH NO MAN THAN THIS,
THAT A MAN LAY DOWN HIS LIFE FOR HIS FRIENDS"

The right hand panel bears the inscription: "I AM HE THAT LIVETH AND WAS DEAD" and the left hand panel: "AND BEHOLD I AM ALIVE FOR EVERMORE". Each corner of the side panels was embellished with a Royal Engineer grenade or 'bomb flash'. The triptych was designed by Martin Travers, ARCA and dedicated by the Reverend E A Fitch, the Assistant Chaplain General, Aldershot Command on 26 April 1936. The directors of the civilian railway companies who attended the inauguration conceived the notion of installing stained glass windows in the church. The combined efforts of Mr Gilbert Szlumper[63] of the Southern, Mr (later Sir) Michael Barrington of the London and North Eastern and Mr R Carpmael of the Great Western would bring the idea to life. Martin Travers was again commissioned to undertake the work. 'The problem of producing suitable church windows to represent each of the Railway Companies gave much food for thought, but finally it was decided to include in each window the patron saints of two cathedrals on each railway system, and to incorporate the coats of arms of representative cities and towns.'[64] There were eventually ten windows in all, each featured two saints connected with the route of the railway company concerned. The arms of London, the headquarters of each company appears on each window, with the representative coats of arms of the cities and towns associated with the railway concerned. In the case of the London, Midland and Scottish Railway window, St Mungo (representing Glasgow) and St Alban appear. In the case of the London Passenger Transport Board window, St Paul and St Edward the Confessor feature. After the Second World War the Canadian Railway window featuring St Lawrence was added. In 1977 the Army School of Transport (now the Defence School of Transport) moved from Longmoor to Leconfield, East Yorkshire and took the contents of St Martin's, triptych, windows and all, with it. This ended the association between the railway companies of the Corps of Royal Engineers and their successors the Royal Corps of Transport with Longmoor that dated back to 1905. St Martin's had stood at Longmoor since 1931 as a place of worship. The Garrison Church of St Martin at Leconfield is now housed in a former parachute packing shed on the camp. All of the memorials previously sited at Longmoor were incorporated into the fabric and design of the new church. It was dedicated in the presence of Princess Alice, Duchess of Gloucester, Colonel-in-Chief of the Royal Corps of Transport on 31 May 1978.

---

[63] Gilbert Savil Szlumper CBE (1884-1969). Later Major General Gilbert S Szlumper.
[64] *The Institution of the Royal Army Service Corps and the Royal Corps of Transport: Memorials Register –* Camberley 1998.

# LONDON TRANSPORT

The London Underground War Memorial may be found in the lobby of Transport for London at 100 Petty France, London and was sculpted by Phoebe Stabler.[65] It was inaugurated by Field Marshal Sir William Robertson and dedicated by Dr Winnington Ingram, the Bishop of London. 'This memorial is in the form of a bronze-gilt statue of St. George, carried out in a very 1920s avant garde style. Flanking oak panels list the names of the dead - 1,514 are given but this includes the various tram and bus companies then associated or owned by the underground.'[66] The role of the bereaved at such ceremonies was of considerable importance. A good illustration may be taken from the inauguration of this memorial on 10 June 1925. 'Among those who attended this service and the unveiling ceremony were Lord Ashfield and the Directors and Officers of the Underground Companies; about 500 widows, mothers and other near relations of the fallen; and 150 ex-Servicemen, representing the various departments of the Companies.'[68]

*The Times* of 12 December 1927 reported that General Sir Herbert Lawrence unveiled a stained glass memorial window in St Mark's Church, Kennington, to commemorate the London County Council tramwaymen killed in the war. The window depicted a tramcar and two figures, one in tramway uniform and another in military uniform. The memorial was lost when St Mark's was bombed in the Blitz during the Second World War.

---

[65] Phoebe Stabler née McCleish. Noted pottery modeller. Studied at Liverpool University and Royal College of Art. Died 1955. Married Harold Stabler in 1906, sculptor, jeweller, teacher, silversmith, inventor of 'Pyrex' and close friend of Frank Pick; 'The man who invented London Transport'.
[66] *Underground News*, November 2000, No 467.
[67] *Backtrack* Vol. 10 (1996) p. 689.
[68] *T.O.T. Staff Magazine,* 1925, Vol III, No 45, July, p. 182.

# STREET MEMORIALS

The Cyprus Street War Memorial.

Having earlier in this study mentioned the spontaneous erection of street memorials, in a number of rare cases this would be the final form the memorial took and this form bears further examination. 'Ten street memorials in the Abbey parish of St Albans commemorate the dead of the 1914-18 War from those streets. It is believed that these street memorials are unique survivals. Wall plaques record the names of more than 100 men, including nine pairs of brothers, who from a small group of streets around the Abbey left their homes to fight for King and Country, never to return.'[69] These small memorials mounted on the walls of the houses of St Albans detail the fallen of each street by name and may be seen *in situ* to this day.

Another good example may be seen at Cyprus Street in London's East End (photograph above). The memorial tablet incorporates the names of the men of Cyprus Street who died in both the Great War and the Second World War, a Union Flag flies from the flagpole and a plaque underneath has the fourth verse of Laurence Binyon's poem *For the Fallen*:

> "THEY SHALL GROW NOT OLD, AS WE THAT ARE LEFT GROW OLD:
> AGE SHALL NOT WEARY THEM, NOR THE YEARS CONDEMN.
> AT THE GOING DOWN OF THE SUN AND IN THE MORNING
> WE WILL REMEMBER THEM."

---

[69] Alice Goodman *The Street Memorials of St Albans Abbey Parish*.

# THE CROSS OF SACRIFICE

'In the autumn of 1919 the Royal Academy arranged a War Memorial Exhibition to assist promoters of such memorials and an advisory scheme was offered to all who wished to apply. All the works and designs exhibited had a direct reference to the war, and no utilitarian scheme was examined. There were models, photographs, designs and sketches, and actual statues, tablets, rolls of honour and stained glass. Works by Sir Edwin Lutyens and Sir Reginald Blomfield appeared several times in the catalogue, and, in the quadrangle, there was a model of the Great War Cross by Blomfield which was to be erected by the Imperial War Graves Commission in the war cemeteries abroad'. 'The place of Christianity, and of the soldiers belonging to that faith, in the Great War is further emphasised by the large white stone Cross of Sacrifice, bearing a Crusader's sword, which stands conspicuously in each cemetery'.[70] Blomfield wrote: 'I took immense pains with the design, working it out on a carefully adjusted system of proportions so that in the four sizes in use, the relative proportions of the design were maintained. The Cross has been set up in all the War Cemeteries throughout the Empire. It has also been adopted in many places in England as the local War Memorial, and though some antiquaries may have regretted the absence of cusps and crockets, it has undoubtedly pleased the majority of English speaking people. I have had applications for its use from every part of the Empire'.[71]

    Clearly the distinctive design of Blomfield's Great War Cross (also known as the Cross of Sacrifice) caught the imagination of many of the war memorial committees who attended the exhibition. It would be widely copied and imitated, sometimes inexpertly. Blomfield, having viewed the efforts of the local stonemason at Aylesbury, Buckinghamshire lamented: 'the local man has done his best, but he has simply murdered my Cross'. On mainland Great Britain, the names of the fallen from the local community were usually inscribed on the octagonal base of the cross. The above photograph is of the base of the Chislehurst War Memorial, Kent.

---

[70] *The Burdett-Coutts Paper.*
[71] Sir Reginald Blomfield *Memoirs of an Architect.*

# STAINED GLASS

Stained glass has been a highly popular form of memorialisation since the late 19th century and a particularly fine example may be found in the parish church of St John, Great Clacton, Essex. Here the window dating from the Boer War depicts a Zulu Chief, a Red Cross nurse, a sailor and a soldier complete with bushwhack hat.

Many of the finest memorial windows in Britain's churches date from the Great War. The illustration above is a particularly fine example. This 'Armistice Window' is in St Michael and All Angels Church, Bugbrooke, Northants. It depicts a wounded soldier, supported by a sailor, both in Great War uniform. They kneel at the foot of the Crucified Christ. Behind the figures trenches are depicted and further back are burning ruins, graphic wartime images rarely seen in stained glass imagery. The window is surmounted by an image of the Paschal Lamb. (In Western iconography the Paschal Lamb represents Jesus Christ).

Another fine example can found at Canterbury University, New Zealand. The War Memorial Window there has in its bottom left hand a depiction of a large red dragon being bayoneted by the serried ranks of Allied troops. Should the viewer have any difficulty in interpreting what all this is supposed to represent, there are scrolls in the design which helpfully bear the words "BRUTALITY" and "IGNORANCE" in the bottom left corner and "HUMANITY" and "JUSTICE" in the top half of the window.

# ROLLS OF HONOUR

At the end of the Great War, such was the scale of British losses, rolls of honour and books of remembrance were compiled by schools, universities, churches, boroughs, cities, breweries, banks and other businesses as a means of paying tribute to the sacrifice of the fallen. Good religious examples may be found in the British Jewry Roll of Honour and the Catholic Officers' Roll of Honour. The information contained in rolls can vary widely, but may include a record of war service, a short biographical sketch, or a photograph; in most cases the roll simply consists of a list of names. Often it formed part of a community's war memorial and a good example of how this worked may be taken from St Saviour's War Memorial at Borough in London. Sculpted by Philip Lindsay Clark, the memorial bears no names, instead these are to be found on the St Saviour's Parish Roll of Honour held by the nearby St Saviour' Church. In a number of cases, such as the City of Aberdeen War Memorial, the Woolwich War Memorial and the Civil Service Rifles War Memorial at Somerset House in London, the original roll of honour was embedded in the war memorial itself. Unlike the Second World War, at the end of the Great War, no British civilian Roll of Honour was compiled and in 2005 work on this immensely complex task was underway. Initial indications were that the number of civilian deaths from enemy action in the Great War was far larger than anticipated. In recent years much work has been carried out in compiling rolls and the recent completion of two rolls is a good illustration: The Fleet Air Arm Roll of Honour may be found in St Bartholomew's Church at Yeovilton, Somerset. It contains the names of all who died since the beginning of naval aviation. The Royal Naval Volunteer Reserve Roll of Honour containing the names of all 6,200 Officers and Ratings of the Empire and Commonwealth Naval Volunteer Reserves who died during the Second World War may be found at The Naval Club at Hill Street, London. The photograph above is of the Norwich Roll of Honour in Norwich Castle designed by Sir Edwin Lutyens in Norwich Castle. In recent years the Roll has been augmented by a touch-screen database. And it would appear that technology is the way forward, a number of rolls of honour are now available on CD (most specifically the Irish) and a considerable number may also be found on the worldwide web. A particularly good website containing the details of the fallen alumni of the University of Birmingham may be found at www.firstworldwar.bham.ac.uk/memorial/ww1/intro.htm

## GENERAL JAMES WOLFE

In June 1759 the struggle between the British and the French for the control of Canada was nearing its peak. Admiral Charles Saunders sailed from Louisburg with a small army aboard commanded by Brigadier-General James Wolfe (1727-59). It disembarked on Orléans Island, just below Quebec. For two months the Marquis Louis Joseph de Montcalm de Saint-Véran in his impregnable fortress thwarted every attempt by Wolfe to gain a foothold. On the morning of 13 September, astonished French sentries on Quebec's walls watched as a British force of some 4,800 men formed up on the Plain outside the city, having scaled the Heights of Abraham. The French lost the ensuing battle and the British captured Quebec. Wolfe was mortally wounded on the field of battle and lingered until, informed of his victory, he said: 'Now God be praised, I will die in peace' and expired. Montcalm died the next morning. Wolfe's body was brought back to England and lay at McCartney House, his mother's home, until burial at St Alphege under the hill, Greenwich. (Nicholas Hawksmoor 1712-14). His cloak is in the collection of HM Tower of London. His statue was sculpted by the Canadian Dr R Tait MacKenzie (1867-1938). It stands on the crest of a ridge in Greenwich Park and commands a fine view over the Thames. The 10 ft tall sculpture was funded by the Canadian People. It took MacKenzie and the architect A S G Butler nearly two years of wrangling with the Board of Works and the Fine Art Commission to get agreement as to the form the plinth would take and its siting. The rear of the plinth has cannon shell damage (probably British in origin) dating from the Blitz. It bears the following inscription:

"THIS MONUMENT
THE GIFT OF
THE
CANADIAN PEOPLE
WAS UNVEILED ON
THE FIFTH OF JUNE 1930
BY
LE MARQUIS DE MONTCALM"

# CHAPTER III

# OVERSEAS MEMORIALS OF THE GREAT WAR

# THE NATIONAL BATTLEFIELDS MEMORIAL COMMITTEE

'Towards the end of 1919 Winston Churchill persuaded the Cabinet that Britain should pay for general memorials to the Army as a whole to be erected on the principal battlefields of the war - at Ypres, Mons, Arras, the Hindenburg Line and on the Somme, at Gallipoli and Jerusalem. The result was the formation of a National Battlefield Memorial Committee, chaired by the Earl of Midleton and it included the Dominion High Commissioners. The terms of reference of this committee were: 'To consider and report on the forms of National War Memorials and the sites on which they should be erected, together with estimates of cost'.[1] On 29 July 1920 Churchill produced a memorandum for circulation to the Cabinet.[2] It was duly circulated on 4 August 1920. On 13 December Sir Alfred Mond, the First Commissioner of Works produced a memorandum that bears quoting in full:

'In view of the revision of expenditure which is now taking place I wish to draw the attention of the Committee to the cabinet approval of the expenditure of £300,000 on the erection of Memorials on Battlefields, half of this sum being devoted to the erection of a Memorial Gateway at Ypres. (Cabinet 45/20, Conclusion 4). My Department has been in no way consulted on this matter, nor has any kind of Parliamentary sanction been obtained and, inasmuch as the expenditure will fall on my Votes, I feel I must ask the Committee to reconsider the sum allotted, more especially in regard to the Ypres Memorial which seems to me far to exceed what would appear reasonable in view of the fact that the Government do not propose, so far as I know, to erect any War Memorial in this country beyond the Cenotaph'.[3]

The PRO file contains an undated Cabinet Office minute[4] that shows a Cabinet meeting was called probably in January 1921 to specifically discuss the points made in this memorandum. Both Lieutenant General Sir GMW MacDonogh, the Adjutant General and Lord Midleton attended. In view of subsequent developments the points agreed in this meeting also bear quoting:

'After a full discussion the Cabinet agreed:-

(a)     That the sum of £100,000 required for the British share of the cost of the Ypres Memorial should be granted.

(b)     That a sum of £100,000 should be allotted to be divided between the Royal Navy and Army for the other Memorials, in the proportion of £60,000 to the Army and £40,000 to the Navy.

(c)     That the Committee should advise the Cabinet as to the best manner of utilising the sum of £60,000 referred to in (b). They should consider, inter alia, the following proposals, which were suggested at the meeting:-

(i)     A Memorial in Paris, which might perhaps be a replica of the Whitehall Cenotaph, and which should record the total of British casualties. This should be conditional on the French Government granting a satisfactory site in a conspicuous position in the capital.

(ii)    A memorial in Gallipoli, in regard to which the Committee should get in touch with the Australian and New Zealand Governments, with a view to a joint Memorial, if possible at the entrance to the Dardanelles.

---

[1] National Memorials on the Battlefields. PRO file Adm 116, Case 1160.
[2] Churchill's Memorandum appears at the Appendix to this study.
[3] Memorandum C.P. 2291 by the First Commissioner of Works. PRO file Adm 116, Case 1160.
[4] Undated Cabinet Office Minute CABINET 12 (21). Minute 8, probably January 1921.

(d) That the Admiralty should consider the suggestion to erect a striking monument on Dover Cliffs to be seen from ships passing up and down the Channel'.[5]

Lord Midleton's committee duly produced its report, which incorporated these helpful suggestions on 24 February 1921.[6]

## THE COMMITTEE

### Chairman

The Rt Hon The Earl of Midleton, KP[7]

### Members

Colonel the Hon Sir James Allen, KCB (New Zealand)
The Rt Hon G N Barnes, MP[8]
Rear Admiral Sir R W Bentinck, KCMG
Sir R A Blankenberg, KBE (South Africa)
Sir Lionel Earle, KCB, KCVO, CMG
The Rt Hon A Fisher (Australia)[9]
Mr D S MacColl, MA, LLD[10]
Lieutenant General Sir G M W MacDonogh, KCB, KCMG (Adjutant General)
Lieutenant Colonel Thomas Nangle (Newfoundland)
The Hon Sir George Perley, KCMG (Canada)[11]
Sir M G Ramsay, KCB (The Treasury)
The Rt Hon the Lord Riddell[12]
Mr J S Sargent, RA[13]
Major General the Rt Hon J E B Seely, CB, CMG, DSO, MP
Sir Aston Webb, KCVO, CB, PRA

### Secretary

Mr K Lyon, OBE (The War Office)

---

[5] The Monument to the Dover Patrol at Leathercote Point, St Margaret's Bay takes the form of a granite obelisk 83 feet 9 inches tall. It was unveiled by the Prince of Wales (later King Edward VIII) on 27 July 1921. A matching memorial at Cap Blanc Nez in France was destroyed by the Germans in the Second World War.
[6] Report of the National Battlefields Memorial Committee.
[7] William St John Fremantle Broderick (1856-1942). MP for Surrey West 1880-85 and Guildford 1885-1906. PC 1897. Secretary of State for War 1900-03. Secretary of State for India 1903-05. Knight of the Order of St Patrick 1916. Spokesman for Southern Irish Unionists. Created Viscount Dunsford and Earl of Midleton 1920.
[8] George Nicoll Barnes (1859-1940). Leader of Labour Party 1910-11. Minister for Pensions 1916-17. Served in Lloyd George's coalition government as Minister without Portfolio 1917-20.
[9] Andrew Fisher (1862-1928). Born Kilmarnock, Scotland. A coalminer, he emigrated to Australia. Prominent Labour politician at the forefront of Australian social reform. Prime Minister of Australia 1910-15.
[10] Dugald Sutherland MacColl (1858-1948). Initially trained for the church, he became an art historian, then art critic for the *Spectator*, *Saturday Review*, *The Studio* and *Weekend Review*. Keeper of the Tate 1906-1911.
[11] Sir George Halsey Perley (1857-1938). Canadian statesman, businessman and philanthropist. Canadian High Commissioner in London 1914-22. Knighted 1915. Canadian Signatory to the Treaty of Sevres 1920.
[12] Sir George Allardice Riddell, later Lord Riddell (1865-1934). Newspaper proprietor. 1906 Secretary of the Newspaper Proprietors' Association. Noted diarist.
[13] John Singer Sargent (1856-1925). Arguably the most distinguished portrait painter of his age. Born in Florence of American parents, he spent most of his life in London. He studied painting in Florence and in Paris under Carolus Duran. He refused the offer of a knighthood from King Edward VII.

## FRENCH MEMORIAL TABLETS

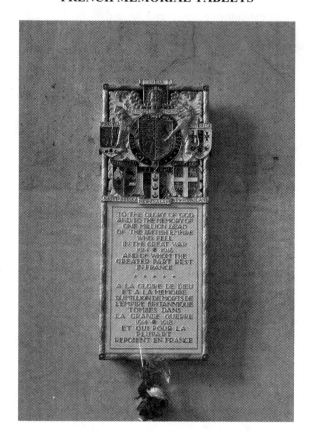

Earl Midleton's National Battlefield Memorial Committee suggested that commemorative tablets be erected in the great cathedrals and churches of Belgium and France.[14] The Commission undertook the task. Lieutenant Colonel Cart de Lafontaine was commissioned to design the tablets and to negotiate with the ecclesiastical authorities. Reginald Hallward[15] made them. The standard tablet displays the Royal Coat of Arms, those of India and the Dominions. These surround an inscription in French and English, which told of Britain's million dead. The tablets cast in gesso were gilded and coloured, then set in a surround of stone. The prototype (with only the Royal Coat of Arms) with the dedication to those who fell in the Diocese of Amiens was installed in the south transept of Amiens Cathedral in 1923. These tablets serve to remind all who see them of the sacrifice made in defence of the freedom of the French People. Replicas of the Amiens and standard French tablets flank the entrance to the main conference room at the Head Office of the Commonwealth War Graves Commission at Maidenhead.

The standard tablets were erected in the following cathedrals or churches: Amiens, Arras, Bayeux, Beauvais, Bethune, Bolougne-sur-Mer, Cambrai, Laon, Le Mans, Lille, Marseilles, Meaux, Nancy, Nantes, Noyon, Orleans, Paris (Notre Dame), Reims, Rouen, St Omer, St Quentin, Senlis and Soissons. The photograph above is of the Memorial Tablet in Beauvais Cathedral.

---

[14] Paragraph 34 (iii.) Report to the Cabinet of the National Battlefields Memorials Committee, 24 February 1921.
[15] Reginald Hallward (1858-1948). Noted stained glass artist.

## BELGIAN MEMORIAL TABLETS

In Belgium the inscriptions on the tablets were slightly different. Due to Belgium's linguistic divide between French-speaking Wallonia in the south, Dutch-speaking Flanders in the north and also a substantial German-speaking minority, it was decided that the tablets would be inscribed in both English and Latin. The inscriptions read:

"TO THE GLORY OF GOD
AND TO THE MEMORY OF
ONE MILLION DEAD
OF THE BRITISH EMPIRE
WHO FELL IN THE GREAT WAR
1914 1918 MANY OF WHOM
REST IN BELGIUM


AD MAJOREM DEI GLORIAM
ET IN MEMORIAM
MILLIENS MILLIUM NOSTRORUM
QUI EX IMPERIO BRITANNICO
UNDIQUE COORTI
ANNO DOMINI
MCMXIV MCMXVIII
IN BELLO PRÆTER OMNIA
MEMORANDO
VITAM PRO PATRIA
PROFUDERUNT
QUORUM PARS MAGNA
IN TERRA BELGICA DORMIUNT

HOC MONUMENTUM EXSTRUXERE
TOTIUS IMPERII GENTES
ATQUE COMMUNITATES"[16]


The tablets were erected in the following cathedrals and churches: Antwerp, Brussels, Malines, Mons and Ypres.

---

[16] This monument was erected by the peoples and communities of the Empire.

# THE LOCHNAGAR CRATER MEMORIAL

'At seven o'clock in the morning of July 1 the British and French armies rose from their trenches steel-helmeted, gas-masked, equipped with all the latest apparatus of war, bombs, mortars, machine-guns light and heavy, and supported by all their artillery, marched against the enemy on a front of 45 kilometres. Fourteen British Divisions and five French divisions were almost immediately engaged.'[17]

The Lochnagar Crater is at La Boisselle near Thiepval on the Somme and was created by two charges of ammonal, of 24,000lb and 30,000lb that were detonated along with 16 others at 0728 hours on the morning of 1 July 1916 as a prelude to General Sir Douglas Haig's ill-fated Somme Offensive intended to relieve the pressure on French Army at Verdun. There was no chance of surprising the Germans, as the British assault was preceded by a massive artillery bombardment that lasted a week. The Crater measures 300 feet across wide and 90 feet deep. RFC pilots airborne at the time of detonation observed that debris from the explosion rose some 4,000 feet into the air. After the crater was blown, the German line was charged by the Northumberland Fusiliers. The Tynesiders gained and held the crater and the trenches around the 'Schwaben Hohe' strongpoint. The Worcestershire Regiment finally captured the village of La Boisselle on 3 July. 'On the first day of the Somme Offensive, the British Army suffered 57,000 casualties - the biggest loss ever suffered by any army in a single day. And yet, as one historian has put it, to see the ground gained one needs a magnifying glass and a large-scale map.'[18] The later stages of the offensive marked the debut of Britain's secret weapon, the tank, which was deployed by General Haig in numbers too few to be effective, but the aggressive qualities of this new weapon were clearly demonstrated and a thousand were ordered. The Army Council cancelled the order and David Lloyd George intervened and cancelled the cancellation.

In October 1998 the remains of Private George James Nugent of the 22nd (Tyneside Scottish) Battalion of the Northumberland Fusiliers were discovered near the Crater. He had been posted missing on 1 July 1916 and his name inscribed on the Memorial to the Missing at Thiepval. With the assistance of John Sheen, an expert on the Tyneside Scottish and Irish battalions, - and the presence of a razor found on the body with his service number on it, he was positively identified. He was buried in Ovillers Military Cemetery after a military funeral attended by family members on 1 July 2000.

There are several memorials at the site of the Lochnagar Crater. Each year at 0728 on 1 July a well-attended Service of Remembrance commences at the Crater to commemorate the first day of the Somme offensive. At its commencement a maroon is fired, an address given, wreaths are laid, the hymn *Abide with Me* is sung, the *Last Post* is sounded, followed by the two minutes' silence. *Reveille* is then sounded, followed by the scattering of a third of a million petals by both British and French schoolchildren. This is followed by the piping of a lament. The ceremony is noticeably well-attended by the local population. The crater receives around 75,000 visitors a year and is one of the most popular visitors' sites on the Western Front. It is privately owned by Richard Dunning, an Englishman. He purchased it in 1978 to save at least one of the original Somme craters from being filled in and reclaimed for agricultural purposes. In 2004 he wrote: 'There is nowhere in the world quite like the Lochnagar Crater. Once a place of such suffering, sacrifice and courage, it is now a poignant memorial to the men of all nations who fell during the Battles of the Somme. It is said to be the largest crater ever made by man in anger, yet this simple 'corner of a foreign field' has an extraordinary quality to bring people together in an atmosphere of peace and friendship. To young people especially, its impact can powerfully convey the horrors of war in a way that today, few places can.' Website at www.friendsoflochnagar

---

[17] Winston S Churchill *The World Crisis 1911-1918* p. 1073.
[18] Norman Dixon *On the Psychology of Military Incompetence* p. 82.

# HILL 60

The Memorial to the 1st Australian Tunnelling Company.

Hill 60 was the scene of ferocious hand-to-hand combat in May 1915, but was captured and held by the Germans until June 1917. It was a prominent feature on the edge of the Ypres Salient and gave the Germans a commanding view of British activities within it. The loss of this strategically important objective did not deter the British. On the contrary, it only served to spur them to even greater efforts. Soon Hill 60 and another feature close by called the Caterpillar were honeycombed with underground galleries 90 feet below ground. In November 1916 the 1st Australian Tunnelling Company arrived and took over operations. They packed the galleries under Hill 60 with 53,500lbs of high explosive and another 70,000lbs under the Caterpillar. The highly dangerous nature of this work included destroying German galleries by camouflet (counter-mining).[19] The charges in the British galleries were detonated at 0310 on 7 June 1917 and the force of the explosion was felt in Downing Street. There followed a massive artillery barrage by the guns of the British 2nd Army lasting 15 minutes and a rapid assault which took both positions effortlessly. 'The craters which were left after the eruption can still be seen today all along the line of the Messines-Wytschaete Ridge (the southern arc of the Salient) - most of them are small ponds now used by farmers. In 1917, the Hill 60 crater was 60 feet deep and 260 feet wide at the rim, and the Caterpillar position disappeared into a hole 90 feet deep and 260 feet wide at the brim. The German 204th Division, which held the two positions, lost 10 officers and 677 men killed by the explosions'.[20] As some measure of the endeavours of the tunnellers, four Victoria Crosses were awarded to the men who tunnelled under Hill 60. The bronze tablet on the memorial (pictured above) surmounted by the 'Rising Sun' of the Australian Commonwealth Military Forces badge has two bullet holes in it dating from the Second World War, no doubt the response of enraged German soldiery having read and translated the inscription.

---

[19] John Brophy & Eric Partridge *The Long Trail: What the British Soldier Sang and Said in the Great War of 1914-18,* London, Andre Deutsch Ltd 1965.
[20] Rose EB Coombs *Before Endeavours Fade.*

## THE TASK

'The architects who worked for the IWGC created a network of monuments which symbolically appropriated the landscape in which they were placed in the name of the British Empire, an appropriation both subtle and effective. As much through his response to landscape and environment as by his command of Classical forms, Lutyens achieved in his commemorative architecture on the Western Front a truly poetic quality which successfully fused patriotism, religion and grief'.[21] The Commission's architects of course recognised 'the Pagan sources for the funerary tradition in architecture. A compromise was essential, and it was that each cemetery should have both the Great War Stone and a free standing Cross of Sacrifice'.[22] 'The Commission had always tried to avoid the possibility of any ambiguity in its memorials to the missing. It had set its face against buildings of practical utility, knowing that ultimately they must invite association with their function rather than with the sacrifices the dead had made'.[23] 'In the disciplined classicism favoured by the Commission, sculpture is always secondary to the architectural conception; as Blomfield justly observed, "many of us had seen terrible examples of war memorials in France and we were haunted by the fear of winged angels in various sentimental attitudes". Baker and Blomfield used the most sculpture, Lutyens least; the latter required little beyond carved stone wreaths, flags or sarcophagi. Nevertheless, some fine sculpture was done for the Commission by Gilbert Ledward, Charles Wheeler, William Reid Dick, Ernest Gillick, William Gilbert, Laurence Turner and, above all, Charles Sargeant Jagger'.[24]

However, all was not going well at the Menin Gate in Ypres. The Earl of Crawford and Balcarres wrote in a secret memorandum to the Cabinet on 23 May 1921: 'Australia refuses to subscribe to the Archway to be erected as the Central Memorial of British gallantry. Other Dominions may act likewise. I gather that Sir Reginald Blomfield R.A., was commissioned to make a design which has now been discarded, and that he has entered a substantial claim for services rendered. As this will fall on my Votes I invite protection from this kind of embarrassment'. With an eye to foundations, Blomfield had asked the Ypres Town Architect what the town stood on and was told clay. His test bores for the foundations revealed that it stood on sand, the worst of all foundations. The engineer Sir Maurice Fitzmaurice designed a concrete raft that successfully overcame the problem and the memorial was completed in 1927. Touchingly, Blomfield wrote: 'With me the Menin Gate is perhaps the only building I have ever designed in which I do not want anything altered, and if I am ever remembered I hope it may be by the Menin Gate'. [25]

Each of the Dominions built a National Memorial to their fallen on the battlefield. With tragic inevitability they stand on the site that has most meaning for the country involved. These memorials stand that future generations might understand the sacrifice made in their name.

The New Zealand National Memorials are at Longueval, France and Polygon Wood, Belgium. New Zealand lost more than 18,000 men in the Great War and the participation of the New Zealanders was unique in that they fought the entire war as a single formation without being merged or amalgamated. New Zealand built memorials to its missing at all the locations where their troops had fallen in significant numbers. By the end of the war they knew exactly who had fought where, who had died where, who was missing and needed commemorating - unlike the mammoth task the Commission faced and for this reason there are no New Zealand names on the Menin Gate.

---

[21] Hopkins and Stamp Editors, *Some Corner of a Foreign Field: Lutyens, Empire and the Sites of Remembrance*. Essay by David Crellin.
[22] Gavin Stamp *Silent Cities*.
[23] Philip Longworth *The Unending Vigil*.
[24] Ibid.
[25] Reginald Blomfield *Memoirs of an Architect* p. 189.

## NEUVE CHAPELLE

The Indian National Memorial at La Bombe crossroads was designed by the eminent architect Sir Herbert Baker: 'Because of my interest in Indian art and history I specially welcomed the commission to design the Indian Memorial at Neuve Chapelle, which enshrines the names of the soldiers who fell on the battlefield there and on other fields. It consists of a circular space of green turf with stone paths surrounded by a high stone wall, solid at one end where the names are inscribed, and pierced elsewhere and carved with symbols like the railings of Buddha's Shrine at Budh Guaya and those surrounding the great Sanchi topes - low domes preserving sacred relics of Buddha. In the centre, opposite the names, is an Asoka Column raised on high and guarded on either side by sculptured tigers. The entrance is through a small domed Chattri with pierced redstone grilles or jaalis - a familiar feature of Indian buildings; another Chattri opposite forms a shelter'.[26] The Asoka Column bears the inscription in English, Hindi and Urdu at its base:

"GOD IS ONE
HIS IS THE
VICTORY"

This site selected was of special significance because the Indian Corps, commanded by Lieutenant General Sir James Willcocks (1857-1926) had only been in France for four weeks, when on 27 October 1914, the Corps was responsible for retaking Neuve Chapelle after it had been captured in the German advance. 4,847 names are inscribed on the memorial. Indian troops suffered greatly in the winter of 1914, due to their being unused to the cold European climate. More sensible counsel eventually prevailed and they were used in other theatres, most notably the East African Campaign and in Mesopotamia 'Mespot'. Despite there being no conscription in India during the course of the Great War, a total of 1,338,620 men enlisted in the Indian Army and more than 72,000 died in it. The above photograph is of the chattri.

---

[26] Herbert Baker *Architecture and Personalities*.

# THE THIEPVAL MEMORIAL TO THE MISSING

Designed by Lutyens and built between 1928 and 1932, this redbrick and stone memorial stands on the ruins of Thiepval Château, one of the strongest positions in the German line. Slightly larger than the Arc de Triomphe, it was the largest memorial ever built by the Commission and dominates the landscape. It stands in its own grounds of 40 acres on a spur overlooking the battlefield. It takes the form of a massive stepped arrangement of intersecting arches that increase in height and proportionate width and culminate in a central arch 80 feet high. The total structure is 150 feet high. Its sixteen piers are faced with Portland stone on which are carved the names of 72,085 soldiers who were killed on the Somme and Ancre up to February 1918 and have no known grave, many bodies having been lost entirely in the pulverised battlefield, and many others not found until battlefield clearance took place some years after the war, by which time all trace of identity had disappeared. The memorial was inaugurated by the Prince of Wales on 31 July 1932, in the presence of M Albert Lebrun, President of the French Republic. The brickwork had to be replaced in the 1980s. Surprisingly, Lutyens had incorporated drainage into his design, which fell foul of the law of nature that makes frozen water expand. In addition to being a memorial to the missing, the Memorial is also a Battle Memorial commemorating the Anglo-French offensive on the Somme in 1916. A small cemetery in front of the memorial contains 300 British and 300 French graves, a symbol of the united effort of the two allies. Organised by the Royal British Legion, the annual British memorial service to the fallen of The Somme takes place at Thiepval on 1 July each year, the anniversary of the first day of the Battle in 1916. Website at www.thiepval.org.uk Near the summit of the memorial the following words are inscribed;

> "AUX ARMEES FRANÇAISES ET
> BRITANNIQUES L'EMPIRE
> BRITANNIQUE RECONNAISSANT"

# THE MENIN GATE

Ypres (now known as Ieper) is one of the old towns of Flanders and, eight centuries ago it was the greatest of them. By 1914 it was one of the smaller towns of the province of West Flanders. Nearby are the landmarks and battlefields of the Ypres Salient. Hundreds of thousands of British and Empire soldiers marched through the old Menin Gate on their way to the battlefields of Flanders. The battles that were fought for Ypres symbolised the British refusal to yield this last unconquered corner of Belgium and resulted in its total destruction.

The memorial was designed by the architect Sir Reginald Blomfield and faced with Euville stone. Sir William Reid Dick executed the sculpture. The dominant feature is a "Hall of Memory", 36.5 metres long and 20 metres wide, covered by a coffered half-elliptical arch in a single span. At either end is an archway 9 metres wide and 14.5 metres high, with flat arches on either side of it 3.5 metres wide and nearly 7 metres high. The inscription in the main hall reads "Here are recorded names of officers and men who fell in the Ypres Salient but to whom the fortune of war denied the known and honoured burial given to their comrades in death". In the centre of the sides are broad staircases, leading up to the ramparts and to loggias running the whole length of the building. The names of 54,986 officers and men are engraved on Portland stone panels fixed to the inner walls of the Hall, up the sides of the staircases, and inside the loggias. Each of the four straight arches is flanked on either side by an engaged Doric column and surmounted by an entablature. Over the central arches are large panels for dedicatory inscriptions; and above these panels is a recumbent lion on the east side, and a sarcophagus, with a flag and a wreath, on the side facing the town.

On 1 July 1928, the practice of sounding *Last Post* by the town fire brigade each night at the Memorial was instituted at the suggestion of Superintendent Vandenbraambusche of the Belgian Police and the tradition has been observed at 2000 hours each evening ever since. (During the Second World War it was observed daily in Brookwood Cemetery, until Ypres was free once more). 31 October 2001 marked the 25,000th sounding. There is no direct Army equivalent to the RN or RAF memorials of the Great War in this study, but the Menin Gate is perhaps the nearest to one. Field Marshal Viscount Plumer ('He is not missing, he is here!') inaugurated it in the presence of the King of the Belgians on 24 July 1927.

# MAMETZ WOOD

Despite being initially rebuffed by Field Marshal Earl Kitchener in October 1914, David Lloyd George did eventually get his way and an all-Welsh formation was established. At the start of the war the chapels of North Wales held that soldiering was sinful, but with the inexorable rise of Wales' favourite son, they changed their minds, unlocked their manpower and a total of 272,924 Welshmen eventually enlisted in the army during the war. Robert Graves who served as an officer in the Royal Welch Fusiliers, noted in his best-selling autobiography *Goodbye to All That* that the phenomenon of non-English speaking Welshmen made for interesting times in the battalion orderly room. Graves was so seriously injured by a shell splinter whilst serving with on the Western Front that he got to read his own obituary in *The Times*. His own recollection of events was limited to the laconic comment of a nearby soldier: 'Old Gravy's 'ad it'. Lloyd George's son served as aide de camp to the commander of the 38th (Welsh) Division and on 7 July 1916 it was ordered to attack Mametz Wood. The Wood was finally cleared on 12 July and when the Division regrouped on the Bazentin Ridge, they discovered the cost had been 4,000 casualties. After the success of General Ludendorff's Spring Offensive in 1918, the Wood was lost and the Welsh had to capture it again in August 1918. After the Great War, the communities of Mametz and Llandudno formed a 'twinning' arrangement. Erected in 1991 by the Western Front Association the memorial (pictured above) commemorates those men of 'Lloyd George's Welsh Army' who fell on the Somme in July 1916. It stands facing Mametz Wood. In 2002 the South Wales Branch of the WFA added two new features to the memorial. These were new steps for easier access and a multi-lingual information plaque, which tells the story of the battle in Welsh, French and English.

# THIEPVAL

The Ulster Memorial Tower stands on what was the German front line during the Battle of the Somme, which took place from July to November 1916. It is opposite Thiepval Wood from where the 36th (Ulster) Division made their historic charge on 1 July 1916, two Victoria Crosses being won that day. Men of the Division were eventually to win a total of 9 VCs and it served on the Western Front until Armistice Day.

The Tower itself is a replica of the well-known Ulster landmark, Helen's Tower designed by William Burn, which stands on the Dufferin and Ava Estate at Clandeboye, County Down. On completion of the tower in 1867, Lord Dufferin dedicated it to his beloved mother Helen, Baroness Dufferin, granddaughter of the playwright Richard Brinsley Sheridan. It was in the shadow of the tower that the men of the 36th (Ulster) Division trained at the outbreak of the Great War. When demands grew for a monument on the Western Front to Ulster's fallen it was a natural choice. The architects chosen for the task were Messrs Bowden and Abbot of Craven Street, London. This was the first national memorial to be erected on the Western Front and it was inaugurated by Field Marshal Sir Henry Wilson on 19 November 1921. On 1 July 1989 Princess Alice, Duchess of Gloucester rededicated the memorial. The principal room inside the Tower is a sixteen-foot square memorial chamber, faced throughout in stone, with a marble tablet. The inscription on the tablet reads:

"THIS TOWER IS DEDICATED TO THE GLORY OF GOD, IN GRATEFUL MEMORY OF THE OFFICERS, NON-COMMISSIONED OFFICERS AND MEN OF THE 36TH ULSTER DIVISION AND OF THE SONS OF ULSTER IN OTHER FORCES WHO LAID DOWN THEIR LIVES IN THE GREAT WAR, AND OF ALL THEIR COMRADES-IN-ARMS, WHO BY DIVINE GRACE, WERE SPARED TO TESTIFY TO THEIR GLORIOUS DEEDS"

# THE CARIBOU

During the Great War 9,826 Newfoundlanders enlisted in the army and another 2,000 served in the Royal Navy. Lloyd George would write: 'Newfoundland sent over a regiment, which took part so unyieldingly in the conflict that it used up reinforcements far quicker than they could be sent along to it. It fought at Suvla Bay in 1915, on the Somme in 1916, at Monchy and Cambrai in 1917; and by the end of 1917 its death-roll alone was more than a quarter of all the men sent over from Newfoundland. Casualties had wiped out the regiment twice over'.[27] The Dominion of Newfoundland became a province of Canada in 1949.

During that war, the sculptor Captain Basil Gotto served as a musketry instructor at The Depot, Winchester. He dramatically improved the shooting skills of a number of regiments that passed through his hands, one of which was the Newfoundland Regiment and he struck up a friendship with their padre, Major (later Lieutenant Colonel) the Reverend Thomas Nangle. After Gotto's discharge from the army in January 1919, he sculpted the bronze statue *The Fighting Newfoundlander* at the Winchester School of Art using Corporal Thomas Pittman DCM MM of the Newfoundland Regiment as his model. Pittman had been wounded four times in the Battle of Beaumont Hamel. He was summoned from Hazley Down Camp and closely scrutinized by Gotto who told him: 'All right, you'll do.' The statue got its name from the ironic sense of humour of Pittman's comrades who would visit 'The Fighting Newfoundlander' each day over the two months he spent posing for Gotto. Cast in Belgium, the sculpture was commissioned and donated to the City of St John's, Halifax by Sir Edgar Bowring and was inaugurated on 13 September 1922 in Bowring Park. (During the Second World War, Pittman was in Bowring Park admiring the memorial with his wife, when a stranger came up to him and said: 'Whoever posed for the sculptor, he must have been a very untidy soldier.' Only then did Pittman realise that Gotto had accurately captured every single last detail of his dress right down to his badly worn boots). Father Nangle subsequently contacted Gotto and told him that the Newfoundland Government was considering a proposal to erect a memorial at the scene of each battle in which the Newfoundland Regiment (later the Royal Newfoundland Regiment) had fought on the Western Front and asked him to think about what form these might take. Gotto noted in his unpublished memoirs: 'One had to avoid flamboyance and whilst trophies of arms might have been appropriate they would have been monotonous. I was puzzling over the question as I walked across St James's Park when the idea struck me of elevating the caribou into the national emblem for the Dominion. I would propose a caribou standing on a hilltop bellowing defiance. The idea was enthusiastically received and in due course the sites were acquired, the artificial hills raised and crowned by my colossal caribous. At Beaumont Hamel a Park of Remembrance was acquired and the original trenches maintained as on the day of the battle and it was there that Field Marshal Earl Haig supported by Maréchal Fayolle, unveiled the Memorial in June 1925.' At the ceremony on 7 June, Gotto was presented to Fayolle who asked him in French: 'How it was that the English sculptors always struck upon a happy motif for their work whereas our French sculptors, alas!' Gotto paused to frame a suitably diplomatic reply that would not offend his French artistic colleagues, but before he could do so Haig intervened, having misinterpreted Gotto's pause as signifying that he could not speak the French language. He then embarrassingly translated the Marechal's question into English for what he assumed was Gotto's benefit. Much to Haig's chagrin, Gotto's reply was in fluent French.[28] The erection of each of the caribous was superintended by Father Nangle and each site was landscaped by the Dutch architect Rudolph Cochius. The five memorials stand at Beaumont Hamel (July 1916), Gueudecourt (September 1916), Monchy-le-Preux (April 1917), Masnières (November 1917) and Courtrai (October 1918). They cost approximately £1,000 ($35,000) each.

---

[27] David Lloyd George *War Memoirs of David Lloyd George* Volume II.
[28] Gotto had trained as a painter under both Bougereau and Fleury at the Académie Julian in Paris and was a friend of both the artist Theodore Roussel and the sculptor Rodin. Needless to say he spoke French like a native.

# BEAUMONT HAMEL

One of Gotto's caribous was designated as The Newfoundland National Memorial and it stands in the 84 acre Newfoundland National Memorial Park at Beaumont-Hamel, some nine miles north of Albert. It was here on 1 July 1916 that the Newfoundland Regiment made their famous charge into a hail of German machinegun bullets and in less than half an hour was annihilated. When Roll Call was held the next day, only 68 out of 801 men were not casualties. The final figures were 255 killed, 386 wounded and 91 missing. Every officer was either killed or wounded. The bronze panels at the base of the caribou at Beaumont Hamel bear the names of 820 Newfoundland soldiers and sailors who fell in the Great War. The Park in which the Beaumont Hamel memorial stands was also inaugurated by Field Marshal Earl Haig on 7 June 1925. The Park also contains memorials to the 29th Division, the 51st (Highland) Division, the Commonwealth War Graves Commission cemeteries Hawthorne Ridge Cemetery No 2, Hunter's Cemetery and Y-Ravine Cemetery.

A sixth caribou sculpted by Gotto was also erected in Bowring Park. In 1924 working once again in collaboration with Father Nangle, Gotto sculpted the *Newfoundland National War Memorial* at St John's. The memorial was erected at King's Beach on Water Street, where some 350 years earlier Sir Humphrey Gilbert had claimed Newfoundland for England. Gotto's design was replete with symbolism and at the summit stands a nine-foot maiden with a sword and a torch, she represents the spirit or morale of Newfoundland. Below are a soldier and a sailor and between them literal figures representing the Newfoundland Mercantile Marine and the Forestry Corps. It was inaugurated by Field Marshal Earl Haig on 1 July 1924.

Regrettably, Basil Gotto is not as well-recognised a sculptor of war memorials as he should be, probably because only three of those he sculpted are resident in the UK, the other eight being in Canada or situated on the Western Front.

# VIMY RIDGE

The Canadian Army arrived on the Western Front in January 1915. In March the 1st Canadian Division took part in the Battle of Neuve Chapelle. In April they also took part in the Second Battle of Ypres. This formation was later expanded into the Canadian Corps with the arrival in France of the 2nd and later the 3rd Division. The Corps fought from April to August in defence of Ypres. It took part in the Battle of the Somme. On 9 April 1917 the Corps captured Vimy Ridge, which had remained in Germans hands against all assaults for two years.

The Canadian Memorial stands seven miles north of Arras. It overlooks the Douai Plain and was built by the Canadian Battlefield Memorials Commission. The design was chosen from 160 submissions and sculpted by the Toronto architect Walter S Allward. The two pylons represent France and Canada. The 250 acres on which it stands was the 'free gift in perpetuity of the French nation to the people of Canada'. Inscribed on the ramparts of the memorial are the names of 11,285 Canadian soldiers from the Great War to whom the fortune of war denied a known and honoured grave. King Edward VIII inaugurated the memorial on 26 July 1936. There is a visitor's centre nearby. 'Visible from a distance of forty miles, the two massive irregular pylons, stretching toward the sky like white bone needles or remarkable stalagmites, even the skeleton of the memorial had become a feature of the French landscape. The Italian carvers were beginning to work on the figures Allward had cast in plaster in his London studio. The names of the eleven thousand missing were being collected and the complicated mathematics necessary to fit these names into the space available on the base was being undertaken. The most recent set of figures had suggested that it would likely take four stone carvers two years to chisel the hundreds of thousands of characters into the stone. Lines, circles and curves corresponding to a cherished remembered sound called over the fields at summer dusk from a back porch door....'[29]

---

[29] Jane Urquhart *The Stone Carvers*.

## CANADA MOURNS HER SONS

At the base of the memorial the following inscription appears in both French and English:

"TO THE VALOUR OF THEIR
COUNTRYMEN IN THE GREAT WAR
AND IN MEMORY OF THEIR SIXTY
THOUSAND DEAD THIS MONUMENT
IS RAISED BY THE PEOPLE OF CANADA"

*The Times* newspaper reported: 'Just before their famous attack on Vimy Ridge in April 1917, men of the Canadian Corps 'of their own initiative and with the assistance of the Directorate, marked out the land, dug trenches, and made all the arrangements for the burial of the killed in the forthcoming action' and within 24 hours of the attack all the graves were marked and recorded'. 619,636 men enlisted in the Canadian army during the war and more than 65,000 died in it.

# DELVILLE WOOD

A large number of South Africans sailed for UK upon the outbreak of the Great War and they joined various British regiments to get into the war before it was over, but the South African Brigade commanded by General Henry Lukin (1860-1925) did not go into action on the Western Front until July 1916 and its blooding would be horrific. The four South African Regiments that made up the Brigade represented each of the four Provinces of the Union of South Africa. It came under command of the 9th (Scottish) Division during the Battle of the Somme. Delville Wood stands in the Bois d'Ellvile, twenty miles south of Arras. The Brigade consisting of 121 officers and 3,032 men, less one battalion sent to assist the clearing of Longueval, went into action on the morning of the 15th. Under heavy bombardment by the defending force, the battalions fought their desperate way into the wood and, despite heavy losses, had taken all the wood except the north-west corner by July 17'.[30] 'The South Africans nearly succeeded. They had taken most of the wood when the German army pulled their soldiers out - so they could bomb the place into oblivion. Up to 400 shells a minute crashed down on one square mile of wood, including one six-hour period where 20,000 fell, along with buckets of rain, turning the place into an impassable quagmire. When they were finally relieved after six days, less than 150 South Africans walked out of the wood. The rest were killed, wounded or missing in action.'[31] The South African National War Memorial honours all South Africans who fell in the Great War and it bears no names. The group on top of the memorial consists of two figures leading a warhorse into battle. These figures were based on Castor and Pollux and symbolise the British and Boer Peoples, the Horse represents South Africa. The memorial was designed by Sir Herbert Baker with sculpture executed by Alfred Turner. It was inaugurated on 10 October 1926 by Mrs Botha, widow of General Louis Botha. The ceremony was attended by Maréchal Joffre and Field Marshal Earl Haig. 136,074 South Africans enlisted in the army during the war and more than 21,000 lost their lives. The Stone of Remembrance (which was added after the Second World War to commemorate South Africa's dead from that war) can be seen in front of the arch and the Delville Wood Commemorative Museum at its rear was opened on 11 November 1986.

---

[30] Rose EB Coombs *Before Endeavours Fade*.
[31] *TNT Magazine* 10 November 2003 p. 23.

# ST GEORGE'S MEMORIAL CHURCH, YPRES

St George's Memorial Church was built as a memorial to the quarter of a million men who died in the Ypres Salient and the architect was Sir Reginald Blomfield. He was also responsible for the design of a considerable number of cemeteries in the area. Field Marshal Lord Plumer laid the foundation stone and the Bishop of Fulham dedicated the church on 24 March 1927. The altar was given in memory of the fallen of the Royal Army Medical Corps. The windows were designed by the London firm of Clayton and Bell. At the insistence of Blomfield they are of clear glass with small regimental crests and coats of arms in the centre of each. The three windows in the northern elevation commemorate the dead of the three Air Services. The Guards window is notable, carrying the crests of all the Guards regiments and formations of the Great War. The window given by the Monmouthshire Regiment carries the red dragon, the regimental badge and the Welsh motto: "GWELL ANGUA NA GWARTH".[32] There are also windows that commemorate individuals; most notably the Grenfell brothers. Every item in the church, the plaques on the walls and the chairs, the windows, the banners and the church furniture are all there in memory of someone who gave their life in the cause of freedom. A portrait bust of Field Marshal French, 1st Earl of Ypres, by the American sculptor Jo Davidson[33] is in the church. As Chairman of the Ypres League he was responsible for getting the appeal to build the church under way in 1924.

During the Second World War the locals removed all items of value from the church and hid them before the Germans arrived. The exterior of the church suffered bomb damage. The Germans did however borrow the church's chairs for their soldiers club in the Rijselstraat. All valuables were restored after the liberation of Ypres. Each year the church is visited by thousands of students, servicemen and veterans. It remains a fully functioning church and is used to give Christian burial to remains of the British and Empire fallen discovered on the battlefields of the Ypres Salient. The 75th anniversary of the church was celebrated by the Bishop of Gibraltar in Europe, the Right Rev Geoffrey Rowell, and the church's chaplain, the Reverend Ray Jones on 21 April 2002.

---

[32] In English: 'Better dead than cowardly'.
[33] Jo Davidson (1883-1952). Born New York, USA. Studied sculpture at the Art Students League, New York and at École des Beaux-Arts. He worked in a variety of media including terracotta, marble and bronze. He was famed as a sculptor of portrait busts. His subjects included: Woodrow Wilson, Franklin D Roosevelt, Anatole France, Maréchal Ferdinand Foch and Albert Einstein.

## VILLERS-BRETONNEUX

The Australian National Memorial (at the top of the photograph) stands in the British Cemetery 20 miles south of Arras, on the site captured by the Germans on 24 April 1918. The Australians recaptured it that same night, halted General Ludendorff's Spring offensive and prevented the German capture of Amiens.

'The Sub-Committee were unanimous in the choice of Villers-Bretonneux as the most suitable spot to commemorate the actions of 1918. It was here that the 4th Army under General Sir Henry Rawlinson (1864-1925) checked the German Advance in April, 1918 within 8 miles of Amiens and subsequently drove them out on 8 August, 1918, a day specially marked by Ludendorff in the German Military Calendar. There is an admirable site in the centre of the town at the junction of the Corbie-Villers-Bretonneux and Villers-Bretonneux - Amiens road'.[34] 'The Australian Government turned to Lutyens after the winning design for its memorial by W. Lucas had been set aside; the last to be built, this Memorial.... was only completed in 1938'.[35] It carried the names of 10,866 Australians who died for freedom and to whom the fortune of war denied a known grave. Only two years later it was to sustain considerable damage from the German invader whilst being used by the French army as an artillery observation post. The door of the locker that holds the cemetery register has a bullet hole in it to this day. The Sir William Legatt Museum stands nearby. 416,809 Australian men enlisted in the army during the Great War and 61,919 lost their lives.

With the agreement of the Commonwealth War Graves Commission, in November 1993 an unknown Australian soldier was exhumed from Adelaide Cemetery, placed in a simple Tasmanian blackwood coffin and taken to lie in state at Villers-Bretonneux, from where an Honour Guard from the Australian Defence Force took him home to Australia. He lay in state for three days at the Old Parliament House in Canberra. Finally, on 11 November 1993 - the 75th anniversary of the Armistice which ended fighting on the Western Front, the remains of the Unknown Australian Soldier were interred in the Hall of Memory at the Australian War Memorial, Canberra. The eulogy at his funeral was delivered by Australian Prime Minister Paul Keating. The empty grave at Adelaide Cemetery (Grave 13, Row M. Plot 111) is now marked with a special headstone.

---

[34] Report of Lord Midleton's Battlefield Memorials Committee 28 February 1921.
[35] Gavin Stamp *Silent Cities*.

## THE AUSTRALIAN MEMORIAL TABLET

In Amiens Cathedral a tablet was also placed to commemorate the role played by the Australians in the Defence of Amiens. On 8 August 1918, they would also perform a significant role in the Battle of Amiens. On that date the German Army underwent its first major collapse, with entire regiments surrendering to the Allied armies. That day the Germans lost 27,000 men, including 15,000 prisoners and 400 artillery pieces. So began the 'Advance to Victory'. History records that on this date known to the Germans as 'Der Schwarze Tag', both General Erich Ludendorff and the Kaiser noted that Germany would eventually have to sue for peace. - The end was in sight. Surmounted by the Australian Imperial Force badge, the text in English and French reads:

"TO THE GLORY OF GOD
AND TO THE MEMORY OF
THE SOLDIERS
OF THE AUSTRALIAN IMPERIAL FORCE
WHO VALIANTLY PARTICIPATED IN THE
VICTORIOUS DEFENCE OF AMIENS
FROM MARCH TO AUGUST 1918.
AND GAVE THEIR LIVES FOR THE CAUSE
OF JUSTICE, LIBERTY AND HUMANITY
THIS TABLET IS CONSECRATED BY
THE GOVERNMENT OF THE
COMMONWEALTH OF AUSTRALIA"

# ANZAC SQUARE, BRISBANE

ANZAC Square is located in the middle of the bustling modern city of Brisbane in Queensland, Australia. The square is dedicated to Australia's military heritage. The Shrine of Remembrance with its Eternal Flame is the Square's focal point. The Brisbane *Daily Standard* reported on 12 November 1930: 'The Queensland National Anzac Memorial in Brisbane has an ideal position right in the very centre of Brisbane, being situated on the highest point of the Ann Street level of Anzac Park, which has been created right at what might be termed Brisbane's front door, namely the Central Railway Station.' This central city site was chosen as the location for Queensland's memorial to Australia's service men and women, as it was highly visible to the citizens of the 1930s who travelled to the city to carry out their daily activities. The memorial is the focus of Brisbane's Dawn Service which is held every year on 25 April. The service commences at 0428 hours, this being the exact time the ANZACs went into action at Gallipoli. The 18 columns in the Shrine's Doric colonnade represent the year of peace 1918. Also encoding that date is the number of stairs leading up to the Square, 19 in the first row and 18 in the second. The Square contains memorials to all conflicts in which Australia's men fought in the 20th century, including Vietnam and Korea.

It would appear that the acronym ANZAC was invented in early 1915 by two Australian staff clerks named Millington and Little who were administering the Antipodean elements of General Hamilton's forces from Shepheard's Hotel in Cairo. It was then quickly taken into official use. The convention is that the word 'ANZAC' should always be written in upper case and permission to use the name for commercial or official purposes rests with the Australian Minister for Veterans' Affairs. Website at anzacday.org.au

# THE CANADIAN NATIONAL WAR MEMORIAL, OTTAWA

The funeral of Canada's Unknown Soldier on 28 May 2000 at the Canadian National War Memorial, Confederation Square, Ottawa, Ontario.

After the Great War, Canada decided to erect a memorial to commemorate all 60,000 Canadians who died. The design competition for the memorial was announced in 1925. Its rules stated: the design was to be: 'Expressive of the feelings of the Canadian people as a whole, to the memory of those who participated in the Great War and lost their lives in the service of humanity' and 'While the spirit of heroism and self-sacrifice should be commemorated, there should be no attempt to glorify war.' The competition was open to architects, sculptors and artists resident in the Empire, who were British subjects by birth, but residing elsewhere, or subjects of Allied nations. A total of 127 entries were received - 66 from Canada, 24 from England, 21 from France, seven from the United States, five from Belgium, two from Italy, one from Scotland and one from Trinidad. Seven finalists were then chosen to submit scale models of their designs. The Board of Assessors selected the design submitted by the English sculptor Vernon March for his concept of 'The Great Response of Canada'. March based his design on Sir William Goscombe John's *The Response* at Barras Bridge, Newcastle upon Tyne in England, (page 87 of this study). The March family of six brothers and a sister, all of whom were artists or sculptors lived in a house named 'Goddendene' at Locksbottom, Farnborough, Kent. They turned out a large number of war memorials in their workshop after the Great War and notable examples of their work are the St Peter and St Paul Church War Memorial at Bromley and the Bromley War Memorial, both in Kent. March's dramatic design consisted of 22 bronze soldiers and a 13 pounder field gun passing through a granite arch under the guidance of the allegorical figures of Peace and Freedom. March's conception was undoubtedly one of the most impressive war memorials of the Great War period. The project was delayed for years by site problems, compounded by March's death. Poignantly, the memorial was inaugurated by King George VI on 21 May 1939. In 1982 the bronze numerals '1939-1945' and '1950-1953' were added to the memorial to honour the fallen of the Second World War and the Korean War. The memorial is the focus for the National Ceremony to remember all Canada's war dead held there each 11 November. Website at www.cdli.ca/monuments/

## THE FALLEN MADONNA

A form of memorialisation often overlooked is the mural and whilst rare on mainland Great Britain, a variety of examples can be found in Northern Ireland. Usually these are interestingly proportioned equestrian portraits of 'King Billy'[36] painted on gable ends and are usually employed by the communities in which they may be found as a means of marking their territory and of advertising their allegiance to the Crown. King William's victory over King James II at the Battle of the Boyne on 12 July 1690 (1 July old style) ensures that this date has considerable significance in the Loyalist calendar. 1 July 1916 marked the opening day of the Battle of the Somme, in which the 36th (Ulster) Division played such a heroic role. At the Donegal Pass in Northern Ireland may be found an impressive mural of a lone soldier of the 36th Division, head bowed contemplating the grim Somme battlefield. At Albert on the Somme in France can be found a large mural painted in the 1990s on the gable end of a street. The date "1916" is painted on it in large white numbers and the heads and shoulders of three British 'Tommies' are depicted. In the background, amidst the smoke of war is a representation of the Basilica of Notre Dame de Brebieres at Albert topped off by the gilded Virgin and Child perched forward horizontally and this mural refers to a most remarkable story: 'Even before the war, the golden Virgin, triumphantly holding the infant Child in her uplifted arms on the soaring heights of Albert's Cathedral had been a landmark. Now it was the very symbol of the war itself. Early in 1915 an unlucky shot from a German gun had struck the cathedral tower fair and square and the Virgin had fallen forward to lie precariously horizontal, face downwards above what had once been the market-place and was now the bustling centre-point of troop movements through Albert. It was an awesome sight. As the shellfire intensified and the cathedral itself became more and more battered and knocked about, the tower with its leaning Virgin remained intact. A superstition grew up among the French troops and it was adopted in their turn by the British when they came to the Somme. When the Virgin fell the war would end - and the Germans would have won! As the Virgin looked likely to fall at any time, an event which would be distinctly bad for morale, French engineers were ordered to secure the statue with strong steel hawsers. So, there she hung, sorrowing or, according to the various imaginations of the troops, protecting or blessing them as they passed beneath'.[37] Had they known it, the French could have saved their energies as the German artillery would not fire upon the statue, because the German version of the superstition held that the side which shot the Virgin down from the Basilica would lose the war. The golden Virgin would remain suspended over Albert's market-place until General Ludendorff's Spring Offensive of 1918. 'When Albert fell to the Germans in March 1918, the British were determined that their enemies should not use the tower of the basilica for artillery observers as they themselves had used it for so many months earlier in the war, and British heavy guns were turned onto it. The tower was destroyed and the golden Virgin finally fell into the square below. It has been estimated that the church had been struck by some 2,000 shells since 1914. The statue was lost; rumour had it that the Germans took it away for its scrap metal value. The soldiers' legend that the fighting would end only when the Virgin fell had been true, for within a few months the war was over.'[38] In 1927 Albert commenced the restoration of its battered Basilica which had only been completed some thirty years earlier. The restoration was completed by 1929. At the bottom of the street in which the mural appears is the fully repaired Basilica with the upright golden Virgin and Christ Child restored to its original pristine condition on its summit.

---

[36] William of Orange (1650-1702). Born at The Hague, Netherlands. He married Princess Mary in 1677. At the secret invitation of England's aristocracy, he landed at Torbay 5 November 1688 and dispossessed his Roman Catholic father-in-law King James II of the British throne in 'The Glorious Revolution'. He took the title of King William III and ruled jointly with Queen Mary (1662-94). He was victor of the Battle of the Boyne and for that reason is an enduring hero to the Loyalist community in Northern Ireland.
[37] Lyn Macdonald *Somme* pp 105-106.
[38] Martin Middlebrook *The First Day on the Somme*.

# CHAPTER IV

# THE SECOND WORLD WAR

# THE SECOND WORLD WAR

At the end of the Second World War, parish councils often added the names of the fallen to existing Great War memorials. Building on lessons learned, the War Department decided that they needed to produce a complete list of all who had died, reasoning that such a list would be required both by the Imperial War Graves Commission and the Registrar General. The printing of lists after the Great War was costly and had not commanded a large sale. The War Department's solution was to produce a 'Hollerith' card index system, from which details could be extracted upon demand, in the format required. War Memorial Committees actively addressed the issue of commemoration from a utilitarian perspective. They balloted their communities to determine which projects would be well supported. Strong evidence of a sea change in the public's attitude towards traditional modes of commemoration may be taken from a survey carried out by Mass-Observation in November 1944. The question asked of the public was: 'What form should war memorials take to commemorate the fallen of World War II? Practically no one wanted the memorials of this war to take the form they often did after the last - that is, costly erections in stone. Most people wanted 'a memorial which would be useful or give pleasure to those who outlive the war'.[1] In the words of a chemist interviewed by the researchers: 'The only point on which my mind is fully made up is that they should not take the form of stone monstrosities on every street corner and village green and not one penny would I willingly contribute to any scheme to erect such'. 'The Second World War produced no new architectural vocabulary. Essentially the same forms were used as in the First'.[2] The rarity of memorials commemorating the fallen of this war can also be understood from the widely held point of view that both World Wars were essentially the same conflict. Support for this view can be found in a letter Admiral of the Fleet Lord Chatfield[3] wrote to the Maintenance Commander at the Nore, Chatham on 24 October 1944: 'As time goes on, these two wars will settle down in their true perspective in history, and will appear more like one war in two parts.... Where, however, no appropriate suggestions are forthcoming, I submit that the extension of the last War's Memorial is the best way of commemorating this war'.[4] When Sir Edwin Lutyens was asked in January 1940 by Colonel Kenyon of the Imperial War Graves Commission what forms of commemoration should be employed for the fallen Servicemen of the Second World War, he gave pretty much the same response.

In a paper submitted to the Royal Society of Arts on 22 February 1944, Major Walter Irvine of Warrington wrote with some asperity on the subject of Gardens of Memory: 'After the last war as we all remember only too well, every city and nearly every community in the country expressed a wish to commemorate those of the locality who had given their lives in the war. There could have been no finer thought, there can have been none more generally disastrous in execution. Here and there one has seen the craftsmanship of the artist, but in the large majority of instances there sprung up some pathetic pseudo-realistic figure which remains an eyesore in nearly every public place in Britain'.[5] Major Irvine had a point, much of the statuary that was erected after the Great War was unimaginative, derivative and some of it downright ugly. Apart from Blomfield's Cross of Sacrifice, the usual form employed by communities was that of the archetypal bronze 'Tommy' in marching order complete with rifle and tin helmet. Artistically, this offered a limited range of possibilities. It would take the genius of sculptors such as Sir William Goscombe John ('The Response' at Barras Bridge, Newcastle upon Tyne and the Port Sunlight War Memorial on The Wirral), Francis Derwent Wood (Ditchingham War Memorial) and inevitably, Charles Sargeant Jagger (Hoylake and West Kirby War Memorial) to overcome the limitations of this form.

---

[1] Arnold Whittick *War Memorials*.
[2] Conversation with David Crellin 4 October 2002.
[3] President of the War Memorials Advisory Council.
[4] Royal Society of Arts archive PR.GE/117/10/3.
[5] Royal Society of Arts archive PR.GE/117/10/4.

# THE BLITZ

After the failure of the Luftwaffe to gain mastery of Britain's airspace in the Battle of Britain, they turned their attention to the bombing of Britain's ports and cities (including neutral Dublin on 31 May 1941). Plymouth, Newcastle, Southampton, Coventry, Bath, Bristol and Belfast were all subjected to major attacks. London was singled out for special treatment and this phase of the war would become known as 'the Blitz'. This war of terror against Britain's civilian population would be intensified by the arrival of the unmanned 'V' weapons. The Vergeltungswaffe 1 FZG-76 (V1) known as the Flying Bomb or Doodlebug was the first modern unguided missile used in wartime. The fact that these projectiles were unmanned meant that they could be used regardless of the human or meteorological factors that often limited air operations. The first V1 fell on Grove Road, Bow in London's East End on 13 June 1944 and its arrival is marked by an English Heritage Blue Plaque. The 'Flying Bomb Blitz' began in earnest on 15 June 1944, with 244 fired at London and 50 fired at Southampton. 144 crossed the English coast, 73 reached London. Some were shot down, but most of the rest landed south of the Thames and a few hit Southampton. One malfunctioned and landed in Norfolk. There are currently some 120 memorials in UK to the civilian casualties of the Second World War. Many of these are in London and the approaches to the capital, reflecting the targeting of the city. The first V2 rocket to land in Great Britain wrecked Staveley Road in Chiswick, West London and 1,115 rockets were fired at England in the period 8 September 1944 - 27 March 1945, killing 2,754 people and seriously injuring 6,523. The last V2 landed on Hughes Mansions, Bethnal Green, killing 134 on 27 March and two days later, the last V1 weapon aimed at Britain was destroyed in flight over Sittingbourne, Kent. The V2 was 45 feet long, 6 feet wide and weighed some 14 tons. It carried a one-ton warhead. It arrived silently because it travelled at supersonic speed. Such was the confusion the rockets caused, that the resulting explosions were initially thought to be exploding gas mains, before the true nature of the weapon was ascertained. The rocket sites in Northern France were singled out by the RAF and USAAF for special attention and were regularly attacked to prevent them from carrying out their mission. The invasion France in June 1944 and the reconquest of France pushed the rocket sites further and further away from mainland Britain and consequently diminished the effectiveness of the V weapons. Many of the missile and space rocket technology developments after the war - especially the American Apollo programme, were based on the work of Werner von Braun's team at Peenemünde.

At 2140 on 19 April 1941, a parachute mine was dropped on Essex Road, Romford, Essex. Seventeen houses were demolished in the explosion and 38 people killed. At the spot where houses were mere piles of rubble, a small triangular piece of wall stood, with a short length of picture rail attached. Hanging from it was a glass-fronted unharmed copy of William Holman Hunt's portrait of Jesus Christ: *The Light of the World*. Amid the carnage, the picture and the portion of wall remained untouched. For those who believe in such things, no explanation is necessary. For those who do not, none is possible. Today the picture may be seen in St John's Church, Romford with the Book of Remembrance to those who died.

Another good example of the bringing of the battlefield to the civilian environment may be taken from the fact that Liberty and Co, the department store in London's West End has on one of its staircases two war memorials, one commemorating the store's 44 men who died in the Great War and another commemorating the 16 civilian members of staff who were killed in the Blitz. A plaque let into the pavement outside Marks and Spencer's department store at Lewisham Market in south east London commemorates a strike by a V-1 on 28 July 1944 that demolished 20 shops, damaged 30 more, killed 51 people and injured 313.

On 18 July 1944, Elmers End Bus Garage in Beckenham sustained a direct hit from a V1 flying bomb. 16 staff were killed and 39 vehicles destroyed. The garage was later rebuilt, but closed in 1986. The memorial to those who died that day is in London's Transport Museum Reserve Collection at The Depot, Acton and may be seen by appointment.

# THE ROYAL GARRISON CHURCH OF ST GEORGE

The Royal Garrison Church of St George at Woolwich Barracks in South East London was destroyed by a flying bomb on 13 July 1944. It had been built by Thomas Henry Wyatt and was modelled on his Italianate church at Wilton near Salisbury in Wiltshire. It was consecrated on 3 November 1863. Its unusual design would make it a remarkable building in its own account. However, elements of its marble and mosaic interior remain and although open to the elements, it is retained as a memorial garden and occasionally used for open-air services. After the Second World War, the Regiment adopted St Michael and All Angels in the nearby Royal Military Academy as their new church. Notwithstanding, St George's consecrated ground remains the spiritual home of the Royal Regiment of Artillery and is preserved as a memorial garden. The ashes of serving and former gunners are scattered in its grounds. Here the names of gunners, bombardiers, warrant officers and colonels can be found commemorated on brass plaques on the interior walls of the church in the equality of death. The interior fabric of the building having been exposed to the elements for 60 years is in the process of deterioration. The photograph above shows the Victoria Cross Memorial of the Royal Artillery on the rear wall of the church. It takes the form of a mosaic of St George killing the Dragon flanked on either side by panels listing the name of every gunner VC. As can be seen in the photograph above, the right hand panel is suffering from severe damp.

The church's condition serves as a particularly good example of the absurdity of current government policy in this field. St George's is not eligible for lottery funding to restore it, as long as it remains within the defence estate and given the continuous downward pressure on the Ministry of Defence's budget, funding is unavailable, or unlikely to be so to repair it, or to protect it from the elements. The mosaics have suffered over the years from exposure and this important relic of Britain's military heritage continues to decay for the want of common sense. The fallen pieces of mosaic are regularly and painstakingly collected by army cadets from 97 Cadet Battery (RA) and handed to the Depot Quartermaster against that day when steps can be taken to conserve what remains of this jewel of Britain's military history. In a further disturbing development, in consequence of the radical downsizing of the British Army in recent years, the Royal Artillery is due to leave Woolwich, its home for three centuries in 2006 and move to Salisbury Plain in Wiltshire, thus further distancing the Regiment from its past.

# ST MICHAEL'S CATHEDRAL, COVENTRY

On the night of 14 November 1940 the city of Coventry was bombed by 449 German aircraft on *Operation Moonlight Sonata*. The city was an important centre of Britain's aircraft production and was devastated by fire. St Michael's Cathedral was gutted. On the 16 November King George VI visited the bombed city. A form of memorialisation not so far considered in this study was Coventry's decision to leave its 14th century cathedral as a permanent memorial to the 568 civilians who died that night and to build a new cathedral at a right angle to the devastated ruins and in so doing consciously join the past to the present. Coventry's new cathedral was not without controversy, but was eventually brought to a happy conclusion. Its rebuilding was not only of national interest but drew the attention of the entire world, for rising phoenix-like it would be symbolic of Britain's rebirth. Within one year of the destruction of the cathedral a commission met to plan its rebuilding. Many Coventrians wanted to restore the interior of the old cathedral, but the commission asked Sir Giles Gilbert Scott to design a new one. His design involved the destruction of the old and a new building with a central altar. The design was accepted by the Coventry's Cathedral Council, but rejected by the Royal Fine Art Commission. In 1950 the Cathedral Council conducted an open competition and received 219 entries from architects all over the world. The winner was Basil Spence (1907-1976) who was later knighted for his work. He visited the ruins and had had a vision of the new rising out of the old, a huge tapestry of Christ and saints cut into glass. Spence's plans were initially condemned as a monstrosity, he was pilloried in the press and received hundreds of letters opposing his plans. His commissions began to dry up and brought him to the verge of bankruptcy. Coventry City Council objected to the building of the Cathedral, believing that the city should be concentrating its resources on rebuilding itself. The Minister of Works overturned the council's objections. In 1954 permission was granted to Laing Construction to build the Cathedral and work began on 8 June on the huge undercroft, which during construction would serve as a place of worship. As the building began to rise, the world was gripped with interest and Spence's reputation soared. He commissioned the most eminent artists of the age to produce the finest examples of their work - and they rose to meet the challenge. Over the High Altar, Graham Sutherland designed the largest tapestry in the world *Christ in Glory in the Tetramorph*, measuring some 74 ft 8in by 38 ft it was woven by the Frères Pinton at Felletin, France. The glass *West Screen* with its eight rows of full-size figures of saints and angels is also the largest of its kind in the world. It was designed and engraved by the outstanding New Zealand glass engraver John Hutton. The *Baptistry Window* was designed by the artist John Piper and executed by Patrick Reyntiens. It was made of 195 panels and is considered by experts to be one of the finest pieces of 20th century decorative glasswork. Dame Elizabeth Frink sculpted the bronze lectern. On the exterior of the Cathedral and above its steps, is the sculptor Sir Jacob Epstein's last great work *St Michael and the Devil* symbolising the triumph of good over evil. The new cathedral cost some £1,250,000 and was consecrated on 25 May 1962 by Dr Cuthbert Bardsley, Bishop of Coventry. Queen Elizabeth II signed the documents of consecration. The first performance of Benjamin Britten's *War Requiem* was conducted in the Cathedral by Meredith Davies (1922-2005) that same year.

Reconciliation is a recurrent theme at Coventry and in 1956 the cities of Coventry and Dresden were twinned. In 2004 the gilt orb and cross placed atop the rebuilt Frauenkirche in Dresden was donated by Coventry. After the war, the *Reconciliation Altar* was erected in the apse of the (still consecrated) ruined Cathedral and prayers for reconciliation are conducted there each Friday at midday. In 1995, on the 50th anniversary of the end of the Second World War the businessman Richard Branson donated the *Statue of Reconciliation* which can be seen in the grounds of the old cathedral (with copies in Berlin and Stormont). It was sculpted by Josefina de Vasconcellos at the age of 90. A replica was donated by Coventry to the Peace Garden of Hiroshima, Japan. The International Centre for Reconciliation is based at Coventry Cathedral. Website at www.coventrycathedral.org

# BOMBED OUT CHURCHES AS WAR MEMORIALS

In the Second World War, as in the Great War, churches presented significant landmarks to enemy pilots operating over Britain and for that very reason suffered considerable damage. A good example of how this was handled by communities may be taken from St Luke's Church on the corner of Leece Street and Berry Street in Liverpool, which was bombed and gutted by fire in May 1941. After the war ended, the shell of the structure was reinforced with girders and cables and the church was left in ruins as a memorial to those Liverpudlians who lost their lives in the Blitz and this is exactly the state in which it may be seen today. The Guards Chapel at Wellington Barracks, Birdcage Walk in London was hit by a V1 flying bomb in the middle of the singing of the *Te Deum* during Divine Service on 18 June 1944, killing 119 worshippers and seriously injuring 102. Due to the limitations of the site and its proximity to Buckingham Palace, the Guards Chapel was rebuilt on the same site after the war.

The lychgate at St James Parish Church, Bushey in Hertfordshire was bombed and destroyed during the Blitz. By coincidence, it was the parish's Great War memorial and there are many other instances of war memorials from the Great War situated in churches, or on church ground being destroyed in the Blitz. In Great Britain sculpted depictions of Jesus Christ as a form of memorialisation are comparatively rare. A particularly good example may be found on the outside wall of the Church of St Peter, Hobart Place, Eaton Square, London. It was originally the Great War Memorial at St John's Church in Wilton Road. St John's was destroyed by enemy action on 11 October 1940. As it was the daughter church of St Peter's, the war memorial was moved there and re-erected on the outside wall of the church, where it may be seen to this day.

By 1944, one church in the City of London had been destroyed and 18 others burned out. The utilisation of their shells for memorialisation purposes was discussed by the various bodies involved in their keep and a letter from the 'great and good' published on 15 August 1944 in *The Times* sparked a lively debate in their letters page over the period 17 August - 23 September, of which the newspaper published 13 letters. These included opinions on the subject from such distinguished individuals as Sir Herbert Baker, Professor Gilbert Ledward, Lord Faringdon and A E Richardson, (who wrote on behalf of the Friends of City Churches). Sir Herbert Baker objected to the proposal on the grounds that 'retained ruins would foster hate and revenge'. Ledward's intervention was the most interesting of all, given what would follow. He stated: 'Re-creation not retrospection should be the theme for all memorials of this war, the symbol should be that of the phoenix rather than the collector of antiquities.' (His letter certainly leads one to muse as to whether he had seen one of the few remaining complete mosaic panels in the Royal Garrison Church of St George at Woolwich Garrison which had been bombed and gutted a month earlier, the surviving panel depicted a phoenix rising from the flames). Also of note was a letter from Dr E F Armstrong, President of the Royal Society of Arts drawing the attention of interested parties to the inaugural meeting of the War Memorials Advisory Council which had been called for 18 September 1944. A booklet entitled *Bombed Churches as War Memorials* with a foreword by the Dean of St Paul's was produced on the subject by the Architectural Press in 1945.

On 15 August 1944 *The Times* newspaper printed the following letter which was signed by: Lady Allen of Hurtwood (1897-1976) Vice President of Institute of Landscape Architects 1939-46, Lord David Cecil (1902-1986) literary critic, biographer and Fellow of New College, Oxford 1939-69. Sir Kenneth Clark (1903-1983) Baron Clark 1969, art historian and patron of the arts, Director of the National Gallery 1934-45. The Rev F A Cockin (1888-1969) Canon of St Paul's 1938-44, Chaplain to the King 1937-46, Bishop of Bristol 1946-58. T S Eliot (1888-1965) poet. H S Goodhart-Rendel (1887-1959) Architect. Julian Huxley (1887-1975) scientist, knighted 1958. Lord Keynes (1883-1946) better-known to history as the economist John Maynard Keynes. E J Salisbury (1886-1979) knighted 1946, Director Royal Botanical Gardens, Kew 1943-56.

'Sir, - We should like to invite your attention to a proposal first advocated, we believe, by the *Architectural Review*, that a few of our bomb-damaged churches should be preserved in their ruined condition, as permanent memorials of this war. Already the authors of 'A Plan for Plymouth' have taken up this idea to the extent of selecting the ruined church which, they feel, would symbolise the city's grief....' And on April 28 your correspondence columns contained a specific suggestion for London.

There will probably be a wide measure of agreement that many of the memorials put up after the last war were unworthy of the men whose sacrifice they commemorate. That a vast gulf of feeling should have lain between the experience and the memorials was in any case inevitable. In this war conditions have been different. England has itself been in the battle and London is still in it. Could there be a more appropriate memorial of the nation's crisis than the preservation of fragments of its battleground ?

It is proposed that work on the selected ruins themselves should be confined to the minimum essential to preserve them from further decay, but that they should be surrounded by lawns, flower-beds and flowering trees, with seats for those in search of quietness and rest. The churches themselves would in many cases also permit the use for open-air services in the summer months, for which the climate of this country is far more favourable than is sometimes supposed. Thus in addition to the commemoration of this war's dead through the preservation of a few tangible fragments of distinction, we should be able to provide in some measure for the needs of our successors for spiritual refreshment and physical and mental relaxation.

If the general proposal which we are advocating is accepted, the question, which are the most appropriate ruined churches to preserve should at once be faced. The final choice, will, of course, rest with the church authorities and the appropriate committees. It is hoped that the Fine Arts Commission will also be consulted. Those churches which have not been too severely damaged will no doubt be restored. Others, more seriously injured, will in many cases be restored too, on account of their local or national prestige. But others again have been so far destroyed that their restoration could be nothing more than a mockery of their former selves. Such churches must either be removed altogether or remain as ruins. If the former course were too widely adopted we believe that a potent source of emotional experience would be lost to future generations.

The time will come - much sooner than most of us to-day can visualize - when no trace of death from the air will be left in the streets of rebuilt London. At such a time the story of the blitz may begin to seem unreal not only to visiting tourists but to a new generation of Londoners. It is the purpose of war memorials to remind posterity of the reality of the sacrifices upon which its apparent security has been built. These church ruins, we suggest, would do this with realism and gravity. While being kept as gardens suitable for meditation or relaxation, in the heart of the city, each could act at the same time as a specific memorial, one to the seamen of the convoys, another to the men of the 8th Army, a third to the air crews of the RAF, a fourth to the women in the services, a fifth to a regiment; the names of the fallen being inscribed on their ruined stones. And in the City of London one church at least should be set aside for a memorial to the thousands of Londoners who died in the blitz for whom those walls of calcined stone were once not monuments, but tombs.

Yours Faithfully,

MARJORY ALLEN OF HURTWOOD, DAVID
CECIL, KENNETH CLARK, F A COCKIN,
T S ELIOT, H S GOODHART-RENDEL,
JULIAN HUXLEY, KEYNES, E J SALISBURY.

August 12.'

## THE WAR MEMORIALS ADVISORY COUNCIL

The Council was established under the auspices of the Royal Society of Arts in September 1944, after it had organised a conference on 27 April that year on the subject of war memorials. The speakers at the conference included Major General Sir Fabian Ware, Paul de Labilliere, Dean of Westminster, Sir Noel Curtis-Bennett and Admiral of the Fleet Lord Chatfield. It was decided that: 'The opinions of the men and women in the Services as to what form memorials should take deserves foremost consideration. Judging from letters published in the press recently, these men and women are, in the main, determined to break away from the purely monumental memorials which appeared all over the country after the last war'. This statement was adopted by the committee as an article of faith and determined the manner in which they sought to commemorate the fallen of the Second World War. The conference also undertook to ensure that the memorials of the Second World War were better than the First. Lord Chatfield was nominated President. As many as fifty leading societies connected with social welfare and the arts, together with a similar number of distinguished individuals from the arts, industry, education, the church, letters, etc placed their resources and experience at the disposal of the council. It functioned as a clearing house for the guidance of those committees commemorating the fallen. Correspondence requesting advice was received from the length and breadth of the Empire. Requests were also received from as far afield as Mexico and the American Battle Monuments Commission in the USA. Ware's involvement is surprising, as the Council actively promoted the concept of utilitarianism in its advice. 'The Commission had always tried to avoid the possibility of any ambiguity in its memorials to the missing. It had set its face against buildings of practical utility, knowing that ultimately they must invite association with their function rather than with the sacrifices the dead had made'.[6]

The Council noted in a minute dated 1 March 1946: 'Sir Fabian Ware, on behalf of the Imperial War Graves Commission invited the Council to submit suggestions as to the form which commemoration abroad to the fallen of the British Forces should take. The Committee greatly appreciates the response to this request from associated societies and individual members, all of whose suggestions were conveyed to the War Graves Commission. Sir Fabian Ware has sent a cordial acknowledgement of the suggestions submitted and further consultations between the Executive Committee and Sir Fabian are taking place'.[7]

It is worthwhile illustrating this change, by quoting a leader in *The Times* newspaper on the debate on war memorials that took place in the House of Lords on 14 February 1945: 'The debate upon war memorials, which Lord Chatfield initiated in the House of Lords yesterday, will have served a useful purpose if it leads those whose duty it may be to find concrete forms in which to express the wishes of the community to reflect a little upon the first principles of this matter. The essence of a war memorial, whether national or local, is that it should be an abiding reminder of the lives and sacrifices of those whom it commemorates. Any other quality, whether utility, amenity, or beauty, which it may possess should be secondary to that, and should be so disposed as to remind the living, even while ministering to their needs, of the debt which they owe to those who gave their lives in order that the British way and purpose might survive. Thus it is important that war memorials, though they may well go beyond a cenotaph or sculptured monument, should have something ceremonious or stately about them, and should not take the form of supplying a service which State or municipality might be expected to provide in the ordinary course of events. Archbishop Lord Lang indeed deprecated any strictly utilitarian tendency in war memorials, and favoured 'gardens of memory' as places of quiet rest, beauty, and meditation. Replying for the Government Lord Munster gave general approval to the report lately prepared by the committee of the Royal Society of Arts and issued by the War Memorials Advisory Council, a body consisting of representatives of a number of societies as well as of individual members

---

[6] Philip Longworth *The Unending Vigil*.
[7] Royal Society of Arts archive PR.GE/117/10/1.

distinguished in public affairs and the arts. This report is likely to be of much value since, besides discussing the elements of the problem, it tabulates, with comment, many of the forms which memorials may take. These include memorial gardens, parks and open spaces, avenues of trees, the acquisition of hill-tops or view-points, playing fields, the preservation of historic buildings, community centres, and village halls. But whatever their form, it is important that memorials should be planned with careful regard for design and maintenance, and that in every case a worthy record of the names of those commemorated, whether in a finely carved inscription or in a 'book of remembrance,' should be part of the scheme. It is the dead who are to be remembered and honoured in these memorials, even though it is the lives of those who survive that are enriched and perhaps ennobled by the act and form of commemoration'.[8] This development gave voice to the Puritan or utilitarian tradition which demanded that memorials should take a practical form. Structures such as hospitals, cottages for retired soldiers and village halls would all feature. 'However, with such utilitarian architecture the commemorative purpose is almost inevitably forgotten after a few years unless, as is rare, there is something in the design to communicate poignancy or higher purpose'.[9] The Council learned at the beginning of 1946 that Herbert Morrison, Lord President of the Council (the post then responsible for the organisation of government business) had called a meeting for 13 February to consider the question of a national war memorial. They hastily sent out a questionnaire to the member societies asking: 'Is there, in the Council's view, any widespread demand for a national war memorial, apart from steps such as the rededication of the Cenotaph to commemorate to commemorate the dead of both wars?' Three of the replies to this question were revealing: the Dean of Westminster replied: 'But inasmuch as most people realise that the two wars were fundamentally one, I fancy that they would also feel that a rededication of the Cenotaph would be singularly appropriate'.[10] Sir Fabian Ware responded: 'My personal view is that new dates only should be added to the Cenotaph, and I should deprecate any competing monument or any structural addition to the Cenotaph (which would be aesthetically unpardonable). At the same time, it seems to me almost impossible to pick out a beneficient object which would command universal assent'.[11] Although Sir Edwin Lutyens had died on New Year's Day 1944, Ware was well aware of his wishes as regards the Cenotaph and his opinion carried great weight with the Council. He had founded the Imperial War Graves Commission and had made it his life's work to commemorate the sacrifice of the British Empire's war dead. Colonel Lord Wigram replied: 'The dates 1939-1945 could be inscribed on the present Cenotaph'.[12] The shortness of notice given to the Council's member organisations obviously precluded them from properly consulting their membership.

On 9 April 1946 Hugh Dalton, Chancellor of the Exchequer announced in the House of Commons the establishment of a National Land Fund as a memorial to Britain's war dead from the Second World War, (of which a great deal more later).

Lord Chatfield tabled a motion in the House of Lords on 22 January 1947. It was not well supported. Peers who had expressed their willingness to support it were not present. Viscount Hall in replying for the Government stated: 'If at any time an expression of public opinion of sufficient magnitude to warrant further consideration of this matter should emerge, together with a scheme which could be regarded as a suitable National War Memorial, His Majesty's Government would then be prepared to give further thought to the question. I regret that it is impossible to accept the Motion in the form in which it is on the Paper, but I can assure your Lordships that His Majesty's Government will give very careful consideration to the points which have been raised in all speeches'.[13] Lord Chatfield withdrew his Motion.

---

[8] House of Lords *Hansard* Volume CXXXIV Columns 1016–1054. See also *The Times* 15 February 1945.
[9] Gavin Stamp *Silent Cities*.
[10] Royal Society of Arts archive PR.GE/117/10/4.
[11] Royal Society of Arts archive PR.GE/117/10/14.
[12] Royal Society of Arts archive PR.GE/117/10/14.
[13] House of Lords *Hansard* 22 January 1947 Column 57.

The Council held a Special General Meeting on 30 April 1947 and speaker after speaker voiced their outrage, disappointment, etc. However, none could answer the two exam questions: What form should such a memorial take? and where should it be sited? The Council wrote to the Prime Minister on 28 May recording their dismay. Prime Minister Clement Attlee replied on 10 June: 'I can assure you that the Government are in no sense opposed to the idea of a national war memorial nor are they unwilling to give a lead in this matter if this would help crystallise a general public sentiment in favour of the project. The difficulty is that there is little sign of public feeling on the matter and no scheme has been put forward which commands a general measure of acceptance'.[14] On 1 October 1947 the Council sent a deputation to see the Prime Minister at 10 Downing Street. He received them courteously and heard what they had to say. He wrote to them again on 29 January 1948 doubting that there was 'real public demand for such a memorial….the general public tend to think of the two wars as one defence against aggression'.[15] As a last attempt to force the Government's hand, a question was tabled in the Commons for the Lord President of the Council on 28 July 1948. This elicited the same response as before. However, the supplementary questions arising from the question are worth repeating in full, as they illustrate the variety of opinions in Parliament on this subject:

**Mr Medland:** Will the Lord President give an undertaking that neither the committee nor the War Graves Commission will continue to take large tracts of open spaces, such as that they propose to do at Plymouth Hoe, for the erection of ghastly memorials?

**Mr Ivor Thomas:** Does my right hon. Friend think that St Paul's Cathedral would have been built if Sir Christopher Wren had waited for public opinion to express itself?

**Mr Morrison:** That is a bright observation, but it really does not help us in examining this matter.

**Mr Emrys Hughes:** Would not the best memorial to the victims of the last war be for us to keep out of another one? [16]

Its task complete, the War Memorials Advisory Council was disbanded in 1948 and in time-honoured fashion its leaders were duly thanked and honoured. In consequence of the Council's lead, utilitarian modes of commemoration would feature strongly in the post-war period. As will be seen elsewhere in this study, the downside of this mode was, unless the form employed quite categorically denoted a memorial, the original purpose could be forgotten with the passage of time, or superseded by its function. For that very reason the Imperial War Graves Commission had always rejected this mode of commemoration.

In September 2003 The United Kingdom National Inventory of War Memorials had records of 536 war memorial halls, of which 236 had been erected after the Second World War, 88 war memorial hospitals, of which 20 were erected after that war. 313 war memorial chapels, of which 139 commemorated the fallen of the Second World War, and 31 examples of war memorial housing, of which 9 related to that war.

It was also notable that many memorial funds were established to build hospitals or better existing healthcare facilities. This was in the period immediately before the institution of the National Health Service by the Labour Government in 1948. A good example may be taken from Northampton General Hospital, which founded a war memorial appeal that by October 1946 had raised the phenomenal sum for that time of £145,000.[17]

---

[14] Royal Society of Arts archive PR.GE/117/10/16.
[15] Royal Society of Arts archive PR.GE/117/10/17.
[16] *Hansard* 28 July 1948 Column 1535.
[17] Royal Society of Arts archive PR.GE/117/10/13.

# THE DESTRUCTION OF WAR MEMORIALS

The destruction and defilement of the statuary of opponents has a long history. During the Great War, on 17 July 1916, to the fury of the Germans, bluejackets of the Royal Navy pulled down and decapitated the statue of 'The Iron Chancellor' Prince Otto von Bismarck at Tanga, German East Africa.[18] In a useful illustration of the nature of evil, during the 1930s the Nazi Party carefully erased from Germany's war memorials the names of the 12,000 German Jews who had died fighting for the Kaiser. During the Second World War the Germans destroyed many British memorials in the Blitz and made a point of destroying those on the Western Front they deemed unacceptable to German sensibilities. Most notable among these were Paul Landowski's equestrian statue of Earl Haig at Montreuil-sur-Mer in 1940, the Zeebrugge Memorial celebrating the assault on The Mole there on St George's Day 1918 which the Germans dynamited in 1942 [19] and the 2nd Australian Division Memorial at Mont St Quentin, which depicted a 'Digger' bayonetting a German eagle.[20] They also blew up the memorial to Admiral Saumarez on the Channel Islands, supposedly for strategic reasons. As part of the process of de-Nazification after the war, the Allied Powers determined that war memorials in Germany that celebrated militarism, or which had connections to the Nazi era should be destroyed. On 23 May 1946, Lord Saltoun rose in the House of Lords and called attention to the statement made by the Parliamentary Under-Secretary of State for War in the House of Lords on 15 May on the directive issued by the Allied Control Commission in Germany that 'certain war memorials including those of the 1914-1918 war shall be destroyed or mutilated'. Lord Saltoun tabled a Motion that this policy be reversed. He spoke at length, averring that such an act was ignoble, un-English, no better than the Nazis and that he suspected that the Government had been misled by 'a pack of wily foreigners' (our allies). He was strongly supported by a number of speakers, all of whom spoke of their horror at such a prospect. Lord Nathan, the Under-Secretary of State replied by reminding the Members that: 'It must be remembered that the general background out of which this directive has emerged is provided by the decisions taken by the great Allied Powers at Potsdam regarding the elimination of all forms of German militarism, the destruction of the National Socialist Party and of Nazi institutions, and the prevention of all Nazi and militarist activity and propaganda, leading finally to the eventual reconstruction of German political life on a democratic basis.'[21] He then went on to explain the measures that were being undertaken by the Allied Powers to dismantle the Nazi regime. He further explained why the directive included memorials from the Great War. Tellingly, he then informed the House that the ultimate decision on the removal or destruction of memorials would be placed in the hands of German officials. He then dilated on the type of memorials that would have to be removed which included street names such as Adolf Hitlerplatz, statues of Hitler and other Nazi leaders, statues of Ludendorff and Kaiser Wilhelm II - all of which were present within the British Zone. 'All that is intended to erase from war memorials Nazi emblems or offensive wording which glorifies the ideals of the Nazi leaders or war as such. Apart from those there is no question of removing or destroying monuments to the memory of formations or individuals who fell in a battle. The same refers to tombstones or plaques in churches that serve a similar intention. There is no intention to interpret the directive in a way which would be repugnant to decent feeling, and our officers in charge in Germany have been so instructed'. Nonetheless Lord Nathan recognised the strength of feeling of the House on the issue and stated that he would bring it to the attention of the Government. Lord Saltoun thanked the noble Lord for the conciliatory nature of his reply and withdrew his Motion.

---

[18] Charles Miller *The Battle for the Bundu.*
[19] A new, smaller, memorial commemorating the heroic events of St George's Day 1918 was erected in 1983.
[20] Replaced by the Australian Government with a new less dramatic sculpture in 1993.
[21] House of Lords *Hansard* 23 May 1946. Column 485.

# THE ROYAL NORFOLK'S REGIMENTAL CHAPEL

The Bishop of Norwich, Dr Bertram Pollock spoke at the graveside during the re-interment of 'the dear form of Edith Cavell' on 15 May 1919. He informed the throng that they were close to the ruins of the 13th Century Lady Chapel that was soon to be rebuilt as a memorial to 'Norfolk's sailors and soldiers who gave their lives for us in the Great War'. Much of the credit for its establishment rested with The Dean of Norwich, Herbert Somerset Crannage (Dean 1928-45). After long discussion, St Saviour's Chapel was commenced to a design produced by the cathedral architect Sir Charles Nicholson in 1931. It was consecrated by Bishop Pollock in the presence of Prince George[22] in 1932. A desk behind the entrance (through the twin arches of the 13th Century chapel) contains the Roll of Honour for the Great War of 1914-1918. Later another containing the names of Norfolk's war dead from the 1939-1945 war joined it. Each day a page is turned in these two volumes. In 1947 the chapel received a gift of a small 18th century Snetzer organ. In 1954 the County Regiment was invited by the Dean and Chapter to make the chapel their own. The Royal Norfolk Regiment accepted wholeheartedly and set about beautifying the chapel. The altar rails and screen gates (dedicated to the memory of Canon Busby) were constructed in wrought iron by the Wroxam blacksmith Eric Stevenson to a design by the cathedral architect Sir Bernard Fielding. In 1958 Queen Elizabeth the Queen Mother was present at the re-dedication of the chapel and unveiled the newly acquired reredos. This consisted of five 15th century painted panels chosen from eight, which were formerly in St Michael-at-Pleas Church, Norwich. Until the 1960's no subscription list had been raised and all funds were derived solely from gifts given by the Regiment and family members. In order to further beautify the chapel, the Dean of Norwich, the Very Reverend Norman Hook with Brigadiers F P Barclay, F Bassett Horner and F W Clowes launched an appeal to raise £4,000. The design by the cathedral architect Mr Dykes Bower, has college stalls with oak wall panels facing inwards fronting the two memorial floor tablets. That closest the altar is inscribed to: "THE 36 OFFICERS AND MEN OF THE 1st BATTALION ROYAL NORFOLK REGIMENT, WHO DIED FOR THE UNITED NATIONS IN KOREA, 1951 - 52'. The other, larger stone, commemorates: "ALL THE RANKS OF THE IX FOOT WHO SINCE THE RAISING OF THE REGIMENT IN 1685, HAVE IN MANY LANDS GIVEN THEIR LIVES FOR THEIR COUNTRY."[23] Each stall and wall panel in the chapel was sponsored by an individual, group or business and is carved with the name of a regimental campaign commencing with 1702. In nearly 50 years of regimental use the chapel has indeed been beautified. Regimental Colours including the 1st Battalion Royal Norfolk's laid up when new colours were presented to the 1st East Anglian (Royal Norfolk & Suffolk) Regiment, bedeck the chapel. The people of Norfolk presented the silver chalice and patten on the return of the 1st Battalion from Korea. Stained glass was provided by the Walpole family for the South windows and these represent notable East Anglian saints. In 1984 a special service in the chapel saw the unveiling of a bronze panel inscribed with the names of 103 ranks (plus one missing) of the 2nd Battalion who fell at the Battle of Kohima, Burma in 1944. This panel was a fortunate survivor of those on the 2nd Division's Kohima memorial (the majority having been stolen). It was replaced by engraved stonework on that memorial. In 1994 it was discussed and touched with much reverence and not a little sadness by those present at the 50th Anniversary Memorial Service. The chapel is now, through the inexorable progress of amalgamations of East Anglia's infantry regiments since the Second World War, the regimental chapel of The Anglian Regiment, successors to that illustrious line begun in 1685.

---

[22] George Edward Alexander Edmund Saxe-Coburg Gotha (Windsor 1917) 1902-42. Fourth son of the Prince and Princess of Wales (later King George V and Queen Mary). Duke of Kent 1934. Air Commodore RAF 1940. Killed in an air crash at Caithness on 25 August 1942.

[23] The regiment got its nickname: 'The Holy Boys' from a Spaniard who saw Britannia on the Regimental Colour during the Peninsular War and (to the delight of the Army) believed it to be an image of the Virgin Mary.

# THE CHINDIT FORCES MEMORIAL

The Chindits were a force founded and led by Major General Orde Wingate (1903-44). The two Chindit campaigns *Operation Longcloth* in 1943 and *Operation Thursday* in 1944 carried out long-range penetration in the rear of the Japanese Army trying to break into India with considerable success. The origin of the word Chindit is attributed to Wingate hearing one of his Burmese officers use the word 'Chinthe' in conversation. Wingate misheard it as Chindit, the name stuck in his mind and the rest is as they say history. The Chinthe is a mythical beast that can often be found standing guard outside Burmese temples. The Chinthe atop the plinth of the memorial was sculpted by Frank Forster, the architect was D Price. This memorial stands in odd contrast to the nearby statues of Portal and Trenchard on Victoria Embankment, London. Every regiment and formation that served in the Chindits is listed on it and it was unveiled on 16 October 1990 by Prince Philip, Duke of Edinburgh. The Chindit Chaplain, Lieutenant Colonel Eric Noble then inaugurated it. There followed a march past of the Chindit Old Comrades accompanied by veterans of 1st Air Commando and 194 Squadron RAF. Air Vice Marshal Sir Bernard Chacksfield, Chairman of the Burma Star Association wrote: 'The memorial itself is excellent in conception and execution. Another handsome, permanent and historic monument for the edification of future generations.' The inscription on this memorial reads; "THE BOLDEST MEASURES ARE THE SAFEST".

The large wreath at the base of the memorial in the photograph above is noteworthy, as it bears an extract from the text on the stone raised in memory of the fallen of the 2nd Division at Kohima in the Assam Hills. It is perhaps the most poignant of all such inscriptions:

> "WHEN YOU GO HOME
> TELL THEM OF US, AND SAY
> FOR YOUR TOMORROW
> WE GAVE OUR TODAY"

# THE WESTMINSTER THEATRE

War memorial theatres are extremely rare, the only surviving example in 2004 being Frome War Memorial Theatre in Somerset dating from the Great War. However, until recently there was another, the Westminster Theatre at Palace Street, Westminster:

The original building on the site was erected in 1766 for private worship by Dr William Dodd,[24] chaplain to King George III and was known as Queen Charlotte's Chapel. In 1922 Lord Lascelles converted it into the St James' Picture Theatre at the request of King George V, for the private viewing of films by the Royal Family. It was converted in 1931 for theatre use.

Frank Buchman (1878-1961) was born in Pennsburg, Pennsylvania and educated at Muhlenberg College. He was ordained into the Lutheran ministry in 1902 and was successively pastor of a church in Overbrook, Pennsylvania, a YMCA missionary to the Orient and a lecturer at the Hartford (Connecticut) Theological Foundation. During a visit to Oxford University in 1921, he founded an evangelical religious fellowship which became known as the Oxford Group. Its principles were based on four absolutes; honesty, purity, unselfishness and love. In an age in which dictatorships were fashionable, the Oxford Group sought to remake the world under the dictatorship of God. Buchman had an abiding interest in sin and being an American, this inevitably meant the sins of others. Unsurprisingly, the Oxford Group was instrumental in the founding of Alcoholics Anonymous and in 1939 the Group renamed itself Moral Re-armament (MRA). Buchman was a fairly controversial figure in his day: 'I thank heaven for a man like Adolf Hitler' is one of his more memorable quotes.

In 1946 MRA established a memorial fund through which to commemorate friends and family who had died in the Second World War. A prime mover behind this initiative was the author Peter Howard. The Westminster Theatre and its freehold site were purchased in April 1946, for the sum of £132,500.[25] The money was contributed in 2,857 individual gifts. Gifts in kind were also donated to equip it. The building was faced in Welsh slate donated by communities in the Valleys where MRA had toured a number of plays. Many returning Servicemen and Servicewomen donated their gratuities. The theatre was dedicated on Remembrance Sunday 1946, in the presence of men and women of all ranks. British, Empire and Allied troops took part in the ceremony. In the years that followed the theatre staged many productions with a Christian or improving theme. Upon the death of Buchman in 1961, he was succeeded by Howard, who unfortunately died in 1965. From that point onwards the fortunes of MRA declined. In 1991 they decided to sell the site on which the theatre stands. In 1998 it was acquired by a property developer who proposed developing the site to include residential accommodation, car parking and a substantially reduced theatre space. However, the developer faced considerable opposition from interested parties concerned at the dilution of the original intention and that Westminster would no longer have a theatre that could mount amateur productions, (the Portcullis Theatre having been discreetly demolished in 1986). In 2002 MRA rebranded itself as 'Initiatives of Change UK'. In June 2002 local residents reported that the plaque on the front of the building, proclaiming its existence as a memorial had been removed. Subsequent investigation revealed that the Roll of Honour had also disappeared. The building then in time-honoured fashion 'went on fire', destroying many of the original internal features and clearing the way for a development more suitable to the wishes of the developer. A Local Enquiry was held by Westminster Council on 10 and 11 December 2002. The decision of the inspector chairing the enquiry, and subsequently ratified by the Deputy Prime Minister, was that there was no impediment to the developer razing the site to the ground if he chose. This decision brought the whole sad story to an end.

---

[24] Convicted of forging a bond for £4,200 in the name of his patron the Earl of Chesterfield, he was hanged at the King's Gallows, Tyburn in London on 27 June 1777. Dr Johnson observed of him: 'When a man knows he is to be hanged in a fortnight, it concentrates the mind wonderfully'.

[25] At the time of writing in 2003, the purchasing power of £132,500 was £3.500,000.

## THE CASE OF THE VANISHING WAR MEMORIAL

As already mentioned, in 1946 Chancellor Hugh Dalton made the sum of £50 million available from the sale of war surplus, for the purpose of establishing a national fund as a war memorial to Britain's fallen of the Second World War. The National Land Fund was set up to purchase land, property and works of art for the nation. It was established by the Finance Act 1946 and placed under control of HM Treasury to use for the purposes specified in the Act 'and for such other purposes as Parliament might thereafter determine'. In his budget speech on 9 April 1946 Dalton said: 'It is surely fitting in this proud moment of our history, when we are celebrating victory and deliverance from overwhelming evils and horrors, that we should make through this Fund a thank-offering for victory, and a war memorial which, in the judgement of many is better than any work of art in stone or bronze. I should like to think that through this Fund we shall donate some of the loveliest parts of this land to the memory of those who died in order that we might live in freedom, those who for our sake went down to the dark rivers, those for whom already "the trumpets have sounded on the other side". Thus let this land of ours be dedicated to the memory of our dead, and to the use and enjoyment of the living for ever'. In the post-war years the fund was used primarily to make payments to the Commissioners of Inland Revenue for property accepted in lieu of tax. The House of Commons Public Accounts Committee Report 1953-54 recommended 'the desirability of legislation to return to the Exchequer some part of a large and growing balance of the National Land Fund'. J Enoch Powell MP, Chief Secretary to the Treasury arranged by means of the Finance Act 1957, for the holdings of the fund to be reduced from £50 to £10 million. Frankly, given his outstanding war record, Powell should have known better. 'He was one of only two instances during the whole war of a private soldier rising to the rank of brigadier; and for a few weeks he was the youngest holder of that rank in the army'.[26] On 7 November 1977 Field Marshal Sir Gerald Templer (1898-1978) wrote to the Expenditure Committee of the House of Commons. He copied his correspondence on 26 November to his friend General Jack Harman, Adjutant General of the Army. He made the not unreasonable point that the fund was not being used for the purpose Dalton originally intended. He attached to his letter a summary of the facts he had discovered. With a flippancy only a field marshal could get away with, he amusingly headed his synopsis: *The Case of the Vanishing War Memorial*. This correspondence caused deep breathing at the Ministry of Defence, a falling out between the three Services and their Ministry and embarrassment at HM Treasury. Sir Arthur Hockaday (1926-2004), Second Permanent Under Secretary at the Ministry of Defence carefully examined all the evidence and came to the same conclusion as Templer. Hockaday's report and recommendations were forwarded to the Expenditure Committee, which asked the Royal British Legion for their opinion on the matter. Surprisingly, they declined to become involved. In 1978 following the failure of the Fund to acquire Mentmore Towers, the Earl of Rosebery's stately home for the nation, the *Daily Telegraph* commented: 'The Mentmore saga revealed also that the Treasury saw the fund as subject to public expenditure restrictions with the severe implication that payments from it were at the cost of saving elsewhere. Almost unanimously, the art world has seen the Treasury's handling of the affair as a breach of trusteeship. It should be removed from Treasury control and put under independent trustees; perhaps in the form of a Heritage Commission or Council'.[27] 'The creation of the National Heritage Memorial Fund in 1980 as the successor to the Land Fund revived the original idea and since its inception the NHMF has been instrumental in saving or preserving a whole range of items from works of art to the nesting sites of bats'.[28] In April 2004 a donation of £1.8M from the fund was instrumental in keeping the famous Doncaster-built LNER locomotive No 1472 (later 4472) *Flying Scotsman* in Great Britain.

---

[26] Simon Heffer *Like the Roman: The Life of Enoch Powell* 1998, p. 93.
[27] *Daily Telegraph* 18 January 1978.
[28] Alan Borg *War Memorials*.

## BETHNAL GREEN AND BOUNDS GREEN UNDERGROUND STATIONS

At 2017 on 3 March 1943 in the East End of London, a loud explosion was heard. No German planes were overhead and no bombs were dropped. The explosion was a volley of rockets being fired by an anti-aircraft battery in Victoria Park, Hackney. This alarmed civilians in the immediate area, who feared a new German type of bomb and it triggered a panic-stricken stampede of men women and children down the stairs of Bethnal Green tube station. 'In just 15 seconds, more than 300 bodies were trapped in a stairwell 15ft by 11ft wide'.[29] In less than a minute 173 people were trampled to death. The government suppressed news of the disaster for 48 hours fearing that news of it would cause panic. A plaque commemorating those who died in the worst civilian disaster of the Second World War was installed above the entrance of the station in 1993. 168 of those who died that evening are commemorated in the Commission's Civilian War Dead Roll of Honour in Westminster Abbey. Bounds Green Tube Station on the Piccadilly Line has a large simple bronze plaque affixed to the wall on one of its platforms that commemorates those who were killed when the Station was bombed during the Blitz in 1940. The inscription reads:

> "IN MEMORY OF
> THE SIXTEEN BELGIAN REFUGEES AND THE THREE BRITISH CITIZENS
> WHO DIED ON THIS PLATFORM DURING THE AIR RAID OF
> 13 OCTOBER 1940
>
> LONDON UNDERGROUND LIMITED
> 13 OCTOBER 1994"

---

[29] *Metro* 4 March 2003 p. 32.

## THE SPECIAL OPERATIONS EXECUTIVE

SOE was founded in July 1940 shortly after the fall of France and it set about implementing Churchill's directive to 'set Europe ablaze'. It came under political control of the Ministry of Economic Warfare which was initially headed by the Socialist intellectual Hugh Dalton and from February 1942 by the Earl of Selborne. Agents were conveyed to France by the RAF or inserted into unoccupied southern France by the Free Polish Navy based at Gibraltar. SOE sabotaged German communications, forged documents, blew up trains and provided material support to the Maquis in their resistance to the German Occupation. SOE's French operations were conducted by two sections controlled from Baker Street in London, F Section and RF Section. Violette Reine Elizabeth Bushell was born in 1921. Her father was English, her mother French and she was brought up in Stockwell, South London. In 1940 she met Captain Etienne Szabo, of the Free French Forces and they married in August that year. Two years later he was killed in action in North Africa. Violette Szabo's fluent French made her a natural candidate for recruitment by SOE and she was trained at Christmas Pie, near Normandy, Surrey. In June 1944 she was captured by the Germans, interrogated and revealed nothing. She was executed at Ravensbrück Concentration Camp in January 1945 and cremated there. She was posthumously awarded Croix de Guerre and on 7 December 1946 the George Cross. She is commemorated on the Brookwood Memorial at the CWGC's cemetery in Surrey and also on their *Debt of Honour* website. Her story was told in the book *Carve Her Name With Pride* (1956) and the film of the same name (1958). An English Heritage Blue Plaque marks her home at 18 Burnley Road, Stockwell. Subsequently the SOE heroine Odette Hallowes GC[30] unveiled a plaque to both her and Noor Inayat Khan GC [31] at Ravensbrück. In the 1980s a committee was formed to erect a memorial to commemorate the sacrifice of those who had died serving in F Section of SOE. This committee was headed by Jean-Bernard Badaire, President of the Federation Nationale Libre Résistance. The F Section Memorial at Valençay, Indre Département, commemorates by name the 91 men and 13 women of F Section of the SOE who were killed in action, or more usually, under torture in the concentration camps of the Third Reich. F Section's operatives were drawn from Canada, France, Great Britain and USA. The architect was J P Callideau and construction took place between December 1990 and April 1991. The memorial was unveiled by André Méric, French Secretary of State for Veterans Affairs in the presence of Queen Elizabeth the Queen Mother on 6 May 1991. Both the location and the date are of particular significance. The first F Section agent successfully dropped in France was Georges Bégué, codenamed BOMBPROOF (and he was) on the night of 5-6 May 1941, between Valençay and Levroux. Bégué was followed by more than four hundred agents including 39 women. The F Section Memorial cost £50,000 and the town of Valençay donated the site on which it stands. 'The monument was designed under the title 'Spirit of Partnership' by Elizabeth Lucas Harrison, herself a refugee from Hitler, resident in London and the design of other works on similar themes, notably the Royal Air Force's Escaping Society Memorial in the crypt of St Clement Danes Church in London.'[32] The design took the form of two columns, one black, one white. This design symbolises the partnership between SOE and the Resistance. Black represents the night and secrecy, white represents the shining spirit which eventually brought forth victory. The two columns are joined by a circular disc which for obvious reasons represents the moon. The memorial additionally commemorates those members of the RAF and USAAF and also the sailors of the Allied navies who died on operations whilst in support of the Resistance.

---

[30] Odette Marie Céline Hallowes GC (1912-95). Entered Special Forces 1942. Captured by the Gestapo 1943. Liberated from Ravensbrück Concentration Camp April 1945.
[31] Princess Noor Inayat Khan GC, Hon Assistant Section Officer, Women's Auxiliary Air Force. Landed in France June 1943 as a member of the CINEMA/PHONO circuit. Captured October 1943. Killed by the Nazis on 13 September 1944 in Dachau Concentration Camp.
[32] *The F Section Memorial: Valençay* Hart Books Welwyn 1992.

# MALTA

'Nothing is better known than the siege of Malta' - Voltaire.

The history of this small island in the Mediterranean, eighteen miles long by nine wide, is the inevitable consequence of its geographical position. It is the key to Sicily, which in turn is the door to mainland Italy. This much was apparent to Suleiman the Magnificent in 1565 and no less so to Adolf Hitler in 1940. Both great sieges were unsuccessful. The island was the gift of the Holy Roman Emperor Charles V in 1530 to the Knights Hospitaller of the Order of St John of Jerusalem, after Suleiman had evicted them from Rhodes. By the 18th century the martial capabilities of the knights had declined. They were deposed and the island ransacked by Napoleon on his way to conquer Egypt on 12 June 1798. Admiral Nelson recognised the island's strategic importance, captured it on 5 September 1800 and for the next 160 years Malta enjoyed the fruits of British hegemony in the Mediterranean. The island was HQ of the British Mediterranean Fleet, an overseas garrison and until 1964 an important military staging post for military operations. On 10 June 1940 Italy entered the Second World War as a partner of Nazi Germany and Malta was besieged by the Axis Powers from 1940-1943. The stoic defence of the island by the Maltese and the British is perhaps best symbolised by the endeavours of the three airborne 'stringbags' Faith, Hope and Charity and the miraculous survival of the oiler OHIO during *Operation Pedestal*. What is less well-known is the heroic role played by the Royal Navy Submarine Service. Its presence would decisively influence the outcome of the war in both the Mediterranean and North Africa. Submarines operating out of Malta sank more than 1.35 million tons of Axis shipping between Italy and North Africa during this period. This intervention slowly strangled Rommel's Afrika Korps. In consequence, the submarine base at Lazaretto was bombed by the Axis air forces more than 1,000 times during the course of the siege and submarine crews returning from patrol had to sleep in their submarines on the bed of Lazaretto Creek. Malta was also re-supplied during the siege by large mine-laying submarines operating out of Alexandria in Egypt, nick-named 'The Magic Carpet Service'. General Bayerlein, Rommel's Chief of Staff commented after the war: 'We should have taken Alexandria and reached the Suez Canal but for the work of your submarines'. The resistance of the beleaguered Maltese was recognised by the award to the Island of the George Cross by King George VI on 15 April 1942. On 3 May 1954 The Queen inaugurated the first overseas memorial of the Second World War in the Floriana district of Valetta. The memorial took the form of a golden eagle atop a column designed by Hubert Worthington. At the base of the column are bronze panels listing every member of the RAF killed in the Mediterranean. There are seven CWGC cemeteries on Malta. These are: Santa Maria Addolorata, Imtarfa, Pembroke, Cappucini, Pieta, Marsa and Malta Memorial. They contain not only military burials from the two World Wars and non-World War graves, but also civilians, Service dependants and those with military connections. Malta has other cemeteries that also contain burials of British Service personnel and dependants.

Din l-Art Ħelwa (The National Trust of Malta) was founded in 1965 with the aim of creating a new awareness of Malta's natural, historic and cultural environment. The main work of this non-governmental organisation has been restoring historic buildings, such as chapels and towers. The Trust has also restored both Msida Bastion and Ta'Braxia cemeteries, both of which contain a considerable number of graves of British Service personnel. An unusual feature of the cemeteries and memorials on Malta is the significant amount of bomb damage from the enormous quantity of ordnance dropped on the island by the Axis Powers during the 2,740 air raids of the siege. Cast by Morris Singer, the Memorial Siege Bell at Valetta was designed by Professor Michael Sandle. It was inaugurated by The Queen and the President of Malta in May 1992. It commemorates all who died during the siege of 1940-43 and the 50th anniversary of the award of the George Cross. The 13 ton bronze bell is rung every day at mid-day to honour the memory of those who died.

# MALTA

A memorial in Ta'Braxia Cemetery to the victims of a cholera outbreak amongst the men, women and children of 1st Battalion of 14th Regiment shortly after their arrival on the island in 1867.

The Memorial Siege Bell.

## PEGASUS BRIDGE AND THE CAFÉ GONDRÉE

One category of memorial not so far considered, is where an existing structure becomes a war memorial because of the part it played in momentous events. Immediately before D-Day, on the night of 5/6 June 1944, D Company of the Oxfordshire and Buckinghamshire Light Infantry, commanded by Major John Howard, landed in five Horsa gliders and seized the Bénouville Bridge over the Caen Canal in France, (later renamed the Pegasus Bridge). The first Allied soldier to land in France on D-Day was probably Sergeant Jim Wallwork of the Glider Pilot Regiment. He arrived headfirst on French soil at 0016 hours, catapulted through the perspex windscreen of his glider by the impact of landing. Although rendered unconscious, he survived. The bridge was not blown by the Germans, as they had with Teutonic efficiency removed the explosives for the night to prevent them being stolen by the French Resistance. Once Howard's men had captured the bridge, a German fighter-bomber fired a rocket at it which hit one of the spars without exploding, - probably because the rocket did not have enough time to arm itself. The gash on the spar can be seen on the bridge to this day. During the course of the action, Howard's men knocked out a tank and a gunboat. The British landed successfully on Sword Beach as planned at 0700 hours the next morning. Howard's *coup de main* prevented Lieutenant General Edgar Feuchtinger's 21st Panzer Division from attacking the left flank of the invasion and assisted it in getting off the beaches. The Ox and Bucks were relieved by the Royal Warwickshire Regiment on 7 June.

Both the Pegasus Bridge and Café Gondrée, the first household liberated in Occupied France, became war memorials because of their part in this remarkable feat of arms. In June of each year Ranville is the rendezvous for thousands of airborne veterans who come to remember and meet old friends. The local population takes an immense pride in the achievements of 6th Airborne Division and frankly, the entire area can be considered one living memorial. Pegasus, the powder-blue winged horse on a purple ground, symbol of 6th Airborne can be seen everywhere. Pegasus Bridge was purchased for one franc in 1994 and installed at the rear of *Memorial Pegasus* which was opened by the Prince of Wales (Colonel-in-Chief of the Parachute Regiment) on 4 June 2000. The museum stands in Avenue du Major Howard and illustrates the role of 6th Airborne Division in the invasion of Europe. Website at www.normandy1944.com

# THE BAYEUX MEMORIAL

What strikes the first-time visitor as decidedly odd about the Bayeux Memorial is that both it and Bayeux War Cemetery are bisected by a main road. Quite why this should be so only becomes apparent when one learns that during the desperate fight for Normandy after D-Day the British Army's supply element discovered that it was unable to cope with the limitations of the narrow winding streets of Bayeux and requested the Royal Engineers to build a road to the south of the town. In so doing, the sappers inadvertently constructed the first ring road in France. Sections of it were named after Allied generals, such as Eisenhower and Montgomery. However, the south-western stretch that separates the memorial from the cemetery is named after a British general with whom the reader will be entirely familiar. It was named Rue Fabian Ware after 'The Great Commemorator'. The memorial was designed by the architect Philip Hepworth and unveiled by the Duke of Gloucester, President of the Imperial War Graves Commission on 5 June 1955. The land on which the memorial stands was donated by the town of Bayeux, in memory of those who are honoured there. On it were inscribed the names of the 1,801 soldiers of the British and Commonwealth who fell on the beaches, or in the 'Sweep to the Seine', but to whom the fortune of war denied a known and honoured grave in the period 6 June - 29 August 1944. Bayeux War Cemetery is the largest Commission cemetery from the Second World War in France. It contains 4,144 graves and as one would expect is kept in immaculate condition. Given the close links between English and Norman history, the Latin inscription on the frieze of the memorial is of particular interest. It reads:

> "NOS A GULIELMO VICTI
> VICTORIS PATRIAM
> LIBERAVIMUS"[33]

---

[33] 'We, once conquered by William, have now set free the Conqueror's native land.'

# BURMA

The Rangoon Memorial, Taukkyan War Cemetery, Myanmar (Burma) was built by the Imperial War Graves Commission with 2,000 tons of granite shipped from India. Taukkyan is some 20 miles north of Yangon (Rangoon).[34] It records the names of over 20,000 Indians, 4,000 British, 2,000 from East and West Africa and 50 South Africans who have no known grave. This was to be the largest memorial built by the Commission after the Second World War, being designed by Henry Brown and taking the form of two long colonnades at the centre of which is an open rotunda (pictured). The names of the missing are inscribed on the walls of the colonnade. This memorial was inaugurated by General Sir Francis Festing.[35] Commander-in-Chief British Far East Land Forces, in the presence of the Honourable U Nu, Prime Minister of Burma on 9 February 1958. Some indication of just how tough the war that was fought by General 'Uncle Bill' Slim's 14th Army in Burma actually was, may be taken from the fact that 29 Victoria Crosses were awarded during the campaign, (20 to the Indian Army) compared with 27 in North Africa, 22 in North Western Europe and 20 in Italy.

    The Catholic Church of Our Lady and St Thomas of Canterbury at Wymondham, Norfolk, is the Far East Prisoner of War Memorial Church and is a permanent memorial not only to all those who lost their lives whilst incarcerated in Japanese Prisoner of War camps in the Far East during the Second World War, but also to those who died later as a result of their ordeal. It was built in 1951 by the late Father Malcolm Cowin, himself a former prisoner of war, in fulfilment of a vow he made during captivity. The side chapel holds the Books of Remembrance containing the names of 26,900 who died from six nations. The building was largely funded by former POWs and their families. Each year on the nearest Sunday to the date of the relief of Rangoon on 2 May 1945, a memorial service is held for all denominations and nationalities, to commemorate all those who died and those who have died since. Those of all faiths and none are welcome. Website at www.fepow-memorial.org.uk/fmc_prom.html

---

[34] The name 'Yangon' meaning 'The end of enmity' was given to the city after the conquest of Lower Myanmar by King Alaungpaya in 1755. The British annexed Burma in 1886 and changed the name to 'Rangoon'.
[35] Field Marshal Sir Francis Wogan Festing. (1902-76). East Lancashire Regiment. Distinguished service in Far East in the Second World War. Chief of the Imperial General Staff 1958-61. ADC to the Queen 1958-60.

# KOHIMA

The Cross of Sacrifice on the Deputy Commissioner's tennis court at Kohima.

With the invasion of Burma by the Japanese in 1942, the British Army retreated some 1450 km to Imphal in the Assam Hills, India. There General Slim[36] decided to make his stand. The Japanese 15th Army under General Mutaguchi crossed the Chindwin River on 7 March, with 100,000 men and lay siege to both Imphal and a garrison town some 65 km to the north called Kohima. The town was entirely invested by 6 April. After intense fighting, 2,500 Commonwealth troops fought off the Japanese 31st Division. They were then relieved by elements of 2nd Division. 'That was 20 April. The garrison had been relieved. The siege of Kohima was over. But the battle for Kohima was about to begin'.[37] This was one battle the Japanese would not win and Mutaguchi ordered a general retreat on 8 July thus ending the Japanese attempt to co-opt India into its 'Greater East Asia Co-Prosperity Sphere'. The Cross of Sacrifice in the Commission's cemetery at Kohima stands on the tennis court where the Japanese invasion of India was halted. The cemetery contains the burials of 1,100 British, 330 Moslem Indians and five Canadians. There is also a cremation memorial, which commemorates the 900 Hindu Indians who in accordance with the tenets of their faith were cremated. 'High above Kohima, in Naga Village, stands the memorial to the Cameron Highlanders with its proud lament, 'Lochaber no more'. Beneath it lies the miniscule perimeter defended to the death by The Queen's Own Royal West Kent Regiment, and there, too is the simple Cenotaph of 2 (British) Division with its infinitely moving inscription:

> When you go home
> Tell them of us and say
> For your tomorrow
> We gave our today'[38]

---

[36] 1st Viscount Slim (1891-1970) Second Lieutenant 1914. Served Gallipoli, France, and Mesopotamia. Transferred to Indian Army 1920.Participated in conquest of Italian East Africa 1940. Commander 1st Burma Corps 1942. He masterminded the British retreat from Burma and halted the Japanese invasion of India. GOC Allied Land Forces, South East Asia 1945. Recalled from private life by Prime Minister Attlee in 1949, promoted Field Marshal and appointed CIGS. Governor-General of Australia 1952-1960. KCB 1944, GBE 1946, GCVO 1954, GCB 1950, KG 1960. Author: *Defeat into Victory* (1956) and *Unofficial History* (1959).
[37] Louis Allen *Burma: The Longest War.*
[38] Ronald Lewin *Slim: The Standardbearer* p. 273.

# THE UNITED KINGDOM FIREFIGHTERS NATIONAL MEMORIAL

The United Kingdom Firefighters National Memorial stands in Change Court, in the shadow of St Paul's Cathedral in London. The site is most appropriate, as the famous photograph of the dome of St Paul's rising above the smoke and flames during the Blitz is one of the most enduring images of the Second World War. The photo was taken during a major raid on 29 December 1940 by Herbert Mason whilst standing on the roof of the *Daily Mail* building in Fleet Street. During the raid Prime Minister Winston Churchill, with his unerring sense of Britain's history sent a note post-haste to the St Paul's Watch at the Cathedral which read: 'St Paul's must be saved at all costs'.

The bronze maquette that became the memorial was originally commissioned in 1984 by C T Demarne, OBE, ex-Chief Officer of West Ham Fire Brigade, as a personal memorial to his colleagues who had died during the Second World War. The maquette may be seen in the Hall of Remembrance at London Fire Brigade Headquarters, Lambeth. The idea of commissioning a full-scale sculpture took a while to germinate and the Firefighters Memorial Trust was established in 1990 for the purpose of commissioning and erecting a National Memorial to the men and women of the United Kingdom Fire Service, who had made the ultimate sacrifice in the Second World War. The Trust secured a site at the top of the New City Walkway to the Millennium Bridge, (otherwise known to posterity as 'the Wobbly Bridge'). On 4 May 1991 Queen Elizabeth the Queen Mother inaugurated the memorial. This was followed by a service in St Paul's Cathedral. Sculpted by John W Mills, the bronze memorial depicts an officer directing two firefighters. The octagonal base commemorates by name all 974 firemen and 23 firewomen who died in the Second World War.

In December 1996, the Board of Trustees accepted a proposal to create and maintain a database of all UK firefighters who had lost their lives in the execution of their duties. In 2003 the plinth was raised and the names of all other firemen and firewomen who have died on duty were added. This listing commences with the name of an insurance fireman who died in January 1723. The refurbished memorial was unveiled by the Princess Royal on 16 September 2003. The photograph above is of the raised memorial. Each September a Service of Remembrance followed by wreath laying ceremony is held there.

# CHAPTER V

# THE POST WAR PERIOD

# BONNIE PRINCE CHARLIE

Prince Charles Edward Stuart, 'the Young Pretender' landed on Eriskay in the Western Isles of Scotland from France on 23 July 1745 and embarked on an adventure to usurp the Hanoverian throne that would last eight months. On 19 August he raised the standard of rebellion at Glenfinnan and gathered about him an army of some 4,000 disaffected Scots, most of whom were adventurers, bored apprentices or those compelled to turn out by their clan chiefs. Significant elements of Scotland's leadership refused his call to arms. The Scots had been taught a sharp lesson after the failure of the Jacobite Rebellion of 1715 and smarted from it still, most accepted that Scotland's future was Hanoverian, not Stuart. Their lack of support should have given the Prince and his advisers some inkling of what would follow. 'Thus began one of the most audacious and irresponsible enterprises in British history. Charles had made scarcely any preparations. He could command support only in the Highlands, which contained but a small proportion of the whole population of Scotland.'[1] Intending to take London, both seat of Government and the Monarchy, he marched south to Derby via Carlisle, Preston, Manchester and Macclesfield, but the English did not flock to his banner either. With armies commanded by General Wade and the Duke of Cumberland menacing his flanks, he held a Council of War at Derby. At this stormy meeting, his plan to march on London was overruled by his War Council led by Lord George Murray. His poorly-equipped army turned about and set out on the long retreat back to Scotland. The great adventure would end in tragedy at the Battle of Culloden Moor on 16 April 1746, followed by five months in hiding, then the escape and flight of the 'Young Pretender' back to France. Bonnie Prince Charlie died of apoplexy in Rome on 30 January 1788.

In the garden at the rear of the Crewe and Harpur Arms public house in Swarkeston, Derbyshire stands a cairn. It marks the furthest point south reached by his army on 4 December 1745. It was erected by the Charles Edward Stuart Society and the Marston Brewery on the occasion of the 200th anniversary. Inside the pub is a reproduction of the declaration signed by Derbyshire's nobility, including Devonshire and Hartington against the 'Popish Pretender'. A bronze equestrian statue of the prince sculpted by Anthony Stones was unveiled in Derby on the 250th anniversary. Website at www.royalstuartsociety.com/

---

[1] Winston S Churchill *A History of the English-Speaking Peoples* Vol. 3.

# FIELD MARSHAL JAN SMUTS

Jan Christiaan Smuts 'Jannie' was born in Cape Colony in 1870. Trained as a lawyer, he was State Attorney to President Kruger in Pretoria at the outbreak of the Second Boer War (also known as the South African War) in 1899. He served as General commanding Boer forces in Cape Colony. By the war's end, he had become a zealous convert to the Imperial Ideal and served as Minister of Defence for the Union of South Africa from 1910-20. At the start of the Great War he commanded the Empire forces that cleared the Germans out of South West Africa and annexed it to South Africa's interest. He was however less successful in rounding up the Germans in East Africa under General von Lettow-Vorbeck, who ran rings round both the British and Boer generals and remained undefeated at the time of the Armistice in 1918. Smuts represented South Africa at the Imperial War Conference in 1917 and Prime Minister Lloyd George recognising that the war effort needed another smart lawyer like himself, appointed him to his War Cabinet. The author Professor Norman Dixon called Smuts a: 'great operator of fraudulent idealism' and it is certainly true that he was instrumental in whitewashing the British generals in the enquiry into the collapse of 3rd British Army at Cambrai in 1917.'[2] Upon the death of General Louis Botha, Smuts became Prime Minister of South Africa (1919-24). He was Minister of Justice (1933-39) and would serve as Prime Minister again (1939-48). In 1941 he was appointed Field Marshal. He lost his Standerton constituency seat (whilst in office) in the South African General Election of 1948 and died on 10 September 1950. Standing in London's Parliament Square, the bronze statue of him was sculpted by Sir Jacob Epstein and cast by the Art Bronze Foundry at Fulham, London. A man with the common touch, Epstein pressed a white five pound note into the hands of each of the foundrymen as a tip, a fortnight's wages in those days. The statue was personally inspected at the foundry by the Prime Minister and was unveiled by W S Morrison, Speaker of the House of Commons on 7 November 1956. Epstein's portrayal drew the tart observation from David Piper, critic and Director of the Ashmolean Museum at Oxford that Smuts seemed: 'to skate on very thin ice and to be unsuitably dressed for the occasion'.

---

[2] Norman Dixon *On the Psychology of Military Incompetence*.

# THE PASSING OF SIR WINSTON CHURCHILL

In the mid 1950s Queen Elizabeth II granted approval for Churchill to be accorded the honour of a state funeral when he died. The Duke of Norfolk, Earl Marshal of England was accordingly informed and *Operation Hope Not* prepared at HQ London District. Churchill died on 24 January 1965 at the age of 90 and Prime Minister Harold Wilson announced: 'It is with great regret that I have heard of the death of Sir Winston Churchill. He will be mourned all over the world by all who owe so much to him. He is now at peace after a life in which he created history and which will be remembered as long as history is read. Our thoughts and sympathy are with his family.' Churchill's body lay in state for three days in Westminster Hall. On 30 January the bell of Big Ben was silenced from 0945 until the close of day. That morning, the catafalque was removed from Westminster Hall by a bearer party found from 2nd Battalion Grenadier Guards. As Major Churchill MP he had served with the battalion in the trenches on the Western Front in 1915. Under the command of the General Officer Commanding London District, 7,083 officers and other ranks were on parade. The coffin was borne on a gun carriage drawn by a Gun's crew of naval ratings. The carriage built in 1880 had been kept at HMS EXCELLENT, the naval gunnery school at Portsmouth. It was first used for Queen Victoria's funeral and later the bodies of Edward VII, George V and George VI were carried on it. As the cortege processed from Westminster to St Paul's, King's Troop, Royal Horse Artillery fired minute guns in St. James's Park. Officers of the Household Division wore mourning armbands, standards and colours were draped and drums muffled. That bitterly cold morning huge crowds assembled to watch the cortege pass. Churchill had planned his funeral and told Harold Macmillan: 'There will be lively hymns' These would include: *Fight the good fight with all thy might; Mine eyes have seen the glory of the coming of the Lord* and, as the coffin was carried out of St Paul's *O God our help in ages past*. The funeral was attended by four kings, three queens, eight princes, four princesses, three dukes, three duchesses and five presidents. The 12 pall bearers were former prime ministers Clement Attlee, the Earl of Avon, Harold Macmillan, Sir Robert Menzies of Australia and Field Marshal Sir Gerald Templer, Field Marshal Viscount Slim, Field Marshal Earl Alexander of Tunis, Lord Bridges, Lord Normanbrook, Lord Ismay, Marshal of the RAF Viscount Portal of Hungerford and Admiral of the Fleet Lord Mountbatten. The River Procession from Tower Pier to Festival Pier was commanded by the River Superintendent and Harbourmaster of the Port of London Authority. 'For some, the most memorable and unexpected moment of the stately ceremonies that marked the end of the Churchillian era then occurred, making the hairs bristle on the napes of the necks of those present. All the cranes on Hay's Wharf on the opposite bank started dipping their long necks, like dinosaurs bowing, in a eerie, unforgettable civilian salute.'[3] On arrival at Festival Hall Pier, the coffin was taken by hearse to Waterloo Station. Here a bearer party was provided by the Queen's Royal Irish Hussars, the regiment to which he was gazetted when they were the 4th Hussars in March 1895. The Battle of Britain Class locomotive *Winston Churchill* drew the funeral train to Long Handborough, Oxfordshire. In a private ceremony he was then buried at Bladon Churchyard. The two wreaths on the coffin were from his wife Clementine, Lady Churchill and The Queen. On 30 November 2004, the 130th anniversary of Churchill's birth, a bronze and steel screen was unveiled in the crypt of St Paul's. 'Designed by the master blacksmith James Horrobin in his Somerset forge, the memorial screen was commissioned by the Chapter of St Paul's. Composed of a pair of centre gates and two smaller gates, it is emblazoned with bronze reminders of Churchill's life, the Garter, the Order of Merit and the shield of the Cinque Ports.'[4] Although Churchill had been buried at Bladon rather than in the crypt of St Paul's, it was entirely fitting that he be commemorated in the same place as Britain's two other greatest wartime leaders, the Duke of Wellington and Admiral Viscount Nelson.

---

[3] Philip Howard, *London's River*
[4] *Daily Telegraph* 29 November 2004.

## SIR WINSTON CHURCHILL

Since his death, Sir Winston Churchill has been memorialised more comprehensively than any other British leader since the Iron Duke. These memorials would take a wide range of forms and the following list is by no means exhaustive. The two British National Memorials to Churchill were: The Winston Churchill Memorial Trust (travelling fellowships), together with Churchill College, Cambridge University. The Valiant class nuclear submarine HMS Churchill was commissioned on 15 March 1970 and the American guided missile destroyer USS WINSTON S CHURCHILL was commissioned on 10 March 2001. In 1976 Ivor Roberts-Jones sculpted the brooding monolithic Churchill in London's Parliament Square (pictured above). Another bronze statue of Churchill by Oscar Nemon (1906-85) stands in the Members Lobby of the House of Commons with a very shiny foot, it being a tradition for MPs making their maiden speech to rub it for good luck. Nemon was very particular and could not stand the shiny foot, so borrowed a metal chaser/patinator (skilled craftsman) from the Art Bronze Foundry in Fulham to dull it down. However, the parliamentary authorities *did* like it and responded by withdrawing Nemon's House of Commons pass. Sculpted by Jean Cardot, another statue of Churchill stands on the Champs Elysée in Paris and was unveiled by The Queen on 11 November 1998. Yet another by David McFall, was erected in Woodford Green, Essex in 1959 and others may be found in Toronto, Canada, Oslo and in Upper Barrakka Gardens at Valetta on Malta. The Winston Churchill Memorial Forest is in Israel. Given his wartime role and Anglo-American parentage, Churchill is well remembered by America. A statue of him stands in the grounds of the British Embassy in Washington DC, with one foot on American soil and the other on British soil. Buried beneath it is a time capsule, due to be opened by the US President in 2063 on the 100th anniversary of the award of Churchill's honorary US citizenship. The *Churchill Porch* may be found in the National Cathedral, Washington DC. The sculpture of him and Lady Churchill titled *Married Love* by Nemon is situated on The Plaza in Kansas City, Missouri USA. At Mougins in France a tribute to Churchill can be found in the form of a huge bronze hand raised in Churchill's trademark 'V for Victory' sign. Lawrence Holofcener's bronze statues of President Roosevelt and Churchill sit on a bench in London. The life-size bronze, a tribute to the partnership between the two great statesmen, was purchased by The Bond Street Association and unveiled in 1995 by Princess Margaret and placed in the pedestrian area in New Bond Street. Churchill's London home at 28 Hyde Park Gate, bears an English Heritage Blue Plaque.

# THE KOREAN WAR MEMORIAL, SAINT PAUL'S CATHEDRAL

Following an initiative by the British Korean Veterans Association (BKVA) the primary memorial in Britain, to those British Servicemen, who died in the Korean War, was placed in the crypt of St Paul's Cathedral, London alongside the memorials to those killed in other post-war conflicts. It was unveiled by The Queen on 11 March 1987. The inscription reads:

"REMEMBER THE BRITISH SERVICEMEN
WHO DIED IN THE FIRST WAR FOUGHT IN THE NAME OF
THE UNITED NATIONS
THANK GOD FOR THEIR COURAGE AND ENDURANCE
AND PRAY FOR PEACE AND RECONCILIATION
AMONG THE PEOPLES AND NATIONS OF THE WORLD
KOREA 1950-1953

*Not one of them is forgotten before God*"


At the same time, a Book of Remembrance was dedicated. This book currently contains the names of 1,083 servicemen killed in the war, listed by Service and Regiment. A second edition was rededicated at the Royal Hospital, Chelsea on 30 July 1993, and is on display in the National Army Museum in Chelsea, London, where a facsimile can be inspected. Another facsimile is held in the Anglican Cathedral at Seoul in South Korea.

On 26 July 1998 a memorial was dedicated in the regimental chapel at Llandaff Cathedral, Cardiff to the 32 soldiers of The Welch Regiment who were killed in the Korean War.

In 2002 veterans of the Royal Regiment of Fusiliers gathered in the Chapel Royal of St Peter ad Vincula in HM Tower of London, for the dedication of a Roll of Honour listing the names of the 40 Fusiliers from the Regiment's 1st Battalion who died in the Korean War. This memorial was subsequently set into the north wall of the chapel.

The official history concludes: 'The British may draw satisfaction from their part in a distant obligation honourably discharged' - which is a very real and fitting tribute to the 1,135 British Servicemen who gave their lives for Korea's freedom. The British Korean Veterans Association website may be found at www.bkva.co.uk/

## OTHER KOREAN WAR MEMORIALS

There is a move to add the names of the dead of the Korean and other wars to existing memorials. A good example is the recent addition of the name of a member of the Black Watch to the war memorial at Edderton on Dornoch Firth, Scotland.

There is a British Korean Veterans Association memorial garden in the National Memorial Arboretum at Alrewas in Staffordshire. The plaque bears the following inscription:

> "BRITISH KOREAN VETERANS ASSOCIATION
> TO HONOUR THOSE BRITISH SERVICEMEN
> WHO FOUGHT IN THE KOREAN WAR
> 25 JUNE 1950 TO 27 JULY 1953
> ESPECIALLY THE 1078 KILLED IN ACTION
> 2674 WOUNDED IN ACTION
> 1060 HELD AS PRISONERS
> FREEDOM IS NOT FREE
> THIS PLAQUE AND GARDEN
> DEDICATED
> ON 2 JULY 2000"

The British Commonwealth Memorial at Pusan.

Sited in the centre of the town of Kapyong, close by the site of the Battle of Kapyong fought from 22 to 24 April 1951 by 27 Commonwealth Brigade, the British Commonwealth Memorial is the sole memorial in Korea to commemorate all British Servicemen who fought and died in the Korean War. It is the location for the annual Commonwealth Service of Remembrance for the Commonwealth dead of the Korean War, which takes place on the weekend closest to the anniversary of the battle. Further up the valley are individual National Memorials to the war-dead of Australia, Canada and New Zealand.

# THE FALKLAND ISLANDS MEMORIAL CHAPEL

On 9 March 2000 The Queen officially opened the Falkland Islands Memorial Chapel in the grounds of Pangbourne College, Berkshire, to commemorate the 255 Servicemen and three Islanders who died during the Falklands Conflict in 1982. All who fell have their names recorded on the memorial plaque in St Paul's Cathedral, London and on the memorial in Port Stanley, Falkland Isles. Her Majesty's son Prince Andrew who had piloted a Sea King helicopter during the conflict wrote in the *Sun* newspaper on 10 March 2000: 'The Falkland Islands Memorial Chapel at Pangbourne is a permanent reminder of the ultimate sacrifice made in the defence of our freedom and democracy. We forget the sacrifice at our future cost. I, for one, will never forget the ultimate sacrifice made by my colleagues and friends'. The chapel was built in recognition of the bravery of those who fell in the Falklands Conflict and in memory of their sacrifice. It stands in a school environment, in the hope that their deeds will act as an inspiration for future generations who come to worship. It seats 600 and cost £1.6 million. It was designed by the Crispin Wride Architectural Design Studio, which beat 72 other entries in a design competition run by the Royal Fine Art Commission.[5] An annual service of remembrance is held each June. In 2003 a memorial cairn was being built next to the chapel. Among the stones was one sent by Mr Donald Lamont, Governor of the Falkland Islands on behalf of The Queen. Another form of memorialisation may be taken from the presentation to The Queen by SAMA82[6] of a solid gold replica of the South Atlantic Medal on the 20th anniversary of the campaign in December 2002. Website at www.sama82

---

[5] In 1999 the British Government disbanded the Royal Fine Art Commission (founded 1924, eight staff), after claims that it was 'cliquey'. The RFAC was replaced by the Commission for Architecture and the Built Environment, (CABE) with 80 staff. This new organisation lost its chairman in June 2004, after an audit found a potential conflict of interest with his role as chairman of a property development company. There had been a number of written complaints to DCMS about a number of CABE's design review rulings. It subsequently transpired that seven out of CABE's 15 Commissioners were linked to the same company - *plus ça change*.

[6] The South Atlantic Medal Association 1982.

# WESTMINSTER ABBEY

As can be seen from The Old Contemptibles Memorial (1993) above and from a considerable number of mentions elsewhere in different chapters of this study, Westminster Abbey has historically functioned as a repository for a significant number of new war memorials commemorating the sacrifice of those Service personnel who fell in the conflicts of the 20th century. However this does not meet with the approval of all. Historically war and religion have made uneasy bedfellows and the relationship between the two is complex.

On 2 December 2002, the *Daily Telegraph* published a letter from a reader which echoed the sentiments of the English poet and essayist Joseph Addison in his *Spectator* article some 290 years earlier. (The full story of Admiral Cloudesley Shovel and his memorial in Westminster Abbey appears in the naval chapter of this study). Insofar as this subject goes, clearly, you can please some of the people some of the time....

'Sir - While applauding a national memorial to honour recipients of the Victoria and George Crosses (report, Nov.28), is Westminster Abbey really the best place for it? The Abbey is already stuffed with many large and ugly memorials to long-dead and forgotten heroes, statesmen and builders of empire, and it is high time to call a halt. It is, after all, primarily a place of worship, but too much of its floorspace is dedicated to the greater glory of individuals, some of whom barely command a footnote in our history. Give the Abbey back to God and the memorials to a museum. James Buchanan - Barrowden, Rutland'.

# RECENT MEMORIALS

The Felix Memorial Garden is at Thiepval Barracks, Lisburn, Northern Ireland. It was created in memory of the 20 Officers and soldiers of 321 EOD Squadron RLC, who lost their lives carrying out bomb disposal operations in Northern Ireland. The specially commissioned mural on the far left of the photograph was by the military artist Kelvin Hunter. There is an individual plaque for each life lost and a memorial stone of Rhodesian marble. Website at www.palacebarracksmemorialgarden.org

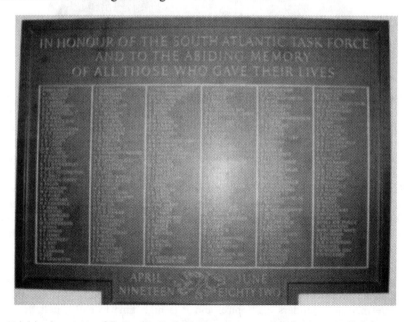

This memorial in the crypt of St Paul's Cathedral commemorates by name, all those members of the South Atlantic Task Force who were killed in the campaign to recapture the Falkland Islands in 1982.

## THE BROOKWOOD RUSSIAN MEMORIAL

Standing in the CWGC's Brookwood Cemetery in Surrey, the Brookwood Russian Memorial was completed in 1984. It commemorates all those from the British and Commonwealth Service personnel (620 British, 26 Canadians and one Australian) who died in Russia or the Soviet Union in either the Great War or the Second World War, whose graves are either unknown or, if known, unmaintainable. The Union of Soviet Socialist Republics suffered from a continuing paranoia about the Commission, being unable to accept its innocuous bona fides. By refusing to permit access to Commission officials they made the maintenance of the Commission's graves within the USSR impossible. This was a rare (if not unique) case of the Commission accepting dual commemoration, as the grave markers were left standing in situ. The Commission as ever, sensitive to both the feelings of the relatives of the fallen and the diplomatic niceties involved did not hold a formal unveiling ceremony for the memorial.

But even then, matters were not that simple. In June 1940, in accordance with the secret codicils to the Molotov-Ribbentrop Pact concluded between Nazi Germany and the USSR, the Soviets occupied the independent Baltic republics of Estonia, Latvia and Lithuania. The graves of 20 British Servicemen who had died on land in the Russian Civil War were in the Garrison Cemetery, Tallinn, Estonia, hard by the wall adjoining that city's army barracks. In 1961 the cemetery keeper was ordered by the Soviet Military Authorities to remove the graves - and subsequently suspended from work without pay for refusing to do so. Her staff then covered the graves with manure and vegetation to prevent the Soviets from removing them. The Soviets eventually lost interest in the plot and the graves remained for thirty years under the cemetery's compost heap, an insoluble problem for the Commission. With the disintegration of the Russian version of communism in 1991, Estonia regained her independence, the CWGC uncovered the graves, refurbished them with new headstones and Her Majesty's Government awarded Mrs Linda Soomre the Order of the British Empire.

## ANNE FRANK'S TREE

'Otto Frank, Anne's father, was a Jewish businessman in Germany, but when the Nazis seized power in 1933, the family left for Amsterdam. The German invasion in 1940 made life increasingly dangerous for Jews and by 1942 it was clear that they would have to go underground. The Franks hid with another family in secret rooms behind Otto Frank's offices; food was brought by employees. Anne Frank wrote her diary until August 1, 1944, days before the family was betrayed and arrested. Anne and her 19-year old sister Margot were taken to Auschwitz.'[7] She was arrested on 4 August 1944 and died of typhus aged 16 years in Bergen-Belsen Concentration Camp in March 1945. Her notebooks were subsequently discovered by Otto Frank's secretaries hidden on his office premises and were returned to him after the war. The diary Anne Frank wrote between 1942 and 1944 was published in English in 1952 as *Anne Frank: The Diary of a Young Girl*. It was subsequently translated into more than 55 languages and became a worldwide best-seller. On the 10th anniversary of the Anne Frank Trust (UK), Anne Frank's Tree was planted on 22 October 2001 by the actress Hannah Taylor Gordon and dedicated by the actor Sir Ben Kingsley. It stands by the Roundhouse Public House in New Row WC2, opposite London's Covent Garden. The Tree can be seen in reflection in the photograph of the brass plaque in the photograph above. The inscription reads:

> "Anne Frank has served as an inspiration to millions around the world, and
> Her life warns us of the dangers of intolerance
> This tree is dedicated as a place to reflect on all the children who have
> died owing to the wars and persecution in the last century, and
> This site serves as an inspiration to us all to work together towards a
> better world free from bigotry in this century."

---

[7] *The Times* 12 June 2004 p.15.

## THE KINDERTRANSPORT MEMORIAL

In the period shortly before the outbreak of the Second World War, 10,000 Jewish and other children were evacuated from Nazi occupied territories in the *Kindertransport*. They began new lives in Britain with foster carers. Many of the unaccompanied Kinder (children) disembarked at the port of Harwich and travelled by train to Liverpool Street Station, London.

In a ceremony on 16 September 2003 a sculpture by the Venezuelan-born artist Flor Kent was unveiled at the station to commemorate the place of their arrival and the beginning of their new lives in Britain. The Kindertransport Memorial was commissioned by the Central British Fund for World Jewish Relief, in conjunction with the Museum of London and the Imperial War Museum. The artefacts on show are stored in museum-quality conditions and are cared for jointly by the Imperial War Museum and the Museum of London. The sculpture has two main elements. A large glass box created in the shape of a suitcase carried by one of the children. Inside it, surviving personal belongings brought by the Kinder from various European countries are displayed. The title of the sculpture, *Für das Kind* (For the Child), is taken from the inscription on one of these objects - a coat hanger. The design of the memorial only becomes apparent at a distance and is thought-provoking. Part of the inscription on a bronze plaque on a nearby wall reads:

'WHOSEVER RESCUES A SINGLE SOUL IS CREDITED
AS THOUGH THEY HAD SAVED THE WHOLE WORLD

TALMUD'

In the same ceremony on the forecourt of the station, two of the rescued Kinder, Harry Heber and Erich Reich, assisted 94-year old Sir Nicholas Winton, the rescuer of many Czech Kinder, in unveiling the bronze statue of a child refugee standing next to the transparent case containing some of the few items of clothing, toys, family photographs and other memorabilia which the children were permitted to take with them. The bronze statue is a life cast of a descendant of one of the Kinder. The ceremony was addressed by the Home Secretary and the Chief Rabbi. Guests included many of the Kinder and the ambassadors of Germany, Austria, Czechoslovakia, Poland and Israel. Website at www.kindertransport.org/

# THE WALLENBERG MONUMENT

In 1944 as the tide of fortune turned against the 'Thousand Year Reich' a young Swedish diplomat was posted on 9 July 1944 to Budapest, Hungary. Raoul Wallenberg was born in Stockholm on 4 August 1912 and he would find fame as the man who thwarted one evil, only to be consumed by another. By issuing false Swedish passports he saved thousands of Hungarian Jews from deportation and death in the Nazi concentration camps. When Budapest was liberated by the Russians in 1945 they arrested him and he disappeared into the maw of the Soviet prison system and they consistently denied holding him. The evidence of a number of former prisoners of the Soviet Union finally forced them to admit in 1957 that Wallenberg had been detained. They added without producing any proof that he had died in the Lubyanka Prison, Moscow in 1947. Evidence from former prisoners of the USSR suggests that he was still alive in the 1950s, or even as late as the 1970s.

The Wallenberg Monument stands outside the West End Great Synagogue, Cumberland Place, London. At the express wish of his family, it is a monument and not a memorial - as his death has never been confirmed. He stands bareheaded in a greatcoat with a bundle of Schutz-Passes in his right hand. The entire rear of the monument is composed of sculpted representations of bundles of Schutz-Passes draped at the top with a representation of the Swedish flag. Sculpted by Philip Jackson, the architects were Donald Insall Associates. The monument was unveiled by The Queen in the presence of Princess Christina of Sweden, the UN Secretary General and the President of Israel on 26 February 1997. The inscription on the north-west side of the monument tells Wallenberg's story:

"IN 1944 ARMED ONLY WITH DETERMINATION AND COURAGE, RAOUL WALLENBERG ARRIVED IN BUDAPEST AS A MEMBER OF THE NEUTRAL SWEDISH LEGATION AND SET ABOUT RESCUING THE 230,000 JEWS WHO REMAINED, SNATCHING MANY FROM NAZI AND HUNGARIAN DEATH SQUADS. HE DEMANDED THE REMOVAL OF OTHERS FROM TRAINS DEPARTING TO THE GAS CHAMBERS AT AUSCHWITZ. HE PLACED TENS OF THOUSANDS UNDER THE PROTECTION OF THE SWEDISH CROWN BY ISSUING THEM WITH FALSE PASSPORTS, "SCHUTZ-PASSES", SHELTERING THEM IN SAFE HOUSES FROM WHICH HE FLEW THE SWEDISH FLAG".

Website at www.raoul-wallenberg.net/

# THE COMMONWEALTH GATES, CONSTITUTION HILL

On 6 November 2002, The Queen unveiled a striking set of giant memorial gates and a pavilion to commemorate the contribution and sacrifice of Service personnel from the nations of the Indian sub-continent, Africa and the Caribbean, who served during the two World Wars. It is often forgotten that the Indian Army in the Second World War was the largest volunteer military force raised in history. Website at www.mgtrust.org/

An inscription records that Queen Elizabeth the Queen Mother laid the foundation stone on 1 August 2001. However, The Queen laid it, as her mother was ill that day and unable to attend the ceremony. Veterans from around the world gathered for the event. The Booker Prize-winning poet Ben Okri read a specially composed poem at the inauguration. The names of these nations are inscribed on the four piers constructed from Portland stone weighing 60 tons each and standing 8 metres high. Each is topped with an African bronze urn. The ceiling of the cupola (pictured) of the pavilion lists by name 62 Commonwealth personnel awarded the Victoria Cross and 12 awarded the George Cross. The idea for this memorial was originally conceived by Lord Weatherill, former Speaker of the House of Commons along with Viscount Slim, son of the commander of the 'Forgotten' 14th Army. The memorial cost £2.7 million, £1.1 million of which was obtained by a grant from the National Lottery and the project was organised by the Memorial Gates Trust, which was chaired by Baroness Flather. The project took five years to bring to fruition. The memorial was designed by the architect Liam O'Connor and bears the inscription:

> "IN MEMORY OF
> THE FIVE MILLION
> VOLUNTEERS FROM
> THE INDIAN
> SUB-CONTINENT
> AFRICA AND
> THE CARIBBEAN
> WHO FOUGHT WITH
> BRITAIN IN THE TWO
> WORLD WARS"

## THE GURKHA SOLDIER

Field Marshal Lord Bramall, Lord Lieutenant of London, pays his respects before the statue of the Gurkha Soldier, which stands at the junction of Horse Guards Avenue and Whitehall Court, London. The memorial was commissioned and funded by the Gurkha Brigade Association. The 9 ft tall bronze statue was sculpted by Philip Jackson. The architect was Cecil Denny Highton and the masonry was carried out by Stonewest Ltd. The memorial cost some £17,000 which was subscribed by the public and former Gurkha officers. The Queen unveiled the memorial in a ceremony on 3 December 1997. The east and west sides of the Portland stone plinth contain bronze plaques detailing all the campaigns in which the Gurkhas have served and at the south side, a list of all the Gurkha formations and battalions which have existed since they first entered service with the British Army in 1815. The proud recipients of 13 Victoria Crosses, some 200,000 Gurkhas served in the two World Wars. On the north face of the plinth underneath crossed kukris is the inscription:

"THE GURKHA
SOLDIER

BRAVEST OF THE BRAVE
MOST GENEROUS OF THE GENEROUS
NEVER HAD COUNTRY
MORE FAITHFUL FRIENDS
THAN YOU"[8]

---

[8] These lines were written in 1931 by Colonel Sir Ralph Turner MC (1888-1983) and also appear on the Gurkha Memorial inaugurated in 1996 at the British Embassy in Kathmandu, Nepal. Turner was Adjutant of 2nd Battalion, 3rd Queen Alexandra's Own Gurkha Rifles in the Gallipoli Campaign and subsequently Professor of Sanskrit at the University of London 1922-54. Director, School of Oriental & African Studies, London 1937-57.

## THE TANK CREWS MEMORIAL

The Tank Crews Memorial stands in Whitehall Court, London. It was inaugurated by the Queen (Colonel-in-Chief of the Royal Tank Regiment) on 13 June 2000. The funds for its erection were raised by public appeal and generous donations from Vickers and British Aerospace. It was produced by Vivien Mallock working from a maquette produced by the Scottish Academician George Henry Paulin ARSA RBS RI in 1953 and it was cast by the Morris Singer Foundry. The architect was Cecil Denny Highton. The nine feet tall group depicts five crew members of a Comet tank. The base bears countersunk bronze badges of the Machine Gun Corps and the Royal Tank Regiment with both male and female crowns. The inscription on the base reads "FROM MUD THROUGH BLOOD TO THE GREEN FIELDS BEYOND". (The colours of the Royal Tank Regiment are brown, red and green). The memorial was dedicated to all 'Tankmen' who have served, since tanks were first used in combat in the Battle of Flers-Courcelette on the Somme on 15 September 1916. A Military Medal, the first decoration to a tank operator, was awarded to Private A Smith that same day.

As early as December 1914, Colonel Maurice Hankey as Secretary of the Committee for Imperial Defence was lobbying for the development and use of such a weapon. A demonstration of the Killen-Strait tractor took place at Wormwood Scrubs on 28 June 1915. Both David Lloyd George and Winston Churchill attended and were most impressed, but the army's 'top brass' was not. Churchill as First Lord of the Admiralty sponsored the development of this 'land ship' and it was initially crewed by sailors. The codename given to this new secret weapon was the 'tank'. As the fire-eating Admiral Sir Murray Sueter would accurately record for posterity: 'The Tank as employed in the Great War and the forerunner of present Mechanised Armament, was developed from the Armoured Car Experiments of the Royal Naval Air Service'.[9] Website at www.army.mod.uk/armcorps/firsttan/

---

[9] Rear-Admiral Sir Murray Sueter *The Evolution of the Tank* Hutchinson, 1937.

# THE ANZAC MEMORIAL, BATTERSEA PARK

The ANZAC Memorial takes the form of a sandstone boulder weighing three quarters of a ton which was brought to England from Bondi Beach in Australia. It contains an inlaid bronze relief map of the Gallipoli Peninsula designed by Dr Ross J Bastiaan and sculpted by Ray Ewers. The explanatory legend is in both Turkish and English. There were a number of copies produced and the original was installed at Chunuk Bair at Gallipoli. At the instigation of Robert Rhodes James MP, an authority on the campaign, a copy (now at Churchill College, Cambridge) was presented to the Speaker of the House of Commons in 1991 in honour of the three British MPs who served at Gallipoli. The transportation of the boulder from Australia was paid for by the media tycoon Rupert Murdoch, (his father, the war correspondent Keith Murdoch was responsible for blowing the lid off the mismanagement of the campaign). It was unveiled on ANZAC Day 1999 by the Australian poet, wit and raconteur Clive James.

Prior to 11 November 2003, when the Australian War Memorial was inaugurated by The Queen in Hyde Park, London's Dawn Service in honour of those who fell at Gallipoli conducted on ANZAC Day was held at the memorial in Battersea Park. ANZAC day falls on 25 April each year, the anniversary of the Australian and New Zealand Army Corps Landings on the Gallipoli Peninsula, Turkey in 1915 and is kept as a national public holiday in both Australia and New Zealand. On that day, the Gallipoli Association hold a wreath laying ceremony in the crypt of St Paul's Cathedral, London. The High Commissioners of Australia and New Zealand accompanied by Commissioners from the CWGC then attend a wreath laying ceremony at 1100 hours at the Cenotaph in Whitehall, followed by a service at Westminster Abbey. A notable feature of ANZAC Services in recent years has been the attendance of Turkish diplomatic representatives. On ANZAC Day 2004, the Lesson at the Service in the Abbey was read by Valerian, 3rd Baron Freyberg.

Events at Gallipoli were a defining moment of nationhood for the Antipodean Peoples. Australia sustained 26,111 casualties including 8,141 deaths and New Zealand suffered 4,275 injured and 2,721 dead. Mustafa Kemal who commanded the Turks at Gallipoli (and who later as Kemal Atatürk would become Turkey's first president) wrote: 'You, the mothers who sent their sons from far away countries, wipe away your tears; your sons are now lying in our bosom and are in peace. After having lost their lives on this land, they become our sons as well.' Website at www.gallipoli-association.org

# THE AUSTRALIAN WAR MEMORIAL

On Armistice Day 2003 The Queen inaugurated the Australian War Memorial in Hyde Park. The £3 million memorial commemorates the 102,386 Australians who died in the two World Wars. 'In her role as Queen of Australia, she led a 3,000-strong crowd, including 25 Australian war veterans who had flown to Britain for the event'.[10] The ceremony commenced with the arrival of the Queen and the Duke of Edinburgh, who then inspected Australia's Federation Guard. The Queen's Personal Flag for Australia was flown. On the stroke of 11, the thunder of a salute fired by King's Troop, Royal Horse Artillery in Hyde Park announced the commencement of the two minutes silence. It was ended by a flypast of Jaguar aircraft from 54 Squadron, RAF. The Prime Ministers of both Great Britain and Australia were present and each gave an address. Prayers of dedication were then offered by the Principal Chaplains to the Australian Army, Air Force and Navy. The Queen stated in her address: 'Twice in the space of a generation Australia and Britain stood side by side in two of the bloodiest wars in human history. The struggle was bitter but by sheer resistance and dogged courage the forces of tyranny were defeated but the cost in human life and misery was immense'. The followed a moving rendition of the hymn *O Valiant Hearts* by Yvonne Kenny, the audience joining in after the first verse. The Ode of Remembrance[11] was then recited by Rear Admiral Guy Griffiths, followed by the sounding of the *Last Post*, a one minute silence, *Rouse* and the final blessing. The ceremony ended with the singing of *God Save The Queen* and lastly *Advance Australia Fair* which was belted out with gusto by the Australians present.

    The memorial was constructed from grey-green granite quarried at Jerramungup, Western Australia. It takes the form of a curved wall bearing in large letters the names of the 47 battles in which the Australians fought in both World Wars. Beneath these, in a carefully textured design are the names of the 24,000 hometowns of Australian men and women who served in the two World Wars. The general inscription reads: "WHAT EVER BURDEN YOU ARE TO CARRY WE ALSO WILL SHOULDER THAT BURDEN".[12] A design competition for the memorial conducted by invitation only was won by Tonkin Zulaikha Greer Pty Ltd (architects) in association with the artist Janet Laurence. The CWGC undertook to care for the memorial in perpetuity. Website at www.dva.gov.au/commem/oawg/memorials/london/

---

[10] *Daily Telegraph* 12 November 2003 p 11.
[11] Also known as the Act of Remembrance, - the fourth verse of Laurence Binyon's poem *For the Fallen*.
[12] Robert Menzies, Prime Minister of Australia 1941.

## THE ROYAL PIONEER CORPS

Although pioneers have always existed in the British Army in one form or another and they performed sterling work in both the Crimea and in the Great War, in modern times the Royal Pioneer Corps was only granted that title in 1946. 8,600 pioneers were killed in the Second World War. The Corps was disbanded in 1993, when it was amalgamated with four other corps to form the Royal Logistics Corps. On 14 November 1963 in a ceremony on platform 6 at St Pancras Station in London, the Royal Pioneer Corps joined with British Railways to name a diesel engine THE ROYAL PIONEER CORPS. The Corps of Drums and a detachment of recruits from the Corps Depot, under command of Lieutenant J B Snowdon, gave the General Salute on the arrival of the official party. Lieutenant General Sir John Cowley performed the naming ceremony at the invitation of Mr M C B Johns, Divisional Manager of the London Midland Region of British Railways. The other official guests were Major General A Jolly, Vice Quartermaster General at the War Office; Brigadier C R Nicholls of the War Office; Brigadier H G L Prynne, Vice President and Chairman of the RPC Association Council; The Rev G P H Rowson, Chaplain of the RPC Depot; Mr T R Barron, Assistant Divisional Manager, British Railways and Mr J G Handley, Station Master of St Pancras, resplendent in top hat and tails and with a scarlet carnation in his buttonhole. After inspecting the detachment and the Corps of Drums the Colonel Commandant was introduced to the old comrades. An address was given by Mr Johns, during the course of which, he presented General Cowley with a framed photograph of the giant diesel. General Cowley responded by stating: 'It was significant that only fifteen years ago the latest type of steam engine was named THE ROYAL PIONEER CORPS and now it had been honourably retired. He said: 'This is a measure of the effort needed to keep a railway system up to date. A similar effort is required to keep the Army up to date and the Royal Pioneer Corps of today looks very different to the Corps in 1948. Then it consisted largely of National Servicemen doing their two years of compulsory service. Now it is a Corps of volunteers who have chosen soldiering as their profession - a smaller Corps but more efficient and better equipped. Like the new engine, in the words of Mr Johns, it has the ability of working many more hours a day with less attention, and the Army also is taking every advantage it can of these important capabilities, and is operating this Corps more intensively and for longer periods than its predecessor. Declaring that he wished the engine many years of good service and expressing confidence that when it was eventually honourably retired it would have travelled about one and half million miles, or 6 times the distance to the moon, he then named the engine 'THE ROYAL PIONEER CORPS' and unveiled the name plates. The locomotive was then blessed by the Rev G P H Rowson. General Cowley then mounted the foot plate and with the controller key started the engine for the first time under its new name. After the unveiling ceremony the Colonel Commandant was introduced to the driver, Mr J A Graham and the Secondman, Mr J Ratcliffe and presented them with suitably inscribed tankards on behalf of past and present members of the Corps, in commemoration of the ceremony. The guests were invited to lunch at the Kings Cross Hotel during which General Cowley thanked Mr Johns and his colleagues on behalf of the Corps and its Association. The 2500 hp engine D54 was the first of the London Midland Region's fleet of mainline diesel locomotives to carry the name of a Corps of the British Army. Weighing more than 135 tons and with an overall length of nearly 68 feet, it was capable of speeds of up to 90 miles per hour while pulling the heaviest of passenger trains. D54 was built at Crewe and operated between St Pancras and Manchester, Leeds, Bradford, Sheffield, Nottingham and Derby. Two hours after the ceremony, D54 pulled the 3.25 pm train out of St Pancras to Manchester. The engine replaced the Patriot Class steam locomotive No. 45506 which was named the 'ROYAL PIONEER CORPS' by Field Marshal Viscount Montgomery in a ceremony at Euston Station on 15 September 1948, and was retired after covering over 1,280,000 miles during its working life. Its name plates are now in the Corps Museum. Website at www.royalpioneercorps.co.uk/

## LOCOMOTIVE 48773

The above photograph is of a Stanier 8F Class goods locomotive built in 1940 in Glasgow. Passenger engines may have names, goods engines generally do not, and therefore this locomotive is known only by its number 48773. It was consigned for service in France, but when that country fell in the summer of 1940, the locomotive was sent instead to Iran where it served with the Corps of Royal Engineers and ran for three years on the Trans-Iranian Railway, it then being sent to Egypt. It spent most of its working life in the Middle East. The engine was saved from the scrapyard in 1968 by the Stanier 8F Locomotive Society.[13] No. 48773 was one of the first locomotives ever acquired by the Severn Valley Railway. It currently runs on the 16 mile Bridgnorth to Kidderminster steam line, but has worked from Penzance to Carlisle. The class was built to last and apart from periods out of service for overhaul, 48773 has been a constant and reliable performer. She has over 100,000 miles on the clock and is still going strong. On 27 September 1986 No. 48773 was dedicated by the Dean of Hereford as the National War Memorial to all British Railwaymen who fell in the Second World War in a ceremony at Highley, near Bridgnorth. The locomotive carries a memorial plaque with the badge of the Royal Engineers proclaiming its status as the memorial to all British sappers who died operating trains in the Second World War.

The Roll of Honour listing the names of all 354 Army railwaymen who died in the Second World War was unveiled at Kidderminster Station by the Chief Royal Engineer, Lieutenant General Sir Scott Grant, on 3 November 2002. Two Books of Remembrance were also dedicated and these were deposited at both the Museum of Army Transport at Beverley in East Yorkshire and at the Royal Engineers Museum, Chatham. The full list of names commemorated can be viewed on the society's website at www.8fsociety.co.uk

---

[13] The Stanier 8F Society was named after Sir William Stanier, who designed the locomotive for service on the pre-War London, Midland and Scottish Railway Company (LMS). The 'F' in the title means freight. On a scale of 1 - 9, '8' denotes that the locomotive was capable of hauling very heavy freight.

# THE ESSEX REGIMENT

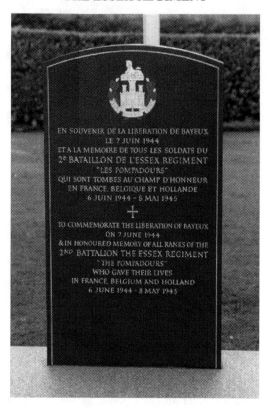

On 7 June 2002, 58 years after they landed in Normandy on D-Day in 1944 and liberated the town of Bayeux, the men of the 2nd Battalion, the Essex Regiment, who died in the liberation of Europe were remembered with a new memorial in the Norman town. Over thirty veterans gathered with their French counterparts at a service at Bayeux. Local councillors represented communities from all over the Battalion's recruiting area in Essex and London. The Essex Regiment earned their nickname 'The Pompadours' by adopting purple facings to their red coats, purple being the favourite colour of Madam de Pompadour, mistress of King Louis XV of France. The Royal Anglian Regiment, modern-day successors to the Essex Regiment, sent their Colour Party to the ceremony, whilst music was provided appropriately enough by the Army's Normandy Band. The Lord Lieutenant of Essex unveiled the memorial which was carved from Welsh slate. The Chief of the General Staff, General Sir Michael Walker, Regimental Colonel of the Royal Anglians, delivered the address. The Mayor of Bayeux presented each of the veterans with a medal from the town marking its lasting gratitude. The Normandy Band closed the day by Beating Retreat.

Apart from the events that took place there in the Second World War, Bayeux has other significant links with England's history. The 231 foot long *Bayeux Tapestry* is on display in the *Centre Guillaume le Conquérant* in Bayeux, having survived being used as a wagon tarpaulin cover during the French Revolution. Commissioned by William the Conqueror's half-brother Odo, Bishop of Bayeux and probably created by the nuns of Canterbury in Kent, it tells the story of the successful invasion and conquest of England by the Normans in 1066. Its modern-day counterpart *The Overlord Embroidery* is on public display in the D-Day Museum in Portsmouth. Its 34 panels tell the story of the Normandy Landings on 6 June 1944.

# THE EXPLOSIVE ORDNANCE DISPOSAL MEMORIAL

This memorial stands opposite the main entrance to Marlborough Barracks at Kineton in Warwickshire. It is dedicated to the memory of the 23 officers and soldiers who since 1945 have been killed working in bomb disposal. It also serves to remind the men and women who pass through those gates, who hold the aspiration of qualifying as an Ammunition Technician or Ammunition Technical Officer, of the sacrifices made by their predecessors and the personal commitment they are being asked to make. The central feature of the monument is an EOD operator in a bomb suit carrying an EOD helmet. It is hewn from Cotswold stone and stands some 8 ft high. The names of those who have died whilst undertaking bomb disposal are engraved on polished green slate plaques affixed to the inner walls of the memorial. The memorial was dedicated in a ceremony in June 1991. Its original cost was £33,000 and was raised by individual subscription and from generous donations from both industry and commerce, of particular note was the support given to the project by the Worshipful Company of Gold and Silver Wyre Drawers. After atmospheric erosion of the stonework was observed, the memorial was refurbished in 1999 at a cost of some £10,000 with additional work to refurbish the plaques at a cost of £2,000 which was donated by the Royal Army Ordnance Corps and Royal Logistic Corps Charitable Trusts.

Since 'The Troubles' began in Northern Ireland in 1969, 321 Explosive Ordnance Disposal Squadron has responded to 55,000 call outs and neutralised some 6,000 live devices. On 12 May 2005 Prime Minister Tony Blair presented a letter to officers of 321 EOD at Downing Street in honour of the men and women who he said have: 'put themselves in harm's way to safe lives and property.' At the presentation he said that: 'while Northern Ireland had made real progress towards peace, the gallantry and dedication of the British Army Ammunition Technical Officers should not be forgotten.' In the letter he handed to Lieutenant Colonel Mark Wickham, Chief Ammunition Technical Officer, Northern Ireland, the Prime Minister said the death toll and devastation would have been much higher without the sacrifice of members of the 321 EOD. Even though there have never been more than 100 soldiers in its ranks, it is the most decorated peacetime unit in the British Army.

The Association of Ammunition Technicians marches as a contingent in the March Past following the National Ceremony at the Cenotaph each Remembrance Sunday.

## THE NORFOLK LANDMINES CLEARANCE MEMORIAL

In June 1940, following the collapse of France after just six weeks of war and the surrender of Belgium and the Netherlands, in *Operation Dynamo* the badly beaten British Expeditionary Force was miraculously evacuated from the beaches and harbour of Dunkirk. Adolf Hitler expected Winston Churchill to recognise Britain's defeat, that she stood alone against the most powerful war machine the world had ever seen and to sue for peace. Churchill responded on 4 June by making his most famous speech of all on the floor of the House of Commons: 'We shall go on to the end, we shall fight in France, we shall fight in the seas and oceans, we shall fight with growing confidence and growing strength in the air, we shall defend our island whatever the cost may be, we shall fight on the beaches, we shall fight on the landing grounds, we shall fight in the fields and in the streets, we shall fight in the hills; we shall never surrender'. This defiance enraged Hitler and on 16 July he issued Fuehrer Directive No 16 ordering the German High Command to prepare a plan to invade and subjugate Britain. The planners insisted, that notwithstanding the menace posed by the Royal Navy, for a seaborne invasion to succeed, firstly the skies over Britain needed to be cleared of the RAF. The British removed signposts from roads, defaced a number of war memorials to prevent them giving away their location, raised the Home Guard and laid thousands of land mines on Britain's eastern coastline as part of the defence plan. In the summer of 1940 the heroic endeavours of 'The Few' against the might of the Luftwaffe in the Battle of Britain postponed the invasion indefinitely and *Operation Sealion* would be consigned to the 'what if' chapter of history. In 1944 Churchill and his War Cabinet decided that the possibility of invasion had receded sufficiently for the mines to be lifted. 'When they were laid the mines were set to be detonated by a pressure of at least 50 lbs but over the years they had become ultra sensitive and unstable because of rust and general deterioration. The job of locating and clearing the mines was made more difficult because the landscape had changed due to cliff falls, soil erosion and the natural movement of sand and shingle. Although mines were laid all along the Norfolk coast, the minefield between Trimingham and Sidestrand was considered to be the most dangerous in the country.'[14] In the UK, responsibility for bomb disposal above the high tide line usually falls to the Royal Engineers and below it, to the Royal Navy. Needless to say bomb disposal of any kind is a highly skilled and extremely dangerous occupation. The first fatalities occurred at Yarmouth on 5 January 1944 when three sappers were killed in an explosion and the last was at Trimingham on 6 May 1953, when two more were killed. Norfolk's beaches were finally declared clear and reopened for public access in 1966. However, on the night before Christmas 1971, RE Bomb Disposal were called post-haste to Sheringham, where a scouring tide had revealed eight mines.

The erection of a memorial to commemorate the 26 men killed in lifting the mines was the idea of Mr Noel Cashford MBE, who was a wartime Royal Navy Bomb Disposal Officer. On 30 April 2003 he was interviewed on air by John Mills of *BBC Radio Norwich* about the role of the Army's bomb disposal teams in clearing Norfolk's coastline after the war. Due to the public response to the broadcast, a committee of Norfolk residents was formed which immediately set about raising funds to erect a memorial to commemorate the 26 brave soldiers who died. Designed by the Royal Engineers at Chatham, the memorial at Mundesley-on-Sea takes the form of an inverted 1,000 lb bomb case fins uppermost, mounted on a brick-faced square plinth with stainless steel plaques supplied free of charge by Keith Shepherd of Kaliber Engineering, Derby, which carries the names of the men, beneath the badge of the Royal Engineers. The dedication ceremony on 2 May 2004 was conducted by the Lord Lieutenant of Norfolk and attended by some 500 people including relatives of those killed, the Commanding Officer and Regimental Sergeant Major of 33 Engineer Regiment (EOD), the Mayor of Yarmouth and local representatives from BLESMA.

---

[14] *BLESMAG* Summer 2004. (With acknowledgements and grateful thanks to both Noel Cashford MBE and John Philips DSC).

The inauguration of the Norfolk Landmines Clearance Memorial on 2 May 2004.

# JOHN CONDON

John Condon was born at No. 2 Teapot Lane in Waterford City in 1901. He was the son of John and Mary Condon. His mother died in 1912 and he found work as a boy bottler. With the outbreak of war in 1914 he enlisted in the British Army and was posted to the 2nd Battalion of the Royal Irish Regiment which was serving in the Ypres Salient in Belgium. 'At 2 a.m. on May 24th, 1915, the Royal Irish were stood to arms near Mouse Trap Farm. Twenty minutes later, the gas rolled in yet again from the German positions. Some of the Irish soldiers had respirators. Most didn't. In the final action of what we now know as the Second Battle of Ypres, the second battalion of the Royal Irish Regiment was all but wiped out.'[15] Seven years after John Condon's death, his remains were found. He was identified from the heel of a boot which bore his regimental number 6322 and his remains were buried at Poelcappelle Cemetery. The portion of the boot was forwarded to the Condon family on 8 January 1924.

Substantial progress has been made by the Irish in recent years in recognising the contribution of the 500,000 Irishmen who served in Britain's armed forces in the Great War and in October 2001 Waterford City Council passed the following resolution: 'That this Council agrees to set up a Committee to investigate the possibility of erecting a memorial to the memory of John Condon, a native of Waterford, who, at 14 years of age, was the youngest Allied soldier to die in the First World War and in doing so to remember the 50,000 Irish men and women who died in that war and also to remember all Irish men and women who died in conflict at home and abroad.' The John Condon Memorial Committee was composed of members of Waterford City Council, representatives of the Organisation of National Ex-Servicemen and Women, the Royal British Legion and other interested parties. The Committee invited a number of local architects to submit designs for a memorial and in June 2003 it selected that submitted by Anne Harpur and Patrick Cunningham. The design was subsequently approved by the Council and a site to erect it was granted on Waterford's Quay. The Council's resolution was denounced by Councillor Billy McCarthy of the Workers Party who condemned it as: 'offensive' and 'militaristic.' He stated: 'This has no Celtic or Irish connection whatsoever. It doesn't fit, it won't fit and is a throwback to an imperial past.'[16] His concerns were duly noted by Waterford City Council. The design selected by the Committee was highly original in conception and took the form of four bronze sculptures positioned within a circular stepped limestone structure. The four figures were conceived as one form and then separated to create an inner sanctuary. The figures were created as universal forms using familiar elements from early Celtic art such as a head, a torso and legs. The cape shape which enfolded the forms, added to the sense of anonymity. The figures were poised with heads bowed as a mark of respect. The shape that crowns the figures is the only indication of any military connection and is deliberately understated. The inner surface of the sculpture is finished with a golden patina, which encircles the inner sanctuary. The word "PEACE" is inscribed on the inner face and is echoed on each of the gold surfaces of the sanctuary. A high-powered spotlight concealed within the base of the inner sanctuary illuminates the night sky. The illumination of the golden chamber acts as a metaphor for the symbolic presence of all souls who lost their lives in armed conflict. The use of the square and circle juxtaposed in the design has its origin in ancient Celtic tradition in which these two primary geometric shapes represent the symbolic relationship between the human and the divine, the physical and spiritual worlds and the equilibrium between heaven and earth. The passageways leading to the sculpture are inscribed in embedded bronze with the inscriptions: "24/05 - 074'" "WATERFORD 1901" "YPRES 1915" AND "POELCAPPELLE".[17]

---

[15] Kevin Myers *The Irish Times* 23 March 2004 p.17.

[16] *Daily Telegraph* 12 November 2003.

[17] On 24 May, the anniversary of John Condon's death 74 degrees is the alignment of the rising sun and the memorial. The sculpture has been positioned to allow the beams of the sun to penetrate the inner sanctuary. 24 May is also the date marking the end of the Irish Civil War in 1923.

## THE ANIMALS IN WAR MEMORIAL

Located at Brook Gate, Park Lane, London, the Animals In War Memorial was erected to recognise the contribution of animals in Britain's wars. They included mules, donkeys, horses, dogs, oxen, elephants and canaries. Some 300,000 carrier pigeons served Britain in both World Wars. The Patron of the Appeal was the Princess Royal, Colonel-in-Chief of the Royal Army Veterinary Corps, President of the Animal Health Trust and President of the International League for the Protection of Horses. She unveiled the memorial on 24 November 2004. The original Animals In War charity was formed in 1996 by the author Jilly Cooper, Brigadier Andrew Parker Bowles and the then Director of the RSPCA, Major General Peter Davies. The memorial cost some £1.4 million. Eluned Price of the *Daily Telegraph* wrote: 'The sculptor David Backhouse has designed the Portland stone memorial to symbolise the arena of war, with the different animals depicted in bas relief on a broken wall through which struggle two bronze mules, heavily laden; beyond, a bronze horse and dog look to the future. Inscriptions detail the theatres of war and the animals lost.'[18] Interviewed by the *Telegraph* the Princess Royal said: 'We always underestimate how creatures manage to survive and adapt, what is peculiar is how animals have adapted to what human beings want them to do. But they wouldn't do it unless they wanted to please them or unless they were interested. If you have a relationship with an animal, you can train it any damn way you like but you can't make it do something it doesn't want to do.'

The journalist A A Gill wrote flippantly in his column in the *Sunday Times* on 14 November 2004: 'Don't you simply worship Jilly Cooper? The best damn columnist this paper ever had. She has finally managed to get a war memorial for animals that made the ultimate sacrifice. I heard her on *Today* waxing sentimental for the millions of horses, thousands of dogs, dozens of camels, the odd goat and the pigeons. "The pigeons," she said, voice cracking, "with their little beaks shot off, their legs hanging, bringing messages from the front." And the glow worms: "Glow worms that soldiers used to read maps with." Sorry Jilly, but you lost me with the glow worms. They shall glow not old as we that are left glow old. Does this memorial also honour the cows that made the boots and bully beef, and the pigs in the Spam? If we can have war hero animals, can we also have war criminal rats? Can we have trials for mosquitoes and lice? While we're at it, let's have a memorial for the trees that have suffered in conflicts. Let's have a Poppy Day for poppies.'

---

[18] *Daily Telegraph* 1 November 2004.

# THE NATIONAL MEMORIAL ARBORETUM

On 16 May 2001 the Duchess of Kent opened the National Memorial Arboretum at Croxall Road, Alrewas in Staffordshire. The inspiration for the memorial came from Group Captain Geoffrey Leonard Cheshire VC OM DSO** DFC, 1st Baron Cheshire of Woodall (1917-92), who expressed the wish to create a permanent national living tribute to the wartime generations of the 20th century and a gift in their memory for present and future generations to reflect upon and enjoy. In the words of Commander Childs, the director of the arboretum: 'My generation had done little to acknowledge the great sacrifice that a whole nation had been willing to make to guarantee that we would live in peace and freedom. Fifty years after the end of the Second World War it seemed right to create a living tribute that would forever acknowledge that unrepayable debt'.

The appeal to create the arboretum was launched by Prime Minister John Major in 1994. The land was provided by the generous gifting of 82 acres of reclaimed gravel workings along the banks of the River Tame. Financially, the project was supported by contributions from the non-public funds of individual units of Britain's armed forces and donations provided by veterans' organisations.

The first planting in 1997 was funded from a grant by the National Forest, within whose boundary the arboretum lies. The initiative was shortlisted for a Millennium Commission grant of £1.8M provided such a sum could be match-funded. It was, and the result was the Visitor Centre and the country's only Millennium Chapel. Every day at 1100 hours The Silence is observed to remember all those lost in the wars of the twentieth century. The site now comprises over 150 acres. By February 2003, some 40 military and 20 civilian memorials had been erected. Since March 1997 over 40,000 trees have been planted in over 60 plots and groves. Website at www.nationalmemorialarboretum.co.uk

## THE ROYAL BRITISH LEGION

On 2 July 2002 it was announced that the Royal British Legion and the National Memorial Arboretum had begun negotiations for it to be acquired by the Legion. Brigadier Townsend, the Legion's Secretary General stated: 'As the nation's de facto custodian of Remembrance, we are very pleased to deepen our relationship with the Arboretum. The Arboretum is a national symbol of Remembrance - an inclusive tribute which invites the visitor to think about all who have, and those who will, don a uniform in the service of their country. The Arboretum currently attracts visitors of every age and background, reflecting the public's increasing interest and support for Remembrance'. He added: 'The future development of the site could produce many new opportunities for the Legion to reach an even wider audience, raising awareness of the meaning and ethos of Remembrance and reinforcing the connection between the Legion, our work for ex-Service people and our two main symbols - The Two Minute Silence and the Poppy. The Arboretum could become the focus for all year round Remembrance - enhancing our schools, Remembrance Travel and fundraising programmes as well as helping to recruit volunteers to help our welfare work'. Geoff Hoon, Secretary of State for Defence stated: 'I warmly welcome the agreement between the National Memorial Arboretum and the Royal British Legion. Earlier this year I announced that the new Armed Forces Memorial would be located in the National Memorial Arboretum and I strongly believe that the Arboretum should be promoted as a site of national importance for commemoration. A strengthened relationship with The Royal British Legion will do much to further that aim'. David Childs, Director of the Arboretum said: 'We are delighted to be in discussion with The Royal British Legion. The Arboretum provides a beautiful and tranquil location for thought and reflection. It is a celebration of those who have sacrificed so much in order to preserve our freedom and enhance the quality of our lives. This is clearly in line with the Legion's Remembrance message. This move enlists the strengths of a larger, long established and much respected charity and helps ensure that the Arboretum remains true to its goal to be a living gift for future generations to reflect on and enjoy'. The photograph above is of the model of the proposed Armed Forces Memorial released in May 2005.

# THE QUEEN'S GOLDEN JUBILEE VISIT TO THE ARBORETUM ON 3 JULY 2002

The Queen with Commander Childs to her left.

Standard Bearers of the Royal British Legion on parade.

# THE TON CLASS MEMORIAL

The Ton Class Association was founded in 1987 by the late Jack Worth MBE. Membership of the Association is restricted to those who have served at any time in a ship of the Ton Class. It currently has some 1,300 members. The Prince of Wales, who commanded HMS BRONNINGTON in 1976, is Patron of the Association.

These wooden minesweepers were built in response to the threat posed by the mine warfare capability of the Soviet Union. They were equipped to deal with contact, magnet and acoustic mines. To protect these ships from the magnetic and acoustic influence of modern mines they were built of non-ferrous metals, their hulls being constructed of double mahogany and the superstructure of aluminium alloy. All other materials used in their ingenious construction were of the lowest magnetic content. Designed in Bath and built between 1950 and 1960, these 153 ft long vessels were crewed by a complement of 5 officers and 32 ratings. Known universally as happy ships, they are remembered with much affection by those who sailed in them. An important weapon in the Royal Navy's armoury, they served the Royal Navy worldwide for 40 years, mostly on low intensity operations,

The origin of the name 'Ton Class' may be found in that all the vessels of the Class were named after villages and hamlets ending in 'ton' - whose names appeared in the Domesday Book.[19] They were usually affiliated to the community after which they were named. *Ton Talk* is the association's bi-monthly magazine which features comings and goings, lists those who have 'crossed the bar' and details the significant amount of research being undertaken by the association to document and research the complete history of all 118 vessels of the Class. Website at www.tca2000.co.uk

The Ton Class Memorial at the Arboretum (pictured above) lists the name of every ship of the Class and on the right is a depiction of HMS FITTLETON, and below that, the name of every member of her crew who perished when she was in collision with HMS MERMAID during a NATO exercise off the Netherlands and sank on 20 September 1976. Twelve sailors, mostly members of the Royal Naval Volunteer Reserve lost their lives.

---

[19] A record of the lands of England compiled in 1086 by order of William the Conqueror.

# THE BURMA STAR

On 20 May 2004 the Burma Star Memorial Grove at the Arboretum was dedicated. It commemorates the heroism, self-sacrifice and devotion of the armed forces of Britain, the Commonwealth and members of other services, including the Merchant Navy, who fought and fell in the Burma Campaign 1942-45. The Grove comprises a mixture of some one hundred native trees and a small avenue of Scottish beech, flanked at either end by elephant grass and bamboo. Within the plot is a circular garden of shrubs and a 14 foot tall granite pillar that carries the badge of the Burma Star and the inscription:

> "WHEN YOU GO HOME
> TELL THEM OF US
> AND SAY
> FOR YOUR TOMORROW
> WE GAVE OUR TODAY"

Over 1,000 veterans attended with their families. Also present were Countess Mountbatten of Burma, Viscount Slim (son of Field Marshal Viscount Slim), President of the Burma Star Association, Captain Paddy Vincent, Chairman of the Burma Star, Colonel Bathia from the Indian High Commission and Mr Ivor Caplin MP, Minister of Veterans' Affairs. The service of dedication was conducted by the Right Reverend Hugh Montefiore, former Bishop of both Coventry and Birmingham (and holder of the Burma Star). There was a flypast of two Tornado jets (31 Squadron, RAF Marham), two Chinook helicopters (27 Squadron, RAF Odiham) and a Dakota from the Battle of Britain Memorial Flight.

## THE BURMA STAR MEMORIAL AT THE ARBORETUM

Captain Vincent said: 'It gives us great pride to have this plot in the National Memorial Arboretum, to provide a worthy and permanent memorial for all those of the many nations who fell and who fought on land, air and sea in the Burma Campaign.' Ivor Caplin stated in his address: I am glad to have the opportunity to pay tribute to the veterans of the Burma Campaign and to join them in this ceremony to commemorate a new permanent memorial. I believe that we should continue to remember the bravery of British and Commonwealth forces during the Second World War. Without their efforts and sacrifices our lives today would be very different.' South East Asia Command was formed in 1943 under Lord Louis Mountbatten and in October of that year, General William Slim was appointed commander of the 'Forgotten' 14th Army that would fight its way back into Burma and recapture Rangoon on 2 May 1945. Earl Mountbatten accepted the surrender of all Japanese forces in South East Asia on 29 August 1945. Earl Mountbatten and Field Marshal Viscount Slim founded the Burma Star Association on 26 February 1951 with 2,000 founder members drawn from those who had served in the Burma Campaign who had been awarded the campaign medal, the Burma Star. Viscount Slim was first President of the Association until his death on 14 December 1970. He was succeeded by his son, the second Viscount Slim. Earl Mountbatten was the Association's Patron until his assassination by the IRA on 27 August 1979.[20] He was succeeded by the Duke of Edinburgh. The Association was established to relieve need, hardship and distress among all holders of the Burma Star, of all HM and Allied forces, the Nursing Service and the Merchant Navy and to promote the continuing comradeship of all who fought in the theatre and in the bitter fighting in the jungles of Burma. It currently has some 10,000 members in 160 branches, both in UK and overseas. Its Benevolent Fund provides respite care and assistance to all veterans from the Burma Campaign, whether members of the Association or not. Valuable work is also carried out in the field of applications and claims for war pensions and war widows' pensions. Website at www.burmastar.org.uk/

---

[20] In 1976 a plaque to Slim's memory was unveiled in St Paul's Cathedral, London - a tribute from the Burma Star Association. Mountbatten's statue by Franta Belsky stands at the foot of the Horse Guards Parade Ground.

# THE RAF REGIMENT MEMORIAL

In the years following the Great War the RAF under its Chief of the Air Staff, Sir Hugh Trenchard fought for survival, as HM Treasury sought huge savings in the armed forces budget. Initially it looked as if the fledgling air force would be consumed by either the navy or the army. In 1920 Winston Churchill, as Secretary for War and Air detailed the RAF to suppress a revolt in Somaliland using only air operations. The success of this campaign in less than a month decided Churchill that the RAF had a future as a separate entity. As post-war peace treaties dismembered the Ottoman Empire and carved out the new nations of the Arab World, in 1921 he, (by now Colonial Secretary) convened a meeting in Cairo between his Department, the Air Ministry, the War Office and the Treasury. At this meeting, he put forward the argument that the RAF rather than the army should be used to police the vast territories of the Middle East which had passed to Britain under League of Nations mandates. To the delight of HM Treasury, he advanced this argument on the grounds of cost. The outcome of this conference ensured that by the end of 1922 the RAF became responsible for the security of all the former Ottoman territories. In October of that year they took over Iraq from the army and found themselves running armoured trains, Rolls Royce armoured cars, gunboats and a large force of native levies, as well as carrying out air operations. The precedent of the RAF carrying out land-based operations, with or without air support was established. The Air Ministry had been studying the need to defend its airfields from air attack as early as 1935. However, the threat was not clearly understood. It took the Battle of Britain in 1940 and the fall of Crete in 1941 to clarify the issue. In the debate in the House of Commons that followed the loss of Crete, Colonel R J R MacNamara, MP for Chelmsford, raised the issue of the formation of specialised airfield defence force. His well-supported call led the Air Ministry to convene a committee under Sir Findlater Stewart. Churchill as Prime Minister took a direct interest in its deliberations. The committee's conclusion proposed the establishment of a force of 79,000 airmen to guard 590 airfields and Cabinet approval was granted on 25 December 1941. The unwieldy title initially proposed was the 'Royal Air Force Aerodrome Defence Corps'. By the time King George VI signed the Royal Warrant on 6 January 1942, the name had been changed to the Royal Air Force Regiment and under that title it continues to this day carrying out the vital role for which it was originally founded.

# THE BERLIN AIRLIFT MEMORIAL

Following rising tension between the Soviet Union and the Allied Powers, in 1948 the Soviet dictator Josef Stalin cut all road and rail links to Berlin. The improvised solution to this situation was produced by Air Commodore Rex Waite RAF. He believed that the 2.1 million people of Berlin could be sustained by the operation of an air bridge. Events were to prove him right. The humanitarian effort required to sustain this population resulted in what is now known as the Berlin Airlift. In the course of eleven months 2,325,800 tons of vital foodstuffs and fuel were delivered to the beleaguered city, ensuring its survival in the face of the Soviet blockade. Both military and civilian British aircraft flew more than 30 million miles and spent more than 200,000 hours in the air between 26 June 1948 and 12 May 1949. The largest part of the effort was shouldered by the Americans. At the height of *Operation Vittles* aeroplanes were landing in Berlin at the rate of one a minute. British aircraft consumed over 35 million gallons of aviation fuel. 39 British aircrew, 31 Americans and 15 Germans were killed during the airlift which lasted from June 1948 to October 1949. Their names are inscribed on the Berlin Airlift Memorial at Tempelhof Airfield in Berlin.

On 12 May 2001 Air Chief Marshal Sir Peter Squire unveiled the Berlin Airlift Memorial at the Arboretum. He was accompanied by Air Marshal Sir John Curtis (President of the Berlin Airlift Association) and Air Vice Marshal GC Lamb (Vice President). The service was held by the Venerable J Hewitt Wilson, former Chaplain in Chief of the RAF, assisted by the Reverend Peter Furness (Chaplain to the Berlin Airlift Association). Colonel Hasso Kortgé, the German Air Attaché laid a wreath on behalf of the people of Berlin.

# SERVICE AND FORTITUDE

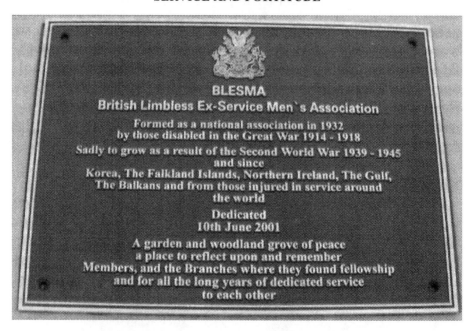

In the Great War, the use of high explosive and high velocity small arms, combined with infection and frostbite produced more than 41,050 British amputees. The British Limbless Ex-Servicemen's Association (BLESMA) was founded as a national charity in 1932 for the express purpose of providing them with support and practical assistance. The Second World War produced another 11,500 British amputees. Given its depth of knowledge and experience, the Association also carries out a significant advocacy role in the field of disabled rights and functions as a centre of expertise on disabled and ex-Service issues.

On 10 June 2001 a dedication service was conducted in the Millennium Chapel by the Reverend Tim Goode, a former RAF chaplain. It was attended by BLESMA Members, Officers of the Association, spouses and widows from all corners of the British Isles. Following the service, all assembled in the BLESMA Memorial Garden where Captain (Rtd) Bob McQueen RN, National Vice Chairman removed the Union Flag to reveal the BLESMA plaque mounted on a stone plinth in the centre of the Garden. Surmounted by BLESMA's coat of arms,[21] the inscription on the plaque celebrates and remembers the fellowship of BLESMA's Members and their years of dedicated service to each other. Captain McQueen then read the Remembrance Exhortation and the *Last Post* was sounded. A white dove was released to symbolise everlasting peace and prayers were said. Whilst the Garden is as yet sparse, a number of saplings sponsored by members have already been planted and it remains only for Mother Nature to do her work.

In an ideal world, there would be no need for an organisation like BLESMA. Sadly the day is not yet with us when armed conflict ceases to be the means nations employ to resolve their differences and until such time as that day arrives, the work of BLESMA must continue. Website at www.blesma.org

---

[21] The motto on BLESMA's coat of arms reads: Service and Fortitude.

## MEMORIALS AT THE ARBORETUM

Standard Bearers of the Royal British Legion at the dedication ceremony of the Staffordshire Regiment Memorial.

The Polar Bear, symbol of the 49th (West Riding) Division.

# THE ARMED FORCES MEMORIAL

The vast majority of war memorials in UK commemorate those who have died in the two World Wars. However, Britain's armed forces have sustained casualties in one form or another every year since 1945, though there was no national memorial that acknowledged their sacrifice. The issue of an Armed Forces Memorial was raised in a question to Geoff Hoon, Secretary of State for Defence, in the House of Commons on 10 November 2000. He announced that he had considered ways in which the recognition of members of the Armed Forces who gave their lives in the service of their country might be enhanced. He concluded that the most appropriate way would be through the erection of a memorial bearing the names of those killed on duty and by terrorist attack since the end of the World War II. Funds would be raised by public subscription and public donations. Further consultation would take place with the ex-Service organisations and other interested bodies. An Armed Forces Memorial Project Team was established and extensive consultation was carried out with both the Services and ex-Service organisations. They were asked to consider options for the criteria for inclusion and the siting of the memorial. It should be noted that the memorial will commemorate personnel from all three Services - the Royal Navy (including the Royal Marines), the Army and the RAF. There was general agreement that the memorial should also include those members of the Royal Fleet Auxiliary and Merchant Navy who were killed in conflict zones while in direct support of the Armed Forces. On 20 March 2002 the Secretary of State made the following statement to the House of Commons: 'A project team was appointed early last year to look at potential sites for the memorial and to consider the qualifying criteria for those to be commemorated. Extensive research was carried out on suitable sites both in and outside London. There has been wide consultation with the Services and ex-Service organisations on both the siting and criteria issues and there is general support for the proposals. I am delighted to be able to confirm that the Armed Forces Memorial will be sited at the National Memorial Arboretum in Staffordshire. The names of those commemorated will either be engraved on the memorial or in Rolls of Honour that will be kept close by in the Millennium Chapel at the Arboretum. The design of the memorial will be decided following an architectural competition that will be held later this year'. The qualifying criteria for inclusion on the memorial were: 'All those Service personnel who were killed on duty whilst performing functions attributable to the special circumstances and requirements of the Armed Forces, or as a result of terrorist attack, and all those who died whilst deployed on designated operations. An additional part of the project will be to erect a memorial plaque in the Cloisters of Westminster Abbey to those members of the Armed Forces killed in conflict since the end of the Second World War. Finally, there will be Rolls of Honour recording the names of all members of the Royal Navy and the Army who have died in Service during this period. These will be kept in suitable churches in London and will be similar to those for the Royal Air Force that are kept in the Church of St Clement Danes. Trustees of the Armed Forces Memorial Trust will now be appointed to take this project forward. They will take on the ownership of the memorial and will be responsible for its funding and construction. Funds will be raised by public subscription. This is a very important National project that will also provide a platform to help educate our younger generations about the value of our Armed Forces'. In January 2005 Ian Rank-Broadley was appointed sculptor to the project and on 6 April at the Imperial War Museum it was announced that the names of 16,000 sailors, soldiers and airmen would be individually carved in chronological order into the stone of the memorial. Liam O'Connor was appointed architect and his design comprised a 140 foot diameter circle of stone on a mound next to the River Trent. A slit in the south east wall will allow a beam of sunlight to fall on the centre stone at 1100 on 11 November. Veteran war correspondent John Simpson said: 'Not everyone who dies, dies a hero. That doesn't mean that their families are any less devastated by their loss and do not need somewhere to go to mourn their loss.' Website at www.forcesmemorial.org.uk

# PIPERS AND MEMORIALISATION

Pipers have existed in the Scottish and Irish regiments in the service of the Crown for as long as the regiments themselves have existed. Despite repeated attempts throughout the 19th century by senior officers to remove them from their regimental establishments, these efforts met with resolute opposition by the regiments concerned and pipers became a permanent and popular feature. The pipes were even taken up by the Brigade of Gurkhas and pipe bands continue to this day in the armies of India, Pakistan, Jordan and Egypt. Some 500 British Army pipers were killed in the Great War and over 600 wounded. In a long-standing tradition, pipers played their companies into action and their exploits are the stuff of legend. The last such recorded occasion was the Battle of Ava Fort in Burma in 1945, where Piper Jock Laidlaw played the Cameron Highlanders into battle. On the modern battlefield, these highly-trained musicians are employed first and foremost as infantrymen.

For this unique, singular, brotherhood their forms of memorialisation would include challenge cups and shields to be competed for. Airs have always been composed to commemorate great events, great men and battles - and in time these tunes take their place in the piping canon. The reel *General Stewart of Garth* first appeared in William Ross's collection of tunes in 1869. Pipe Major Ross of the Black Watch composed *The Battle of Alma* in 1854, shortly after the battle of that name. *Paardeburg* commemorates the surrender of General Piet Cronje after the battle of that name in the Boer War. From the Great War compositions would include: *Battle of Arras* by Pipe Major McLean, *The Highland Brigade at Mons* by Pipe Major Laurie and *The Balkan Hills* by Piper Gillon. The tradition endures still. The composition of *The Crags of Tumbledown Mountain* by Pipe Major James Riddell commemorates the role played by the Scots Guards in taking that feature on the night of 13/14 June 1982, during the Falklands Conflict. In the savage hand-to-hand fighting on the Mountain, nine Scots Guards were killed and 43 wounded.

In recent years, the Piobaireachd Society (the governing body of the piping fraternity) has arranged for the erection of benches to commemorate celebrated pipers. Two have been dedicated to Pipe Major Willie Ross and Captain John McLellan at Edinburgh Castle in recognition of their work at the Army School of Piping there. Benches have also been dedicated at Fort George in the Highlands in memory of Captain D R McLellan and Pipe Major Donald McLeod in recognition of their services with the Seaforth Highlanders. The Society was also responsible for placing of a memorial plaque on a house at 5 Perceval Road, Inverness in memory of Pipe Major John MacDonald, who lived and taught there.

A piper is featured in the bronze frieze around the shrine in the Scottish National War Memorial atop Castle Rock in Edinburgh. In Princes Street in that same city, a pipe band leads a similar frieze behind the figure which forms the centrepiece of the Scottish American War Memorial by the Canadian sculptor Dr Tait Mackenzie.

On the North Inch at Perth is the memorial to the fallen of the 51st Highland Division of the Second World War. On this memorial a Dutch girl is depicted offering a bouquet to a piper. On 20 July 2003 after a service of dedication, The Pipers Memorial was dedicated at Longueval, France. This unique memorial which took the form of a piper playing the pipes was unveiled by Lieutenant General Sir Peter Graham and Major General Corran Purdon. There were 105 pipers present in the massed bands that attended the inauguration.

After the Second Gulf War in 2003, £3,500 was raised by a public house in South East London, another in Edinburgh and by the staff of Harrods for pipe maker Pipe Major Brian Donaldson to craft a silver and ivory set of bagpipes to be donated to the Irish Guards in honour of the Zimbabwean Piper Christopher Muzvuru and L/Cpl Ian Malone, two Irish Guards pipers who were killed in the assault on the southern city of Basra in Iraq on 6 April 2003. The presentation of the 'Muz and Molly Pipes' took place on ANZAC Day 2004 and were gratefully received by Pipe Major Rod Allan of the Irish Guards. The entwined shamrock and the African palm were prominent in the engraving on the silverwork.

## THE ENVIRONMENT

Another form of permanent memorialisation that is not often considered is our physical environment. However, such links are not always immediately apparent.

In 1698 the Palace of Whitehall burned down, the only surviving structure being that great monument to Stuart megalomania, the Banqueting Hall. Opposite, William Kent completed the Horse Guards building in 1706, which until Cardwell's War Office Act of 1870 housed the Headquarters of the British Army. The clock tower on the top of the Horse Guards building is noteworthy. The keen-eyed visitor to Whitehall will note that the Roman numeral II on the clock face has a black dot above it, denoting the time of King Charles I's execution immediately opposite, at two of the clock on 30 January 1649.

Unlike some capital cities, London does not have almost every street or square named after a general or battle. Trafalgar Square and Waterloo Station being notable exceptions and that area of London named Maida Vale, which commemorates the victory of General Sir John Stuart's army at Maida against a superior French force in Italy on 4 July 1806. Street names in metropolitan London also feature as a form of permanent memorialisation and these include: Blenheim, Plassey, Balaclava, Sevastopol, Prince Imperial, Moodkee, Baden Powell and Kitchener. Croydon has a Wellesley Road, Chelsea has a Burnaby Road and South Norwood has an Armistice Gardens. Sometimes the historical events being commemorated run into each other and this can produce odd results. The Guards Crimean War Memorial stands in Waterloo Place, London and THE HERO OF THE ALMA public house stands in Alma Square in Maida Vale. Putney Vale Cemetery in London has seven roads within it all named after winners of the Victoria Cross and Manor Park Cemetery in East London has both a Remembrance Road and a Cornwell Crescent. The vast majority of VC Cross winners are not commemorated by local authorities in UK by the naming of roads or streets after them. Current research in this field indicates that at least 116 are commemorated in this manner. After the Great War, the Geographical Society of Alberta, Canada decided to name an entire mountain range in Jasper National Park after individual Canadian VC winners. Significant street naming opportunities occurred in UK after the Blitz. The Isle of Dogs in London's East End which was heavily bombed, has both an Arnhem Place and an Arnhem Wharf. Unlike London, The city of Portsmouth is noteworthy in that almost every street and public house in the centre of that historic naval port is named after a great British admiral, historic event, or naval engagement. Eleven thoroughfares in the West Midlands bear Nelson's name and other examples illustrate Britain's shared history with other countries. Good examples being: Coventry Straat in Rotterdam, the John Frost Bridge, Arnhem, Churchill Park, Den Helder - all in the Netherlands, Cambrai Avenue in Chichester and Verdun Road in Plumstead, London. After the Second World War, the French renamed the Normandy seaside town of Colleville, Colleville Montgomery in honour of Field Marshal Viscount Montgomery.

Now that the Corps of Royal Engineers no longer runs railways and locomotives, it tends to name the bridges it constructs worldwide after sapper VC winners. In recent years the Durrant Bridge constructed over the Vrbas River at Jajce in Bosnia was named after Sergeant Thomas Frank Durrant VC (the first soldier to win the VC in a naval engagement). The Dundas Bridge, built by sappers on the road across the Shermali Plain that links Kabul to Bagram airfield in Afghanistan was named in 2003 in honour of Captain James Dundas VC, who fell in action at Sherpur Cantonment near Kabul on 23 December 1879.

The name Valour Road in Winnipeg, Manitoba, Canada commemorates that fact that three Canadian soldiers who earned the VC, all lived there within one block of each other. As a general rule, in the UK memorialisation usually takes place posthumously. The author can only recall three exceptions to this rule (and two of these are in France), these being: Avenue Captain Portéus in Belleville-sur-mer, Dieppe, Avenue du Major Howard at Ranville, Normandy and Speakman Street in Slough, Berks which commemorates Sergeant Bill Speakman of the Black Watch who earned his VC in the Korean War on 4 November 1951.

# WOMEN AND WAR MEMORIALS

Since the Crimean War, women have featured in the nation's wars, primarily in the field of nursing. Notwithstanding the efficient humanitarianism of Florence Nightingale and all that she achieved, the British Army in 1898 employed only 92 female nurses. The real breakthrough was to come with the Boer War in 1899. The Boer War Memorial Plaque in St Helens Town Hall, Lancashire was the first British war memorial to carry a woman's name, it carries that of Nursing Sister Clara Evans of the Army Nursing Service Reserve. 31 nurses of the Army Nursing Service and Army Nursing Service Reserve who died in that war are commemorated in town halls, churches and hospitals across the UK and in South Africa.[22] This was the first conflict in which women served in the field and became casualties. Most died from disease. Only after this war and reform of its medical services did the British Army begin to recruit substantial numbers of female nurses. In 1902 Queen Alexandra's Imperial Military Nursing Service replaced the Army Nursing Service. The mass mobilisation of Britain's menfolk for war service in the Great War led to women taking up many civilian roles in their stead. There were openings in public transport, munitions factories, arsenals, the Voluntary Aid Detachment and draughtswomen posts in the Admiralty. The use of female labour to replace men in fields that were hitherto the preserve of men would have a direct impact on the post-war employment of both sexes. At least 32,000 women served as military nurses in the Great War. In that period over 2,500,000 sick and wounded soldiers were treated in hospital in the UK. There were also roles for women in the First Aid Nursing Yeomanry and the British Red Cross. Despite being rebuffed by a War Office official who told her: 'My good lady, go home and sit still' Dr Inglis set up the Scottish Women's Hospitals for Foreign Service which was formed in Edinburgh. Aged from 17 to 65, these 1,000 volunteers set up and served in 14 hospitals overseas. They served as surgeons, doctors, nurses, auxiliaries, drivers, cooks, administrators and fundraisers. 17 of them gave their lives. Winston Churchill would write of them: 'The record of their work in Russia and Rumania will shine in history. Their achievements in France, Serbia, in Greece and in other theatres (of war) were no less valuable and no body of women has won a higher reputation… The record of their work lit by the fame of Dr Inglis will shine in history'. Memorials specifically commemorating the women who fell in the Great War were erected at both St Paul's Cathedral in London and at York Minster. Mostly due to technological developments, the Second World War provided women with a far broader range of opportunities than the Great War and some 640,000 served in the Armed Forces. As well as nursing, there were roles in the Home Guard, Air Raid Precautions, Fighter Command control centres, in the Auxiliary Territorial Service, in mixed-sex anti aircraft batteries of the Royal Artillery, the Royal Observer Corps, the Women's Land Army and Timber Corps, the Women's Voluntary Service, Queen Alexandra's Imperial Military Nursing Service, the Women's Transport Service of the First Aid Nursing Yeomanry, the Special Operations Executive, code-breaking at the Government Code and Cipher School at Bletchley Park, aircraft manufacture and the fire brigades. To date, 93rd Searchlight Regiment RA was the only all female regiment in the history of the British Army. The war also provided women with a previously unavailable range of shore-based duties in the fleet and in flying aeroplanes across the Atlantic and Europe for RAF Transport Command. After the Second World War a noteworthy memorial was erected at Devizes, Wilts to commemorate the farmers' appreciation of the work of the Women's Land Army during the war. On 4 March 2000 The Queen unveiled the Home Front Memorial at Coventry Cathedral. Most unusually, this memorial does not commemorate those who died in war, instead it commemorates those 'who also served', in the dockyards, the aircraft and munitions factories, down the mines and on the land.

---

[22] Sir James Gildea *For Remembrance and in Honour of Those Who Lost Their Lives in the South African War 1899-1902.*

# FIELD MARSHALS

In the 17th century the British Army utilised the title of Captain General as its senior army rank and the title is still in use. With the arrival of the Hanoverian dynasty on Britain's throne, the equivalent continental title in common usage in the Holy Roman Empire, of which the Electorate of Hanover was a constituent member, was taken into use and the office of Field Marshal of the British Army can be dated from the appointment to that rank of Lord George Hamilton, 1st Earl of Orkney (1666-1737) by King George II in 1736. Field Marshal appointments were made for life and the rank was also bestowed on senior members of the British, or closely allied royal families - sometimes unwisely, as in the cases of Kaiser Wilhelm II and the Japanese Emperor Hirohito. British Monarchs were traditionally appointed Field Marshal, but Queen Elizabeth II does not hold that rank. In all, a total of 138 appointments were made to the rank, the Duke of Wellington holding it longest at 39 years. The rank was suspended under a streamlining recommendation made by a team of management consultants to the Ministry of Defence and announced in the House of Commons on 20 February 1996. The decision resulted in five star appointments to the equivalent ranks of Admiral of the Fleet and Marshal of the Royal Air Force also falling into abeyance.

In Britain, commemorative statuary does not normally appear in the lifetime of the individual concerned and this is generally true of all forms of memorialisation. However, statues do not always appear nearly contemporaneously. General Wolfe had to wait some 170 years before his statue by Dr Tait MacKenzie took its place in Greenwich Park in 1930. In our own time, after the death of the individual concerned, the relevant regimental association or arm of Service will usually take the matter in hand. The scale normally employed is usually one third larger than life size, (as a rule of thumb usually nine feet). In the Whitehall area, the group of statues on Raleigh Green outside the Ministry of Defence is particularly noteworthy. Since the rustication of William McMillan's diminutive Sir Walter Raleigh to Greenwich in 2001, the group now consists of three Second World War Field Marshals, these being; Slim (1990), Alanbrooke (1993) and Montgomery (1973). Slim and Alanbrooke were sculpted in the literal manner by the celebrated Welsh sculptor Ivor Roberts-Jones and the poses are evocative of both these two great commanders. However, the interesting statue in the group is the 14 foot tall sculpture of Montgomery which was sculpted by Oscar Nemon in the impressionist style, with only the face being rendered in the literal manner, the surface of the rest of the statue being rough cast with little detail apparent. Although 'Monty' was known for his unorthodox dress sense, quite why he should be presented to posterity wearing a battledress that looks as though it is being attacked by mange, is in itself a fairly interesting question. Nemon's sculpture of Marshal of the Royal Air Force Viscount Portal (1975) on Victoria Embankment behind the Ministry of Defence is in the same style.

Another recent form of memorialisation may be found in the practice of installing memorial windows in the chapel at Royal Military Academy, Sandhurst. Here windows can be found designed by the noted stained glass craftsman Alan Younger (1933-2004) which commemorate Field Marshals Cassels and Carver.

The crypt of St Paul's Cathedral in London contains a memorial to each of Britain's field marshals who served in the Second World War. They were erected in the late 1970s and included one to Field Marshal Sir Claude Auchinleck. Notwithstanding his stormy relationship with Prime Minister Churchill, who interfered relentlessly in the conduct of the war in North Africa and sacked him in 1942, Rommel considered 'The Auk' to be one of the greatest generals of the Second World War. In retirement, Auchinleck settled in Marrakesh, Morocco where he lived quietly in a modest flat for many years. The 'powers that be' at St Paul's Cathedral soon discovered that that the long-lived Field Marshal was still alive and a letter of apology speedily sent. The Auk drily responded that he: 'felt certain that time would rectify the mistake'. He was in old age cared for by Corporal Malcolm James Millward (a serving soldier) and full of years, the Field Marshal died in 1981.

## MORRIS SINGER

The impetus for the establishment of Morris Singer's foundry may be found in the Victorian mania for erecting statuary to public figures to military leaders, ecclesiastics, reformers and colonial administrators. John Webb Singer (1819-1904) was apprenticed to E G Pitt of Eagle Lane, Frome, Somerset as a watchmaker. In 1841 he undertook the first of 51 trips to Europe then worked in London and Blandford. In 1843 he was appointed manager of Pitt's business. In 1848 he set up the Frome Art Metal Works. The religious upsurge accompanying the Oxford Movement afforded him considerable opportunities in the field of ecclesiastical furnishing, so he diversified into brasswork and began to engage craftsmen. The appointment of the influential Sir William Bill (Member of LCC and later MP) as chairman of the company in 1897 ensured it received plenty of commissions. In 1899 John Webb Singer relinquished control to his sons whom he had wisely sent to the South Kensington Art Schools to learn their trade. That same year the firm became a private limited liability company, with shares being offered to the craftsmen. Although the requirement for ecclesiastical furnishing at the start of the 20th century was in decline, the death of Queen Victoria in 1901 and the end of the Boer War led to a considerable number of statues and memorials being cast. During the Great War 'Singers of Frome' was converted to war work and produced millions of cartridge cases and artillery shells. In common with other foundries, Singers then worked flat out in the golden age of war memorials 1919-1926. The increasing interest in bronze sculpture after the Great War encouraged Singers to move to London after merging with the Morris Art Bronze Foundry in 1927. The Foundry at Dorset Road, Lambeth had been founded in 1921 by William Morris.[23] During the Depression Morris Singer laid off most of its staff, its workforce declining at one point to five men and an apprentice. The firm eventually recovered and was purchased as a going concern by the Pollard Group in 1935. The outbreak of war in 1939 delayed the completion of a number of commissions and after the Second World War, figurative statuary continued to be the largest part of Morris Singer's output until its modern sculpture phase began in 1960 when Dame Barbara Hepworth began sending her work and since that time the foundry has cast every great modern sculptor from Sir Jacob Epstein to Sir Eduardo Paolozzi. Examples of the quality and craftsmanship of 20th century architectural works Morris Singer has cast may be found in the doors of Washington Cathedral in USA, the Bank of England and the RIBA. In 1967 the firm moved from London to purpose-built premises at Basingstoke, where among a number of monumental projects, it cast the 56ft high bronze and wall sculpture for Montreal's Notre Dame Cathedral by Charles Dauderin and in recent times, many major works for corporations and companies in England and abroad including Philip Jackson's *The Yomper* in Portsmouth, *The Horses of Helios* in the Haymarket in London by Rudy Weller, *St George and the Dragon* by Professor Michael Sandle and countless others. Morris Singer specialises in casting sporting monuments and these include: *Sir Matt Busby* at Old Trafford, *Sir Garfield Sobers* in Barbados and *Shergar* in Ireland. A further move was made in April 1999 to a purpose-built location at Lasham in Hants. For a century and a half, skilled craftspeople at Morris Singer have worked with artists to create works of art, large and small, from maquettes to the magnificence of metal sculptures and statues, monuments, memorials and architectural metalwork. The firm has cast many historically important monuments all over the world - from the Lions and Fountains in Trafalgar Square (1867) and Frederick Pomeroy's *Figure of Justice* atop the Old Bailey (1906) in London, to the *Victory Arch* in Baghdad (1988) and the Holocaust Memorial in Toronto (1991). Major 20th century commissions in London cast by Morris Singer include *Boadicea, Oliver Cromwell, F D Roosevelt* in Grosvenor Square and Philip Jackson's 1997 *Monument to Raoul Wallenberg*. Website at www.morrissinger.co.uk/

---

[23] Despite his reticence (which can have done business no harm), he was unrelated to William Morris (1834-96), pioneer of the Arts and Crafts movement and arguably the most influential designer in British history.

# BRITISH GOVERNMENT POLICY ON WAR MEMORIALS

*Apollo* sculpted by Sir Bertram MacKennal in the grounds of Taplow Court in Berkshire commemorating the Grenfell brothers.

In the UK, it has been the policy of successive governments that the cost of erecting war memorials and associated projects are not usually met from public funds, but from private donations or public subscription. Officially, the only war memorial erected and funded by the British tax-payer is the Cenotaph in Whitehall, which functions as the national memorial to the fallen of both World Wars and it is unique for that reason. It cost the British tax-payer £7,325. The only exceptions to the rule of which the author is aware, have been the Waterloo Memorial which stands in Everè Cemetery, Brussels, to which the British Government donated £500 in 1878 and the Falklands Memorial in the crypt of St Paul's Cathedral, London which at the strident insistence of the then Prime Minister, was funded by the tax-payer, despite the existence of the policy. The MOD does not have responsibility for either the funding or maintenance of war memorials. It receives many requests from individuals, ex-Servicemen's groups and charitable organisations seeking assistance with various projects. It would be invidious to be seen to support one project rather than another. The vast majority have worthy goals and can make an equally compelling case for support. It would be divisive and open to criticism from unsuccessful applicants, if Government were to pick and choose which projects to support. Whilst unable to assist financially with the cost of funding new war memorials, MOD will assist in identifying a suitable site and will provide advice on fund raising. It will also endeavour to provide Service representation at any dedication ceremony for new war memorials, once funding has been raised and the memorial erected. This policy was announced by the then Parliamentary Under Secretary of State for Defence in May 1997 and despite regular letter-writing campaigns to Members of Parliament, it remains in force. Another interesting aspect of this policy has in recent years been the regular announcement by ministers of various government departments that they are going to spend tax-payers money on funding of memorials to the victims of this or that train crash, or to the victims of the conflict in Northern Ireland. The ongoing cross-government 'policy tension' in this area serves as a clear indication that a number of politicians and senior civil servants (the real culprits) remain oblivious to this long-standing policy.

## THE CHURCH OF ENGLAND

War memorials situated in Church of England churches or churchyards are subject to the faculty jurisdiction system, which ensures that churches and their contents and churchyards are properly cared for by requiring a faculty (special permission from the church authorities) for works or other changes to them. Such memorials remain the property of the person, community, association, regiment, or other body that erected them, or the heirs, legal successors of that person or body. A parochial church council has the power, subject to faculty permission, to repair any such memorial within the precincts of a church or churchyard, but may look to others, for example the owners, or the local authority to accept or assume responsibility for its upkeep. Any proposal to remove a war memorial would require a faculty, which would only be granted if there were strong reasons for the change of location and following consultation. As part of that process the church authorities would need to be satisfied about the arrangements for the future of the memorial.

Under the Disused Burial Grounds (Amendment) Act 1981 and the Pastoral Measure 1983, if a disused Church of England church or churchyard, or a disused Non Conformist burial site is made the subject of a redundancy scheme, relatives of those commemorated or buried there, or the Commonwealth War Graves Commission must be given the opportunity to make alternative arrangements for any war memorials on that site. Responsibility for deciding what happens to these items rests with the bishop, after consulting his Diocesan Advisory Committee (DAC). If it is not feasible for the memorial to remain in place, the bishop will often direct that the memorial is relocated to another church in the parish, or to an appropriate public building. Given the public's natural sensitivity about the disposal, of memorials of any kind, the DAC would be expected to make enquiries locally before advising the bishop on the form his direction should take. A public notice will usually be placed in a local newspaper explaining what is intended. If the next of kin of those commemorated indicate that they would prefer to deal with the memorials in some other suitable way, the church will assist such an endeavour financially. The Pastoral Measure does not differentiate between memorials to individuals and those to the fallen of the community concerned. Where monuments or memorials remain in a redundant church following disposal, the new owner will be prohibited by covenant from removing or disturbing them without the prior approval of the relevant church authorities. Removal of a war memorial from a listed church will also require secular listed building consent in addition to any negotiation with the church authorities under the terms of the covenant placed on the building. Neither local authorities nor the church are however, compelled to arrange a suitable resting-place, to which the memorial can be transferred. In such cases, details of the memorial to be removed, including a copy of the inscription, as well as the date and manner of disposal are to be lodged with the local council and copied to the Registrar General. War memorials in Scotland are not covered by similar legislation. Responsibility for policy dealing with disposal of war memorials from disused churches or burial grounds belonging to a church in England rests with the Home Office, but there is no governmental responsibility for the disposal of war memorials from other locations e.g. memorial halls. Further evidence of the intimate link between organised religion and memorialisation may be taken from the fact that of 118 Grade I listed war memorials in England in September 2003, 113 of them were situated in churches. The acquiring of churches and chapels by regiments, corps and different arms of service over the last century serves to emphasise the continuing connection between organised religion and memorialisation.

Another interesting aspect of the ecclesiastical theme may be taken from Britain's highest war memorial at Fort William in the Scottish Highlands. The Fort William-Dudley (Worcs) Cairn of Remembrance was erected on VJ Day in 1945 by members of the Vicar Street Bible Class of Dudley, Worcestershire who were on holiday in the Highlands on the day the Second World War officially ended.

## THE WAR MEMORIALS TRUST

The Friends of War Memorials was founded in 1997 by ex-Royal Marine Ian Davidson in response to growing public concern over the condition of many war memorials. The organisation changed its name to the War Memorials Trust on 1 January 2005. The aims and objectives of the organisation are:

- To monitor the condition of war memorials and to take steps to ensure that local authorities and other relevant organisations are alerted to such condition with a view to their undertaking any necessary restoration, essential maintenance, repairs, renovations and cleaning.

- To liaise with the public, ecclesiastical authorities, regiments ex-service organisations, and other responsible bodies with a view to their accepting responsibility for, and undertaking repairs to and restoration of, war memorials.

- To publicise and to educate and inform the public about the spiritual, archaeological, artistic, aesthetic and historical significance of war memorials as part of our national heritage; to encourage support groups and to inspire young people to cherish their local war memorials and the memory of those who sacrificed their lives in the cause of freedom.

In pursuing these objectives the organisation seeks to heighten public interest in and awareness of memorials, their spiritual, artistic, archaeological, aesthetic and historical significance, thereby ensuring that the country's memorials are maintained in the best condition. The Trust has a network of 200 regional volunteers who act as its eyes and ears. Life membership costs £100 and at 31 December 2003 the Trust had approximately 1,300 members. It offers conservation and funding advice and administers both its own Small Grants Scheme (which can furnish grants up to £250). It also administers the English Heritage Grants for War Memorials Scheme. Dr Pedro Gaspar, the charity's Conservation Officer interviewed by *Heritage Today* in August 2004 stated: 'There is money available, and interest is growing fast,... When we issued a press release about the English Heritage grants scheme this March, we had 250 new requests for information packs within one or two months'.[24] To be eligible for a grant, a memorial must be free standing. There are no conservation area or listing criteria. The Scheme awards grants of up to 50% of eligible costs up to a maximum of £10,000. The types of work which may qualify for grant aid include:

- Repairs to fabric.
- Recutting and recarving of eroded inscriptions and detail.
- Relettering, releading and regilding.
- Cleaning where appropriate and clearly beneficial.
- Reinstatement of lost elements, particularly decorative features.
- Works to associated hard landscaping, where this forms part of the overall design.

The War Memorials Trust is a voluntary organisation and relies exclusively on voluntary support and donations. It does not receive any statutory funding. If you would like to receive further information about the charity's work, contact www.warmemorials.org.

---

[24] *Heritage Today* September 2004.

# THE UNITED KINGDOM NATIONAL INVENTORY OF WAR MEMORIALS

As long ago as 1921 the newly-founded Imperial War Museum appealed for photographs of war memorials. However, little systematic attempt was made by any organisation after the Great War to record the unparalleled construction of memorials which has been described as the UK's greatest flowering of public art. Conscious that no comprehensive record existed and that in time memorials could disappear, in 1987 Dr Alan Borg, the Director General of the Imperial War Museum, approached Stephen Croad of RCHME (now merged with English Heritage) with a detailed proposal for the two organisations to co-operate on the creation of an inventory of war memorials. On 5 March 1988 *The Times* published a letter from Dr Borg, pointing out the 'urgent national requirement for an inventory of war memorials', as many were 'suffering from the ravages of time and pollution, with inscriptions becoming illegible and details of sculpture destroyed.' Following an enthusiastic response, a meeting was convened at the Imperial War Museum on 10 June 1988 at which a number of representatives of organisations sharing Dr Borg's concerns agreed to the founding of the National Inventory of War Memorials. Some of the participating organisations provided representatives to form a committee to oversee the project, which was jointly supervised by the IWM and RCHME, and in January 2001 representatives from heritage organisations in Northern Ireland, Scotland and Wales joined the Committee to reflect the changes brought about through devolution. At the same time, the Inventory was re-titled the United Kingdom National Inventory of War Memorials (UKNIWM). Most recently, the Inventory was granted charitable status in March 2005 to aid its work. Independently funded, the UKNIWM is based at and administered by the IWM. The aim of the Inventory is to record all physical objects, other than graves, located in the British Isles (excluding the Irish Republic) created or installed to commemorate those who both served and died as a result of conflict. The information is used to educate the public, assist historical research and to promote good citizenship as well as assist in the finding, restoration and maintenance of such memorials and in the establishment of new memorials. To assist those interested in the preservation of war memorials the UKNIWM produced a booklet entitled *The War Memorials Handbook*. It provides a concise summary of the subject and contains advice for those wishing to undertake maintenance of war memorials.

In June 1989 Dr Catherine Moriarty was appointed full-time project co-ordinator, with the task of establishing a recording system and overseeing the many volunteers contributing records. In conjunction with RCHME she devised a standard recording form for use by the volunteer fieldworkers, and by the summer of 1990 a specialised computer database was operational. The memorial to the earliest conflict on the database dates from the Roman occupation of England and commemorates soldiers stationed at Vindolanda Roman Fort in Northumberland during the Roman occupation of Britain, but other records bring the database right up to the present day and include Iraq in 2003. In March 2005 the database contained more than 53,000 records, each recording information about a memorial's type, inscription, artistic details and materials, background history and condition. The database forms a central source of information for those interested in commemoration, military history, local or family history and art history. Access to the UKNIWM database is currently available IWM Reading Room or by application to the Inventory but from November 2005 will be available on the Internet.

At the launch of the fundraising drive on 3 February 2005 to achieve this and other project developments, Alderman Michael Savory, Lord Mayor of London noted in his speech at the Mansion House in London: 'From Battle Abbey to Park Lane, from Cornwall to Norfolk, from Skye to Salcombe this land commemorates its lost sons and daughters, and animals as well, in memorials magnificent and gleaming, in memorials humble, almost forgotten, honouring men and women of many nations who confronted evil and tyranny at the cost of their own lives. And when the memories of those who knew them fades, the stones, the iron, the bronze, the glass will carry on their witness to generations new'.

## THE MAINTENANCE OF WAR MEMORIALS

'After the First World War, the sheer scale of the losses had meant every community wanted to build its own monument to the dead. With further memorials being added after the Second World War, the UK now had between 50,000 and 70,000, standing in churches, parks, private gardens, village and town halls, scout huts and railway offices'.[25] Because of their architectural or historical significance, in July 2002 1,409 war memorials were protected, 114 of them listed as grade I and 183 grade II,[26] the most notable example of a grade I listing being the Cenotaph in Whitehall. The Department for Media, Culture and Sport is responsible for compiling lists of those that are protected and the listing system only applies to UK.

During the 20th century a large number of war memorials erected by private subscription, were handed over to parish councils, urban councils and boroughs to maintain. In order to ensure that every form of local council had the ability to raise appropriate funds to preserve these war memorials, the War Memorials (Local Authorities' Powers) Act 1923 was passed. Under the terms of this Act, as amended by Section 133 of the Local Government Act 1948, the Parish Councils Act 1957 and the Local Government Act 1972 responsibility for the overall control of war memorials was vested with local authorities, who were empowered to incur reasonable expenditure for the maintenance, repair and protection of war memorials within their control.[27] Those powers also extend to the alteration of a memorial to enable the fallen of any subsequent war, to that for which it was originally intended, to be commemorated. The Local Government (Scotland) Act 1973 and the Local Government and Planning (Scotland) Act 1982 applies to war memorials in Scotland.

Attitudes of different councils can vary. On some memorials the names of Service personnel who fell in Korea, Suez, Aden, Malaya, Northern Ireland, the Falkland Isles and the Gulf have been added. In some cases it has been discovered that names that should have been on a war memorial in the first place were, for one reason or another omitted. Whilst the above Acts empowered local authorities to care for war memorials, they did not compel them to do so. Responsibility for the provisions of the War Memorials (Local Authorities' Powers) Act 1923 rests with the Home Office. Responsibility for the maintenance, repair and protection of individual war memorials lies with the owner, or the body in which ownership is vested. Concern for the condition, maintenance and future of war memorials has increased significantly in recent years and there have been reports in the national press concerning the disposal of war memorials where churches, memorial halls and other buildings have been closed or redeveloped. These memorials, which have on occasion been sold to scrap yards and architectural salvage yards, have tended to be rolls of honour, plaques or marble slabs attached to churches and other buildings, rather than the traditional public war memorial.

In recent years it became apparent that the most vulnerable war memorials were those that had been erected by firms, factories and businesses. As firms closed down, amalgamated or moved premises, it became evident that memorials were being discarded or lost. The timely founding of both the War Memorials Trust and the United Kingdom National Inventory of War Memorials ensured that memorials under threat could be identified and relocated. The quarterly *Friends of War Memorials Newsletter* carries a regular feature on stolen and recovered war memorials and draws on the knowledge of its readership in identifying memorials. SALVO was founded in 1990 to promote ethical practice in architectural salvage. It takes a direct interest in war memorials and carries a 'Theft Alerts' column in its magazine *Salvo News* free of charge and also on its website at www.salvoweb.com

---

[25] *The Guardian* 11 February 1998 p. 9.
[26] *Daily Telegraph* 4 July 2002 p. 12.

# CHAPTER VI

# ROYAL NAVY MEMORIALS

# COMMODORE SIR WILLIAM JAMES

William James was born the son of a miller near Haverfordwest, Pembrokeshire, Wales in 1721. At the age of 12 he abandoned an unpromising career as a ploughboy and ran away to sea. Examination of his early naval career reveals something of a chequered existence, during the course of which he would appear to have contracted matrimony with the landlady of the Red Cow Public House at Wapping in London. In 1738 he is recorded as serving under Admiral Sir Edward Hawke in the West Indies

In 1747 James entered the service of the Honourable East India Company and after two years as Chief Mate was appointed Captain of THE GUARDIAN. In 1751 he was appointed Commodore and Commander-in-Chief of the Company's marine forces with the 44 gun PROTECTOR as his flagship. Piracy was the scourge of the Malabar Coast (the western coast of India) and it was costing the HEIC the enormous sum of £50,000 a year to police it. James' principal antagonist was the improbably named pirate chief Conagree Angria, whom he first encountered whilst escorting a convoy of 70 trading vessels along the coast. James successfully repelled his attack and forced him to take cover under the guns of his stronghold on the island of Severndroog, (not to be confused with Savandroog in Mysore, a mountain stronghold captured by Lord Cornwallis in 1791). Mahratta Rajah, the local leader was unable to check the depredations of Angria and appealed to the British for help. Aware of the mettle of his adversary, Angria then built a further fort with forty guns on the mainland to cover the approaches to Severndroog. On 1-2 April 1755 James successfully attacked Severndroog with four warships, assisted by an attack on the mainland mounted by 10,000 of Mahratta Rajah's men. He cleaned out the pirates' nest, took the mainland fort and then Bankot. Forewarned, the pirate fleet had set out to sea before the attack, but now had no base to repair to and sailed south. The Mahrattas anxious to pursue their advantage then offered James two lakhs of rupees to cooperate with them, but he had already exceeded his instructions and refused to do more without permission from Bombay. This, the Governor and Council declined to give, judging the season too late. Severndroog was then handed over to the Mahrattas. In November that year James joined forces with Vice-Admiral Watson's Royal Navy squadron and in February 1756 mopped up the pirate forts 100 miles further down the coast at Gheriah. On that occasion James and Watson acted in conjunction with the land forces of Robert Clive (Clive of India), but the success of the operation was said to have owed much to James' skilful reconnaissance and pilotage. In 1759 having amassed a fortune in prize money from his adventures in India, James returned to England, married Anne, daughter of Edmond Goddard of Hartham in Wiltshire and settled at Park Farm Place, Eltham in South East London. He then became a Senior Director of the HEIC, an Elder Brother and Deputy Master of Trinity House, a Governor of Greenwich Hospital and Member of Parliament for West Looe in Cornwall. In 1778 he was created baronet. Commodore Sir William James died of apoplexy on 16 December 1788 during the festivities celebrating his daughter Elizabeth's wedding to Thomas Boothby Parkyns (1755-1800) later 1st Baron Rancliffe.

His widow erected Severndroog Castle as a monument to both her husband's memory and his audacious exploit. Originally labelled by the locals: 'Lady James' Folly', it was built in 1784 by R Jupp (1728-99), who was from 1768 until his death, architect to the HEIC. The design of the castle took the form of a 63 foot tall triangular 'Gothick' tower with a stone spiral staircase, three floors, each with a main room, battlements and hexagonal corner turrets.[1] 'Its walls are built of a mix of red and brown bricks, much repaired, with two-centred, pointed arched windows of two widths. The fenestration is the same on all faces with the symmetry sustained by the use of trompe l'oeil windows to the turrets and blind quatrefoils to the turret tops.'[2] Standing in Castle Woods near the summit of Shooters Hill in South London, Severndroog Castle stands taller than the dome of St Paul's Cathedral.

---

[1] B Cherry and N Pevsner *Buildings of England Series (London & South)*.
[2] *Royal Commission on the Historical Monuments of England NBR 90838.*

# SEVERNDROOG CASTLE

In 1797 the tower was used to enact Major General William Roy's[3] plan to link up England and France trigonometrically and for that purpose the 36 inch theodolite made by the renowned instrument maker Jesse Ramsden[4] and presented by King George III to the Royal Society was installed on its summit. Lady James died in 1798 and Severndroog then passed through the hands of a succession of private owners. In 1848 it survived a proposal to erect a 10,000 catacomb cemetery on the site and it was used again that year for survey purposes by the Corps of Royal Engineers. Over the years, the various artefacts, models and memorabilia that Lady James had collected gradually disappeared. Upon the death of the castle's owner, Mr E Probyn Godson in 1921, he bequeathed the LCC an option on his estate and in 1922 the property was purchased for £6,000 with contributions being raised from the metropolitan borough councils of Bermondsey (£250), Deptford (£500), Greenwich (£500), Lewisham (£500) and Woolwich (£2,000) and was then transferred to LCC management in November that year and run by them as a tea room.

During the Second World War, the tower was manned night and day by two special constables, who kept constant lookout for enemy aircraft flying up the Thames. In the 1950s it would cost a penny to see the view from the top, a penny for an ice lolly and tuppence for a cup of tea. Various London landmarks could be identified by looking along wooden grooves carved into the edge of the observation gallery, each labelled with the landmark to which they pointed. With the abolition of the Greater London Council in 1986, the castle was boarded up, but in 2004 there was a well-supported local campaign underway to restore this important reminder of Britain's maritime history to its former glory.

---

[3] Major General William Roy (1726-1790). Born Carluke, Scotland. Mathematician and army surveyor. Surveyed Scotland 1746. His work laid the groundwork of the trigonometrical survey of the three kingdoms. Shortly after his death, his work at the Board of Ordnance led directly to the creation of Ordnance Survey.

[4] Jesse Ramsden (1735-1800). Born Halifax. Instrument Maker and Optician to King George III. The King once complained that Ramsden had appeared at Buckingham House at the appointed day and hour, but a year late.

## ADMIRAL SIR CLOUDESLEY SHOVEL

Cloudesley Shovel (also spelt Clowdisley Shovell) was born at Cockthorpe, Norfolk and is recorded as having been baptised there on 25 November 1650. He first went to sea in 1664 under the care of Admiral Sir Christopher Myngs and is recorded as having served bravely in the Second Dutch War. He subsequently served with Admiral Sir John Narborough (and married his widow in 1691). In 1677 he was appointed Captain of the SAPPHIRE and fought Barbary pirates in the Mediterranean. Shovel was knighted after the Battle of Bantry Bay in 1689. He was promoted Rear Admiral in 1690 and Admiral of the Fleet in 1705. He was a trusted friend of John Churchill, 1st Duke of Marlborough and his ability and seamanship brought him to prominence during the War of the Spanish Succession. He fought against the French at Barfleur and played a significant role in the capture of Gibraltar in 1704. He generously contributed monies to erect the Corn Exchange at Rochester and his coat of arms may be seen displayed on the clock there. 'In 1707 Admiral of the Fleet Sir Cloudesley Shovel was leading 21 ships of the line from Gibraltar to Plymouth after blockading the French fleet at Toulon. Because of bad weather in the Bay of Biscay, the Admiral got lost and ran his flagship the *Association*, plus the *Eagle, Romney* and *Firebrand* onto the Scilly Isles rocks, with the loss of more than 2,000 sailors. The Admiral took to his barge but was shipwrecked again and washed up at Port Hellick on St Mary's. Barely alive, he was found by a woman who stole the emerald ring from one of his fingers before finishing him off by strangling him on the beach. Thirty years later on her deathbed, the woman confessed and delivered up the ring to a clergyman, who passed it on to the Admiral's old friend, the Earl of Berkeley. The Admiral's body now lies in Westminster Abbey while a stone on that Scilly Isles beach marks the spot where he was washed ashore and cruelly murdered.'[5] Admiral Shovel was initially buried in the dunes behind the beach where he met his end. On the orders of Queen Anne, his body was exhumed, identified and embalmed at Plymouth. It was transported to London, where it lay in state at his townhouse at Frith Street in Soho. His funeral took place with great ceremony in Westminster Abbey on 22 December 1707.

Controversy in the matter of public sculpture is not new the 20 foot tall marble monument to Shovel's memory in the south choir aisle of Westminster Abbey was sculpted by Grinling Gibbons. It depicts Shovel disporting himself on a couch dressed incongruously in Roman armour and a large wig. At the summit of the monument, a winged boy holds the shield of arms awarded him in 1692 in recognition of his victories over both the Turks and the French. A voluminous inscription extols his virtues. The monument was erected by order of Queen Anne and its flamboyant style incensed Joseph Addison, the English essayist and poet. He wrote in the 30 March 1711 edition of *The Spectator*: 'As a foreigner is very apt to conceive an idea of the ignorance or politeness of a nation from the turn of their publick monuments and inscriptions, they should be submitted to the perusal of men of learning and genius before they are put in execution. Sir Cloudesley Shovel's monument has very often given me great offence. Instead of the brave rough English admiral, which was the distinguishing character of that plain gallant man, he is represented on his tomb by the figure of a beau, dressed in a long periwig, and reposing himself upon velvet cushions under a canopy of state.'

Jodocus Crull, author of the 1711 guide to Westminster Abbey, eulogised Shovel as: 'a person of uncommon courage, esteemed by the kings of Spain and Portugal, as well as Queen Anne.' With considerable cheek, Crull also commended Admiral Shovel for his un-naval-like virtues of temperance, humanity and affability in conversation.

Admiral Shovel's full-length portrait (1702) by the talented Swedish portraitist Michael Dahl (2223 mm x 1422 mm) may be seen at the National Portrait Gallery in London. In 1969 divers located the wreck of his ship the ASSOCIATION.

---

[5] *Daily Mail* 10 July 2004 (with grateful thanks to G E Clark of Orpington, Kent).

# ADMIRAL HORATIO VISCOUNT NELSON

Horatio Nelson was born in Burnham Thorpe, Norfolk on 29 September 1758. He entered the Royal Navy in 1770, serving under his uncle Captain Maurice Suckling. He was promoted Captain in 1779. In 1793 whilst serving under Admiral Hood, he assisted in the occupation of Toulon. After the British were driven out by Napoleon, Nelson assisted in operations on Corsica and its capture in 1794. At Calvi he was wounded in his right eye and eventually lost use of it. He was promoted commodore in 1796. The following year he played a prominent part in the victory off Cape St Vincent, Portugal, of the British fleet under John Jervis, over the Spanish. In July 1797 he led an attack on Santa Cruz de Tenerife in the Canaries. The attack failed and Nelson lost his right arm to amputation after injury. The following year he was sent to investigate the French fleet at Toulon. Nelson's ships were scattered by a storm and the French escaped. Nelson learned that they had sailed east carrying an army to invade Egypt. The French landed their troops before Nelson caught up with them in Aboukir Bay. In the Battle of the Nile on 1-2 August 1798 he destroyed the French fleet. His victory ended Napoleon's adventure in the Middle East. Nelson then went to Naples and assisted in the restoration of the Neapolitan Royal Family which had been expelled. In 1801 at the Battle of Copenhagen, Nelson famously ignored Admiral Hyde Parker's signal for the British ships to withdraw, by placing a telescope to his blind eye and declaring that he could see no signal. Later that year he was created viscount. When war broke out again in 1803 he commanded the Mediterranean fleet. He blockaded Toulon, where a French fleet under Amiral Pierre Charles de Villeneuve was preparing to invade England. Nelson's vigilance forced the French to remain in port for two years. They escaped in 1805 and bolted for the West Indies. Nelson set off in pursuit, but they doubled back to Europe and took refuge in Cadiz. The British blockaded the city, but Villeneuve's Franco-Spanish fleet finally broke out and gave battle off Spain. At the Battle of Trafalgar 16 miles off Cape Trafalgar on 21 October 1805 Nelson led the attack in his flagship HMS VICTORY. His famous signal to the fleet that day was: 'England expects that every man this day will do his duty'. During the course of the battle Nelson fell mortally wounded, shot by a sniper. He was carried below to the cockpit by Sergeant Major Secker RM and lingered for three hours with a musket ball lodged in his spine. Having been informed that the battle had been won, he expired at 1630 in the arms of Captain Hardy. The Battle of Trafalgar was one of the most decisive victories in the history of naval warfare, with 18 of the 33 French and Spanish ships present being captured or sunk and more than 4,400 enemy sailors killed. British losses were 449 men.

## THE OBSEQUIES

Nelson had a presentiment of his own death at Trafalgar, for he remarked to his officers before the battle:

> 'To-morrow I will do that which will give you
> younger gentlemen something to talk about and
> something to think about for the rest of your lives.
> But I shall not live to know about it myself!'

News of his death and victory would be carried to Falmouth by Lieutenant John Lapenotiere RN on the schooner PICKLE and thence to London in 37 hours by post chaise. Nelson's body was preserved in a cask of French brandy and conveyed to England for a state funeral and burial in St Paul's Cathedral, London. His body was conveyed to London in the coffin, which he kept behind his desk on HMS VICTORY. The coffin was presented to him by one of his captains and made from the mainmast of the French warship L'ORIENT which had blown up at the Battle of the Nile on 1 August 1798. Each time Nelson saw the coffin it must have moved him, for he knew the story of ten year-old Giacomo Jocante Casabianca's devotion to duty. Nelson was not buried in the coffin: Robert Southey records that it was 'cut in pieces, which were distributed as relics'. At Gibraltar, his coffin was transferred into a lead-lined casket and steeped in distilled wine. When the pickled remains reached England, they were put in two more coffins before burial. Nelson's tomb rests immediately below the centre of the Cathedral's great dome close by to that of his friend Vice-Admiral Collingwood and those of Admirals Beatty and Jellicoe, finally reconciled in death. Nelson's massive stone sarcophagus was originally the property of Cardinal Wolsey (c1465-1530), King Henry VIII's disgraced Lord Chancellor, who died at Leicester Abbey on 29 November 1530 whilst on his way to the Tower of London to face a charge of treason. The unused tomb was then stored at Windsor Castle. Upon Nelson's death, the tomb was brought out of store, dusted down, the cardinal's biretta on its top was replaced by a viscount's coronet and under the supervision of Benedetto da Rovezzano (also known as Benedetto di Bartolomeo de' Grazini) the tomb was prepared for use at St Paul's. The mosaic floor around both the tombs of Admiral Nelson and the Duke of Wellington was made by the women prisoners of Woking Gaol. Nelson was one of only two men (the other being Churchill) to be honoured by a funeral procession on the River Thames, his body being borne from Greenwich to Whitehall.

At his funeral, the 35 ft by 25 ft White Ensign that had flown from the flagstaff of HMS VICTORY at the Battle of Trafalgar was placed on his coffin. In an unscripted departure from the ceremony, as the coffin was lowered into the crypt and Sir Isaac Heard, Garter King at Arms (1731-1822) read out Nelson's many titles in sonorous tones, the attendant sailors, instead of folding the Ensign reverentially and placing it in the coffin, ripped a large strip out of it, which they further subdivided as mementoes of their commander. In September 2004 two fragments came up for auction at Bonhams in London and fetched £47,800. That same year, during the course of a 'clear out' at the Headquarters of the Sea Cadets in London, a buff envelope marked 'Nelson's Flag' was discovered in a locker. It contained what appeared to be two tea towel-sized fragments of the Ensign. Experts were called in to examine the two fragments and after having compared them against an authentic fragment held by the National Maritime Museum at Greenwich, analysed the thread-count, weave and dye of the newly-discovered portions, pronounced them genuine.

Notable memorials to Nelson were erected at Birmingham (1810) and Great Yarmouth (1817). Nelson's Pillar in Dublin was inaugurated in 1808. The Irish Republican Brotherhood unsuccessfully attempted to blow it up three times during the Easter Uprising in 1916. At 0200 on 8 March 1966 the IRA blew up the top half of the Pillar. The Irish Army completed the job two days later and as an added extra blew out most of Central Dublin's windows. Nelson's Portland stone head may be seen on display in Dublin Civic Museum.

# TRAFALGAR SQUARE

In 1820 Trafalgar Square was laid out by the Regency architect John Nash, as part of his Charing Cross Improvement Scheme. It was constructed it on a slope with a terrace on the north side and is situated at the intersection of St Martin's Lane, The Mall, Pall Mall, Charing Cross Road, Whitehall, Northumberland Avenue and The Strand. It was originally intended that the square be named after King William IV but the name 'Trafalgar Square' was adopted at the suggestion of George Ledwell Taylor. Nash's original layout was remodelled by the celebrated Victorian architect Sir Charles Barry (1795-1860) in 1840. Barry created the northern terrace and installed the flights of stairs on either side leading down into the Square. The original fountains were added by Barry in 1845 and remodelled by Sir Edwin Lutyens in 1939. These were populated by copper mermen, mermaids, dolphins and toothy sharks designed by the famous partnership of Sir Charles Wheeler and William McMillan.

Dominated by Nelson's Column, Trafalgar Square is London's most famous landmark and also its most impressive war memorial. Since the great Chartist Rally of 1848, it has been the venue for occasions of national rejoicing, rallies and political protests. Women's Suffrage, Suez, CND, the Vietnam War, animal rights and the Poll Tax have all featured in demonstrations held there. Courtesy of London's Mayor, the Square experienced its first rock concert on 29 April 2001 with the band REM topping the bill. The Square is also the venue for revellers wishing to 'see in' the New Year in freezing cold conditions in Central London. Each December, an enormous Christmas tree stands in the Square, donated by the Norwegian People in enduring gratitude for the role played by Britain in her struggle and liberation from Nazi occupation during the Second World War. On the west side of the Square stands Canada House by Sir Robert Smirke (1781-1867) with its Corinthian columns (constructed 1824-7). Admiralty Arch (1910) by Sir Aston Webb was constructed as part of the National Memorial to Queen Victoria and it forms the processional entrance to The Mall. To the east stands South Africa House (1935) designed by Sir Herbert Baker with sculpture by Wheeler, and in the north-east corner stands St Martin's in the Fields.

To the north is the National Gallery (1832-8) designed by William Wilkins (1778-1839). Lord Leighton PRA wrote of Wilkins' design: 'The original building has remained unaltered as to its exterior; but on the rear of one of its flanks loom now into view, first an appendage in an entirely different style of architecture, and further on, an excrescence of no style of architecture at all: the one an Italian tower; the other a flat cone of glass surmounted by a ventilator - the whole resulting in a jarring jumble and an aspect of chaotic incongruity, which would be ludicrous if it were not distressing.' In 1986 the Sainsbury Wing designed by Robert Venturi was added to the Gallery, Ahrends, Burton and Koralek, the original winners of the architectural competition having withdrawn, after the Prince of Wales condemned their design as: 'a monstrous carbuncle on the face of a much-loved elegant friend'.

In 1996 following an international competition, a team of consultants headed by Foster and Partners was commissioned to develop the area around the Square. The purpose of the scheme was to produce a detailed plan to improve access and enjoyment of the area, whilst preserving and enhancing the heritage settings of the buildings and monuments. During the debate in the Greater London Assembly on the works, Ken Livingstone, London's Mayor - always keen to demonstrate his ignorance, helpfully suggested that the statues of General Sir Henry Havelock and General Napier and others that he that he did not recognise: 'should be removed to an empire theme park on the outskirts of London'. The development proposals were made available for public consultation in November 1999 and work commenced in April 2001. The traffic flow in the Square was slowed to a snail's pace by the re-phasing of the traffic lights and the north side of the Square was pedestrianised. Whilst the cost of these works at £25 million might seem excessive to the reader, one would certainly need to add to the cost the tearing up the paving in Northumberland Avenue three times during the course of the works.

## THE STATUARY IN THE SQUARE

Barry's plan for the Square included the elevation of a statue on each plinth, three of which are occupied. The north-east plinth is occupied by an equestrian bronze of King George IV sculpted by Sir Francis Chantrey and erected in 1843. Commissioned by King George IV in 1829, it was originally intended for installation on Marble Arch, but Robert Peel argued eloquently for the more public Trafalgar Square site, given that the public had paid 9,000 guineas for it, which was at that time by far and away the largest sum paid for a statue. Its position in Trafalgar Square was meant to be temporary and it is considered by experts to be Chantrey's finest work.

The south-east plinth is occupied by a bronze statue of General Sir Henry Havelock sculpted by William Behnes. Erected in 1861, the statue was specifically designed for the square. The statue was strongly criticised after installation for its lack of vitality.

The south-west plinth is occupied by a bronze statue of General Sir Charles Napier sculpted in 1856 by George Gannon Adams. Napier figured large in events in India, being Commander-in-Chief 1870-76. He was responsible for the annexation of Scind in 1841-3 and as a Parliamentary Radical was sympathetic to the Chartists. He was victor at the Battle of Magdala in Ethiopia in 1868 and plundered the treasury of Emperor Theodore II. He was Governor of Gibraltar (1876-82) and later Field Marshal 1st Baron Napier of Magdala.

It was originally intended that the fourth plinth would be occupied by a statue of King William IV, but this proposal failed due to lack of funds. In 1936 a proposal was made to place a statue of Cecil Rhodes on it, but this proposal was opposed by the Royal Fine Art Commission. In the late 20th century a number of proposals were made to erect statues of Winston Churchill, Earl Kitchener, Earl Mountbatten, Alan Turing and Queen Elizabeth the Queen Mother. Use of the fourth plinth is in the gift of London's Mayor and is used for periodic displays of modern sculpture in accordance with his own taste for vulgarity.

On the north side of the Square, outside the National Gallery stand two statues. George Washington (1921) by Jean Antoine Houdon is a bronze copy of his marble statue in Virginia, USA. There is also a well-travelled life-sized bronze statue of arguably the worst monarch ever to occupy the British throne. King James II (1686) tricked out as a Roman emperor (alluding to Roman virtue) complete with the inscription: "JACOBUS SECUNDUS" is ascribed to the studio of Grinling Gibbons. It was 'temporarily' erected outside the Gallery in 1948. On the front of the east facade of the National Gallery is John Flaxman's statue of Minerva which was originally sculpted for the Marble Arch.

In keeping with the naval theme, on the wall of the terrace at the north side of the square are portrait busts of the famous Great War Admirals Jellicoe and Beatty (1947) also sculpted by Wheeler and McMillan. In 1967 to their number was added, a bust by Franta Belsky of the Second World War Admiral, Lord Cunningham (1st Baron Cunningham of Hyndehope). The Standard Imperial Measures in brass are mounted on the north wall and were placed there by Act of Parliament in 1876. They illustrate the obsolete English measurements of the inch, foot, yard, rod, pole, and perch. In 1943 Sir William Hamo Thornycroft's statue of General Charles Gordon originally situated on the north side of the square was supplanted by a Lancaster Bomber placed there during 'Wings for Victory Week' and General Gordon was rusticated for the duration of the war to Mentmore Towers. The statue was finally resited on Victoria Embankment in 1953 after Queen Elizabeth II's coronation. The site allocated having been previously occupied by a massive grandstand erected for spectators of the coronation procession. The well-travelled bronze statue of General Charles Gordon on a camel sculpted by Onslow Ford was erected in 1902 on the location now occupied by the patriot Edith Cavell. Gordon's statue was subsequently sent to Khartoum in the Sudan and in 1957 was removed to Gordon's School, Woking, Surrey. The statue of the physician Edward Jenner by William Calder Marshall (1818-1878) was briefly situated in the Square from 1858 to 1862, it then being resited to Kensington Gardens.

# NELSON'S COLUMN

In the apocryphal story, a schoolboy was asked: 'What is Britain's highest award for valour?' His unexpected reply was: 'Nelson's Column' and he certainly had a point. The column was designed by the architect William Railton and erected in 1839-42. Its Devon granite Corinthian column stands 170 feet 2 inches high. The design of the column is believed to be based on that of Trajan in Rome. The bronze capital was cast from the cannon of the ROYAL GEORGE which sank at Spithead in 1782 when heeled over for examination of her underwater timbers. Admiral Richard Kempenfelt and 800 crew were drowned. The 17 foot tall statue of Nelson on top was sculpted by Edward Hodges Baily. (The original model of his sculpture stands in the foyer of the Office of the Deputy Prime Minister, barely a stone's throw away in Whitehall). The cost of the column quickly outstripped the original estimates which the organising committee refused to pay, the contractors went on strike and blacklegs were brought in to finish the job. After completion of the column, it is recorded that 14 members of the organising committee held a dinner party at the summit. The four reliefs on the base depict Nelson's victories and were executed by I E Carew (Trafalgar 1805), J Ternouth (Copenhagen 1801), M L Watson (St Vincent 1797) and W F Woodington (Nile 1798). Carew's relief faces south into Whitehall and in the far left of it, he has clearly depicted a Black sharpshooter on the deck of HMS VICTORY at the Battle of Trafalgar, as the mortally wounded Nelson is carried off the deck.

After a series of false starts, embarrassing delays and a great deal of mocking in the press, Nelson's Column was belatedly guarded by four bronze lions designed by Sir Edwin Landseer (1802-73). They were cast by his founder Baron Carlo Marochetti from both British and French cannon. 'The lions were put in place without ceremony in February 1867. It was nearly thirty years after the first meeting of the Nelson Memorial Committee, most of the members of which were now dead. Railton was sixty-eight and living in Brighton, and did not even bother to attend'.[6] They cost a total of £17,183 rather than Railton's original estimate of £3,000 - such disparities being something of a recurrent theme in Marochetti's affairs. Despite the well-known antipathy of London's Mayor to the military figures commemorated in the Square, on 1 December 2003 - World Aids Day, he utilised the Column's 'phallic' properties after nightfall as a backdrop on which to project 'safe sex' messages.

---
[6] Rodney Mace *Trafalgar Square: Emblem of Empire* London 1976, Lawrence and Wishart.

# HMS VICTORY

HMS VICTORY is the oldest commissioned warship in the world and is manned by officers and ratings of the Royal Navy. The flagship of the Second Sea Lord and Commander-in-Chief Naval Home Command, she lies in No 2 Dry Dock at Her Majesty's Naval Base, Portsmouth. Designed by Thomas Slade, Senior Surveyor of the Royal Navy, her keel was laid down in Chatham on 23 July 1759 and she was launched on 7 May 1765, but not commissioned until 1778. This long period of weathering meant that her hull timbers were well seasoned, which is probably the main reason why she has survived so long. She cost £63,176. Once commissioned, she became the most successful First Rate ship ever built. Her excellent sailing qualities made her a popular choice for use by several admirals as their flagship. Admirals Keppel, Kempenfelt, Howe and Jervis all used her prior to Nelson, who used her when he was appointed Commander-in-Chief, Mediterranean Fleet. A total of 26 miles (41.9 km) of cordage was used to rig the ship. 768 blocks, made from elm or ash, were used for the rigging and a further 628 for the guns. Many other blocks were carried for the ground tackle, the ship's boats, storing and spares. 216 deadeyes were also used on the standing rigging. VICTORY could spread a maximum of 37 sails and her total sail area was 6,510 square yards. (Only her original fore topsail survives and despite being mislaid twice over the years, having 90 bullet holes in it and a rent in the middle went on display in 2005). She was one of the fastest first rate ships of the line at her time and had excellent handling abilities. In good wind conditions she could reach a top speed of 11 miles per hour. 6,000 oaks were consumed in her construction. In March 1780 her hull was sheathed with 3,923 sheets of copper to protect against shipworm (Teredo Navalis). Each copper sheathing plate measured 4 ft x 14 ins (1.22 m x 35.6 cm). Her armament consisted of: Lower gun deck 30 x 32 pounder, Middle gun deck 28 x 24 pounder, Upper gun deck 30 x 12 pounder (long), Quarter gun deck 12 x 12 pounder (short), Forecastle 2 x 12 pounder (medium), 2 x 68 pounder carronade. HMS VICTORY played a major role as the Flagship of Admiral Lord Nelson at the Battle of Trafalgar on 21 October 1805. The two fleets joined battle off Cape Trafalgar, Spain. 'A deathly silence fell upon the fleet as the ships drew nearer. Each captain marked down his adversary, and within a few minutes the two English columns thundered into action. The roar of the broadsides, the crashing of masts, the rattle of musketry at point-blank rent the air. VICTORY smashed through between Villeneuve's flagship BUCENTAURE, and the REDOUTABLE, the three ships remained locked together, raking each other with broadsides.'[7] At 1.15 p.m. Nelson fell mortally wounded, shot by a sniper high in the rigging on the French ship REDOUTABLE whilst pacing the quarterdeck. 'Partial firing continued until 4.30, when a victory having been reported to the Right Hon. Lord Viscount Nelson, K.B. and Commander-in-Chief, he then died of his wound'.[8] This victory would establish Britain as the greatest maritime power in the world, a position she would occupy until overtaken by the Americans during the Second World War. HMS VICTORY continued her career after Trafalgar and was involved in two Baltic campaigns under Admiral Saumarez. Her active career ended on 7 November 1812, she was then moored in Portsmouth Harbour for 110 years fulfilling a number of roles.

By 1921 she was in a poor state of repair and it was at that point the Government, supported by the Society for Nautical Research agreed that she should be saved and become a lasting reminder to the nation of Nelson, the Battle of Trafalgar, and the Royal Navy's supremacy in the days of sail - and she is therefore also a form of memorialisation. She was moved to her present dock on 12 January 1922 and since then has been undergoing restoration by the Royal Navy with assistance from the Society for Nautical Research, to return the ship to her Trafalgar design and condition. As well as her naval role, HMS VICTORY is also a major heritage attraction and she attracts over 350,000 visitors each year. Website at www.hms-victory.com

---

[7] Winston S Churchill *A History of the English-Speaking Peoples* Vol 3.
[8] Ship's Log HMS VICTORY.

# THE ADMIRALTY CHURCH - ST MARTIN'S IN THE FIELDS

A church has stood on the present site, on a corner of what is now Trafalgar Square since the Middle Ages. The current is the fourth to stand there. It was designed by James Gibbs (1682-1754) and completed in 1726. It was named for St Martin and there are a number of representations in it of him dividing his cloak to give half to a beggar and his example is the enduring inspiration for the church's work amongst London's homeless community.

The earliest record of an intimate connection between the Admiralty and St Martin's in the Fields can be dated from the operation of the provisions of the Test Act of 1672. Under this Act, all government officials were required to take communion 'after Divine Service and Sermon' to demonstrate proof of adherence to the established Anglican Church. Those employed by the Admiralty would have carried out this duty at St Martin's, which was their parish church. In 1689 both the communion plate and the alabaster font were presented to St Martin's by William Bridgeman, Joint Secretary of the Admiralty.

The church's bells have traditionally been rung to mark naval victories. It had for this purpose the first dual and triple ring of 12 bells in the world. These were installed in 1727 replacing an earlier ring of eight. These were replaced in 1988, with the originals being presented to the City of Perth, Australia to mark the Australian Bicentennial.

On 30 May 1726, the Board of Admiralty passed the following minute: 'The Navy Board are to be directed to cause a Standard to be supplied out of His Majesty's Stores to St Martin's Church, to which Parish are the Royal Palaces of Whitehall and St. James's.' The Royal Navy has been providing flags at intervals to the church since that date. In 1772 the church requested a replacement: '26 May 1772. We the Churchwardens of the Parish of St Martins (sic) in the Fields beg to inform you that flag used and hoisted from Parish Church upon King's Birthday and on all other publick occasions being quite worn out and rendered unfit for further service, and it being the constant custom of Their Lords of the Admiralty to provide the Parish with such flag being the King's Parish. We therefore take the liberty to request the favour that Their Lordships will be pleased to order a new flag for the above purpose of such dimensions as shall be judged fit and necessary in granting of which they will much oblige the Parish and in particular Senders. Your most obedient and humble servants, etc..'[9] Since 1790 the flag supplied has been the White Ensign. In 1866 the Admiralty supplied a new 40 foot flagstaff for the church and 1867 the Lords of the Admiralty subscribed to the large stained glass window depicting the Ascension of Christ. The Board of Admiralty were granted the distinction of their own pew in the church which still exists. A number of naval flags hang inside the church. The White Ensign can be observed flying over St Martin's on Trafalgar Day and on other special occasions and is the most obvious outward sign of the church's enduring connection with the Royal Navy. Over the years, many special services have been held there with a particular naval theme. Traditionally a Trafalgar Day Service was held each year until the outbreak of the Great War in 1914.

There are a number of war memorials in the church, most notably the Sharpshooters Memorial to those members of the County of London Imperial Yeomanry who fell in the Boer War (1899-1902), The Far East Prisoners of War Memorial (Second World War) and also a memorial to HMS FITTLETON, a Ton Class Minesweeper which sank whilst on a NATO exercise in 1976. The crypt of the church houses the Old Contemptibles Chapel.

The link with the Admiralty was somewhat diminished with the formation of the Ministry of Defence (MOD) on 1 April 1964; this new tri-Service organisation incorporated the work of the Admiralty, War Office, and Air Ministry. The Admiralty then became the Admiralty Board of the Defence Council. However, the Navy remained in residence at the Old Admiralty until 1996, when MOD removed its rapidly diminishing naval staff to Portsmouth and handed the building over to the burgeoning Cabinet Office and the ever-expanding Foreign and Commonwealth Office.

---

[9] PRO File ADM 1/5117/16.

## THE ROYAL MARINES MEMORIAL

'On 28 October 1664, during the early months of the Second Dutch War, a new regiment was formed on the Artillery Ground by Bunhill Fields in the City of London. Drawn mostly from the Trained bands of the City Militia and designated the Duke of York and Albany's Regiment of Foot, but also known as the Admiral's Regiment, it was armed with flintlocks and had a parade strength of 1200 land sodjers raysed to be in rediness to be distributed in his Mat's Fleet prepared for sea service.'[10] So commenced the illustrious history of that corps of sea-borne soldiers which would in 1802 be redesignated the Royal Marines.

The Royal Marines Memorial stands at the Admiralty Arch end of The Mall in London, immediately opposite Sir Thomas Brock's statue of Captain James Cook. It was erected in 1903 to commemorate the Royal Marine casualties sustained in defending the foreign legations during the Boxer Rebellion in China (1900) and the South African War. It was designed by Sir Thomas Graham Jackson, (notable designer of a number of Oxford colleges) with the sculpture being executed by Captain Adrian Jones. In bronze, it depicts a figure of an heroic Marine with fixed bayonet defending a fallen comrade. The names of the fallen are carried on the reverse and on the front is the Corps badge and the motto "PER MARE PER TERRAM"[11] On 25 October 2000 the refurbished memorial was rededicated by the Chaplain to the Fleet in the presence of Prince Philip, Duke of Edinburgh (Captain General of the Royal Marines). The Grade II listed Memorial is the scene of the annual Graspan Parade held on the second Sunday in May. This ceremony commemorates a desperate action in the Boer War at Graspan Hill on 24 November 1899. The Royal Marine Artillery and Royal Marine Light Infantry, supported by seamen of the Naval Brigade, sustained 88 casualties out of a total of 206 men in taking the kopje. The central feature of the parade is an Act of Remembrance. Wreaths are then laid by the President of the City of London Branch of the Royal Marines Association and by an officer representing the Commandant of the United States Marine Corps. Website at www.cityroyal.co.uk

---

[10] Robin Neillands *By Sea and Land.*
[11] In English: 'By sea and by land'.

# CAPTAIN JAMES COOK

James Cook was born on 27 October 1728 at Marton, south of Middlesborough, the son of an agricultural labourer. He left agriculture at 17 to work in a grocers shop, but found the call of the sea too strong. He left the shop and learned his seamanship on colliers working the London - Newcastle route. He joined the Royal Navy as a seaman in 1755 and worked his way up through the ranks. His outstanding abilities as a navigator and cartographer were early recognised by his ship's captain, Hugh Palliser. Cook laid the basis of his formidable reputation during the Seven Years War, by nightly charting the St Lawrence River under the guns of the French during the campaign to remove them from Canada in 1758-59, a task that was accomplished without the Royal Navy losing any of the 200 ships involved. He was commissioned First Lieutenant in 1768. He would lead three expeditions that established him as the father of modern marine survey. Whilst on the third expedition, he was clubbed to death by natives on the beach at Kealakakua Bay, Hawaii on 14 February 1779. Parts of his body were handed over by a native priest six days later and these were committed to The Deep by his friends to the accompaniment of minute guns firing. The botanist Joseph Banks, who had accompanied Cook on the first expedition called him: 'The greatest man I ever knew'. It is recorded that King George III wept upon being informed of his death. 'At his own expense Sir Hugh Palliser erected a handsome and moving memorial to Cook on his estate at Vache Park, Chalfont St Giles, Buckinghamshire. Since then statues, memorials and obelisks have proliferated where Cook had been - from the bleak coast of Newfoundland to Point Venus, Tahiti; from the Yorkshire Moors to Queen Charlotte's Sound, New Zealand. At a rough count there are known today about two hundred. Oddly enough perhaps the best-known is also one of the most recent - the bronze statue by Sir T Brock, RA, which was erected in 1914 in The Mall[12], Admiralty Arch and within sight of the statue of that other famous seaman, Horatio Nelson'.[13] Cook also has a statue on Hawaii, under the terms of its gift from the Queen of Hawaii, responsibility for its maintenance is vested in the British Defence Staff at the Washington Embassy, USA. Cook's portrait by John Webber (artist on Cook's third expedition) hangs in the National Art Gallery, Wellington, New Zealand.

---

[12] Inaugurated on 7 July 1914 by Prince Arthur of Connaught on behalf of the Empire League.
[13] Rex and Thea Rienits *The Voyages of Captain Cook* Paul Hamlyn 1968.

# THE ADMIRALTY CIVILIANS MEMORIAL

On 27 October 1919 in reply to a groundswell of staff opinion expressed through the Admiralty Staff Committees, the Director of Contracts at the Admiralty wrote a paper setting out a proposal to commemorate in some way the 110 permanent civilian members of the Admiralty who had been killed in the Great War. A small committee was convened. It canvassed the different departments for a suitable form of commemoration. Personnel Branch were instructed to correspond with the War Office and compile a list of the fallen. This committee determined that contributions were to be limited to a maximum of one guinea. Sheets were drawn up for each department detailing the contribution given by each member of staff. Mr W A Hartnett was appointed by the Admiralty Whitley Council to administer the fund. A total of £351 and 9 shillings was collected. The form of commemoration chosen by the majority of committees was a tablet. Sir Vincent Baddeley, First Principal Assistant Secretary of the Admiralty wrote to Sir Lionel Earle at the Office of Works seeking agreement to proceed. Permission having been granted, Mr J G West of the Office of Works furnished detailed technical advice on 19 December 1919. The tender submitted by the monumental masons W Aumonier & Son of Fitzroy Square, London was accepted at a price of £264. After surveyors' fees, the surplus of £63 8 shillings and 11d was donated to the Civil Service Benevolent Association (Orphans Fund). A survey of staff via their local committees had determined that this was deemed to be of most benefit to civil servants. In due course, a large light brown stone tablet with carved flags and anchors either side was erected and inscribed with the names of the fallen. It was situated over the mantelpiece of the entrance hall of the Admiralty Building (Ripley Block) in Whitehall. 'The site selected as being the best as regards its position and as being capable of treatment on lines which will harmonise with the artistic merits of the Old Hall'.

The date for the inauguration was fixed. Unfortunately First Sea Lord was called away at short notice to a Cabinet meeting and it was postponed. The ceremony was eventually held on 26 February 1920. Given the restrictions on space and security considerations, the only guests at the inauguration would be the subscribers. Despite the care with which the names of those to be commemorated had been collected, on 3 March it came to light that a name had been missed off. Assistant Constructor A K Stephens had been killed at the Battle of Jutland on board HMS QUEEN MARY on 31 May 1916. Although in uniform, he was still technically a civilian employed by the Admiralty. The following week, Admiralty Salary Branch was instructed to obtain the addresses of all next of kin and to write, informing them that they were welcome to call and inspect the memorial tablet and to bring the invitation with them. The Office Keeper was then instructed that the letter of invitation was to be accepted as a pass for admission to the Admiralty. The list of names and home addresses on the file in the National Archive at Kew bears a pencilled comment next to the name C H Smith: 'This man (formerly a Boy Messenger) was reported by the Army authorities as having died on 24/10/16. It is now understood however, that he is alive and has been seen by Messenger Goodhew of the Naval Stores Dept'. On 10 March 1921 Corporal Smith called at the Admiralty and a subsequent note on the file archly records: 'He has satisfied the Office Keeper that he is still alive'. Baddeley's minute of 11 March notes with considerable understatement: 'The resurrection of Corporal Smith affords a happy way out of the little difficulty which had arisen'. Without altering the alphabetical sequence, the change was effected by letting in a new slip of stone with the name of Assistant Constructor Stephens already carved on it. The memorial is still present in its original site over the fireplace in the foyer of Ripley Block,[14] but times have moved on and so has the Royal Navy. Ripley Block was refurbished in 2001-03 and the grade I listed building then became the Office of the Deputy Prime Minister. The foyer also contains the original maquette of the statue on the top of Nelson's Column executed by Edward Hodges Baily in 1844.

---

[14] Built by the architect Thomas Ripley 1723-6.

# THE ADMIRALTY CIVILIANS MEMORIAL

The Admiralty Civilians Memorial in the foyer of the Office of the Deputy Prime Minister.

## THE MERCHANT NAVY MEMORIAL ON TOWER HILL

12,674 sailors lost in the Great War from the Merchant Navy were commemorated by a memorial on the south side of the garden of Trinity Square on Tower Hill. It was built of Portland stone and was designed for the Imperial War Graves Commission by Sir Edwin Lutyens. The inauguration was carried out by Queen Mary on 12 December 1928 in place of her husband King George V who was seriously ill at that time.

Major General Sir Fabian Ware wrote: 'On the historic site of Tower Hill, London a memorial has been erected to the officers and men of the Merchant Navy and Fishing Fleets who lost their lives through enemy action and whose graves are not known. In this service - responsible for carrying by sea the necessities of warfare and those of civil life, for supplying and recruiting the Royal Navy, and for the mine-sweeping which alone made their other tasks practicable - twelve thousand officers and men sank without a trace, and 3,300 vessels were destroyed by raiding cruiser or by submarine'.[15] Britain declared war on Nazi Germany on 3 September 1939. That date also marks the start of the Battle of the Atlantic, the longest campaign of the Second World War. On that day SS ATHENIA, a liner en-route from Liverpool to Montreal was sunk by the U-boat U-30 some 200 miles west of the Hebrides, with the loss of 19 crew and 93 passengers. 28 were American. Britain being an island, required immense quantities of foodstuffs and materials to prosecute the war and the Convoy System was again instituted. More than 51,000 Royal Navy sailors and 30,000 Merchant Navy seamen lost their lives on the convoys bringing food, equipment and supplies from North America and ferrying aid to Russia on the Arctic Convoys. More than 20,000 Royal Navy and Merchant Navy personnel participated in almost 80 convoys to the Soviet Union between 1941 and 1945. Some 3,000 men perished in the Barents Sea after their ships were torpedoed. Survival in the freezing waters was measured in minutes. Arctic Convoy memorials may be found in the crypt of St Paul's Cathedral in London and at the Chapel of the Royal Naval College, Greenwich. National Merchant Navy Day falls each 3 September and the memorial is the site of the annual Merchant Navy Day Memorial Service on that date.

The nearest church is All Hallows by the Tower which traditionally has strong links with the Merchant Navy. In a rededication ceremony held on 15 July 1949 and attended by Queen Mary, it was the first bombed City of London church to be reopened after the war. The British Maritime Foundation's Memorial Book containing the names of all those lost at sea in time of war was dedicated in a ceremony at All Hallows on 25 March 1987.

---

[15] Fabian Ware *The Immortal Heritage*.

## THE UNVEILING OF THE MEMORIAL BY THE QUEEN

On 1 March 1955 *The Times* reported 'The Queen is to unveil the Merchant Navy Memorial on Tower Hill on November 5 this year, and the dedication will be by the Archbishop of Canterbury, The next-of-kin of those commemorated on the memorial will receive invitations to the ceremony which are being posted on March 21. The memorial, being built by the Imperial War Graves Commission to the design of Sir Edward Maufe, RA, honours 24,000 officers and men of the Merchant Navy and Fishing Fleets, and is an extension of the 1914-18 memorial in the form of a garden on the walls of which will be fixed bronze panels bearing the names. Two sculptured figures of sailors stand at the garden entrances and between the bronze panels are sculptures of the Seven Seas.' 'In the garden on the Tower Hill in which already stands a memorial to 12,000 merchant seamen who died in the First World War the Queen on Saturday unveiled a new memorial to nearly 24,000 men of the Merchant Navy, the fishing fleets, and the lighthouse and pilotage services who lost their lives between 1939 and 1945 and whose only grave is the sea. Around the two memorials, now an impressive whole, were gathered some 16,000 relatives of those commemorated. They had come from all parts of Britain and some from the Commonwealth. They carried wreaths and flowers which later - until after dusk had fallen and the memorial had been floodlit - they were to place on the sunken lawn near the names inscribed in relief on bronze commemorative panels. The memorial was lit with sunshine when the Queen unveiled it. *Last Post* was sounded by buglers of the Royal Marines, and the memorial was then dedicated by the Archbishop of Canterbury, Dr Fisher. After *Reveille* the Moderator of the General Assembly of the Church of Scotland, the Rt Rev G D Henderson, gave thanks "for these our brothers whose names are graven on this stone, and who in the day of peril gave their lives for our safety and defence." With the Queen were the Duke of Edinburgh, in the uniform of Admiral of the Fleet; the Duke of Gloucester, President of the Imperial War Graves Commission, in the uniform of Master of the Elder Brethren of the Corporation of Trinity House; and Mr Head, Chairman of the Imperial War Graves Commission and Secretary of State for War. Among the guests were representatives of the Governments of the United Kingdom and the Commonwealth, including Sir Anthony Eden, senior officers of the three Services, and many representatives of shipping companies and organisations. Speaking before the unveiling the Queen praised the men whose names were commemorated. 'They were members,' she said, 'of a splendid company of brave men and women, from many nations and all countries of the Commonwealth, who served in fellowship under the Red Ensign, and who maintained the great traditions of their service wherever the war was waged at sea.... To sustain the life of a nation at war they endured the dangers of their great calling, and in that cause they laid down their lives. The true memorial of these men was to be found in the lives of those who now, and in the years to come, would hold fast to those ideals for which they died. It rests with us, and with those who will come after us, to give to their heroism that enduring memorial which shall far outlast this garden and these stones.' 'The Queen, the Duke of Edinburgh, and the Duke of Gloucester later laid wreaths, followed by Ministers of State and the High Commissioners of countries of the Commonwealth. After inspecting the memorial the Queen walked among the relatives. The memorial was designed by Sir Edward Maufe, RA and has been built by the Imperial War Graves Commission. It extends the existing memorial and takes the form of a sunken garden. The bronze-faced surrounding wall records a total of 23,765 names, shown alphabetically under the ships in which the men served. The commemorative panels are relieved by seven stone allegorical figures, representing the Seven Seas. The approach to the garden from the 1914-18 memorial is flanked by pylons on which the Merchant Navy badges and wreaths are carved in relief; the main dedicatory inscription between these pylons is guarded by the sculptured figures of an officer and a seaman of the Merchant Navy.'[16]

---

[16] *The Times* 7 November 1955.

# HMY IOLAIRE

The story of the erection of the memorial at Stornoway to the Lewismen who fell in the Great War appears elsewhere in the study, but sadly that's not the full story. On New Year's Eve 1918, 250 sailors coming home to Lewis were at the Kyle of Lochalsh awaiting passage across The Minch. They were boarded onto HMY IOLAIRE and she set sail at 2000. In the early hours of 1 January, as she neared the light on Arnish Point which marks the entrance to Stornoway Harbour, she encountered rocks in high seas. The impact of an almighty crash hurled 50 sailors into the sea. It was impossible in the pitch dark to see land and these men were dashed to death against the rocks barely 20 feet from safe harbour. IOLAIRE listed heavily at an angle of 40 degrees and took three quarters of an hour to sink. News spread through the island like wildfire and by the time townsfolk arrived at Holm, the ship was lying between the Beasts of Holm and the shore with only her mast showing. 'On the grass were laid out the bodies that had been recovered from the sea, and below the crews of eight row-boats proceeded in silence with their work of dragging round the wreck. At very short intervals the grappling irons brought another and another of the bodies to the surface, and the crew proceeded with them to the ledge where they were being landed. Here they were placed on stretchers and slowly and laboriously the bearers clambered up with them to be laid out reverently on the grasslands above. Scarce a word was spoken, and the eyes of strong men filled with tears as the wan faces were scrutinised with hope and fear of identification'.[17] The Admiralty held its own board of enquiry in January and a public enquiry was held by Stornoway Council in February. In his evidence to the public enquiry, Lieutenant Commander Morris RN stated that HMY IOLAIRE had 284 men on board, of whom 79 survived. 138 bodies were recovered and 67 were missing. All her officers were lost. The public enquiry concluded that in the darkness she had overrun her course by a few minutes, and it was this that had made the difference between shipwreck and safety. Those who lost their lives that night are commemorated by a cairn at Holm.

In 1970 divers diving for clams recovered the IOLAIRE's bell and nameplate and these were handed over to Stornoway Town Council.

Rudyard Kipling would write:

> There dwells a wife by the Northern Gate
> And a careworn wife is she;
> She breeds a breed o' rovin men
> And casts them over the sea.
>
> And some are drowned in deep water
> And some in sight o' shore,
> And word goes back to the weary wife,
> And ever she sends more.
>
> And some return by failing light.
> And some in waking dream,
> For she hears the heels of the dripping ghosts
> That ride the rough roof-beam.
>
> Home they come from all the ports,
> The living and the dead;
> The good wife's sons come home again
> For her blessing on their head!

---

[17] *Sea Sorrow: The Story of the Iolaire Disaster* published by the *Stornoway Gazette* 1972.

## THE THREE NAVAL MEMORIALS

After the Great War the Royal Navy posed unique difficulties when it came to the erection and siting of memorials. It could not erect them at the scene of its exploits, neither would it make any sense to erect them in the nearest land-based location, such as Jutland in Denmark or the Falkland Islands. Added to which, unlike the army, the navy did not consist of well-defined permanent units, the only exceptions to this rule being the Submarine Service and the Royal Naval Division, both of which eventually erected their own memorials. (The Royal Marines Memorial by Adrian Jones already stood in The Mall in London).

On 2 June 1919 the Imperial War Graves Commission wrote to the Admiralty, setting out the pressing need to raise memorials to commemorate those naval personnel who had lost their lives in the war.[18] This initiated a body of correspondence within various departments of the Admiralty, a study of which, indicates that the exam question had not been clearly understood. Eastwood, Assistant Secretary to the Naval Law Branch wrote to the Commission on 31 March. This letter indicates that he may have confused the issue in his mind with the Committee on Battlefield Memorials to which the Admiralty appointed Rear Admiral Bentinck the next day. The Commission replied and spelled out in some detail the terms of their Royal Charter and what they expected of the Royal Navy.[19] Consequently, in September 1920, the Admiralty appointed a Naval Memorials Committee chaired by Captain Loring, RN to advise the Commission on the most suitable form of monument to commemorate the 25,567 officers and ratings of the Royal Navy who had lost their lives at sea in the war. It was decided that there would be three identical monuments designed by the Commission's architect for the UK the celebrated Scottish architect Sir Robert Lorimer. The Committee examined a number of different proposals of types of commemoration and examined three sites at Portsmouth, Plymouth and Chatham, which were the three principal manning stations of the Royal Navy. The Committee's report was signed, sealed and delivered on 9 November 1920. Having been considered and endorsed by the Navy Board, it was communicated to the Commission on 27 January 1920. Lord Arthur Browne wrote to the Admiralty on 28 February 1921, stating that the report had been laid before the last meeting of the Commission, had been approved and instructions were being issued to Sir Robert. Henry Poole was appointed sculptor.

Lists of the missing were requested. 'It is understood that these memorials will contain the names of all officers and men of the Royal Navy who lost their lives at sea during the war in every part of the world, and that the lists to be supplied will not include the names of any who have known graves'. The Admiralty already had this task in hand, as they were required by the Registrar General to produce a full list of all those who had died in the War.

In March 1921 Sir Fabian Ware wrote to the Secretary of the Admiralty: 'Sir Robert Lorimer came to see me yesterday morning. He has visited the sites and made a sketch design of the three memorials to the officers and men of the Royal Navy who were lost at sea, in accordance with the recommendation of your committee'. He went on: 'An architect of this calibre must of course be given a very free hand in his designs.... it occurs to me that the simplest and quickest way of setting to work would be to appoint a small committee here consisting of Sir Frederic Kenyon, and Sir Robert Lorimer, to whom you should add some representative of the Admiralty'.[20] Captain Washington, RN was duly appointed to undertake this duty by the Admiralty on 5 April. A meeting chaired by the Chancellor of the Exchequer was held at the Treasury on 22 July 1921. At this meeting 'it was decided accordingly that all general War Memorials abroad and general Naval Memorials in this country should be erected by and under the responsibility of the War Graves Commission'.[21]

---

[18] Talbot, Principal Assistant Secretary IWGC to the Admiralty 2 June 1919.
[19] Lord Arthur Browne, Principal Assistant Secretary IWGC, to the Secretary of the Admiralty 23 June 1920.
[20] Major General Sir Fabian Ware to H Eastwood Esq 22 March 1921, PRO File Adm116, Case 1160.
[21] Naval War Memorial, PRO File Adm116, Case 1160.

In August the Commission wrote to the Admiralty informing them that 'the Government of Newfoundland has expressed the wish to commemorate the missing of Newfoundland Royal Naval Reserve at a Dominion port' and this requirement was duly incorporated.[22]

On 7 Sept 1921 Colonel Durham of the Commission wrote to Captain Washington: 'The question of the inscription has been laid before Mr Kipling, who always advises the Commission on the correctness of the text.... With regard to the progress of the work, Sir Robert Lorimer is now detailing the drawings, and we are having trial holes made on the various sites in order to find out about the foundations'. After correspondence between the IWGC and the Fourth Sea Lord, the inscription was arrived at for all three memorials:

> "IN HONOUR OF THE NAVY AND TO THE ABIDING MEMORY OF THOSE RANKS AND RATINGS OF THIS PORT WHO LAID DOWN THEIR LIVES IN THE DEFENCE OF THE EMPIRE AND HAVE NO OTHER GRAVE THAN THE SEA"

In December Captain Littlejohns RAN of the Australian High Commission in London wrote to the Admiralty informing them: 'the Department of the Navy desires that Ranks and Ratings who lost their lives during the Great War may be commemorated on one of these memorials, and it is understood verbally that this would meet with Their Lordships' approval, and in view of the fact that Devonport was the base to which H.M. Australian Fleet was attached whilst with the Grand Fleet &c., it is understood that there would be no objection to the inclusion of their names on the Memorial to be erected at that Port'.[23] This request was communicated by the Admiralty to the Commission on 27 January 1922, with the recommendation that the missing of New Zealand and Canada also be included and these were also incorporated. Each of the monuments took the form of a stone obelisk, which serves as a leading mark for shipping. The tower being supported by four corner buttresses, each with a lion couchant. Towards the top the tower branches out in the form of four ships' prows. Above these are representations of the four winds, which in turn support a large copper sphere symbolising the globe. The sculpture was undertaken by Poole in the period 1923-24.

The bronze statuary on the Plymouth Memorial undergoing refurbishment in 1993.

---

[22] Director of Works IWGC to the Admiralty 2 August 1921, PRO file Adm116, Case 1160.
[23] Captain AS Littlejohns RAN, Commonwealth of Australia to the Secretary of the Admiralty 20 December 1921, PRO file Adm116, Case 1160.

# THE MEMORIALS

'Owing to the situation of the Port of Chatham - differing as it does from that of Portsmouth and Plymouth, in that it is up a river - it has been found impracticable to select a suitable site for a memorial which fulfils the double requirement of being in a frequented public place, and of being of use for a Leading-mark, or other Navigational purpose'.[24] Eventually a suitable site was found and the memorial at Great Lines, Chatham was in fact the first memorial completed. The land on which it stands was donated by the War Department. The bronze panels were inscribed with 8,541 names. The Prince of Wales inaugurated it in April 1924. Website at www.stephen-stratford.co.uk/chatham.htm

The memorial on Southsea Common at Portsmouth (pictured above with US Navy warship) was inscribed with the names of 9,666 sailors. Its position provided a leading mark for the Swashway when in line with St Jude's Church spire, and a leading mark for ships rounding the Spit Refuge Buoy when in line with the Clock Tower on the Clarence Barracks.[25] It was the last of the three to be inaugurated. The Duke of York carried out this duty on 15 October 1924. The Portland stone figures at the base of the Portsmouth memorial were renewed in 2002. They were exact replicas of the originals and were carved by Rob Humphreys of Cambridge's Fairhaven Stonemasons at a cost of £70,000. Website at www.memorials.inportsmouth.co.uk/southsea/naval.htm

The Plymouth memorial stands on the north side of the Hoe between the Drake Statue and the Armada Memorial, the site at which legend tells us, Sir Francis Drake played bowls whilst he awaited the appearance of the Spanish Armada in 1588. Initially it had 7,256 names inscribed on its bronze panels. The memorial was given extra height and included South African and Australian names. Prince George inaugurated it on 29 July 1924. As can be seen in the photograph on the opposite page, the globe has a distinct dent on its seaward side, the result of being thumped by the trailing cable of a runaway barrage balloon during the Second World War. Website at www.webrarian.co.uk/rnwm/

The names of soldiers lost at sea were inscribed on memorials in cemeteries closest to their point of embarkation. The most notable of these was the Hollybrook Memorial at Southampton, which commemorates 1,857 soldiers, including Field Marshal, Earl Kitchener who perished when HMS HAMPSHIRE struck a mine off Scapa Flow on 5 June 1916. His name may be found alongside that of Private Paraffin, (indeed that was his name, for he had no other) of the South African Native Labour Corps. A third of the names on the memorial relate to men who drowned in the sinking of the SS MENDI in the English Channel on 21 February 1917. Website at www.navy.mil.za/newnavy/mendi_history/mendi_hist.htm

---

[24] Report of the Naval Memorials Committee dated 9 November 1920. PRO file ADM116, Case 1160.
[25] Commander-in-Chief Portsmouth Yard 31 December 1922. PRO file Adm116, Case 1160.

## THE MEMORIAL THAT NEVER WAS

The foregoing story had an interesting postscript. In 1921 the Admiralty convened a committee to consider the erection of a general Naval War Memorial in London. This committee comprised representatives from each of the departments of the Admiralty including the Royal Marines. 'The First Meeting of this committee took place in the First Lord's room on Tuesday 24 May 1921 at 3.30pm, with the First Lord in the chair and all the members present. The First Lord explained that the Cabinet had allocated £40,000 to the Admiralty to be expended on the erection of a permanent War Memorial, to commemorate the part played by the Royal Navy and the Mercantile Marine in the war 1914-1918'.[26] The committee spent much of its energy in its first two meetings pursuing the notion of a memorial in Trafalgar Square, but were frustrated in their choice of site by both General Gordon's statue,[27] and the new First Commissioner of Works, the Earl of Crawford and Balcarres.[28] The minutes of their second meeting on 31 May 1921 noted: 'The committee then visited Trafalgar Square. The general opinion was that the ideal site in the Square for a Naval Memorial would be that occupied by General Gordon's statue, but that a site against the North parapet of the Square immediately behind the Gordon statue on a line drawn from the centre of the Nelson Column through the Gordon statue towards the centre of the façade of the National Gallery, was practicable and had much to recommend it. The First Lord repeated to the committee his view that they were inclined to under-estimate the indignation which was invariably aroused by any proposal to move an existing statue from a desirable site, adding that the partisans of General Gordon might be expected to prove formidable'.[29] They spent the rest of 1921 looking at and discussing a site opposite Temple Gardens on Victoria Embankment. The First Lord approached the King to see if he would agree to the removal of the Duke of York's statue in The Mall and in due course received a less than enthusiastic response from His Majesty. On 1 June 1922 Eastwood wrote to the First Lord to notify him of an 'awkward situation' that had arisen. He had discovered that the Royal Navy Submarine Service, 'the Silent Service' had approached one of the Royal Princes to unveil their memorial on the very site the Admiralty believed belonged to them. It soon became apparent that the site had indeed been acquired by the submariners, who had successfully concluded negotiations with London County Council, the owners of the land without breathing a word of their plans to the Admiralty. Permission to erect their memorial had been granted by the LCC on 18 February 1921.[30] Indeed matters were so far advanced, their memorial was ready for casting. This intelligence was received badly at the Admiralty. Subsequent enquiries established that the LCC had seen no need to communicate their offer to the Office of Works, which believing the site available, had offered it to the Admiralty for their memorial and was actively consulting the eminent architects Sir Reginald Blomfield and Sir Aston Webb on their behalf. Needless to say, there was a well-documented history of antagonism and non-cooperation between the LCC and central government. However, there was no reason why the Office of Works should not in the course of its duties have read the minutes of the Local Government Committee of the LCC, where the matter was clearly documented from the original proposal initiated by the Submarine Memorial Committee as far back as August 1920.[31] On 31 October 1922 Captain H Douglas King RN MP also wrote to the LCC requesting the same site, on which he proposed to erect a memorial to the fallen of the Royal Naval Reserve. He was in turn duly informed that it had been allocated to the submariners and that was that. Bloodied but unbowed, the Naval War Memorial Committee ploughed on.

---

[26] Naval War Memorial, PRO File Adm116, Case 1160.
[27] As mentioned elsewhere in this study, Gordon's statue was removed from the square during the Second World War and replaced by a Lancaster Bomber publicising 'Wings for Victory Week'.
[28] Naval War Memorial, PRO File Adm116, Case 1160.
[29] Ibid.
[30] Minutes of meeting of LCC Local Government Committee 18 February 1921. LCC/MIN 8165.
[31] Letter from Submarine Memorial Committee to LCC Local Government Committee dated 14 August 1920.

In July 1923 Sir Aston Webb wrote to the First Lord about Admiralty Arch, Trafalgar Square, which he had designed, informing him: 'There was never any intention of crowning it with a statuary group, and I fear neither the design nor the construction are suitable for such a feature'.[32] At this point the Committee became resolved that the memorial would be sited on the north side of Trafalgar Square and they consulted the Commissioner of Police to ascertain that he had no objections. In November Sir Aston, with the active encouragement of Sir Lionel Earle, Permanent Secretary of the Office of Works, suggested that designs be sought from the most eminent sculptors of their age: Charles Sargeant Jagger, William Reid Dick, Professors Gilbert Ledward and Francis Derwent Wood. On 2 November Eastwood wrote to Sir Norman Warren Fisher at the Treasury requesting funding for the memorial, which the Committee had resolved would be constructed on the North Wall of Trafalgar Square. This letter elicited a bombshell by way of response. Sir George Barstow wrote on 22 November in the following terms: 'This letter comes to me as a great surprise, since it entirely ignores the agreed settlement reached at a Conference held at the Treasury on 22 July 1921 which was duly noted by the Cabinet on 6 August 1921 and which superseded the earlier arrangements approved by the Cabinet in the previous March. At that conference it was agreed: 'that all general war memorials abroad and general naval memorials in this country should be erected by and under the responsibility of the Imperial War Graves Commission', being combined with their memorials to the Missing, and that all proposals for the erection of general memorials otherwise should be abandoned. In pursuance of this decision no general memorial has been erected to the Army and Air Force dead at the expense of public funds other than those which commemorate the Missing and I understand that 3 Naval Memorials are in fact being erected by the Commission at Chatham, Portsmouth and Plymouth at an estimated cost of about £77,000 and that the Commission are also taking steps with a view to the erection of a memorial to the Mercantile Marine. In these circumstances it appears to me that your claim is completely met and that there can be no question of erecting any further naval memorial at the cost of public funds'. Clearly in some difficulty, on 8 December 1923 Eastwood sat down to pen another one of those letters no civil servant likes to write, to apprise the First Lord of this unexpected development: 'First Lord, A very embarrassing situation has arisen with regard to the general Naval War Memorial....' There followed a blow by blow account of every decision made. A good deal of hand wringing ensued, followed by the search for the guilty. Sir O A R Murray of the Admiralty wrote to the First Lord (Mr Leopold Amery) on 8 December informing him that his predecessor (Lord Lee) had had in his possession a document (C.P.3162) of which no trace could be found in the files. Neither had it been passed to his Principal Private Secretary. As Lord Lee was in India at the time, the facts could not be established with any certainty, but it seemed likely that he had misinterpreted the various decisions made by the Cabinet in respect of the various national memorials that were to be erected, and that the memorials being erected by the Commission were in fact the only three that were to be erected to the officers and men of the Royal Navy in the Great War. On 11 December Murray wrote to Colonel Sir Maurice Hankey,[33] Secretary to the Cabinet to see if he could 'throw any light on what seems to be a curious difference of interpretation of this document between Lord Lee and the Treasury'. Hankey replied on the 12th confirming that Murray's suspicions were correct, but advising that 'the pressure of Cabinet business was so great at that time, that it was entirely possible that a misunderstanding could have arisen'. The Navy Board recognised that without the cooperation of the Treasury, there was no future in pursuing the proposal and quietly abandoned it at their meeting on 12 May 1924. On 29 May Mr Connolly of the Office of Public Works wrote, enquiring as to progress and cheerily announcing that paving works on the north side of Trafalgar Square were about to commence.

---

[32] Sir Aston Webb to The Rt Hon Lord Lee of Fareham, First Lord 5 July 1922, PRO file Adm116, Case 1160.
[33] Maurice Pascal Alers Hankey (1877-1963). Educated Royal Naval College, Greenwich. Royal Marine Artillery 1895-1901. Naval Intelligence 1902-06. Secretary to the Committee of Imperial Defence 1912-38. Knighted 1916. Secretary to the Cabinet 1916-18. Secretary to the Cabinet 1919-38. 1st Baron Hankey 1939.

On 27 September 1943 Leopold Amery, Secretary of State for India, wrote to the Rt Hon A V Alexander, First Lord at the Admiralty: 'After the last war we had endless discussions on the Board of Admiralty as to the best way of utilising the £40,000 promised by the Treasury for a Central Memorial to the Navy. Arthur Lee wanted something for the crypt of St Paul's. Beatty began by suggesting that the Duke of York should be taken off the top of his column and replaced by Britannia to match Nelson on the other column! Later, he and others of the Board thought something on the Embankment near HMS PRESIDENT might be more appropriate. In the end we all agreed upon an idea of my own which was to utilise the whole length of the back wall of Trafalgar Square for a bas relief of the Navy's work. Nothing less spacious than that would afford the opportunity of showing something to future generations of the types of ships used in the war. The centre was to be occupied by a standing figure of Britannia with her trident, and after considerable discussion we agreed with the Royal Academy that she should not be tall enough, trident and all to break the line of the Academy roof.[34] It was also tentatively arranged that the Royal Navy Division might have a memorial at the end of one wing. I forget whether we got as far as selecting the architect before I left the Admiralty. Anyhow the thing presently reached the point of further discussion with the Treasury, who blandly replied that it was all a mistake and that they had never promised the £40,000 or any sum at all! Would it be possible to revive the idea at the end of this war and have a Central Memorial for the Navy in both Wars? After all, I doubt if there would be much point in repeating Memorials for the Navy at each of the three Naval ports, and that their case might be met by simply adding the dates of the present war to the last. But for a really good Central Memorial the Treasury might very well cough up a good deal more than the £40,000 we once talked about! I should indeed like to see the whole of Trafalgar Square consecrated to the Navy, and Gordon and others, who now inhabit it, transferred to some more appropriate locality.'

The Admiralty staff were asked to prepare a brief to enable the First Lord to respond to Mr Amery and given the foregoing, their advice makes interesting reading:

'I attach the papers containing the decision referred to by Mr Amery; they are entitled "Case 1160". It will be seen that after the expenditure of a very great deal of time and effort it was ascertained that the Cabinet had decided, as a result of a conference at which the First Sea Lord (sic) was not present, that all general war memorials abroad and general Navy memorials in this country should be erected by and under the responsibility of the War Graves Commission., and that all proposals for the erection of such memorials otherwise than through the Imperial War Graves Commission should be abandoned. It seems to me that if a similar fiasco is to be avoided, we should first ascertain who will be in charge of the erection of the proposed Naval memorial. So far as the site in Trafalgar Square is concerned, it is I think the general view of the navy that Trafalgar Square should be regarded entirely as a naval square, and that the military and other statues there should be transferred elsewhere. Considerable discussion on this took place on the Private Office papers numbered 8457 which are attached, and among other things approval was obtained in the highest quarters to remove the statue of George IV to a site at Virginia Water. In fact, however, the proposals then made were abandoned in favour of the fountains. I think it would be safe to say to Mr Amery that there is a considerable body of Naval opinion in sympathy with his proposal to navalise Trafalgar Square completely, and that (if such be the case) the First Lord is in favour of his proposal; but that the first step, if we are to avoid the troubles which occurred before, is to ascertain beyond a doubt who is going to be responsible for the erection of the war memorials'.[35] Alexander replied to Amery to this effect on 16 October.

---

[34] The above letter contains a number of howlers. The Royal Academy was at that time, and is still situated at Burlington House, Piccadilly. The National Gallery occupies the north side of Trafalgar Square. The sum of money quoted in the letter is also incorrect. First Sea Lord as senior ranking naval officer would not ordinarily attend meetings of the Cabinet. However, the First Lord of the Admiralty, as a Minister of the Crown *would*.
[35] PRO file ADM1/14977.

# THE NATIONAL SUBMARINERS MEMORIAL

Situated just outside the City of London boundary and below Temple Gardens, this bronze memorial on a stepped monolithic granite plinth stands set into the Thames Embankment Wall. It was designed by the architect A Heron Ryan Tennison FRIBA and was inaugurated on 15 December 1922. The sculptor was F Brook Hitch and the memorial was cast by the E J Parlanti foundry at Parson's Green in London. British submarines at that time did not have names, but numbers and the memorial lists by number every submarine lost in the Great War. The memorial was rearranged in 1959 by the Morris Singer foundry to accommodate the Second World War inscription. The names of missing and dead submariners are inscribed on the wall of the chapel at HMS DOLPHIN in Portsmouth. The 40 bronze anchors on the memorial are for the hanging of wreaths at remembrancetide. They are an unusual feature, but not unique. (Such anchors may also be found on the Scottish National War Memorial in Edinburgh). After eighty years of being exposed to carbon monoxide fumes on a busy central London thoroughfare, the patina of the memorial has suffered from its location. The memorial is the venue for the annual Act of Remembrance by the veterans of the Submarine Service in the week before the National Ceremony at the Cenotaph. The general inscription reads:

"ERECTED TO THE MEMORY OF THE OFFICERS AND MEN OF THE BRITISH
NAVY WHO LOST THEIR LIVES SERVING IN SUBMARINES 1914 – 1918"

The plaque at the base of the memorial reads:

"NATIONAL SUBMARINE MEMORIAL (1922)
THIS PLAQUE COMMEMORATES THE MEMORIAL'S SEVENTIETH
ANNIVERSARY AND THE CONTRIBUTION BY THE MEMBERS OF THE
SUBMARINER'S OLD COMRADES LONDON. IN THEIR DEVOTION TO THE
UPKEEP OF THIS MEMORIAL
UNVEILED BY PETER P. RIGBY
CBE JP 1st NOVEMBER 1992"

# THE DRUMS AND FANFARE TRUMPETS OF THE ROYAL MARINES BAND SERVICE

After the Great War each member of the Royal Naval School of Music[36] donated a day's pay towards a memorial to their fallen comrades. The form chosen comprised a set of five silver side drums and a wooden bass drum. Each silver drum carried the inscription: 'In Memory of the one hundred and forty-three WOs, NCOs and men of the RM Band Service who lost their lives in the Great War, 1914-1918, whilst serving in the following ships and theatres of war: HMS BULWARK; HMS MONMOUTH; HMS INFLEXIBLE; HMS LION; HMS NATAL; HMS INVINCIBLE; HMS INDEFATIGABLE; HMS QUEEN MARY; HMS CORNWALLIS; HMS VANGUARD; HMS GLORY; HMS MONARCH; HMS CARNARVON; HMS CAESAR; HMS PRINCESS ROYAL; HMS BRITANNIA; HMS CONQUEROR; Drake Battalion of the Royal Naval Division at Gallipoli and with the West African Frontier Force. The bass drum has the names of the 143 men emblazoned upon it. The drums were dedicated and presented in a ceremony held on the 5 March 1921 when some 400 members of the School were on parade. Following an inspection, the Royal Marine Artillery Chaplain conducted a short religious dedication. After a brief address, the Adjutant-General handed over the drums to the RNSM percussionists and the band marched through the ranks prior to the National Anthem being played. A Roll of Honour, also paid for by the men, comprised four oak panels decorated with the Service crest surmounted by the Admiralty coronet with a carved laurel decoration and a scroll with the carved motto *Sans Peur et Sans Reproche*. After the Second World War a memorial committee was appointed to collect donations and to determine an appropriate form of memorialisation. They settled on the purchase of 14 fanfare trumpets and their bells are inscribed with the names of the ships in which the men died. The banners are of Royal blue velvet with gold lace fringes. The rules relating to these trumpets were set down in 'The War Memorial Charter' of 1949 with a Book of Remembrance being the third part of the Memorial. It is of parchment, bound in blue leather and tooled in gold. It is the Roll of Honour of the two hundred and twenty-five Royal Marine Band Ranks who lost their lives in the Second World War. In the centre of its cover is the fouled anchor with the letters RNSM. The whole design surmounted by a Royal Crown. On 1 June 1949 the Massed Bands were paraded before a dais bearing the Book of Remembrance and the stands bearing the Memorial Trumpets. During the Dedication Service the Commandant General read the Lesson and the Book of Remembrance was blessed. All ranks were called to attention and, during The Silence the School Chaplain handed one of the trumpets to the Chaplain of the Fleet for Dedication. 'In memory of those who gave their lives in the service of their country'. The Commandant received the trumpets and with the Musical Director, handed each of them to those who had the honour of receiving them on behalf of the Royal Marines Bands. The fanfare *To Comrades Sleeping* was sounded. It was composed by Leon Young, a wartime survivor of HMS HERMIONE. The Musical Director then passed responsibility for the 'Act of Memorial' by the Massed Bands of the Royal Naval School of Music to Lieutenant W Lang. What followed was an original marching display, designed by Lieutenant Lang, which became the pattern for what would in 1950 become the annual Beating of Retreat on Horse Guards Parade Ground.

In 1973 the Commandant General agreed to the suggestion that both the Memorial Silver Drums and the Memorial Silver Trumpets should be transferred to, and permanently laid up in, the Royal Marines Museum at Eastney. When they were withdrawn from service, instructions were issued that 'The Memorial Silver Trumpets of the Royal Marines School of Music', as they had been officially re-titled, should never be played again.

---

[36] After a highly critical report on the Italian and Maltese musicians employed by the Royal Navy was produced in 1902, the Royal Marines Band Service was formed in 1903. At that point, all Royal Navy musicians became Royal Marines. The RN Band Service and the three divisional bands of the Royal Marines were amalgamated on 1 September 1950 and the RNSM was renamed the Royal Marines School of Music.

# THE ROYAL NAVAL SCHOOL OF MUSIC

The original War Memorial Charter of 1949, which also covered The War Memorial Silver Drums 1914-1918 was worded as follows:

1.     The Book of Remembrance. The Book of Remembrance will form the permanent Roll of Honour and will be placed in the Chapel of St Cecilia at the Royal Naval School of Music.

2.     The Trumpets and Banners. These shall be called 'The Memorial Trumpets of the Royal Naval School of Music' and this title shall on no occasion be abbreviated.

3.     Custody. The War Memorials shall be in the custody of the Quartermaster (Music) at the Royal Naval School, who shall keep them in safe storage and issue orders covering their safety when in use.

4.     Usage of the Trumpets. The Trumpets are never to be played by any but RN School of Music personnel and when performing in public will always be conducted by a RN School of Music Officer.

5.     Fees. Fees will normally be charged even if the object of the function is to raise money for charity.

6.     Fanfare Trumpeters. Trained Fanfare Trumpeters will be maintained continuously at the Royal Naval School of Music as far as is possible. If circumstances prevent the maintenance of a team of the highest class, no engagements will be accepted, since the trumpets reflect the reputation of all ranks, past and present.

7.     Dress. The dress for the Fanfare Trumpeters will be Royal Marine Band Ceremonial Dress with the addition of dress cords and white gloves. Caps will be worn as it is not possible to play the trumpets when wearing Royal Marine uniform helmets.

8.     Insurance. The Memorials are to be covered by a comprehensive Insurance Policy the cost of which will be met by the RN School of Music Band Fund.

9.     The War Memorial Silver Drums 1914-1918 It is hereby decreed that all or any charter, rules or regulations drawn up in connection with the Silver Drums shall be cancelled and the provisions of this Charter, in so far as they shall apply, shall also govern the usage of the Silver Memorial Drums 1914-1918.

10.     Deciding Authority. Subject to the provisions of this Charter, the Commandant of the Royal Naval School of Music will be vested with final decision as to the use of the Instruments mentioned herein. In this connection, it is hereby recorded that they belong collectively to the Royal Naval School of Music, as opposed to being public property, and, as a War Memorial, they shall be used only with dignity and pride.

11.     Memorial Day. The War Memorial Committee recommend that the 'Dedication Fanfare' composed by Mr Leon Young shall be sounded with due ceremony by the Fanfare Trumpets on the First of June each year.

Website at www.royalmarinesbands.co.uk

## SS CURACA

On the morning of 6 December 1917, the French merchantman MONT BLANC loaded with ammunition bound for France collided with the merchantman IMO outside Halifax Harbour, Nova Scotia, Canada and caught fire. The consequent explosion devastated South Halifax, killed some 2,000 civilians on shore, injured 10,000 and rendered some 20,000 people homeless. SS CURACA was a merchantman out of London in the vicinity of the explosion and lost with all hands. Her mostly British crew of 45 included: 3 Chinese, 1 Finn, 1 American, 1 Filipino, 8 Canadians, 8 Liverpudlians and 5 men from the Isle of Barra. The force of the explosion hurled MONT BLANC's anchor two miles and it remains as a monument where it stands to this day to those who died that day in the disaster.

A black marble obelisk was subsequently erected in Fairview Cemetery, Halifax by the ship's owner the New York and Pacific Steamship Company, to the memory of the crew of SS CURACA. In 2001 William Fairbrother, the grandson of one of the crew, discovered that the names of the crew were not recorded on the memorial, or indeed anywhere and he set out to establish their identities in order that they should be commemorated in a fitting manner. He commenced his research at the National Records Office at Kew in England and examined the Return of Deaths of Seamen reported to the Registrar of Shipping in February 1918. He then approached the Fairview Cemetery authorities to ask for permission to have the names engraved and was informed he needed the consent of the owner, which was the shipping line. He eventually established that the line had been sold in 1970 and no longer existed. This satisfied the cemetery authorities and the task of cutting the names was undertaken by a Halifax stonemason and completed in time for a service of rededication held in the cemetery on 6 December 2001.

# THE ROYAL NAVAL DIVISION

In addition to the role of the Royal Navy at sea during the Great War, it had a less well-known, but major participation in the struggle on land. The Royal Naval Division was formed on 16 August 1914 by Winston Churchill, First Lord of the Admiralty, as an intervention and raiding force. It drew its manpower from surplus Royal Marines and naval reservists. Forced at an early stage to provide its own officers, the Division supplemented the existing cadre of high-calibre Royal Marines with officers promoted from within, including a surprisingly high proportion from the ranks. Every promotion was based on merit, or as a result of performance in battle, and this contributed greatly to the quality of leadership. The cosmopolitan origin of many of the Division's officers may be explained by the fact that Churchill's Private Secretary Edward Marsh was deeply involved in the world of the arts. His network of contacts included poets, artists, civil servants, publishers and prominent members of London society, all of whom were keen to get into uniform before the war was over. The ratings were a tough bunch of customers, with a preponderance of Scots, Yorkshire and Durham miners. Two of the Division's finest leaders were Arthur Asquith and Bernard Freyberg.

The Division saw action in the defence of Antwerp in October 1914 and in April 1915 it landed at Gallipoli. It possessed a fierce *esprit de corps* and an indication of its fighting qualities may be taken from the Second Battle of Krithia, (4-6 June) where the Division lost 40 officers and 600 men. Two battalions, Benbow and Collingwood, were disbanded, the men being absorbed into the Anson, Hood and Howe. In 1916 the Division came under army command and was renamed the 63rd (Royal Naval) Division. Army troops were added to its establishment and it was posted to the Western Front, where it would fight until the Armistice. To the end, the majority of its battalions were manned by sailors and marines and the Division retained its peculiarly naval character. Units flew the White Ensign, sailors spoke of 'going ashore' when leaving camp, toasted the King sitting down, wore beards and persisted in all those sea-borne traditions calculated to get under the skin of army officers posted to serve with the Division.

On 17 October 1916 General Shute replaced General Archibald Paris as commander of the RND. Upon arrival, his first act was to issue a bizarre instruction that all non commissioned officers would wear army rank on one sleeve and naval rank on the other. 'Shute was a proper Army bloke. He never really liked the naval tradition stuff and when he took over he came and inspected us. We'd only just gone into the line in the Souchez Sector and we'd taken it over from the Portuguese. Of course it was in a bloody mess, but we hadn't had time to clear it up or anything. Well Shute was furious. He went back and wrote an absolute stinker about the disgusting state of our trenches and really created the most awful fuss.'[37] In consequence, A P Herbert's highly amusing poem about General Shute, (which for reasons of both brevity and common decency does not appear here) entered the folklore of the British Army.[38] General Shute lasted four months before wangling a transfer elsewhere.

More than 40% of all Royal Navy and Royal Marine casualties in the Great War were sustained by the Division on land, although at any given time, its strength was rarely more than 5% of the Royal Navy's total manpower. The disparity between these two figures reflects both the Division's fearsome fighting reputation and the fact that it was in action from the earliest days of the war. The Royal Naval Division was disbanded at a parade on Horse Guards Parade Ground in 1919 and the Prince of Wales took the salute. In five short years it had earned the battle honours ANTWERP, GALLIPOLI, ANCRE, ARRAS, YPRES, WELSH RIDGE and HINDENBURG LINE. Written by Captain Chris Page (Retd) RN, Head of the MOD's Naval Historical Branch, what follows is certainly the most unusual and comprehensive account of any British war memorial anywhere:

---

[37] Lyn Macdonald *Somme*. Told by Sub-Lieutenant William Marlow MC (RNVR) Howe Battalion RND.
[38] Sir Alan Patrick Herbert (1890-1971). Educated Winchester, read Law at New College, Oxford. Served RND, Author, *Punch* contributor and librettist. Knighted 1945. Independent MP for Oxford University (1935-1950).

# THE ROYAL NAVAL DIVISION MEMORIAL

Some years ago, whilst researching a biography of Brigadier-General Arthur Asquith[39] of the RND, I came across some documents relating to the original procurement of the memorial. I discovered that almost immediately after the war, a committee led by Asquith was set up by the survivors to erect a suitable monument to their fallen comrades. At first, there was some discussion and correspondence with the Admiralty as to whether the memorial would be part of a proposed national memorial to naval forces, to include the Merchant Marine. The Admiralty believed that the Cabinet had sanctioned £60,000, a huge sum in today's terms, on the basis that the north wall of Trafalgar Square would be the site. The erection of the three separate memorials at the main home ports by the Imperial War Graves Commission as detailed elsewhere in this study was the outcome of this scheme. At a fairly early stage, the RND, previously associated with this idea, decide to press ahead with their own monument to be sited, preferably, near the Admiralty. Provisional approval for the memorial to be erected at the foot of the Duke of York's Steps on the Mall was granted by the Government Sites Committee of the Office of Works, but this offer was quickly withdrawn. In January 1922 Asquith was advised to liaise with the great architect of war memorials, Sir Reginald Blomfield with a view to erecting a monument on one of the buttresses of the Victoria Embankment, near Waterloo Bridge. The introduction to Blomfield did not work out, possibly because the site was rejected by the RND Committee, who were advised to consult with the sculptor Charles Sargeant Jagger, creator of the magnificent Royal Artillery Memorial at Hyde Park Corner. On 30 January 1923 Asquith wrote to Sir Lionel Earle, Permanent Secretary to the Office of Works, asking for 'a site in Trafalgar Square or in the immediate neighbourhood of the Admiralty'. Asquith even specified the preferred option, in the middle of the nine panels into which the north wall of the Square was divided. The memorial would take the form of an inscription of the crests of the units or a bas-relief. He helpfully pointed out that this would involve the removal of the Standard Measures sited there. At the end of April 1923 Asquith wrote to the First Lord, Leopold Amery, complaining that no site had been allocated, either in the Square itself, or along one of the walls. He pointed out that his committee had had the money in hand for about three years, but still had no memorial to show for it. The Naval Memorials Committee suggested to Earle that the existing statue of King George IV might be moved to accommodate the monument, a proposition that received short shrift from the Office of Works. The consultations with Jagger also came to nothing, and with no decision forthcoming, Asquith asked to see the First Lord. In his briefing for Amery on 7 March 1924, Eastwood, the Secretary of the Naval War Memorials Committee finally mentioned 'that excellent site, the triangle patch of the Cambridge enclosure opposite the Secretary's window'. By then, Asquith had engaged the service of Sir Edwin Lutyens, who wrote to the Sites Committee of the Department of Works, on 16 April 1924 - he was on first name terms with Earle - formally providing an alternative to Trafalgar Square, the corner of the Admiralty where the balustrade followed the south west rounded corner looking on to the Horse Guards Parade. In his own hand he drew a small sketch to illustrate his proposal. Concluding that the best site remained Trafalgar Square, he finished, again in manuscript, 'They have little money so whatever is done will have to be modest'! Earle replied doubting that 'so important a site as the North Wall of Trafalgar Square could be allocated to so small a Memorial as that of the Royal Naval Division - small, I mean, not in merit but in expenditure', and suggesting that the west wall might be possible. It seems that it was Earle himself who put into Asquith's mind a fountain as a memorial, remarking that it would have to be 'a purely sylvan piece of architecture, and not in any way a way memorial, as that would not be tolerated in any of the Royal Parks'.

---

[39] Arthur Melland Asquith (1883-1939). Son of Prime Minister Herbert Asquith, served in Sudanese Civil Service 1906-11. In business 1911-14. Sub-Lieutenant RND 1914. Served Antwerp, Dardanelles and Western Front and wounded four times. Brigadier-General 1917.

The reader might be left wondering how the Guards Memorial in the Horse Guards Approach Road ever received approval. Lutyens pressed on and produced drawings of a fountain to be sited on the Admiralty balustrade. His proposals were accepted by the Royal Fine Art Commission (RFAC) in July 1924. It was decided that the words of one of the RND's most famous members, Rupert Brooke, would be inscribed on one of the faces of the square supporting plinth. Even then, Sir Vincent Baddeley, the First Principal Assistant Secretary to the Admiralty, still found points to object to in the proposals: having seen the Lutyens drawings, he wrote to Earle again on 11 July complaining that the proposal was different from that originally agreed. A meeting with the architect was quickly arranged and most of Baddeley's concerns were allayed. The Admiralty, one week later, after further badgering in a hand-written note from Asquith, gave grudging consent to the design. Baddeley wrote to Earle concluding, 'I ought to say that if there had been any scheme for a memorial more directly connected with the Royal Navy than this one of the Royal Naval Division, the Admiralty would have given it priority.....' This summed up pretty well the attitude of the Admiralty at that time to the RND. Earle quickly passed on the design to Buckingham Place, and in a note of the 21 July, Lord Stamfordham, the King's Private Secretary, wrote: 'The King quite approves of the design for the fountain and the site where your Department propose to erect it'. Pre-empting the King's decision, presumably having had the nod from Stamfordham, Lord Chelmsford, the First Lord of the Admiralty, wrote to Asquith on 18 July, 'Go ahead with your memorial'. He concluded, illogically: 'I understand that it will be somewhat more conspicuous than originally contemplated, but that is not a reason for turning down an approval which I gave to the less conspicuous scheme'. Asquith at last had permission to erect the monument. Lutyens completed his drawings for the memorial in August 1924, and the contract was let to Nine Elms Stone Masons of Lambeth, and the work started. While the fabric was under construction, it was belatedly realised that the monument, being a fountain, would require water, and that there would be an ongoing requirement for maintenance. At that point, no estimate of the cost for such provision had yet been made. Mr G L Barstow of the Treasury wrote to the Office of Works on 8 August 1924, concluding: 'My Lords [Commissioners of HM Treasury] agree that you should in due course accept responsibility for this memorial. They note that you will endeavour to obtain a contribution from the [RND] committee towards the cost of maintenance. Eventually, it was agreed that the RND Memorial Fund would contribute £100, the sum estimated by the Chief Engineer to Mr Heasman, the Director of Works for 'current, water, repairs etc...'.

The memorial bore the general inscription:

"BLOW OUT. YOU BUGLES, OVER THE RICH DEAD!
THERE'S NONE OF THESE SO LONELY AND POOR OF OLD,
BUT, DYING, HAS MADE US RARER GIFTS THAN GOLD.
THESE LAID THE WORLD AWAY; POURED OUT THE RED
SWEET WINE OF YOUTH; GAVE UP THE YEARS TO BE
OF WORK AND JOY. AND THAT UNHOPED SERENE,
THAT MEN CALL AGE; AND THOSE WHO WOULD HAVE BEEN,
THEIR SONS THEY GAVE, THEIR IMMORTALITY

RUPERT BROOKE 1887-1915

Hood Battalion"

The Memorial was dedicated on Horse Guards Parade on 25 April 1925, 10th anniversary of the Gallipoli Landings, and six years after the initial proposal was mooted. It was unveiled by the first commander of the Division, Major General Sir Archibald Paris,[40] who ended his address: 'It will remain a permanent record of noble deeds and duty accomplished'. After the dedication, Paris's moving piece was followed by a typical masterpiece of rhetoric from the creator of the RND, the former First Lord of the Admiralty, Winston Churchill: 'Everyone, I think, must admire the grace and simplicity of this fountain, which the genius of Lutyens had designed. The site is also well chosen. Here, under the shadow of the Admiralty Building, where, eleven years ago, the Royal Naval Division was called into martial life, this monument now records their fame and preserves their memory. Their memory is thus linked forever with the Royal Navy, whose child they were, of whose traditions they were so proud, and whose long annals, rich with romantic and splendid feats of arms, contain no brighter page then theirs. But if the place is well chosen, so also is the day. This is April 25, and ten years ago the astonishing exploit of landing on the Gallipoli Peninsula was in full battle. And we here, who have so many memories in common, almost seem to hear the long reverberations of the distant cannonade, and we certainly feel again in our souls the awful hopes and awful fears of those tragic hours. A mellow light seems to the mind's eye to surround this monument. The passer-by who in other days pause to drink of its water or to examine its design will be held by something else. The famous lines of Rupert Brooke inscribed upon its panel will make their own appeal and tell their own story to anyone who loves this island or speaks the English tongue. These verses, and others given in the order of service, have brought comfort to many who sought it so long and wearily, and whose spirit seemed broken, but who nevertheless found relief in reading and repeating their noble utterance. Their high, calm peace rises confidently above the tumult and the carnage, and beyond all error and confusion; it reigns by right divine over men and over centuries, we meet his verses everywhere. They are quoted again and again. They are printed in newspapers, written in books, blotted by tears, or carved in stone. But they belong to us, to the Royal Naval Division, to the memory of Rupert Brooke and his comrades and companions. They were the inheritance he bequeathed to them, and through them to us all. They are inscribed on this memorial because it is their proper home, and from here, while these stones endure, they will carry to the ears of generations differently attuned from ours, the chant of valiant youth entering willing and undaunted into the Valley of the Shadow of Death. Ten years and more have gone by since this parade ground used to be thronged by bands of volunteers marching off to join the Army amid the blare of music and at their country's call. Nearly seven years have gone since the victory was won; since all the kings and emperors against whom we warred were driven into exile, and all their mighty armies shattered and dispersed. Those years have not been years of joy or triumph. They have been years of exhaustion, despondency, and bickerings all over the world, and we are often tempted to ask ourselves what we have gained by the enormous sacrifice made by those to whom this memorial is erected. But this was never the issue with those who marched away. No question of advantage presented itself to their minds. They only saw the light shining clear on the path of duty. They only saw their duty to resist oppression, to protect the weak, to vindicate the profound but unwritten law of nations, to testify to truth and justice and mercy among men. They never asked the question, 'What shall be gain?' They only asked the question, 'Where lies the right?' It was thus that they marched away for ever, and yet from their uncalculating exaltation and devotion, detached from the considerations of material gain, we may be sure that good will come to their countrymen and to this island they guarded in its reputation and safety so faithfully and well. Bold indeed will be the tyrant who seeks again to overthrow by

---

[40] Archibald Paris (1861-1937). Entered Royal Marine Artillery 1879. Column commander in Boer War. Forced to surrender after most of his troops ran away. He was promoted Lieutenant Colonel for bravery in the field. Major General Commanding the Royal Naval Division October 1914. In 1916 he was severely wounded by an artillery shell in France, losing a leg. He was knighted that same year.

military force the freedom they established. After the confusion has passed away and the long period of reconstruction has been closed it will be perceived by all that the freedom, not only of individuals, but also of States, has been established upon a stronger and broader foundation. Humanity, for all its sufferings and disappointments, has yet moved forward through the Great War at least one stage towards the realisation of its ideals. And this country and Empire, saved by its sons from the worst perils which have confronted it in its long history, remains still able to guide, to encourage, and in a large measure to inspire the peoples of the world. Doubts and disillusions may be answered by the sure assertation that the sacrifice which these men made was not made in vain. And this fountain to the memory of the Royal Naval Division will give forth not only the waters of honour, but also the waters of healing and the waters of hope.'

The cost of the memorial was met from private subscription, reputedly largely through donations by survivors of the Division and the relatives of those killed. While the final sum raised cannot now be ascertained with certainty, the figure of £3,000, about £150,000 in today's terms has been mentioned. There was sufficient left over for Asquith and Donaldson (a winner of the DSO for conspicuous gallantry in 1918) to establish a charitable trust for the purposes of maintaining the RND Memorial at Beaucourt, France, and other divisional or battalion memorials. The £3,000 bequeathed was administered by the Commandant General Royal Marines and it formed the basis of the fund on which the reinstatement of the memorial back to Horse Guards Parade in 2003 was based. The erection and dedication of the memorial was not the end of the story. The installation was not quite perfect, with the result that the bowl of the fountain was not horizontal, a crucial requirement for this sort of fountain, otherwise the water cascaded from only one side of the bowl. After about one year of use it was discovered that the gravel area around the memorial tended to become soggy, particularly when the wind blew water from the fountain, which led to the two open sides around the base being paved, for which the RND Committee paid. The RND Committee also fended off a proposal from Earle that the fountain should not be used in the winter as it 'was cold and cheerless'. Asquith quickly made his strong objections known. By 1928, the Ministry of Works realized that the subvention of £100 provided by the Committee was insufficient: water alone was costing between £7 and £11 per year. No repairs had yet been required, but the Office of Works kept the memorial clean, and removed dead leaves from the water basins. In 1934 it was found to require £200 of underpinning, as it was moving and had to be stabilized. The Office of Works again paid for the work, albeit with bad grace: one of their officers, the aforementioned Mr Heasman, wrote in February 1934: 'I'm afraid this memorial was a bad bargain for the Dept, but I suppose that there is no alternative to this underpinning if it is clear that movement is still going on'. By October 1938, the Royal Naval Division Association, who had taken over the mantle of the RND Memorial Committee, complained of the deterioration of the carvings on the memorial and invited the Office of Works to repair them at an estimated cost of about £35. In a minute of 25th, an unknown official in Works accepted that his Department bore 'the cost of all ordinary maintenance', and so reluctantly the work was completed at a cost of £21, although it took until 30 August 1939 before it was declared finished. The memorial was the focus for many reunions of the survivors of the RND, particularly on Regimental Day, 13 November, the anniversary of their fine attack on the Ancre in 1916. This event was well supported, not only by those who had served in the Division, but also by the Royal Navy Volunteer Reserve units, notably that of the London Division. The memorial was jealously guarded by the RNDA, who resisted the intentions of senior Admiralty officials to place chairs around it so that they could have a better view of the King's Birthday Parade. They also lobbied to prevent people parking their motorcars right up against the monument. Nevertheless, the memorial's days in the heart of the capital were numbered. Early in the Second World War it was decided to erect a massive extension to the Admiralty at the rear of the Old Building. This building in time would become known as the Citadel.

As a precaution, the memorial was dismantled by Messrs Holloway, of the Nine Elms Masons Company, and initially stored in their Battersea yard, together with the Royal Marines Memorial and the pedestal of the statue of King James II. The firm made no charge for the storage, but accepted no responsibility for the memorials in their care. In April 1942 the memorial was inspected by Heasman and found to have suffered no damage. It seems that the inspection alerted Holloways to the fact that they should not have been storing the memorials for free, for in November 1942 Heasman questioned that the £178 quoted by the firm was 'reasonable' and sought a cheaper place. Eventually, on 6 May 1943, the memorial was moved to the grounds of Gordon House, the Royal Hospital, Chelsea.

By now the secretary of the RNDA was Captain Michael Isaacs, who had earned his Military Cross in France whilst serving with Drake Battalion. He wrote to Heasman some time in July 1943 at the Ministry of Works, complaining that he had never been officially informed what had happened to the memorial, and asking when it was to be re-erected. The reply informed Isaacs of the new storage location of the memorial, and informed him that: 'no decision will be taken during the period of the war', and there the matter rested for nearly two more years. By June 1945, discussions had begun about demolishing the Citadel, but by December it became clear that it was unlikely that it would be pulled down. A short minute dated 13 December, to the Director of Works signed by J Burgess of AS 23 - a section of that Department - has been traced as the key reason why the monument was simply not restored to its original location. He wrote: 'The sites of two statues, the Royal Marines Memorial and the Royal Naval Division Memorial, were: 'built over when the Admiralty fortress was erected. As it seems unlikely that this building will be pulled down, at any rate perhaps for years to come, perhaps you would kindly suggest alternative sites for these two statues'. This minute reveals that the author had no idea of the form of the memorial, or the fact that the original plinth for the RND memorial was still available, unbuilt on, where it was originally erected in 1925. It was this unfortunate minute which started the Ministry of Works on its wild goose chase to find another site for the fountain. The first proposal, discarded by June 1946, was to the triangular grass area behind the Citadel, known as Cambridge Green to be used for both the Royal Marines and RND memorials. The Deputy Secretary of the Ministry, H L Davis, agreed that this part of St James's Park was a possibility. By December of that year, this proposal too had been dropped, and a meeting was held on the 10th, chaired by W A Procter, of the Ministry of Works, attended by a representative of RFAC. The Admiralty were reported as being: 'anxious that the Royal Naval Division Memorial should be sited near the Admiralty'. Once again, however, its original site was not considered, and there was talk of another, at 'the Lambeth Bridge end of Victoria Tower Gardens, near the children's sand-pit'. Nothing happened for six months, when Procter and Rutter, the Chief Architect of the Ministry of Works, decided that the Lambeth Bridge option was a non-starter, and a position on 'the plot of grass near the Foreign Office', or 'at the end of Downing Street facing Horse Guards Parade' was suggested. The latter looked like a good option, so on 26 June Procter wrote to his Deputy Secretary for the go-ahead. Earle's successor Sir Eric de Normann's reply began: 'I think it would be a pity to waste (sic) this fine site, the only remaining good site at our disposal, on the Royal Naval Division Memorial'. He then told Procter to go back to the drawing board, and involve the Minister of Town and Country Planning, who, on 11 August 1947, in an unhelpful reply wondered whether the Ministry of Works could 'wait for several years'. An exasperated Works officer, Brock, finally, by the middle of November 1947, and the Town and Country Planners, came up with a choice of the Foreign Office or a space inside the Admiralty Courtyard. In despair, the planners added that a move to Greenwich (either the College or the National Maritime Museum) or the Imperial War Museum might be necessary. Tower Hill and alongside the Guards Memorial were also suggested as a possibilities. By now it was November 1947. De Normann's inclination was for the National Maritime Museum, and he planned a visit there. A proposal for the memorial to be sited in front of the Queen's House at Greenwich, accompanied by a photo-montage of the site, was rejected in horror by

Mr Chettle, the Inspector of Ancient Monuments, at the end of January 1948. De Normann eventually got round to visiting Greenwich on 26 April 1948, and discussed with the Director of the College a location near Greenwich Pier. It took him fourteen days to minute this in the file. Matters were hastened by the arrival in June 1948 at the Ministry of Works of a letter from the Secretary of the RNDA, now Edward Burton, enquiring where and when it was proposed to re-erect the memorial. Procter replied that there were hopes of finding a site near the Royal Naval College, Greenwich, and listing all the others considered. Delighted at last to have some light at the end of the tunnel, Burton, on 30 August, asked for details of the proposal to site the memorial near Greenwich Pier, now aware that Works were already cooling on this site and all the others at Greenwich. By November, the patience of the RNDA was wearing thin. As a result of their pressure on the Admiralty, Gerald Hayes, the Head of Welfare and Accommodation wrote on the 18th to Procter, asking what progress there was on finding a site at Greenwich. Hayes concluded: 'The First Lord [Viscount Hall] is taking a personal interest in the matter and has asked for a report ... He had been approached more than once by distinguished persons who were connected by the RND and would like to give them some more definite reply than the rather vague hope that this has been all that has been possible up to the present'. A later note reveals that Sir A P Herbert was one of those pressing the First Lord. The Chief Inspector of Ancient Monuments was contacted in December and he advised that he had practically decided that the memorial would be moved to Greenwich, either behind the Queen's House, or in one of the Courts of the College. Thus, nine years after its removal, and three and a half years after the end of the Second World War, we have the first reference to the site finally chosen for the relocation. By now the Deputy Secretary of the Ministry of Works, de Normann, realized that he had to solve this problem, and requested his chief architect, Rutter, to provide him with a template of the monument so that he, de Normann could personally decide on a site. It was minuted that he was 'not anxious to consult the Royal Fine Art Commission'. As he was writing this, Chettle at last came up with his final recommendation: to site the memorial in the grounds of the College in the area west of King William Block. Suddenly, previous objections on the grounds of the clash of architectural styles between Wren's masterpiece, and one of Lutyens' finest works were quietly shelved. The Office of Works then discovered that they had no photograph of the memorial. The only one they could find had been stuck together, having been torn in half, annotated on the back 'Negative loaned from the Imperial War Museum, the only one in existence'. The latter statement was incorrect.

By April, a full-scale mock up had been produced, and the intention was for all interested parties to be present at the inspection on 21 April 1949. Even now, the model was only to be erected on the south side of the Queen's House, ignoring the advice of the IAM. Burton was written to, but he had moved and could not be contacted, and the inspection took place without him, but with the Captain of the College and his Secretary present. Both the Queen's House site, and the proposed location west of King William Block were rejected in favour of a site in the northeast corner of the grounds. Having finally bitten the bullet, de Normann invited a final inspection of the mock-up on the proposed site. He wrote to his Minister on 4 May, and having asked him to attend the inspection went on: 'It is a divisional memorial and I have never understood why it was erected in the centre of London in such a prominent position. There were many other famous divisions of the 1914-18 war who might have claimed equal rights and we should never have been able to find sites for them'. It is uncertain whether de Normann was writing purely to influence his Minister, or if he had not read the previous correspondence on the matter. He neglected to point out that the original site had been approved by the King himself, and the project was supported by Churchill. Moreover the Division was indeed unique, and it was perfectly appropriate that it stood on the corner of the Admiralty, from where the Division was 'called into martial life', in the words of Churchill. Nor did he point out that the Guards Memorial, a few yards from the Admiralty, was a divisional monument.

The meeting took place on 13 May 1949, with the RNDA represented by their Vice Chairman, Colonel Sir Leslie Wilson. It was agreed the area in the northeast corner of the College would probably be the best possible site, and that the model should be re-erected on 18 June when the RNDA was having a function there. There is no final statement of approval for the memorial to be resited in this part College grounds, but, by July, it was pretty well assumed, at least by the Office of Works and the Divisional Engineers, who had costed the pumping arrangements for the fountain at £250. A short item appeared in the London *Evening Standard* on 24 August reporting that a new home had been found for the monument. By 18 August 1949, Works had started to worry about the cost: the estimate provided was £2,500. During the whole of the process of finding a new site, the Office of Works had, as a matter of policy, excluded the Royal Fine Art Commission from any input to the debate and as late as October 1949, the officials concerned, led by their Deputy Secretary de Normann, decided to press ahead and present not only the RFAC, but even to a certain extent, the RNDA, with a fait accompli. In fact, on 22 October, Burton was contacted by Miss Olivia Cockett at the Office of Works, and left in no doubt as to what was expected of him. Miss Cockett's report of the conversation with Burton states: 'I ... made it quite clear that we do not expect to have any but approving comments from him after the annual reunion on November 12 as we regard the proposals for the re-erection of the memorial as having been settled at the meeting on the site last summer. To this he agreed'. In fact, after the meeting, Burton returned the drawings lent to him with no comments, favourable or otherwise, on the proposals. Replies to invitations to tender for the work were received in April 1950, and were judged to be too high. Someone in the Office of Works now thought to advise the Admiralty of the situation, and received the unwelcome reply that the Director of the Greenwich Hospital should agree the proposals before formal Admiralty consent. As their Lordships of the Admiralty Board were the Trustees of the Greenwich Hospital, this seems to be unnecessarily diligent, but on 14 July they were rewarded with a reply from the Director of the Greenwich Hospital, who remarked that he did not wish the old Hospital to become a home for memorials, and then solemnly gave Their Lordships approval to the proposal, adding two conditions, that the Ministry of Works undertook:

a. Full responsibility for the maintenance, and
b. To remove it, if asked by their Lordships

These conditions were accepted by Roland Barker, Assistant Secretary of the Office of Works, in an undated note in July. A minor stir occurred later that month when the lowest estimate for the work, by Galbraith Bros, arrived at £3,245, i.e. £100 more than the original Works estimate, but at least nearly £1,300 cheaper than the next lowest. The contract was let and work started on 18 August 1950, 'scheduled' to last for 4 months. Also in that month, the wisdom of presenting the RFAC with a fait accompli was revealed when in answer to a query from them on progress with the memorial, Barker nonchalantly informed them that a site had been agreed after discussion with 'the RNDA, the Trustees of Greenwich Hospital, and the Admiralty etc' (sic). He chose not to highlight the fact that the Fine Art Commission was bypassed, and that the last two authorities consulted were in fact one and the same entity; nor did the RFAC appear to notice. The work was inevitably delayed, and by January the RNDA, planning the rededication ceremony, were becoming concerned that their late April function might not be able to take place. It was with some relief, therefore, that Burton was told on the 22 February that the memorial would be completed by 24 March. The service of rededication was scheduled for 26 April 1951, by the First Sea Lord, Admiral Lord Fraser. A new inscription was added to the memorial on one of the previously empty sides: 'This Memorial designed by Sir Edwin Lutyens was unveiled on Horse Guards Parade at the corner of the Admiralty on 25 April 1925, the tenth anniversary of the landing on Gallipoli, and re-erected on this site in 1951.' The final recorded cost was £3,918.

The memorial was unveiled on 26 May 1951 by the Second Sea Lord, the First Sea Lord being unavailable, and thereafter it formed the centrepiece for the annual reunions of the survivors at the Royal Naval College. Looking back, one cannot but be struck by the enormous support given to the Royal Naval Division Association by the College over many years. The Admirals Superintendent went out of their way to provide accommodation for the members of the Division, while the Captain of the College took great pains to ensure that the ceremonial was always first class. Relations were so cordial that the Captain often dined with the RNDA. Slowly and inevitably, the Association's numbers declined. In October 1980 it was finally disbanded and the RNDA Colour was laid up at the entrance to the chapel at Greenwich. On 31 May 1981, 65th anniversary of the Battle of Jutland, the final parade of the survivors was held at Greenwich and the Royal Naval Division marched into history.

The memorial remained at Greenwich, regrettably in an area of the College not on the prime tourist route, and whilst one of the aims of siting it in the College grounds was to be a reminder of the RND's achievements, few of the naval students who passed through the College understood its significance. The defects of the site also became apparent: the memorial began to be dominated by the trees among which it had been set, and these dropped leaves and detritus into the fountain, and in winter dripped lichens on to the stonework. At the unveiling ceremony in 1951, the Second Sea Lord had accepted the memorial 'into the special care of the Royal Navy, who are deeply gratified and immensely proud to have it'. Unfortunately, no-one in the College could determine exactly who was responsible for its maintenance, and so the local staff of the Ministry of Works were commissioned on an ad hoc basis, thus putting into practice what should have been the formal arrangement, and one that had been accepted by them as long ago as 1924. With the closure of the College as a naval establishment in the early 1990s, it became apparent that the reasons for siting the memorial at Greenwich were no longer appropriate: no survivors were left to take advantage of the facilities and the generosity of the College, and the significance of the memorial would be largely lost on the new population of students on the campus of the University of Greenwich. Early attempts were made for the memorial to be moved as part of the closure procedure of the College, but these came to nought when it was decided by the Ministry of Defence that, notwithstanding the Second Sea Lord's declaration at the 1951 unveiling, they did not *'own'* the memorial, and therefore it would be improper to use public funds to reinstate it. A judgement was made that the monument was 'owned' by those who paid for it, or their survivors and descendants. Without exception, all of those contacted were strongly in favour of its reinstatement on Horse Guards Parade. A committee was set up under the patronage of the Prince of Wales and the chairmanship of Lieutenant General Sir Robin Ross, a former Commandant General of the Royal Marines, to raise the necessary £250,000 to restore the memorial to its original site on the corner of the Old Admiralty Building. Amazingly, the plinth still existed, beneath which, was much of the old pipework installed to provide water for the fountain. The Charity Commissioners agreed to the remit of the RND Memorial Charity, administered by the Commandant General Royal Marines being extended to cover the resiting of the fountain. All the necessary permissions to remove the memorial and re-site it were received by 2003.

With the assistance of generous funding from among others, the Rothermere Foundation, the fund raising phase of the project was completed in 2003. 'Lord Rothermere, Chairman of the Daily Mail and General Trust, said: "My great grandfather was one of the instigators of this memorial, as he had lost his son Vere at the Battle of Ancre whilst he was serving with the Royal Naval Volunteer Reserve. I was delighted for the Rothermere Foundation to support this striking monument moving back to Horse Guards Parade, as it was clearly designed for that position. That after so many years people felt it was appropriate to move the memorial to its original platform reflects on the continued recognition of the gallant and sustained contribution the men of the RNVR made to the Great War."[41]

---
[41] London *Evening Standard* 12 November 2003.

A rededication service in the presence of Prince Michael of Kent (Honorary Commodore of the Royal Naval Reserve) and the First Sea Lord took place on Horse Guards Parade on 13 November 2003. (The RND's Divisional Day). The well-attended ceremony commenced with a band of the Royal Marines playing a most moving piece entitled: *Elegy for Rupert Brooke* composed by Lieutenant Commander Frederick Septimus Kelly, RNVR of Hood Battalion who was killed on the Somme in November 1916. Prayers were led by the Chaplain of the Fleet, followed by the hymn *O God Our Help in Ages Past*. The memorial was then rededicated by the Chaplain of the Fleet. During the course of the ceremony, Winston Churchill MP delivered the speech originally given by his grandfather on 25 April 1925. After the wreath laying by Prince Michael, the Naval Hymn *Eternal Father, Strong to Save* was sung. After a long, eventful journey the Royal Naval Division Memorial had finally come home to its rightful place to continue as a visible public reminder of a unique and honourable part of the history of the Royal Navy and to stand as a monument worthy of the pride and gratitude of the nation. Website at www.cwgc.co.uk/RNDmem.htm

The Royal Naval Division Memorial reinstated on Horse Guards Parade.

# BEAUCOURT

In Max Arthur's 2002 book *Forgotten Voices* he quoted Sergeant Major Richard Tobin of Hood Battalion of the RND who recalled: 'Colonel Freyberg said, 'Hello Tobin, how are you?' and I said, 'All right, sir.' He said, 'We'll get a VC today,' so I replied, 'You can have mine as well.' He got his. Our final objective was the village of Beaucourt, but we hadn't sufficient men to take it so we dug in and waited for reinforcements to come up.'

The memorial to the 63rd Royal Naval Division stands at Beaucourt, scene of Freyberg's exploit.[42] It takes the form of a truncated obelisk and the bronze tablet on its front is decorated with the cap badges of all the regiments and RND battalions that comprised the Division. The tablet bears the inscription:

"IN MEMORY OF  
THE OFFICERS AND MEN  
OF THE  
ROYAL NAVAL DIVISION  
WHO FELL  
AT THE BATTLE OF  
THE ANCRE  
NOVEMBER 13$^{TH}$ - 14$^{TH}$  
1916"

---

[42] Later Lieutenant General Lord Freyberg VC GCMG KCB KBE DSO*** (1889–1963). He was born in Richmond, Surrey and his family emigrated to New Zealand in 1891 when he was two years old. He was educated there at Wellington College. In the Great War he served in the Royal Naval Division and was wounded so many times Churchill nicknamed him: 'The Empire's Salamander'. He was awarded the Victoria Cross for leading the capture of Beaucourt on 15 November 1916. He was C-in-C New Zealand forces in the Second World War and knighted in 1942. Governor General of New Zealand 1946–52, created baron in 1951 and appointed Deputy Constable and Lieutenant Governor of Windsor Castle in 1953.

# THE JAPANESE NAVAL MEMORIAL – CAPPUCINI, MALTA

Given Turkey's role as a Central Powers belligerent in the Great War, the presence of an Austro-Hungarian submarine base at Pola and the importance of Britain's lines of communications with Egypt, the Mediterranean was an important theatre of operations and the Allies did not have it all their own way. A tablet in Mikra British Cemetery, Salonika commemorates the 135 nurses and men who died when the transport MARQUETTE was torpedoed on 23 October 1915, the 80 British and Indian Servicemen killed when the transport IVERNIA was torpedoed on 1 January 1917, the 8 officers and men of the Royal Army Medical Corps who died when the hospital ship BRITTANIC was sunk by a mine on 21 September 1916 and two men killed when the hospital ship BRAEMAR CASTLE was sunk by a mine on 23 November 1916. The general inscription reads "ALL THESE HAVE NO OTHER GRAVE THAN THE SEA. "HE DISCOVERETH DEEP THINGS OUT OF DARKNESS AND BRINGETH OUT TO LIGHT THE SHADOW OF DEATH".

In the CWGC's Cappucini Naval Cemetery on Malta can be found a memorial to 66 Japanese sailors who died on escort duty. Japan fought on the side of the Allies in that war and in 1917 a Japanese naval squadron under the command of Vice-Admiral Kozo Sato undertook convoy duties in the Mediterranean, escorting nearly 800 Allied troopships and merchantmen. The sailors were buried in a low vault below the memorial, which took the form of an obelisk. This combined tomb and memorial is both a rare and unusual form of memorialisation. The thought-provoking general inscription on the base of the memorial reads:

"SACRED TO THE MEMORY OF THE OFFICERS AND MEN BELONGING TO HIS IMPERIAL JAPANESE MAJESTY'S 2ND DETACHED SQUADRON WHO GLORIOUSLY FELL IN THE MEDITERRANEAN DURING THE GREAT WAR
1914 - 1918"

# HMS THETIS

The Triton patrol class submarine HMS THETIS[43] was laid down on 21 December 1936 by Cammell Laird of Birkenhead. Her initial sea trials on 18 April 1939 would have given any submariner pause for thought. When Lieutenant Commander Bolus gave orders to steer to starboard she turned to port. Quite how the steering gear could have been reversely connected and passed by the Admiralty Overseer was the cause of some conjecture by the crew. Submariners are a superstitious breed and what followed fully confirmed their fears. On 1 June 1939 in Liverpool Bay, she sank in 160 feet of water during her acceptance trials. On board there were 53 officers and crew, 9 officers from other submarines, 32 technicians from Cammell Laird and associated contractors, two staff from a Liverpool catering company and a Mersey Pilot. Four men managed to escape. Those lost left 192 dependants who formed themselves into the Thetis Families Association. The report of the Tribunal of Enquiry was presented to Parliament in April 1940. It did not apportion blame, but lamented the unfortunate series of circumstances that led to the loss of life that day. It concluded that Lieutenant Woods had tested each torpedo tube via its test cock. The test cock on tube number five had been painted over with bitumastic paint and although that tube was full of water, when tested it registered as dry. When the tube was opened it flooded the forward compartment. THETIS was subsequently salvaged and taken into service by the Royal Navy. In November 1939 she joined the 3rd Submarine Flotilla as HMS THUNDERBOLT. She was commanded by Lieutenant Commander Cecil Crouch and every man who served on her knew her story. On her sixth Mediterranean patrol, she was sunk by enemy action off Sicily on 12 March 1943 whilst attacking an Italian convoy. There were no survivors from the 60 crew.

The memorial to the crew of HMS THETIS is of Welsh granite and was unveiled by Vice Admiral J M Mansfield, Flag Officer Submarines on 7 November 1947 in Maeshyfryd Cemetery, Holyhead. In keeping with naval tradition, the crew were buried in a communal grave. Their names are on the raised slate plaque at the front of the memorial. Three survivors attended the ceremony, the fourth having been killed in a traffic accident. The 13 foot headstone bears a cross in the form of a sword above the Admiralty anchor.

---

[43] In Greek mythology, Thetis was the daughter of the sea divinities Nereus and Doris. She was wooed by both Zeus and Poseidon until they learned of the prophecy that she would bear a son who would be mightier than his father. She was then given to Peleus of the Myrmidons, considered the most deserving mortal by the gods. By him she bore Achilles.

# THE THREE NAVAL MEMORIALS

After the Second World War it was decided that the naval memorials at the three principal manning stations should be extended to provide space for commemorating the dead without graves of that war, but since the three sites were dissimilar, a different architectural treatment was required for each. The architect for the extensions was Sir Edward Maufe (1882-1974) Principal Architect for the Commission in the UK. Additional sculpture at all three sites was carried out by the famous partnership of Wheeler and McMillan. Plymouth had 15,935 names added (comprising nearly a quarter of a million letters) and Portsmouth 14,921. The Plymouth extension was inaugurated by the Duke of Edinburgh in October 1952. Portsmouth's extension took the form of a sunken garden on the walls of which were mounted 78 bronze panels bearing the names of the sailors from the port that had died in the war. It was inaugurated by Queen Elizabeth the Queen Mother on 29 April 1953.

On 2 October 1952 *The Times* reported: 'The Chatham Naval Memorial Register, which has now been published by the Imperial War Graves Commission, the first of a series of 600 memorial and cemetery registers that will contain the names of all of the member of the forces of the British Commonwealth and Empire who lost their lives during the years 1939-45. The Chatham Register, which records the names of the men and women from the great manning port of the Royal Navy who "have no other grave than the sea" is published in seven parts. Copies of the part containing the name in which relatives and others are interested will be supplied by the Commission (7s. 6d.) with a separate volume, an introduction to the registers which has been written under the literary supervision of Mr. Edmund Blunden. The introduction describes all the naval memorials being erected in Britain by the Commission, with a brief but moving synopsis of the naval war and Commonwealth losses. A paragraph preceding a chronological table of the most noteworthy actions of the sea war sets the ship losses of the Royal Navy at 1,500 of all classes, apart from 20 landing ships and more than 1,300 landing craft and barges. The Royal Canadian Navy lost 22 ships, the Royal Australian Navy 12 (including three cruisers), the Royal Indian Navy two, the Royal New Zealand Navy three small ships, and the South African Naval Forces four. Germany lost more than 1,600 of all classes, many of them scuttled or destroyed in the last days of the war, Italy 613, and Japan 713.' Invitations to inauguration ceremonies were issued by the Commission, basing their information on the Next of Kin forms that had been completed and returned by relatives.

On 16 October 1952 *The Times* reported: 'The Duke of Edinburgh unveiled the 1939-45 extension to the Chatham naval memorial in Great Lines at Gillingham this afternoon. The extension commemorates 9,946 men and women of the Royal Navy, Royal Marines, WRNS and the maritime regiments who lost their lives at sea in the last war. About 8,000 relatives of the men who died attended the ceremony.

Before the service the Duke who was in the uniform of a commander Royal Navy, inspected a Naval guard of honour. In a short address he said: 'These men paid the greatest sacrifice, and it was not in vain. England remained inviolate, and who is there who would not gladly give his life that England might stay free. It is now our duty to work with all our strength to prevent another war from shaking the world.'

The service was conducted by the Chaplain of the Fleet, the Ven. F Noel Chamberlain and the dedication was performed by the Bishop of Rochester, Dr Chavasse. When the Duke released the White Ensign which covered the memorial plaque, Royal Naval signallers simultaneously unveiled 50 bronze tablets bearing the names of the fallen.

The extension takes the form of a high semi-circular wall in Portland stone, surrounding the memorial obelisk and finishing in two pavilions in which will be stored the seven volumes of the memorial register. The extension was designed by Mr Edward Maufe, RA, and the sculpture was by Mr Charles Wheeler RA, and Mr W McMillan RA.

The first wreath was laid by the Duke; others were laid by Admiral Sir Cecil Harcourt, Commander-in-Chief The Nore, and Mr Head, Secretary of State for War and Chairman of the Imperial War Graves Commission.'

In an interesting postscript, on 22 October 1952 *The Times* reported: 'After receiving letters and telephone calls from next-of-kin, the Imperial War Graves Commission has decided the replace part of the screen wall forming the extension to the Chatham Naval War Memorial, which was unveiled by the Duke of Edinburgh last Wednesday. Correspondents pointed out that the name Philippines among the naval battle honours inscribed on the wall was incorrectly spelt as Phillipines. An official of the Commission said to-day that it had not been established how or at what stage the mistake occurred, but fortunately it was discovered before it could be duplicated on similar memorials at Portsmouth and Plymouth. He said that the portion of Portland stone bearing the inscription would be cut out and replaced with the name correctly spelt as soon as possible.'

Those seamen lost from the Merchant Navy who served under command of the Royal Navy in the Second World War under the terms of what was known as the T 124 agreement were commemorated by name on the Liverpool Memorial that stands on the banks of the River Mersey. This monument, the collaborative effort of the architects Stanley Harold Smith, Charles Frederick Blythin and the sculptor George Herbert Tyson Smith consists of a circular column, faced in Portland stone, on a raised, semi-circular platform; on its summit is a device of reflective lenses suggestive of a beacon. The platform is approached from the promenade by a flight of steps, and is surrounded by a wall; at the head of the steps, at each end of the wall there is a globe, that on one side being a celestial globe ornamented with the signs of the zodiac, and that on the other being a terrestrial globe depicting the countries and seas of the world. Set in recesses in the wall are bronze panels that carry 1,390 names. The Memorial Register consists of a single volume. In it the names are arranged in alphabetical order, whereas on the Memorial they appear under the names of the ships on which the men served. At the base of the column, facing the steps and the promenade, beneath the badge of the Naval Crown, wreath, and fouled anchor, is carved the inscription:

"THESE OFFICERS AND MEN OF THE MERCHANT NAVY DIED WHILE SERVING WITH THE ROYAL NAVY AND HAVE NO GRAVE BUT THE SEA 1939 – 1945."


The Royal Navy Fleet Air Arm at Yeovilton had enjoyed a close friendship with the parish church of St. Bartholomew which began in 1940 with the commissioning of RNAS (Royal Navy Air Station) Yeovilton (HMS HERON). During 1940-42. 15 victims of air accidents were buried in the churchyard before the opening of the Naval Cemetery on the church's southern boundary in 1942. By 1988 much of the church structure having become unsafe, it was made redundant. It was then that the oft discussed idea of using St. Bartholomew's as the Anglican Church for RNAS Yeovilton was put into action. The Royal Navy seized the opportunity and bought the 'job-lot' for £1. This triggered a series of national and international appeals to restore the church to its former glory under the guardianship of the newly formed Trustees. An Order in Council signed by the Prince of Wales and Queen Elizabeth the Queen Mother formally sealed this process. St Bart's, as it has come to be affectionately known, passed from the local Diocese of Bath and Wells to assume the mantle of Fleet Air Arm Memorial Chapel - effectively a private chapel housing the Fleet Air Arm Memorial Record Book and a fitting focal point for those lost in conflict and other events. On 11 November 1993, after much restoration work, it was dedicated for use as such. Its appeal is worldwide and many visitors are struck by its beauty and upkeep. The site had been in use as a place of worship at least as far back as the Norman era. The chapel contains a Roll of Honour listing all those who have died in British Naval Aviation since 1908.

# OTHER NAVAL MEMORIALS FROM THE SECOND WORLD WAR

The memorial pictured above was erected by the Imperial War Graves Commission at the principal base of the Fleet Air Arm, at Lee-on-the-Solent. It commemorates all those lost from the Fleet Air Arm with no known grave in the Second World War. Its Westmoreland slate panels carry 1,928 names. It was jointly designed by J C Smith and L K Pallister of Newcastle and inaugurated by the Duchess of Kent on 20 May 1953.

The memorial erected at Lowestoft commemorated those lost from the Royal Naval Patrol Service. It was erected on that site, as it was from the Depot of the Royal Naval Reserve Trawler Service at Lowestoft that the new Service was raised. The memorial took the form of a fluted column rising from a circular base and was surmounted by a bronze ship device. Around the base were arranged 17 bronze panels containing the engraved names of 2,385 seamen, including 49 Newfoundlanders.

The Jack Mantle, VC Naval Gunnery Trophy is awarded twice a year to the Royal Navy warship with the best record in close range bombardment. It is awarded in memory of Leading Seaman Jack Mantle who died when HMS FOYLEBANK came under air attack whilst she lay off Portland on 4 July 1940. He was manning the starboard pom-pom. 'Early in the action his left leg was shattered by a bomb but he stood fast at his gun and went on firing... his great courage bore him up till the end of the fight when he fell by the gun he had so gallantly served'.[44]

---

[44] Extract from Victoria Cross citation for Leading Seaman Jack Mantle, VC.

# THE BINNEY MEMORIAL MEDAL

The Goldsmiths' Company is one of the twelve Great Livery Companies of the City of London. Its roots go back to the trade guilds of the Middle Ages and since 1300 it has been responsible for hallmarking gold and silver articles. It continues to this day to carry out this statutory function by operating the London Assay Office. The Worshipful Company of Goldsmiths gained their first Royal Charter from King Edward III in 1327 and they have occupied their present premises at Foster Lane in the City since 1339. The Company also promotes excellence in the design and craftsmanship of silverware and jewellery.

'On 8th December, 1944, a case of shopbreaking occurred at 23, Birchin Lane, City, E.C., when jewellery to the value of £2,563 was stolen. This crime was effected by several men using a stolen motor vehicle. They stopped outside the shop, broke the window with an axe, stole jewellery displayed in the window, entered the car and drove away. The offence was witnessed by Captain Binney, who in an effort to prevent the thieves driving away, jumped in front of the car. The driver drove at Captain Binney who was caught underneath the car and dragged for a considerable distance (over London Bridge) to Bermondsey. Captain Binney was found suffering from multiple injuries from which he later died. Enquiries were made by Metropolitan Police Officers in conjunction with City of London Police Officers and although several arrests were effected, sufficient evidence was obtained to convict only two of them, viz.: Ronald Hedley (the driver of the car) and Thomas James Jenkins. Hedley was convicted of murder and sentenced to Death; Jenkins was convicted of Manslaughter and sentenced to eight years' Penal Servitude. Hedley appealed against Conviction and Sentence of Death but his appeal was dismissed. The Death Sentence was later respited and commuted to Penal Servitude for Life.'[45] Captain Ralph Douglas Binney, CBE RN served in the Royal Navy in the Great War and was brought out of retirement during the Second World War to command HMS YEOMAN. After discussion with Captain Binney's friends and colleagues, in December 1946 Admiral Harold Tom Baillie-Grohman wrote to the Commissioner of Police for the Metropolis suggesting the institution of an award for bravery in his memory. After consultation between the Admiralty, the Home Office, the Treasury and the City of London Police, the Commissioner set in hand the institution of an award which would commemorate his bravery in a manner that would carry forward his example in perpetuity. They founded a trust fund to strike a medal which could be awarded for acts of bravery by civilians who were not members of any police force. Posthumous awards were not excluded (the headmaster Philip Laurence was the recipient of the award in 1996). The medal was designed by Gilbert Bayes and cast in bronze. The obverse has a relief portrait of Captain Binney and his dates, "1888-1944". The reverse has the inscriptions: "FOR COURAGE" and "IN SUPPORT OF LAW & ORDER AWARDED TO". An English Heritage Blue Plaque marks 23 Birchin Lane. The Selection Committee comprises the Chief Metropolitan Stipendiary Magistrate (Chairman), The Commissioner of Police for the Metropolis, the Commissioner of Police for the City of London, Second Sea Lord and the Clerk of the Goldsmiths' Company, (Secretary). Only one medal is awarded each year. If, in the opinion of the Selection Committee no act of sufficient merit had been performed in the year in question, then no award is made. A number of Certificates of Merit are also awarded each year to civilians for similar acts of courage for which the medal cannot be awarded, but which are judged deserving of special recognition. These arrangements were promulgated in Metropolitan Police Orders on 22 July 1947 and the first meeting of the Selection Committee duly took place at the Goldsmiths' Hall on 15 April 1948. Each December the Binney Memorial Awards ceremony is hosted by the Prime Warden and Wardens of the Worshipful Company of Goldsmiths. It is attended by the Commissioners of Police for both the City of London and the Metropolis, an Admiral of the Fleet, the Clerk of the Goldsmiths' Company and previous recipients of both the Binney Memorial Medal and Certificates. The awards are presented by London's Lord Mayor.

---

[45] Albert Pierrepoint *Executioner: Pierrepoint* 1974.

## ABLE SEAMAN DAVID VIGILAND RN

Able Seaman P/JX 643264 David John Vigiland served in the Royal Navy on HMS CHITRAL. He was born in West Ham, in the East End of London on 9 December 1926 and was the only son of John Vigiland, a successful businessman. At the start of the 20th century, the Vigilante family had migrated to England from Italy and anglicised their name to Vigiland.

David Vigiland died of peritonitis at the tragically young age of 20 in the Station Medical Hospital, Mombassa, Kenya, on 20 December 1946. The Imperial War Graves Commission did not permit repatriation of the bodies of dead Servicemen in the period for which it was responsible in either World War and he was buried in the naval plot at Mombassa. The Commission's remit for the Second World War ran up to and including 31 December 1947. John Vigiland refused to accept this state of affairs, reasoning that his son had not even died in wartime. After six years of correspondence between the family and the Commission and after the intervention of Sir Philip Euen Mitchell, Governor of Kenya, David Vigiland's body *was* eventually repatriated from Africa and interred with ceremony in the City of London Cemetery at Manor Park, East London on 9 December 1952.

# THE VIGILAND MEMORIAL

The Vigiland family were Roman Catholic and the design of the memorial over their son's grave was based on *The Descent from the Cross* - a magnificent altarpiece in Notre Dame Cathedral, Antwerp painted by Peter Paul Rubens in 1612.[46] The top of the cross bears Pontius Pilate's inscription: 'INRI' - 'Iesvs Nazarenvs Rex Ivdaeorvm' (Jesus of Nazareth, King of the Jews). The nine figures in the group are marginally smaller than life-size. The two figures leaning over the top of the cross are unnamed helpers. The figure holding Jesus Christ's right arm is St Joseph of Arimathea.[47] The male figure standing on the second and third steps of the right ladder is Simon of Cyrene. St Mark's Gospel records that he was stopped by Roman soldiers on the road to Jerusalem and compelled to carry Christ's cross to Golgotha. The figure with his back to the viewer, his right foot on the bottom rung of the ladder, is St John the Evangelist. The standing female figure on the far left is the Virgin Mary. The figure kneeling in front of her is her sister-in-law Mary Cleophas. The female figure kneeling with her back to the viewer is Mary Magdalene. The memorial took four years to carve from a 25 ton block of marble in Rome's Pietrasanta studio. It was imported to England as a work of art and dedicated as a memorial in 1955. John Vigiland purchased nine separate burial vaults from the cemetery to enable the memorial to be erected. Framed photographs of David Vigiland, his mother and father can be seen on the rear of the memorial. David Vigiland's mother, Lucy May died aged 63 on 8 February 1962 and his father John aged 72 on 7 February 1969. On the reverse of the memorial can be found the inscription in Italian: "E IN MEMORIA DELLA MIA CARA ADORATA MOGLIE" (AND IN MEMORY OF MY DEAR BELOVED WIFE). In the half century the Vigiland Memorial stood in the cemetery, it suffered weathering and discolouration. In 2003 the Corporation of the City of London decided to undertake its restoration and contracted Ron Knee of RK Conservation and Design to carry out the work. After being successfully cleaned, it was rededicated in a ceremony in the cemetery on 13 April 2003. Website at ww.cityoflondon.gov.uk/cemetery

---

[46] Peter Paul Rubens (1577-1640). Born Siegen, Westphalia. Studied under Tobias Verhaecht, Adam van Noort and Otto van Veen. He was court painter to Vincenzo Gonzaga, Duke of Mantua and subsequently to Archduke Albert and the Infanta Isabella of the Spanish Netherlands. In 1629 he was appointed Ambassador to the Court of St James by King Philip IV of Spain. In 1635 in Antwerp he painted *The Apotheosis of King James* which can be seen mounted on the ceiling of the Banqueting House, Whitehall. He was knighted by King Charles I.

[47] According to St Matthew's Gospel, St Joseph of Arimathea obtained the release of Christ's body from Pontius Pilate and buried it in a tomb in a garden. According to legend, he travelled to Glastonbury in AD 63 and evangelised the English. His journey from the Holy Land contains the seed of the *Sang Raal* or Grail legend.

## THE ROYAL NAVAL VOLUNTEER RESERVE

In 1903 the Royal Naval Volunteer Reserve (RNVR) was established to provide a body of trained men to supplement the Royal Naval Reserve (RNR), who were professional merchant seamen and the Royal Navy in times of crisis. Large numbers served with distinction throughout the Great War, particularly in the Royal Naval Division in France and Gallipoli. In 1919 the RNVR (Auxiliary Patrol) Club was founded to arrange periodical reunions, to form a Welfare Fund and to keep members in touch with the Volunteer Movement, but it had no premises. During the Second World War, the RNVR was again expanded and by 1945 there were 58,000 RNVR Officers or 80% of the naval officer strength. The idea of a Club where all RNVRs could meet in London and make their temporary home had long been in the minds of a number of people, but it was not until 1943 that the idea of forming an RNVR Officers' Association and a Club was suggested and much supported amongst the RNVR community, although not at first by the Admiralty, which suspected that such an association might be a front for 'subversive trade union type activity'. Owing to the good offices of Captain J N Pelly CBE RN and Commander Harry Vandervell RNVR, several interested people were able to get together at a meeting presided over by Commander Peter Frai RNVR (Sussex Division). Following the meeting, Vice Admiral Sir Godfrey Blake KCB DSO then Flag Officer to Admiral Harold Stark USN, took great interest in the project and owing to his influence, the official blessing of the Admiralty was obtained and the work was put in hand forthwith. The next problem was to raise money. Although the Admiralty intimated that certain funds might be made available, it was felt that private subscription would enable future members to feel that the Club was their very own. Accordingly, certain officers both RNVR and otherwise were approached for their support. This was given most generously and led by Lieutenant W Reynolds Albertini RNVR enough money was raised to enable a start to be made. At this time London had been badly blitzed and few buildings were available for conversion. Londonderry House in Park Lane was one of the places discussed, but was found to be too badly damaged to be of any practical use. Lieutenant R Nesbitt RNVR then reported that the Marlborough Club premises at 52 Pall Mall were vacant and negotiations were started with Lord Clarendon, Chairman of that Club to rent the premises. Construction and alteration work was put in hand and proceeded satisfactorily if spasmodically, owing to shortage of both labour and materials. By the beginning of February 1944, the premises were almost ready. The Germans however, not having been offered membership, demonstrated their resentment by dropping a stick of bombs on the premises on the evening of 23/24 February 1944 and reduced it to rubble. Fortunately the War Damage Commission were most helpful and with the assistance of two RNVR Lieutenants, Lennox-Boyd and Astor both of whom were also Members of Parliament, work was put in hand again and the Club was finally opened on 20 September 1944 by Mr A V Alexander, First Lord of the Admiralty, and named the King Alfred Club. It incorporated the old RNVR (Auxiliary Patrol) Club but the two Clubs maintained separate Officers. The object of the Club was to provide a residential Club in central London to furnish accommodation, meals, amenities and a common meeting ground for RNVR Officers living in, or passing through. London. The needs of Junior Officers were of primary importance. The Club was open to all Officers of all branches of the Service, including Dominion Officers, who had been mobilised for war service and who held commissions in the RNVR and had been confirmed in rank. The premises at Pall Mall provided accommodation for up to 50 members, two bars, a lounge and reading room, and a dining room. It was subsequently realised that the wartime function of the Club would soon be overshadowed by the demands of peacetime, and a new policy was required to maintain the interest and needs of both past and present RNVR Officers, many thousands of whom would return to their 'Civvy Street' occupations. Although adequate for wartime, the facilities would need to be improved to provide all the advantages of a West End club, for those who might not be able to afford the subscriptions of such clubs.

# THE NAVAL CLUB

It would be necessary to achieve and maintain a very large membership and obtain premises, which would enable the Club to expand. In October 1945 the first anniversary dinner was held and the Club was renamed The RNVR Club. In June 1946 a letter from the two Chairmen of the RNVR Club and the RNVR (Auxiliary Patrol) Club, respectively Commodore Earl Howe, RNVR, and Commander Harry Vandervell RNVR, was sent to all RNVR Officers. This letter announced that the two Clubs would combine to form one RNVR Officers' Association. The Association would:

a) Maintain a Clubhouse in London as the headquarters of the Association.
b) Continue and extend the RNVR (Auxiliary Patrol) Welfare Fund.

It also announced that the lease on 52 Pall Mall would expire on 31 December 1946 and a Commemoration Fund was being launched to purchase and refurbish a property at 38 Hill Street. As time was short, the property had already been bought by four individuals who had lent the necessary funds of £50,000. The Commemoration Fund sought to raise the £50,000 to repay the loan, plus a further £25,000 to convert and equip it as a Club and another £25,000 to create an Endowment Fund. Any surplus funds would go to the Welfare Fund. Although the sums were large, so was the RNVR and only £2 per head was needed to raise the funds. All RNVR Officers were invited to join. The RNVR Club, with a membership of 10,000, opened its doors to members in Hill Street on 9 December 1946. In 1949 The King granted his patronage to the Association, and this has been continued by The Queen. Also in 1949, with membership down to 8,000, members of the RNR, RMR, and Cadets of Worcester, Pangbourne and Conway were invited to join. By January 1950 membership had increased again to 10,655. The RNVR, RNV(S)R, RNV(W)R and all other Reserves were all amalgamated under the title RNR in October 1958 and the Club continued to prosper through the 1950s with membership reaching an all time peak of 12,114 in December 1959. However the 1960s saw a dramatic fall in membership and by January 1966 numbers were down to 5,220. The decision was then made to extend membership to all Naval Officers and others interested in the sea and maritime affairs in general, and the Club was renamed The Naval Club. In 1954, to mark the Golden Jubilee of the RNVR, the building was designated as a War Memorial to all RNVR Officers who had died in the two World Wars, and a Commemorative Tablet was unveiled by Admiral of the Fleet Lord Cunningham. A charity known as WAVE Heritage Trust was subsequently established to maintain the building as a war memorial in perpetuity. In November 2000, the Duke of Edinburgh unveiled the RNVR Roll of Honour containing the names of 6,200 RNVR personnel killed during the Second World War, from all the countries of the Empire and Dominions. The memorial cabinet occupies pride of place in the inner hall. In December 2003 to mark the centenary of the formation of the RNVR the Prince of Wales unveiled a Commonwealth Commemorative Plaque showing wartime ships particularly connected to the Volunteer Naval Reserves from Australia, Canada, India, New Zealand, South Africa and the UK.

Today the Naval Club continues to be open to all those who have an interest in the sea and maritime affairs in general, whether or not they have served in any branch of the Royal Navy. Members have the use of the Club's public rooms including the beautiful oak panelled bar, an elegant Reading Room, and up the magnificent grand staircase is the Dining Room where all meals are served. Private function rooms are available for hire for receptions, conferences, meetings, lunches and dinners. Reciprocity is established with over 60 Clubs world-wide, enabling members to have access to first class facilities in many countries. During the last four years £500,000 has been spent on refurbishing and modernising the building and the accommodation. In 2004 the Club underwent a substantial restoration which was completed in August that year. Website at www.navalclub.co.uk

# HILL STREET

The Club.

The commemorative tablet.

# THE ROYAL NORWEGIAN NAVY AND MERCHANT MARINE MEMORIAL

Just north of the Serpentine in London's Hyde Park stands an ice-age boulder placed by the Royal Norwegian Navy and the Norwegian Merchant Marine in thanks for the assistance and succour afforded them by the British People in the struggle against the Nazis in the Second World War. The memorial was the initiative of the Chief of the Norwegian Naval Staff and cost 25,000 Kroner which was funded by the Norwegian Government. The cost of its transportation from Norway was borne by the Norwegian Merchant Marine. It was inaugurated by the Chief of the Norwegian Naval Staff and accepted by the First Sea Lord on 20 September 1978. A Guard of Honour was furnished by both the British and Norwegian Armies. Two hundred invited guests attended the ceremony and the reception at the Norwegian Embassy afterwards. The front of the boulder carries the inscription:

"THIS STONE WAS ERECTED BY THE ROYAL NORWEGIAN NAVY
AND THE NORWEGIAN MERCHANT FLEET IN THE YEAR 1978
WE THANK THE BRITISH PEOPLE FOR FRIENDSHIP
AND HOSPITALITY DURING THE SECOND WORLD WAR
YOU GAVE US A SAFE HAVEN IN OUR COMMON STRUGGLE
FOR FREEDOM AND PEACE"

The reverse face carries the inscription:

"THIS BOULDER WAS BROUGHT HERE FROM NORWAY
WHERE IT WAS WORN AND SHAPED FOR THOUSANDS OF YEARS
BY FORCES OF NATURE - FROST, RUNNING WATER, ROCK, SAND AND ICE –
UNTIL IT OBTAINED ITS PRESENT SHAPE"

## THE BATTLE OF MAY ISLAND

A tragic series of accidents occurred during a night exercise during the Great War and cost the lives of more than 100 Royal Navy sailors. 84 years after the so-called 'Battle of May Island' - in which no enemy was present, their loss was commemorated by a cairn erected in Anstruther Harbour on the Forth shore opposite May Island. The tragedy centred around the K-class of submarines. 'These huge vessels were the most bizarre submarines ever built and K-3, laid down by the King in 1915, was the first to commission on 4 August 1916. Although 28 were ordered in batches, only 17 were completed'.[48] Vickers built six at an estimated cost of £340,000. Others were built by Fairfield, Armstrong-Whitworth, Scotts, Beardmore, Portsmouth and Devonport Dockyards. British admirals of the period were keen to have their battle fleets supported by the new weapon; it seemed logical to have submarines accompany the fleet on the surface, diving to attack the enemy fleet when it was spotted. But diesel engines of the period simply could not provide enough speed on the surface for a submarine to keep up even with battleships. The K-class was Admiral 'Jackie' Fisher's answer: huge submarines, with powerful steam-driven propulsion on the surface, normal electric motors whilst submerged. Fisher[49] had written a prophetic paper on the likely German use of the submarine in 1913, which had been disregarded. With the coming of war in 1914 his conclusions were proved correct. From which point on, Fisher became the Admiralty's acknowledged guru on the subject of submarines.

From the start the K-boats were plagued with misfortune. Built with great haste during wartime, and pushing submarine technology to the limits, they had a poor reputation for mechanical reliability. The steam-propulsion complete with funnels took a long time to prepare for a dive. One, K-13, confirmed the worst fears of the superstitious by sinking on her maiden dive on 29 January 1917 with the loss of 30 lives. But the submarines were fast on the surface, and the Royal Navy determined to use them for Fleet work, including K-13, salvaged and hastily renamed K-22.

On 31 January 1917 Admiral Beatty took the Grand Fleet to sea for an intensive exercise to ensure it remained at full efficiency whilst waiting for the German High Seas Fleet to risk battle. Nine K-boats sailed from Rosyth that evening, along with the battlecruiser squadrons. A U-boat was thought to be in the area, so all ships increased speed as they approached May Island, to offer a more difficult target. In the dark, two small patrol boats wandered into the path of the K-boats of 13th Flotilla. Turning to avoid them, the rudder of K-14 jammed. She ended up broadside on to the unlucky K-22, which spotted her too late in the dark and the ensuing collision left both submarines dead in the water, with lights only showing dimly and their silhouettes almost impossible to spot. They were nearly run over and sunk by the battlecruiser HMS AUSTRALIA, but were narrowly missed. It seemed as if disaster had been averted. However, the light cruiser HMS ITHURIEL and the other three K-boats of 13th Flotilla had turned back to help. Unfortunately, the 12th Flotilla K-boats, led by the light cruiser HMS FEARLESS, were unaware of the accident ahead and ran straight into their sister Flotilla. HMS FEARLESS rammed K-17, and the submarine sank with all hands in a matter of minutes. K-6 hit K-4 and nearly cut her in half. The two submarines sat locked together, but K-7 was approaching fast astern. Spotting K-6, she just managed to avoid her, but was totally unaware of K-4 lying across her path, and a further collision ensued. The second hit proved fatal for K-4, and she sank. Only nine men were subsequently pulled from the water, and one of these died before he could receive medical treatment. Over 100 men were lost that night. Two submarines were sunk and four damaged, along with a light cruiser.

---

[48] Reginald Longstaff *Submarine Command*.
[49] John Arbuthnot Fisher (1841-1920). Born Ramboda, Ceylon. Entered Royal Navy 1854, gunnery specialist. Rear Admiral 1890. First Sea Lord 1904-10. Admiral of the Fleet 1905, Baron 1909, retired 1911. Reappointed First Sea Lord by Churchill in October 1914. Resigned (for the ninth time) after disagreeing with Churchill's Gallipoli policy in May 1915. ('Lord Fisher In the King's name I order you at once to return to your post'. Prime Minister Asquith's note to Admiral Fisher 15 May 1915). Chairman Admiralty Inventions Board 1915-16.

## THE MEMORIAL CAIRN

The cairn in front of the lifeboat house at Anstruther Harbour in memory of those lost was unveiled on 31 January 2002.

The inauguration ceremony attended by members of Fife Council, representatives of the Royal Navy Submarine Service and veterans.

# ESTONIA

In June 2000, a little-known theatre of operations involving the Royal Navy in the Baltic in the period 1918-1920 was honoured. British sea power played a crucial role in securing Latvian and Estonian independence from the Bolsheviks immediately after the Great War. The waters of the Baltic had during the course of that war been sown by the belligerents with more than 60,000 mines and this hazard would take its toll of British crews. British Government nervousness that naval crews might become infected with communism meant ships spent only six weeks at a time on station. Lloyd George's government was fully aware that British involvement in the Baltic was unpopular at home and actively opposed by socialist elements among Britain's workforce. However, the greatest loss sustained by the Royal Navy in the Baltic would not be a ship. HM Submarine L55 commanded by Lieutenant C M S Chapman was sunk on 4 June 1919 by a British moored mine whilst attempting to torpedo the Red cruiser *Gavriil*.[50] Bolshevik propaganda insisted that she had been sunk by one of their destroyers.[51] But given the offensive capabilities of the Red Navy at that time, this is unlikely. On 11 August 1928 she was raised by the Soviets who were keen to learn her secrets. The Admiralty via the Swedish Government requested that the bodies of the crew be returned. The Soviets acceded to this request, but stipulated that no British warship would be allowed to enter any Russian port. The British merchantman TRURO commanded by Captain W Dearing took the 42 coffins on at Kronstadt, the naval base that guarded Leningrad. They were transferred to HMS CHAMPION at Reval, (now Tallinn) Estonia on 15 August. Captain Dearing wrote in his diary: 'An Estonian naval and military guard of two hundred marched on to the jetty. They saluted the coffins as they passed and halted in line, and in three ranks, opposite CHAMPION. The reception of floral tributes then began. One tribute drew particular attention; a poorly clad elderly peasant woman made her way quietly to the quarter-deck where she placed a bunch of wild flowers on a coffin before moving away sobbing. In spite of the adverse weather conditions a large crowd gathered for the official ceremony. Government, military, naval and other dignitaries passed along the row of coffins saluting the dead and depositing wreaths. When this part of the ceremony had been completed, the visitors left CHAMPION and stood on the jetty while an Estonian military band played *Nearer My God to Thee*. CHAMPION's crew stood smartly to attention and those on the jetty bared their heads. The Estonian naval and military guard then fired three volleys. Royal Marine buglers sounded the *Last Post* to complete the ceremony.' All shipping in the port and government offices lowered their flags. The ceremony ended with HMS CHAMPION leaving the jetty with her Royal Marine band playing Chopin's *Funeral March*. The coffins were buried in a communal grave in the Royal Naval Cemetery, Haslar on 7 September. A single large headstone marks their grave with the names of all the crew members inscribed upon it.

General Johan Laidoner, Chief of the Estonian General Staff would write: 'I am sure that without the arrival of the British fleet in Tallinn in December 1918, the fate of our country and our people would have been very different - Estonia and I believe, other Baltic states would have found themselves in the hands of the Bolsheviks'.

The Baltic Battle Squadron was initially commanded by Rear Admiral Edwyn Alexander-Sinclair and he was succeeded by Rear Admiral Walter Cowan. Richard Hough described 'Titch' Cowan in his review of *Cowan's War* as: 'short, sharp-faced, highly strung, belligerent and thoroughly difficult'. Cowan would go on to fight with the Commandos in North Africa in the Second World War, in 1944 earning a bar to his (1898) DSO at the age of 72. *L55* was subsequently commissioned into the Soviet Baltic Fleet and was again lost with all hands whilst undergoing sea trials. She was recovered once again and served in the Soviet Baltic Fleet without further mishap until being scrapped in 1953.

---

[50] *The Salvage of HM S/M L55 by the Soviet Navy: The Reason Why* Przemysław Budzbon and Boris Lemachko *Warship* Number 45, January 1988, p. 4.
[51] Geoffrey Bennett, *Cowan's War* Collins, London 1964, p. 119.

# THE MEMORIALS IN THE PULAVAIMU CHURCH

In the 13 month campaign in the Baltic, 128 British service personnel were awarded the Vabodus Rist (Estonian Freedom Cross) for their role in Estonia's War of Independence. Recipients included King George V and the Unknown Warrior. In June 2000 a memorial listing their names was unveiled in the Pulavaimu (Holy Spirit) Church, Tallinn by Rear Admiral Tarmo Kõuts, Commander of the Estonian Defence Forces, accompanied by Admiral Sir Michael Boyce, First Sea Lord. It was designed by Mr Priit R Herodes, Chairman of the Estonian Heritage Society and Heraldry College. It cost £1,000 and was funded by the Estonian Government. A Royal Navy White Ensign was donated to the church on that occasion. At the ceremony, the Very Reverend Gustav Peeter Pir, Dean of Tallinn, invited the Earl of Carlisle (Patron of the Baltic Council) to assist in identifying the names of all the British Service personnel who had died in Estonia's War of Independence, that they might be commemorated in like manner. Through the Earl's efforts and with the assistance of the CWGC and MOD's Naval Historical Branch, a complete list of all who had died in the campaign was arrived at. The unveiling and dedication of the memorial to the 14 Royal Navy officers, 92 ratings, 4 RAF officers and one airman who were killed in action in the Baltic 1918-19, took place in the Church on 20 July 2003. The ceremony was performed by Admiral Sir Alan West, First Sea Lord and Vice Admiral Kõuts. (The religious dignitaries and First Sea Lord are pictured above). In his address Admiral West noted: 'One December day nearly 85 years ago there appeared on the horizon in the Bay of Tallinn a British fleet - three light cruisers, nine destroyers and the PRINCESS MARGARET, carrying ammunition. This was to be the beginning of a partnership which brought hundreds of British ships, planes and men to this theatre of war. Their presence achieved a breakthrough in the Estonian War of Independence. It ensured that the fighting spirit and the will of the Estonian Army and Navy were able to operate so effectively in the liberation of this land. But for many of the British Servicemen who came to these northern waters this campaign was their last. And today we remember those gallant men, of the Royal Navy and the Air Force who died in this campaign. In placing a memorial today in this historic building, in the heart of Estonia's capital we commemorate for all time the sacrifice they made. We remember by name 111 who died. We remember the grief of their loved ones. And we give thanks that the values which they died for once again bind our two countries so closely. We remember them. Me maletame neid'.[52]

---

[52] In Estonian: 'We remember them'.

# THE COMMANDOS

The first Royal Marines Commando was formed at Deal, Kent on 14 February 1942. 'The concept of Combined Operations had been accepted by the British military hierarchy by the middle of 1942, and Combined Operations Headquarters, under the leadership of Lord Louis Mountbatten, was seen as the focal centre for developing the techniques and equipment needed for the eventual invasion of German-occupied Europe'.[53] Planning for the invasion of Europe commenced even as the British Army was being evacuated from the beaches at Dunkirk and the Commandos would play a key role. In consequence, the Commando Basic Training Centre was established at Achnacarry, on the estate of Sir Donald Cameron of Lochiel near Fort William in the Highlands. Troops arriving for the 12 week course would de-train at Spean Bridge, put their baggage on the motor transport and then speed-march the seven miles to the camp in full kit with weapons. Any man who fell out on the march was immediately RTU'd. (Returned To Unit). This served merely as a curtain-raiser for what would follow. In Charles McNeill's words: 'Reveille at Achnacarry was at six or thereabouts, when a piper marched right through the Nissen hut, leaving all the doors open. That's no joke in March in the Highlands, and most of the training was physical. You ran everywhere at Achnacarry, even when off duty, even to the sick bay to have the blisters cut off your feet. Officers had to do the same, and all exercises used live ammo. It was a very fit unit that marched out a few weeks later'. More than 20,000 commandos of all nationalities were trained at Achnacarry and their memorial (pictured above) stands at Spean Bridge. It consists of three commandos in battle dress wearing cap-comforters on their heads, standing on a plinth. Designed by Scott Sutherland, (1910-84) and made by the firm of H H Martyn and Co, the memorial was inaugurated by Queen Elizabeth the Queen Mother on 27 September 1952.

The Commando Memorial sculpted by Gilbert Ledward in the cloister of Westminster Abbey was unveiled by Winston Churchill on 21 May 1948. It is the venue for the annual service of remembrance held there on the Saturday preceding Remembrance Sunday. In St George's Chapel in the Abbey, under the Commando Association Battle Honours Flag, is an inscribed Roll of Honour which contains the names of all 1,706 Commandos, both Army and Royal Marine, who died in the Second World War.

---

[53] Robin Neillands *By Sea & Land: The story of the Royal Marines*.

## THE FLEET AIR ARM MEMORIAL, VICTORIA EMBANKMENT

The Fleet Air Arm Memorial was inaugurated by the Prince of Wales on 1 June 2000. He was accompanied by his brother the Duke of York (a former naval helicopter pilot). The First Sea Lord, Admiral Sir Michael Boyce, attended with senior FAA Officers, Rear Admiral Iain Henderson, Commodore Christopher Clayton and Commodore Tony Hogg, and Admiral of The Fleet Sir Benjamin Bathurst, President of the FAA Memorial Trust Committee. The unveiling, at Victoria Embankment Gardens near MOD Main Building in London was watched by thousands of veterans from Fleet Air Arm Associations, widows and relatives of those who lost members of their family both in war and flying accidents. The memorial commemorates the 6,000 naval personnel who have died in the service of the Fleet Air Arm and its precursor, the Royal Naval Air Service. Architect Tim Kempster designed the bronze sculpture and it was executed by James Butler RA. He also sculpted *Alex* which stands outside the Guards Chapel at Wellington Barracks, Birdcage Walk, London and the Green Howards Memorial at Crepon in Normandy. This memorial takes the form of a striking bronze figure of Daedalus. In Greek mythology, Daedalus and his son Icarus escaped on wax-coated wings from the labyrinth on Crete, where they had been imprisoned by King Minos. Ignoring Daedalus' warning, Icarus flew too close to the sun. His wings melted and he plunged into the sea. Daedalus stands on a Portland stone column with a distinctive curved base. The battle honours of the Fleet Air Arm are incised on the column and the gold 'wings' insignia of the Fleet Air Arm and the dedication appear on the reverse face. Daedalus has a special resonance for both the Fleet Air Arm and the Fleet, with five ships having been named after him since the C18. The memorial bears the following inscription:

"TO THE EVERLASTING MEMORY OF ALL THE MEN AND WOMEN FROM THE UNITED KINGDOM, THE BRITISH COMMONWEALTH AND THE MANY ALLIED NATIONS WHO HAVE GIVEN THEIR LIVES WHILST SERVING IN THE ROYAL NAVAL AIR SERVICE AND THE FLEET AIR ARM"

# THE RECENT PAST

On 20 September 1976 during a mail transfer, the Ton Class minesweeper HMS FITTLETON was in collision with the 2,500 ton type 41/61 frigate HMS MERMAID some 80 miles north of Texel, off the Frisian Islands, during the NATO exercise *Teamwork '76* and sank. 12 sailors, mostly members of the Royal Naval Reserve, lost their lives. 32 survivors were rescued. One of the memorials to those who died that day took the form of a stained glass window at HMS PRESIDENT, St Katharine's Dock, London (pictured above). The window contains a scroll listing by name each man who died that day. A memorial plaque was placed in the village church of Fittleton and another in St Martin's in the Fields Church, Trafalgar Square, London. Subsequently HMS FITTLETON was also commemorated on the Ton Class Memorial erected at the National Memorial Arboretum at Alrewas in Staffordshire. A memorial service is held each 20 September in the steepled medieval village church at Fittleton in Wiltshire to commemorate those who died.

The discovery in 2001 of the location of 44,600 ton, 860 foot long HMS HOOD in the Denmark Strait between Iceland and Greenland by a team led by the American marine archaeologist David Mearns on the research vessel *Northern Horizon*, gives food for thought on the subject of future modes of commemoration for the Royal Navy. In a ceremony to remember those who perished, a brass plate was laid on the deck of the HOOD it contained an embedded microdot listing the names of 1,415 men who lost their lives when she was sunk by the German battleship BISMARCK on 24 May 1941. She went down in less than four minutes. That the mechanical claw that laid the plate on HOOD's deck should have been released by Mr A E Briggs, one of three men, who survived the sinking of the world's largest warship that day was poignant, and a new chapter in the history of memorialisation for the Royal Navy.

# CHAPTER VII

# ROYAL AIR FORCE MEMORIALS

## THE ROYAL AIR FORCE MEMORIAL

Although the origins of the modern Royal Air Force can be discerned as far back as the experiments conducted by the Royal Engineers in the Balloon Equipment Store at Woolwich Barracks in 1878, the Royal Flying Corps was only constituted by Royal Warrant on 13 April 1912. During the Great War, on the recommendation of a committee chaired by Lieutenant General Jan Christiaan Smuts which considered the issues of air power and home defence, the RFC and the Royal Naval Air Service were amalgamated on 1 April 1918 into a new organisation titled the 'Royal Air Force'. On 23 February 1921 the Royal Air Force Memorial Fund wrote to the Local Government Committee of London County Council requesting a site on Victoria Embankment for the purpose of erecting a memorial to commemorate all those who fell in the service of their country in the RNAS, RFC and RAF in the Great War. This was duly granted on 15 April and the memorial was inaugurated in 1923. The architect Sir Reginald Blomfield designed it and it took the form of a pylon surmounted by a golden eagle sculpted by Sir William Reid Dick. The eagle looks out across the River Thames. The general inscription is on the Embankment side, reading:

"IN MEMORY OF ALL RANKS OF ROYAL NAVAL AIR SERVICE, ROYAL FLYING CORPS, ROYAL AIR FORCE AND THOSE AIR FORCES FROM EVERY PART OF THE BRITISH EMPIRE WHO GAVE THEIR LIVES IN WINNING VICTORY FOR THEIR KING AND COUNTRY 1914 – 1918"

On the bottom plinth is the inscription when the memorial was rededicated in 1946. It was unveiled by Marshal of the Royal Air Force Lord Trenchard:

"THIS INSCRIPTION IS ADDED IN REMEMBRANCE OF THOSE MEN AND WOMEN OF THE AIR FORCES OF EVERY PART OF THE BRITISH COMMONWEALTH AND EMPIRE WHO GAVE THEIR LIVES 1939 - 1945"

# THE FLYING SERVICES MEMORIAL

After the Great War, at Fauborg d'Amiens Cemetery at Arras, Sir Edwin Lutyens designed a memorial with a repeating colonnade nearly 400 feet long. The memorial carries 35,942 names of the missing. The largest numbers are from the Royal Fusiliers (City of London Regiment) with 1,422 and the Northumberland Fusiliers with 1,378. There are 2,600 graves in the cemetery.

Although the Royal Air Force was only founded on 1 April 1918, by the close of the Great War it had more than 50,000 men serving on the Western Front. 9,352 airmen lost their lives during the war and of these, some 4,000 were killed in action. Lutyens modified his design of the Arras Memorial to incorporate a pylon to commemorate the 1,000 pilots of the Royal Flying Corps, Royal Naval Air Service and the Royal Air Force who died on the Western Front and have no known grave. Sir William Reid Dick's design for the memorial took the form of a free standing pylon, surmounted by a winged globe oriented as the Earth was poised in Space at 1100 on 11 November 1918, Armistice Day. Five winged comets representing the five years of war encircle the globe symbolising the forces of the air. The memorial lists by name each pilot who did not return and includes the names such illustrious figures in military aviation history as Major Lance Hawker VC (also commemorated by a stained glass window in his local church at Longparish in Hants) and Major 'Mick' Mannock VC who was shot down flying from St Omer on 26 July 1918. The memorial was unveiled by Marshal of the RAF Lord Trenchard,[1] the Father of the Royal Air Force, on 31 July 1932.

---

[1] Hugh Trenchard (1873-1956). Born in Somerset, he was commissioned into the Royal Scots Fusiliers, served in the Boer War and subsequently in Nigeria. In 1910 he gained a pilot's licence and during the Great War he commanded the Royal Flying Corps. In January 1918 he was appointed Chief of Staff of the new Air Ministry, but returned to France to command the Allied Air Force. On 1 April 1918 he became Chief of Staff of the RAF. In 1927 he was appointed first Marshal of the Royal Air Force. He served as Metropolitan Police Commissioner 1931-1935 and was created 1st Viscount Trenchard in 1936.

## THE SECOND WORLD WAR

At the end of the war, the RAF recognised that its need for commemoration far outstripped the forms it employed after the Great War and it showed considerable ingenuity in selecting the forms it would adopt. The Air Council agreed with the Commission's proposal to commemorate airmen alongside their Army comrades on the memorials at Singapore and El Alamein and adopted the church of St Clement Danes and laid plans for its resurrection. However, given that this was an Anglican church, the Board recognised that this would not serve the interests of all faiths and determined to find a means of commemorating all with equal honour. 'It was decided to build a separate memorial to airmen who had died in Britain, north-west Europe and over the north Atlantic, but while some wanted this to be in London, others, notably Sir Arthur Longmore, now the air force representative on the Commission, wanted to preserve a closer association with aircraft that would continue to fly, and favoured a position near Heathrow, London's airport. Lieutenant Colonel Reginald Murphy, the Chief Officer for the United Kingdom, took many a long investigatory walk along Thameside near Windsor and eventually came upon a site on Cooper's Hill, part of a wooded ridge that swept down to the river at Runnymede, with broad views toward Windsor and Heathrow. Maufe and Longmore were delighted with it, and by the autumn of 1949 the owners had donated the site and the Commission and the Air Council had given their approval'.[2]

The Richard Ormond Shuttleworth Remembrance Trust commemorates Richard Shuttleworth. He was the only son of a wealthy family from Bedfordshire and an aviator of considerable experience and ability. He collected airplanes which he stored at his own private airfield. He joined the RAF on the outbreak of war and was killed flying night-fighters in 1940. His mother founded the Trust to perpetuate his name through the medium he loved and the Shuttleworth Collection can still be seen at Biggleswade Airdrome in Bedfordshire.

Another form of memorialisation is the Arthur Barrett Memorial Prize. Air Chief Marshal Sir Arthur Barrett served in both the RFC and the RAF. His career spanned the very beginnings of military aviation to the jet age. When he died in 1966, it transpired that he had endowed a fund in his memory. It was decided that the prize, an engraved piece of silverware, would be awarded each year on the recommendation of an adjudication panel of senior RAF officers to that member of the RAF selected as having shown the greatest degree of outstanding skill and proficiency in performing aircrew duties the previous year.

In the early hours of 16 May 1944 a Lancaster bomber from 576 Squadron RAF was 'bounced' by a German nightfighter over Denmark. The bomber began to disintegrate in the air and crashed into the village of Gamtofte in eastern Denmark. 'Bomber Command records show that Lancaster ME576 UL-X2 took off from RAF Elsham Wolds in North Lincolnshire at 10 pm on May 15, 1944. Under *Operation Gardening*, the Lancaster's mission was to lay mines in Denmark's Little Belt seaway.'[3] The village church was seriously damaged and its presbytery demolished. Most of the village was destroyed and two farms were burned to the ground in the subsequent conflagration. All eight crew perished in the crash and were buried by the occupying Germans in the cemetery at nearby Assens. Miraculously and despite the damage caused to the village, no Danes were killed. In 2004 the villagers made an appeal through the *Daily Telegraph* newspaper seeking to contact the relatives of the aircrew to enable them to attend a memorial service being held in the village church on 16 May 2004. Six years after the war, the villagers of Gamtofte raised a commemorative stone carrying the names of the crew. It also bore the inscription:

"DENMARK THANKS THESE SONS OF ENGLAND
WHO FOUND THEIR DEATH HERE ON MAY 16th 1944"

---

[2] Philip Longworth, *The Unending Vigil*.
[3] *Daily Telegraph* 21 April 2004.

# THE BATTLE OF BRITAIN CLASS OF LOCOMOTIVES

The former Southern Railway was one of the pre-Nationalisation 'Big Four' of independent railway companies who preceded the former British Rail (along with the Great Western Railway, London, Midland and Scottish Railway and the London and North Eastern Railway after grouping in 1923). With the assistance of the Air Ministry, the company decided to name 40 of its Bulleid light pacifics (4-6-2 wheel arrangement) to commemorate the Battle of Britain. Fully laden, a West Country/Battle of Britain pacific locomotive tipped the scales at 133 tons 5cwt. Unrebuilt engines had something of a reputation with train crews and shed fitters, but were speedy when running well. Their original colour scheme was malachite green with yellow lining, with nameplate with coat of arms or badge on each side of the original streamlined casing. From August 1949 this was changed to standard British Railways express passenger loco Brunswick Green, lined in black and orange. It took until March 1953 to repaint the whole class. A few briefly received an experimental apple green livery.

Following introduction in 1946, the locomotives operated throughout the area covered by the Southern Railway, from the London terminals at Waterloo (London's last steam terminus in 1967) for the West Country and south coast, and the Kent coast expresses from Victoria, Charing Cross (to Ramsgate) and Cannon Street. Construction of the West Country/Battle of Britain class continued after nationalisation, until January 1951. Other than the nameplates, the 'West Countries' and 'Battle of Britain's' were virtually identical, with their distinctive 'air-smoothed' boiler casing (hence their nickname 'spamcans' or 'streaks') and Bulleid-Firth-Brown 'Boxpox' driving wheels. Their chain-driven valve-gear in its oil bath between the frames could fail, and the oil proved to be a fire hazard on occasions when leaks reached the hot boiler. The class was designed by the highly idiosyncratic Oliver Vaughan Snell Bulleid, Chief Mechanical Engineer of the Southern Railway, and all but six were built at Brighton Locomotive Works, the others being built at Eastleigh.

The nameplates are of brass with raised letters on a pale sky-blue background, each with the wording Battle of Britain Class in small lettering at the base; badges were vitreous enamelled within a gunmetal surround, with the appropriate badge or crest again on an air force pale blue background. On air-smoothed casing engines the nameplate was applied above the badge, with the badge above the nameplate mounted on the running plate of rebuilt locos. Squadrons of the RAF have their own crest and where none was available, as in the case of Croydon and the Hurricane, the Arms of the Royal Air Force was used.

After much correspondence with the Air Ministry, names were allocated, some being taken from Fighter Command's Order of Battle for No.11 Group on 3 November 1940, (the end of the Battle).The names included famous airfields, personalities, aircraft and squadrons as a tribute to the part they played in defeating the Luftwaffe, fighting for the most part, over territory served by the Southern Railway. The names included: *Hurricane; Fighter Command; Air Vice Marshal Sir Keith Park; Air Vice Marshal Sir Trafford Leigh-Mallory; Royal Observer Corps; Croydon; No 46 Squadron; No 141 Squadron; No 219 Squadron; No 222 Squadron; No 229 Squadron; No 249 Squadron; No 253 Squadron; No 264 Squadron; No 501 (County of Gloucester) Squadron Royal Auxiliary Air Force; No 602 (City of Glasgow) Squadron, Royal Auxiliary Air Force; No 603 (City of Edinburgh) Squadron* and *No 615 (County of Surrey) Squadron Royal Auxiliary Air Force.*

Most of the nameplates were presented by British Rail to the RAF and by the mid 1960s many locomotives had their name and number plates removed while they were still in service to prevent theft as these items climbed in value. The frequently filthy locomotives saw out their final days with cabside or smokebox numbers crudely painted or chalked on.

With the radical downsizing of Britain's armed forces throughout the 1980s and 1990s, many of the nameplates and crests slowly found their way to the Royal Air Force Museum at Hendon, (not all are on display). A number of them may also be seen displayed in the entrance portico of the Officers Mess at RAF Bentley Priory.

# RAF BENTLEY PRIORY

The stained glass window pictured above may be found beneath the vaulted ceiling of the entrance portico of the Officers Mess at RAF Bentley Priory. Topped by a gilt RAF crest, in the window a spitfire is superimposed on a green map of Great Britain whilst an RAF pilot in flying gear and wearing a Mae West life jacket scrambles. Airborne spitfires can be seen in the top left portion of the window. The portico's other window depicts a hurricane. These two fighters were the weapon with which Fighter Command fought the Battle of Britain and prevailed. The window commemorates the critical role played by Bentley Priory.

By the summer of 1940 Bentley Priory had been fitted out as HQ of Fighter Command and was it was from the Operations Room here that Air Marshal Sir Hugh Dowding directed the RAF's fighter squadrons in the Battle of Britain. Given that the RAF did not have enough aircraft to mount standing patrols to defend Britain's airspace, the Operations Room performed the function of a brain, with appreciations of threat being made and instructions being passed to Group and Sector levels to direct Fighter Command's operational units onto attacking formations of German aircraft. The first stage in the process was the Filter Room. 'Information on incoming raids was passed, via land lines, into the room from various different sources including the Chain Home Radar sites, Royal Observer Corps observation posts and anti-aircraft battery sites. The function of the Filter Room was to collate, classify and record the information before passing it, in a concise form, to the appropriate desk in the Operations Room which was next door.'[4] 'Here sat Dowding, the Chief of Fighter Command, together with the General in charge of Anti-Aircraft Command, the Commandant of the Observer Corps, liaison officers from Bomber and Coastal Commands, the Admiralty, the War Office and the Ministry of Home Security. Here was the map of operations, attended by WAAF plotters with their croupier rakes.'[5]

Heavily camouflaged, the Sir John Soanes' designed Priory was never identified by the Germans as being HQ Fighter Command and it survived the war practically unscathed, which might strike the reader as somewhat surprising, given that the Luftwaffe 'top brass' had been entertained there in October 1937. The Priory was subsequently used as the HQ from which the D-Day Landings were directed in 1944.

---

[4] *An Illustrated History of RAF Bentley Priory*. Published by HQ Strike Command, RAF High Wycombe.
[5] David Beaty *Light Perpetual*.

# THE BATTLE OF BRITAIN COMMEMORATIVE LACE PANELS

In 1851 a lace panel depicting scenes from the life of St Joan of Arc was manufactured for the Paris Exhibition. It remains the largest pictorial lace work in existence and it would serve as the inspiration for what would become the Battle of Britain Commemorative Lace Panel.

The Panel was manufactured in the period 1942-46 by the Nottingham lace making firm of Dobson and Browne Ltd: 'To perpetuate this glorious epic in our history and as a tribute to those who gallantly saved this island'. 'The panel measures 15 feet long by 65 inches wide and depicts various scenes witnessed during the bombing of London, the principal Allied and Axis aircraft in the battle, and the badges of the Allied Air Forces involved, together with the names of the craftsmen who created this masterpiece. Sir Winston Churchill's immortal words, 'Never was so much owed by so many to so few', are also woven into the panel.'[6] Harry Cross, the firm's chief designer spent two years designing it and he worked from a wide variety of sources including photographs, drawings and postcards. His design includes a cottage and a castle at the centre of the panel to show that rich and poor alike suffered together. His finished design was passed to the draughtsmen to translate the drawing on to squared paper with each square corresponding with the different coloured threads to be used on the loom. This immensely intricate task was carried out by draughtsmen Mr W Herod and Mr W R Jackson and took 15 months. The pattern made on the loom was controlled by a jacquard, which is a set of cards on which individually punched holes control the varying threads. The draught was then transferred to the jacquard by Mr Alf Webster, who punched a total of 40,000 cards with a combined weight of more than a ton. These were then sewn together to make a continuous strip hundreds of feet in length with a width of 18 inches. These tasks depended heavily on the skills of the craftsmen involved, as there was at that time no means of checking their work for errors. A total of 26,000 miles of fine Egyptian cotton was used in each panel requiring 4,200 threads and 975 bobbins. One panel was produced each day. It was taken off the loom and checked against the jacquard, with any errors found being corrected by hand. The panels were then passed to the 'Brown Curtain' department where they were inspected by expert hand menders who repaired any damaged threads and lastly the panels were washed and treated to withstand the passage of time. The loom used to produce the panels was manufactured in about 1880 by Swift and Wass Co Ltd of Nottingham. When the panels were completed the jacquard was destroyed.

It is thought that between 25 and 30 copies of the panel were produced and the whereabouts of all them is not known. Recipients are known to have included: King George VI, Sir Winston Churchill, Westminster Abbey, the Air Council, the Royal Air Force Association and the councils of Sheerness, Croydon and Southampton. Croydon's panel is on display at the Croydon Museum, that of Sheerness is on display at the Sheppey Leisure Complex and Southampton's is at St Mary's Church. One panel is on display at the RAF Museum, Hendon. The museum holds a second panel and Harry Cross's original design sketches. Another is on display at the foot of the main staircase of the Officer's Mess at RAF Bentley Priory. The Royal New Zealand Air Force Museum at Christchurch, New Zealand has another. The Canadian Air Council purchased two panels in 1983 and 1990 at auction at Sotheby's in London. One of these is on display in the Billy Bishop Building in Winnipeg. Nottingham Council has a panel which is on display at the Museum of Costume and Textiles. A privately purchased panel is held by the museum at Perth, Australia. Dowding House RAFA Sheltered Housing Project in Dumfriesshire was presented with a panel in 1947 which is on display. After the war the Burgermeister of Apeldoorn in Holland was presented with a panel and it may be seen on display in the Historical Museum at Marialust, Apeldoorn. A panel was also presented the Member of Parliament for Nottingham, who presented it to Beckenham Council. It may be seen on display at Bromley Civic Centre. Yet another is held by Southwell Minster, and is displayed there each year on Battle of Britain Sunday.

---

[6] *An Illustrated History of RAF Bentley Priory* published by HQ Strike Command, RAF High Wycombe.

# SAINT GEORGE'S RAF CHAPEL OF REMEMBRANCE, BIGGIN HILL

'The gratitude of every home in our island, in our Empire, and indeed throughout the world, except in the abodes of the guilty, goes out to the British airmen who, undaunted by odds, unwearied in their constant challenge and mortal danger, turned the tide of the world war, by their prowess and by their devotion. Never in the field of human conflict was so much owed by so many to so few'. - Winston Churchill, 1940.

This chapel stands at Biggin Hill on the site of one of the most famous airfields, 'The Bump', from which the RAF flew from in the summer of 1940 to fight the Battle of Britain. The erection of a memorial chapel was the idea of the South African fighter ace 'Sailor' Malan. It was built in 1943 on the South Camp, but burned down in 1946. It was rebuilt and Air Chief Marshal Lord Dowding laid the foundation stone on 25 July 1951. The Bishop of Rochester rededicated it on 10 November that same year. The architects were Messrs Beasley, Harper and Williams. Hugh Easton designed the 12 stained glass windows in the main chapel. The chapel's reredos contains the names of 454 aircrew who were killed flying from Biggin Hill Sector. These were from 14 different countries: Australia, Austria, Belgium, Canada, Czechoslovakia, France, Holland, New Zealand, Norway, Poland, South Africa, Sweden, UK and USA. The architects were Messrs Beasley, Harper and Williams. Housed in a former aircraft hangar, with a plain brick interior, it is still a Service chapel and is used by all Christian denominations. The lectern was donated by the Belgian Air Force and the cross and the candlesticks were presented by the Royal Australian Air Force on the 25th anniversary of the Battle of Britain. Plaques in the chapel commemorate the Polish and Canadian pilots. There is a Delftware plaque donated by the People of The Netherlands. The Book of Remembrance contains the name of every pilot who served in the Biggin Hill Sector and was killed in the cause of freedom. Every day a page is turned. Either side of the altar is a board that lists every single commanding officer of the Station from its origins as a Wireless Experimental Establishment in 1917 until its closure as an RAF establishment in 1992.

## STAINED GLASS

Pictured above are two of the stained glass memorial windows in St George's Room in St George's RAF Chapel. These were designed and installed by Goddard and Gibbs of Shoreditch in 1985. The three medals in the bottom right-hand corner of the window on the right commemorate the award of three Military Medals to members of the Women's Auxiliary Air Force, as a result of their bravery during two attacks on the airfield in 1940.

'The RAF lost 70,253 aircrew killed or missing, by far the largest share of these casualties was borne by Bomber Command, which lost 47,268. The US 8th Army Air Force flying from Britain lost 44,472, again most of these being borne by bomber squadrons.'[7]

Once the war was over, the RAF consciously chose stained glass for many of its memorials and the forms employed would range from the simple engraved window in the church at Thorney Island, to the ornate beauty of Harry Stammers' stained glass windows in Lincoln Cathedral. RAF stained glass windows usually commemorate squadrons, wings and individuals and can often be found in churches situated close by what were RAF bases during the war. However, other examples can be found on air stations, at Rolls Royce's Derby works and in Britain's cathedrals. This form was also adopted by the United States Army Air Force which flew from airbases in East Anglia. Careful examination of stained glass windows in churches in Essex and the Fens will often reveal this connection.

Hugh Easton's work in this field would take the stained glass form to new heights and the most impressive examples of his art may be found in Westminster Abbey. The Battle of Britain Memorial Window in the Royal Air Force Chapel in the Abbey consists of 48 individual stained glass windows. The Islip Chapel in the Abbey was dedicated as The Nurses Memorial Chapel in 1950. It commemorates the nurses and midwives from the Commonwealth who died during the Second World War. Easton's remarkable window there depicts Our Lady standing on a crescent moon carrying the Christ Child, blessing the figure of a nurse kneeling below. Above the nurse is the figure of St Luke standing on a rainbow.

---

[7] David Beaty *Light Perpetual*.

# THE BATTLE OF BRITAIN MEMORIAL, CAPEL LE FERNE

Prime Minister Winston Churchill in his speech to the nation on 18 June 1940 stated: 'Hitler knows he will have to break us in these islands, or lose the war'. The invasion of Britain could not be launched until the Luftwaffe had shot the RAF out of the sky and gained complete air superiority over the Channel. With 2,600 aircraft opposed to the RAF's 642, the Luftwaffe can be forgiven for pre-judging the outcome of this unequal contest. The Battle commenced on 10 July and raged until 31 October. During those long summer months, 2,953 RAF aircrew and some Fleet Air Arm aircrew, flew operationally under Fighter Command control; 500 of these were from Australia, New Zealand, Canada, South Africa, Southern Rhodesia, Jamaica, Ireland, USA, Poland, Czechoslovakia, Belgium, France and Palestine. Over a third of the pilots and aircrew who took part became casualties, including 507 killed in action. In the period 8 August - 3 November, the Luftwaffe lost 2,433 aircraft and more than 6,000 airmen killed. Unable to sustain this level of casualties, they switched their attentions from the RAF's airfields to bombing Britain's cities. This victory in the air would change the course of the war and grant Britain the breathing space it needed to refit its armies and prepare for the next phase of the war against Hitler in North Africa. On the cliffs at Capel le Ferne near Folkestone on the site of a former coastal artillery battery stands the only national memorial to the titanic struggle. The late Wing Commander Geoffrey Page, - himself a veteran of the battle, believed that there should be a permanent national memorial, and the clifftop location was ideal. The memorial itself takes the form of an immense three bladed propeller, each blade 38 metres long, cut into the hillside. The stone figure of a lone pilot sits on a sandstone base in the centre of the propeller. The badges of the squadrons and units that fought in the battle are carved on the base of the memorial. It commemorates all those who flew and those who died in the battle. Nearby stands the visitors' centre Hunting Lodge and a flagpole originally from RAF Biggin Hill. On 9 July 1993 Queen Elizabeth the Queen Mother unveiled the Memorial on the annual Memorial Day and met Battle of Britain veterans, many of whom were known to her from wartime. Each year on Battle of Britain Sunday, the Sunday nearest to 10 July, the date in 1940 which officially marks the start of the battle, a memorial service is held at the site. Website at www.spitfire-museum.com/capel.htm

# THE ASTRONOMICAL CLOCK MEMORIAL - YORK MINSTER

This ingenious memorial commemorates the airmen from Britain, the Commonwealth and the Allies who gave their lives in the Second World War flying from air stations in the north east. It was dedicated in 1955 by Dr Eric Milner-White (1884-1963) Dean of York Minster. The movement was designed by Dr Robert d'Escourt Atkinson of the Royal Observatory and was made at their workshops in Greenwich. The walnut case was designed by Sir Albert Wilson RA and built by Messrs Ratee and Kett of Cambridge. The names of some 18,000 airmen are recorded in the Book of Remembrance in the glass case in front of the clock. A page of the Book is turned four times a year. Visitors can request to view names at any time.

    Whilst beyond the author's meagre understanding, the following explanation of the workings of the clock is included in the sure knowledge that it will assist the reader appreciate the unique nature of this memorial: 'As a mechanism, the Astronomical Clock is immensely complicated. Suffice to say that it indicates the stellar and solar time used by aeronautical navigators in the days before on-board computers. The large green disc facing into the body of the transept displays a gilded map of York as seen by a flyer approaching from the north and looking south. The silver band showing behind and above the disc represents the southern sky. The sun, on the end of a gilt pointer, travels along this band and is always in the correct position for the time of day, rising and setting as appropriate, at the correct point on the horizon. The amount of visible *sky* varies seasonally - more showing in summer than winter. Zodiacal signs representing the very constellations through which the sun is passing are engraved on the silver band. On the other side of the case there is a blue astral dial, indicating *star* or sidereal time. The Pole Star is in the centre, and those constellations which appear to revolve around it (and are always visible from York's latitude of almost 54 degrees north) are indicated in gold leaf. The entire disc turns slowly, in accordance with the earth's actual rotation.'

# THE AIR FORCES MEMORIAL RUNNYMEDE, SURREY

The Royal Air Force saw some of the earliest action of the Second World War in what would become a world-wide struggle to gain mastery in the air upon which victory depended. It was a struggle that would last the war through and would cost the lives of more than 116,000 men and women of the Air Forces of the Commonwealth. The Air Forces Memorial commemorates by name the 20,352 missing airmen lost in the Second World War during operations from bases in the UK and North and Western Europe to whom the fortunes of war denied a known grave. They served in Bomber, Fighter, Coastal, Transport, Flying Training, Maintenance Commands and on special operations. They came from all parts of the British Empire. In addition, some came from those countries of continental Europe that had been over-run by the Nazis, but whose airmen continued the fight against the Axis Powers by serving in the ranks of the RAF.

The Air Forces Memorial stands on a spur of Cooper's Hill at Englefield Green between Windsor and Egham. It overlooks the riverside meadow where the Magna Carta was sealed on 15 June 1215 enshrining man's basic freedoms under law. The land was donated by Sir Eugen and Lady Effie Millington-Drake. As British consul at Montevideo, Sir Eugen (1889-1972) had played an important diplomatic role in the heady events on the River Plate which led to the scuttling of the German pocket battleship *Graf Spee* on 17 December 1939.

The memorial was inaugurated before a gathering of 24,000 invited guests by The Queen on 17 October 1953. The key, presented to her by the architect and graciously returned, is preserved in a case in the shrine. The text of the Queen's dedicatory address is displayed inside the entrance loggia and the following is extracted from it: 'It is very fitting that those who rest in nameless graves should be remembered in this place. For it was in these fields of Runnymede seven centuries ago that our forefathers first planted a seed of liberty which helped to spread across the earth the conviction that man should be free and not enslaved. And when the life of this belief was threatened by the iron hand of tyranny, their successors came forward without hesitation to fight, and, if it was demanded of them, to die for its salvation. As only free men can, they knew the value of that for which they fought, and that the price was worth paying'.

# RUNNYMEDE

The memorial was designed by Sir Edward Maufe, the Imperial War Graves Commission's principal architect for the United Kingdom after the Second World War and it remains in their care. It consists of a shrine embraced by a cloister in which the names of the 20,352 dead are recorded. These, grouped according to the year of death, are inscribed on the stone reveals and mullions of the narrow windows giving the impression of partly opened stone books. The coats of arms of the Commonwealth countries are represented on the cloister ceilings. The sculpture was executed by Vernon Hill and the coats of arms were painted by the New Zealand-born artist John Hutton. He also carried out the all the glass engraving on the windows. On the Great North Window overlooking the valley is engraved the Airman's Psalm:

> "If I climb up into heaven, thou art there.
> If I go down into hell, thou art there.
> If I take the wings of the morning,
> And remain in the uttermost parts of the sea;
> Even there also shall thy hand lead me,
> And thy right hand shall hold me".
>
> (Psalm 139 verses 8,9 & 10 KJVI)

On 17 October 2003 The Queen attended a special commemorative service at the Air Forces Memorial, Runnymede to mark the 50th anniversary of the unveiling of the Memorial. The Commission's Vice-Chairman, General Sir John Wilsey said: 'The Commonwealth War Graves Commission is honoured to welcome Her Majesty back to the Air Forces Memorial, Runnymede, for this momentous occasion.'

# SAINT CLEMENT DANES

This church stands on an island in The Strand in London, just outside the city boundary. It was originally built by the Danes. Legend has it that when King Alfred the Great (871-901) expelled the Danes from London, he permitted those with English wives to settle just outside the city wall. The church was named for St Clement, the fourth pope. During the reign of the Roman Emperor Trajan, Clement was exiled to the Crimea and martyred there in AD 100 by being tied to an anchor and thrown into the sea. He thus became the patron saint of mariners and since the Danes were a nation of seafarers, this was the name they chose for their church.

The church was rebuilt by William the Conqueror and rebuilt again by Sir Christopher Wren in 1681, after the Great Fire of London in 1666. James Gibbs added the steeple in 1719. The church was immortalised in popular culture by the age-old children's nursery rhyme *Oranges and Lemons*. It was gutted on 10 May 1941 by the Luftwaffe. Although the Battle of Britain Memorial Chapel in Westminster Abbey was dedicated in the presence of King George VI on 10 July 1947, the RAF felt the need for a place to worship that they could call their own and they adopted St Clement Danes in 1956. The church was reconsecrated in the presence of The Queen on 19 October 1958 as the Central Church of the Royal Air Force. On the forecourt stand statues by Faith Winter of Air Chief Marshal Lord Dowding, Commander of Fighter Command 1936-1940, and Air Chief Marshal Sir Arthur Harris, Commander of Bomber Command 1942-1945. Books of Remembrance record the names of over 155,000 men and women who, while serving with the RAF, made the supreme sacrifice.

The pulpit of the church was reputedly carved by the wood carver Grinling Gibbons (1648-1721), as were the cherubs in the sanctuary. Nearly 800 unit and squadron badges sculpted from Welsh slate are embedded in the floor and the church contains memorial gifts of great beauty from the air forces of many countries. Set in the floor half way down the north aisle is a memorial to all the Polish squadrons who flew with the RAF in the Second World War. The pew ends facing the aisle are decorated with the coats of arms of deceased Chiefs of the Air Staff and the Colours of the RAF Regiment are laid up in the church.

# THE ROYAL AIR FORCE ESCAPING SOCIETY MEMORIAL

The Royal Air Force Escaping Society existed in the period 1945-1995 and was founded as an organisation to commemorate the fellowship of those who escaped after being shot down over occupied territory and in remembrance of the selfless assistance rendered by the European civilians who helped Allied aircrew behind German lines gain safety. This bronze memorial cast by the Art Bronze Foundry is in the crypt of St Clement Danes and was designed by Elizabeth Lucas-Harrison, who was later awarded the MBE for her dedication and service as Secretary of the RAFES. The plaque depicts an airman being helped by a girl and an older man, as another airman parachutes down nearby. Copies of it may be seen in the RAF Museum at Hendon, the War Museums at Ottawa, Canada and Canberra, Australia, the Musée de l'Armée at the Hôtel des Invalides, Paris, the National Resistance Museum, Overloon, Netherlands and the Basilique Nationale du Sacre Coeur at Koekelberg, Brussels, Belgium. Website at www.rafinfo.org.uk/rafescape

The memorial bears the following inscription:

" ON THE 21ST JUNE 1981 THIS PLAQUE WAS DEDICATED TO THE COUNTLESS BRAVE MEN AND WOMEN OF ENEMY OCCUPIED COUNTRIES WHO, DURING WORLD WAR TWO (1939-45) WITHOUT THOUGHT OF DANGER TO THEMSELVES, HELPED 2803 AIRCREW OF THE ROYAL AIR FORCE AND COMMONWEALTH AIR FORCES TO ESCAPE AND RETURN TO THIS COUNTRY AND SO CONTINUE THE STRUGGLE FOR FREEDOM. MANY PAID WITH THEIR LIVES, MANY MORE ENDURED THE DEGRADATION OF CONCENTRATION CAMPS. THEIR NAMES ARE REMEMBERED IN EQUAL HONOUR WITH THOSE WHO WERE SPARED TO FIGHT A LONGER BATTLE. TO MARK ITS DEBT OF GRATITUDE THE ROYAL AIR FORCES ESCAPING SOCIETY ERECTED THIS MEMORIAL AS A LASTING TRIBUTE AND ALSO TO SERVE AS AN INSPIRATION TO FUTURE GENERATIONS."

## THE UNITED STATES

Before the entry of the United States into the war, three squadrons of American volunteers flew against the Germans with the RAF and these three 'Eagle Squadrons' were numbered 71, 121 and 133 Squadrons of RAF Fighter Command. From the time the first Eagle Squadron was formed in September 1940, until all three were disbanded and incorporated into the USAAF in September 1942, they accounted for 73 German planes, 77 American and 5 British pilots were killed. Erected by the Hearst Corporation in 1985, the Eagle Squadron Monument may be found in Grosvenor Square, London. In St Clement Danes, the Central Church of the Royal Air Force, a Roll of Honour commemorates by name the 19,000 American airmen of the Eighth and Ninth Air Forces who died on active service flying from Great Britain.

Immediately behind the High Altar of St Paul's Cathedral in London is the American Memorial Chapel. Financed by a national appeal that raised £57,000, it commemorates the 28,000 Americans who were killed either on their way to, or while stationed in the UK during the Second World War and as can be seen from the figures above, the vast majority of these were airmen. The Roll of Honour is housed in a glass case in front of the Chapel's altar. Its marble plinth bears the inscription:

"THIS CHAPEL COMMEMORATES THE COMMON SACRIFICES OF
THE BRITISH AND AMERICAN PEOPLES DURING THE SECOND
WORLD WAR AND ESPECIALLY THOSE AMERICAN SERVICE MEN
WHOSE NAMES ARE RECORDED IN ITS ROLL OF HONOUR
THIS TABLET WAS UNVEILED BY H.M. QUEEN ELIZABETH II
ON 26 NOVEMBER 1958 IN THE PRESENCE OF RICHARD M. NIXON
THE VICE PRESIDENT OF THE UNITED STATES OF AMERICA"

The marble floor of the chapel bears the inscription: "TO THE AMERICAN DEAD OF THE SECOND WORLD WAR FROM THE PEOPLE OF BRITAIN". On 1 September 1951 *The Times* newspaper reported: 'President Eisenhower paid a brief visit to St Paul's Cathedral yesterday morning to be shown for the first time the completed American memorial chapel by which the people of Britain have commemorated more than 28,000 Americans who were based here and gave their lives during the Second World War. For the President it was a return visit to the cathedral to which he said he had much looked forward. On Independence Day, 1951, in the name of his countrymen General Eisenhower presented to the Dean of St Paul's the Roll of Honour, which consists of 473 pages of bound vellum. President Eisenhower, accompanied by Dr Wand, former Bishop of London, and Lord Ballieu, chairman of the executive committee of the memorial chapel fund, paused to inspect the book, which had been opened at a page on which all the names began with the letter D.' One page of the Roll of Honour is inscribed with the words written by General Eisenhower on 23 August 1946: 'Each name inscribed in this book is a story of personal tragedy and a grieving family; a story repeated endlessly in white crosses girdling the globe. Fittingly, this Roll of Honour has been enshrined by the Mother Country of all English-speaking democracies in this special Chapel of St Paul's, once a target of barbaric attack.'

On 4 July 1941 a tablet in honour of Pilot Officer William Meade Lindsley Fiske III, of 601 Squadron RAFVR was unveiled in St Paul's crypt. It carries the inscription: "AN AMERICAN CITIZEN WHO DIED THAT ENGLAND MIGHT LIVE". At the unveiling, Sir Archibald Sinclair, Secretary of State for Air said: 'Here was a young man for whom life held much. Under no kind of compulsion he came to fight for Britain. He came and he fought, and he died.' Fiske died on 16 August 1940 and was the first American pilot to be killed in the Battle of Britain. He was buried at Boxgrove Abbey, near RAF Tangmere. Lieutenant Colonel J T C Moore-Brabazon (later Lord Brabazon of Tara) would write of him: 'We thank America for sending us the perfect sportsman. Many of us would have given our lives for Billy.'

# THE UNITED STATES ARMY AIR FORCE

There are many instances of commemoration of American flyers dating from the Second World War in Great Britain and these memorials can usually be found on former RAF airfields or in local churches. Careful examination of stained glass windows in the churches of East Anglia will often reveal this connection. Particularly good examples may be found at Chelmsford Cathedral and in the RAF/USAF Chapel at RAF Mildenhall.

The Cambridge American Cemetery at Madingley is sited on a hilltop, three miles from the centre of Cambridge, within sight of the fens and the airbases where many of the Servicemen flew from. Here are buried 3,811 war dead, a high proportion of whom were members of the United States Army Air Force. At the cemetery is a 'Wall of the Missing', 472 feet long on which are inscribed the names of the 5,125 whose fate is unknown'.[8] Among the names of those missing in action listed on the Wall is Glenn Miller, the American bandleader who disappeared on a flight to Paris on 15 December 1944. The cemetery is maintained by the American Battle Monuments Commission.

The memorial in the photograph above can be found at the roadside at Greatstone-on-Sea in Kent. It commemorates four aircrew of the USAAF Liberator Bomber 42-95191 who died whilst engaged on a mission to bomb the V1 launch sites in the Pas-de-Calais. The nose of the bomber was blown off by German flak during the raid and the bombardier and navigator killed. As the crippled bomber approached the Kent coast, the only working engine out of four began to lose power and two crew members baled out and were killed instantly by the impact of landing on the sands, as the aircraft was too low for their parachutes to deploy. The bomber crashed into rough seas off the coast and a desperate effort to rescue the remaining crew was conducted from the shore. This was ultimately successful and a young RAF doctor, Sqn Ldr Morrell was appointed OBE for 'outstanding courage and initiative'.

Another aspect of this subject can be found in the story of the US 9th Air Force flying from the airfield at Little Walden, Essex in 1944: 'On 27th May, as the aircraft were departing on a mission, one of the A-20s had just taken off when it collided with a low-flying P-51 from a nearby airfield. The Mustang disintegrated and the A-20 crashed into a field to the south of the airfield near Church End. A farmer's widow, Mrs Betty Everitt, who was walking her dog, witnessed the accident and rushed across to the crashed A-20. With little thought for her own safety she immediately dragged one airman out of the aircraft and, whilst she was attempting to save another crewman, part of the bomb load exploded, killing her and the airman. There is a memorial in Ashdon church to this courageous lady, as well as another plaque in her honour in the old control tower. Within days the USAAF set up a fund to help and support her orphaned son'.[9]

---

[8] David Beaty *Light Perpetual*.
[9] G Smith *Essex Airfields in the Second World War* (1996).

# ALAN BLUMLEIN

Alan Dower Blumlein was born in Hampstead, London on 29 June 1903. He was the only son of Semmy Joseph Blumlein, a naturalised Briton. His mother was Jessie Edwards, daughter of the Reverend William Dower, a Scottish missionary to the East Griquas in Africa. Blumlein's father died in 1914. This event, combined with the outbreak of the Great War and the consequent unpopularity of those with German names and accents made him a solitary and withdrawn figure. In 1917 he entered Highgate School where he exhibited considerable intelligence and an exceptional memory. He was unpopular at school because he hated games. In 1921 he obtained a scholarship to commence studies in electrical and telephony engineering at the Imperial College of Science and Technology. For financial reasons he took the shortened two-year course and passed out with a first class honours degree. In 1924 he and Edward Mallett presented their paper 'A New Method of High-Frequency Resistance Measurement' to the Institution of Electrical Engineers and caused a sensation. That same year he commenced work with the International Standard Electric Corporation. 'He was sent to Switzerland, France and Spain to cure electrical interference plaguing telephone lines. Successful, he returned to England and invented a telephone crosstalk reduction circuit, which was adopted internationally from 1927 under a joint patent with J P Johns. He invented and patented the 'closely coupled inductor ratio arm bridge', a measuring instrument of great accuracy with numerous variations, including the low-level altimeter he developed in 1941 for the Royal Air Force'.[10] In 1929 he qualified as a private pilot and flew regularly. That same year he joined the Columbia Gramophone Company. They sought to manufacture a new recording system that would remove their royalty obligation to Western Electric for the existing semi-mechanical technology. A keen music-lover, Blumlein produced the revolutionary electrical disk recording system. His patent granted in 1931 made 70 claims and established the two-channel stereo record adapted as the international standard in 1958 and anticipated the development of quadrophonics. 'In 1931, under the direction of (Sir) Isaac Shoenberg of the newly formed Electric and Musical Industries (EMI) research laboratories, Blumlein was appointed chief engineer to head a multi-disciplinary team charged with research and development of a purely electrical television system. They produced the 405-line 50 fields per second interlaced, high-definition, versatile and reliable equipment preferred by the BBC as the standard in 1937, when the Baird system was rejected. Within a year, a miniaturized lightweight airborne version was built for British and French air-force experiments'.[11] In the late 1930s, with war clouds gathering once again, many 'boffins' found themselves working on cutting-edge projects in the field of defence technology. 'From 1938 television pulsed circuit and other sophisticated techniques were of increasing interest for the development of essential defence innovations. Blumlein's team was contracted to expedite development of - among other devices the ultra-secret H2S or 'bomber's eye' airborne earth-surface, cockpit screen display equipment, immune to darkness or weather.'[12] By the outbreak of war he was working for the top secret Telecommunications Flying Unit based at RAF Defford in Worcestershire. On 7 June 1942 Halifax Bomber V9977 housing his airborne laboratory crashed at Welsh Bicknor, Ross-on-Wye. The crash was caused by failure of the starboard outer engine, and all 11 civilians and airmen aboard were killed. In his short career, Blumlein was awarded a total of 128 patents and his pioneering work formed the basis of many of the post-war developments in the fields of both modern electronics and telephony. He is commemorated by the CWGC's Civilian War Dead Roll of Honour in Westminster Abbey, on their *Debt of Honour* website, by the RAF Defford Memorial on the Village Green at Defford, by the Memorial Window designed in 1992 by W H Sleigh at Goodrich Castle and by an English Heritage Blue Plaque on his house at The Ridings in London.

---

[10] *Dictionary of National Biography* Oxford University Press.
[11] Ibid.
[12] Ibid.

# THE CZECHOSLOVAK ARMY AND AIR FORCE MEMORIAL

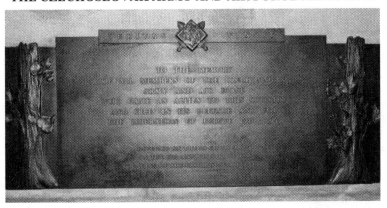

This bronze memorial plaque in the west cloister of Westminster Abbey was designed by Franta Belsky (who fought with the Czechoslovak forces). It remembers all those who came to Britain and: 'DIED IN ITS DEFENCE AND FOR THE LIBERATION OF EUROPE 1940-1945'. It was unveiled on 28 October 1993, the 75th anniversary of the founding of the Czechoslovak Republic. The names of the 20 Czechoslovakian pilots who died while serving with the RAF during the Battle of Britain are recorded on the Roll of Honour in the RAF Chapel at the east end of Henry VII's Chapel. A stained glass window, designed by Hugh Easton, includes the furled flag of Czechoslovakia together with those of other Allied nations.

Slovakian involvement in the Royal Air Force effort against Hitler was formally recognised on 6 December 2000 with the presentation of the Battle of Britain diptych or painting showing wartime aircraft and volunteers. This was presented at the Slovak Embassy in London. The ceremony followed a thanksgiving service at St Clement Danes Church to commemorate the 60th anniversary of Czechoslovak volunteer forces arriving in Britain. Presenting the diptych to the Slovakian Ambassador Frantisek Dlhopolcek, Air Chief Marshal (Retd) Sir David Cousins, controller of the RAF Benevolent Fund, said: 'We will never forget the brave actions of our Slovak and Czech friends alike in the battle against the common enemy in World War II. I am delighted to recognise their outstanding contribution with the presentation of this diptych'. The Slovak contribution to Britain's war effort had not been distinguished from that of the far more numerous Czechs with whom they shared a common homeland. Czechoslovakia was dismembered by the Nazis but reunited from 1945 until 1993, when Slovakia and the Czech Republic went their separate ways. Although Slovakia remained outside the Western Alliance and the Czech Republic became a NATO member, in 2002 15 veterans or widows were still in receipt of support from the RAF Benevolent Fund in Slovakia compared with 238 in the Czech Republic. Around 3,500 Slovak and Czech military personnel escaped to Britain with the fall of France in June 1940 and a formal agreement was signed with the Czech Government-in-exile on 25 October 1940 under which Czechoslovak airmen were enlisted or commissioned into the RAF Voluntary Reserve for the duration of the war, while officially remaining members of a Czechoslovak airforce. Many returned, together with their RAF aircraft and ground equipment, to re-establish the Czechoslovak airforce in 1945. Slovak pilots who took part in the Battle of Britain included Jan Ambrus, commander of 312 Squadron, Otto Smik DFC, and Anton Prvonic and Anton Vanko, both killed in action. Rudolf Husar was among the first RAF bomber pilots to attack Berlin, later flying a Mosquito on night reconnaissance and interception. Navigators and telegraphers included Ivan Schwarz and Aladar Berry-Pkory of 311 Squadron; technicians included the radar expert Nikulas Grofcik and the pilot/technician Ludovit Ivanic.

# THE FOREIGN CONNECTION

Whilst the Second World War took place 60 years ago and it might appear that the endeavours of the RAF's aircrew that died in such great numbers are by and large forgotten by the British, this is certainly not the case of the foreign communities where they perished. A good example may be taken from a letter written by Amiral Brac de La Perriere, who was President of the French Committee organising the 60th anniversary of the Normandy Landings in France in 2004. In May 2003 he wrote to the Veterans Affairs Secretariat at the UK Ministry of Defence seeking next of kin details of two British airmen who had been shot down and killed there on 6 August 1944. Subsequent enquiries by MOD established that the Mayor of Montmartin sur Mer had written to the Amiral requesting information on the next of kin, as his community planned to erect a memorial in the airmen's honour.

In May 1942 a German Dornier 217 flying from Holland to bomb Sunderland in England's north east was attacked by RAF fighters and the pilot in his desperation to escape their onslaught jettisoned his bomb load at tree-top level. One of his 1,100 lb bombs punched through the wall of St Andrew's Church at Bolam near Morpeth in Northumberland and slid across the floor of the church but did not explode, as it had insufficient time in which to arm itself. On 12 July 2004 Willy Schludecker, the pilot who dropped the bomb returned to Bolam to apologise to the locals in person. He said: 'The people here are very friendly and forgiving. They have accepted that dropping those bombs on their church was a mistake. It is very nice to see that they have made the most of the damage to the church wall, by making a remembrance plaque.' A clear glass window fills the hole where the bomb pierced the wall. It bears the inscription:

> "This window marks the place where,
> on 1st May 1942, a bomb dropped from
> a German aircraft entered the Church
> but did not explode."

Perhaps the most remarkable of all aviation memorial stories is that of 18 year old Luftwaffe rear gunner Gunther Anton. He was shot down over Southampton in 1944 whilst on a bombing raid, sent to a POW camp at Houndstone, Yeovil and put to work on a farm. There he became aware of the mass bombing raids the Allies were carrying out on Germany's cities and feared for the survival of his parents at home in Stuttgart. He prayed at the church of the Blessed Virgin Mary at East Chinnock, found consolation there and vowed to install a window in the church. He subsequently learned that both his parents had survived the war and he returned home to what was then West Germany in 1948. There, he worked with his father designing stained glass windows and in time became a master glazier. Before his father died, he reminded him of his vow and begged him not to forget it. Gunther Anton returned to East Chinnock in 1962 bringing the window with him and installed it in the church. In the following years he installed windows on the themes of the Holy Family, the archangels, the life, passion, crucifixion, resurrection and ascension to heaven of Jesus Christ. In 1969 his windows that year were impounded by HM Customs and Excise which refused to believe that they could be a gift. Eventually they were released and installed in the church. 'Finally in 1988 Gunther created a screen of glass bricks with the 'Agnus Dei' superimposed, to fill the open arch between the chancel and the bell tower. This completed twenty-six years of Gunther's generous gifts of his work and skill which he described as a thanksgiving to God for the kindness shown to him by the people of East Chinnock, for his safe return from the war, and as an act of reconciliation. His own little bit of peace in the world today. Six months later he died. Friends in Germany said he felt that his work was done.'[13]

---

[13] David Beaty *Light Perpetual*.

# THE COMMONWEALTH AIR FORCES MEMORIAL

At the end of the Second World War, the Imperial War Graves Commission sought a means of commemorating the airmen who had died in the Mediterranean Theatre and eventually settled on Malta as being the most suitable location at which to erect the Commonwealth Air Forces Memorial. Sir Hubert Worthington was selected as architect and a site selected at Floriana overlooking the old Knight's Harbour. Worthington's design consisted of a fifty foot tall column of travertine marble, from the Tivoli area near Rome, incised with a light reticulated pattern. The pylon stands on a circular plinth to which 20 bronze panels are affixed. 19 carry the names of the airmen and the 20th the general inscription. The memorial bears 2,301 names of which 1,545 are RAF, 286 Royal Canadian Air Force, 211 Royal Australian Air Force, 85 Royal New Zealand Air Force, 171 South African Air Force and 3 from the British Overseas Airways Corporation. On top of Worthington's column perches a gilded bronze eagle 7 foot 9 inches tall sculpted by Sir Charles Wheeler. He exhibited it at the 1953 Royal Academy Summer Exhibition, before it was shipped to Malta.

    The date for inauguration was set as 3 May 1954. The Royal Air Force Association swung into action to provide assistance to the next of kin and the SS MEDITERRANEAN was chartered to transport them from Venice to Malta. The memorial was inaugurated by The Queen and although the ceremony was of a secular nature, the day before being a Sunday, a Requiem Mass for the 2,301 airmen was celebrated in St John's Co-Cathedral by Monsignor Michael Gonzi, Archbishop of Malta, and later a Memorial Service was held at St Paul's Anglican Cathedral conducted by Canon Alan S Giles, Chaplain General of the Royal Air Force. Many of the families and Commonwealth Air Force officers attended both services.

# THE AIR FORCES MEMORIAL - PLYMOUTH HOE

'The charge of the Light Brigade at Balaclava is eclipsed in brightness by these almost daily deeds of fame' - Winston Churchill, August 1941

The idea for the monument at Plymouth was conceived in the early 1980's by former Warrant Officer James (Jim) Davis, who had served as a rear gunner with 83 Squadron RAF during the Second World War. He realised that there was no single monument in existence which collectively commemorated those men of all the allied air forces who had given their lives, either in the air or on the ground and in 1984 he enlisted the support of Air Vice Marshal Don 'Pathfinder' Bennett[14] , under whose typically energetic direction they rapidly developed the idea into a firm proposal and subsequently persuaded Plymouth City Council to support the project. This they did by allocating the site alongside the Armada Monument on Plymouth Hoe and by arranging that the office of Lord Mayor of Plymouth would become patron of the memorial. Following the death of Air Vice Marshal Bennett in 1986, there were many who were sceptical that the necessary funding could be raised to complete the task, but with the help of the local business community, Plymouth City Council and some generous personal contributions they were, and the idea born in the early part of the decade was brought to completion in its last year.

Surmounting the granite column stands a bronze figure, sculpted by Pam Taylor, of a typical aircrew member in full flying kit, looking resolutely out over Plymouth Sound, (which coincidentally, but fittingly, was used as an 'airfield' by RAF and RAAF Sunderland crews of Coastal Command during the Second World War). The figure was cast by the Art Bronze Foundry at Fulham in London. He was anonymously christened the 'Unknown Airman' is seldom alone, and at almost any hour of the day visitors can be seen reading the names of all the allied countries, the tributes and various facts and figures engraved on his plinth.

The unveiling of the monument and dedication took place on 3 September 1989, the 50th. anniversary of the start of the Second World War, in the presence of 300 invited guests including official representatives of 15 of the allied air forces: Australia; Belgium; Canada; Czechoslovakia; Denmark; Greece; India; the Netherlands; New Zealand; Norway; Pakistan; Poland; South Africa; the United States and the former USSR. After unveiling the monument, Air Marshal Sir John Curtiss paid tribute to the decisive role played, in all theatres, by members of the allied air forces and referred particularly to the efforts of Bomber Command and the US 8th Air Force in carrying the war to the enemy. In paying tribute to the ground crews, in his address Sir John said that: 'without them the gallant allied airmen would have been unable to fly or fight and that it was therefore only right that the monument should also commemorate them.' He went on to say that: 'no one who has been involved in war had any illusions about its beastliness, its terrible waste and destruction and that no one with such experiences would ever want to resort to war again unless there was no alternative. In 1939 there was no alternative, and the awful losses and destruction that ensued was the price that we had to pay to preserve our freedom and way of life.' The memorial commemorates all those airman of the Allied air forces who did not return. It also records the British nation's gratitude to the USA for the major part played by that country in the air war, particularly over Europe, the substantial losses sustained by them and those of the USSR. The casualty figures of 107,000 RAF, 84,000 USAF, and 42,000 Russian airmen are carved into the column. The ashes of Air Vice Marshal Don Bennett were subsequently interred beneath the memorial.

---

[14] Air Marshal Donald Clifford T Bennett 1910-86. Born Toowoomba, Australia. Joined Royal Australian Air Force in 1930, served with the Royal Air Force 1931 to 1935. In 1936 he joined Imperial Airways and piloted *Mercury*, a Short Mayo seaplane, on record non stop flights from Iceland to Canada and from Scotland to South Africa. He rejoined the RAF in 1941, and was Air Officer Commanding Pathfinder Force from 1942 to 1945. The elite Pathfinders led the massed night-bombing raids on targets in Germany.

# THE ST OMER MEMORIAL

On 11 September 2004 the St Omer Memorial in France was unveiled by Air Chief Marshal Sir Brian Burridge, Commander–in-Chief Headquarters Strike Command, RAF High Wycombe and Lieutenant General Jean Patrick Gaviard of the Armee de l'Air. Air Vice-Marshal Ron Hesketh, Senior Chaplain to the RAF, led the prayers. The ceremony was attended by the relatives of those who had served at St Omer during the Great War. Mr Henry Allingham, a 108 year old veteran of the Royal Naval Air Service and a founder-member of the Royal Air Force returning to France for the first time, was also present and laid a wreath. The unveiling marked the 90th anniversary of the arrival of the first British aircraft at St Omer and the 100th anniversary of the Entente Cordiale. The airfield the British established there in October 1914 eventually became the most important British air base in France. It was both an operational station and a major maintenance depot and housed a number of headquarters including Headquarters Royal Flying Corps commanded by Major General Hugh Trenchard. More than 50 squadrons were based at St Omer at some point during the war. Upon the formation of the Royal Air Force on 1 April 1918 more than 4,000 personnel were based there, out of a total of some 50,000 airmen serving on the Western Front. A total of 293,522 men served in the RAF and its predecessor formations during the war.

The memorial was the inspiration of Air Commodore Peter Dye who said: 'I welcome this opportunity to commemorate the many thousands of men and women from the Royal Flying Corps, the Royal Naval Air Service, the Australian Flying Corps and the Royal Air Force, who served on the Western Front during the First World War. Their selfless efforts and personal sacrifice provide the Royal Air Force with a proud legacy and offer an inspiration and example to us all'. The £60,000 cost of the memorial was funded by personal and private donation and the architect and designer was Tim O'Brien. Generous contributions were made by Cross and Cockade International, the RAF Historical Society, BAe Systems, Airbus Military, VT Group and Messier-Dowty International Ltd. The memorial was erected on land provided in perpetuity by the French authorities and it was the first permanent monument to personnel from the British Air Services who served on the Western Front in the Great War.

## THE BATTLE OF BRITAIN MONUMENT

The British and Allied pilots who flew at least one authorized sortie with an accredited unit of RAF Fighter Command in the period 10 July to 31 October 1940 during the Battle of Britain are known to British history as: 'The Few' and the story of this monument to commemorate them by name is not without controversy. The story began in 2001 when the Battle of Britain Historical Society ran a competition to select a design for a memorial to 'The Few'. The winner was the Scottish neo-Classical sculptor Alexander Stoddart. His design consisted of two naked male figures either side of a pyramid. This allegorical concept did not meet with the approval of the appointed architects Donald Insall Associates and after consultations with Westminster Council, a new design and new sculptor emerged. The site suggested by English Heritage for the memorial was on Victoria Embankment between Hungerford and Westminster bridges, where it would be placed on a granite plinth, which was formerly an 80 foot long smoke vent for the District Line underground railway dating from the days of steam. The Morris Singer Foundry was appointed to cast the three bronze panels. In March 2003 *RAF News* announced: 'An appeal has been launched to fund the first memorial in London to those who fought and died in the Battle of Britain in 1940. The monument, in bronze and granite will be sited alongside the Thames on Victoria Embankment. It will list all 2,953 airmen from 16 countries who fought in, and with, the RAF in the battle. The organisers led by the Battle of Britain Historical Society, need to raise £1.6 million to complete the tribute by the target date of September 2004. The appeal was launched at the RAF Club with Lord Tebbit, the chairman of the monument's organising committee, actor Edward Fox, who starred in *The Battle of Britain* film and a number of surviving veterans of the battle'.[15] The new sculptor Paul Day commenced work at his studio near Dijon, France and by May 2004, two of the three panels had been completed in clay ready for casting. Interviewed by Lewis Smith of *The Times* he said: 'I've tried to put across in a simple snapshot something of what the people then were going through - the determination, the courage, the fear, the pounding hearts and the bursting blood vessels.' 'High relief sculpture' is an interesting form which consists of figures emerging 'face on' from the relief. However, his use of this form did not meet with universal approval and it was condemned by 'Piloti' - architectural critic of the magazine *Private Eye* who wrote: 'It is like something out of a cartoon strip, like "Paddy Payne - Fighter Pilot" in the old *Lion* boy's comic. Why such trite vulgar realism is necessary in the age of photography and film is hard to understand.'[16] Whilst 'Piloti' appears elsewhere in the pages of this study under his real name and his opinion on the subject of war memorials is generally sound, in this case the author does not concur with his viewpoint.

On 15 May 2004 *The Times* reported; 'The Chairman of the Heritage Lottery Fund was accused yesterday of "spitting in the faces" of The Few who won the Battle of Britain. Lord Tebbit launched his scathing attack on Liz Forgan and the fund after being told that there was no chance of the organisation contributing to the £1.5 million cost of a Battle of Britain Memorial. He is furious that the fund has pledged £1 million to a Women at War memorial but will not honour the men and women who saved the nation during the Battle of Britain... Lord Tebbit, a former RAF pilot who is leading the fund-raising campaign said he was shocked at being given the "brush-off" by Ms Forgan and the fund's refusal to help. "I'm amazed that she's not prepared to talk to me and even listen to the case," he said. "I regard it as spitting in the face not merely for the pilots but all the others who took part in the battle.... Ms Forgan said she had explained to Lord Tebbit that the lottery did not fund new memorials but that Women at War was an "exceptional national monument". She said the Battle of Britain Memorial was an "admirable project".[17] The monument was due to be inaugurated in 2005. Website at www.bbm.org.uk

---

[15] *Royal Air Force NEWS* 7 March 2003 p. 13.
[16] *Private Eye* No' 1115, 17 September - 30 September 2004.
[17] *The Times* 15 May 2004 p. 16.

# CHAPTER VIII

# VICTORIA CROSS AND GEORGE CROSS MEMORIALS

# THE VICTORIA CROSS

The Victoria Cross is the highest honour that can be awarded to members of Britain's armed forces for valour. It was established by Royal Warrant on 29 January 1856, to be awarded to officers and men of the Royal Navy and British Army who, whilst serving in the presence of the enemy, should have performed some signal act of valour or devotion to their country. It could not be earned any other way. The medal is awarded only after the most searching enquiries into the circumstances of the action for which it has been recommended. The Victoria Cross is classless and open to all ranks, taking precedence over all other honours, awards and decorations. Its award is the sole prerogative of the Sovereign. During the course of the Crimean War it became apparent that other nations had instituted medals to recognise acts of bravery on the battlefield, but the British had no equivalent award. The proposal for such a medal was resisted by the War Office, which believed that the institution of such an award would lead to men breaking ranks to try and earn it and would therefore be detrimental to good order. They were overruled by Prince Albert who was an original thinker on military themes, and for that very reason deeply unpopular at the War Office. Queen Victoria chose the design of the medal and it took the form of a 'Cross Paty' or 'Cross Formy' ensigned with the Royal Crest and a scroll inscribed 'For Valour'. (The medal's patent states it is a Maltese Cross, which it manifestly is not). It is connected by a V-shaped link to a bar engraved on the face with laurel leaves. There is space on the rear face for the inscription of the recipient's name and the date of the deed involved. The medal weighs just over three ounces and is worn on the left breast suspended from a crimson ribbon. The medal is cast from the sawn off cascabels of two bronze Chinese 18 pounder cannon captured at Sevastopol and its simple inscription reads: "FOR VALOUR". The institution of the medal was backdated to the start of the Crimean War. The first awarded was to Mate Charles Lucas from County Armagh, who won his on 21 June 1854 during the bombardment of the forts at Bomarsund in the Baltic by heaving a fizzing live shell over the side of HMS HECLA. To date, a total of 1,354 have been awarded. 634 were won in the Great War and 182 in the Second World War. Twelve have been awarded in campaigns since. 50% of the awards made in the Korean War and 100% of those in the Falkland Conflict were posthumous. Due to Prince Albert's intervention, the original Royal Warrant contained a surprisingly democratic feature, in that it provided for a situation whereby the valour of a body of men is adjudged to have collectively earned the award, the recipient of the medal could be determined by the drawing of lots. No posthumous awards were permitted until the Boer War, although a number of individuals who had earlier died in action would clearly have been granted the award had they survived. To rectify what was clearly an injustice, on 15 January 1907 King Edward VII authorised six posthumous awards. Only three men have won the award twice. In the early years there were a number of instances of confiscation of the medal after the conviction of recipients for bigamy and theft, on one occasion, police officers redeeming a pawnbroker's ticket to return a confiscated medal to the War Office. In 1920 King George V issued a Supplemental Royal Warrant which stated that once the medal had been awarded, it could never be removed - even if the person to whom it was awarded were sentenced to hang, he could wear it on the scaffold. The CWGC has in its care the graves of 377 recipients of the Victoria Cross: 262 from the Great War and 112 from the Second World War; and three non World War recipients. Usually their VC is engraved on their headstone. Uniquely, in the case of Captain Noel Chavasse VC and bar, both his VC's are engraved side by side on his headstone in the Commission's Brandhoek New Military Cemetery, Belgium. The Victoria Cross and George Cross Association preserves the memory of those who have earned either medal and it organises a bi-annual reunion of surviving medal-holders at the Union Jack Club in London. At the time of writing in 2004, 358 ounces of the metal remain, sufficient to cast a further 85 medals.

# THE VICTORIA CROSS AND MEMORIALISATION

Interrogation of the UKNIWM database in February 2004 revealed 498 instances of commemoration in UK of VC winners and most were in churches, cathedrals or educational foundations. The forms adopted varied widely, with plaques and memorial windows in churches much in evidence. As in times past, famous generals are commemorated in Cathedrals and St Paul's Cathedral in London is where Field Marshals Earl Roberts, Sir Evelyn Wood, Lord Gort and Lieutenant General Freyberg are commemorated, whilst General Sir Redvers Buller and Brigadier-General Gough are commemorated in Winchester Cathedral. Private Anderson has an alms dish named for him in Beverley Minster. The tenor bell in St Margaret's Church, Lowestoft is named 'the VC Bell' and dedicated to the memory of Skipper Thomas Crisp. Roads and buildings featured strongly. Sergeant Ablett has Ablett Close in Weybread, Suffolk, Flight Sergeant Aaron a road in Poole, Dorset (and an architectural scholarship), Captain Ackroyd a road in Royston, Herts, Sergeant Angus a road in Carluke, Lanarkshire, Captain Barter Barter Road and Barter Close in Hightown, Wrexham. Corporal Bates has a street in Norwich, Lieutenant George Ingram a street in Sydney and Captain Borella roads in Canberra and Albury, New South Wales. Private Clare has Clare Street, Chatteris, Cambridgeshire. Company Sergeant Major Stan Hollis has Hollis Crescent at Strensall Barracks, York and a memorial statue sculpted by James Butler at Crepon, Normandy which was unveiled in October 1996 by the King of Norway, Colonel-in-Chief of the Green Howards. Lance Corporal Jarvis has Jarvis Place in Carnoustie and Jarvis Street in Fraserburgh. Sgt Harris has Harris House, a retirement home in Halling, Medway named for him. The Albert Ball VC DSO MC Memorial Homes can be found at Lenton, Nottingham and Major Francis Harvey RMLI is commemorated by Harvey House at the Royal Marines Museum, Eastney, Hants, Lieutenant General Halliday is commemorated at Eastney in the same manner. Company Sergeant Major William Gregg is commemorated by the William Gregg Memorial Baths and Gregg Street at Heanor, Derbyshire. Charles Upham, one of only three men to win the VC twice, had a warship of the Royal New Zealand Navy named after him on 18 October 1995. Lieutenant Combe had a lake in Northern Saskatchewan named for him and Lieutenant Colonel Grimshaw one in Western Australia. Mount McBeath in the Jasper National Park in Canada was named after Lance Corporal Robert McBeath. Educational foundations also feature, with both scholarships and annual prizes being awarded in the name of VC winners. Brigadier Andrew has 'the Les Andrew VC Scholarship' at Horowhenua College, Levin, New Zealand named for him. The sale of Midshipman Boyes' VC in 1998 was used to fund a scholarship to Cheltenham College. Sergeant Cairns had the Hugh Cairns VC Elementary School, Cairns Avenue, Saskatchewan, Canada named for him. Eton College, Harrow School, Wellington College, Haileybury College, Sedbergh School and Bedford School all have memorials that list the names of their 'old boys' who have won the VC. The Anson Memorial Prize is awarded three times a year to the officer cadet with the best military scores at RMA Sandhurst in memory of Lieutenant Colonel the Honourable Augustus Anson. There are also many instances of clubs, pubs, messes or veteran's social facilities being named after VC winners. Liverpool takes great pride in the memory of Captain Noel Chavasse, where he has Chavasse Court, Church Street named for him. It contains a mural of him and his twin brother and there is a Blue Plaque on the outside wall of his childhood home in Abercromby Square. He is also commemorated in the Anglican Cathedral, The Liverpool Scottish Regimental Museum, and Liverpool College. He is further commemorated at St Peter's and Magdalen Colleges, Oxford. And the memorialisation process goes on. In January 2004 an English Heritage Blue Plaque was unveiled to Private 1362 Frederick Hitch (of Rorke's Drift fame) in Chiswick, the ceremony being attended by the Royal Regiment of Wales and the Professional Association of Cab-drivers (Fred Hitch's occupation after he left the army), together with his descendants.

# THE REVEREND THEODORE BAYLEY HARDY VC

Theodore Bayley Hardy was born in London in 1863 and educated at the City of London School. He was Assistant Master at Nottingham High School between 1891 and 1907. He was then appointed Headmaster of Bentham Grammar School, resigning to become Vicar of Hutton Roof, Kirkby Lonsdale. 'A country clergyman over fifty years old might have been excused for thinking he was not called upon to play an active part in the Great War. However, he applied for a chaplaincy and waited for two years (because younger men were waiting for vacancies) but in August 1916 he applied again and was successful in being appointed to a Chaplaincy to the Forces'.[1] He was attached to the 8th Battalion of the Lincolnshire Regiment, (37th Division). His fearless attitude to the recovery of wounded soldiers and the tending of their wounds ensured that in his two years service on the Western Front, he earned the highest gallantry awards available to an officer of Britain's armed forces. In turn, he earned the Distinguished Service Order, the Military Cross and on 12 July 1918 the Victoria Cross.

'After it was believed that all our men had withdrawn from the wood, Chaplain Hardy came out of it, and on reaching an advanced post asked the men to help him get in a wounded man. Accompanied by a serjeant he made his way to the spot where the man lay, within ten yards of a pill-box which had been captured in the morning, but was subsequently recaptured and occupied by the enemy. The wounded man was too weak to stand, but between them the chaplain and the serjeant eventually succeeded in getting him to our lines. Throughout the day the enemy's artillery, machine-gun and trench mortar fire was continuous and caused many casualties. Notwithstanding, this very gallant chaplain was seen moving quietly amongst the men and tending the wounded, absolutely regardless of his personal safety'.[2]

Hardy was appointed Chaplain to King George V on 17 September 1918. The King asked him to return to Britain, but he declined and was killed on 18 Oct 1918, just three weeks before the Armistice. He was buried in St Sever Cemetery Extension, Rouen, France. He has plaques to his memory at both the City of London School in EC4 and Carlisle Cathedral (pictured above).

---

[1] *The City of London School: London Open House 2000.*
[2] Extract from Victoria Cross citation for the Reverend Theodore Bayley Hardy in *The London Gazette No 30790* dated 9 July 1918.

# CAPTAIN LEEFE ROBINSON VC

In the early hours of Sunday 3 September 1916 Captain Leefe Robinson RFC[3] was flying his BE2c plane over Cuffley, Herts. He was headed back to Hornchurch, when he spotted a German Navy Schutte-Lanz airship, SL11, commanded by Kapitan Schramm. It was trapped in searchlight beams, having that night bombed Finsbury Park, Tottenham and Enfield. Attacking from underneath at 11,500 ft and risking being shot down by both ground fire and the airship, he emptied a drum of incendiary bullets into the airship's gas envelope. It began to glow, burst into flames and crashed into a field behind the Plough Inn, Cuffley. Millions of Londoners watched it come down. All 16 crew were killed and buried at Great Burstead Churchyard on 27 September. The inquest was held in the public bar of the Plough Inn. In 1966 the bodies were exhumed and reinterred in the Deutscher Soldatenfriedhof (German Military Cemetery) at Cannock Chase, Staffordshire, which is maintained by the CWGC on behalf of the Volksbund Deutsche Kriegsgräberfürsorge (its German equivalent). For shooting down the first airship over the UK, Robinson was awarded the Victoria Cross by the King at Windsor Castle on 7 September 1916 - the only such award in the Great War for an act of bravery in the UK. He subsequently served in France and was captured after being shot down behind German lines at Douai, France, (now twinned with Harrow). He was held as a POW, but after attempting to escape was held in solitary confinement until the Armistice. There is evidence that he was maltreated in captivity at Holzminden by Commandant Niemeyer, a friend of the late Kapitan Schramm. He died aged 23 of influenza at his home in Stanmore, on 31 December 1918, just 17 days after returning home. He was buried in All Saint's churchyard extension, Harrow Weald and is commemorated by having a restaurant named after him. Opened in 1954, rebuilt and reopened in 1991, it was named *The Leefe Robinson VC*. His grave is just 100 yards from the site and in a civic ceremony a wreath is laid on it by the Mayor of Harrow each remembrancetide. There is also a memorial in the form of an obelisk to him on The Ridgeway, Cuffley which was erected from funds subscribed by readers of the *Daily Express* and inaugurated on 9 June 1921.

---

[3] William Leefe Robinson. Born at Kaima Betta, Tollideta, South Coorg, India 14 July 1895. Captain Vth Battalion Worcester Regiment, attached to 39 Squadron Royal Flying Corps.

# BOY 1st CLASS JOHN TRAVERS CORNWELL VC

Jack Cornwell resigned his position as a delivery boy with the Brooke Bond Tea Company in October 1915 and joined the Royal Navy. His father was a tram driver who had joined Kitchener's Army and was fighting in France. At the age of 15 Jack carried out his basic training at Keynsham Naval Barracks, Plymouth. Because of his eye for detail and quick wit, he was selected for further training as a Sight Setter or Gun Layer, a responsible position on board a ship of war. In Nelson's day this would have been the job of a Gun Captain, who was usually a mature, seasoned sailor. The intensive training was difficult for a boy barely out of school, but he passed out as Boy Seaman First Class and was posted to HMS CHESTER.

The Royal Navy's state of preparedness at the outbreak of war was in no small part due to Churchill's ability as First Lord of the Admiralty and they got off to a flying start with Rear-Admiral David Beatty trouncing the German Fleet at Heligoland within days of the outbreak of war. Three German ships were sunk. Britain then imposed a blockade of the continent to prevent supplies and foodstuffs reaching Germany. Her response would be the adoption of submarine warfare. In turn, the effectiveness of this form of warfare would be reduced by the British adopting the convoy system. The defeat of Admiral Cradock's two cruisers at the hands of Admiral Von Spee off Cape Horn on 1 November 1914 would be avenged on 8 December by Admiral Sturdee. He sank 4 German cruisers including Von Spee's flagship the GNEISENAU. 'In both encounters the braver actions were in the defeated vessels. In naval battles of this period a ship that went into action against a vessel with superior armament could expect only to be sunk, usually with all hands. Cradock was brave, if ill-advised, to attack Von Spee with only two cruisers against five. The Germans, at bay off the Falklands, also turned on a more powerful squadron and tried to close with them so that their lighter guns could be brought to bear, but the British stood off and pounded the smaller vessels to pieces at long range'.[4]

Room 40 in the Admiralty contained the Royal Navy's code-breakers and they had been reading the German navy's signal traffic since the start of the war. On 30 May 1916 they intercepted a signal to the German High Seas Fleet ordering a sortie up the coast of Denmark. The British Grand Fleet commanded by Admiral Jellicoe[5] set sail from their base in Rosyth to intercept them and what followed would go down in history as: the Battle of Jutland.

---

[4] John Percival *For Valour: The Victoria Cross Courage in Action.* Thames Methuen 1985.
[5] John Rushworth Jellicoe (1859-1935). Joined RN 1872, Captain 1897. Knighted 1907. Vice-Admiral 1910. Second Sea Lord 1912-14. Commander In Chief Grand Fleet 1914-16. Admiral 1915. First Sea Lord 1916-17. Chief of the Naval Staff 1917. Viscount 1918. Admiral of the Fleet 1919. Governor General of New Zealand 1920-24, Earl 1925.

At 2.32 p.m. the following day Beatty[6] turned his battle group for the Horn Reef having heard the guns of HMS GALATEA in action. The 5th Battle Cruiser Squadron under command of Rear-Admiral Evan Thomas continued to sail in the opposite direction, and by the time they turned, they were ten miles behind. Their heavy armament would be out of range when Beatty needed it most. HMS CHESTER was operating as a forward piquet for Admiral Hood's 3rd Battle Cruiser Squadron. Distant gunfire was heard by her lookouts and Captain Robert N Lawson RN ordered full speed. Action Stations sounded through the ship as HMS CHESTER sliced through the grey waves. Jack Cornwell was standing by his 5.5 inch gun on the forecastle, listening intently into his earphones for orders from the Gunnery Officer high up in the control tower. At 5.36 p.m. HMS CHESTER encountered the German 2nd Scouting Group consisting of three German light cruisers. She heeled to port to bring her broadside armament to bear and opened fire. In return she received accurate, sustained fire, found herself outgunned and took severe punishment. In all she was hit seventeen times by major calibre shells - four of which struck the turret housing the 5.5 inch gun that was Jack Cornwell's position. The ship was reduced to a shambles, with only one gun remaining operational. All around Jack, men lay dead and dying. He himself had felt a red hot shard of steel penetrate his chest. With grim determination he stood to his post, patiently awaiting orders. At 5.55 p.m. Admiral Hood's HMS INVINCIBLE arrived on the scene. Her 12 inch guns crippled one German cruiser and inflicted severe damage on the other two.

Upon being informed that HMS PRINCESS ROYAL had blown up, Beatty on his flagship HMS LION turned to his Flag Captain and said: 'Chatfield, there seems to be something wrong with our bloody ships today'. And his remark was addressed to exactly the right man. The highly dangerous practice of keeping the entire route open from the shell room and the magazine to the gun turrets was specifically forbidden by naval regulations. By pinning back blast doors, it was intended to increase the speed at which ammunition could be replenished. However, any explosion would be catastrophic. This danger was compounded by the stockpiling of charges in turrets. 'These potentially lethal shortcuts were connived at by everybody in the ships concerned; except in LION, where the Chief Gunner, Warrant Officer Grant, successfully defied Chatfield and refused to allow these highly dangerous drills'.[7] After 8 minutes in action, HMS LION received a direct hit on her 'Q' turret from the LÜTZOW. The 12 inch shell blew the roof off, killing or mortally wounding everybody within it. Major Francis Harvey RMLI, hideously burned, with both legs blown off, shouted the order: 'Close magazine doors and flood magazines'. The magazine party opened the valves controlling the flooding system, and sea water poured in. 'The shell of the LÜTZOW wrecked the turret and set the wreckage on fire. The shock flung and jammed one of the guns upwards, and twenty minutes later the cartridge which was in its breech slid out. It caught fire and ignited the other charges in the gun-cages. The flash from these passed down the trunk to the charges at the bottom. None but the dead and dying remained in the turret. All had been finished by the original shell burst. The men in the switchboard department and the handling parties of the shell-room were instantly killed by the flash of the cordite fire. The blast passed through and through the turret in all its passages and foundations, and rose 200 feet above its gaping roof. But the doors of the magazines were closed'.[8]

Major Harvey's swift action averted disaster, saved Admiral Beatty's flagship and in due course he was awarded a posthumous Victoria Cross. Winston Churchill would later write: 'In the long, rough, glorious history of the Royal Marines there is no name and no deed which in its character and its consequences ranks above this'.

---

[6] David Beatty (1871-1936). Entered Royal Navy 1884. Rear-Admiral 1910. Churchill's Naval Secretary 1912. Commander 1st Battle Cruiser Squadron 1913-16. Knighted 1914. Vice-Admiral 1915. Commander-in-Chief of Grand Fleet 1916-18. Created Earl Beatty and Admiral of the Fleet 1919. First Sea Lord 1919-27.
[7] Julian Thompson *The Royal Marines: From Sea Soldiers to a Special Force.*
[8] Winston S Churchill *The World Crisis 1911-1918* p. 1028.

Rear-Admiral Sir Robert Arbuthnot in his Flagship HMS DEFENCE crossed LION's bows in pursuit of the WIESBADEN. 'In a moment the DEFENCE struck by a succession of shells from the heaviest guns, blew up in a terrific explosion and at 6.19 p.m. vanished with nearly 800 men in a huge pillar of smoke.'[9] HMS CHESTER was ordered post-haste to the Humber and the Port of Immingham. As she steamed into the river, tugs waited to remove her wounded. Jack Cornwell was being lowered into a tug when Captain Lawson appeared on deck, having been wounded in the action. He looked at Jack and exclaimed: 'A cheer for the Royal Navy, Hip Hip, Hurrah' to which all responded. George Ball, a Grimsby seaman, stated that it was the proudest moment of his life. Jack was rushed to Grimsby General Hospital and was tended there by Dr Stephenson, to no avail. He found the boy to be brave when told that nothing could be done for him. The Matron asked him how the action had been and he replied: 'We carried on OK'. Later, before he died, he said to her: 'Give my love to my mother, I know she is on her way here'. He died on 2 June 1916, and was buried in Scartho Road Cemetery, Grimsby. Admiral Jellicoe's cautious handling of the Grand Fleet at Jutland enabled the Germans to escape into the gathering gloom to fight another day. They fired faster and more accurately, lost eleven ships and the British 14. 6,000 British seamen and 2,500 German sailors had been killed. Both sides claimed victory and in a sense they were both right. The Germans sank more ships than they lost, but the realisation that the Royal Navy could have landed the killer-punch, had they got their heavy guns within range, led the High Seas Fleet to remain in port until it mutinied in the Schillig Roads on 1 November 1918.

Three months later at the Admiralty, Captain Lawson related HMS CHESTER's part in the action. The story of Jack Cornwell's devotion to duty resulted in an immediate recommendation for an award of the Victoria Cross. Jack Cornwell's coffin was exhumed from Scartho Road Cemetery and taken by train to London for re-burial with full military honours. The *Grimsby Evening Telegraph* reported: 'With full naval and civic honours the remains of John Travers Cornwell, the 16 year old hero of the Jutland Battle, were borne to Manor Park Cemetery on Saturday, and laid to rest in a pleasant corner, under the shade of a plane tree. Dr Macnamara MP attended to represent the Admiralty. Sir John Beshell MP, and the Mayor and Corporation of East Ham were present. The boy's father Mr. Eli Cornwell, in khaki, as a reservist of the 10th Battalion of the Essex Regiment, accompanied by Mrs Cornwell and 3 sons were the chief mourners, while other relatives included two of the boy's uncles and several of his cousins. The funeral procession formed up at East Ham Town Hall, and headed by a firing party of the Royal Naval Division with full band, moved off shortly after 3 o'clock. The oak coffin covered with the Union Jack and bearing several magnificent floral tributes, was placed upon a gun carriage and drawn by a naval gun crew. Eighty of Cornwell's old school mates from the Walton Road School, the Band of St Nicholas School, the local Boy Scouts and Ilford Naval Cadets walked in the procession. Tremendous crowds witnessed the funeral, the whole route of two miles to the cemetery being lined by dense masses of people. Dr Macnamara spoke at the grave side, 'I am here,' he said, 'to pay my tribute of respect to the memory of a hero, and in the name of the Royal Navy to lay at his grave, a wreath of tender loving thoughts. He died inscribing his name imperishably upon the roll of British honour and glory. His grave will be the birthplace of heroes, from which will spring an inspiration that will make the spirit more dauntless and the purpose more noble for generations of British subjects yet unborn, the wide world over.' The epitaph on the monument over Jack Cornwell's grave reads:

> "IT IS NOT WEALTH OR ANCESTRY,
> BUT HONOURABLE CONDUCT AND A NOBLE DISPOSITION,
> THAT MAKETH MEN GREAT"

---

[9] Winston S Churchill *The World Crisis 1911-1918* p. 1043.

Alice Cornwell, Jack's mother received his Victoria Cross from the King at Buckingham Palace on 16 November 1916. The citation read: 'Mortally wounded early in the action, Boy, First Class, John Travers Cornwell remained standing alone at a most exposed post, quietly awaiting orders, until the end of the action, with the gun's crew dead and wounded all around him. His age was under sixteen and a half years'. Eli Cornwell did not live to see his son's VC, dying on 25 October 1916. He had previously served in Egypt and South Africa and had volunteered at the outbreak of the Great War as a Private in 57th Company, Royal Defence Corps. Alice Cornwell died at the family home in Commercial Road, Stepney on 31 October 1919, aged 54. Admiral Lord Beresford, with the approval of Jack's family decided that that his national memorial would take the following forms: the endowment in perpetuity of a Jack Cornwell Ward to be reserved for disabled sailors in the Star and Garter Home at Richmond, Surrey, towards which every boy and girl attending school throughout the Empire would be invited to donate a penny.; the provision of Jack Cornwell cottage homes for disabled and invalided sailors and their families; Naval Scholarships for deserving boys and a suitable monument on Cornwell's grave to be erected by the school children of East Ham. Jack's half-sister presented, on loan his VC to the Imperial War Museum on 27 November 1968. The 5.5 inch 'Cornwell Gun' from HMS CHESTER is also on display there. Jack Cornwell is commemorated in Chester Cathedral and the Scout Movement named a badge after him. The Victoria Cross Public House and the Jack Cornwell Community Centre both stand in Jack Cornwell Street in Manor Park, East London. In 1997 the *Collected Poems* of the Cornish naval poet Charles Causley were published by MacMillan and these included *The Ballad of Jack Cornwell*. The Yorkshire artist F W Elwell painted Jack's portrait in oils and donated it to Grimsby General in 1916, where it hung in the ward where he died. It now hangs in Grimsby Town Hall. The old hospital was demolished, but the new Diana, Princess of Wales Hospital has a Bader-Cornwell Ward which faces across Scartho Road to the cemetery where he was first buried. His grave in Cornwell Crescent in Manor Park Cemetery is cared for by the CWGC. In the popular mind, Cornwell's heroic death echoed that of Giacomo Jocante Casabianca, ten year old son of Amiral Louis de Casabianca, commander of Napoleon's warship L'ORIENT at the Battle of the Nile on 1 August 1798. His death was immortalised by Felicia Hemans in her poem *The Boy Stood on the Burning Deck*.

The gateposts of Cornwell Cottages at Hornchurch, Essex.

# THE ROYAL MILTARY ACADEMY WOOLWICH

The Royal Military Academy Woolwich was founded in 1741 to train officer cadets for the Royal Regiment of Artillery and Corps of Royal Engineers. Officers in these formations could not purchase their commissions and promotion could only be had by strict turn of seniority.[10] Given the highly technical nature of these professions, the Academy was nick-named 'the workshop' or simply 'the shop'. It closed its doors as a training establishment in 1947 and its function was transferred to the Royal Military Academy Sandhurst. The present Academy was designed by the architect James Wyatt in 1796 and at the time of writing in 2004, the Grade II listed building was awaiting sale to a property developer by the Ministry of Defence and the Victoria Cross and George Cross Association were actively seeking to rehome the memorial.

    Ornamented only by a single carved wooden Victoria Cross above it, the simple granite memorial over the fireplace in the oak-panelled Mess Hall was installed in 1900 and it has carved into it the names of all gunner and sapper officers who won the Victoria Cross in the period 1854-1942. On it can be found some of the most famous names in the annals of the British Army. All entering or leaving must pass it and it dominates the Hall.

    The plain grey stone with 40 names on it picked out in gold paint has little in the way of artistic merit and that was not its purpose, far from it. There is some powerful psychology at work here and its unspoken significance to every young officer cadet who trained at the 'shop' and saw it in the mess hall three times a day must have been immediately apparent. Its message is both daunting and at the same time quite straightforward: 'These are the illustrious names of those who have gone before you. This is the standard of your calling - uphold it.'

---

[10] Commission by purchase in the British Army was abolished by Royal Warrant on 17 July 1871.

# THE RAF VC10

From early on in the VC10's career as a commercial airliner the Royal Air Force was interested in the aircraft, but it was not until after the commercial airlines had sold off their aircraft that the main career of the VC10 in the service of the RAF started and the VC10 still flies each day as a tanker or transport aircraft in service with either 10 Squadron RAF or 101 Squadron RAF, both based at RAF Brize Norton. The link between the RAF and the VC10 was strong from the beginning, as the RAF originated the requirement for the V.1000, Vickers was well aware of their requirements. Several developments in the commercial VC10s were of interest to the RAF, especially the cargo door that Vickers had developed. The type 1106 that the RAF eventually ordered was different in many ways compared to the Standard VC10s that had been built until then. It had the fuselage length of the Standard but incorporated many changes that were designed for the Super VC10, such as the fin fuel tank and the uprated Conway engines. The wing planform was similar to the type 1102/1103 wing but, as on the Super, may have incorporated a different profile, optimized for a higher cruise mach number. With the higher thrust from the more powerful Conways, but without the performance penalties incurred in the Super because of the stretched fuselage and therefore increased take off weight, the RAF VC10s are even more impressive performers than the Standards. The design includes a strengthened cabin floor with a loading system, and this combined with the cargo door in the forward fuselage means that the VC10s are capable load carriers.

The RAF ordered 5 airframes initially in September 1961, followed by 6 more a year later and the final three in July 1964. The first aircraft was delivered to 10 Squadron RAF in 1966 and training flights were speedily scheduled to get the squadron operational as quickly as possible.

The VC10 has proven itself a very capable refueling platform. Because of its configuration the receiving aircraft is well away from the tailplane and the engine exhausts, which means less risk in turbulent weather. A major demonstration of the effectiveness of this capability was demonstrated by the 'Black Buck' missions flown by the RAF during the Falklands War in 1982, which saw Vulcan bombers fly from UK to the Falkland Islands and back without landing. The RAF's original VC10's were all named after winners of the Victoria Cross, all of whom had served in either the Royal Flying Corps or the Royal Air Force.

| Aircraft Serial Number | Name |
| --- | --- |
| XR806 | George Thompson VC |
| XR807 | Donald Garland VC and Thomas Grey VC |
| XR808 | Kenneth Campbell VC |
| XR809 | Hugh Malcolm VC |
| XR810 | David Lord VC |
| XV101 | Lance Hawker VC |
| XV102 | Guy Gibson VC |
| XV103 | Edward Mannock VC |
| XV104 | James McCudden VC |
| XV105 | Albert Ball VC |
| XV106 | Thomas Mottershead VC |
| XV107 | James Nicholson VC |
| XV108 | William Rhodes-Moorhouse VC |
| XV109 | Arthur Scarf VC |

# THE GEORGE CROSS

The George Cross was instituted by a Royal Warrant on 24 September 1940 and its creation published in the *London Gazette* of 31 January 1941. King George VI established the award 'for acts of the greatest heroism or of the most conspicuous courage in circumstances of extreme danger'. At the time of the award's inception, 108 living recipients of the Empire Gallantry Medal (EGM) and the next-of-kin of 4 further recipients were eligible to exchange the EGMs for the GC. The EGM then became obsolete. In 1971 surviving holders of the Albert Medal (65) and the Edward Medal (68) also became eligible to exchange their decorations for the George Cross.

The medal was designed by Percy Metcalfe (1895-1970). He was also responsible for the design of the crowned head of King George VI used on the George Medal and the 1939-45 War Medal. The depiction of Saint George and the Dragon is based on the work of the Royal Mint's Italian master engraver Benedetto Pistrucci (1784-1855), and his design has appeared on a number of British coins. The medal is struck by the Royal Mint and consists of a plain silver cross, with the initials 'GVI' in the angle of each limb. In the centre is a circular medallion depicting St George slaying the Dragon, and surrounded by the inscription "FOR GALLANTRY". The reverse of the medal is plain and bears the name of the recipient and the date of the award. The George Cross, which is worn before all other decorations except the Victoria Cross, is suspended from a dark blue ribbon threaded through a bar adorned with laurel leaves. The ribbon is 38mm wide and its colour is officially described as dark blue. Ladies not in uniform wear the medal suspended from a wide bow of dark blue ribbon, below the left shoulder. Recipients are permitted to use the post-nominal letters 'GC' after their name. Although award of the medal is recommended by the Prime Minister, the decoration is bestowed by the Sovereign.

The first investiture of the George Cross took place at Buckingham Palace on 24 May 1941. Recipients included the three armed services as well as the civilian services. King George VI presented the first George Cross to Mr Thomas Alderson, Detachment Leader, ARP Bridlington, Yorkshire with the words: 'You are the first recipient of the George Cross. It gives me very great pleasure to hand it to you.' To date, there have been 401 awards of the George Cross. Bomb disposal experts, miners, lifeboatmen, railwaymen, policemen and SOE agents all feature prominently, as do men and women from all three armed services. There have been two collective awards, to the Island of Malta in April 1942 and to the Royal Ulster Constabulary in November 1999. Recent recipients include: Air Stewardess Barbara Harrison who was posthumously honoured in 1969. She helped many passengers escape, after a fire crippled a BOAC jet at Heathrow Airport before perishing in the wreck. Several soldiers serving in Northern Ireland have received the George Cross, including in 1979, Captain Robert Nairac of the Grenadier Guards and bomb disposal expert Warrant Officer Barry Johnson, who was seriously injured in 1990 whilst attempting to defuse a mortar bomb in Londonderry. A posthumous award was made in 1992 to Sergeant Stewart Guthrie of the New Zealand Police, who displayed great courage whilst attempting to apprehend a gunman in the town of Aramoana. On 31 October 2003 Trooper Christopher Finney of the Blues and Royals was awarded the medal for outstanding bravery after a 'friendly-fire' incident near Basra in Iraq.

In the Autumn of 1990, a service of thanksgiving for the 50th anniversary of the George Cross was held at St Martin in the Fields Church in London and was attended by Queen Elizabeth the Queen Mother. There was no provision for the payment of any annuity contained in the original Royal Warrant. However, from 4 February 1965 living holders of the award were granted a tax-free annuity of £100. The figure remained unchanged until 15 August 1995 when it was raised to £1,300. This was further increased to £1,495 from 1 April 2002. The annuity is paid to all holders of the Victoria Cross and George Cross.

## A DRIVER'S REPORT

'I, BENJAMIN GIMBERT, aged 41 years, check No. 1525, am a driver on the London and North Eastern Railway Company stationed at March, having entered the Company's service at that depot in August 1919 as a cleaner, made a passed cleaner in March 1920, a fireman in February 1921, a passed fireman in May 1939, and a driver in July 1942.

Having signed off duty at 12.40 a.m. on 1 June 1944 at March, I signed on at 10.10 p.m. the same date to work the 11.40 p.m. from Whitemoor to Goodmayes with Fireman J. Nightall, engine No. W.D. 7337, eight wheels coupled, load class 7. The starting-point of the train was diverted to March to start at 12.10 a.m. on 2 June for White Colne. The train started at 12.15 a.m. and consisted of fifty-one wagons, and the guard said they would be via Marks Tey and Ipswich to destination. I noticed nothing amiss with the engine and wagons and did not have to work the engine heavily. On approaching Ely West Junction I had signals against me and was stopped there for a short time and again on the Ely Up Reception Road where I took water. I should say I arrived at water crane about 1.13 and left at 1.24 a.m. At neither place did I notice anything wrong with any of the wagons. On getting the 'right away' I proceeded to Barway Siding, obtaining the key token as I passed Ely Dock Junction box. I checked the train at Barway in order to let my mate exchange the key token and again I noticed nothing amiss.

After passing the Soham distant signal, which was off, I thought I noticed some steam coming from the injector and looked out and saw that the wagon next to the engine was on fire. The flames appeared to be getting all over the bottom of the wagon and seemed to be spreading very rapidly which seemed to suggest that something very inflammable was alight. I sounded the engine whistle to notify the guard and immediately took steps to stop the train carefully, knowing what the wagons contained, and stopped the train by the station end of the goods shed, where my mate, under my instructions, uncoupled the wagon from the remainder of the train. I told him to take the coal hammer with him in case the coupling was too hot to handle. On his having done this and rejoined the engine, I proceeded with the wagon which was on fire intending to get it well clear of the station and surrounding buildings, and leave it there and proceed to Fordham. The signalman came from his box onto the platform and I said: 'Sailor have you anything between here and Fordham? Where is the mail? I did not get a reply from him as the explosion occurred at that moment. The engine and wagon were moving slowly at that time and the regulator was shut. I did not notice if he had a bucket, which I understand was found outside the box. I should estimate that from the time when I first saw the fire in the wagon to time of the explosion would be about six or seven minutes. The fireman uncoupled and was back on the engine very quickly. On approaching the station I gave a second touch on the whistle to draw the signalman's attention and as my engine rolled towards him on the platform I went over to my mate's side, namely to the right hand side of the engine, and shouted to him to stop the mail and asked if the road to Fordham was clear.

At that moment a terrific explosion occurred and I was blown off the engine on to the down platform, which is the right-hand side of the engine and nearest the signal box.

At no part of the journey was there any jerking of the train or application of the brake. All the Soham signals were off. I should say as near as I can my speed between Barway and Soham would be between fifteen and twenty miles per hour.

I did not notice whether the sheet was over the top of the wagon or was wrapped around the contents. My anti-glare sheets were fastened down on both sides of the back of cab.'

# THE EXPLOSION AT SOHAM

The wagon next to the locomotive contained forty 500 pound bombs. The train's other 50 wagons contained both bombs and detonators. The explosion left a crater 15 feet deep, 66 feet in diameter and demolished Soham Station. Signalman Bridges and Fireman Nightall were killed in the explosion. 700 houses were damaged and Civil Defence workers had to dig a number of families out of the wreckage of their homes the next morning, but no Soham residents were killed. No trace of the wagon was ever found. Ben Gimbert's life was saved on the operating table by Professor Maxwell in Newmarket Hospital after 30 pieces of metal were removed from his back. He would have lumps of metal and glass regularly removed from his body for the rest of his life.

In recognition of their heroism that night, both Ben Gimbert and James Nightall (posthumously) were awarded the George Cross by King George VI. [11] Ben Gimbert was invested with the medal by the King at Buckingham Palace on 10 October 1944. Both were also awarded the LNER Medal and the *Daily Herald* Order of Industrial Heroism. Both sets of medals are on display at Soham Village College. Gimbert Road, Soham, Gimbert Square, March, Nightall Road, Soham and Nightall Drive, March were named after them. A memorial plaque was erected at Soham Station by the LNER Company and subsequently removed to Soham Village College after the closure of the station in the late 1960s. A memorial was placed in St Andrew's Church, Soham and a framed scroll in the booking hall of March Station. James Nightall had started his working life on a chicken farm and later joined the railways. Ironically when war broke out he was refused permission to enlist in the army, because he was in a 'reserved' occupation. He was buried in the churchyard at Littleport and to this day flowers are laid on his well-tended grave by railwaymen. Ben Gimbert presented the Gimbert Cup to Soham Village College in 1972. It is awarded annually to the year eleven pupil judged to have made the greatest overall contribution to the ethos of the College. The first presentation was made by Ben Gimbert himself. In time, he would become a great-grandfather and he died at home in March at the age of 73 on 6 May 1976 and was buried in Eastwood Cemetery, March on 12 May.

On 21 September 1981 in a ceremony at Euston Station hosted by Clement Freud MP, two class 47 locos were named 47577 "BENJAMIN GIMBERT GC" and 47579 "JAMES NIGHTALL GC". On the evening of 1 June 2004, a vigil was held at St Andrew's Church, Soham to remember the events of 60 years before and to give thanks for the saving of the town. The following day, a ceremony was held at the Whitemoor Yard in March to name two new class 66 locomotives. It was hosted by Lew Adams (late General Secretary of the railway union ASLEF) of the Strategic Rail Authority and attended by the Gimbert and Nightall families, the Mayor of March, civic dignitaries and Richard Bowker, Chairman and Chief Executive of SRA. March's oldest railwayman aged 92 was present as was its youngest aged 60 who was born on the night of the explosion. An address was given by Councillor Barry Hewlett, a former railwayman. Mr Norman Steward representing the Nightall family then unveiled locomotive 66079 "JAMES NIGHTALL GC" and it was blessed by the Reverend Tim Alban-Jones, Vicar of Soham. Mr Graham Smith, Planning Director of EWS, Britain's largest rail operator, then presented a copy of the locomotive's nameplate to Richard Munns, Vice Chairman of March and District Museum. After an address by Richard Bowker, Ben Gimbert's daughter Mrs Joyce Dedman then unveiled locomotive 66077 "BENJAMIN GIMBERT GC" and it was blessed by Father Eric Willett. A copy of the nameplate was also presented to Mr Munns. Poignantly, the ceremony concluded with an unscripted flypast by RAF Tornado jets. The attendees then adjourned for speeches, reminiscence and refreshment at March's BRAZA Club.

---

[11] Since its institution in 1856, five Victoria Crosses were awarded to civilians, and with the advent of the Second World War it became apparent that an equivalent civilian award should be instituted. This was the George Cross.

# THE VICTORIA CROSS AND GEORGE CROSS MEMORIAL

On 14 May 2003 in Westminster Abbey, a congregation of some 2,000 people gathered to witness the dedication of the Victoria Cross and George Cross Memorial. The assembled congregation included some 1,600 descendants of those who had been awarded the Victoria Cross and George Cross. The Antiphon used in the service was commissioned by the Dean and Chapter specially for the occasion. The sermon was preached by the Archbishop of Canterbury and the Act of Remembrance recited by Dr George Bonello Du Puis, High Commissioner for Malta. The lessons were read by Lieutenant Ian Fraser, VC DSC RD and Colonel Stuart Archer, GC OBE ERD.

Colonel Archer, Chairman of the Victoria Cross and George Cross Association then invited The Queen to unveil the memorial. It was carried by representatives from the three Services and the Metropolitan Police from the Sacrarium to the West End of the Abbey preceded by the Flags of the Nations. It consisted of a nabresina stone tablet with enlarged bronze and silver crosses inlaid with enamelled ribbons in the appropriate colours. It was engraved with the words: "REMEMBER THEIR VALOUR AND GALLANTRY" and was installed near the Tomb of the Unknown Warrior. Although various suggestions had been put forward about forming a VC Association, it was not until after the Centenary Celebrations in 1956 that such a body was finally founded. The 1956 Centenary gathered 299 VCs from all over the world, the focal point being a review of holders in Hyde Park by The Queen on 26 June. Other events included a party at Marlborough House, attended by Queen Elizabeth the Queen Mother; a Thanksgiving Service in Westminster Abbey, when the Address was given by the Archbishop of Canterbury; and receptions at Guildhall, and in Westminster Hall given by HM Government. With a large proportion of surviving holders together in London over several days there was discussion of forming an association, and Sir John Smyth, VC MC agreed to be the Founder Chairman. At the second committee meeting it was decided to invite George Cross holders to become associate members; this was felt to be in accord with King George VI's wish that the George Cross (awarded for gallantry when not in direct contact with the enemy) should be of equal standing with the VC. It was also felt that future awards of the GC were likely to be rather more frequent than the VC, since warfare on the scale of the two World Wars could not be envisaged. In 1961 it was decided it would be appropriate for GC holders to be full members, and the Association was re-named The Victoria Cross and George Cross Association. In December 2003, membership of the Association consisted of 15 holders of the VC and 30 holders of the GC.

# THE VICTORIA CROSS AND GEORGE CROSS MEMORIAL, MOD

On 2 November 2004, military Victoria Cross and George Cross recipients were honoured when ministers unveiled Britain's first permanent memorial for Service recipients at a dedication ceremony at the Ministry of Defence. The dedication service was led by the Reverend John Whitton, Deputy Chaplain General to the Forces. The Secretary of State for Defence Geoff Hoon, Under Secretary of State Ivor Caplin and Vice Chief of the Defence Staff, Air Chief Marshal Sir Anthony Bagnall were present to honour the bravery of Victoria Cross and George Cross recipients. The memorial is at the heart of MOD's refurbished Main Building in Whitehall and consists of an imposing bronze statue and stained glass window. Mr Hoon said: 'I am honoured to be here to mark the bravery and courage of recipients of the Victoria Cross and George Cross. It is right to remember their contribution with a memorial at the very centre of our military and civilian headquarters as a permanent reminder of the values we should all strive to uphold.' The art nouveau style stained glass window is 3 metres high and 1.6 metres wide. It was produced by Rachel Foster and a group of pensioners from Eastwood and Broxtowe in Nottinghamshire. The ESCAPE Group of pensioners produces stained glass windows in order to provide opportunities for Nottinghamshire pensioners to meet people and develop new skills. The oldest member of the group was 90 and the youngest 71. The statue was sculpted by Marcus Cornish and the architect was Liam O'Connor RIBA. There is an engraved tribute under the window (engraved by Richard Kindersley) which reads:

"IN MEMORY OF THE SERVICE MEN AND SERVICE WOMEN
OF THE ARMED FORCES WHO HAVE BEEN AWARDED
THE VICTORIA CROSS OR GEORGE CROSS
FOR CONSPICUOUS GALLANTRY IN THE COURSE OF THEIR DUTIES"

Mrs Didy Grahame, Secretary of the Victoria Cross and George Cross Association said: 'The actions of holders of the Victoria Cross and George Cross represent the finest of all human qualities and it is fitting they should be remembered in the Headquarters of the Ministry of Defence. Now the Memorial is blessed, it can start living in its space and with luck will help inspire some who pass by.' At Buckingham Palace on 27 April 2005, with the words: 'You're very special', The Queen presented a Victoria Cross to Private Johnson Beharry of 1st Battalion, the Princess of Wales's Royal Regiment, for twice saving the lives of his colleagues, whilst under enemy fire in Iraq, the first award to a living recipient for 35 years.

# CHAPTER IX

# BRIEF BIOGRAPHIES

## JOHN BACON THE YOUNGER

John Bacon was born at Southwark in South London on 24 November 1740. He was the son of a Somerset cloth-weaver. At the age of 14 he was apprenticed to a Lambeth manufacturer of porcelain, where he was at first engaged in painting ornamental pieces of china and later promoted to the position of modeller. His observation of the models executed by different sculptors of eminence, which were sent to be fired at an adjacent pottery, determined the direction of his genius. He imitated them with so much success that in 1758 a small figure of *Peace* sent by him to the Society for the Encouragement of Arts received a prize, and the highest premiums given by the Society were awarded to Bacon nine times between the years 1763 and 1776. Bacon first attempted working in marble in 1763 and during the course of his early efforts in this art was led to improve the method of transferring the form of the model to the marble 'getting out the points' by the invention of a more perfect instrument for the purpose. This instrument took exact measurements in every direction, was contained in a small compass, and could be used on either the model or the marble. In 1769 he was awarded the Royal Academy's first Gold Medal for Sculpture for his bas-relief *The Escape of Aeneas from Troy*. In 1770 he exhibited his figure of *Mars*, which gained him the Gold Medal of the Society of Arts and election as ARA. As a consequence of this success, he was engaged to execute a portrait bust of *King George III*, originally intended for Christ Church, Oxford. It was exhibited at the RA in 1774 and pleased His Majesty so much, that it may be found at Windsor Castle. In consequence, Bacon retained the King's favour throughout his life, although he was often criticised for his ignorance of the classic style. This charge he refuted with his head of *Jupiter Tonans*, and many of his figures were in perfect classical taste. Bacon was a prolific sculptor and examples of his art may be seen in St Paul's Cathedral, London, Christ Church Cathedral and Pembroke College, Oxford, Bath Abbey and Westminster Abbey. Bacon's grand marble *Monument to Sir William Blackstone* (1784) may be found at All Soul's College, Oxford. Bacon's statue *Dr Samuel Johnson* (1796) may be found in St Paul's Cathedral. His dramatic white marble *Monument to General Sir John Moore* in St Paul's Cathedral, London depicts Moore's corpse being lowered into his grave by two allegorical figures. William Pitt the Elder, Earl of Chatham (1708-1778) was twice Prime Minister and is buried in the north transept of Westminster Abbey. His large white marble monument was sculpted by Bacon and stands nearly 33 feet high. It cost more than £6,000. At the base, sits *Britannia* holding her trident, and below her are the reclining figures of *Ocean* (Neptune) with a dolphin and the female figure of *Earth*, with a globe, fruit and flowers. Above, on a sarcophagus, sit the figures of *Prudence* and *Fortitude*. At the very top, in a niche is the standing figure of *Chatham* with arm outstretched delivering an oration. In the Church of St Mary at Paddington Green he sculpted the *Wall Monument to General Charles Crosbie* (1807). Bacon sculpted the portrait statue *Charles, Marquess Cornwallis* for the directors of the HEIC in 1793 (now in the FCO, Whitehall). A copy stands in the East Quadrangle of the Victoria Memorial, Calcutta. For a fee of 5,000 guineas, he also sculpted the life-sized marble statue of *Cornwallis* which now stands in gardens of the Victoria and Albert Museum, Mumbai - minus its head and right arm, which were removed by the locals during civil unrest in 1965. Bacon competed against Rossi and won the commission for the marble portrait statue *Richard, Marquess Wellesley, Earl of Mornington*. It was exhibited at the RA in 1808 and shipped to Calcutta. It may be seen in the collection of the Victoria Memorial, Calcutta. He was subsequently to sculpt the marble portrait statue of *Wellesley* for Mumbai, most of the work apparently being carried out by Bacon's business partner Samuel Manning the Elder. It having been shifted a number of times and decapitated in 1965, it may now be found in the grounds of the Dr Bhau Daji Lad Museum, Mumbai. Bacon died on 4 August 1799 and was buried at Mr Whitfield's Tabernacle in Tottenham Court Road, London. A medal by J S Wyon was commissioned in 1864 by the Art Union of London. It depicts a bust of Bacon on the obverse and his statue of Dr Johnson in St Paul's on the reverse.

# JOHN NASH

John Nash was born in September 1752. He was the son of a millwright, but chose not to follow his father's trade and was apprenticed to the architect Sir Robert Taylor (1714-1788). Nash quickly wearied of learning and set up his own practice. His first major enterprise was a speculative project, building houses in London of brick which were faced with stucco painted to look like stone. The venture miscarried and Nash was declared bankrupt in 1783. He moved to Wales and subsequently inherited a large sum of money, which he lost in a series of unwise investments. In 1792 he was forced to return to work and established a partnership with the distinguished landscape architect Humphry Repton (1752-1818). Together they designed more than 40 country houses in a variety of styles. In 1802 the partnership was dissolved and Nash returned to London. In 1798 Nash designed a conservatory at Brighton for the Prince of Wales (later Prince Regent and subsequently King George IV) and became an intimate member of 'Prinnie's' circle. In 1809 Nash designed Blaise Hamlet near Bristol. He employed Repton's sons John Adey Repton, and George Slaney Repton on the project, but offended their father by poaching his clients. In 1811 the Prince Regent asked three architects including Nash for their ideas on developing the farmland called Marylebone Park and its surrounding areas. Nash's ambitious plans included a 'garden city', with villas, terraced houses, crescents, a canal and lakes. The focus of the development was a proposed avenue from Prince Regent's Park to Carlton House in the Mall. The area covered by Nash's scheme covered the present Regent's Park, Trafalgar Square, St. James's Park and Regent Street. The Prince Regent threw his support and money behind Nash's vision and for the next 23 years Nash laboured to bring it to life. Several elements of his original scheme had to be abandoned, including a summer palace in Regent's Park and the present day Regent's Street has since been altered. As the work in London proceeded, Nash took on other projects for the Prince, including the remodelling of Brighton Pavilion (1815-22). The villa there was originally designed by Henry Holland and the Prince asked Nash to turn it into a palace. This he did, commencing in the Moghul style and as the work progressed, incorporating further Eastern elements. The result has been described as: 'Indian Gothic with a flavour of Chinese'[1] In London, Nash remodelled Carlton House as Carlton House Terrace (1827-1833) and built the Royal Mews (1825); Haymarket Theatre (1820) and All Soul's Church in Langham Place (1822-25). Cumberland Terrace (1827) is one of his most impressive achievements, it being the last in a sequence which included Cornwall Terrace (by Decimus Burton, under Nash's supervision), Hanover Terrace, Chester Terrace and York Terrace. Through his friendship with the Prince 'the first gentleman of Europe', who was a most generous patron of the arts, Nash - along with the celebrated wit and clotheshorse George Bryan 'Beau' Brummel (1778-1840) helped define the style of the Regency Era. Nash also laid out what is now Trafalgar Square. In contrast, his other major project at Buckingham Palace did not fare so well. When Nash began work on redesigning it in 1825 it was still Buckingham House. King George IV decided that it was: 'antiquated, rundown, and decrepit', and decided to create a palace on the site of the Duke of Buckingham's former villa. Nash was dilatory in his work there however and erected then pulled down several wings of the building according to whim. After the death of King George IV in 1830, Nash was dismissed from the project and replaced by Edward Blore (1790-1879). All that remains of Nash's endeavours there is the west wing. He worked in a range of architectural styles from Gothic to Italianate, Palladian, Greek and the picturesque. He was enthusiastic, impatient, yet blessed with great talent and creative vision and whilst he was given nothing like the free hand in London that Baron Haussman would be in Paris, the palatial grandeur of his work is with us still. (In recent years, based on descriptions of Nash's personality, it has been suggested by experts that he may have suffered from a variant of Asperger's Syndrome). Nash built East Cowes Castle (1798) on the Isle of Wight and died there on 13 May 1835 and is buried in St James's Churchyard.

---

[1] Doreen Yarwood *Encyclopaedia of Architecture* 1993.

# PROFESSOR JOHN FLAXMAN

John Flaxman was born on 7 December 1755 at York. His father was a farmer who also carried on the trade of moulder and seller of plaster casts at the sign of the Golden Head in Covent Garden in London. Within six months of his birth the family returned to London and he spent an ailing childhood in his father's back shop. He would appear to be almost entirely self-taught and developed an interest in drawing and modelling from the shop's stock. His father's customers took a shine to him and encouraged him, helping him with books, advice and eventually commissions. Aged twelve he won the first prize of the Society of Arts for the design of a medal and became a public exhibitor in the gallery of the Free Society of Artists. In 1770 at the age of 15 he won a second prize from the Society of Arts and began to exhibit at the Royal Academy of Arts, then in the second year of its existence. That same year, he entered the RA as a student and won their Silver Medal. In the competition for the Gold Medal of the RA in 1772, although confident of victory, he was defeated, the prize being awarded by Sir Joshua Reynolds to another competitor named Engleheart. This rebuff cured him of a tendency to conceit, which made Thomas Wedgwood later say of him: 'It is but a few years since he was a most supreme coxcomb'. To the RA he contributed a wax model of *Neptune* (1770); four portrait models in wax (1771); a terracotta bust; a wax figure of a *Child;* a figure of *History* (1772); a figure of *Comedy*, and a relief of a *Vestal* (1773). He was the first British sculptor to achieve an international reputation. In the period 1775 to 1787 he worked for the potter Josiah Wedgwood as a modeller of classic and domestic friezes, plaques, ornamental vessels and medallion portraits. By 1780 Flaxman had begun to branch out and produce sculpture of monuments for the dead. Three of his earliest are those of *Chatterton* in the church of St Mary Redcliffe (1780) at Bristol, of *Mrs Morley* (1784) in Gloucester Cathedral and of the *Reverend Thomas and Mrs Margaret Ball* (1785) in Chichester Cathedral. In 1782 he married Anne Denman and set up house in Wardour Street, Soho. In the period 1787 to 1794 he worked in Rome for Wedgwood. Although initially intending only to spend two years there, he ended up spending seven and was detained by a commission for the marble group *Fury of Athamas*. In Rome, he became a member of the Academy of St Luke and illustrated *The Iliad, The Odyssey* and Dante's *Divine Comedy*.

Back in England, Flaxman sculpted many monuments, including that in Westminster Abbey to *William Murray, 1st Earl of Mansfield* (1801). His figures of *Comedy* and *Tragedy* adorn the façade of the Covent Garden Opera House. He sculpted the marble funerary plaque in St George's Cathedral, Penang commemorating *Charles, Marquess Cornwallis.* (destroyed by enemy action in the Second World War). Flaxman was elected ARA in 1797 and RA in 1800. In 1810 he was appointed the first Professor of Sculpture at the Royal Academy Schools. He undertook the frieze *Peace, Liberty* and *Plenty* for the Duke of Bedford's sculpture gallery at Woburn and the heroic group *St Michael Overthrowing Satan* for Lord Egremont at Petworth. He produced the monument to *Mrs Baring* (1805-1811) in Micheldever Church, the richest of all his monuments in relief and that for the *Worsley Family* at Campsall church, Yorkshire which is his next richest. His neoclassical memorials of *Sir Joshua Reynolds* (1807); *Admiral Earl Howe* and *Viscount Admiral Horatio Nelson* may all be found in St Paul's Cathedral, London. An engraving of his *Nelson Monument* may be found in the collection of Sir John Soane's Museum at Lincoln's Inn Fields, London. Flaxman also sculpted the memorials to *Captain Beckett* (1811) for Leeds and *General Sir John Moore* (1813) for Glasgow. In 1816 he appeared as an expert witness before the parliamentary commission investigating the Elgin Marbles and recommended their purchase for the nation. In 1822 he delivered the memorial lecture at the RA on the art of his great friend and contemporary Antonio Canova (1757-1822).

On 3 December 1826 Flaxman caught a cold in church and died four days later. An English Heritage blue plaque marks his house at 7 Greenwell Street, Westminster and a collection of his casts may be found in the Flaxman Gallery at University College, London.

# PROFESSOR SIR RICHARD WESTMACOTT

Richard Westmacott was born in 1775, son of the sculptor of the same name. He was trained by his father in his art and sent to Rome in 1793 to train under Canova. In 1795 he was awarded the first Gold Medal of the Academy of St Luke by Pope Pius VI for his bas-relief *Joseph and his Brethren*. That year he was elected Member of the Academy of Florence. In 1797 he fled Rome in haste upon the approach of Napoleon's army and set up his studio in London. Westmacott produced a substantial body of work, much of it in the neoclassical manner, notable amongst which were: *Sir William Chambers* (1797) for Westminster Abbey; *Addison* (1806); *General Villettes* (1809); *Pitt* (over the west entrance door); *Charles James Fox; Spencer Perceval* and *Duc de Montpensier* (1830). For St Paul's Cathedral, London he produced the white marble statues of *Sir Ralph Abercromby; Admiral Viscount Duncan* (behind the servery in the cafeteria in the crypt); *Admiral Collingwood; Captain Cook; General Gibbs* and *General Pakenham*. He produced a splendid bronze *Lord Nelson* (1810) which stands in the Bullring at Birmingham with another at Bridgetown, Barbados (1813). Other works are *The Fifth Duke of Bedford* (1809) in Russell Square, London; *Canning* in Parliament Square; *Charles James Fox* (1814) in Bloomsbury Square; *A Nymph* (1814); *Hero and Leander* (1820); *Maternal Affection* (1820); *Resignation* (1821); *The Distressed Mother* (1822); *Psyche* (1822); *Cupid* (1823); *Horace's Dream* (1823); *Afflicted Peasants* (1825); *Madonna and Child* and *Cupid Made Prisoner* (1827). His Diploma Work *Jupiter and Ganymede* (1811) may be seen at the Royal Academy.[2] In the years 1828 and 1829 he worked on segments of the monument to *Warren Hastings* for Calcutta Cathedral and produced a bust of *Wellington* for the Almeida Gardens, Gibraltar. In 1813 he cast the Matthew Cotes Wyatt's monument to *Lord Nelson* in Liverpool. In 1822 he cast the controversial colossal *Achilles* in Hyde Park as a tribute to the Iron Duke.[3] That year, he produced *The Equestrian Monument to George III* for Liverpool. This was also based on a theme from antiquity, the Capitoline *Marcus Aurelius*. 'Although he was not as highly skilled as many continental founders, Westmacott's role in the development of casting monumental bronzes in England should not be underestimated. With the exception of John Bacon the Elder (1740-99), Westmacott was the only English sculptor of the late eighteenth and early nineteenth centuries to undertake bronze casting until Sir Francis Chantrey opened his own foundry in Pimlico in the early 1830s'.[4] He produced *Lord Erskine* (1826) now in Old Hall, Lincoln's Inn and *The Gypsy* (1832). He sculpted the statue of *the Duke of York* on top of Benjamin Dean Wyatt's column at Waterloo Place (1833). He produced *Locke* for University College, London (1834); *Devotion* (1835); *Euphrosyne* (1837) and *Lord Penrhyn* at Penrhyn, North Wales. He produced the statues *Warren Hastings* (1828) and *Lord William Bentinck* (1839) both of which now stand in the grounds of the Victoria Memorial, Calcutta. Westmacott was elected ARA in 1805 and RA in 1811. In 1827 he succeeded Flaxman as Professor of Sculpture at the RA and was knighted by Queen Victoria on 19 July 1837. He produced the recently re-gilded ornamental group *The Progress of Civilisation* (1847) which may be seen on the portico of the British Museum at Bloomsbury in London. Westmacott died on 1 September 1856. The National Portrait Gallery has a chalk drawing of him by Charles Benazech (1792); a pencil drawing by Charles Hutton Lear (1845); a chalk/pencil drawing by William Brockedon (1844) and a medal cast in 1868 by Leonard Charles Wyon and Richard Westmacott (son). An English Heritage Blue Plaque marks his house at 14 South Audley Street, Westminster.

---

[2] According to Emerson: 'An institution is the lengthened shadow of one man.' In the case of the Royal Academy of Arts the man in question is the noted English portrait painter Sir Joshua Reynolds (1723-92). He founded the RA in 1768 and it is governed by 80 Royal Academicians who are usually eminent painters, sculptors, architects and print makers. They elect officers from their number. A Diploma Work is usually deposited with the RA when a member achieves full status as a Royal Academician and these may be seen in the Diploma Gallery at Burlington House, London. The Loggia there houses the Artists Rifles Great War Memorial.

[3] *Gentleman's Magazine* Frontispiece Vol XCII part II (1822).

[4] *The Burlington Magazine* Vol 130 (1988).

# SIR FRANCIS CHANTREY

Francis Legatt Chantrey was born at Norton near Sheffield on 7 April 1782, the son of a carpenter. His father died when he was eight and his mother remarried. Aged 15 he was on the verge of being apprenticed to a grocer in Sheffield, when having seen some wood-carving in a shop-window, he requested to become a carver and was placed with Mr Ramsey, a woodcarver in Sheffield. The mezzotint engraver Raphael Smith was a frequent visitor to Ramsey's shop. He took a liking to young Chantrey and gave him drawing lessons. Chantrey started to paint portraits, and moved from portrait painting to wood carving and back again before making his first attempts at clay modelling. He obtained the cancellation of his indentures and went to try his fortune in Dublin, then Edinburgh and finally London in 1802. In 1807 he married his cousin Miss Wale. The £10,000 she brought to the marriage helped to establish his studio and funded the purchase of several houses. In 1809 he exhibited his *Head of Satan* at the Royal Academy, which led to the commissions of four colossal busts of admirals *Duncan, Howe, Vincent* and *Nelson* for Greenwich Hospital. His bust of *Lord Nelson* nearly 3 feet tall and weighing three quarters of a ton was originally sculpted in 1834 for the guardroom of Windsor Castle and was reinstated there in 2005. In 1815 Chantrey executed the statue *Dr James Anderson* for the vestibule of Madras Cathedral and it was exhibited at the RA that year. In 1827 he sculpted his youthful *Stephen Babington* of that long line of illustrious judges for Mumbai Town Hall. He sculpted the portrait statue *The Honourable Mountstuart Elphinstone* in the Grand Assembly Room of Mumbai Town Hall. At the request of Lady Raffles he produced the statue *Sir Stamford Raffles* for Westminster Abbey in 1834. He produced portrait statues of *Bishop Reginald Heber* (who drowned in the bath in 1833) for St Paul's Cathedral, London (1835) and St Paul's Cathedral, Calcutta. He sculpted the marble statue *Major General Sir John Malcolm* (1836) for Old Town Hall, Mumbai. He spent ten years sculpting the bronze equestrian statue *Major General Sir Thomas Munro* (1838), which stands on the Island in Madras. His equestrian *George IV* sculpted originally for Marble Arch may be seen in Trafalgar Square. His *Monument to Lieutenant Colonel the Honourable Henry Cadogan* may be found in St Luke's Church, Chelsea. His *George Washington* is in Boston State House, USA and his equestrian statue the *Duke of Wellington* stands in front of the Royal Exchange. Critics hold that his finest works are his busts and his representations of children. His figures of *Sleeping Children* (1817) in Lichfield Cathedral have long been praised for their simplicity and grace. Chantrey travelled to Paris in 1814 and in 1819 to Rome where he visited the studios of Canova and Albert Bertel Thorwaldsen and bought marble at Carrara. Chantrey was elected ARA 1815, RA 1818 and knighted in 1835. He was a man of warm and genial temperament and is said to have borne a noticeable resemblance to portrayals of William Shakespeare. He died after a brief illness on 25 November 1841 and was buried in a tomb constructed by himself in the church of his native village. He had no heirs and had built up a large fortune, which he willed be devoted to the purchase of works of fine art of the highest merit for the nation. The Chantrey Bequest permitted the Royal Academy to purchase works of art executed in Britain for the National Collection (later the Tate Gallery). Up to 1905 inclusive, 203 works had been bought, all except two from living painters at a cost of nearly £68,000. Of these 175 were oil-colours, 12 water-colours, and 16 sculptures (10 in bronze and 6 marble). Galleries in the Victoria and Albert Museum at South Kensington were at first adopted as the depository of the works acquired, until in 1898 the Royal Academy arranged with HM Treasury, on behalf of the government for the transference of the collection to the National Gallery of British Art, which had been established by Sir Henry Tate at Millbank. The RA's administration of the Bequest was repeatedly attacked in the press by the art critic D S MacColl and in 1903 a debate in the House of Lords led to the appointment of a Select Committee of the House of Lords, which sat from June to August 1904. Their report made recommendations with a view to the prevention of former errors of administration held to have been proved, but dismissed all other charges.

# EDWARD HODGES BAILY

Edward Hodges Baily was born at Bristol in March 1788, son of a carver of figureheads for ships. 'He was sent to grammar school, but showed the common artistic repugnance to the regular studies. Young Baily would carve strange portraits of his schoolfellows, and showed no capacity for ordinary school work. At 14 he entered a merchant's office, and remained there for two years. During this time he obtained some instruction from a modeller in wax, and greatly improved his opportunity. Soon he forsook commerce, and began taking portraits in wax. By virtue of some studies which he made from the antique, he obtained an introduction to Flaxman, in whose studio, in 1807, he became a pupil, and there he remained for seven years. In 1809 he entered the Academy Schools, gaining silver and gold medals in quick succession.'[5] In 1811 he won the RA Gold Medal for his *Hercules Restoring Alcestis to Admetus*. He exhibited *Apollo Discharging his Arrows against the Greeks* in 1817 and was elected ARA. He was elected RA in 1821. His Diploma Work was the bust *John Flaxman*.

A prolific sculptor, Baily produced a substantial body of high quality work. His output consisted of groups, portrait busts, statues and memorial tablets. In 1825 he executed the frieze for the portico of the Masonic Hall in Bristol and in 1826 the relief for *General Picton's Monument* at Carmarthen. The figure that established his reputation was *Eve at the Fountain* for Bristol Art Gallery exhibited at the RA in 1818, (a copy is in the Glyptotek, Copenhagen). His statues included: *Jenner* (1825) Gloucester Cathedral; the gilded *Minerva* for the Athenæum (1830) and *Jebb, Bishop of Limerick* (1836) for Limerick Cathedral. For St Paul's Cathedral he sculpted in white marble *Earl St Vincent* (1826); *Admiral Sir Pultney Malcolm* (1838) and *General Sir William Ponsonby*, all of which stand in the cafeteria in the crypt. He sculpted *Eve, Listening to the Voice* (1842) at Bethnal Green Museum; *The Duke of Sussex* (1846) in the Freemasons' Hall; *Professor Owen* (1846) Royal College of Surgeons; *Chief Justice Tindall* (1847) Chelmsford; *Flaxman* (1849) University College, London; *Sleeping Girl* (1850) Bristol Art Gallery; *Alderman Donkin* (1851) Newcastle Public Library; *Joan Lever* (1851) Guy's Hospital; *Sir Robert Peel* (1852) Old Market Place, Bury; *The Morning Star* (1854) Mansion House, London; *The Circassian Slave* (1855) in the Royal Collection; *Charles James Fox* and *Earl Mansfield* (1857) in the Palace of Westminster. His *Genius* (1858) at the Mansion House was destroyed by enemy action on 29 November 1940. In 1831 Baily and Westmacott jointly wrote to HM Treasury protesting that fees for sculpture commissioned by the Government that they had carried out had not been paid: 'the greatest part of these works have been executed nearly three years ago'.[6] He sculpted *Lord Nelson* on top of Railton's column in Trafalgar Square. He designed the *Doncaster Cup* in 1843 and the *Ascot Gold Cup* in 1844. With Flaxman and Westmacott he carried out the sculpture for the Marble Arch at Buckingham Palace. He also carried out both exterior and interior work at the Palace. He executed the statues on the façade of the National Gallery. His busts included: *Lord Byron* (1826) Harrow School; *Duke of York* (1827) Freemasons' Hall; *Thomas Campbell* (1827) Glasgow Art Gallery; *Michael Faraday* (1830) University Museum, Oxford and *Lord George Bentinck* (1842) at the Russell-Cotes Museum, Bournemouth. Facsimiles of his most popular works were commissioned by the Crystal Palace Company and included: *JMW Turner, George Stephenson, Earl of Egremont,* and *Apollo*. Baily retired in 1863, was soon embarrassed by his financial extravagance and by application was granted a pension by the RA. He died at Holloway, London on 22 May 1867 and his grave may be found in Highgate Cemetery. 'The years of his prolonged life were actively passed in upholding the dignity and purity of his art, and in its annals his name must always be referred to as one of the most successful sculptors of the nineteenth century.'[7] There is a drawing of him by Charles Hutton Lear and a medallion by Benjamin Wyon in the collection of the National Portrait Gallery.

---

[5] *Dictionary of National Biography* Oxford University Press 1997.
[6] PRO Works T.1/3489.
[7] The *Art Journal* July 1867.

# PROFESSOR CHARLES COCKERELL

Charles Robert Cockerell was born in London in 1788 and despite begging his father Samuel Pepys Cockerell to allow him to train as an artist he was trained in his father's practice as an architect. Later he assisted Sir Robert Smirke in the rebuilding of Covent Garden Theatre (1809-10) and would never shake off his stylistic influence. In the period 1810-17 Cockerell toured southern Europe and the Levant. Whilst excavating at Bassae, Aegina, and other sites in Italy, Greece, and Asia Minor, he studied the remains of ancient architecture and designed restorations for the temple of Zeus at Agrigento, Sicily. His stunning panoramas of Ancient Rome and Athens were exhibited at the RA and may be found in the British Architectural Library Drawings Collection. On his return to London, he established his own practice and in 1819 was appointed Surveyor of St. Paul's Cathedral. He designed the Hanover Chapel in Regent Street (1823-25) and built the Office for Sun Life Assurance in Threadneedle Street, (pulled down in 1970). In 1833 Cockerell succeeded Sir John Soane as Architect to the Bank of England and built banks at Courtney Street, Plymouth (1835); Broad Street, Bristol (1844-7); King Street, Manchester (1845) and Castle Street, Liverpool (1851-4). Also in Liverpool, Cockerell completed the Assize Courts and St George's Hall after the death from consumption of Harvey Lonsdale Elmes (1814-47). Cockerell was architect of the Ashmolean Museum, the Taylorian Institute (1839-42) at Oxford and the Cambridge University Library (1837-40). Cockerell was a good friend of the Iron Duke and after his death in 1852, Cockerell superintended the arrangements for his lying-in-state at the Royal Hospital, Chelsea. With his assistant William Henry Playfair (1790-1857) he designed the National Monument to Scotland's Dead from the Napoleonic Wars and his unusual design was based on the Acropolis in Athens. £24,000 was raised by a committee for its construction and its incomplete appearance was intentional, but did not please the Scots. Its foundations were laid during the visit of King George IV to Edinburgh in 1824. Work came to an end in 1829 when the money provided by public subscription finally ran out. Controversy in the matter of war memorials is not new and Cockerell's design would later be labelled 'Scotland's Shame'. Given that he was a standard-bearer of the Greek Revival, it was hardly surprising that his work and that of other architects such as Alexander 'Greek' Thompson resulted in Edinburgh subsequently being described as the 'Athens of the North'. In the 19th century the Neoclassical Movement in art, architecture, and design was characterized by the revival of classical Greek and Roman styles and apart from Cockerell, its leading figures were the architects Claude-Nicolas Ledoux, John Soane and Robert Adam; the painters Jacques-Louis David, Jean Ingres and Anton Mengs; the sculptors Antonio Canova, John Flaxman, Bertel Thorvaldsen and Johann Sergel; the designers Josiah Wedgwood, George Hepplewhite and Thomas Sheraton. Cockerell's abiding interest in antiquity led him to exhibit restorations of classical buildings at the Royal Academy, he also wrote extensively on the subject and discovered the reliefs from the temple of Phigalia, which are now in the collection of the British Museum. His Monument to Admiral Collingwood may be seen in the Cathedral of St Nicholas, Newcastle-upon-Tyne. In 1836-37 Cockerell sat as member of a committee that included Jacques Ignace Hittorff, and Thomas Leverton Donaldson which convened in London to determine whether the Elgin Marbles had originally been coloured, (they decided they had not). In 1853 he designed the obelisk memorial to the fallen of the 24th Regiment of Foot at Chillianwallah, which stands in the grounds of the Royal Hospital, Chelsea. Cockerell was elected ARA in 1829, RA in 1836 and President of the Royal Institute of British Architects in 1860. With the assistance of the Heritage Lottery Fund, a pencil portrait of him (1817) by Jean Ingres was purchased by Oxford University in 1999 and may be found displayed at the Ashmolean in Beaufort Street, Oxford. Cockerell's lecture notes dating from his tenure as Professor of Architecture may be found in the Royal Academy Library at Burlington House and other of his papers at Trinity College, Cambridge. Cockerell died in London in 1863. His memorial may be found in the crypt of St Paul's Cathedral in London.

# WILLIAM BEHNES

William Behnes was born in London in 1794. He was the son of an emigre Hanoverian pianoforte-maker and his English wife. William's early years were spent in Dublin, where after a false start in the field of piano manufacture, he commenced studying art at Dublin Academy. After the Behnes family returned to London, he continued his artistic training, studying at the Royal Academy School of Art from 1813, and in the years 1816-19 winning successive silver medals. To critical acclaim, he first exhibited at the Royal Academy in 1815 and success duly followed. In 1819 the Society of Arts awarded him their Gold Medal for inventing an instrument for transferring points from models to marble. He continued to pursue his interest in sculpture and demonstrated considerable facility in his busts of children.

Behnes would quickly establish himself a master of the white marble portrait bust. Of his prolific output, a number are in the collection of the National Portrait Gallery. These include: *George Tierney* (1822); *Judge William Scott, Baron Stowell* (1824); *Henry Addington, 1st Viscount Sidmouth* (1831); *William Charles Macready* (1844) and *1st Earl Camden* which may be found at Bayham Abbey at Lamberhurst in Kent. His bust *Dr Thomas Arnold* (1849) may be found in the Temple Reading Room and Museum at Rugby School in Warwickshire; *Lord Lyndhurst* in Trinity College Library at Cambridge University; *Richard Porson* at Eton College in Bucks; *Sir Joshua Reynolds* on a base of scagliola may be seen in the Cottonian Collection at the Plymouth City Museum & Art Gallery and *Robert Vernon* (1849) is in the collection of the Tate. In 1837 recognition arrived and Behnes was appointed Sculptor in Ordinary to Queen Victoria. His pupils included such notable figures as: George Frederic Watts; Thomas Woolner; William Mossman II and Benjamin Waterhouse Hawkins. Behnes' *Monument to Major General Sir John Thomas Jones* may be found in St Paul's Cathedral, as may his statue *Dr Babington*, considered by the experts to be his finest work. His bronze statue *Sir Robert Peel* (1855) cast by Robinson and Cottam of Pimlico, (originally erected on a plinth of Peterhead granite at Cheapside in London) is at the Police Training School, Hendon, with copies at Peel Park in Bradford (1855) and at Leeds (1852). His much criticised bronze statue of *Major-General Sir Henry Havelock* is believed to be the first statue sculpted from a photograph. Two casts were made - one occupies one of the plinths in Trafalgar Square, London, the other is in Mowbray Park, Sunderland. His *Monument to Dr Andrew Bell* may be seen in Westminster Abbey. His *Memorial to Joseph Nollekens* may be found in Paddington Parish Church, that to *Mrs Botfield* in All Saints Church at Norton in Northamptonshire. His bust of *George Cruikshank* (1855) may be found in the collection of the National Portrait Gallery. The *Every-Day Book* of the diarist William Hone (1825-26) records: 'On the 10th of March, 1820, died Benjamin West, esq., President of the Royal Academy, in the eighty-second year of his age. It was his delight to gently lead genius in a young artist; and Mr. William Behnes, the sculptor, was honoured by the venerable president with the means of transmitting his parting looks to an admiring world, upon whom he was soon to look no more. Mr. West's sittings to Mr. Behnes were about two months before his death. Expressing himself to his young friend in terms of high satisfaction at the model, he encouraged him to persevere in that branch of art which Mr. Behnes has since distinguished, by admirable power of design and use of the chisel. To speak of Mr. Behnes's model as a mere likeness, is meagre praise of an effort which clearly marks observation, and comprehension, of Mr. West's great mental powers. The bust, as it stands in marble, in Sir John Leicester's gallery, is a perfect resemblance of Mr. West's features and an eloquent memorial of his vigorous and unimpaired intellect in the last days of earthly existence. If ever the noblest traits of humanity were depicted by the hand of art, they are on this bust. Superiority of mind is so decidedly marked, and blended, with primitive simplicity, and a beaming look of humanity and benevolence, that it seems the head of an apostle.'

Behnes was by nature financially improvident and he was declared bankrupt in 1861. He died in poverty in 1864 and his grave may be found in Kensal Green Cemetery in London.

# BARON CARLO MAROCHETTI

Carlo Marochetti was born in 1805 at Turin, Italy. That city was capital of Piedmont and part of Napoleon's empire. In 1814 after Napoleon's abdication, his father settled in Paris to practice law. Carlo was educated at the Lycée Napoleon and commenced studies under the sculptor Baron Bosio. Marochetti resided in Rome 1822-1830 working in the Academy of French Artists at the Villa Medici on the Pincio. In 1827 he exhibited *A Girl Playing with a Dog* and was awarded a medal by the École des Beaux-Arts. His first equestrian sculpture was *Emmanuel Philibert of Savoy* which he presented to Turin. He was created baron by Carlo Alberto, King of Sardinia. He subsequently produced the equestrian statue *Carlo Alberto*. He sculpted the *Fallen Angel* and a bust of *Mossi* for the Turin Academy. He returned to France, found favor at the court of King Louis Phillipe and executed *Napoleon's Tomb* in Les Invalides in 1841 a design which the *Art Union* noted was a direct crib of Goldicutt's design for the *Nelson Monument* in St Paul's Cathedral. He produced the statue *Duke of Orleans* for the courtyard of the Louvre with copies for Lyons and Algiers. He produced the relief *The Assumption* for the high altar of the Madeleine and the tomb of the composer Vincenzo Bellini in Père Lachaise Cemetery. Upon the outbreak of revolution in France in 1848 Marochetti fled to England. In 1850 he competed for Sir Robert Peel's statue in Bury, but lost out to Baily. That same year Marochetti exhibited *Sappho* at the Royal Academy and his busts *Prince Albert* and *Lady Constance Gower* in 1851. For the Great Exhibition that year he produced the equestrian *Richard Cœur de Lion* which was later executed in bronze by public subscription and stands outside the Palace of Westminster, its bent sword a legacy of the Blitz. Marochetti produced a wide variety of work. He sculpted the *Coldstream Guards Inkerman Memorial;* the *Cavalry Division Crimean War Memorial* both in St Paul's Cathedral; *The East Devonshire Regiment Crimean War Memorial;* the *Monument to the 9th Queen's Royal Lancers* in Exeter Cathedral; the bronze statue *Joseph Locke* (1866) in Locke Park, Barnsley; the bust *W M Thackeray* in Westminster Abbey; the statue *Lord Clive* at Shrewsbury; the *Duke of Wellington* at both Leeds and Stratfield Saye; *Lord Herbert* at Salisbury; *Field Marshal Lord Clyde* (1867) at Waterloo Place; London, the sheep breeder *Jonas Webb* (1876) at Market Place, Cambridge and the *Duke of Wellington* (1884) which stands in front of Glasgow's Gallery of Modern Art usually ornamented by an orange traffic cone. He produced the seated statue of *Sir Jamsetjee Jejeebhoy* at Mumbai and the memorial to *Lord Melbourne* in St Paul's Cathedral. He executed the controversial *Scutari Monument* in granite for Haidar Pasha Cemetery in Turkey. A facsimile in imitation granite was erected at Crystal Palace. He recycled this design for his *Angel of the Resurrection* (1865) at Cawnpore. He produced Aberdeen's bronze statue of *Prince Albert* and Queen Victoria unveiled it on 13 October 1863. He produced the memorial to *Princess Elizabeth Stuart* (1856) in the Parish Church of St Thomas, Newport. 'Marochetti's handsome figure and engaging manners rendered him popular with his fashionable patrons in England and on the continent. As a sculptor he introduced a great deal of vitality into the somewhat stiff and constrained manner then prevalent in England. His equestrian statues command attention, even if they invite criticism, and are - especially at Turin - a conspicuous ornament to the place where they are erected.'[8] Marochetti designed the recumbent marble effigies of both Queen Victoria and Prince Albert in the Royal Mausoleum at Frogmore. The sarcophagus was made from a single piece of grey Aberdeen granite, the largest block of flawless granite in existence and the fourth to be quarried for the purpose, the first three having been found flawed after cutting from the quarry at Cairngall. Despite the antipathy of his fellow sculptors, Marochetti was elected ARA in 1861 and RA in 1866. He died at Passy, France on 29 December 1867 and was buried in the cemetery at Vaux-sur-Seine. There is a chromolithograph of him by Vincent Brooks, a portrait by Sir Anthony Coningham Sterling and a statuette of him by Gabriele Ambrosio all in the collection of the National Portrait Gallery.

---

[8] *Dictionary of National Biography* Oxford University Press 1997.

# JOHN BELL

According to the DNB John Bell was born at Hopton, Suffolk in 1811, (*Men of Our Times* in 1862 gives his year of birth as 1812). He was educated at Catfield village school and on the recommendation of H Sass entered the RA Schools in 1829. He exhibited his first work, a religious group at the RA in 1832 and would exhibit there for 47 years. He produced *A Girl at a Brook* and *John the Baptist* (1833); *The Quarterstaff Player* (1833); *Ariel* (1834); *Psyche feeding a Swan; Youth, Spring* and *Infancy; Psyche and the Dove* (1837); *Amoret Captive* (1838); *The Wounded Clorinda* (1841) and *The Eagle Shooter*. In 1837 he produced the busts *Amoret* and *Psyche* which were exhibited at the British Institution and *The Babes in the Wood* (1839). In 1839 he exhibited *Dorothea* at the RA and this work would subsequently be reproduced by Minton in Parian porcelain. Bell was the first British sculptor to produce a large number of reduced sized works for sale and *Dorothea* would be the most popular piece he ever produced. He sculpted again *The Eagle Shooter* (1841) (Bethnal Green Museum). In 1848 he executed the figures on the Corn Exchange at Newark.[9] He produced the bronze and ormolu figures *Queen Victoria* and *The Prince Consort* for the Great Exhibition (1851). In 1853 he produced the colossi *Australia, California, Birmingham* and *Sheffield* for the terrace of the Crystal Palace at Sydenham. In 1854 he produced *Lord Falkland* and *Sir Robert Walpole* for St Stephen's Hall, Westminster. He sculpted *Armed Science* (1855) for the Royal Artillery Officers Mess at Woolwich. A modified terracotta version was fired by Doulton for the *Soldiers Memorial* (1878) in Norwich Cemetery. He produced The *Wellington Monument* (1856) at the Guildhall, London and *Lalage* (1856). In 1859 he was awarded a medal by the Society of Arts for his treatise *The Origination of the Principle of Entasis as Applied to the Obelisk*. He sculpted the *Guards Crimea Memorial* (1860) in bronze at Waterloo Place, London which earned mixed reviews. One journal lamented: 'We have tried in every possible way to like this work and consider it the right thing, but we have failed signally.'[10] Bell also produced *The Royal Artillery Crimean War Memorial* (1860) on the Parade Ground at Woolwich. He produced *The Cross of Prayer* (1864); *A Cherub* (1865); *The Foot of the Cross* (1866); *Mother and Child* (1867); the medallion portrait *John Croome* (1868) in St George's, Norwich and for the Albert Memorial he produced his remarkable 27 ton work in Campanella marble *The United States Directing the Progress of America* (1869). A large terra cotta copy is in Washington DC. *The Times* wrote: 'Mr Bell's America is undoubtedly the finest conception and composition of the four groups, and the boldest and most vigorous in every way... The sense of action and progress and power which radiates from the whole group makes us aware that we are in the presence of a really great work'.[11] He produced the *James Montgomery Monument* (1861) in Sheffield Cemetery and *Cursetjee Manockjee* (1875) at Mumbai. His busts included: *Sir Robert Walpole* (1858) Eton; *Dr Clarke* (1866) Anatomical Museum, Cambridge; *Dr Hugh Falconer* (1867) Madras; *Monument to Lady Waveney* (1871) Flixton Church, Suffolk, and *Lord Byron* (1877). One critic noted: 'His early works of sculpture had shown vigour and imagination, but his later groups exhibited at the Academy were remarkable for nothing but bad taste and sickly sentimentality.'[12] In retirement Bell wrote poetry and presented his models to Kensington Town Hall. It took a direct hit in the Blitz and they were destroyed. Kensington and Chelsea's Rate Records show that he occupied a studio at Little Camden House (also demolished in the Blitz) from 1851 until his death. 'In private life Bell endeared himself to all who knew him. He had retired from the active exercise of his profession for many years before his death, which took place on 14 March 1895 at Douro Place, Kensington, where he had resided for more than forty years'.[13]

---

[9] *Builder* 1848 p. 391.
[10] *Art Journal* 1861 p. 158.
[11] *The Times* 2 July 1872.
[12] R Gunnis *Dictionary of British Sculptors 1660-1951* London 1968.
[13] *Dictionary of National Biography* Oxford University Press 1997.

# COUNT VICTOR GLEICHEN

Prince Victor Ferdinand Franz Eugen Gustaf Adolf Constantin Freidrich of Hohenlohe-Langenburg was born at Langenburg Castle in Württemberg on 11 November 1833. He was the third son of Prince Ernest of Hohenlohe-Langenburg and Princess Féodore, only daughter of Emich Charles, reigning prince of Leiningen, by Princess Victoria of Saxe-Coburg-Saalfeld, afterwards Duchess of Kent. His mother was therefore Queen Victoria's half-sister. Young Prince Victor was sent to school at Dresden, from which he ran away. Queen Victoria then arranged for him to enter the Royal Navy. After basic training, he was posted as a Midshipman to HMS POWERFUL. He then served on HMS CUMBERLAND, flagship of Admiral Sir George Francis Seymour (1787-1870) on the North America Station. In 1854 during the Crimean War, Prince Victor took part in the bombardment of the Russian forts at Bomarsund in the Baltic and was injured in that action. He subsequently served on HMS JEAN D'ACRE off Sevastopol and also in the Naval Brigade. He took his turn in the trenches before Sevastopol. He served as ADC to Admiral Sir Harry Keppel at the Battle of Tchernaya and in 1856 served under him again in China, during which service his bravery under fire earned him a recommendation for the Victoria Cross. In 1861 Prince Victor contracted a morganatic marriage with Laura Williamina, (1833-1912) daughter of his old commander Admiral Seymour. Under the laws governing the succession of members of German reigning houses, he married beneath his station and his wife was therefore disqualified from using or sharing his title. He then assumed the title Count Victor Gleichen and despite his changes of title, this is the designation by which he is known to posterity. Repeated illness prevented Count Victor from progressing in his Royal Navy career and he retired on half-pay in 1866. That same year he was granted the appointment of Governor and Constable of Windsor Castle. In retirement he pursued his interest in the arts and studied sculpture for three years under the outstanding William Theed the Younger (1804-91), who was a favourite of Queen Victoria. Count Victor was granted a suite of apartments at St James's Palace by the Queen, set up his studio there and regularly competed for sculptural commissions. In 1887 Count Victor was promoted admiral on the retired list and appointed GCB. He is known to have executed a number of busts including: *Queen Victoria* and *Mary Seacole* (at the Royal College of Nursing, with a terracotta copy in the National Institute, Kingston, Jamaica). 'He executed several imaginative groups, as well as memorials and portrait busts. Some of the busts were very successful, notably those of the *Earl of Beaconsfield, the Marquis of Salisbury,* and *Sir Harry Keppel*. His most important work was his colossal Sicilian marble statue of *Alfred the Great*, executed for the town of Wantage, where it was erected. He was enabled by his success as a sculptor to build himself a small house near Ascot. In 1881 Count Victor designed and sculpted the ingenious monolithic granite Afghan/Zulu War Memorial for the Royal Artillery which may be seen at Napier Lines, Woolwich. 'In 1885 Count and Countess Gleichen were permitted by Queen Victoria to revert to the titles of Prince and Princess Victor of Hohenlohe-Langenburg. Prince Victor died on 31 Dec 1891.'[14] An 1872 lithograph of him by Carlo Pellegrini is in the collection of the National Portrait Gallery. Count Victor's eldest daughter was the talented sculptor Countess (later Lady) Feodora Gleichen (1861-1922). She studied under Alphonse Legros (1837-1911) and executed the *Diana Fountain* in Rotten Row, Hyde Park, the *Florence Nightingale Memorial* outside Derby Royal Infirmary and the *37th Division Memorial* at Monchy le Preux in France. She was posthumously appointed Member of the Royal Society of British Sculptors, the first woman to be accorded such an honour. Count Victor's only son was Major General Count Albert Edward Wilfred Gleichen (1863-1937) of the Grenadier Guards and he commanded the 37th Division on the Western Front in the Great War. In response to anti-German feeling during the Great War, in 1917 and following the lead of the British Royal Family, the English branch of the Gleichen family changed their titles from the German to the English style.

---

[14] *Dictionary of National Biography* Oxford University Press 1997.

# SIR JOSEPH BOEHM

Joseph Edgar Boehm was born in Vienna on 4 July 1834. His father Joseph Daniel Boehm was Director of the Imperial Mint, a collector of antique sculpture and the Boehm's were Hungarian in origin. In 1848 Joseph travelled to England and worked mostly at the British Museum for three years where he sketched and fell under the spell of the Elgin Marbles. He then studied sculpture in Italy, Paris and Vienna, where at the age of 22 he won the First Imperial Prize in 1856. His father arranged a job for him, but Joseph had by that point decided he was going to be a sculptor and departed for Paris. He married Louise Francis Boteler of West Derby, Liverpool in 1860 and settled in London in 1862. 'In the year of his arrival he made his début at the Royal Academy with a bust in the then unfamiliar material, terra cotta. In 1863 he exhibited statuettes in the same material of Millais and his wife. Boehm's work soon became popular, and, from about 1865 to the end of his life, commissions came to him in an unbroken stream from fashionable patrons as well as from government. For some years he had almost a monopoly in providing statues of public men and of members of the royal family.'[15] Boehm's large output included: *St George and the Dragon*; the marble statue *Queen Victoria* at Windsor Castle; *The Duke of Kent* in St George's Chapel; *Lord Stratford de Redcliffe*; *Queen Victoria at the Spinning Wheel*; the recumbent figure *Archbishop Tait* in Canterbury Cathedral; *Benjamin Disraeli, Earl of Beaconsfield* in Westminster Abbey and the German *Emperor Frederick* also at Windsor. In 1880 he executed the stone figures of Queen Victoria and the Prince of Wales on the Temple Bar Memorial in Fleet Street. Boehm sculpted *Carlyle* on Chelsea Embankment, *William Tyndale* in Embankment Gardens, London and the *Wellington Memorial* at Hyde Park Corner. Among his busts were: *Gladstone, Huxley, Lord Rosebery, Lord Napier, Lord Russell, Francis Drake, Lord Wolseley, John Ruskin, Lord Shaftesbury, Millais* (in the Diploma Gallery in Burlington House) and *Thomas George Baring, Earl of Northbrook* (now in the library of Mumbai University). A representative selection of his busts is in the collection of the National Portrait Gallery. To critical acclaim, he executed the sarcophagus of *Dean Stanley* in Westminster Abbey, his memorial to *General Charles Gordon* in St Paul's Cathedral met with less approval. In 1877 he produced *Field Marshal Sir John Fox Burgoyne* (cast by H Young of Pimlico) for Waterloo Place. That same year he completed the colossal bronze *King Edward VII* at Byculla, Mumbai. He sculpted the equestrian statue of *Lord Napier*, which was erected in front of St George's Gate, Fort William, Calcutta in 1880 and removed in the 1970s to the Temple of Fame, Barrackpore. (After Boehm's death, a copy was executed by Alfred Gilbert, now at Kensington Gore). Boehm sculpted the well-travelled *Baron Lawrence of the Punjab* lately resident in London, Lahore and Foyle College, Londonderry. In 1887 he executed the head of Queen Victoria for the Royal Mint and the Official Jubilee Medal. In 1865 he became a naturalised Briton; was elected ARA in 1878, RA in 1880 and created baronet on 13 July 1889. He was a member of several foreign academies, lectured at the RA and was appointed Sculptor in Ordinary to Queen Victoria. Boehm was rumoured to have been the lover of Queen Victoria's daughter, the talented artist Princess Louise (1848-1939) and she was believed to have been with him at the time of his sudden death in his studio on 12 December 1890. Boehm's chief assistant Lantéri would go on to play an important role in British sculpture and the early days of the RBS. Two stipple engravings of Boehm by George J Stodart and also a bronze medallion by Lantéri may be seen in the National Portrait Gallery.

The critic Sir Walter Armstrong (1850-1918) wrote Boehm's DNB entry in 1901 and in it offered the following gem of patronising snobbery: 'As a practical sculptor Sir Edgar Boehm takes a high place in the English School, but as an artist he scarcely deserved the patronage he received. In the large bronze population with which he endowed his adopted country, it would be difficult to find a single true work of art, while some of his productions, notably the Wellington group at Hyde Park Corner fall lamentably short of their purpose'.

---

[15] *Dictionary of National Biography* Oxford University Press 1997.

## CAPTAIN ADRIAN JONES

Adrian Jones was born at Ludlow, Shropshire in 1845 the fourth son of James Brookholding Jones, and educated at Ludlow Grammar School. His artistic talents were apparent at an early age. In his youth he excelled at equestrian pursuits and when his father discouraged his artistic leanings, he joined the 3rd Hussars and qualified as a veterinary officer. He fought in the Abyssinian Campaign, the First Boer War and served on the Nile Expedition. After leaving the army, he studied sculpture under C B Birch ARA and inevitably his work in that field would be dominated by his equine knowledge. In 1891 Jones exhibited the group *Triumph* at the RA which caught the eye of the Prince of Wales, who sent for him and discussed with him the need for Decimus Burton's Wellington Arch to be crowned by a suitable sculptural group. The project would be delayed for many years by the inability of the Board of Works to set in hand the necessary funding. In response to criticism by Sir Frederick Leighton PRA[16] of his suitability for the commission, Jones undertook *Duncan's Horses* (1892) which was exhibited at the RA. The theme was taken from a line in Shakespeare's play *Macbeth*. The resounding acclaim for this work was not shared by his fellow sculptors, who resented Jones's preferment. In 1893 he was commissioned by Earl Spencer to undertake the sculpture of his favourite foxhound *Forager*. That same year he exhibited the equine group *Maternal Care* at the RA. In 1894 he exhibited *Rape of the Sabines* at the RA. He also sculpted King Edward VII's racehorse *Persimmon* (Derby winner 1896) at Sandringham. In 1903 he exhibited the equine study of a crusader entitled *For the Faith* at the RA and also executed the *Royal Marines Memorial* which stands in The Mall. In Whitehall, outside the Old War Office stands his equestrian sculpture *Field Marshal HRH the Duke of Cambridge* (1907). The curious choice of location should be noted, as C-in-C of the British Army for 39 years, the Duke had fought the War Office tooth and nail over army reform and political control of the army. Jones was awarded the MVO by his grateful sovereign for this work. He then undertook a number of commissions related to the Boer War. He produced *The Soldiers National Memorial* (1904) at Adelaide to the Australian fallen; *Captain Sturt* (the Australian explorer) in Adelaide; the *Queen's Bays* (portable) *War Memorial;* the delightful orange brick and bronze *Carabiniers Boer War Memorial* (1905) to the fallen of the 6th Dragoons, on Chelsea Bridge Road in London, and the equestrian statue *General Redvers Buller VC* at Exeter. In 1907 Jones began work on modelling *Peace Ascending* and *the Quadriga* for the Wellington Arch. The Prince of Wales, by now King Edward VII took a direct interest in the project and upon asking Jones what the allegorical figure in the chariot was supposed to represent, received the reply 'peace', - an answer the architect of the *Entente Cordiale* took as a personal compliment. The King died some 18 months before the completion of England's largest bronze sculpture and although Jones received no formal recognition for the Quadriga, praise from the likes of Goscombe John and George Frampton must have assuaged his feelings to some degree. Jones lived next door to the Chelsea Arts Club, was a regular attender there, and from the accounts of his contemporaries, was agreeable company. After the Great War he produced the *Bridgnorth War Memorial* to the fallen of the King's Shropshire Light Infantry, the *Uxbridge War Memorial* (1924) and the *Cavalry Memorial* in Hyde Park. A painter of no little ability, Jones also produced equine portraits of *Lord Roberts, General Smuts, Lord Annally, Lord Kitchener* (Ipswich Town Hall), *Lord Allenby* and, with J Watts, *Persimmon*. Jones was elected MRBS 1913, FRBS 1923 and HFRBS 1931. Despite his manifest talent, he was never elected to membership of the RA. He ascribed this to professional jealousy of his friendship with King Edward VII. In 1933 he produced his *Memoirs of a Soldier Artist* with a foreword by Lieutenant-General Lord Baden-Powell. Jones died in 1938.

---

[16] Frederick Leighton (1830-1896). Created Baron Leighton of Stretton the day before his death. Born at Scarborough, a prodigy, he commenced studies in Rome at the age of ten. He studied in Berlin, Dresden, Florence and London. He raised the Artists Rifles in 1859, was elected RA in 1868 and PRA in 1878. First painter to be honoured with a baronetcy. Leighton House in Holland Park Road, London is open to the public.

## SIR THOMAS BROCK

Thomas Brock was born on 1 March 1847 at Worcester, where he studied at the Government School of Design. From 1867 he studied at the Royal Academy Schools and was trained in his art in the studio of the talented Irish sculptor John Henry Foley (1818-1874). He first exhibited at the RA in 1868 and the following year won the RA Gold Medal. On Foley's death, Brock completed a number of his commissions, took over his studio and would go on to become one of Britain's most prolific sculptors of high quality public monuments and statuary. Brock's output included the statue of the administrator and imperial meddler *Sir Henry Bartle Frere* and the founder of the Sunday school movement *Robert Raikes* (1889), both in Victoria Embankment Gardens, London; the *Tomb of Lord Leighton* in St Paul's Cathedral (1900) and the statue of the actor *Sir Henry Irving* on Charing Cross Road, London. His *Captain Cook* (1914) stands in The Mall and his *Gainsborough* may be seen on the staircase of the Royal Academy at Burlington House. His bronze portrait statue of the zoologist *Sir Richard Owen* (1896) may be found clutching a symbolic bone at the Natural History Museum in London and his statue *Sir J E Millais* (1904) stands in the grounds of the Tate Gallery. Outside London his equestrian statue of the *Black Prince* (1902) was produced for Leeds City Square; *Sir Rowland Hill* is at Kidderminster; *Bishop Philpott* is in Worcester Cathedral; *William Ewart Gladstone* at St George's Hall, Liverpool and *Bishop Hervey* is in Wells Cathedral. His busts *Joseph Lister; Michael Faraday* and *Frederick Leighton* can all be found in the Primary Collection of the National Portrait Gallery. His bust of *Longfellow* is in Westminster Abbey and his 1887 bust *Sir Isaac Pitman* was subsequently produced in Parian. Brock's *Lister Memorial* stands complete with sculpted lamp posts and bollards (all cast by the Morris Art Bronze Foundry in 1922) at Portland Place in London. Brock produced the bronze statue *Brigadier General John Nicholson* originally erected at the Kashmir Gate in Delhi. After Foley's death, Brock completed the bronze equestrian statue of *Earl Canning* (1874). It now stands in the Police Hospital Grounds at Barrackpore, India. He sculpted the marble statue *Sir Richard Temple* (1884) which now stands in the grounds of the Dr Bhau Daji Lad Museum in Mumbai. The death of Queen Victoria in 1901 led to a mass outbreak of patriotism across the Empire and Brock must have thought it was Christmas. In front of the main entrance of Belfast City Hall in Northern Ireland stands his marble statue *Queen Victoria* with bronze side figures symbolising *Shipbuilding* and *Spinning*. It was paid for by public subscription and unveiled by King Edward VII on 27 July 1903. That year, he executed a copy of his statue of *Queen Victoria* at Hove for Queen's Park, Cawnpore (now at residing in the basement of the State Museum, Lucknow). A further copy may be found situated in a compound behind the same museum. He produced another version of *Queen Victoria* with a sculpted group for the Queen Victoria Memorial Committee of Agra in India in 1905 originally situated in MacDowall Park, Agra, (it may now be found in the Police Lines at Muttra). Other copies of this work may be found at Brisbane, Cawnpore and Carlisle. In 1905 he completed his sculpture of *Queen Victoria* for Bangalore which now stands in Cubbon Park, Mumbai. Copies were erected at Worcester, Capetown and Belfast. His colossal *Victoria Memorial* stands in front of Buckingham Palace (1906-24) and earned him a knighthood in 1911. After the death of King Edward VII in 1910, Brock was chosen by a joint Indian/British Memorial Committee to sculpt his memorial in bronze. It was cast by A B Burton's foundry at Thames Ditton and inaugurated in Cubbon Park by King George V on 8 December 1911. Brock was elected ARA in 1883 and RA in 1891, his Diploma Work was the bust *Frederick Leighton PRA* which is in the collection of the National Portrait Gallery. He designed the portrait head of Queen Victoria for the Royal Mint in 1893. In 1904 Brock was one of the nine founder members of the Society of British Sculptors and was elected their first President in 1905.[17] He served again in the same role during the war years 1914-19. He was appointed KCB in 1911 and died on 22 August 1922 in London.

---

[17] From 1911 by Royal Warrant the Royal Society of British Sculptors.

## PROFESSOR ÉDOUARD LANTÉRI

Édouard Lantéri was born on 1 November 1848 at Auxerre, Burgundy, France. His parents sent him to Paris to study music, but he quickly discovered his vocation lay in the field of figurative sculpture and was trained in his art in the studio of the sculptor Aimé Millet, at the Petite École de Dessin and the École des Beaux-Arts. After spending 18 months mending furniture damaged in the German bombardment of Paris in 1871, he left France to escape civil unrest and settled in Beaufort Street, London. Due to the influence of Aimeé-Jules Dalou, he obtained a position in the studio of Sir Joseph Boehm and would eventually become his chief assistant. After Boehm's death in 1890, Lantéri obtained the position of Sculptor Master at the Royal School of Art, South Kensington (Royal College of Art 1896). The appointment caused a furore in the art world and was relentlessly mocked in print by the critic Edmund Gosse as 'The Dalou-Boehm Job'. Nevertheless, Lantéri would speedily establish a reputation as an outstandingly popular teacher and although passionate, he evinced none of the histrionics of Dalou, who had a tendency to destroy the work of students with whom he disagreed. The only works Lantéri ever destroyed were his own, due to his driven perfectionism. In high dudgeon, Gosse deleted all reference to Lantéri from his influential 1894 *Art Journal* essay *The New Sculpture*. Regardless, Lantéri's 1899 class attracted an unheard of 105 students and he would influence an entire generation of British sculptors. The New Zealander Francis Shurrock would write: 'Lantéri was more than a teacher, he was an inspiration'. Among Lantéri's star pupils would be: Albert Toft, Gilbert Ledward, Charles Sargeant Jagger and Charles Wheeler.

    A prolific sculptor in his own right, Lantéri exhibited 70 works at the RA in the period 1887-1917, exhibited at the New Gallery in London, the Royal Scottish Academy, the Glasgow Institute of the Fine Arts, the Royal Society of Artists in Birmingham and the Walker Art Gallery in Liverpool. His *Beatrice* may be found at the Victoria and Albert Museum, *Paysan* at Tate Britain and *Landau* at the Laing Art Gallery in Newcastle. An insight into Lantéri's rapport with his students may be gained from Basil Gotto's memoirs in which he noted the events of an evening in 1903 on which members of the Arts Club in Dover Street held a dinner at the Café Royal in honour of Rodin, then staying in London with John Tweed: 'After many drinks had circulated and many toasts had been honoured, we found that the Café was besieged by excited students from South Kensington Arts School. The sculptor master there Monsieur Lantéri, a friend of Rodin's, had evidently enthused them. They seized a four-wheel cab, took the horse from the shafts, put Rodin, George Wyndham and Sargent inside, and with John Tweed on the roof, pulled the lot round to Dover Street, where we all thronged into the Club, which to my amazement, produced a supper as if by magic.' In 1887 young Francis Derwent Wood arrived at South Kensington and he would in time become both Lantéri's assistant and his successor. Lantéri was an early member of the Society of British Sculptors and a force for good in their affairs until his death. In 1905-07 he was one of the 21 sculptors engaged by Sir Aston Webb to execute the sculpture on the southern façade of the Victoria and Albert Museum in London. There he supervised the work of his students, sculpted *Fame* in marble at the top of the tower near the entrance and executed the Portland stone allegorical figures of *Sculpture* and *Architecture* in the niches at the base of the tower. His bronze statuette *Ludwig Mond*, the bronze medallion *Sir Joseph Edgar Boehm* (1891), the marble bust *Sir Walter Sendall* (1902), the bronze plaque *Ludwig Mond* (1909) and the bronze statuette *Sir Robert Ludwig Mond* (1912) may all be found in the Collection of the National Portrait Gallery. Lantéri's influence on British sculpture endures. His books: *Modelling - A Guide for Teachers and Students*, *Modelling and Sculpting the Human Figure* and *Modelling and Sculpting Animals* are still in print. Lantéri' coined the maxim: 'The artist is nothing more nor less than an observer, and he is the greater or lesser artist according to the perfection or imperfection of this power of observation.' Lantéri died at home in East Acton on 22 December 1917. A portrait photograph of him taken in 1902 by Charles George Beresford may be found in the collection of the National Portrait Gallery.

## SIR ASTON WEBB

Aston Webb was born on 22 May 1849 at Clapham, London. He was educated in Brighton then articled in 1866 for five years to the architects Banks & Barry of London, whilst attending classes at the Architectural Association. He toured Europe and Asia Minor. Upon his return to England in 1873 he established his own practice. His earliest works were the Church of St John, Kingston Blount, Oxfordshire (1875), the Almshouses (in the Arts and Crafts style) at Worcester (1878) and the Granary at Deptford (1880). He was soon joined by Edward Ingress Bell (1836-1914) who became his business partner. Their first large-scale venture was their successful competition design of 1885 for the Victoria Law Courts in Birmingham, a structure clad in terracotta with rich detailing completed in 1891. In 1890 Webb commenced the restoration of St Bartholomew the Great at Smithfield in London and built Yeaton-Peverey House (1890-92) near Shrewsbury in Shropshire described by Pevsner as: 'an astonishing Jacobean fantasy'. There followed a series of smaller commissions in London at 23 Austin Friars, the Metropolitan Life Assurance building at 13-15 Moorgate (1890-93) in the Franco-Flemish style and the French Protestant Church, Soho Square (1891-93). In 1890 he designed the reredos of St John's Church, Notting Hill. He designed the Royal United Services Institute for Defence Studies in Whitehall (1893-5) with its cherubic figures sculpted by William Silver Frith. At the same time, he carried out refurbishment of Inigo Jones' Banqueting Hall. By the turn of the century Webb's practice was the largest in the country and in 1900 he designed the Royal Naval College, Dartmouth. His works outside London included Christ's Hospital School, Sussex (1893-1902), the brightly coloured Victoria Law Courts in Birmingham and the University of Birmingham buildings at Bournbrook, Edgbaston (1900-09), although the visual impact of his achievement there is diminished by the brutalist ugliness of the office blocks added to the site in the 1960s. He also designed the complex of Government Buildings at Merrion Street, Dublin. Webb designed three major buildings in South Kensington, London; in 1891 he competed for and won the commission to design the extension to the Victoria and Albert Museum with its façade on the Cromwell Road. His other buildings were the Chemistry and Physics Building (1898-1906) (destroyed by enemy action) for the Royal College of Science and Technology, and the Royal School of Mines (1908-13) in Prince Consort Road. Webb's Admiralty Arch (1910) incorporated an archway joining The Mall and Trafalgar Square. It was commissioned by King Edward VII in memory of his mother Queen Victoria, although he did not live to see its completion. In 1923 Webb dissuaded the Admiralty from adding a naval memorial to it. In the period 1912-30 Webb laid out the gardens at Dunecht House in Aberdeenshire. In 1913 he redesigned the eastern facade of Buckingham Palace as a setting for Sir Thomas Brock's Queen Victoria Memorial. As the sun set on the British Empire, Webb's every endeavour met with unstinting success and his practice was renowned for running a 'tight ship'. He was the very model of Victorian moral rectitude and recognition duly arrived by way of honours. He joined the RIBA in 1883 and served as PRIBA 1902-04. In 1904 he was knighted and in the period 1919-24 was President of the Royal Academy, the first architect elected to the post since 1805. He introduced a number of permanent changes in the running of the RA and was instrumental in establishing the Royal Fine Art Commission. In 1921 he designed both the Stock Exchange War Memorial in London and the Hertford War Memorial in Herts. He retired from the active exercise of his profession in 1924 and died at home at 1 Hanover Terrace, London on 21 August 1930. The Memorial Tablet to his memory by William McMillan may be found in the crypt of St Paul's Cathedral. The Great Hall of the University of Birmingham is known as the Aston Webb Building and he designed the University of Birmingham War Memorial there. The Aston Webb Room on the second floor of the RA also perpetuates his memory. Unusually, the walls of the room are lined with leather, a material rarely used outside lunatic asylums for interior decoration in the UK. His portrait in oils painted by Solomon Joseph Solomon is in the collection of the National Portrait Gallery.

## SIR (WILLIAM) HAMO THORNYCROFT

William Hamo Thornycroft was born on 9 March 1850 in London and spent much of his youth in Cheshire. His father was the sculptor Thomas Thornycroft (who sculpted *Boadicea* on Westminster Bridge). His mother, the sculptor Mary Francis, was the daughter of the sculptor John Francis and she taught sculpture to Princess Louise, daughter of Queen Victoria. Hamo was educated at Macclesfield Grammar School and at University College, Gower Street, London. He entered the RA Schools in 1869. In 1871 he exhibited the bust *Professor William Sharpey* (now at University College, London). That year he visited Italy and was profoundly influenced by the work of Michelangelo. He exhibited at the RA from 1872 onwards. Upon his return to London he worked with his father on the *Poets Fountain* in Park Lane, London and executed the figures of *Shakespeare, Comedy* and *Fame*. The fountain was unveiled to critical acclaim in 1875. The same year he was awarded the RA Gold Medal for his group *A Warrior bearing a Wounded Youth from the Field of Battle*. In the period 1872-75 he worked with his brother Thomas on the equestrian statue *Richard Southwell Burke, 6th Earl of Mayo* (now at Barrackpore). In 1878 he exhibited *Lot's Wife* and in 1880 *Artemis*, executed in marble, commissioned by the Duke of Westminster for Eaton Hall. In 1881 he exhibited his bronze *Teucer* which was purchased by the Chantrey Trustees for £1,000 and is in the Tate. 'In his work up to this time, Thornycroft had, as regards subject, kept more or less within the convention of the antique, although in vitality of form and treatment he had advanced well beyond the formula of neo-classicism. Thenceforward he brought within the range of his art the subjects affected by the contemporary realism of painting, exhibiting in 1884 'The Mower' (now in the Walker Art Gallery, Liverpool) and in 1886 'A Sower', both probably the result of impulses received from the paintings of Jean François Millet'.[18] Miniatures of *A Sower* may be seen at the Harris Art Gallery in Preston and in the Ashmolean. Thornycroft sculpted *General Gordon* (1888) originally sited in Trafalgar Square. Sir Reginald Blomfield reckoned it the best work of its kind in London. He sculpted *John Bright* in Rochdale (1891) and *Oliver Cromwell* (1899) in Old Palace Yard Westminster won him the *Médaille d'Honneur* at the Paris World Exhibition of 1900. He produced *King Alfred* (1901) in Winchester; *Dean Colet and two kneeling scholars* (1902) at St Paul's School, Hammersmith[19] and his *William Gladstone Monument* (1905) stands outside St Clement Danes. He produced the *Durban* and *Manchester Boer War Memorials* and the bronze *Memorial to the Viceroyalty of Lord Curzon* (1912) at the rear of the Victoria Memorial, Calcutta; the *King Edward VII Memorial* (1915) in Karachi; the marble group *The Kiss* (1916) - later purchased by the Chantrey Trustees and now in the Tate; the *Bishop Harvey Goodwin* monument in Carlisle Cathedral; the *Lord Armstrong Memorial* at Newcastle-upon-Tyne and the bronze effigy of *Mandell Creighton, Bishop of London*, in St Paul's Cathedral. He produced the circular bas-relief in stone of *Richard Norman Shaw* (1914) on the Norman Shaw Building, Victoria Embankment. His bronze bust *Earl Roberts* resides in the library of the RUSI in Whitehall. In 1925 he produced the recumbent effigy *Bishop Yeatman-Biggs* for Coventry Cathedral. The sculpture survived the gutting of the cathedral by the Luftwaffe and was exhumed from its crust of molten lead in 1950 by Morris Singer. Thornycroft was elected ARA in 1881, taught sculpture in the RA schools from 1882-1914, was elected RA in 1888, MRBS 1905, knighted in 1917 and elected FRBS in 1923. That year he was awarded the RBS Gold Medal for distinguished service to sculpture and also produced the *Luton War Memorial*. He died at Oxford on 18 December 1925. A retrospective of his work was held at the Burlington House Winter Exhibition in 1927. Thornycroft appears in Reginald Cleaver's pen and ink sketch *Hanging Committee, Royal Academy, 1892*, a pen and ink sketch by Theodore Blake Wirgman and a *Vanity Fair* watercolour of him by Sir Leslie Ward. All are in the collection of the National Portrait Gallery.

---

[18] *Dictionary of National Biography* 1922-1930.
[19] John Colet (c. 1467-1519). Noted theologian, Dean of St Paul's Cathedral and founder of St Paul's School.

# GEORGE WADE

George Edward Wade was born on 2 March 1853, the youngest of six sons and one of 14 children of the Reverend Nugent Wade, Rector of St Anne's Church, Soho. He was educated at Charterhouse and later in Switzerland. As a child he was interested in cricket, fishing, shooting and languages. Whilst reading for the Bar, his health broke down and he was sent to Italy to recuperate. Without the benefit of formal training, there he took up painting generously encouraged by the Crimean War veteran and art patron Sir Coutts Lindsay (1824-1913). In 1869 Wade married Isabella Mary Josephine, daughter of Lieutenant-General J M Macintyre RA and they had two daughters. By his mid-thirties Wade found himself increasingly dissatisfied with his chosen medium, turned his hand to sculpture and quickly discovered that this was the means by which he could express himself best. He first exhibited at the RA in 1889 where he showed the bronze bust *Lieutenant Colonel Myles Sandys MP*. In 1890 he produced the terracotta bust of his father *Canon Nugent Wade*. He subsequently produced a Grenadier Guardsman in terracotta, of which a copy in bronze was purchased by Queen Victoria. He then produced a further 100 copies for the Grenadier Guards. In 1891 he took over the studio of the late Sir Joseph Edgar Boehm and his 1891 bust of the Polish pianist *I J Paderewski* led to orders for a further 500 copies from the American market alone. He went on to produce a large number of portrait busts of which *W E Gladstone*, *Lord Suffield*, and *General William Booth* are noteworthy. His statuettes included: *Il Penseroso; Aphrodite; The Dancer* and *St George and the Dragon*. In a long and varied career Wade's monumental works would include the graceful *Norwich Boer War Memorial* (1904), copies of his bronze statue of *King Edward VII* may be found in Madras, Reading, Bootle and Hong Kong. His marble statue of *Queen Victoria* (1902) now stands in the gardens of the Presidential Residence in Colombo, Sri Lanka. Dr Mary Ann Steggles would write: The Queen Victoria Memorial Committee for Allahabad held a competition to commission a statue of Queen Victoria for Alfred Park. George Edward Wade was awarded £125 for his selected model and was paid Rs17,000 as a fee for his heroic marble seated figure of the Queen. The committee in Allahabad was so successful in raising funds that after paying the model fees and the fee for the final sculpture, they were able to set up an endowment of Rs20,000 for care of the memorial. The completed statue was unveiled by Sir J De La Touche on 24 March 1906.' Wade produced a colossal bronze statue of the *Duke of Connaught* for Hong Kong; *Sir William Rose Mansfield, first Baron Sandhurst* for Bombay and a *Cameron Highlander* for Inverness. He executed the impressive 50 foot tall monument to *Sir John A Macdonald* (1895) which stands beneath its ornate portico at Montreal in Canada. Copies were produced for both Hamilton and Kingston in Canada. For India he produced the portrait statue *King George V* (1911). He produced the monolithic *Pietermaritzburg War Memorial* in South Africa, sculpted the equestrian statues of *Sir Chandra Shamshere Yung* for Nepal and *Field Marshal Earl Haig* for the esplanade of Edinburgh Castle. In 1929 he sculpted *General and Mrs Booth* which stands in Champion Park, Denmark Hill, London. He designed a children's fountain for the Women's World Temperance Movement Association, a copy of which may be seen in Temple Gardens, Embankment, London. 'The popularity of Wade's sculpture was probably due not only to the fact that that it was always comprehensible but that it was both ennobling and restrained in equal measure. In portraiture he obtained at the same time a good likeness, much appreciated by the sitters and their families, and, in these works and in his more fanciful subjects, he engendered feelings of respect and admiration. It might be argued by some that his approach was too prosaic, but it would perhaps be more true to say that he cloaked classical ideals in the trappings of his own environment.'[20] His last work was the *Stourbridge War Memorial* which was inaugurated in 1931. In private life Wade was a keen golfer, designed houses for his friends and pursued his fascination with airplane design. He died at home at Hyde Park Street in London on 5 February 1933.

---

[20] *Dictionary of National Biography* Oxford University Press 1995.

# ALFRED DRURY

Edward Alfred Briscoe Drury was born in London on 11 November 1856. His parents were Richard Drury, a tailor, and his wife Emma Rachel Tombs. Alfred was educated at New College Choir School, Oxford and studied at the Oxford School of Art, then at South Kensington, firstly under F W Moody and then under the gifted French sculptor Aimeé-Jules Dalou (1838-1902). It was evident from the outset of his studies that Drury was highly gifted and his progress through the South Kensington School of Art was considered remarkable. He won a National Scholarship in 1879 which gave him free tuition and maintenance for two years. In the period 1879-81 he won three successive Gold Medals and worked with Dalou on *The Triumph of the Third Republic* at the Place de la Nation in Paris. In 1881-85 he worked as Dalou's studio assistant and then for Sir Joseph Edgar Boehm. Unsurprisingly, his early work demonstrates Dalou's influence and to some extent that of Alfred Gilbert, who also worked for Boehm. A prolific standard bearer of the 'New Sculpture' Drury was highly successful, being commissioned to produce a whole range of public sculpture, including decorative reliefs. Gosse however, criticised Drury as: 'a mannered Kensington student' in his essay *The New Sculpture* in 1894. Drury's work in London includes the eight Portland stone sculpture groups on the Old War Office in Whitehall and the four colossal meditative female figures for Vauxhall Bridge (1905). Commissioned by the Leighton Fund, his bronze *Sir Joshua Reynolds* (commenced 1917) stands in the quadrangle of the RA at Burlington House and his *Lilith* may be seen in the Diploma Gallery. He carved the charming gatepost figures representing *West Africa, Canada* and *South Africa* on Brock's *Queen Victoria Memorial* in The Mall. In the period 1897-98 he carved the twelve busts representing the months of the year, each being mounted on a pier at Barrow Court near Bristol. In 1899 he sculpted the bronze statue *Joseph Priestly* which stands in City Square, Leeds. He sculpted the *Warrington Boer War Memorial* and in 1905 the bronze St George *Clifton College Boer War Memorial*. His bronze *Queen Victoria Memorial* for Bradford was unveiled before a crowd of some 70,000 on 4 May 1904 by the Prince of Wales (later King George V) and copies were produced for both Hove and Wellington, New Zealand. He produced another *Queen Victoria* for Portsmouth and his *Edward VII Memorial* may be seen in Birmingham, Sheffield and Aberdeen. His *Spring* is in City Garden, Auckland, New Zealand. His other prominent works include his life-size bronze statue of *Circe* which earned him the Gold Medal at the Paris Universal Exhibition in 1900 and may be seen in Park Square, Leeds. Versions of his *Age of Innocence* are at Cartwright Hall in Bradford, Newcastle, Manchester, Preston and Blackburn. His *Griselda* (1896) may be seen in The Tate and his *First Lesson* may be seen in the Birmingham Museum and Art Gallery. Drury sculpted the eight *Morning* and *Evening Girls* in Leeds City Square (also known as the Drury Dames), both sets of four statues representing the beginning (right arm raised and holding flowers) and end (left arm raised) of the working day. The statues' original pendant lamps with ball-shaped shades were replaced by torches in the 1960s. Critics have noted the similarity of the girls to the *Stars of Morning* and *Night* outside the Paris Opera House on which Drury worked with Dalou. Drury was one of the 21 sculptors engaged by Sir Aston Webb to sculpt the south façade of the Victoria and Albert Museum His full-length standing figure of *Prince Albert* may be seen inside the tympanum above the main doors. He also sculpted *Knowledge* and *Inspiration* there. Again working with Sir Aston, he sculpted the *Gazing Hart* atop the *Hertford War Memorial* (1921). Drury's *London Troops War Memorial* (1923) outside the London Exchange was strongly criticised for its conservatism. Standing on a pedestal of red Murray Bridge granite, his three ton bronze statue of the Australian statesman *The Right Hon C C Kingston* may be seen in Victoria Square, Adelaide, Australia. The statue was cast by J W Singer & Sons of Frome.

Drury was elected ARA in 1900, MRBS 1905, RA in 1913, FRBS 1923 and HRBS 1942-44. He died at home in Wimbledon on 24 December 1944. He married Phebe Maud Turner in 1900 and one of their two sons was the talented artist Paul Dalou Drury (1903-87).

## SIR REGINALD BLOMFIELD

Reginald Theodore Blomfield was born on 20 December 1856 at Nymet Tracey in Devonshire, where his father was rector of the parish. Reginald was educated at Haileybury and at Exeter College, Oxford. In 1881 he started training as an architect in the office of his uncle, Sir Arthur Blomfield. A year later he was admitted as a student of architecture at the Royal Academy. In 1883 he set up on his own as an architect and became one of the early members of the Art Workers Guild. He struck up friendships with Norman Shaw, Edwin Lutyens, D S MacColl, William Morris and became deeply involved with the Arts and Crafts Movement. In 1892 he published *The Formal Garden in England* and in 1900 *A Short History of Renaissance Architecture in England*. In response to the Boer War, he joined the Inns of Court Mounted Infantry. In 1907 he was appointed Professor of Architecture to the Royal Academy and became a pivotal figure in the transition from apprentices being trained in architects' offices to learning their trade within a degree course at Universities. In his inaugural lectures he praised English Classicism and damned the Gothic Revival. As Professor Sir Charles Reilly subsequently noted, the architectural teaching in the early days at Liverpool University 'was largely based on Sir Reginald's. His books became text-books for professors and students alike.' In 1907-08 Blomfield added a block to Goldsmiths College, Lewisham Way, London. From 1910 onwards he carried out extensive restoration work at Chequers for Sir Arthur Lee (later Lord Lee of Fareham). He published his *History of French Architecture* in 1911. In 1912 he was elected President of the RIBA, was awarded their Royal Gold Medal in 1913 and elected RA in 1914. Upon the outbreak of the Great War, he 'did his bit' with the Inns of Court (which traces its origins back to 1588), by digging trenches all over London in the company of some of the most distinguished legal minds of the British Empire. He attained the rank of sergeant and became a stalwart of the Devil's Own Sergeant's Club. In 1918 he was appointed one of the Principal Architects of the Imperial War Graves Commission and for the next nine years was heavily involved with the design of their cemeteries behind the Western Front. He designed the badge of the Commission and the Cross of Sacrifice[21] which stands in its cemeteries, both the Belgian War Memorial and the RAF Memorial on the Embankment, the memorials at Leeds, Luton and Torquay and the Memorial Chapel at Oundle School. In 1919 he was sent by the War Office to Ypres to design a memorial intended initially to take 40,000 names of those who had no known grave. He chose the site of the Menin Gate and designed the memorial that would be the best known work of his career. The major difficulties involved with its erection were overcome with the help of the engineer Sir Maurice Fitzmaurice (1861-1924) and the King of the Belgians honoured Blomfield for his design. The completion of this commission ended his time with the Commission. In December 1927 Major General Sir Fabian Ware wrote to him: 'I think you will understand it, when I say that everybody working had wished, looking back on the past years, to send you a special message of gratitude for the great work that you have done for the Commission.... We are all deeply grateful to you, and very proud to have been associated with you'. An energetic figure, Blomfield relished a good 'punch up' and engaged in the architectural controversies of his day with gusto. His plans for remodelling John Nash's Carlton Gardens led to a debate in the House of Commons and his resignation from the Royal Fine Art Commission. He designed the façade of the Carlton Club in London and Lady Margaret Hall, Oxford. He was also responsible for remodelling Regent Street and Piccadilly Circus, although it is unlikely Nash would have approved the result. Blomfield designed Lambeth Bridge and St George's Memorial Church in Ypres. In retirement he wrote *Memoirs of an Architect* (1932), *Modernismus* (1934), *Sebastien Le Prestre de Vauban* (1938) and *Richard Norman Shaw* (1940). He died in 1942. A bronze portrait bust of him by Sir William Reid Dick is in the National Portrait Gallery and his portrait by Sir J J Shannon hangs in the South Room of the RIBA at 66 Portland Place, London.

---

[21] Also known as the Great War Cross.

## SIR JOHN BURNET

John James Burnet was born in Glasgow in 1857. He was the son of the distinguished Scots architect John Burnet (1814-1901). John James studied architecture and engineering at the École des Beaux-Arts in Paris and travelled widely in France and Italy, before returning to Glasgow. In 1882 father and son established the architecture practice of John Burnet & Son. In 1886 it became Burnet, Son & Campbell and subsequently the Sir John Burnet, Tait and Lorne Partnership. In an age in which beautification of the building being designed was still part of an architect's repertoire, Burnet was noted for the elegance of his designs and he was responsible for the design of a substantial number of well-known Edwardian Glasgow buildings including: the Athenaeum; the Royal Institute of Fine Arts (later Pettigrew & Stephens); the Clyde Navigation Trust Buildings; the Glasgow Savings Bank; the extensions to Merchants' House; Barony Church; the Cenotaph; Charing Cross Mansions; Atlantic Chambers; the Alhambra Theatre and the Elder Park Library at Govan. The University of Glasgow has some outstanding examples of his work, including its University Chapel, the James Watt Engineering Building, the George Service House and the Thomson Building. In 1882 he designed the Drumsheugh Baths in Edinburgh in the Saracenic style. He rebuilt a fireproof version after it burned down in 1892. In Edinburgh he designed Burtons Department Store, Scotland's first steel framed building; this fine corner building is still in use, but now subdivided into a number of businesses. In the period 1907-14 Burnet carried out a substantial amount of building work at Sir Robert Smirke's British Museum at Bloomsbury in London. He designed the King Edward VII Galleries, fronting Montague Place, which were intended as the first phase of an expansion of the Museum which would replace all the surrounding properties, the freeholds of which had been purchased from the Bedford Estates in 1894-5. The foundation stone was laid by King Edward VII in 1907 and the building was opened by King George V and Queen Mary in 1914. Subsequently, protection orders were placed by the local authority on the surrounding buildings. This development meant that the scheme Burnet originally envisaged for the Museum could never be realised.

In 1918 Burnet was appointed architect for the Imperial War Graves Commission. Arriving on the Gallipoli Peninsula in the Spring of 1919, in concert with the Australian ANZAC veteran Colonel Cyril Hughes, he set to work designing the cemeteries. 'The people of the district were impoverished, and Burnet feared that they might be tempted to carry off any bronze or stone work for domestic purposes. This led him to recommend that the cemetery walls be built at least eight feet high and that 'headstone blocks', very similar to those used in Macedonia, with sloping faces rather like reading-desks be used instead of headstones.'[22] Burnet designed the Helles Memorial which was completed in 1924. The memorial serves the dual function of Commonwealth battle memorial for the Gallipoli campaign and also as a place of commemoration for many of those Commonwealth servicemen who died on the Peninsula and have no known grave. The British and Indian forces named on the memorial died in operations throughout the peninsula and the Australians at Helles. There are also panels for those who died or were buried at sea in Gallipoli waters. The memorial bears more than 21,000 names of the fallen. In 1920 Burnet publicly threw his not inconsiderable reputation behind the Commission's ultimately successful struggle to preserve its Fundamental Principles in the House of Commons. Sir John succeeded Sir Rowand Anderson (1834-1921) as second President of the Institute of Scottish Architects. In that role he inaugurated a collection of busts of celebrated Scottish architects, and the series of portraits of Presidents. In 1923 he designed the Zoology Building at the Hunterian Museum, Glasgow. In 1931 the Sir John Burnet, Tait and Lorne partnership completed the Royal Masonic Hospital (now the Stamford Hospital) at Ravenscourt Park in London. Sir John died in 1938 and the Sir John Burnet Memorial Award Prize is awarded annually in his memory by the Royal Incorporation of Architects in Scotland.

---

[22] Philip Longworth *The Unending Vigil*

# SIR WILLIAM GOSCOMBE JOHN

William John was born in Cardiff on 21 February 1860. His father was a stone mason and woodcarver employed by Lord Bute on the restoration of Cardiff Castle. William was trained in his art at Cardiff and later in London with Thomas Nicholls and C B Birch ARA at the City and Guilds School in Kennington. He assumed the name Goscombe from the name of a Gloucestershire village near his mother's old home. He entered the Academy Schools in 1884 and first exhibited there two years later. He would produce a large body of work, much of it highly original in conception. In 1889 he was awarded the Royal Academy Gold Medal and Travelling Studentship. He took a studio in Paris and made the acquaintance of Rodin. He returned to London in 1891. His works included: *Morpheus* (1892) - Mention Honourable at the Paris Salon of 1892, *Girl binding her hair* (1893); *St John the Baptist* (1894); winner of the Gold Medal at the Paris International Exhibition 1900; *Boy at Play*[23] (1895); *The Elf* (1898) (his Diploma Work); *Joyance* (1899). *Dean Vaughan* at Llandaff Cathedral; *The Seventh Duke of Devonshire* at Eastbourne (Gold Medal at the Paris Salon 1901); the equestrian statue of *King Edward VII* at Liverpool, *Lord Tredegar* at Cardiff (1909); *Lord Minto* Calcutta (1913); *King Edward VII* Cape Town; *King George V* and *Queen Mary* at Liverpool; *Queen Alexandra* at Sandringham Church; *Prince Christian Victor* at Windsor; the *Duke of Beaufort* at Badminton; *Thomas Sutton* at Charterhouse; *David Lloyd George* at Caernarfon and *Sir Stanley Maude* (1921) at Baghdad. He also produced memorials to the *Marquess of Salisbury* in Westminster Abbey and Hatfield Church; the *Earl of Cromer* in Westminster Abbey and Cairo Cathedral and *Sir Arthur Sullivan* in both St Paul's Cathedral and in Victoria Embankment Gardens (1903). He designed the *Memorial Altar* in Hereford Cathedral and produced portrait busts of *Carnegie*; *Edmund Gosse* and *Earl Kitchener*. He designed the regalia used at the investiture of the Prince of Wales at Caernarfon in 1911. 'John's art may be described as a compound of realism and romanticism; it is illustrative, but inspired by fancy rather than imagination. His style underwent little change throughout his long life, apart from a broadening in the treatment of portrait busts. Most of these were in bronze, but in bronze and marble alike he was a convincing portrayer of character and showed notable ability to render the soft surfaces of skin and hair.'[24] 'He was particularly active as a war memorial sculptor after both the Boer and First World Wars, specialising in dramatic compositions. Several of these memorials are naturally enough in his homeland of Wales, but his masterpieces were in Newcastle and Port Sunlight,[25] where he provided two of the finest sculptural ensembles on any British monuments.'[26] He produced the *Royal Army Medical Corps Boer War Memorial* (1905) at Aldershot, the gilt bronze relief *Coldstream Guards Boer War Memorial* (1904) in St Paul's Cathedral, London and the *Journalists Boer War Memorial* also in St Paul's. During and after the Great War he produced the *King's Liverpool Regiment Memorial* at Liverpool, the *Royal Welch Fusiliers Memorial* at Wrexham and *The Engine Room Heroes* (1916) at Liverpool Pier Head. A proud Welshman, Goscombe John also sculpted the war memorials at Lampeter, Llandaff, Carmarthen and Penarth. In 1916 he produced *Saint David Blessing the People* in marble for Cardiff City Hall and in 1918 the bronze statue of *Field Marshal Wolseley* on Horse Guards Parade Ground. A considerable body of his work is in the collection of the National Museum of Wales, Cardiff.

Goscombe John designed the *Jubilee Medal of King George V* (1935) and the *Great Seal of King Edward VIII* (1936). He was elected ARA in 1899, MRBS in 1905, RA in 1909 and knighted at Bangor in 1911. He was elected FRBS in 1928 and HRBS in 1952. He was awarded the Honorary Freedom of Cardiff in 1936 and the Gold Medal of the RBS in 1942. He died in London on 15 December 1952.

---

[23] Purchased by the Chantrey Trustees in 1896.
[24] *Dictionary of National Biography*, Oxford University Press.
[25] This memorial commemorates the 600 employees of Lever Brothers killed in the Great War (1921).
[26] Alan Borg *War Memorials*, p. 78.

## SIR GEORGE FRAMPTON

George James Frampton was born in London in 1860. He studied at the Lambeth School of Art under W S Frith and at the RA Schools 1881-87 where he won the RA Gold Medal and Travelling Scholarship. In 1888 he studied under Marius-Jean-Antonin Mercie and Pascal-Adolphe-Jean Dagnan-Bouveret in Paris. He became Joint Head of London County Council Central School of Arts and Crafts with the architect William Richard Lethaby in 1894. 'He was a leader of the Arts and Crafts movement, as well as a member of the new Sculpture, and like a number of his contemporaries he developed considerable skill as a metalworker'.[27] He produced a substantial body of architectural, memorial and public works in a variety of media. He produced the bronze *Mysteriarch* (1892) which may be seen in the Walker Art Gallery in Liverpool. In 1894 he devised the sculpture schemes for the Glasgow Savings Bank, Ingram Street. He produced *Head of a Girl* (1895), the bronze relief *The Lady of the Lake* (1895), the bronze relief *Alis La Beale Pilgrim* (1896) exhibited at the RA, the bronze relief of *Sir Walter Besant* in the crypt of St Paul's Cathedral, the statue *William Rathbone* (1899) at Liverpool, the remarkable bronze and ivory portrait bust *Lamia* (1900), the silvered bronze against copper panel with enamel disc *Mother and Child* (1900) and the bronze *St Mungo as Patron of Art and Music* (1897-1901) in the Kelvingrove Art Gallery and Museum, at the same time assessing the competition for the pavilion figures for the museum. He produced the bronze *Jubilee Monument for Queen Victoria* (1897-1901) at Calcutta and the *Sailingship* and *Steamship* bronzes (1901) for Lloyd's Registry. That same year he produced the statue of *Queen Victoria* for Newcastle. In 1902 he produced the figures on St Mary's Church Oxford and in 1912 bronze *Peter Pan* in Kensington Gardens, copies of which may be found in Brussels, Halifax, Canada, Camden, America; Perth, Australia and Liverpool. He produced the bronze relief of *W S Gilbert* (1915) in Victoria Embankment Gardens. In 1911 he sculpted the portrait statue *Sir Andrew Henderson Leith Fraser* originally in Dalhousie Square, now in the Victoria Memorial, Calcutta. In 1914 he assessed the competition for the bronze groups on the Kelvin Way Bridge, Glasgow and worked with Charles Rennie Mackintosh on the *Sir James Fleming Memorial Plaque*. After the Boer War, he produced the *Bury Boer War Memorial*. He sculpted the white marble memorial to *Sir George Williams* in the crypt of St Paul's Cathedral. His *Radley School Boer War Memorial* featured St George and this figure would become a recurrent theme. He produced a St George for the *Pearl Assurance War Memorial* (1918) in Holborn, London. Its design is almost identical to that of his *Maidstone War Memorial*. Frampton sculpted two portrait statues of *Queen Mary* for India, one of which is in the Victoria Memorial and the other in the east loggia of the Rashtrapati Bhavan. He produced the much criticised *Edith Cavell* (1920) outside the National Portrait Gallery in London and used his position to block Jacob Epstein's appointment as an official war artist, but he recognised Charles Sargeant Jagger's ability and nominated him to undertake the *Hoylake and West Kirby War Memorial*, at which point Jagger's career took off. Frampton designed the *Wittersham War Memorial* which took the form of an octagonal column on which is perched a cushion, on top of which is a crowned orb. He provided a similar version for Knowlton, Kent. There, the memorial was paid for by *The Weekly Despatch* as the prize for Britain's bravest village. (12 out of a population of 39 enlisted). He produced the memorial, also in the form of a St George, to Captain Francis Mond RAF.[28] He produced the bronze *Death Mask of Sir Herbert Beerbohm Tree* (1918).

Frampton exhibited at the RA from 1884, was elected ARA in 1894 and RA 1902. He was MRBS 1904-14, knighted in 1908, and PRBS 1911-12. He died in 1928. An English Heritage Blue Plaque marks his house at 32 Queen's Grove, St John's Wood, London. There is a self-portrait of him in pencil (1894) in the collection of the National Portrait Gallery.

---

[27] Alan Borg *War Memorials* p. 78.
[28] Killed in air combat over Bouzencourt on the Somme 15 May 1918. He was eldest son of Emile Mond, who also endowed for £20,000 the Mond Chair of Aeronautical Engineering at Cambridge University in his memory.

## ALBERT TOFT

Albert Toft was born in Hunters Lane, Handsworth, Birmingham on 3 June 1862. His father Charles Toft (1832-1909) was principal modeller at the firm of Elkington and later moved the family to Staffordshire to take up a post with the pottery firm of Josiah Wedgwood at Etruria in the Potteries. Young Albert served his apprenticeship at Wedgwood, studying at the art school in Hanley in the evenings and then at Newcastle-under-Lyme. At the age of 17 he won a National Scholarship to the National Art Training School and studied at South Kensington under Professor Édouard Lantéri. He won silver medals in his second and third years. He set up his studio in Abbey Road, London and endured some lean years. He first exhibited at the RA in 1885. He worked in a wide variety of media, producing bas-reliefs, statues, medallions, busts, figurative and monumental sculpture. His portrait busts included: the actress *Ellaline Terriss* (1901); *W E Gladstone* (1888) at the National Liberal Club, London; *Sir Frank Brangwyn* at Brangwyn Hall, Swansea; *Sir Alfred Gilbert RA,* and *George Wallis* (1890), first director of Nottingham Castle Museum. From the late 1880s he sculpted ideal works strongly influenced by his friend Alfred Gilbert (1854-1934). He sculpted *Lilith* (1889); *The Sere and Yellow Leaf* (1892); *The Oracle* (1894); *The Goblet of Life* (1894); *The Vision* (1897) and *Hagar* (1899). His *Fate Led* (1892) may be seen in the Walker Art Gallery, Liverpool. His *Spring* (1894) may be seen in the City of Birmingham Museum and Art Gallery, *Mother and Child* (1899) in Preston Art Gallery and *Spirit of Contemplation* (1901), a remarkable female nude in an Egyptian headdress reclining in an ornately-carved chair in the Laing Art Gallery, Newcastle-upon-Tyne. His sculpture *The Bather* (1914) was acquired by the Chantrey Trustees and is in the collection of the Tate. In 1901 he sculpted the marble statue *HH Rajah Sudhal deb Bahadur of Bamra*. He sculpted the *Queen Victoria Memorial* at Leamington Spa, South Shields and that on Victoria Embankment in Nottingham (formerly in Old Market Square). He also sculpted the statues *King Edward VII* at Birmingham and Warwick and the memorial bust of *King George V* at Eastbourne. In 1911 Toft produced the book *Modelling and Sculpture: A full account of the various methods and processes employed in these arts*. In it he paid tribute to the sculptural legacy of the Italian Renaissance and Alfred Stevens. In 1913 at St Peter's Church, Nottingham he carved from Chilmark stone the altar-piece *The Angel releasing Saint Peter from Prison* which was covered up during alterations in 1950 and only recently rediscovered. 'A notable work in yet another medium is Toft's *Coronation Medal of George V and Queen Mary* (1911); on the reverse, the dramatic use of lines to denote the ship of state again attests to Gilbert's influence.'[29] Toft's working life spanned both the South African War and the Great War and he would be in demand to sculpt war memorials for both. These included: *The Welsh National Boer War Memorial* in Cathays Park, Cardiff, the *South Africa Memorial* (1906) in Cannon Hill Park, Birmingham. He sculpted the *Royal Fusiliers (City of London Regiment) Memorial* at Holborn Bars, an exact copy of which stands as the *41st Division Memorial* at Flers in France. He sculpted the *Chadderton War Memorial* (1921) in Oldham and the monument to *Captain Albert Ball VC* in the grounds of Nottingham Castle. In the years 1923-24 he worked in concert with the Birmingham architects S N Cooke and W N Twist of Paradise Street and sculpted the seated bronze allegorical figures representing the Navy, Army, Air Force and Women's Services as an integral part of the design of the Hall of Memory in Centenary Square, Birmingham.

Socially gregarious, Toft was a stalwart of the Savage Club, figuring prominently in their affairs and frequently presiding over their House Dinners. He was elected to the Art Workers Guild in 1891 and MRBS in 1905. He taught at the Camberwell School of Arts and Crafts and was elected FRBS 1923 and HRBS in 1942. Disappointingly and despite being a regular exhibitor in the years 1885-1947, Toft was never elected to membership of the RA due to the preponderance of sculptors slightly senior to himself during his working life. He died in a nursing home at Downview Rd in Worthing, Sussex on 18 December 1949.

---

[29] *Dictionary of National Biography* Oxford University Press 2004.

# SIR HERBERT BAKER

Herbert Baker was born on 9 June 1862, at Owletts at Cobham in Kent. His family had owned the house since 1794. He was the fourth child in a family of eleven and his parents were Thomas Henry Baker, JP and Frances Georgina Baker. His father was a landowner and farmer. Herbert was educated at Tonbridge School and the Royal Academy School of Architecture. Upon leaving school in 1881, he was apprenticed for three years to his cousin Arthur Baker in London. He then worked as senior assistant in the offices of Ernest George and Harold Peto, where he met the young Edwin Lutyens. In 1890 he became an Associate of the RIBA, having been awarded the Ashpitel Prize for heading the examination lists the year before. In 1891 he went to Capetown, South Africa in the hope of finding a favourable environment in which to practise all that he had learnt. He made the acquaintance of Cecil Rhodes who asked him to restore Groote Schuur - now the South African President's Cape Town residence. Rhodes was so pleased with the results, that he paid Baker to tour the Mediterranean studying classical architecture. Baker also rebuilt Groote Schuur after it was destroyed by fire in 1896. Rhodes was not at home at the time, as he was busy organising Dr Leander Starr Jameson's disastrous invasion of the Transvaal. After Rhodes's death in 1902 and shortly before the end of the South African War (1899-1902), Baker accepted Lord Milner's invitation to go to the Transvaal to help in the work of reconstruction and he designed many grand mansions in the northern suburb of Park Town in Johannesburg. In Bloemfontein he added the lofty tower to the cathedral and at Pretoria, he built Government House. On a natural shelf further along the same ridge he built with a graciously curved frontage, the Parliament Buildings. He also built in Pretoria the first portions of the Anglican cathedral in the Gothic style. In Rhodesia he built a granite cathedral at Salisbury; in Kenya he built Government House at Nairobi. He collaborated with Lutyens on the layout of New Delhi. There he designed the two Secretariat Buildings and the Legislative building. He fell out with Lutyens, returned to London in 1913 and established a practice in partnership with Alexander Thompson Scott. In 1918 he was appointed one of the Principal Architects of the Imperial War Graves Commission. He also undertook the design of the national memorials at Neuve Chapelle for India and at Delville Wood for the Union of South Africa. He designed the war memorials at Harrow, Winchester, King's School Canterbury and Haileybury. Baker accommodated T E Lawrence at his house in Westminster whilst Lawrence wrote *Seven Pillars of Wisdom*. After leaving the Commission, Baker designed the new Bank of England inside Sir John Soane's old curtain wall and he recycled Soane's caryatids in the design of his rotunda there (completed 1939). He designed India House, The Strand (1925) and Rhodes House, South Parks Road, Oxford (1929) as a memorial to Rhodes and permanent headquarters of the Rhodes Trustees. He designed the Scott Polar Research Institute at Cambridge (1933); Church House, Westminster (1934) and the Royal Commonwealth Society building, Northumberland Avenue (1938). He was knighted in 1926, was awarded the Royal Gold Medal of the RIBA in 1927 and elected to the Royal Academy in 1932. He designed South Africa House, Trafalgar Square in 1930. All of the furniture in the High Commission was designed by him and manufactured from stinkwood in Cape Town. Baker presented Owletts to the National Trust in 1937 and lived in it until his death. Gertrude Jekyll (1843-1932) laid out the gardens. The birdbath is one of the Corinthian capitals from the old Bank of England. In 1944 Baker published *Architecture and Personalities* and this book gave his own theory of his art. In later years he was stricken by illness. He died on 4 February 1946. His funeral took place at Westminster Abbey on 13 February and his ashes were buried there. Baker's love for his profession may be found in the scholarships founded in his name during and after his lifetime. A portrait of him by A K Lawrence hangs in the Bank of England, where there is also a marble bust executed by his friend Sir Charles Wheeler. A bronze bust of him by Wheeler, a copy of which is at Owletts, is at South Africa House. His portrait by Sir William Rothenstein may be seen in the National Portrait Gallery.

# SIR BERTRAM MACKENNAL

Edgar Bertram Mackennal was born in Melbourne, Australia in 1862, son of a Scottish architectural sculptor. He studied art initially under his father, then at the Melbourne School of Art. In 1882 he entered the RA Schools, where he first exhibited in 1886. He studied in Paris and Rome in the period 1889-1891. Whilst in Paris he met Rodin and was profoundly influenced by his style. Whilst in Paris, Mackennal set up his own studio at the age of 19 and specialised in rather ideal figures, often female nudes with art nouveau-style faces and also portrait sculpture. Rodin had sculpted *Bellona* in 1879 and it is likely that it was the inspiration for Mackennal's *War* (1906). *War* was displayed for the first time at the RA that same year. In recognition of the bravery of the Australian troops at Gallipoli, MacKennal presented it to the Commonwealth of Australia in 1915. He said: 'In common with all Australians, I have been so moved and proud of the gallantry, extreme courage, and fortitude of our troops at ANZAC. No men have ever made greater sacrifices for honour and duty. I wonder if the Commonwealth Government would accept from me as a small tribute of admiration and pride in my fellow-countrymen, a colossal bronze bust entitled *War*.' The Australian Government did accept the work in the early 1920s but, at that time had no permanent home for it, as the Australian War Memorial didn't open in Canberra until 1941. In the interim, *War* was exhibited at Parliament House in Melbourne until 1927. After that, it was displayed until 1954 on Commonwealth Avenue in Canberra (near Albert Hall). The sculpture had a stint in the foyer of the administrative building near Parliament House and until 1977 in the grounds of Government House. Mackennal also sculpted the remarkable *Apollo* which stands at the rear of the grounds of Taplow Court in Buckinghamshire in memory of the two Grenfell brothers. In 1910 he was appointed Royal Sculptor to King Edward VII. He designed the well-known obverse of the coinage of King George V incised with the initials "BM" at the base of the King's neck. This may also be seen on the coins of the Empire from the period. Mackennal's works included the *Tomb for Edward VII* St. George's Chapel, Windsor a commission he executed jointly with the architect Edwin Lutyens. He also executed the *National Memorial to Gainsborough* at Sudbury, Suffolk. He completed several commissions for the Royal Family. He sculpted the bronze equestrian statue of *King Edward VII* which stands on the memorial arch at the Victoria Memorial in Calcutta. It was exhibited at the RA in 1916 and paid for by the third Aga Khan. In 1916 he produced the marble portrait statue *King George V* (now in the Rashtrapati Bhavan). It was paid for by the Maharaja of Gwalior. 'Mackennal's bronze statue of King George V for Madras shows the King wearing his coronation robes over the costume of the Order of the Garter. The figure was erected at the Flower Bazaar Police Station where it stands today.'[30] MacKennal's 14 foot tall equestrian statue of *King Edward VII* (1921) stands in Pall Mall in London. It cost £10,000 and was cast by Singer's of Frome and was inaugurated in 1921. At the wish of Queen Alexandra, it supplanted Boehm's *Field Marshal Lord Napier of Magdala* which was then removed to Kensington Gore. A copy of Mackennal's *Edward VII* was sent to Australia. His bronze seated statue *Queen Victoria* (1900) may be seen in the garden of the British Embassy in Bangkok. In 1903 he sculpted the *Islington Boer War Memorial* and after the Great War also sculpted both the *Blackburn War Memorial;* the *Members of Parliament War Memorial* in the House of Commons and the *Eton War Memorial*. For Australia House in The Strand, London he completed *Phoebus Driving the Horses of the Sun* (1923). Mackennal was elected ARA in 1909, created MVO (Member of the Royal Victorian Order) in 1912 and KCVO (Knight Commander of the Royal Victorian Order) in 1921. In 1922 he became the first and only Australian sculptor ever to be elected a Royal Academician, he was also the first overseas-born. During his last visit to his homeland in 1926-27, he was lionised by his countrymen and designed the Cenotaph at Martin Place in Sydney. He completed the *Desert Mounted Corps Memorial* for Port Said shortly before his death in London in 1931.

---

[30] Mary Ann Steggles *Statues of the Raj*.

# HENRY ALFRED PEGRAM

Henry Alfred Pegram was born in King Street, Camden Town, London on 27 July 1862. His father was a china shopman (and later a manufacturer of bassinettes and rocking horses). Young Henry studied at the West London School of Art and, sponsored by the gifted art teacher Thomas Heatherley, he entered the Royal Academy Schools in 1881. He was studio assistant to Hamo Thornycroft in the period 1887-91. In 1884 he married Alice Lambert and their happy union produced three sons and three daughters. In 1889 Pegram was awarded a medal at the Paris Exhibition for his sculpture *Death and the Prisoner*. This success would be reinforced by the award of the Gold Medal at Dresden for *The Last Song* in 1897. Pegram worked mainly in marble and bronze and produced work mostly from classical and religious themes. He produced groups, posthumous busts, statuettes and architectural reliefs and medallions. In 1894 he produced *The Bather*. Pegram's early work was strongly influenced by Alfred Gilbert (the sculptor of *Eros* at Piccadilly Circus in London) and oddly Pegram's greatest professional successes came earlier rather than later in his career, with two of his works being purchased under the terms of the Chantrey Bequest: *Ignis Fatuus* (1899) and *Sybilla Fatidica* (1904), both in the collection of The Tate. In 1891-92 he sculpted the reliefs *Industry* and *Britannia* for the Imperial Institute. He sculpted the *Monument to Ninon*, the wife of the 'Randlord' Max Michaelis (1900). In 1898 he produced the heavily criticised bronze candelabra for St Paul's Cathedral in London, described by a contemporary critic as 'deplorable'. Pegram's architectural relief work included friezes at 20 Buckingham Gate, Westminster (1895) and at the United University Club, Suffolk Street, London (1906), as well as the relief at the entrance to the Imperial Institute, South Kensington (1891-2). For Norwich Market Square he sculpted a large seated bronze statue of the philosopher/physician *Sir Thomas Browne*. Pegram's early sculpture included: *A Sea Idyll* (1902); *Into the Silent Land* (1905); *By the Waters of Babylon* (1906); *Nereus and Galatea* (1911); *Chance* (1913) and *Ophelia and the River Gods* (1914). In 1904 Pegram was one of six sculptors who competed for the commission for the *Manchester Boer War Memorial* which, after the most terrific rumpus was awarded to Thornycroft. A keen golfing man and a member of the Mid-Surrey Golf Club, Pegram exhibited two statuettes of the golfer Harry Vardon in 1908 and 1911. In 1913 Pegram was one of ten eminent sculptors controversially selected without competition by the Royal Society of British Sculptors to work on the statuary for the new City Hall at Cardiff. He sculpted in marble the figure of *Llewelyn the Last*. The fall-out from the Society's decision to hand-pick the ten sculptors split the President and Council from its membership. Pegram's *Memorial to Edith Cavell* at Norwich consisting of a bronze bust atop a stone pillar was inaugurated by Queen Alexandra on 12 October 1918. Working with the architect Arthur Davis, he sculpted the bronze *Victory* on the Cunard War Memorial at Liverpool. In 1922 he produced the group *Hylas* which was presented by the RA to the nation and installed in 1933 in the centre of the pool of the rose garden at St John's Lodge, Regents Park. Pegram sculpted busts of *Cecil Rhodes* (1903) in marble for the City of London; *Edmond Halley* (1904); *William Herschel* (1905); *Charles Dickens* (1905); *Rudyard Kipling* (1909); *Earl Jellicoe* (1928) and *Viscount Allenby* (1930 and 1936). Pegram sculpted public statues in bronze of *Sir John Campbell* at Auckland, New Zealand; *Cardinal Newman* at Oriel College, Oxford; *Cecil Rhodes* at Cape Town, South Africa and *Sir Robert Hart* at Shanghai, China. Such large statues were invariably carried to the four corners of the British Empire for free by merchant navy captains glad of the ballast. Interestingly, the records of the Royal Humane Society state that their bronze medal was awarded to Boatman James T Simmons who saved one Henry A Pegram from drowning at Seaford, Sussex, on 3 August 1891. A prolific sculptor, Pegram exhibited more than 160 works at the RA in the period between 1884 and 1936. He was elected ARA in 1904, MRBS 1905-1923 and elected RA in 1922. In July 1936 he was awarded a civil list pension 'in recognition of his services to art'. He died from a cerebral haemorrhage at his home in Belsize Gardens, Belsize Park on 26 March 1937.

# COLONEL SIR FREDERIC KENYON

Frederic George Kenyon was born 15 January 1863 at Lower Berkeley Street, London. He was the seventh son of John Robert Kenyon, grandson of the First Baron Kenyon of Pradoe, Shropshire. From the age of six he lived at Pradoe. He attended Winchester and then New College, Oxford. There, he laid the basis of a considerable reputation as a biblical scholar and took a first in Classical Moderations in 1883 and a first in *Literae Humaniores* in 1886. He obtained a Fellowship at Magdalen College in 1888. The following year, he started work as an assistant at the British Museum, catalogued its collection of Greek papyri and immersed himself in the works of Homer, Hyperides, and Demosthenes. He translated Aristotle's Athenian Constitution of 350 BC. In 1891 he published *Classical Texts from Papyri in the British Museum* followed by three volumes on *Greek Papyri in the British Museum* in 1893, 1898 and 1907. In 1895 he published *Our Bible and the Ancient Manuscripts* and in 1896 *The Brownings for the Young* followed in 1899 by *The Palæography of Greek Papyri*. In the period 1899-1901 he was Commanding Officer of the Roxeth & Harrow Company of the Church Lads' & Church Girls' Brigade. In 1899, in response to the war in South Africa he joined the Inns of Court Regiment[31] (a Territorial Army unit based at Lincoln's Inn in Holborn). He was commissioned in 1906, rising to the rank of Lieutenant Colonel in 1917. In 1900 Kenyon was elected a Corresponding Member of the Berlin Academy. He was deeply involved with the founding of the British Academy in 1901. He became a Fellow in 1903 and served as its President 1917-1921. In 1909 he succeeded Sir Edward Maunde-Thompson as Director of the British Museum. In 1910 he persuaded HM Treasury to underwrite the expenses of T E Lawrence (Lawrence of Arabia 1888-1935) on the archaeological excavation of Carchemish. He was appointed CB in 1912 became President of the Classical Association in 1913 and was appointed GBE in 1915. Although Director General of the British Museum, during the Great War Kenyon served with the regiment on the Western Front, but was recalled home from active service at the request of the Trustees of the Museum. That same year he was contacted by Fabian Ware, founder of the IWGC who requested him to advise on the treatment of the cemeteries to be constructed on the Western Front after the war. The report he wrote formally established the foundation of the work that was to be undertaken by the Commission for the first ten years of its existence. He formed a lifelong friendship with Fabian Ware and for the rest of his life would be heavily involved with all aspects of the Commission's work as their artistic adviser. He was responsible for the appointment of Lutyens, Baker and Blomfield as the first three principal architects to the Commission. 'Kenyon presided over all, ensuring that fine taste would typify everything the Commission produced'.[32] His eagle eye and brilliant mind would serve the Commission for many years. After the Great War Kenyon became a member of the University Grants Committee and was President of the Hellenistic Society 1919-1924. He remained Director of the British Museum until 1930. He then retired to commence a full-time study of biblical papyri. In 1933 as President of the Friends of the National Libraries, he was responsible for leading the public appeal for the British Library to purchase the *Codex Sinaiticus*. He was President of the Society of Antiquaries 1934-39. A prolific author, he then wrote *Recent Developments in the Textual Criticism of the Greek Bible* (1933); *The Text of the Greek Bible: A Student's Handbook* (1937) and *The British Academy: The First Fifty Years* (1952). He died on 23 August 1952 at his home at Oxted in Surrey. Six whole-plate glass negatives taken by Bassano at a sitting on 23 September 1921 may be found in the collection of the National Portrait Gallery. There is a pencil drawing of him by Augustus John in the British Academy and a bronze bust by J A Stevenson in the boardroom of the British Museum.

---

[31] At a Royal Review in Hyde Park 1803, King George III asked an aide which regiment was parading before him. Upon being informed that it was the Inns of Court - a regiment composed of lawyers, he commented: 'The Devil's Own'. A devil riding on a spur is the 'collar dog' worn by all ranks of this unit to this day.
[32] Philip Longworth *The Unending Vigil*.

# SIR NINIAN COMPER

John Ninian Comper was born on 10 June 1864 in Aberdeen. His father, the Reverend John Comper was a leader of the later Anglo-Catholic phase of the Oxford Movement in Scotland. He was educated at Glenalmond, spent an unhappy year at Ruskin's School, Oxford and then attended the Royal School of Art at South Kensington. In 1882 he commenced work as an assistant glass painter to Charles Eamer Kempe and in 1883 he was articled to George Frederick Bodley and T Garner. His life's work would be in the field of ecclesiastical design. From 1882 until his death in 1960, he carried out at least five hundred commissions, the last one being completed in 1966. In Comper's phenomenally long and busy working life he designed at least 408 stained glass windows in churches and cathedrals the length and breadth of the British Isles, including a considerable number in Westminster Abbey. He built 15 churches and concentrated on every conceivable aspect of church design including; altars, stalls, chasubles, lecterns, figures, gravestones, interior fittings, patens, pulpits, banners, cruets, copes, rood screens, fonts, chancels and candlesticks. His ability secured commissions from as far afield as India, New Zealand and the USA. In 1889 he went into partnership with William Bucknall, his brother-in-law and when he died, *his* son and when he died, *his* son. In 1901 Comper was responsible for the design of the hearse and funeral trappings of Queen Victoria. In 1903 he designed St Cyprian's Church, Glentworth Street, London and in 1904 his favourite, St Mary the Virgin at Wellingborough. In 1912-13 he redesigned the interior of the Grosvenor Chapel in Mayfair. In common with other architects Comper designed a number of war memorials. In 1917 he produced the War Memorial Cross at St Erth; in 1919 war memorials at Barnard Castle, Bayford, Benefield, Clifford Chambers, St Paul's Cathedral - Dundee, Devizes, East Malling, Glenalmond, Lytchett Minster, Stanton Broadway and West Keal; in 1920 at Dumbleton, Hopton, Long Eaton, Milborne Port, Rugby, Tintinhull, Westerham, Westwood, Wimbourne St Giles and Wirksworth; in 1921 Caistor, Ufford, Uppingham and the Metropolitan Asylums Board War Memorial; in 1922 Lindfield, the Memorial Cross at Cirencester and the War Memorial Tablet at Stroud Green; in 1923 the war memorial at Merton College, Oxford; in 1926 the War Memorial Tablet at Wymondham. In 1927 he designed the Warriors' Chapel at Westminster Abbey and in 1928 his tour de force, the Welsh National War Memorial at Cathays Park in Cardiff. That year he also designed the extraordinary 8ft 6 in tall silver tabernacle in All Saints' Church, Margaret St, London.[33] This remarkable contraption powered by an electric motor, was the gift of the Duke of Newcastle in memory of the church's choristers killed in the war. In 1935 Comper completed the design of the Suffolk Regimental Chapel at St Mary's, Bury St Edmunds. His last major commission would be at Cosham. Peter Hammond wrote: 'St Philip's, Cosham. Completed in 1938, bears little resemblance to anything the man in the street is likely to associate with functional architecture. Yet, there is no church built in the country since the beginning of the century which is so perfectly fitted to its purpose. It is the work of an architect for whom architecture is essentially the handmaiden of the liturgy, and Christian tradition something more vital than a storehouse of precedents and historical detail. This church functions as the great majority of modern churches - for all their display of contemporary clichés do not. It is a building for corporate worship: a building to house an altar'.[34] Comper was knighted in 1950. In 1952 he designed the Parliamentary War Memorial Window, Westminster Hall. Comper held for his time some unorthodox opinions. He believed that architects needed no formal qualifications and was also of the opinion that there were essentially no doctrinal differences between the Anglican faith and the Roman Catholic Church. He was devoted to the memory of St Pius X. In 1950 he published *Of the Atmosphere of a Church* and *Of the Christian Altar and the Buildings which contain it*. He died at home on Beulah Hill, Sydenham, London on 22 December 1960 and fittingly, his ashes were interred in Westminster Abbey.

---

[33] *The Builder* November 1928 pp 752 and 755.
[34] Peter Hammond *Liturgy and Architecture* 1960.

# CAPTAIN BASIL GOTTO

Basil Gotto was born at Highgate in London on 10 August 1866, the son of Henry J Gotto. He thoroughly enjoyed himself at Harrow School and early demonstrated his artistic talent by winning their drawing competition. The artist George Claussen (1852-1944) persuaded his father to send him to be trained in Paris. There he studied painting at the Académie Julian and had a fairly wild time. In 1887 he returned to London, attempted to enter the RA and was given six weeks in which to produce four months' work. Learning that the entry rules for sculptors were somewhat easier, he arrived at the Ledward studio in Dean's Yard, Westminster. Turned out a creditable clay *Hercules* in three weeks and gained entry. *Victory* his first sculpture exhibited at the RA in 1889 was cast in bronze by Alfred Gilbert and is the first English example of the *cire-perdu* process. Despite his extensive range of interests, Gotto would exhibit regularly at the RA. After the death of his father, he travelled in Italy and returning to London, set up his studio in Glebe Place, Chelsea. His studio backed onto that of John Tweed in Harley Mews. His career was given an unexpected 'leg up' by the critic D S MacColl, who having seen an RA Summer Exhibition, damned in his review the sculptors Brock, Thornycroft et al for their lack of talent and instead praised the foreign exhibitors including Gotto - MacColl assumed he was not an Englishman. In 1899 by an act of subterfuge, Gotto got himself appointed war correspondent of the *Daily News* to cover the war in South Africa. He was subsequently employed by the *Daily Express* newspaper and formed a life-long friendship with its founder, the publisher Sir Arthur Pearson. Gotto was present at the Middlesex Yeomanry's action at Senekal in South Africa and sculpted the *Middlesex Yeomanry Boer War Memorial* in St Paul's Cathedral. In 1913 he married Sibyl Ellis Ashmead Bartlett. They had two sons, Basil and George. In 1915 Gotto sculpted the memorial tablet in St James Church, Piccadilly to his friend and colleague the theatre director Lewis Waller. During the Great War, Gotto served in the army as a musketry instructor at Bisley then at the Depot, Winchester and dramatically improved the shooting skills of the Civil Service Rifles, the London Scottish, the Artists Rifles and the Newfoundland Regiment. After the war, working with Father Thomas Nangle, late chaplain to the Newfoundland Regiment, he sculpted the five caribou memorials which stand on the battlefields of the Western Front to commemorate the fallen Newfoundlanders. A sixth may be seen in Bowring Park at St John's in Canada. In the same park can also be found *The Fighting Newfoundlander* cast in Belgium and donated to the City of St John's by Sir Edgar Bowring. Gotto sculpted it in 1919 at the Winchester School of Art. In 1920 he sculpted the figure of *St Andrew* atop the *Berriedale and Braemore War Memorial* at Caithness for the Duke of Portland. He also sculpted the *Army and Navy Club War Memorial* which takes the form of a six foot tall Greek warrior outside the Club in Pall Mall. In 1924 Gotto sculpted the *Newfoundland National War Memorial* at St John's. When the war memorial commissions dried up in the mid 1920s, he took down his palette once more and painted portraits for a case of port a time. The portrait *Basil Ashmead Gotto* (1927) is in the possession of the Gotto family and *Our Charlady* is owned by Southampton City Council. Gotto was a keen yachtsman, a member of the London Chess Club, the Arts Club, Chelsea Arts Club and over a period of some 15 years, was a director of a number of London theatres. His theatrical connections enabled him to obtain character parts in the early days of British cinema. His unpublished autobiography is full of anecdote, reads like a 'Who's Who' of Edwardian England and makes scant mention of his chosen profession. He counted among his wide circle of friends Mark Twain, Sir Arthur Conan Doyle, James McNeill Whistler, George Sala, Sir J M Barrie, the sculptors Francis Derwent Wood, Frederick Pomeroy, Adrian Jones and Rodin. He was MRBS 1905-21, President of the Chelsea Arts Club 1913-15, ARBS 1923-29 and was responsible for inaugurating the highly successful Chelsea Arts Ball. In 1920 he moved to Twyford near Winchester, continued to paint, immersed himself in the business of local government, sat on numerous committees and died on 19 October 1954.

# JOHN TWEED

John Tweed was born in Glasgow on 21 January 1869, the eldest son of John Tweed, a Glaswegian publisher. He was educated at Hutcheson's Boys Grammar School, Glasgow. Upon the death of his father in 1885, he left his studies and commenced work in his father's business. At the same time he studied drawing and modelling. He obtained a teaching scholarship at the Glasgow School of Art and worked with the sculptors G A Lawson, J A Ewing and J Pittendrigh Macgillivray. In 1890 he left Glasgow and headed for London to take up the offer of a teaching post. The offer came to naught and he was taken on by Hamo Thornycroft's studio. 'During the next two years he received instruction first at the Lambeth School of Art and then at the Royal Academy Schools'.[35] In 1893 he visited Paris and established a life-long friendship with the sculptor Rodin, who would profoundly influence his style. Whilst in Paris, Tweed studied at the École des Beaux-Arts under Jean Alexandre Joseph Falguière (1831-1900). In 1898 Tweed returned to London to undertake his first big commission from Cecil Rhodes, who in the later years of his life discovered culture in a big way, and could certainly afford to indulge his tastes. He would act as patron to a number of important figures in this story. Tweed produced the relief *The Landing of Van Riebeck* which would grace Groote Schuur, Rhodes' residence at the foot of Table Mountain. Tweed subsequently completed *Van Riebeck* (1899) for Cape Town and *Cecil Rhodes* (1902) for Bulawayo. Whilst sculpting a portrait bust of Rhodes, Tweed had a famous 'bust up' with him in his Chelsea studio and Rhodes surprisingly came off second best. In 1902 Tweed accepted the commission to complete the bronze equestrian design for the *Duke of Wellington Memorial* by Alfred Stevens (1818-1875) in St Paul's Cathedral, London. Little did he know at the outset that he would become embroiled in a long-running controversy. He eventually completed this monolithic work in 1912. In that period he also completed a number of memorial statues including *General Lord Chesham* (1910) at Aylesbury, *Captain James Cook* (1912) in bronze at both Whitby and St Kilda, and *Robert Clive* (1912) at the top of Clive Steps, King Charles Street, London. He spent the Great War in London and completed *Joseph Chamberlain* (1916) at Westminster Abbey, the recumbent marble effigy of *Sir William Anson* (1918) late Warden of All Souls, for All Souls College Chapel, Oxford, later he produced *Benjamin Disraeli* (1923) at Aylesbury and *Lord Ronaldshay* (1924) at Mumbai. He made the marble busts *Earl Curzon of Kedleston* for the Oxford Union and *Joseph Chamberlain* in Westminster Abbey and the statue of *General Sir John Moore* at Shorncliffe, and the equestrian statue of *General Sir George White* (1922) in Portland Place, London. He also sculpted *Queen Victoria* at both Aden and Madras. He sculpted the white marble relief of *Admiral Lord Beresford* in the crypt of St Paul's Cathedral. He executed the marble reredos at Holy Trinity, Sloane Street, London and the reredos in Chichester Cathedral. Tweed received a number of commissions to produce war memorials at the end of the Great War. In 1918 he was commissioned by General Smuts to make sketches for the *South African War Memorial* to be erected in France. The project proved abortive, with the commission eventually being completed by Sir Herbert Baker. In all Tweed executed 12 war memorials, notable amongst which would be: the *King's Royal Rifle Corps Memorial* (1922) at Winchester, the *Rifle Brigade Memorial* (1925) at Grosvenor Place, London, and *The National Memorial to Earl Kitchener of Khartoum* (1925) on Horse Guards Parade Ground. He subsequently produced the memorials to *Cecil Rhodes* at Salisbury, Rhodesia (1928) and at Mafeking, South Africa (1932). He sculpted The *Peers War Memorial* (1932) in the House of Lords. In June 1933 a comprehensive exhibition of his work was held at Knoedler's Galleries in London. Tweed was elected MRBS in 1905. He died from a heart condition on 12 November 1933 in London. A memorial exhibition of his work was held at the Imperial Institute, South Kensington in 1934 and *John Tweed Sculptor: A Memoir* was published in 1956. An English Heritage Blue Plaque marks his house at 108 Cheyne Walk in Chelsea.

---

[35] *Dictionary of National Biography* Oxford University Press.

## SIR EDWIN LUTYENS OM

Edwin Landseer (Ned) Lutyens, was born in London on 29 March 1869, son of the soldier turned painter Charles Lutyens. As a child he suffered from rheumatic fever and therefore had little in the way of formal education. He appears to have learned a great deal by observation and the close questioning of his siblings. In 1885 at the age of 16, he was sent to what is now the Royal College of Art at South Kensington to study architecture. Before he completed the course, he had started work as a paying apprentice in the office of the architectural partnership of Ernest George and Harold Peto. There he met Herbert Baker, seven years his senior. They were to collaborate later in their careers designing and building New Delhi, an unhappy partnership that ended in what Lutyens would call his 'Bakerloo'. Lutyens set up his own practice in 1889 and was greatly influenced by the Arts and Crafts Movement. His early works, mostly country houses in Surrey, were in the vernacular revival style, using traditional building methods and materials. He met Gertrude Jekyll when he was 20 and she was 46. They collaborated for many years and he designed her house at Munstead Wood. 'A Lutyens house and a Jekyll garden became an Edwardian status symbol'. [36] Good examples of their work may be found at Le Bois de Moutiers, Normandy, Great Dixter, Surrey and Hestercombe House, Somerset. Lutyens was responsible for some outstanding commissions in England, among which were: Campion Hall at Oxford (1935); the Midland Bank, Poultry, London; Tigbourne Court, Surrey; Castle Drogo, Devon; St Jude's Church, Hampstead Garden Suburb (1909-1911); 36 Smith Square, London (1911); the Catholic Cathedral in Liverpool which was only completed to crypt level (1929-1941) and in Ireland, Howth and Lambay castles. Overseas, his commissions included: the British School of Art in Rome and the British Embassy in Washington DC (1926-1929). He designed the layout of New Delhi, the Rashtrapati Bhavan (Viceroy's Residence) (1912-1931) and the British High Commissioner's residence at Rajaji Marg. In South Africa he designed the Johannesburg Art Gallery (1911) and the Rand Memorial (1911). A man with a delightful sense of humour, he once designed a circular nursery for a client, so that no child could ever be stood in the corner.

Lutyens was appointed Principal Architect for France by the IWGC on 5 March 1918. 'Lutyens strove to make a permanent architectural expression of what he felt, so that for the Imperial War Graves Commission he produced some of his very finest work.[37] He designed the Cenotaph in Whitehall, the Stone of Remembrance which stands in the larger cemeteries of the Commission, the South African War Memorial in Johannesburg, the All-India War Memorial Arch, New Delhi, the Australian National War Memorial at Villers-Bretonneux, France, the Irish National War Memorial at Islandbridge, Dublin, the Merchant Navy Memorial on Tower Hill, the Royal Naval Division Memorial on Horse Guards Parade Ground, the Norwich City War Memorial and the Thiepval Memorial to the Missing. He also designed the delightful Civil Service Rifles War Memorial which now stands at the western end of the terrace at Somerset House in London. A prolific worker, in all, Lutyens designed a total of 133 cemeteries and war memorials. He was elected ARA in 1913, received a knighthood in the New Year Honours list of 1918 and was awarded the Royal Gold Medal of the RIBA in 1921. He was elected PRA in 1934. In 1942 King George VI appointed him to the Order of Merit. He died in London on New Year's Day 1944. His biographer Christopher Hussey wrote: 'his work constitutes the largest and most imaginative addition made by a single mind to the classics of English architecture for two centuries, which will be studied and emulated so long as architecture is conceived as an art.' E V Lucas wrote: 'His friends were legion; his mind was electrically instant to respond to any sympathetic suggestion; he never broke his word; he never let you know if he was tired; and with it all he was out for fun'. Harold Nicholson would write: 'Never since the days of Sheridan and Goldsmith has a man of genius been so widely beloved....' Website at www.lutyenstrust.org.uk

---

[36] Jane Ridley *The Architect and his Wife: A Life of Edwin Lutyens.*
[37] Gavin Stamp *Silent Cities.*

## MAJOR GENERAL SIR FABIAN WARE

Fabian Arthur Goulstone Ware was born at Clifton, Bristol on 17 June 1869. He was educated privately and at the Universities of London and Paris, where he obtained a degree of *Bachelier-des-Sciences* in 1894. Four of the ten years he spent as an assistant master at secondary schools were passed at Bradford, Yorkshire and he was an occasional examiner for the Civil Service Commission and Inspector of Schools to the Board of Education. In 1899 he commenced contributing to the *Morning Post* newspaper. The year after, he was appointed representative of the Education Committee of the Royal British Commission at the Paris World Exhibition. When the Exhibition was over, he obtained a position as Assistant Director of Education in the Transvaal in South Africa. Two years later he became Acting Director of Education for the Transvaal and the Orange River Colony and, after a brief tenure, he entered the Transvaal Legislative Council and was made Director of Education under Lord Milner. In 1905 Lord Glenesk invited him to become editor of the *Morning Post*. He accepted and filled the post with distinction. He resigned in 1911 to join Lord Milner on the Board of the Rio Tinto Company. Upon the outbreak of war in 1914, Ware discovered that at 45, he was too old to be accepted by the Army for active service. He could not have guessed that his entire life had been preparation for what was to follow. With the assistance of Lord Milner, he was appointed to command a mobile unit of the British Red Cross Society and arrived in France in September 1914. He was quickly struck by the absence of any official organisation responsible for the marking and recording of the graves of those killed. He undertook to rectify this state of affairs and in 1915 the organisation he created was transferred from the British Red Cross to the Army. Ware was twice mentioned in despatches, and ended the war as a Major General. From the outset he had been anxious that the spirit of Imperial co-operation, so evident in the war effort should be reflected in his work. This multinational aspect was clearly recognised by the Imperial War Conference and in May 1917 the Imperial War Graves Commission was established with the Prince of Wales as its President and Ware as Vice-Chairman, a post he would hold until his retirement in 1948. As early as 1916 Ware arranged for advice on the horticultural treatment of cemeteries to be provided by the Royal Botanical Gardens at Kew, and under his leadership the most distinguished British architects of the day were engaged to design the war cemeteries and memorials on the Western Front and elsewhere. He was indefatigable in his dealings with foreign governments in obtaining formal agreements to secure recognition of the Commission's duties and to facilitate its work. At the same time he shaped the Commission's organisation to meet efficiently the urgent demands of constructing and maintaining the cemeteries and memorials, of compiling records of all those killed, of publishing registers of those commemorated and of responding to requests for information from relatives. Upon the death of Rudyard Kipling in 1936, Ware deployed his not inconsiderable diplomatic skills to persuade the war poet Edmund Blunden to replace him as the Commission's literary adviser. In 1937 Ware published *The Immortal Heritage*, an account of the work of the Commission during and following the Great War. The outbreak of the Second World War in 1939 saw Ware return to the War Office as Director of Graves Registration and Enquiries, whilst at the same time continuing his duties as Vice-Chairman of the Commission. 'He was appointed CMG in 1917, CB in 1919, KBE in 1920 and KCVO in 1922. He was a chevalier and later a grand officer of the Legion of Honour, and held the Croix de Guerre; he was also a Commander of the Order of the Crown of Belgium, and an honorary LL D (1929) of the University of Aberdeen.'[38]

The 'Great Commemorator' died at home at Amberley in Gloucestershire on 29 April 1949 and is buried there in Holy Trinity Churchyard. His grave is cared for by the Commission and it is marked by a Commission pattern headstone. A tablet was erected to his memory in the Warrior's Chapel at Westminster Abbey and another in Gloucester Cathedral. His monument however, is undeniably the Commission and its works.

---

[38] Dictionary of National Biography 1941-1950.

# PROFESSOR FRANCIS DERWENT WOOD

Francis Derwent Wood was born of Australian and American parentage at Keswick, Cumbria in 1871. He was educated at Lausanne and studied art under Weltring and Götz at the School of Art, Karlsruhe, Germany. In 1887 he arrived at the Royal School of Art, South Kensington and studied under Professor Édouard Lantéri. He then worked as assistant to Professor Alphonse Legros at The Slade (1890-92). He entered the RA Schools in 1894 and became assistant to Sir Thomas Brock. In 1895 he was awarded the RA Gold Medal for his *Daedalus and Icarus*. In 1896 he went to Paris where he gained a *Mention Honourable* at the Salon of 1897 for his group *Maternity*. In 1898 he was one of four sculptors chosen in competition to provide allegorical figures for the pavilions of the Kelvingrove Art Gallery and Museum in Glasgow. He executed *Architecture, Music, Sculpture* and *Painting*. He taught at the Glasgow School of Art from 1897-1905 and was their Visiting Director of Modelling 1898-1900. He worked with Brock on the *Queen Victoria Memorial* Buckingham Palace (1900-1911). In 1910 he was elected ARA. He executed *Psyche* in the collection of the Tate Gallery; *Atalanta* in the collection of the Manchester Art Gallery; *General Wolfe* at Westerham in Kent; *Lord Ripon* in the Spa Gardens at Ripon; *William Pitt* in the National Gallery of Art, Washington DC; *Lord Nunburnholme* at Hull; *Queen Victoria* and *Edward VII* at Patiala, India and *King Edward VII* at Rangoon, Burma. He was famed for his mastery of the female form. 'Wood was gifted with great facility of artistic expression; his work as a sculptor reflects his cultured personality and, as regards style, is perhaps best described as being of a neo-baroque character in its fullness, flexibility, and realism of form. He was an expert at many techniques of craftsmanship and also a draughtsman and water-colour painter of no mean ability.'[39]

During the Great War, Derwent Wood served as an officer in the RAMC and was placed in charge of the department responsible for facial reconstruction. He used his skills as an artist in creating the exquisitely crafted metal masks for soldiers with severe facial disfigurement. He was responsible for modelling the wreaths on the Cenotaph in Whitehall.

In January 1919 Wood became embroiled in controversy when his sculpture *Canada's Golgotha* was exhibited in at the Canadian War Memorials Exhibition at Burlington House. Its appearance resulted in a formal complaint from the German Government, which led to an investigation by the Canadian Judge Advocate General and a formal request from the Canadian Government for its removal. The tale of the crucified Canadian was then categorised as a particularly lurid example of British 'hate propaganda'. 'In April 2001 the *Sunday Express* published an article by journalist Iain Overton which claimed that a Canadian sergeant was crucified near Ypres on April 25 1915, and identified the man as Harry Band of the 48th Canadian Highlanders'.[40] On 12 December 2002 a programme broadcast by Channel 4 Television in the *Secret History* series established that the story was actually true. The sculpture is in the collection of the Canadian War Museum in Ottawa. Derwent Wood also produced the *Ditchingham War Memorial*, in the west end of the nave of St Mary's Church, Ditchingham, Norfolk (1920)[41] and the *Cotton Exchange War Memorial* in Liverpool (1922).

His best-known war memorial was the controversial *Machine Gun Corps Memorial* which took the form of a figure of a 9-foot tall bronze figure of a naked David, leaning on Goliath's sword. It stands at Hyde Park Corner in London. Derwent Wood succeeded Lantéri as Professor of Sculpture at the Royal College of Art in 1918 and was elected RA in 1920. He exhibited at the Royal Society of Arts 1905-1925. He died in London after an operation on 19 February 1926. A copy of his bronze nude *Atalanta* was placed by the Chelsea Art Club on Chelsea Embankment near Albert Bridge and unveiled in 1929. A *Boy David* sculpted by Bainbridge Copnall was placed on Chelsea Embankment as a memorial to Derwent Wood.

---

[39] Dictionary of National Biography 1922-1930.
[40] James Hayward *Myths & Legends of the First World War* (2002).
[41] This brass memorial on a black marble plinth takes the form of a life size soldier in a greatcoat laid out for burial with his head on his pack. Behind, a black marble stele with 30 names and 5 from the Second World War.

# HENRY POOLE

Henry Poole was born in London on 28 January 1873. He attended the RA Schools from 1892 and afterwards trained under Harry Bates and G F Watts. His father had been an architectural carver. Poole won his first major commission in the 1900 Cardiff competition to provide one of the sculpture groups for the scheme designed by Lanchester, Stewart and Rickards. Out of this sprang his friendship with the architect A E Rickards and Poole would profit by it with a series of commissions for architectural sculpture for buildings designed by that practice. In various partnerships they had worked on a succession of similar municipal projects. In 1897 Poole was commissioned to sculpt two caryatids in the New Kent Road for Rotherhithe Public Library (which then occupied space in the old Town Hall). He sculpted the highly impressive decorative naval sculpture ornamenting Deptford Town Hall in London (1902) and the elegant high relief spandrel figures of angels for Methodist Central Hall, Westminster (1905).

In the years 1904-06 in concert with the architect H Fuller Clark, Poole designed the interior of the Black Friar Public House in London. It is London's only Art Nouveau pub and stands on the site of a 13th century Dominican friary. Below an arched mosaic ceiling are such pearls of wisdom as: 'Finery is foolery' and 'Don't advertise, tell a gossip'. The walls, clad in green and red marble, are covered with illustrations of jolly monks and grotesques. Above the fireplace, a large bas-relief bronze depicts frollicking friars singing carols and playing musical instruments. Another titled *Saturday Afternoon* depicts monks gathering grapes and harvesting apples. Poole's attention to detail is outstanding; even the light fittings are of carved wooden monks carrying yokes on their shoulders.

In 1910 Poole carved the Portland stone figure of *Justice* for Bethnal Green Town Hall in Patriot Square. That year King Edward VII died and Bristol's leading citizens established a memorial committee to set up 'a good statue'. Lanchester and Rickards were engaged and Poole sculpted both a fountain and the adjacent statue of the King at Clifton. The fountain arrived first in 1912 and the King's statue was unveiled in 1913. The work was modelled in Poole's Chelsea studio and cast by his founder Alessandro Parlanti. In 1913 Viscount Rhondda, the coal magnate, offered to pay for ten statues of eminent Welshmen in the new City Hall at Cardiff, each statue was to be sculpted by an eminent sculptor, with the intention that the collection should not only commemorate the most famous Welshmen of all time, but also provide examples of the work of leading contemporary British artists. Poole sculpted *Giraldus Cambrensis* in Serravezza marble. In 1916 Poole completed the reliefs on the monument to *Field Marshal Earl Roberts of Kandahar* in Kelvingrove Park, Glasgow which was incomplete, due to Harry Bates' early death. After the Great War, Poole worked with Sir Robert Lorimer on the three naval memorials at the manning ports of Portsmouth, Plymouth and Chatham for the Imperial War Graves Commission. Working with the architect John Campbell, he produced the sculpture for The *Seddon Memorial*, Bolton Street Cemetery, Wellington in New Zealand. The design took the form of a reinforced concrete column faced with Coromandel granite, mounted over a tomb on a square concrete base. Poole sculpted the bronze figure at the top of the column and it was cast by Parlanti. In 1921 he sculpted the *Evesham War Memorial* in Worcestershire. One report read: 'The Tommy is not heroic in the generally accepted sense of the term, but is truly typical of the average British infantryman during the war with a face which still carried the hard-bitten imprint of overseas service. The feature of the figure is its remarkable accuracy with regard to details of military arms and equipment. It is complete even to the cigarette end behind the ear and to the rat-bitten haversack.' He also sculpted the memorials to both William Blake and Anthony van Dyck which may be found in the crypt of St Paul's Cathedral.

Poole was elected MRBS in 1905, ARA 1920, was Master of the Royal Academy Sculpture School 1921-1927, elected FRBS 1923 and RA in 1927. His Diploma Work *Young Pan* may be seen in the Diploma Gallery at Burlington House. Henry Poole died on 15 August 1928.

# ALFRED TURNER

Alfred Turner was born on 28 May 1874, son of the sculptor Charles Edward Halsey-Turner. He entered the Royal Academy Schools in 1894 at the age of twenty, where he won their Gold Medal and Travelling Studentship. Like the vast majority of his contemporaries, he is also known to have studied for a period of time in Paris. Upon returning to England, he worked as assistant in the studio of Harry Bates and taught sculpture at the London County Council Central School of Arts and Crafts at Southampton Row in Holborn (now the Central St Martin's School of Art). He was one of several eminent sculptors who graduated from the City and Guilds South London Technical Art School, Kennington and trained under William Silver Frith (1850-1924), these sculptors often being referred to as: 'The Lambeth Group'. In 1899 Turner married Charlotte Ann Gavin and they had two daughters.

His *Memorial to John Constable RA* may be seen in St. Paul's Cathedral, London. His best-known work in London is the sculpture he executed for the Old Bailey.

Among his public works are his seated *Memorial to Queen Victoria* cast by his founder Alessandro Parlanti. 'The statue was unveiled outside the Town Hall, Delhi, by the Lieutenant-Governor of the Punjab on 26 December 1902. Turner exhibited a bronze statuette of the statue at the Royal Academy in 1903. On 4 February 1905 the crown and the figures of *Justice* and *Peace* were removed by vandals. Today the statue is at the College of Art, Tilak Marg, New Delhi.'[42] Another copy of the statue was produced for North Shields, resulting in a significant saving to the municipal commissioning committee. At a cost of some £1,000 a further replica of the statue was despatched to Tynemouth in 1902 where it was unveiled by the Mayor on 25 October. The records of North Tyneside Council indicate that heavy staining of the stone pedestal by leaching from the bronze was causing concern to them as early as 1909. It is also apparent from the one-sided correspondence in their possession that the sculptor by that point was not answering their letters. Turner's portrait statue of *Queen Victoria* ornamented by the figures of a mother and her children and a Sheffield workman was originally erected in 1905 at Fargate, Sheffield, but may now be found in that city's Endcliffe Park. Website at www.public-art.shu.ac.uk/sheffield/tur79im.html

Turner sculpted the *King Edward VII Memorial* at Lyallpur in India and was one of the ten eminent sculptors controversially selected without competition by the Royal Society of British Sculptors to sculpt the statues in Cardiff's new City Hall and in the period 1910-1916 he sculpted in Serravezza marble the statue of *Owain Glyndwr*. An unintended consequence of the decision of the Royal Society of British Sculptors to select the sculptors without competition was uproar in their affairs. After the Great War, Turner sculpted the war memorials at Fulham, Radyr, Kingsthorp and Northampton. His *Victoria College War Memorial* on Jersey (1924) took the form of a life-size bronze heroic Sir Galahad on an 8 foot granite pedestal commemorating the 127 Old Victorians killed in the war and was exhibited at the RA. In 1926 Turner was selected by Sir Herbert Baker to execute the remarkable *Castor, Pollux* and *Horse* sculptures for the South African War Memorial at Delville Wood in France. This commission led to further South African work and he also carried out sculpture on the war memorials at Cape Town and Pretoria. He sculpted the *Memorial to John Constable* in the crypt of St Paul's Cathedral, London. Turner's graceful marble statue *Psyche* was purchased in 1921 by the President and Council of the Royal Academy under the terms of the Chantrey Bequest and may be seen in The Tate Gallery. In 1936 his sculpted group *The Hand* was also purchased by the administrators of the Chantrey Bequest. The sculpted head of his daughter *Billie* was exhibited at the RA in 1937.

Turner was elected MRBS in 1905, ARA in 1922, FRBS 1923 and RA in 1931. A resident of Fulham in London, he was a popular member of the Chelsea Arts Club. His bronze sculpture *Dreams of Youth* (1932) may be seen in the Diploma Gallery of the Royal Academy. He died aged 66 on 18 March 1940.

---

[42] Mary Ann Steggles *Statues of the Raj*.

# CHARLES HOLDEN

Charles Henry Holden was born 12 May 1875 at Great Lever, Bolton, Lancashire. He was the youngest of five children of Joseph Holden and his wife Ellen Bolton. His father was bankrupted when he was eight and, shortly after, his mother died. He was educated at the village school and then apprenticed to E W Leeson, a Manchester architect. He attended classes at the School of Art and Manchester Technical College. There he made rapid progress and gained first place in the honours examination in construction and design. At that point he was put in charge of the class. Leaving Manchester, he worked briefly for Jonathan Simpson in Bolton before going to London to work for C R Ashbee, who also taught Sir Frank Baines his trade. Shortly thereafter, in 1899, he joined the practice of Percy Adams who decided that Holden should be given a chance to show what he could do. There followed a series of commissions which included: Belgrave Hospital, Kennington (1903); the Law Society in Chancery Lane (1904); the Seamen's Hospital Constantinople; the Women's Hospital, Soho; Edward VII Sanatorium, Midhurst; the Royal Northern Hospital; Tunbridge Wells Hospital and the Bristol Public Library (1905). In 1907 Adams offered him a partnership which he accepted and he went on to design the British Medical Association (now Zimbabwe House) in The Strand, the Bristol Royal Infirmary, New College Oxford, Clifton College, Bristol, the Institution of Electrical Engineers at the foot of Savoy Hill and St Luke's Hospital, Malta. In 1913 Lionel Pearson became a partner. In the Great War Holden served in the London Ambulance Brigade. He joined the Directorate of Graves Registration and Enquiries in 1917. In 1920 he was appointed a Principal Architect of the Imperial War Graves Commission in France. The non-smoking, non-drinking, vegetarian Holden is without doubt the most fascinating of all the Commission's architects and is officially credited with designing 67 of their cemeteries including Corbie, Passchendaele and Louvencourt, but probably designed many more. The architecture critic Gavin Stamp wrote in *Silent Cities*: 'Holden's designs are distinguished by a stripped-down neo-classicism of great power which was sometimes "almost cruelly severe" as well as very military in character'. Holden left the Commission in March 1928. He then designed the Walmer and Deal Memorial Hospital and the Memorial Gateway for Clifton College. Frank Pick commissioned him to design the façade for Bond Street Tube Station in London. Holden then spent fifteen happy years designing stations for the London Underground, He also designed their HQ at 55 Broadway in London (1927-29) and his solution for this problematic diamond-shaped site earned him the London Architecture Medal in 1929. In 1932 he designed the Portland stone-clad London University Senate House, at Malet Street (London's first skyscraper). Unlike Baker and Lutyens, the vast majority of Holden's work was in UK and his buildings displayed the work of the most eminent British sculptors of his day including that of Eric Gill, Jacob Epstein and Henry Moore. During the Second World War Holden turned his attention to town planning; he also advised the Dean and Chapter of St Paul's Cathedral and the University of Edinburgh. In 1947 he was appointed by London County Council as an architectural and planning consultant for the redevelopment of the South Bank of the Thames. That same year he prepared with Professor William Holford[43] a plan for the City of London, which was incorporated into the *County of London Development Plan* (1951). Holden was elected ARIBA in 1906, FRIBA in 1921, Vice-President in 1935-37 and in 1936 was awarded the Royal Gold Medal of the RIBA. He served on the Royal Fine Art Commission from 1933-1937. Remarkably, Holden declined offers of a knighthood in both 1944 and 1951, as he firmly believed to accept would alienate him from ordinary people. He left his mark on London in a way that no other architect had done since Christopher Wren. A good indication of the priorities of our own age may be taken from the fact that whilst Wren designed St Paul's Cathedral and fifty churches, Holden designed 55 Broadway and 50 tube stations. An etching of him by Francis Dodd hangs in the National Portrait Gallery. He died at home at Harmer Green, Welwyn, Herts on 1 May 1960.

---

[43] William Holford (1907-1975) Born South Africa, Rome Scholar, civic designer, PRIBA, later Lord Holford.

## SIR WILLIAM REID DICK

William Reid Dick was born in Glasgow on 13 January 1879. He was educated at the Glasgow School of Art and exhibited at the RA from 1905 onwards. During the Great War he saw active service with the British Army in both France and Palestine. He sculpted the war memorials at both Rickmansworth and Bushey, the lion on the Menin Gate and the eagle atop Blomfield's pylon of the *RAF Memorial* on Victoria Embankment. He designed the *Kitchener Memorial Chapel* at St Paul's Cathedral, London. His prolific output included the statue *Sir John Soane* for the Bank of England, the *Viscount Leverhulme Memorial* (1930) at Port Sunlight, Cheshire and the bronze portrait statue *King George V* for Howard Davis Park, Jersey (inaugurated 2 October 1939). He sculpted the bust of *Canon Alexander* in St Paul's Cathedral in London; the large stone equestrian groups on Unilever House, Blackfriars; the equestrian statue *Lady Godiva* (1949) at Coventry; *Lord Irwin* in Delhi; *Augustus at Nimes* in the Art Gallery of New South Wales, Australia; the stone figures on the New Government Buildings, Edinburgh and the busts of *Sir Edwin Lutyens* and *Isaac Wolfson*. His *George V* stands outside the House of Lords, Westminster, his *Boy with Frog* fountain may be found in Regents Park, London and his bust of *Viscount Bryce* is in Washington, the *Earl of Chatham* in Pittsburg, that of *Dr Parkinson* at Leeds University and those of *Sir Reginald Blomfield* and *Lord Duveen* in the National Portrait Gallery. His statue *King George V* (1953) stands in Parliament Square, Canberra, Australia. The commission for this 14 ft tall, massive three and a half ton statue was originally given to G Raynor Hoff and when he died to J E Moorfield. The commission eventually arrived on Reid Dick's desk in 1951. The statue was so large it had to be let into a pit excavated from the floor of the Morris Singer foundry in Dorset Road, Lambeth. His imposing *Roosevelt Memorial* stands in Grosvenor Square, London. It was inaugurated on 12 April 1948, (a copy was sent to America in 1950). In 1935 he was commissioned to produce two statues in honour of the *Viceroy Lord Willingdon* - 'Dick exhibited a bronze bust at the 1935 exhibition of the Royal Academy and his model for the statue the following year in 1936. The figure wearing viceregal robes and the Order of the Star of India, was originally erected in the grounds of the Viceroy's house. It was removed from this site in the 1980s and placed in the Coronation Durbar Grounds in Old Delhi. Today, the figure is part of a small group, surviving the move to the garden area near the Civil Lines with the pedestal lost. Dick completed a replica of the statue for New Delhi and in bronze for the city of Madras where the statue was originally erected outside the entrance to the Gymkhana Club, the Island. Today, the figure, minus its original pedestal may be found wrapped in a tarpaulin in a storage shed at the Fort Museum in Madras'.[44] In 2004 Reid Dick's graffiti-covered statue of *Doctor David Livingstone* at Victoria Falls was the subject of an international dispute between Zimbabwe and Zambia.[45] The records of Morris Singer show that a copy of it was cast for a Hollywood studio in 1960. He sculpted the tombs of *King George V* and *Queen Mary* in St George's Chapel, Windsor and their memorials in Sandringham church, also the *King George VI Memorial* in the same church. He produced portrait busts in bronze of *George VI* (1942), *Churchill* (1943), *Queen Elizabeth* (exhibited at the Royal Academy 1946) and *Princess Elizabeth* (1947). Reid Dick was elected MRBS 1915, ARA 1921, FRBS 1923, RA 1928, Member RFAC 1928 and PRBS 1933-38. He was a Trustee of the Tate Gallery 1934-1941 and knighted in 1935. From 1938-52 he was Sculptor to King George VI. He was presented with the Albert Medal of the Royal Society of Arts by Princess Elizabeth in 1948. In 1952 he was appointed Queen's Sculptor in Ordinary for Scotland. He was both a Trustee of the Royal Academy and a Member of the Royal Mint Advisory Committee. He died on 1 October 1961 and the memorial to his memory may be found in the crypt of St Paul's Cathedral.

---

[44] Mary Ann Steggles *Statues of the Raj*.
[45] Dr Livingstone's statue stands overlooking the Devil's Cataract, Zimbabwe. It was unveiled by Livingstone's nephew U H Moffat, the former Premier of Southern Rhodesia on 1 August 1934.

## SIR JACOB EPSTEIN

Jacob Epstein was born of Russian-Polish parentage at Hester Street on New York's Lower East Side on 10 November 1880. He studied art there as a teenager, sketching the city and joined The Art Students' League of New York in 1900. In the years 1901-02 he worked in a bronze foundry by day, studying drawing and sculptural modelling at night. Moving to Europe in 1902, he studied in Paris at the Académie Julian and the École des Beaux-Arts where he fell under the spell of Rodin. In 1905 he moved to London, became a fixture on the Bohemian scene and took his place in the Domino Room alongside Eddie Marsh, Wyndham Lewis, Stanley Spencer and W B Yeats. He took out British nationality in 1910.

As a sculptor Epstein worked in a wide variety of media and produced a substantial body of work. He was a pioneer of modern sculpture, often producing controversial works that challenged conventions of what was and was not appropriate for public depiction and his sculpture is distinguished by a vigorous rough-hewn realism. In his enthusiasm for his art, Epstein would sculpt friends, casual acquaintances and even passers-by dragged off the street into his studio. His first major commission was the 18 figures he produced in 1907-08 for the exterior of Charles Holden's British Medical Association Building in The Strand (now Zimbabwe House). The English were not ready for him and his work was condemned as obscene. The figures were mutilated in 1937 having become: 'a danger to the public'. Despite the critical acclaim for his sculpture *The Tin Hat* (1916), Epstein was blocked from obtaining war memorial commissions by senior figures in the arts establishment such as Sir George Frampton in consequence of which, his only war memorial would be the *Trades Unions Congress War Memorial* (1958) which stands on the portico of Transport House, HQ of the TGWU at Bloomsbury in London. During the Great War Epstein was conscripted into the 38th Battalion of the Royal Fusiliers and discharged in 1918 without having left the UK. Unsurprisingly, he always felt an outsider in his adopted country, being continually subject to vilification for pushing the boundaries of public taste. He produced portrait sculptures of the *Admiral Lord Fisher, the Duke of Marlborough, Winston Churchill, Paul Robeson, George Bernard Shaw, Jawaharlal Nehru, Albert Einstein* and *Joseph Conrad*. Notable among his commissions were: his extraordinary Assyrian tomb of Oscar Wilde (1912) at Père Lachaise Cemetery, Paris; his marble *Venus* (1917) may be seen in the Yale Center for British Art, New Haven, Connecticut and his bronze *Christ* (1919) at Wheathampstead, England. He sculpted the W H Hudson Memorial *Rima* figure (1923) in Hyde Park, London. His *Night and Day* (1928-29) may be seen on Holden's London Underground Headquarters at 55 Broadway, London. His *Jacob and the Angel* (1940) is in the Tate Gallery Collection - and was originally controversially 'anatomical'. His *Lazarus* (1947) is at New College, Oxford and his *Madonna and Child* (1950) is in the Convent of the Holy Child Jesus, London. In 1954 he was knighted. Throughout his career he challenged and antagonized both public opinion and the artistic establishment. The people of Liverpool were said to have nick-named his nude male sculpture *The Spirit of Youth* (1956) which stands over the main entrance of the John Lewis Department Store there 'Swinging Dick' and such factors undoubtedly focussed a disproportionate amount of attention on certain aspects of Epstein's career and overshadowed his achievements. His 15 foot tall aluminium *Christ in Majesty* (1957) may be seen at Llandaff Cathedral. His remarkable 19 foot tall, 4 ton *St Michael and the Devil* (1958) may be seen on the exterior of the Coventry's new cathedral. One of his last commissions was *HRH Princess Margaret* (1959) at University College, North Staffordshire (now Keele University).

On 19 August 1959 he was working in his studio at Hyde Park Gate on the *Pan Group* for Bowater House, Knightsbridge. He telephoned Morris Singer to tell them it was ready for collection, went up to bed and passed away in his sleep. Epstein lived in a long-term relationship with Kathleen Garman, whom he married in 1955. The Garman Ryan Collection, including several of Epstein's works was donated by his widow to the people of Walsall in 1973 and is on display in the New Art Gallery, Walsall.

# ERIC GILL

Eric Gill was born in Brighton in 1882, the son of a non-conformist minister. He spent two years at an art school in Chichester and was then apprenticed to an architect in London. He was smitten by the world of calligraphy, which he entered by attending classes given by Edward Johnston. He was strongly influenced by Johnston's dedicated approach to work, soon left his architectural apprenticeship and set up as a self-employed letter carver and signwriter. By 1906 he was married and moved with his wife and family to Ditchling in Sussex. Johnston moved to the village a few years later. Gill began to carve sculpture, undertook several large commissions and in 1913 was received into the Roman Catholic Church. A highly complex individual, Gill's faith influenced both his sculpture and writings and he became a Dominican lay tertiary. Unfortunately, his unconventional sexual attitudes ensured that he was anything but a model Christian. As he took on more work, apprentices and other staff began to join him at Ditchling. Gill first met Stanley Morison in about 1914 and as both were Catholic converts they had much in common. Gill executed a number of wood engravings for the publisher Burns & Oates, for whom Morison worked. Gill wrote prodigiously on his favourite topics: social reform; the integration of the body and spirit; the evils of industrialisation; and the importance of the working man. He designed his first typeface, *Perpetua* for Morison who pestered him for years on the subject. There followed: *Gill Floriated Capitals, Gill Sans, Gill Sans Light Shadowed, Gill Sans Shadowed, Joanna* and *Jubilee*. Of all the typefaces he designed *Gill Sans* is his most famous. It is a clear modern type and it became the typeface of choice for Britain's railways, appearing on their signs, engine plates, and timetables. Gill was together with G K Chesterton, Hilaire Belloc and Father Vincent McNabb, OP one of the founders of the 'Distributist Movement' - an economic and social theory based on Catholic social teaching, regarded as a 'Third Way' between Capitalism and Socialism. A notion of Gill's spirituality may be taken from his aphorism: 'Without philosophy man cannot know what he makes; without religion he cannot know why.' He sculpted the *Stations of the Cross* for Westminster Cathedral (1914-1919) and *Prospero* and *Ariel* for the BBC's Broadcasting House (1932-34). In the period 1918-20 he carved the Portland stone *Chirk War Memorial* at Wrexham, North Wales for Lord Howard de Walden. This simple tapered square obelisk of Portland stone is set on a round nosed low step, with the riser curved back. The top of the obelisk is gabled at 45 degrees on each angle. On the south face is a bas-relief hunched figure of a great-coated and helmeted soldier, holding a rifle. The memorial is one of the most highly original works of its kind dating from the Great War period. In 1920 he executed the lettering on the Angmering War Memorial in Sussex. In 1923 the *Daily Herald* newspaper commissioned Gill to design the *Order of Industrial Heroism*, to be awarded to workers who had saved their fellow workers from danger or death during the accidents that were all too frequent in industry at that time. The award, popularly known as the 'Workers VC' was awarded for the highest levels of civilian bravery with many of the awards being granted posthumously. In many cases the recipients also received awards from the Crown, such as the George Cross, George Medal, Sea Gallantry Medal, British Empire Medal as well as awards by the Royal Humane Society, Liverpool Shipwreck and Humane Society and the Society for the Protection of Life from Fire. Each medal came with a certificate and in all a total of 440 were awarded by the newspaper. Gill died from lung cancer at the age of 58 in 1940 at Uxbridge in Middlesex. By the time of his death, he was famous not only as an artist and craftsman but as a social reformer with views on anything and everything, from the wearing of clothes, to contraception and the sacredness of work. He described himself on his gravestone as 'a stone carver'. His autobiography was published in December 1940, one month after his death and was reprinted eleven times during the Second World War. His Hoptonwood stone torso *Mankind* (1928) may be seen in the Tate Gallery and his Portland stone sculpture *Mother and Child* (1910) in the National Museum & Gallery of Wales, Cardiff. The Eric Gill Collection may be found at the University of Waterloo, Belgium.

## COLONEL CART DE LAFONTAINE

Henri Philip Cart de Lafontaine was born in Switzerland on 30 March 1884. He was educated privately in Italy, France and Switzerland. He was articled to the architect Sir Guy Dawber (1861-1938) and completed his studies at the École des Beaux-Arts in Paris. In 1911 he set up his own architectural practice in London. Very early in his career, de Lafontaine was commissioned to design the Napoleonic Eagle at Norman Cross in Cambridgeshire. It was erected in 1914 by the Entente Cordiale Society to commemorate the 1,770 French prisoners of war who died whilst imprisoned in the Norman Cross Prison Depot during the long years of the Napoleonic Wars. At its peak, the prison held 7,000 French prisoners of war. The *Entente Cordiale* between France and Great Britain was signed on 8 April 1904. The Norman Cross Eagle was the memorial to their captivity. In 1990 the memorial was vandalised and the eagle stolen. The restored memorial with a new eagle sculpted by John Doubleday (born 1947) was inaugurated by the Duke of Wellington on 2 April 2005.

On the outbreak of the Great War, de Lafontaine served in the 4th Battalion of the City of London Regiment (Royal Fusiliers) and was commissioned Second Lieutenant. In the period 1914-17 he served in both Malta, on the Western Front in France and was mentioned in despatches. In 1918 he was appointed Assistant Director of the Graves Registration and Enquiries at GHQ France and promoted Lieutenant Colonel. He was appointed Chief Inspector of Works for the Imperial War Graves Commission on 25 July 1919. He left the Commission on 29 February 1920, was appointed OBE and awarded the Territorial Decoration. He resumed his calling as architect and town planning consultant in 1923 and was later entrusted by the IWGC with the task of designing the memorial plaques which Lord Midleton's Battlefield Memorials Committee proposed to erect in the great cathedrals and churches of France and Belgium. An accomplished polyglot, de Lafontaine was also responsible for negotiating with the French and Belgian ecclesiastical authorities. 'In his final drawings the Royal Arms and those of India and the Dominions surrounded by an inscription in French and English which told of Britain's million dead. The tablets cast in gesso, were gilded and coloured, and set into a surround of stone. They were eventually placed in over thirty French and Belgian cathedrals, including that of Notre Dame in Paris, and have served to this day to remind Frenchmen of British losses in the defence of France.'[46]

In 1926 de Lafontaine was appointed Member of the Council of the Royal Institute of British Architects. In the period 1928-34 he served as Town Planning Adviser to Southampton Corporation. In 1935 he represented His Majesty's Government at the International Congress of Architects in Rome. In 1937 he was appointed Master of the Company of Gold and Silver Wyre Drawers. He was appointed a Member of the Research and Planning Group of the Town Planning Institute in 1940.

In 1947 he was appointed Chairman of the Council of the Royal Drawing Society and Member of the Council of the Town Planning Institute. In 1948 he was appointed President of the Franco-British Union of Architects and was for some years its Secretary General. In 1949 he was appointed Member of the Council of the International Union of Architects and was President of the Town Planning Institute 1950-51. 'He served on several committees engaged on the regulations of international architectural competitions, and was a member of the council of the RIBA 1926-34.'[47] In 1953 he was appointed President of the Old Comrades Association of the Imperial War Graves Commission. That same year he was also responsible for the highly original design of the large circular brass and copper war memorial commemorating the members of the staff of the proprietors of Hays Wharf, London Bridge. Newly restored to the reopened Hay's Wharf, the memorial may be seen on the walkway by the River Thames. Aged 78, Colonel de Lafontaine died suddenly at the Broadway Private Hotel, Dorset Square in London on 2 February 1963.

---

[46] Philip Longworth *The Unending Vigil*.
[47] *The Builder* 15 February 1963.

# CHARLES SARGEANT JAGGER

Charles Sargeant Jagger was born at Kilnhurst, Yorkshire on 17 December 1885. His father was a colliery manager. He was educated at Kilnhurst National School and the Middle Class School, Sheffield. Aged 14 he started work with Messrs Mappin & Webb where he learnt engraving. At the same time, he studied modelling and metal engraving at the Sheffield School of Art and taught drawing there in the evenings. In 1903 he won a scholarship to the Royal College of Art, South Kensington. He became both pupil and assistant to Professor Édouard Lantéri. A travelling bursary enabled him to travel to both Rome and Venice. 'In 1914 he won the Rome scholarship in sculpture but was prevented from taking it up'.[48] Upon the outbreak of the Great War in common with many other artistic types, Jagger joined the Artists Rifles. He was commissioned into the Worcestershire Regiment in 1915. He served at Gallipoli, transferred to their second battalion and then served in France and Flanders. He was wounded three times and awarded the MC. After the war he resumed his calling and was in considerable demand to sculpt war memorials. 'He began work on *No Man's Land* 1919-1920; London, Tate while still convalescing from war wounds'.[49] In the immediate post-war period he carried out a substantial body of work for the cemeteries of the Imperial War Graves Commission on the Western Front. He sculpted the *Anglo-Belgian War Memorial* at Rue des Quatre Bras, Brussels and the *Great Western Railway War Memorial* at Paddington station in London. Jagger was also responsible for the sculpture on the *Royal Artillery War Memorial* at Hyde Park Corner in London (1925). The grim realism of this work was taken directly from his own experience of war. It caused critical controversy, but the Royal Regiment of Artillery was delighted with the result, has always taken great pride in their memorial and it remains the focus of their Act of Remembrance on Remembrance Sunday. In 1926 Jagger was awarded the Gold Medal of the RBS for the work. Subsequently, Father Stephen Bedale, Prior of the Society of the Sacred Mission saw the memorial from the top of a bus at Hyde Park Corner and realised he had found the sculptor who would produce *The Kelham Rood*. Originally commissioned in wood, Jagger's generosity ensured that this powerful work would consist of three life-size bronze figures: *Christ Crucified; the Virgin Mary* and *St John the Evangelist*. Although not a religious man, nor given to flights of fancy, Jagger told Father Bedale that he was visited in his studio by Jesus Christ whilst engaged on this work.[50] In the period 1927-1934 Jagger worked with Lutyens on New Delhi and produced busts and full-sized statues of *Lord Harding* (Viceroy 1912-16) and *Lord Reading* (Viceroy 1921-26). He also sculpted the *Elephants* for the corners of the Rashtrapati Bhavan. Collaborating with Lutyens he produced the extraordinary 18 foot tall marble figure of *King George V* on a pedestal base some 43 foot 6 ins tall adjacent to the All India Memorial Arch in New Delhi, (now in the Coronation Durbar Grounds in the Civil Lines, Old Delhi). 'Jagger was skilled at persuading people to let him do what he wanted (the Royal Artillery War Commemoration Fund minutes reveal instances of this). The fact that many of his patrons also became his friends must have given him much greater flexibility'.[51] In 1931-2 he produced *Sir Ernest Shackleton* for the Royal Geographical Society. In 1932 he was appointed to the Royal Mint Advisory Committee on Coins, Medals, Seals and Decorations. In 1933 he produced a maquette of *Christ the King* for Lutyens' Roman Catholic Cathedral in Liverpool, which was never completed. Jagger was elected MRBS 1921, FRBS 1923 and ARA in 1926. In 1933 the RBS awarded him their Gold Medal again for the stone groups he sculpted for Imperial Chemical House at Millbank. His early death from a heart condition on 16 November 1934 was ascribed to a combination of overwork and his war wounds. An English Heritage Blue Plaque marks his house at 67 Albert Bridge Road, Battersea, London.

---

[48] *Dictionary of National Biography* 1931-1940 Oxford University Press.
[49] *Grove Dictionary of Art.*
[50] *SSM Quarterly* March 1957.
[51] Ann Compton *War and Peace Sculpture* Imperial War Museum 1985.

# WILIAM McMILLAN

William McMillan was born at Aberdeen on 31 August 1887. He studied at Gray's School of Art, Aberdeen and the Royal College of Art between 1908 and 1912 and at the Royal Academy Schools. He also studied in Florence. He served in the Great War and his experience of trench warfare at its worst marked him for life. As a sculptor, McMillan was distinguished by his wide range of subjects, from war memorials (Aberdeen and Manchester, 1919) to medals, curiosity about materials and his marked decorative ability. The last was amply illustrated in his two bronze groups of *Nereid* and *Triton* with dolphins for the *Earl Beatty Memorial Fountain*, Trafalgar Square (1948), which was designed by Sir Edwin Lutyens and exhibited at Burlington House in 1940. He also sculpted the bust *Earl Beatty* (1948) inset on the north wall there. His white marble *Syrinx* (1925) is in Glasgow Art Gallery and Museum. In 1938 he completed the bronze portrait statue *King George V* for Calcutta. Originally positioned opposite the Outram Ghat in Calcutta, it is now at the front entrance of the Temple of Fame at Barrackpore. His *Earl Haig* (1932) may be seen at Clifton College, Bristol. His statue of *King George VI* (1954) in his Garter robes stands in Carlton Gardens, London. His diminutive *Sir Walter Raleigh* (1959) originally stood on Raleigh Green in Whitehall, but has since been rusticated to Greenwich, where it stands in the grounds of the former Royal Naval College. Cast by Morris Singer, his impressive life-size figurative sculpture of *Viscount Trenchard* (1961) stands on Victoria Embankment in London. Other portrait statues included *Goodenough* (1936) in Mecklenburgh Square, London; *Captain Thomas Coram* (1963) of Foundling Hospital fame in Brunswick Square, London; *Sir John Alcock* and *Sir Arthur Brown* at Heathrow were sculpted in 1966 and his *Charles Rolls* and *Henry Royce* (1978) may be seen at the headquarters of Rolls Royce at 65 Buckingham Gate, London. His bronze statue *JMW Turner* is on the staircase of the Royal Academy at Burlington House and his remarkable lightning conductor on the roof of Kensington Town Hall takes the form of a golden figure standing on one foot (1960).

    McMillan sculpted *The Memorial Tablet to Sir Aston Webb* in the Crypt of St. Paul's Cathedral. Among his portrait busts those of *Charles Cundall RA; A R Thompson RA; Vincent Harris RA, FRIBA* and his friend *Sir Edward Maufe RA, FRIBA* were particularly successful. But McMillan's personal qualities, taste and poetical invention, were best seen in the imaginative and decorative pieces in various materials with which year by year he charmed visitors to the RA. Good examples of his art are: *Garden Decoration in Portland Stone* representing *Pan and a Nymph with Frisky Kids* (1926); statuette-group *Two Women with Fruit* in green slate (1927); *Sun and Moon Fountain* - in collaboration with Lutyens and *Mother and Child* (1928); *Swans* a group in alabaster (1930); *The Birth of Venus* in Portland stone which was purchased by the Chantrey Bequest in 1931 and *Night* a group in South African marble (1932). His *Goetze Memorial Fountain* (1950) with triton and dryads may be seen in Regents Park. McMillan found considerable relaxation with water colours and pastels and many of his sketches were exhibited at the RA. In association with his friends Vincent Harris and Sir Edward Maufe, much of his work was of an architectural nature and may be seen on public buildings throughout the Britain. Aberdeen, the city of his birth, elected McMillan as one of its Freemen and its University conferred upon him the honorary Degree of Doctor of Law. In retirement McMillan was elected an Honorary Life Member of the Chelsea Arts Club, where he lunched almost daily until his death. In his younger days, he played a prominent part in the organization of the Chelsea Arts Ball at the Royal Albert Hall. In 1966 McMillan gave up his Chelsea studio and retired from the active exercise of his profession, but continued to paint for pleasure. He was elected ARA in 1925, ARBS in 1927, FRBS 1932 and RA in 1933. In the period 1929-40 he was Master of the Royal Academy Sculpture School. He was elected HRBS in 1964. A few days after his 90th birthday in 1977, McMillan travelled to his Chelsea bank from his home at Richmond in Surrey, was mugged and found in the street badly injured minus his wallet. He died shortly thereafter in hospital.

# PROFESSOR GILBERT LEDWARD

Gilbert Ledward was born on 23 January 1888 at Chelsea in London. He was educated at St Mark's College, Chelsea and then studied sculpture at the Royal College of Art under Professor Édouard Lantéri. Ledward was the first artist to win a scholarship in sculpture to the British School at Rome and during the Great War he served as an officer in the Royal Regiment of Artillery.

Although little-known to our own age, Ledward was much sought after as a sculptor of war memorials after the Great War and carried out commissions in both stone and bronze. In partnership with H Chalton Bradshaw he executed the sculpture on the *Household Division Memorial* on Horse Guards Parade Ground (1922-25). Again with Bradshaw, he carried out the sculpture for both the Malvern and Fordham war memorials. In the years 1926-29 he executed the sculpture on the *Ploegsteert Memorial to the Missing* in Belgium for the IWGC. A particularly impressive example of Ledward's art can be found on the plinth of the obelisk at Blackpool North, Lancashire. Situated in a landscaped sunken basin, it has clustered about it three miniature Stones of Sacrifice, with the names of Blackpool's fallen inscribed on raised bronze tablets. The bronze relief panels were executed by Ledward in 1923. For reasons best known to itself Blackpool Borough Council insist on calling this memorial 'The Cenotaph'. Ledward's sculpture *Awakening* stands on Chelsea Embankment and was cast by the Morris Singer Foundry in 1923. During the 1930s he turned from the established practice of modelling in clay to stone carving. While other artists pioneered the development of modern sculpture, Ledward's work remained obstinately figurative. In 1934 he co-founded the firm Sculptured Memorials and Headstones in an attempt to promote carving by regional artists in native stone. Again working in partnership with Bradshaw he executed the coat of arms on the portal of the tunnel at Penmaenmawr in North Wales (opened 1935). In the years 1936-38 he carried out the sculpture on the exterior of the remarkable Adelphi Building in John Adam Street, London, which in comparison to its surroundings, looks as fresh and striking today as it did in 1938. After the Second World War he was commissioned to undertake three war memorials in the cloister of Westminster Abbey. These were: *The Commando Memorial* (1947): unveiled by Winston Churchill, the original plaster cast of this memorial is in the collection of the National Army Museum at Chelsea; *The Submarine Service* (1948) and *The Airborne Services Memorial* (1948) which was also unveiled by Churchill. He also executed the sculpture in Reichswald Forest War Cemetery in Germany for the IWGC. Ledward designed the fountains in Sloane Square (1952-53) and sculpted the *Cortauld Family Symbols* on the loggia at the rear of Eltham Palace. Cast by Morris Singer, his *King George V* was all but completed in 1939, but did not make the journey out to Hong Kong until 1946. His sculptures of *St Nicholas* (1952) and *St Christopher* (1955) may be seen in the Hospital for Sick Children at Great Ormond Street, London. His sculpted group *The Seer* (1957) is outside Mercury House, Knightsbridge, London. All British monarchs possess a Great Seal of the Realm for official purposes and Queen Elizabeth II has had two during her reign. The first *Great Seal of Queen Elizabeth II* was designed by Ledward and taken into service in 1953. Its replacement designed by James Butler was taken into use in 2001. Artistically, Ledward was one of the most highly skilled sculptors involved in the memorialisation process and his work was consistently of the highest quality. He was an outspoken member of the art establishment and deeply involved in the long-running debate about the place of sculpture in society and the professional standing of the sculptor. In his long and distinguished career, Ledward was a Member of the Council of the British School at Rome 1920, MRBS 1921, FRBS 1923, Professor of Sculpture at the Royal College of Art 1926-29, ARA 1932, RA 1937, a Member of the Advisory Committee of the Royal Mint 1938 and PRBS 1954. He died at home in Pembroke Walk, Kensington on 21 June 1960. In 2003 Ledward's significant contribution to British sculpture received overdue recognition with the publication of Dr Catherine Moriarty's book *The Sculpture of Gilbert Ledward*.

# ERIC KENNINGTON

Eric Henri Kennington was born in Chelsea on 12 March 1888, son of the painter Thomas Benjamin Kennington. He was educated at St Paul's School, the Lambeth School of Art and the City and Guilds School, Kennington. He commenced his artistic career as painter, being strongly influenced by the Italian primitives and Sandro Botticelli. His *Costermongers* (1913) was purchased by Sir William Nicholson and presented to the Musée de Luxembourg, Paris. 'At the outbreak of the First World War, Kennington volunteered, on 6 August 1914, to serve as a private in the 13th (Territorial) Battalion, the London Regiment colloquially known as the 'The Kensingtons'. Private No. 1799 Kennington first entered front line trenches in the valley of the River Lys in north-eastern France, on 21 November 1914. He spent just over two months at the front, frequently under fire from German snipers, trench mortars and artillery. On 19 January he was wounded and evacuated to a hospital in England.'[52] His left foot was saved, but he lost a toe. He was discharged from the army in June 1915. In April 1916 he exhibited his painting *The Kensingtons at Laventie: Winter 1914* at the Goupil Galleries and it caused a sensation. In August 1917 he returned to France as a war artist employed by the Department of Information. Lord Tweedsmuir[53] wrote: 'I am very doubtful about Eric Kennington, his whole style of work is utterly remote from and undescriptive of the western front, and is no use for purposes of record. He might just as well paint his pictures at home.' Notwithstanding, Kennington's extraordinary 1920 oil painting *The Conquerors* (295.9 x 242.5 cm) hangs to this day in the Canadian War Museum, Ottawa. Although not formally trained as a sculptor, Kennington also executed some of the most original war memorials produced in both World Wars. His plaster relief *PBI* (Poor Bloody Infantry) is in the Wolfsonian Florida International University, Miami Museum of Modern Art & Design. He was art editor of T E Lawrence's *Seven Pillars of Wisdom* (1926). He was approached by the architects Gordon Holt and Verner Owen Rees to collaborate in their entry for the competition for the IWGC's *Soissons Memorial to the Missing*. The central sculpture of their winning design was executed in 1927-28 from 22 tons of Euville stone in Kennington's trademark totemic style. It commemorated by name the 3,987 men of the British IX and XXII Corps missing in action and was inaugurated on 22 July 1928 by Lieutenant General Sir Alexander Hamilton Gordon. 'In 1939 he made the recumbent effigy of Lawrence for St Martin's Wareham, of which the Tate Gallery and the Aberdeen Art Gallery later acquired versions in *ciment fondu*. Also in the Tate is a bronze head of Lawrence modelled partly from life and partly from drawings; another cast is in the crypt of St Paul's Cathedral.[54] His sculpture *Earth Child* (1936) is in the Tate. He produced the carvings in the School of Hygiene and Tropical Medicine in Gower St, London, the bronze memorial head *Thomas Hardy* (1929) and the carved decorations on the façade of the Shakespeare Memorial Theatre at Stratford on Avon. Kennington was a friend of both Percy Hobart and Basil Liddell Hart, two of the most original military thinkers of the 20th century. In the Second World War Kennington was again employed as a war artist and a substantial quantity of his work is in the collection of the IWM. He produced the books *Drawing the RAF* (1942), *Tanks and Tank Folk* (1943) and illustrated John Brophy's *Britain's Home Guard* (1945). He sculpted the highly unusual *1940*, his personal memorial to 'The Few'. After being installed at Glasgow Airport, it was removed in 1987 on the grounds that it was too heavy for the concourse floor - and to the lasting shame of Paisley Art Gallery, it remains in storage. His plaster maquette of the *Royal Armoured Corps Memorial* (1950) may be seen at the Tank Museum, Bovington. Kennington was elected ARA in 1951 and RA in 1959. After a remarkable career of some half a century, Eric Kennington died at Reading on 13 April 1960 and was buried at Checkendon. A drawing of him by Sir William Rothenstein is in Manchester City Art Gallery.

---

[52] *Sculpture Journal* Vol XI (2004).
[53] John Buchan (1873-1940). 1st Baron Tweedsmuir, author and statesman. Governor General of Canada 1935.
[54] *Dictionary of National Biography*, Oxford University Press 1995.

# ROBERT MORRISON

Robert Warrack Morrison was born in Aberdeen in 1890, the son of a tailor. Like many other stonecutters, he worked as a young man in the granite yards of the United States before the Great War. It was a letter from his old firm, Morren and Co of Holland Street, Aberdeen which recalled him back to his native city from Vermont in April 1920. David Morren Senior recalled a granite wreath which his young cutter had effortlessly turned out in a lunch hour, confirming his belief that he had a craftsman of rare talent on his staff. Not only was Morrison's attention to detail meticulous, but he was an extraordinarily fast worker. Some said he took tremendous risks. Dispensing for instance with the normal procedure of squaring off a block (a week per face, four weeks per block), he knew instinctively the correct depth to cut to without the use of needles, carving the figure of a soldier in six weeks as opposed to the usual six to nine months. A consummate granite craftsman, he was known in the trade as 'the King of the Carvers'. Only in recent years has Morrison won wider recognition for his work. Fred Watson, a lecturer in sculpture has rated him a genius who used: 'complicated and astonishing trickery'. He has also described the detail on Morrison's war memorial at Rhynie in Aberdeenshire as being: 'virtuoso carving from a man who probably had no formal training in freehand sculpture'. The figure he produced for Rhynie was his first, being unveiled on 30 May 1920 just over six weeks after his return from America. (The photograph of this memorial appears at the beginning of the Great War chapter in this study). Further examples of his work in Aberdeenshire included the obelisk at Clatt and the Celtic crosses at Lumsden and Towie. He executed the soldier figures at New Elgin, Moray and Tarland for other companies, the latter bearing such a strong resemblance to the figures at Ballachulish and Glencoe as to suggest that these may be his work too. He produced soldier figures for Kincardine and Deeside, and as his reputation spread he also executed work for Cumberland, Northumberland and parts of Wales. The great period of memorial-carving lasted from 1919 to 1926, ending with the General Strike, after which they became less ornate and more economical in their use of granite. The Celtic cross at High Spen, Tyne and Wear appears to be from the Morren yard, but may not be of sufficient quality to be Morrison's, but the figure at Blaydon, County Durham, may safely be claimed as his, being an exact replica of that at Rhynie. Morrison became manager of Morren and Co in 1927. He died in 1945 at the age of 55, never having recovered from the death of his beloved wife Annie, the mother of his seven children who died in 1930 at the age of 40. The headstone he carved for her grave in Trinity Cemetery, Aberdeen (above) is reckoned among his finest works.[55]

---

[55] Ian Shepherd. *Gordon: An Illustrated Architectural Guide.*

## SIR STANLEY SPENCER

Stanley Spencer was born at Cookham, Berkshire on 30 June 1891, ninth child of Maria and William Spencer, a music teacher. Stanley had a blissfully happy childhood and was educated by his sisters in the potting shed at the bottom of the garden. In the period 1908-12 he attended the Slade School. Among his contemporaries were Mark Gertler, William Roberts, Paul Nash, Dora Carrington and David Bomberg. They nicknamed him: 'Cookham' or 'Our Genius.' One Slade contemporary noted: 'His pictures have that sense of everlastingness, of no beginning and no end, that we get in all masterpieces'.[56] By the time he left the Slade, he was selling his work and had made his modest mark on the art world by the outbreak of the Great War. In 1915 after rudimentary medical training, he enlisted in the RAMC and served at Beaufort War Hospital, Bristol as a ward orderly, washing patients and scrubbing floors. In 1916 he volunteered for overseas service and was posted to the Army of the Orient in Macedonia. In 1917 he transferred to the 7th Battalion of the Royal Berkshire Regiment and saw active service also in Macedonia. Surprisingly, given his diminutive stature and artistic temperament he acquitted himself well, although the story of him 'dressing down' a captain in front of an apoplectic sergeant major and receiving an apology from the officer rings true. In May 1918 out of the blue he received a letter from the War Office requesting him to undertake an artistic commission for the War Artists' Advisory Commission. He arrived home in December 1918 and commenced work. The War Office failed to communicate their instructions to Spencer's regiment, which sent the military police to arrest him for overstaying his leave. The work he eventually produced was titled: *Travoys Arriving with Wounded Soldiers at the Dressing Station, at Smol, Macedonia* for which he was paid £200. He married in 1925. A prolific painter, much of his output was religiously inspired, all of it intensely personal and often it was set in his beloved Cookham. In 1927 he had a one-man exhibition at the Goupil Galleries in Regent Street. This announced in no uncertain terms to both the art world and the British public that Stanley Spencer had indeed arrived. In the period 1927-32 he worked on the Sandham Memorial Chapel at Burghclere and in 1933 arranged for the art dealer Dudley Tooth to handle his affairs, (probably the soundest decision he ever made).

In 1935 the Hanging Committee of the RA Summer Exhibition rejected two out of the five paintings he submitted that year. Insulted, he attempted to withdraw them, the Academy refused. Spencer resigned from the Academy and ensured the whole row got a good airing in the newspapers. In 1937 his marriage failed and his wife divorced him. He remarried that same year, the second marriage failing immediately. Upon the outbreak of the Second World War, a War Artists' Advisory Committee was formed and Tooth wrote candidly to its head, Kenneth Clark,[57] imploring him to give Spencer a commission. Spencer was offered a choice and undertook a series of seven paintings at the Lithgow Shipyard, Port Glasgow. The results were well received and kept Spencer busy throughout the war years, the last picture in the series being finished in 1946: all are in the collection of the Imperial War Museum. That same period marked Spencer's return to solvency. In 1950 the RA invited him to rejoin them, which he did. In 1955 the Tate held a major retrospective of his work and in 1958 he was knighted. He was diagnosed with cancer in the winter of 1958 and died in the Canadian War Hospital at Cliveden on 14 December 1959. His last great work, the remarkable *Christ Preaching at Cookham Regatta* (1953-59) remained unfinished at his death.[58] It may be seen in the Methodist Chapel at Cookham where he worshipped as a child, which is now the Stanley Spencer Art Gallery. Website at www.stanleyspencer.co.uk

---

[56] Isaac Rosenberg, born Bristol 1891 son of Lithuanian immigrants. Poverty-stricken upbringing in London's East End. Gifted artist and poet, attended both Birkbeck College and the Slade School. Served in King's Own Royal Lancaster Regiment. Killed in action at Fampoux, France on 1 April 1918.

[57] Sir Kenneth Mackenzie Clark (1903-1983) Educated Trinity College, Oxford. Art historian, broadcaster, lecturer and patron of the arts. Director of National Gallery 1934-45. Chairman of the Arts Council 1953-60. 1st Baron Clark of Saltwood 1969. Author: *The Gothic Revival: An Essay in the History of Taste* (1928).

[58] At the time of writing in 2004, the highest price paid at auction for a Spencer painting was £1.5M.

# SIR CHARLES WHEELER

Charles Thomas Wheeler was born at The Cottage, Church Road, Codsall on 14 March 1892 and baptised in Codsall Church by the Reverend Oliver Dunn on St George's Day. His father was a journalist. Charles attended St Luke's Church School and the Wolverhampton Higher Grade School. Aged 15, he won a scholarship to the Wolverhampton School of Art where he studied under Robert Emerson from 1908. He won a scholarship to the South Kensington Royal College of Art and studied under Professor Édouard Lantéri in the period 1912-17. He exhibited for the first time at the RA Summer Exhibition in 1914. Wheeler lived and worked for over 40 years at his studio in Cathcart Road, off Fulham Road in South Kensington. One of his earliest commissions was to produce a bronze memorial tablet to Rudyard Kipling's son, John, who was killed in 1915 at the Battle of Loos. The bronze is in Burwash Church, Sussex. Another early commission was the *Madonna and Child* as part of the War Memorial in the cloisters at Winchester College. The commission was awarded by Sir Herbert Baker and led to Wheeler's close working relationship with him, which lasted more than 20 years. The hand of Baker is evident in Wheeler's subsequent commissions, which included the figures for the Bank of England (1932), five pairs of 20 ft tall bronze doors for the Bank of England (1934-35) and the figure of *Ariel* which surmounts the Sub-Treasury dome. In 1934 he sculpted the decorative motifs (including the gilded bronze springbok) for South Africa House in Trafalgar Square, then the sculpture for India House in The Strand, the sculpture on the Indian Memorial at Neuve Chapelle, also Rhodes House, Oxford, Haileybury College Chapel, the Royal Empire Society and Church House, Westminster. In 1924 he sculpted the winged figure that comprises the *Ilford War Memorial* in Essex and he also produced the *Earl Jellicoe Memorial* on the north wall of Trafalgar Square, the colossal figures *Earth* and *Water* at the North Door of the multi-ministry building that is now occupied by the rapidly diminishing Ministry of Defence in Whitehall. After the Second World War, in partnership with William McMillan and under the supervision of Sir Edward Maufe, he carried out the sculpture on the extensions to the naval memorials at Portsmouth, Plymouth and Chatham. In 1953 he sculpted the bronze gilded eagle atop the Commonwealth Air Forces Memorial at Malta. He also executed sculpture for the Commission in the cemeteries in North Africa and on Malta. He sculpted the statue *Lady Wulfruna* (1974) which stands at the top of the steps leading from the Civic Centre to St Peter's Church, Wolverhampton. His marble busts included *Queen Elizabeth II* commissioned by the RA, the violinist *Yehudi Menuin* and *Lawrence of Arabia*. He produced *Spring* cast by the Morris Singer Foundry in 1927, it was described by critics as one of the most beautiful sculpted works of the 20th century. In 1930 it was purchased by the Chantrey Bequest and it now languishes in the basement of the Tate. His bronze bust *Infant Christ* (1924) was modelled on his son. It also was purchased under the Chantrey Bequest and is in the Tate. Off Lombard Street in London is his *Poseidon* (1969). In the same square is his *Hercules and the Lion* and on the Barclays Building in Lombard Street his *St George and the Dragon*. His *Mary of Nazareth* is in St James, Piccadilly. His *Peter Pan* can be found at Invercargill, New Zealand and it was unveiled there by Queen Elizabeth the Queen Mother in 1966. An immaculately turned out dapper little man who habitually wore a bow tie, Wheeler's hands, (which were the size of shovels, the legacy of many years of hammer and point work) were the only clue to his calling. In his long distinguished career he was elected ARBS in 1926, ARA 1934, FRBS 1935, Vice President RBS 1938-42, RA 1940, PRBS 1945-49. He was instrumental in founding the Society of Portrait Sculptors and became their first President in 1953. In 1956 he became the first sculptor to be elected President of the Royal Academy, a post he occupied until 1966. In 1968 Country Life Books published *High Relief: The Autobiography of Sir Charles Wheeler, Sculptor*. He died aged 82 in 1974 at home in Mayfield, Sussex and was buried in the churchyard at Codsall. In his will, he bequeathed the villagers of Codsall his bronze statue *The Lone Singer* which was unveiled there by his son Robin in 1975. His memorial by Willi Soukop RA may be found in St Paul's Cathedral.

# IVOR ROBERTS-JONES

Ivor Roberts-Jones was born on 2 November 1913 at Oswestry in Shropshire. He was the only son of a solicitor. He was educated at Oswestry Grammar School and Worksop College. In 1932 he commenced studying sculpture at Goldsmiths College, Deptford and from 1935 in the RA Schools. He served with the Royal Regiment of Artillery during the Second World War and fought the Japanese in Burma. He returned to London in 1946 and discovered that his studio in Lillie Road, Fulham had been demolished in the Blitz. His art suffered almost total critical neglect in Britain during the 1950s and 1960s, but in 1971 he was selected to execute the over-life-size bronze figure of *Sir Winston Churchill* for Parliament Square, London. This led to further commissions for figures of Churchill for Oslo (1975) and New Orleans (1977) and a second cast of the London figure for Prague (1999). Papers released from the National Archives in January 2001 revealed that the commission for Churchill's statue in Parliament Square was relentlessly interfered with by officialdom from start to finish. In a letter to Prime Minister Edward Heath dated 25 April 1972, John Tilney MP who chaired the organising committee stated: 'At the moment, the head is undoubtedly like Churchill, but perhaps not quite right of him at the pinnacle of his career. The chin, mouth, and nose can hardly be improved.' But the report added: 'The cheeks, the eyes, the forehead and the top of the head require improvement. I told Mr Roberts-Jones that above the eyes I thought I was looking at Mussolini.' Following this 'harsh comment', the sculptor promised to 'remove the dome of the head which would bring about a lowering of the forehead, which he would then line slightly'. The report went on: 'The eyes remain a problem, particularly the right eye. They convey a rather glowering expression at this stage. Mr Roberts-Jones wants to portray a more resolute expression.' The Churchill Committee also wrote to the Palace suggesting that The Queen unveil the 12ft statue, Buckingham Palace replied: 'There was some reluctance to allow the Queen to unveil a statue of a subject' and suggested it more 'appropriate' if Churchill's widow pulled the string. A handwritten note from Prime Minister Edward Heath stated: 'I am not sure Lady C will wish to do so as she does not like the statue'. But it was duly unveiled by Baroness Spencer-Churchill in the presence of The Queen on 1 November 1973. In the May Day Riots in 2000 the statue acquired a temporary turf Mohican hairstyle and was spray-painted by anti-capitalist protestors with the legend 'FAT TORY BASTARD'. Roberts Jones sculpted the larger than life-size bronze statues *Field Marshal Viscount Alanbrooke* (1993) and *Field Marshal Viscount Slim* (1990) which stand on Raleigh Green in Whitehall. His bronze head of *Oliver Lyttelton (Viscount Chandos)* may be found in the foyer of the Lyttelton Theatre in the South Bank complex in London. His bronze head of *Yehudi Menuhin, Baron Menuhin* (1974); his head of *George Thomas, Viscount Tonypandy* (1982); bronze bust of *Sir Geraint Llewellyn Evans* (1984) and bronze bust of *Sir Nicholas Goodison* (1990) may all be found in the Primary Collection of the National Portrait Gallery. His bronze head on a stone plinth of the artist *Augustus John* may be seen at Bodelwyddan Castle. In 1957 he sculpted the bronze portrait bust of the French poet and playwright *Paul Claudel* based on a series of sketches made during the sitter's lifetime. It may be seen in the Tate. His bronze head of the *Prince of Wales* may be found in the main foyer of St David's Hall, Cardiff. He sculpted the bronze statuette of Robert Falcon Scott's zoologist *Apsley Cherry-Garrard* which may be seen in a niche in the north transept of St Helens Church at Wheathampstead. In 1983 an exhibition of Roberts-Jones's work was arranged for the Royal National Eisteddfod at Llangefni, the exhibition's organisers were surprised to be instructed not to include any of his sculpture of Churchill: 'Set the troops on us, he did!' (a reference to Churchill's role as Home Secretary in the Tonypandy Riots of 1910). Roberts-Jones was Head of the Department of Sculpture at Goldsmiths College 1964-78. He was elected RA in 1973, ARBS 1974, appointed CBE in 1975, elected FRBS in 1975 and was a Member of the Society of Portrait Sculptors. He died at the age of 83 in London on 9 December 1996. A retrospective of his work was held by the Wolsey Art Gallery, Ipswich in 2000.

# FRANTA BELSKY

Franta Belsky was born in Brno, Czechoslovakia on 6 April 1921, son of the economist Joseph Belsky. The Belsky family fled to England following the Nazi dismemberment of Czechoslovakia in October 1938. He volunteered for the Czech exile army, was introduced to Churchill, fought in France as an artilleryman, was twice mentioned in despatches and decorated for bravery. He studied sculpture at the Central School of Arts and Crafts and the Royal College of Art and married Margaret Owen, a fellow student in 1944. She went on to become the well-known, successful cartoonist 'Belsky' and was the first woman to draw a daily front-page political cartoon in Britain. She died in 1989. After the Second World War he returned to Prague and discovered that 22 of his relatives had perished in the Holocaust. He sculpted the *Paratroop Memorial* in Prague and designed a medal in honour of the Olympic athlete Emil Zatopek. Belsky fled Czechoslovakia again following the Communist takeover of that country in 1948. As well as statues and busts, he executed many abstract designs and developed novel techniques. His *Triga* (1958) at Caltex House, Knightsbridge is a 30 foot-high group of three rearing horses in reinforced concrete with a metal coating. In 1969 Westminster College in Fulton, Missouri commissioned Belsky to create the eight-foot tall bronze *Churchill* to mark the twenty-fifth anniversary of his 'Iron Curtain' speech there. Among Churchill sculptors, only Oscar Nemon escaped criticism, either from the subject, from family or friends. Belsky was no exception, although the reception given his statue was not so bad as that which had been given to Jacob Epstein's 1946 bust, David McFall's 1959 statue at Woodford in Essex, or the furore which greeted Ivor Roberts-Jones's 'deformed giant' in Parliament Square. However, when Belsky was able to return to Prague after the 'Velvet Revolution' in 1989, he was commissioned to produce a statue of Churchill for the British Embassy there. In the meantime, he sculpted the portrait bust *Churchill* in the Archive Centre at Churchill College, Cambridge, a copy of which is in the Churchill Hotel, Portman Square, London; and a large and unusual bas relief bronze plaque on the landing of the Conservative Club at Hoddesdon, Herts. Belsky was renowned for his painstaking technique. Most sculptors make a number of working models on the way to developing their finished work, Belsky produced no fewer than nine half-scale models before completion of the Fulton commission. It was his habit to seal inside each of his castings a Guinness bottle, a copy of that day's newspaper, a sixpence and a note declaring that Franta Belsky was the artist. In answer to the suggestion to former US president Harry S Truman that an American sculptor should sculpt his bust, Truman reportedly replied: 'Hell, no, if I ever pose for anybody it will be the guy who did Winston in Fulton'. Belsky duly obliged and the resulting busts may be found in the Presidential Library, Independence, Missouri and at the Truman Dam on the Osage River in Missouri. Belsky sculpted the *Cholmondeley Park Military Monument* in Cheshire, where the Czechoslovak soldiers were initially based after escaping from France. Belsky's bronze heads of *Cecil Day-Lewis* (1952); *Prince Philip, Duke of Edinburgh* (1979); *Queen Elizabeth II* (1981); *Prince Andrew, Duke of York* (1984) and *John Egerton Christmas Piper* (1987) may all be found in the Primary Collection of the National Portrait Gallery. Belsky sculpted the *Czechoslovak Army and Air Force Memorial* (1993) in the west cloister of Westminster Abbey and also the bronze statue *Earl Mountbatten of Burma* (1982) which stands on Foreign Office Green in London. In the 1970s and 80s Belsky was commissioned by the ferry company Sealink to execute large murals for their ships HENGIST, HORSA, SENLAC, ST EDMUND, and ST COLUMBA. In 1996 Belsky married the sculptor Irena Sedlecka. He was for many years prominent in the affairs of the RBS and an active member of their council. He was elected ARBS in 1957 and FRBS in 1961. He was President of the Society of Portrait Sculptors 1996-99. His successor, Anthony Stones, described him as: 'one of the most important sculptors in Britain's post-war history'. Franta Belsky died from prostate cancer at home at Sutton Courtenay, Oxfordshire at the age of 79 on 5 July 2000. His papers may be found in the archives of the Henry Moore Centre in Leeds.

# JAMES BUTLER

James Butler was born on 25 July 1931 in London. He studied at Maidstone School of Art from 1948 to 1950 (where he was introduced to modelling and carving), St Martin's School of Art from 1950 to 1952 and subsequently at the Royal College of Art, London. After two years' National Service with the Royal Corps of Signals, in 1955 he began an association with the City and Guilds of London Art School. Simultaneously he worked for the Giudici Brothers firm of master stone carvers, working on sculptural features such as *The Queen's Beasts* at Kew Gardens and the restoration work on the *Albert Memorial* in Kensington Gore. He spent ten years working as a professional stone carver. In the period 1960 to 1975 he taught drawing and sculpture at the City and Guilds of London Art School. He was also Visiting Tutor to the Royal Academy Schools. In 1972 he was awarded his first major commission by the Kenyan Government and produced the twice life-size statue *President Kenyatta* (1973) for Nairobi. This commission marked a major turning point in his career and he gave up teaching to devote his time to numerous public commissions, as well as to commissions for private collections throughout the world. Butler's prolific output includes: the portrait statue of *James Greathead, Engineer* at Cornhill in London; the portrait statue *Field Marshal Earl Alexander of Tunis* which stands outside the Guards Chapel at Wellington Barracks, Birdcage Walk, London; *Monument to Freedom Fighters of Zambia* at Lusaka in Zambia; the *World Cycling Champion*, National Cycling Centre, Manchester; the bronze portrait bust *Sir Nicholas Bacon* at St Albans School, Hertfordshire; the portrait statue *Thomas Cook* at London Road, Leicester; the bronze portrait busts *Sir Frank Whittle* and *RJ Mitchell* at the RAF Club, Piccadilly, London; the portrait statue of the Wolves footballer *Billy Wright* at the Molineux Stadium, Wolverhampton; the *D Day Memorial* for the Green Howards at Crepon in Normandy; the memorial statue *King Richard III* in Castle Gardens, Leicester; the *Leicester Seamstress* Hotel Street, Leicester; the bronze sculpture *The Burton Cooper* at Burton on Trent; the portrait statue *General Sir John Moore* with its attendant figures of a *Rifleman* and *Bugler* at Sir John Moore Barracks, Winchester; the portrait statue *James Brindley, Canal Engineer* at Canal Basin, Coventry; the memorial portrait statue of *Duncan Edwards* at Dudley town centre; the *Fleet Air Arm Memorial* on Victoria Embankment, London; the sculpted tribute to the racehorse *Thunder Gulch*, winner of the 1995 Kentucky Derby; the memorial statue of *Reg Harris World Cycling Champion* at the National Cycling Centre, Manchester; the sculpture for the National Guard Sports Stadium, Riyadh, Saudi Arabia; the *Anniversary Fountain* Dolphin Square, London; the *Cippico Fountain*, Heriot-Watt University, Edinburgh; the portrait statue of the controversial parliamentary radical *John Wilkes* at New Fetter Lane, London with a second casting produced for Wilkes University, Wilkes-Barre, Pennsylvania, USA and the bronze sculpture *Skipping Girl* at St Ann's Road, Harrow. His remarkable bronze figure *The Stratford Jester* may be seen at Henley Street in Stratford-upon-Avon. He has executed a number of sculptures for Singapore and these include: the *Seagull Sculpture* at Anchorpoint; the sculptures *Girl and Teddy Bear* and *Child and Whale* at KK Women's and Children's Hospital; the life size figures *Ondine*, *Reclining Figure* and *Young Dancer* at Avalon, Pidemco Land. In 2001 Butler executed the second *Great Seal of Queen Elizabeth II*. He sculpted *Scramble* in bronze to mark the 50th anniversary of the Battle of Britain for the RAF Benevolent Fund, ten of which were produced in a limited edition 24 inches tall and a further ten in an edition 12 inches tall. James Butler has cited Classical Greek sculpture, the Italian Renaissance and Andrea Pisano, Donatello, Rodin, Edgar Degas, Aimeé-Jules Dalou, Georges Seurat, Hamo Thornycroft and Charles Sargeant Jagger as being important influences on his work. Warwickshire based, as can be seen from the list of commissions above, much of his work may be seen in the Midlands. He was elected ARA 1964, RA 1972, Member of the Royal West of England Academy in 1980, FRBS in 1981 and is a Member of the Society of Portrait Sculptors. Website at www.jamesbutler-ra.com/

# JOHN W MILLS

John Mills was born in London in 1933. He studied at Hammersmith School of Art 1947-1954 and the Royal College of Art 1956-1960. In 1953 he married Josephine Demarne and they have two children, Dylan and Andrea. He did his National Service as a physical training instructor 1954-56. He first exhibited at the Royal Academy in 1956, and has held solo exhibitions on a regular basis since 1959, showing his work in London and other cities in Great Britain, as well as in Canada, the United States, France, Australia and Germany. In the period 1958-62 he held a number of part time teaching posts in UK. He was senior lecturer at St Albans School of Art 1962-1970, principal lecturer Hertfordshire College of Art and Design 1970-1977. He was Visiting Lecturer Detroit School of Creative Arts 1970 and subsequently Visiting Professor and Artist in Residence at the University of Michigan. He ceased teaching on a regular basis on 1977. His public sculpture includes the memorial to the poet artist and engraver: *The William Blake Memorial* which may be seen at Blake House, London; *Blitz* - the National Memorial to the firefighters who died in the Second World War which stands in Old Change Court, just below St Paul's Cathedral in London. His design for the memorial earned him the RBS Silver Medal in 1991. He sculpted *London River Man* at the Isle of Dogs, Docklands, London; *Family Outing* - Thames Centre, Newton Aycliffe, Durham; *John Jorrocks* (Surtees' creation, the Master of Foxhounds of Handley Cross Spa) at East Croydon in Surrey; *Brother* University Hospital, Ann Arbor, Michigan, USA; *Swimmers* at Cambridge Swimming pool, Cambridge; *St George and the Dragon* in the courtyard of the Windsor Court Hotel, New Orleans; *Diver* University of Eastern Michigan, USA; *Thoughtful Girl* Clark University, Worcester, Massachusetts; *The Thrower* at Ernest Bevin School, Tooting, London; *Lion* at Ward Freeman School, Buntingford, Herts; *The Risen Christ* at Ashwell Church, Herts, *The Jackie Milburn Memorial* (1995) to that great Novocastrian footballer stands at Ashington, Northumberland; the aircraft pioneer *T.O.M.E. Sopwith* at Brooklands Museum, Brooklands and *The Risen Christ* in the Church of Great St Mary at Sawbridgeworth in Hertfordshire. His gallery sculptures include: *Comparison 1990; The Thrower; Lion 1969* (in *ciment fondu*)*; Lion Head Mask; Grande Mastiffs 1990; Mother and Child 1994; Three Kings* (1984)*; Three Kings* (1989) and *Degas Dancing*.

John Mills has been commissioned to execute the sculpture for the *Women in the Second World War* which was originally scheduled to be inaugurated on the site previously occupied by William McMillan's statue of *Sir Walter Raleigh* on Raleigh Green outside the Ministry of Defence. The project was delayed in early 2005 by the discovery of two large gas mains immediately beneath the statue's plinth in Whitehall. Interestingly, the memorial was at the centre of a major development for the future of war memorials construction in the United Kingdom, in that its organisers managed to persuade Her Majesty's Commissioners for Customs & Excise to waive the VAT element of its cost.

John Mills has carried out a wide range of numismatic commissions and in 2003 he produced the *Triple Helix DNA* two pound coin the design of which features Watson and Crick's DNA molecule. That same year he produced the *Letchworth Garden City Centenary Medal*. He also designed the 50 pence coin to celebrate the 50th anniversary of D-Day. His design was voted the best coin of 1994 by the International Numismatic Society in 1996. He was winner of the Royal Mint design competition to design the 25th anniversary of Britain's entry into the Common Market 50 pence coin in 1997. John Mills has written extensively on sculpture and amongst his works are: *The Technique of Casting for Sculpture* (1968); *Modelling the Figure and Head* (1978) and *Encyclopaedia of Sculpture Techniques* (1989). He has held one man exhibitions on a regular basis since 1959, including shows in London and other cities in the UK, Canada, USA, France, Australia and Germany. He was elected FRBS in 1982 and President of the Royal Society of British Sculptors in 1986. In 1993 he became a Fellow of the Royal Society of Arts. In 2000 he was awarded an Honorary Master of Arts Degree by University College, Northampton.

# PHILIP JACKSON

Philip Jackson was born in Scotland during the Second World War. He was educated in England and now lives and works in West Sussex. A prolific sculptor, his interest in history and fascination with religion influences his themes and informs their execution. His work includes figurative sculpture, groups and abstract works. His public sculpture includes: the *Manchester Peace Sculpture* (1988); *Swimmers II* (1992); *Sir Matt Busby* (1996) at Old Trafford; *The Gurkha Monument* (1997) on Horse Guards Avenue; His *Minerva* (1997) stands outside Chichester Festival Theatre and his *Wallenberg Monument* (1997) stands outside the Great West End Synagogue in London with a copy being cast for Buenos Aires in 1998. His bronze *'Sissi' Empress Elisabeth of Austria Monument* (1998) stands on the quayside at Lake Geneva where she was stabbed to death by an anarchist in 1898. His *Jeddah Horses* (1999) are in Saudi Arabia and his bronze *King George VI* (2002) is at Britannia Royal Naval College, Dartmouth. His *Christ in Judgement* (1998) and *Saint Richard* (2000) may be seen at Chichester Cathedral. His seated figure of *Constantine the Great* (1998) is sited outside York Minster. The story of his *Jersey Liberation Sculpture* (1995) is an interesting case study of the need for the sculptor to follow his own conception after research, free from interference. In Jackson's words: 'My task, as the artist, was to design a sculpture that embodied what I saw as the essence of the island's liberation while at the same time taking into account much of the diverse advice given by the islanders. It was not easy.' His design was unveiled by the Prince of Wales on the 50th anniversary of Liberation Day. Jackson's bronze over-life size figure *The Young Mozart* (1994) stands on a plinth in Ebury Street, Chelsea and marks the boy genius's visit to London in 1764. Jackson's background research for this commission included visiting the Mozarteum in Salzburg and interviewing Professor H C Robbins Landon, the greatest living authority on Mozart. His twice life-size sculpture of a Royal Marine, *The Yomper* at Eastney, Portsmouth was unveiled by Baroness Thatcher in 1992. His *In Pensioner* stands in the grounds of the Royal Hospital, Chelsea and was unveiled by the Duke of Westminster in 2000. Other commissions include: the life-size *Mother and Child* (1990) for the Sisters of Mercy, Midhurst; the busts *Dame Kiri Te Kanawa* (1997) for the Royal Opera House; *Dame Edith Sitwell* (1993); *John Treadgold, Dean of Chichester* (2001) and *The Jubilee Statue* unveiled by the Queen in Windsor Great Park in 2003. This sculpture, depicting Her Majesty on horseback as she would have looked in the 1970s is the first public sculpture of the Queen in Britain and was commissioned by the Crown Estate in celebration of Her Majesty's Golden Jubilee. Jackson's statue of *Terence Cuneo* complete with paintbrush and palette was unveiled at Waterloo Station in London by the Princess Royal in October 2004. Jackson's trademark black-robed, gold-masked, elongated gallery sculptures wearing outsized, or exaggerated tricorn hats date from a Venetian commission in the 1980s and marked the commencement of his enduring love affair with the city on the lagoon. These would include: *Sior Maschera* (1990); *Don Ottavio* (1992); *Dangerous Liaison* (1993); *Cloister Conspiracy* (1994); *Capriccio* (1995); *Altar Ego* (1996); *The Sentinels* (1997); *Serenissima* (1997); *The Chaperone* (1998); *The Grandees* (1999); *Seat on the Zattere* (2000); *The Dogerina's Progress* (2000); *Venetian Whispers* (2000); *Moonstruck* (2001); *Mistress of the Ca' d'Oro* (2001); *Full Sail on the Holy See* (2002); *Through a Glass Darkly* (2002) and *Rain on the Rialto* (2002). This recurrent theme consolidated his international reputation and made Jackson's work immensely collectable. His remarkable *Pope Joan* (1999), has a single hand placed on her stomach peeping from the line of her *copa* alluding to the legend that she was with child when elected Pontiff. Jackson was elected FRBS in 1989 and was awarded the Otto Beit Medal for Sculpture in 1991,1992 and 1993. He also holds the Silver Medal awarded by the Royal Society of British Sculptors. In 2004 he was awarded an honorary Master of Arts by University College, Chichester. He cites Epstein, Rodin, Nemon, Kenneth Armitage and Henry Moore as his greatest artistic influences and in recent years has held one-man exhibitions in Italy, Switzerland, the United States, and all over England.

# VIVIEN MALLOCK

Vivien Mallock was born at Hitchin, Herts. Coming from a military family, her childhood education was disrupted by her attendance at some fifteen different schools, as her family regularly relocated to the outposts of the rapidly shrinking British Empire. She worked as a disc jockey and waitress and subsequently married into the Army. A mother of two children, she took up sculpture after being requested to assist in producing dummies for an exhibition to mark the 50th anniversary of the Battle of Britain at the Museum of Army Flying at Middle Wallop. To give her work a personal touch, she sculpted portraits of individual aircrew, including John Cunningham and other celebrated fighter pilots who flew from Middle Wallop in 1940, as part of an exhibition to mark the anniversary. The works have since become a unique feature of the Museum. Her sculpture primarily in bronze, covers a wide spectrum from portraiture and monuments to small figurative pieces of both human and wildlife subjects. Hampshire-based, much of her work may be found in that county. Working from a maquette produced by the Scottish Academician George Henry Paulin (1888-1962), Vivien produced her largest work to date, the remarkable group of five larger than life size figures depicting the crew of a Comet tank, forming the *Royal Tank Regiment Memorial* at Whitehall Court in London. The memorial was unveiled by The Queen on 13 June 2000.

In recent years she has completed a number of sculptures of military figures and her series of five Normandy sculptures depict every level of command in that campaign. She sculpted the 7 ft tall bronze portrait statue *Monty* at Colleville Montgomery, Normandy which commemorates the British commander Field Marshal Viscount Montgomery. A copy of it was cast for Portsmouth and to complement it, she then produced the bronze *Young Soldier of WWII* situated outside the D-Day Museum at Southsea in Portsmouth. In an echo of Jagger's memorial at Paddington Station, he is portrayed seated on a jerrycan reading a letter. Her bronze statue of *Brigadier James Hill* was cast by Morris Singer and stands at Le Mesnil Crossroads near Bavent in Normandy close by the Pegasus Bridge. Brigadier Hill commanded 3rd Parachute Brigade on D-Day. Aged 93 he sat for her at home in Chichester and she said afterwards: 'He is charming, a very gentle man, but I am told he was very steely when he needed to be.' The memorial was inaugurated by the Prince of Wales on 6 June 2004. The Brigadier attended the ceremony and said: 'My thoughts are of gratitude to all those who did not come back. We have not forgotten them. My thoughts are with all those who have come back safely. I was worried at the time but I had to carry on.' Vivien also executed the bust of *Major John Howard*, whose company of the Ox and Bucks Light Infantry seized the Pegasus Bridge in the first hour of D-Day and she executed the bust of *Lieutenant Colonel Terence Otway*, commander of the successful 6 Para assault on the Merville gun battery two hours later and the bust of *Major General Richard Gale* commissioned by the Airborne Assault Normandy Trust. She subsequently produced the *WWI Memorial* at Tidworth commissioned by the Royal British Legion as a memorial to those who had been billeted locally. This four ft tall bronze statue depicts a soldier returning from the front with his kitbag. In 2002 she produced for Portsmouth City Council the 12 foot tall *Golden Jubilee* sculpture sited at Gunwharf Quays, Havant, Hants. Her life size *Dancing Girl* (2003) is in a private collection in England. Her more recent sculptures have featured in a number of exhibitions in London and the Home Counties. In 2003 her 'one-man' exhibition at the Frank T Sabin Gallery in Albemarle Street in London was a notable success. Vivien Mallock was the last artist to complete a portrait bust of *Queen Elizabeth the Queen Mother* unveiled in the Queen Mother Wing of St Mary's Hospital, Paddington on 14 November 2002 by the Earl and Countess of Wessex. She was selected by the Royal Society of British Sculptors to demonstrate the art of ceramic portrait sculpture as part of their *Earth & Fire* Exhibition at the Victoria & Albert Museum in 2002. Vivien Mallock became a member of the Armed Forces Art Society in 1992, a member of the Society of Women Artists in 1993 and an Associate of the Royal Society of British Sculptors in 1998. Website at www.vivienmallock.co.uk

# FAITH WINTER

Faith Ashe was evacuated with her mother to Guildford during the Second World War and in 1944 at the age of 16, attended the Guildford School of Art. That first-rate college was custom-built shortly before the war and the teaching staff who mostly travelled down each day from London, were all of exceptional ability. Her first teacher was Harry Wilson Parker, famed as a designer of medallions and coins. He was followed by Willi Soukop RA (1907-95) a carver in stone and wood who was not only a brilliant sculptor, but an inspirational teacher. Faith's first sculpture accepted at the Royal Academy was a stone carving and her three following works were also accepted. Another exceptional instructor was Fred Brill, later Principal of Chelsea College of Art. He taught drawing in the life class at Guildford and was a forceful character. Faith left the Guildford School of Art in 1948 and on leaving, received the Feodora Gleichen Award, which at that time was presented by the RBS to a female student of promise on leaving art school. She received £100.00 with the award and travelled to Florence. The Guildford School of Art closed a few years later. Despite its excellence, it soon proved too small to cope with the large influx of students in the post-war years. The West Surrey College of Art at Farnham was then built.

Faith married into the Army in 1952 and became Faith Winter, travelled extensively, lived in Singapore and Malaysia and returned to Puttenham in 1973. Army connections resulted in a commission for the 8 foot tall group *The Soldiers* for Catterick Camp, North Yorks (now at the entrance to Blandford Camp in Dorset), which was unveiled by The Queen. Faith's portrait bust of *HRH the Princess Royal* was commissioned by the Royal Corps of Signals and executed in five sittings at Buckingham Palace. During this period she took a number of adult teaching posts, including one at Folkestone Art School before it closed. Her wide variety of commissions have included: her nine foot tall bronze statue *Air Chief Marshal Lord Dowding* (1988) and *Marshal of Royal Air Force Sir Arthur Harris* (1992), both on the forecourt of the Central Church of the Royal Air Force at St Clement Danes in The Strand, London; the 8 foot tall standing figure of the famous botanist *John Ray* at Braintree, Essex; *Archbishop George Abbot* (1993) unveiled by Lord Runcie in Guildford High Street, Surrey; the Second World War Polish commander *General Sikorski* (2000) which stands facing the Polish Embassy at Portland Place, London; the *Memorial for the Liberation of the Falkland Islands* (1984) a 10 foot by four foot bronze relief commissioned by the Falkland Islands Commission, which may be seen at Port Stanley in the Falkland Isles, with a copy at the Fleet Air Arm Museum at Yeovilton; *The Pearce Memorial* (1992) at Thame, Oxon, which takes the form of a boy with carp fountain. She executed the ten foot by four foot *Memorial Plaque - Mulberry Harbour Memorial* (2000) at Arromanches, Normandy; the 15 foot tall coat of arms on the exterior of the Salters' Hall at London Wall; the 24 six-foot wing-span eagles in Tafawa Balawa Square, Lagos, Nigeria and her plaster relief *Dancing Gypsy* (2003) may be seen in the foyer of the Nomad Theatre at East Horsley in Surrey. Her Lennard standing figure *The Spirit of Youth* is in Dundas Park, Ontario, Canada.

Her portrait busts include: *David Devant* (1998) commissioned by the Magic Circle, London; *Daniel Arap Moi, President of Kenya* for the Kenyan Government; *Alan Beckett* (designer of the Mulberry Harbour in Normandy); *Maria Callas* at Renishaw Hall, Sheffield and the Druze leader *Kamal Jumblatt* at the Kamal Jumblatt Museum, Lebanon.

Faith Winter is mother of the sculptors David Winter and Alice Winter; her other son Martin is a solicitor. She was elected ARBS in 1980 and FRBS in 1983. In 1984 she was awarded the Silver Medal of the RBS for her sculpture *The 15 Mysteries of the Rosary* installed in The Church of Our Lady Queen of Peace, Richmond. In 1993 she received the Guildford Society's William Crabtree Memorial Award for her *Archbishop George Abbot* statue in Guildford. Faith is a Member of the Society of Portrait Sculptors. Gallery 27 at Cork Street, London held a one man exhibition of her work in April 2005.

**APPENDICES**

# BIBLIOGRAPHY

Archer, Michael *Stained Glass* published by Pitkin Pictorials.
Barnes, Richard *John Bell: The Sculptor's Life and Works* Frontier Publishing 1999.
Barnes, Richard *The Obelisk: A Monumental Feature in Great Britain* Frontier Publishing 2004.
Beaty, David *Light Perpetual: Aviators' Memorial Windows* Airlife Publishing 1995.
Benson A C *Lest We Forget* Civic Arts Association, London 1917.
Billiere, General Sir Peter de la *Supreme Courage: Heroic Stories from 150 Years of the Victoria Cross* published by Little, Brown 2004.
Black, Harry W. *The Romance of St George's Chapel.*
Black, Jonathan *The Sculpture of Eric Kennington* Lund Humphries, London 2003.
Blomfield, Sir Reginald *Memoirs of an Architect* Macmillan & Co 1932.
Bond, Shelagh M. *The Monuments of St George's Chapel* 1958.
Boorman, Derek *For Your Tomorrow: British Second World War Memorials* published by Derek Boorman 1995.
Boorman, Derek *At the Going Down of the Sun: British First World War Memorials* Ebor Press 1998.
Booth, Philip *The Oxfordshire & Buckinghamshire Light Infantry* Leo Cooper 1971.
Borg, Alan *War Memorials From Antiquity to the Present* Leo Cooper.
Bradford, Ernle *The Great Siege: Malta 1565* Hodder & Stoughton.
Bradley, D L *Locomotives of the LB & SCR Part 3* 1974.
Brentnall, Margaret *John Hutton: Artist and Glass Engraver* Art Alliance Press 1986.
Brown, Sarah *Stained Glass* published by Bracken Books.
Cannon-Brookes Peter *Y Daith i Harlech: The Journey to Harlech* Amgueddfa Genedlaethol Cymru, National Museum of Wales, Llyfrau Trefoil, Trefoil Books 1983.
Clutton-Brock A. *On War Memorials* Civic Arts Association, London 1917.
Collins, Joyce *Dr Brighton's Indian Patients* Brighton Books Publishing.
Colvin, Sir Howard *Architecture and the Afterlife* 1991.
Compton, Ann *Charles Sargeant Jagger: War and Peace Sculpture* IWM 1985.
Compton, Ann, *The Sculpture of Charles Sargeant Jagger* Lund Humphries 2004.
Connelly, Mark *The Great War: Memory and Ritual* Royal Historical Society 2002.
Coombs, Rose E B *Before Endeavours Fade* published by After the Battle Publications 1994.
Corke, James A T *War Memorials* published by Shire Publications 2005.
Crump, Norman *By Rail to Victory: The Story of the LNER in Wartime* London & North Eastern Railway 1947.
Dooner, Mildred *Last Post* Simpkin, Marshall, Hamilton, Kent and Co Ltd 1903.
Gaffney, Angela *Aftermath: Remembering the Great War in Wales.* UWP 1998.
Gardner, Jean *Aviation Landmarks* After the Battle Publications 1990.
Garfield, John *The Fallen: a photographic journey through the war cemeteries and memorials of the Great War 1914–1918* Leo Cooper 1990.
Gibson T A Edwin and G Kingsley Ward *Courage Remembered* HMSO 1989.
Gildea, Sir James *For Remembrance and in Honour of Those who Lost Their Lives in the South African War 1899-1902* Eyre and Spottiswoode Ltd 1911.
Gleichen, Lord Edward *London's Open Air Statuary* London 1928.
Goodman, Alice *The Street Memorials of St Albans Abbey Parish* published by the St Albans and Hertfordshire Architectural and Archaeological Society.
Gregory, Adrian *The Silence of Memory: Armistice Day 1919 – 1946* published by Berg.
Gunnis, R *Dictionary of British Sculptors 1660-1851* London 1968.
Halliday, Sonia and Lushington, Laura *Stained Glass* published by Mitchell Beazley.
Harcourt-Smith, Sir Cecil *Suggested Inscriptions for War Memorials* unpublished monograph 1919, Victoria and Albert Museum Archive.

Harvey, David *Monuments to Courage: Victoria Cross Headstones and Memorials* (two volumes) published by Kevin and Kay Patience 1999.
Hassall, Christopher *Edward Marsh, A Biography* 1959.
Hill, J *Irish Public Sculpture - A History* Dublin 1998.
Hodson-Presinger, Selwyn *Adrian Jones (British Sculptor)* 1996.
Hopkins, Andrew and Stamp, Gavin *Lutyens Abroad* published by The British School at Rome, 2002.
Hussey, Christopher *Tait MacKenzie: A Sculptor of Youth* Country Life 1929.
Hussey, Christopher *The Life of Sir Edwin Lutyens* Country Life 1950.
Imperial War Museum *The Whitehall Cenotaph: An Accidental Monument* Imperial War Museum Review 9. 1994.
James, Duncan S *A Century of Statues: The History of the Morris Singer Foundry* published by Morris Singer 1984.
Jenkyns, Christopher *Westminster Abbey* published by Profile Books 2004.
Jerrold, Douglas *The Royal Naval Division* Hutchinson 1923.
Kernot, C F *British Public School War Memorials* Roberts and Newton 1927.
King A *The Commonwealth War Graves Commission Archive Catalogue* CWGC 1997.
King, Alex *Memorials of the Great War in Britain* Berg 1998.
Laffin, John *Damn the Dardanelles: The story of Gallipoli* published by Osprey 1980.
Lanteri, Édouard *Modelling – A Guide for Teachers and Students* Chapman & Hall Ltd, London 1902.
Longworth, Philip *The Unending Vigil* published by Constable and Co 1967.
McIntyre, Colin *Monuments of War: How to Read a War Memorial* published by Robert Hale 1990.
Mettler, A and Woodcock G, *We Will Remember Them: The Men of Tavistock who died in the First World War* published by Tavistock Local History Society.
Moriarty, Catherine *The Sculpture of Gilbert Ledward* Lund Humphries, London 2003.
Morris, Henry *The AJEX Chronicles: The Association of Jewish Ex-Servicemen and Women: A Brief History* published by AJEX 1999.
Noszlopy, G T *Public Sculpture of Birmingham including Sutton Coldfield* 1998.
Rason, Paul *Bromley War Memorials* 1999.
Ridley, Jane *The Architect and his Wife: A Life of Edwin Lutyens* Chatto & Windus 2002.
Sainsbury, J D *The F Section Memorial: Valençay* Hart Books, Welwyn 1992.
Saunders, Nicholas J *Trench Art* Shire Books 2002.
Sheffield, Gary and Bourne, John *Douglas Haig* published by Weidenfeld 2005.
Smith, David J *Britain's Aviation Memorials and Mementoes* published by Patrick Stephens.
Southey, Robert *Life of Horatio, Lord Nelson* published 1813.
Stamp, Gavin *Silent Cities: An Exhibition of the Memorial and Cemetery Architecture of the Great War* published by RIBA, 1977 (Exhibition catalogue, Heinz Gallery).
Steggles, Mary Ann *Statues of the Raj* Putney: BACSA 2000.
Summers, Anne *Angels and Citizens: British Women as Military Nurses 1854 - 1914* Routledge.
Thorpe, Barrie *Private Memorials of the Great War on the Western Front* published by the Western Front Association 1999.
Ware, Sir Fabian *The Immortal Heritage* Cambridge, 1937.
Weaver, Sir Lawrence *The Scottish National War Memorial* London 1927.
Whittick, Arnold *War Memorials* published by Country Life 1946.
Winter, J *Sites of Memory, Sites of Mourning: The Great War in European Cultural History*.
Wright, Thomas *The Life of Colonel Fred Burnaby* London, Everett & co., 1908.
*Philip Jackson: Sculptures* published by Studio Gallery Publications 2002.
*The Royal Garrison Church of S. George Woolwich 1863-1933: A Brief Illustrated History.*

## LIST OF PLATES

**All images are copyright of the named owner.**

| | |
|---|---|
| 1st Australian Tunnelling Company Memorial, Hill 60 | Vince Webb |
| 14th Regiment Memorial Ta'Braxia Cemetery, Malta | David Edwards |
| 24th Infantry Division War Memorial, Battersea Park | Samuel J Brookes |
| 38th (Welsh) Division Memorial, Mametz Wood | Vince Webb |
| 63rd Royal Naval Division Memorial, Beaucourt | Crown Copyright |
| Aberdeen War Memorial | James Grant |
| Achilles, Hyde Park | Samuel J Brookes |
| Admiralty Civilians War Memorial, Ripley Block | Crown Copyright |
| Air Forces Memorial, Runnymede | CWGC |
| Animals In War Memorial, Park Lane, London | Samuel J Brookes |
| Anne Frank's Tree | Author |
| Annie Morrison's headstone, Trinity Cemetery, Aberdeen | James Grant |
| ANZAC Memorial, Battersea Park | Samuel J Brookes |
| ANZAC Square, Brisbane, Australia | Colin Lathwell |
| Apollo Memorial to the Grenfell Brothers, Taplow Court | Richard Graham |
| Armed Forces Memorial (model) at NMA | Armed Forces Memorial Trust |
| Armed Science, Officers Mess, Woolwich Barracks | Samuel J Brookes |
| Armistice Window St Michael and All Angels, Bugbrooke | Imperial War Museum |
| Astronomical Clock Memorial, York Minster | Dean and Chapter, York Minster |
| Australian Memorial Tablet, Amiens Cathedral | Michael McAloon |
| Australian National Memorial, Villers-Bretonneux | CWGC |
| Australian War Memorial, Hyde Park, London | Samuel J Brookes |
| Battle of Britain Memorial, Capel le Ferne | Battle of Britain Memorial Trust |
| Battle of May Island Memorial, Anstruther Harbour | Crown Copyright |
| Bayeux Memorial, Normandy, France | CWGC |
| Bearsden War Memorial, Glasgow | Bill Ritchie |
| Belgian War Memorial, Victoria Embankment | Samuel J Brookes |
| Berlin Airlift Memorial at NMA | Commander (Retd) David Childs |
| Bethnal Green Underground Station Memorial | Samuel J Brookes |
| BLESMA Plaque at National Memorial Arboretum | BLESMA |
| British Commonwealth Memorial, Pusan, South Korea | Group Capt (Retd) Simon Coy |
| Brookwood Memorial | Richard Graham |
| Brookwood Russian Memorial | Samuel J Brookes |
| Burma Star Memorial, National Memorial Arboretum | Crown Copyright |
| Canadian Memorial, Vimy Ridge | Vince Webb |
| Canadian National War Memorial, Ottawa | CWGC |
| Canada Mourns Her Sons, Vimy Ridge | Vince Webb |
| Captain James Cook, The Mall, London | Samuel J Brookes |
| Captain Leefe Robinson, VC Restaurant | Colin Lathwell |
| Carabiniers (6th Dragoons) Boer War Memorial, Chelsea | Samuel J Brookes |
| Carew's relief on base of Nelson's Column | Samuel J Brookes |
| Cavalry Memorial, Hyde Park, London | Samuel J Brookes |
| Cenotaph, Whitehall on ANZAC Day 2003 | Crown Copyright |
| Chattri at Patcham, near Brighton | Imperial War Museum |
| Chillianwallah Memorial, Royal Hospital, Chelsea | Samuel J Brookes |
| Chindit Forces Memorial, Victoria Embankment | Lt Col Richard Callander |
| Chislehurst War Memorial, detail of base | David Miller |

| | |
|---|---|
| Colne War Memorial, Lancashire | Colne Public Library |
| Commando Memorial, Spean Bridge, Highlands | Penny Nash |
| Commonwealth Air Forces Memorial, Malta | David Edwards |
| Commonwealth Gates, Constitution Hill, London | Samuel L Brookes |
| Cornwell Cottages, Hornchurch, Essex | Peter Roberts |
| Crich Stand, Derbyshire | Colin Lathwell |
| Cyprus Street War Memorial, East End of London | Samuel J Brookes |
| Czechoslovak Army & Air Force Memorial | Crown Copyright |
| Edith Cavell Memorial, Trafalgar Square, London | Ken McCallum |
| Edith Cavell Memorial, Norwich | Clive Brookes |
| Edith Cavell's grave on Life's Green, Norwich Cathedral | Clive Brookes |
| Essex Regiment Memorial, Bayeux, Normandy | Crown Copyright |
| Explosive Ordinance Disposal Memorial, Kineton | Lt Col M I Dolamore |
| Falkland Island Memorial Chapel, Pangbourne College | Trustees of the Chapel |
| Falklands War Memorial, St Paul's Cathedral | Lt Col Richard Callander |
| Felix Memorial Garden, Thiepval Barracks | Sgt Paul Brownbridge |
| Field Marshal Earl Haig, Whitehall, London | Samuel J Brookes |
| Field Marshal Jan Smuts, Parliament Square, London | Samuel J Brookes |
| Field Marshal Lord Napier, Kensington Gore, London | Samuel J Brookes |
| Field Marshal Lord Roberts, Horse Guards Parade Ground | Samuel J Brookes |
| Fleet Air Arm Memorial, Lee-on-the-Solent | CWGC |
| Fleet Air Arm Memorial, Victoria Embankment, London | Lt Col Richard Callander |
| Flying Services Memorial, Arras, France | Keith Machin |
| Fovant Badges | Fovant Badges Society |
| Front Cover, statuary Portsmouth Naval Memorial | CWGC |
| Gallipoli Memorial, St Paul's Cathedral, London | Lt Col Richard Callander |
| General James Wolfe, Greenwich Park | Vince Duquemin |
| Great Eastern Railway War Memorial, Liverpool Street | Samuel J Brookes |
| Guards Crimean War Memorial, Waterloo Place, London | Ken McCallum |
| Guards Memorial, Horse Guards Parade, London | Crown Copyright |
| Gurkha Soldier, Whitehall Court, London | Crown Copyright |
| Guy's Hospital Boer War Memorial, London | Samuel J Brookes |
| Hanoverian Memorial, Waterloo, Belgium | Brian Watts |
| HMS FITTLETON Window at HMS PRESIDENT | Kevin Jackson |
| HMS THETIS Memorial, Holyhead | Crown Copyright |
| Imperial Camel Corps Memorial, Victoria Embankment | Samuel J Brookes |
| IWGC Memorial Tablet, Beauvais Cathedral | Clive Brookes |
| Indian Memorial, Brighton | Imperial War Museum |
| Indian National Memorial, Neuve-Chapelle, (detail) | Vince Webb |
| Japanese Naval Memorial, Cappucini Cemetery, Malta | Ron Wilson |
| John Travers Cornwell VC | Crown Copyright |
| Kindertransport Memorial, Liverpool Street Station | Samuel J Brookes |
| King Alfred's School Lychgate | Martin Pratchett |
| Kohima Cross of Sacrifice on tennis court | Sidney Brookes |
| Korean War Memorial, St Paul's Cathedral, London | Lt Col Richard Callander |
| Lewis War Memorial | Roddy Bain |
| Locomotive 48773 | Clive Blakeway |
| London Underground War Memorial, Petty France | Author |
| London Zoo War Memorial | Samuel J Brookes |
| Machine Gun Corps Memorial, Hyde Park | Samuel J Brookes |
| Major General Charles Gordon, Victoria Embankment | Ken McCallum |
| Marble Arch, London | Samuel J Brookes |

| | |
|---|---|
| Maréchal Ferdinand Foch, Lower Grosvenor Gardens | Samuel J Brookes |
| Memorial Gates, Constitution Hill, London | Crown Copyright |
| Memorial Siege Bell, Malta | David Edwards |
| Memorial Window, Bugbrooke, Northants | Imperial War Museum |
| Menin Gate, Ieper, Belgium | CWGC |
| Merchant Navy Memorial, Tower Hill, London | CWGC |
| National Liberal Club Memorial, Whitehall, London | Trustees of the Club |
| National Memorial Arboretum, Aerial View | Ian Grindlay, Lothian Helicopters |
| National Submariners Memorial, Victoria Embankment | Samuel J Brookes |
| Navy Club, Hill Street | WAVE Heritage Trust |
| Navy Club Memorial Tablet, Hill Street | WAVE Heritage Trust |
| Nelson's Column, Trafalgar Square | Samuel J Brookes |
| Nelson's Tomb, crypt of St Paul's Cathedral | Dean and Chapter, St Paul's |
| Newfoundland Memorial, Beaumont Hamel | Vince Webb |
| Norfolk Landmines Clearance Memorial, Mundesley | Noel Cashford |
| Norwich Boer War Memorial | Clive Brookes |
| Norwich Roll of Honour, Norwich Castle | Clive Brookes |
| Old Contemptibles Memorial, Westminster Abbey | Crown Copyright |
| Oliver Cromwell, Palace Yard, Westminster | Samuel J Brookes |
| Pegasus Bridge & Café Gondrée, Ranville, France | Major Alistair Ross |
| Polar Bear Memorial at NMA | Commander (Retd) David Childs |
| Post Office Rifles badge | Crown Copyright |
| Pulavaimu Church Memorials, Tallinn, Estonia | Crown Copyright |
| Plymouth Naval Memorial, detail of dented globe | CWGC |
| Portsmouth Naval Memorial, Southsea, Hants | CWGC |
| Prince Charles Edward Stuart Cairn, Swarkeston | Colin Lathwell |
| Queen Elizabeth II and Commander Childs at NMA | Ms Jackie Fisher |
| RAF Bentley Priory stained glass window | Crown Copyright |
| RAF Escaping Society Memorial, St Clement Danes | Crown Copyright |
| RAF Regiment Memorial at NMA | Commander (Retd) David Childs |
| RAF Memorial, Victoria Embankment, London | Samuel J Brookes |
| Rangoon Memorial, Taukkyan Cemetery, Myanmar | CWGC |
| Raoul Wallenberg Monument, Cumberland Place | Samuel J Brookes |
| Reverend Theodore Baily Hardy, VC Memorial | UKNIWM |
| Rhynie and Kearn War Memorial, Aberdeenshire | James Grant |
| Rifle Brigade Memorial, Grosvenor Gardens | Samuel J Brookes |
| Roll of Honour, Norwich Castle | Clive Brookes |
| Rorke's Drift Memorial, Natal, South Africa | Sgt Peter Lavery RMP |
| Royal Artillery Afghan/Zulu War Memorial, Woolwich | Samuel J Brookes |
| Royal Artillery Boer War Memorial, The Mall, London | Samuel J Brookes |
| Royal Artillery Crimean War Memorial, Woolwich | Samuel J Brookes |
| Royal Artillery Memorial, Hyde Park | Crown Copyright |
| Royal Fusiliers Memorial, Holborn Bars | Samuel J Brookes |
| Royal Garrison Church of St George, Woolwich | Samuel J Brookes |
| Royal Marines Memorial, The Mall, London | Crown Copyright |
| Royal Marines Memorial (detail), The Mall | Crown Copyright |
| Royal Naval Division Memorial, Horse Guards | Samuel J Brookes |
| Royal Norwegian Navy & Merchant Navy Memorial | Samuel J Brookes |
| Sandham Memorial Chapel, Burghclere | National Gallery |
| Scottish National War Memorial, Edinburgh | Ian Hay |
| Scutari Monument, Haidar Pasha Cemetery, Turkey | CWGC |
| Severndroog Castle, Shooters Hill, London | Samuel J Brookes |

| | |
|---|---|
| Sir Winston Churchill, Parliament Square | Samuel J Brookes |
| South African National War Memorial, Delville Wood | Vince Webb |
| South Atlantic Memorial, Westminster Abbey | Lt Col Richard Callander |
| SS CURACA Memorial, Halifax, Nova Scotia | William Fairbrother |
| St Clement Danes, Reredos | Crown Copyright |
| St George's RAF Chapel of Remembrance, Biggin Hill | Laurie Chester |
| St George's RAF Chapel stained glass windows | Crown Copyright |
| St George's Memorial Chapel, Ypres | The Reverend Ray Jones |
| St Omer Memorial, France | Crown Copyright |
| Staffordshire Regiment Memorial at the Arboretum | Commander (Retd) David Childs |
| Tank Crews Memorial, Whitehall Court, London | Lt Col Richard Callander |
| The Response, Barras Bridge, Newcastle | English Heritage |
| Thiepval Memorial to the Missing, Somme, France | CWGC |
| Tom Webber, former Far East Prisoner of War | Crown Copyright |
| Ton Class Memorial, National Memorial Arboretum | Edward Freathy |
| TRBL standard bearers on parade at the Arboretum | Ms Jackie Fisher |
| Union Jack Club, Waterloo, London | Samuel J Brookes |
| Union Jack Club, Memorial Wall | Samuel J Brookes |
| United Kingdom Firefighters National Memorial | Samuel J Brookes |
| United States Army Air Force Memorial, Greatstone | Bob Whyte |
| Ulster Memorial Tower, Thiepval, France | Somme Association |
| Victoria Cross and George Cross Memorial Inauguration | Didy Graham |
| Victoria Cross and George Cross Memorial, MOD | Crown Copyright |
| Victoria Cross Memorial, RMA Woolwich | Samuel J Brookes |
| Vigiland Memorial, Manor Park | Samuel J Brookes |
| Wagoners Memorial, Sledmere, Yorkshire | Karen Thompson |
| Waterloo Memorial, Everè, Brussels | Samuel J Brookes |
| Wellington Arch, Hyde Park | Samuel J Brookes |
| Wellington Memorial, Hyde Park | Samuel J Brookes |
| Wellington Memorial, St Paul's Cathedral | Dean and Chapter, St Paul's |
| Wellington Monument, Blackdown Hills | Colin Lathwell |
| Welsh National War Memorial, Cathays Park, Cardiff | Imperial War Museum |
| Westminster School Crimean/Indian Mutiny Memorial | Samuel J Brookes |
| Worcester Boer War Memorial, Worcester Cathedral | Clive Watson |

# GREAT WAR CHRONOLOGY

| | | |
|---|---|---|
| 1914 | 28 June | Assassination of Archduke Franz Ferdinand and his wife Lady Sophie Chotek on Apfel Quay at Sarajevo by Serb student Gavrillo Princip. |
| 1914 | 23 July | Austro-Hungarian ultimatum to Serbia. |
| 1914 | 28 July | Austria-Hungary declares war on Serbia. |
| 1914 | 30 July | Russia mobilises. |
| 1914 | 1 August | Germany declares war on Russia and invades Luxembourg. |
| 1914 | 2 August | Winston Churchill orders full British naval mobilisation. |
| 1914 | 3 August | Germany invades Belgium and declares war on France. |
| 1914 | 4 August | Great Britain declares war on Germany. |
| 1914 | 6 August | Austria Hungary declares war on Russia. |
| 1914 | 20 August | Germans capture Brussels. |
| 1914 | 22 August | First British soldier killed (Private Parr of the Middlesex Regiment). |
| 1914 | 23 August | Lieutenant Dease of the Royal Fusiliers wins first VC of war at Mons. |
| 1914 | 28 August | Admiral Beatty trounces German fleet off Heligoland. |
| 1914 | 5 September | First Battle of Marne. |
| 1914 | 8 September | First execution of a British soldier by a court martial. |
| 1914 | 17 September | Beginning of the 'Race to the Sea'. |
| 1914 | 10 October | Germans capture Antwerp. |
| 1914 | 12 October | First Battle of Ypres. |
| 1917 | 27 October | Indian Corps retakes Neuve Chapelle. |
| 1914 | 30 October | Commencement of First Battle of Ypres. |
| 1914 | 1 November | Battle of Coronel. British naval defeat off Cape Horn. |
| 1914 | 2 November | Disastrous British assault on German-held Tanga in East Africa. |
| 1914 | 8 December | Admiral Sturdee avenges Cradock at Battle of the Falkland Islands. |
| 1915 | 2 February | Turks repelled in attempt to seize Suez Canal. |
| 1915 | 10-12 March | Battle of Neuve Chapelle. |
| 1915 | 18 March | Anglo-French fleet fails to force passage at Dardanelles. |
| 1915 | 22 April | Commencement of 2nd Battle of Ypres. |
| 1915 | 25 April | Gallipoli Landings. |
| 1915 | 7 May | Sinking of *SS Lusitania*. |
| 1915 | 9 May | Battle of Aubers Ridge. |
| 1915 | 11 May | Battle of Krithia, Gallipoli. |
| 1915 | 16 May | Fisher's resignation provokes British Government crisis. |
| 1915 | 17 May | Asquith's Liberal administration replaced by all-party coalition. |
| 1915 | 23 May | Italy declares war on Central Powers. |
| 1915 | 4 June | Commencement of Second Battle of Krithia. |
| 1915 | 9 July | Gen. Botha accepts surrender of German forces in South West Africa. |
| 1915 | 6 August | Landings at Suvla Bay, Gallipoli. |
| 1915 | 6 August | Commencement of Australian assault on Lone Pine, Gallipoli. |
| 1915 | 25 September | Commencement of the Battle of Loos. |
| 1915 | 12 October | Edith Cavell executed in Brussels. |
| 1915 | 19 December | Haig replaces Field Marshal Sir John French as BEF commander. |
| 1916 | 8-9 January | Last British forces evacuated from Gallipoli. |
| 1916 | 16 February | First six companies of British tanks formed. |
| 1916 | 21 February | Commencement of German offensive against Verdun. |
| 1916 | 24 April | Easter Uprising in Dublin. |
| 1916 | 24 April | General Townshend surrenders his army to Turks at Kūt al Imāra, Iraq. |
| 1916 | 31 May | Battle of Jutland. |
| 1916 | 5 June | HMS HAMPSHIRE sunk by mine whilst taking Kitchener to Russia. |

| | | |
|---|---|---|
| 1916 | 1 July | Commencement of the Battle of the Somme. |
| 1916 | 27 July | Captain Charles Fryatt executed for 'piracy' by the Germans at Bruges. |
| 1916 | 15 November | Royal Naval Division capture Beaucourt on Western Front. |
| 1916 | 5 December | Bucharest falls to Germans. |
| 1916 | 7 December | Lloyd George replaces Asquith as Prime Minister. |
| 1917 | 31 January | 'Battle of May Island'. |
| 1917 | 1 February | Germany commences unrestricted submarine warfare. |
| 1917 | 3 February | President of USA announces severing of diplomatic ties with Germany. |
| 1917 | 23 February | Arthur Balfour hands Zimmerman Telegram to US Ambassador. |
| 1917 | 14 March | Czar Nicholas II of Russia abdicates. |
| 1917 | 6 April | USA declares war on Germany. |
| 1917 | 9 April | Commencement of Battle of Arras. |
| 1917 | 9 April | Canadian Corps captures Vimy Ridge. |
| 1917 | 16 April | Commencement of French 'Nivelle Offensive'. |
| 1917 | 21 May | Imperial War Graves Commission established by Royal Warrant. |
| 1917 | 6 July | Fall of Turkish-held Aqaba to Arabs. |
| 1917 | 31 July | Commencement of 3rd Battle of Ypres. |
| 1917 | 24 October | Collapse of Italian army at Caporetto. |
| 1917 | 8 November | Bolsheviks storm the Winter Palace, Petrograd. Fall of Kerensky. |
| 1917 | 9 November | Soviet government installed headed by Lenin. |
| 1917 | 9 November | Balfour Declaration: 'A national home for the Jewish People'. |
| 1917 | 20 November | Commencement of Battle of Cambrai. |
| 1917 | 9 December | General Allenby enters Jerusalem. |
| 1918 | 3 March | Russia signs Treaty of Brest-Litovsk with Germany. |
| 1918 | 21 March | Commencement of Ludendorff's Spring Offensive. |
| 1918 | 26 March | Maréchal Foch appointed Generalissimo of the Allied armies. |
| 1918 | 1 April | Royal Air Force established. |
| 1918 | 9-18 April | Battle of the Lys, German gains on the Western Front. |
| 1918 | 22 May | Battle of Chemin des Dames, more German gains. |
| 1918 | 9 June | Commencement of Battle of Noyon, heavy German gains. |
| 1918 | 15 July | Battle of Rheims, German gains. |
| 1918 | 18 July | Commencement of Allied counter offensive on Western Front. |
| 1918 | 24 July | Conference of Allied commanders at Bombon. |
| 1918 | 2 August | Allies occupy Archangel in Russia. |
| 1918 | 8 August | Battle of Amiens, 'Der Schwarze Tag' beginning of German collapse. |
| 1918 | 12-15 Sept | American victory on Western Front at Battle of St Mihiel. |
| 1918 | 15 September | Commencement of Allied offensive against Bulgaria. |
| 1918 | 30 September | Surrender of Bulgaria. |
| 1918 | 1 October | Australian cavalry enters Damascus. |
| 1918 | 4 October | King Ferdinand of Bulgaria abdicates. |
| 1918 | 10 October | Sinking of *RMS Leinster*. |
| 1918 | 26 October | General Allenby captures Aleppo. |
| 1918 | 30 October | Turkey signs Armistice with Allies. |
| 1918 | 1 November | Mutiny of German High Seas Fleet in Schillig Roads. |
| 1918 | 3 November | Italian army occupies Trieste. |
| 1918 | 4 November | Austria-Hungary signs Armistice on Italian Front. |
| 1918 | 9 November | Emperor Karl of Austria-Hungary abdicates. |
| 1918 | 9 November | Kaiser Wilhelm II of Germany abdicates. |
| 1918 | 11 November | Armistice on the Western Front signed at Compiègne. |
| 1918 | 25 November | German forces in East Africa surrender at Abercorn, Rhodesia. |
| 1919 | 21 June | German High Seas Fleet scuttled at Scapa Flow. |
| 1919 | 28 June | Treaty of Versailles signed in Hall of Mirrors, Versailles, France. |

# SECOND WORLD WAR CHRONOLOGY

| | | |
|---|---|---|
| 1939 | 22 May | Germany and Italy conclude 'Pact of Steel'. |
| 1939 | 23 August | Germany and USSR sign non - aggression pact. |
| 1939 | 1 September | Germany invades Poland. |
| 1939 | 3 September | Britain and France declare war on Germany, *SS Athenia* sunk. |
| 1940 | 12 February | Royal Navy sink *U-33* and recover Enigma. |
| 1940 | 9 April | Germany invades Norway and Denmark. |
| 1940 | 10 May | Germany invades France, Luxembourg, Belgium and Holland. |
| 1940 | 10 May | Winston Churchill succeeds Neville Chamberlain as Prime Minister. |
| 1940 | 14 May | Surrender of the Netherlands. |
| 1940 | 27 May | *Operation Dynamo* commencement of British evacuation at Dunkirk |
| 1940 | 28 May | King Leopold III surrenders Belgium. |
| 1940 | 10 June | Italy declares war on France and Great Britain. |
| 1940 | 11 June | British troops invade Italian-held Libya. |
| 1940 | 22 June | France signs terms dictated by Germans and submits to occupation. |
| 1940 | 3 July | *Operation Catapult* destruction of French warships by Royal Navy. |
| 1940 | 10 July | Commencement of the Battle of Britain. |
| 1940 | 7 September | Commencement of Blitz. 337 tons of bombs dropped on London. |
| 1940 | 28 October | Italy invades Greece. Mussolini and Hitler meet at Florence. |
| 1940 | 14 November | 449 German aircraft bomb Coventry. |
| 1941 | 22 January | Italian Garrison at Tobruk surrenders. British take 30,000 prisoners. |
| 1941 | 7 February | Italian army surrenders at Beda Fomm. British take 20,000 prisoners. |
| 1941 | 8 March | US Senate passes the Lend-Lease Bill by 60 votes to 31. |
| 1941 | 27 March | Battle of Cape Matapan. Italian naval defeat at hands of Royal Navy. |
| 1941 | 27 March | Bloodless coup in Yugoslavia. King Alexander replaces Peter II. |
| 1941 | 6 April | Germany invades Yugoslavia and Greece. |
| 1941 | 9 April | 9th Australian Division cut off. Start of Siege of Tobruk. |
| 1941 | 13 April | Belgrade occupied by Germans. |
| 1941 | 13 April | USSR and Japan sign five year non-aggression treaty |
| 1941 | 10 May | Nazi leader Rudolf Hess parachutes into Eaglesham, Scotland. |
| 1941 | 20 May | German airborne and paratroop landings on Crete. |
| 1941 | 27 May | Royal Navy sinks the *Bismarck* off south west Éire. |
| 1941 | 31 May | Last Commonwealth forces evacuated from Crete. |
| 1941 | 22 June | Germany invades Soviet Union and makes rapid gains. |
| 1941 | 23 July | Germans capture Brest-Litovsk. |
| 1941 | 5 August | Germans liquidate Smolensk pocket and take 310,000 prisoners. |
| 1941 | 19 September | Germans capture Kiev and take 600,000 prisoners. |
| 1941 | 7 December | Japan mounts surprise attack on US fleet at Pearl Harbor. |
| 1941 | 8 December | Britain and USA declare war on Japan. Japanese bomb Singapore. |
| 1941 | 10 December | British relieve Siege of Tobruk. |
| 1941 | 10 December | HMS PRINCE OF WALES and HMS REPULSE sunk off Malaya. |
| 1941 | 10 December | Japanese invade Philippines and land on Guam. |
| 1941 | 11 December | Germany and Italy declare war on USA. |
| 1941 | 25 December | Surrender of Hong Kong to Japanese. |
| 1942 | 19 January | Japanese army invades Burma. |
| 1942 | 15 February | Lieutenant General Percival surrenders Singapore to Japanese. |
| 1942 | 8 March | Japanese army enters Rangoon. |
| 1942 | 1 May | Commencement of Battle of Coral Sea off Solomon Islands. |
| 1942 | 6 May | US forces on Philippines surrender to Japanese. |
| 1942 | 27 May | Commencement of Battle of Midway off Japan. |

| | | |
|---|---|---|
| 1942 | 30 May | RAF carry out first 1,000 bomber raid on Cologne. |
| 1942 | 4 June | Reinhard Heydrich dies from wounds sustained in assassination. |
| 1942 | 5 June | USA declares war on Bulgaria, Rumania and Hungary. |
| 1942 | 10 June | German SS massacre 642 French civilians at Oradour-sur-Glane. |
| 1942 | 20 June | Rommel's Afrika Korps attacks Tobruk. |
| 1942 | 21 June | General Klopper surrenders Tobruk. Rommel promoted Field Marshal. |
| 1942 | 27 June | Sevastopol falls to German Army Group South under von Manstein. |
| 1942 | 10 August | *Operation Pedestal* underway to relieve Malta. |
| 1942 | 3 September | Commencement of German siege of Stalingrad. |
| 1942 | 23 October | Commencement of Second Battle of El Alamein. |
| 1942 | 8 November | *Operation Torch* American landings in North Africa. |
| 1943 | 14 January | Field Marshal von Paulus surrenders German 6th Army at Stalingrad. |
| 1943 | 8 February | *Operation Longcloth* first Chindit expedition. |
| 1943 | 12 May | Surrender of Afrika Korps under General von Arnim. |
| 1943 | 5 July | Commencement of German Kursk Offensive against Russians. |
| 1943 | 10 July | *Operation Husky* - Allied invasion of Sicily. |
| 1943 | 25 July | Mussolini dismissed by King Victor Emmanuel and arrested. |
| 1943 | 3 September | *Operation Avalanche* - Allied invasion of Italy. |
| 1943 | 10 September | German army occupies Rome. |
| 1943 | 25 September | Russians capture Smolensk. |
| 1943 | 13 October | Italy declares war on Germany. |
| 1943 | 6 November | Russians recapture Kiev. |
| 1943 | 28 November | Teheran Conference between Stalin, Churchill and Roosevelt. |
| 1944 | 3 March | *Operation Thursday* second Chindit expedition. |
| 1944 | 10 April | Russians capture Odessa. |
| 1944 | 19 April | Liquidation of the Warsaw Ghetto by the Germans. |
| 1944 | 9 May | Russians capture Sevastopol. |
| 1944 | 18 May | Monte Cassino falls. |
| 1944 | 4 June | Liberation of Rome. |
| 1944 | 6 June | *Operation Overlord* - Allied invasion of France. |
| 1944 | 20 July | Attempted assassination of Hitler by Colonel Count von Stauffenberg. |
| 1944 | 15 August | *Operation Dragoon* - Allied invasion of Southern France. |
| 1944 | 25 August | Liberation of Paris. |
| 1944 | 3 September | British army liberates Brussels. |
| 1944 | 17 September | *Operation Market Garden* - Allied attempt to seize Rhine bridges. |
| 1944 | 16 December | Commencement of German Ardennes Offensive. |
| 1945 | 4 February | Yalta Conference between Stalin, Churchill and Roosevelt. |
| 1945 | 27 March | Argentina declares war on Germany. |
| 1945 | 29 April | Unconditional surrender of German army in Italy. |
| 1945 | 29 April | *Operation Manna* - RAF relieve starving Dutch with food supplies. |
| 1945 | 29 April | Mussolini and Clara Petacci executed by partisans at Milan. |
| 1945 | 30 April | Dachau Concentration Camp liberated by American army. |
| 1945 | 30 April | Adolf Hitler and his bride Eva Braun commit suicide. |
| 1945 | 2 May | British army relieves Rangoon. |
| 1945 | 8 May | Unconditional surrender of Germany. |
| 1945 | 27 May | Clement Attlee replaces Churchill as Prime Minister. |
| 1945 | 6 August | *Enola Gay* drops 'Little Boy' on Japanese city of Hiroshima. |
| 1945 | 8 August | USSR declares war on Japan. |
| 1945 | 9 August | *Bock's Car* drops 'Fat Man' on Japanese city of Nagasaki. |
| 1945 | 14 August | Emperor Hirohito announces unconditional surrender of Japan. |
| 1945 | 28 August | Mountbatten accepts surrender of Japanese forces in South East Asia. |
| 1945 | 20 November | Commencement of Nuremberg Trials of Nazi leaders. |

THE WESTERN FRONT ASSOCIATION

# THE WESTERN FRONT ASSOCIATION
## *"Remembering"*

The Western Front Association was formed in 1980 by the military historian John Giles to maintain interest in this key period in British history. Its aim is to perpetuate the memory, courage and comradeship of all those of both sides, who served their countries in France and Flanders. It does not seek to glorify war, is non-political and welcomes members of all ages and backgrounds. The steady growth of its worldwide membership to more than 6,500 since 1980 is strongly indicative of a continuing interest in the events that took place in that band of 70 miles running in a line north west to south east from Belgium to France that constituted the British sector of the Western Front in the Great War. The Association supports remembrance and research projects, and was a prime mover in re-establishing observance of the two-minute silence at the Cenotaph at 11.am on 11 November each year.

Individuals may become members on payment of a subscription, and they are able to attend one of nearly 50 branches in the UK and also branches abroad which conduct their affairs according to democratic principles.

Membership of the Association organisation provides the opportunity to meet like-minded people to learn and exchange information. Benefits include seminars, battlefield tours, help with research, and the opportunity to purchase branded commodities and trench maps and receiving *Stand To!* the journal of the Association which is published three times a year. The Association is interested in all Great War memorials and is able to offer advice on restoration, conservation and research. The Western Front association does not encourage the erection of new memorials.

The WFA is a Registered Charity and is managed by an Executive Committee, which is advised by a President and ten Vice-Presidents. The Association has 14 Trustees and 9 appointed Members who serve on its Executive Committee. The Trustees are subject to annual election and the appointed Members to reappointment. The Committee meets four times per year and its activities are subject to the WFA Constitution and the laws relating to Charities in the UK. All Committee activity is voluntary and unpaid.

Website at www.westernfrontassociation.com

# THE ENGLISH HERITAGE BLUE PLAQUE SCHEME

English Heritage is an NDPB (non-departmental public body) and among its manifold tasks in preserving the fabric of the nation's heritage, it is responsible for erection of the blue ceramic discs which are visible on the façades of a number of buildings throughout London and other parts of the United Kingdom. These plaques mark the houses in which great men and women have lived, or where they have performed or created important works. An English Heritage Blue Plaque is rather special, as only a dozen or so are erected each year and each application undergoes a thorough process of research, scrutiny and approval. They are, in effect a permanent addition to a building, and given that most nominated buildings are in themselves historic, such action is not undertaken lightly. Anybody can propose a blue plaque and English Heritage receives about 100 such suggestions each year. Proposers include experts in specific fields, members of professional societies, relatives of suggested individuals or those who occupy a house once lived in by a famous figure. Proposals may also be inspired by significant anniversaries such as centenaries. The scrutiny process usually takes between six and nine years. The first Blue Plaque was erected to honour Lord Byron in 1866. The fields of endeavour covered by the scheme include: the arts, military affairs, music, the performing arts, politics and statecraft, religion, reform and research, science, engineering, architecture, invention, exploration, thought, history and academia. The criteria for nomination state: 'that the individual is regarded as eminent by a majority of his or her profession', 'has made some important contribution to human welfare or happiness', 'had such an outstanding personality that the well-informed passer-by immediately recognizes his or her name and is deserving of recognition'.[1] In the case of nominations of people from abroad, the person should 'be of international reputation' or 'of significant standing in their own country' and 'have lived in London for a significant period'.

English Heritage state: The Blue Plaque 'celebrates a person's connection with an actual building and transforms bricks and mortar into living history. All sorts of buildings are included in the scheme, from the smartest houses to small flats. Plaques bring a house to life and also draw attention to the irreplaceable heritage of domestic architecture all around us. The selection criteria include: either one hundred years from birth, or twenty years from death, must have passed for a candidate to be eligible, the building associated with them must still exist, and we only commemorate an individual once...' Although at the last count, the poet and mystic William Blake had at least five erected to him and the inventor John Logie Baird had three. There are plaques to poets such as John Keats and Sylvia Plath, writers such as James Joyce and Enid Blyton, scientists such as Charles Darwin, musicians including Mozart, Handel and Jimi Hendrix and wartime figures such as Florence Nightingale, Lord Raglan, Field Marshal Earl Kitchener, General Charles de Gaulle, Admiral Viscount Nelson and Edith Cavell. The official Blue Plaque scheme is managed by English Heritage and sometimes in association with local authorities. It focuses on London and a few other locations such as Liverpool and Merseyside, Birmingham, Portsmouth and Southampton, with plans to extend the scheme to more cities in the future. Some city councils have their own schemes for erecting plaques and these have separate procedures and are not co-ordinated by English Heritage. English Heritage maintain that Blue Plaques are not intended to be memorials, they are specifically intended to draw attention to buildings with special associations, for example the flat where a writer penned a famous work, or a home where a famous figure lived. However, the plaques are by definition a form of memorialisation to a specific individual. In addition to English Heritage's scheme, the Corporation of the City of London and Westminster Council both provide their own distinctive plaques - rectangular blue glazed on the one hand and green on the other. Other London Boroughs also have their own schemes and distinctive plaques.

---

[1] None of the foregoing even comes close to adequately explaining why the infamous American traitor Major General Benedict Arnold has an English Heritage Blue Plaque on his house at 62 Gloucester Place, London.

C.P. 2642.

**Confidential**

123

# THE CABINET

## NATIONAL MEMORIALS ON BATTLEFIELDS.

### MEMORANDUM BY THE SECRETARY OF STATE FOR WAR.

With reference to my predecessor's Memorandum of 28$^{th}$ July, 1920 (C.P. 1705), on the subject of National Memorials on Battlefields, and the Cabinet decision (45/20) of 4$^{th}$ August, I circulate the Report of Lord Midleton's Committee, a summary of which is subjoined.

$$\begin{array}{r} 45 \\ \hline 1 \\ \hline 631 \end{array}$$

L.W.-E.

THE WAR OFFICE
28$^{th}$ February, 1921.

### SUMMARY OF THE REPORT OF LORD MIDLETON'S COMMITTEE

*(The references in brackets are to the paragraphs of the Report.)*

1.   The Committee assume that a sum not exceeding £300,000 will be authorised for expenditure of Memorials, in accordance with the decision of the Cabinet (45/20) dated 4$^{th}$ August, 1920. *(Paragraph 11.)*

2.   In Flanders the Menin Gate at Ypres should be adopted as the site for a Memorial to the Troops of the Empire; its architectural treatment might appropriately be in the form of an archway, the cost of which should not exceed £150,000 ., to which contributions of, say £50,000. In all will be invited from India and the Dominions. *(Paragraphs 5 and 11-12.)*

3.   In France a Memorial to the Troops of the United Kingdom should be erected at La Ferté-sous-Jouarre on the Marne to commemorate the first defeat of the Germans there in 1914, and a second Memorial at Amiens as being the most central point whereat to commemorate the rest of the fighting in France. *(Paragraph 23.)*

4.   Commemorative Tablets should be placed in some of the Cathedrals in the area in which British troops operated, and possibly a somewhat more conspicuous Memorial in the Cathedral at Arras. *(Paragraph 27.)*

5.   With regard to the submission of designs for the Memorials, open competition should be adopted in all cases, and the terms of the competition should be drawn up by an assessor or assessors in consultation with the Office of Works and submitted to the Committee. In this connection the Treasury should arrange for preliminary expenses. *(Paragraph 31.)*

6.   The Office of Works should prepare the necessary surveys of the sites at the Menin Gate and La Ferté-sous-Jouarre, and ascertain what site is available at Amiens. *(Paragraph 34.)*

7.   With regard to Gallipoli, the Committee defer making a recommendation pending a report on possible sites which is awaited from Lieutenant-General Sir Aylmer Hunter Weston, K.C.B., D.S.O., who is proceeding to Gallipoli shortly for private purposes. *(Paragraphs 29 and 30.)*

8.   As arrangements are being made for the erection of Memorials at Salonika and Palestine by troops that fought in these battle areas, and as in Mesopotamia, Memorials have already been erected by the British and Indian troops, the Committee require instructions as to whether other Memorials should be erected in these places at public expense. *(Paragraph 28.)*

9.   An announcement to Parliament should be made by His Majesty's Government.

SECRET

18

# THE CABINET

## NATIONAL MEMORIALS ON BATTLEFIELDS

**MEMORANDUM BY THE SECRETARY OF STATE FOR WAR.**

In continuation of my memorandum of 19<sup>th</sup> November, 1919 (C.P. 123), and of 26<sup>th</sup> May, 1920(C.P. 1344), on the subject of National Memorials on battlefields and the preservation of Ypres, I circulate to my colleagues a memorandum embodying the recommendations of the Committee set up in accordance with conclusion (5) of the Conference of Ministers held on 9th December, 1919.

THE WAR OFFICE
*29<sup>TH</sup> July, 1920*

45
1
518

W. S. C.

In accordance with conclusion (5) of the Conference of Ministers held on 9<sup>th</sup> December, 1919, relating to the erection of memorials on the battlefields a Committee has been set-up "to consider and report on the forms of national war memorials and the sites on which they should be erected together with estimates of cost."

The Committee was composed with the Prime Minister's concurrence as follows:-

*Chairman.*

The Right Hon. The Earl of MIDLETON, K.P.

*Members.*

Colonel The Hon. Sir JAMES ALLEN, K.C.B. (New Zealand).
The Right Hon. G. N. BARNES, M.P.
Rear-Admiral Sir R. W. BENTINCK, K.C.M.G., C.B. (Admiralty).
The Right Hon. ANDREW FISHER (Australia).
Mr. D.S. MACCOLL, M.A. (Wallace Collection).
Lieut.-General Sir G. M. W. MACDONOGH, K.C.B., D.C.M.G. (Adjutant-General).
Major T. NANGLE (Newfoundland).
The Hon. Sir G. PERLEY, K.C.M.G. (Canada).
Sir MALCOLM RAMSAY, K.C.B. (Treasury).
The Right Hon. The Lord RIDDELL.
Major-General The Right Hon. J. E. B. SEELY, C.B., C.M.G., D.S.O.
Sir ASTON WEBB, K.C.V.O., C.B., P.R.A.

Lord Midleton's Committee recommends that:-

(i) It is desirable to erect an Imperial Memorial at Ypres in the form of a gateway at the Menin Gate at a cost not exceeding 150,000. And that the Dominions should be given an opportunity of associating themselves with the scheme should they so wish.

(ii) Suitable memorials, such as a cross, an obelisk, a cenotaph, or a sea mark, should be erected at a total cost not exceeding £150,000. By the United Kingdom on the most memorable battlefields in France and at Gallipoli and Salonika; the questions of Palestine, Mesopotamia and East Africa being reserved for further consideration if necessary.

The effect of these recommendations would be that a single memorial would be erected at Ypres typical of Imperial unity, while the United Kingdom should, like the Dominions, erect other memorials to its own troops elsewhere. Ypres is chosen as the site of the Imperial Memorial because it stands for the troops of the Empire as a symbol of the war in a way unequalled by any other place; practically every unit in the army fought there. The actual sites for other memorials remain to be chosen.

Before further definite steps can be taken it is necessary for the Committee to know whether the requisite funds will be forthcoming. A total expenditure of up to £300,000 (which could not fall upon Army funds and for which a special vote would be necessary) does not appear unreasonable in view of the fact that all the Dominions are spending public money on their own memorials; Australia, for instance, has already erected five memorials on the Western front, Canada has voted a sum of 500,000 dollars for her memorials, while New Zealand, South Africa and Newfoundland are all negotiating for the acquisition of sites for memorials to be erected at their Government's expense.

# REPORT OF THE NATIONAL BATTLEFIELDS MEMORIAL COMMITTEE

1.   In presenting their report the National Battlefield Memorials Committee deem it advisable to explain the causes which led to its formation, arising as they did from certain considerations additional to those of sentiment ant the natural desire to commemorate the battlefields upon which the British Army fought during the late war.   *Origin of the Committee*

2.   So far as United Kingdom troops are concerned, it has hitherto been left to the initiative of individual units to commemorate, if they wish, their own exploits by the erection, at their own expense, of memorials on their battlefields, the necessary negotiations with the French and Belgian authorities being carried out through a committee of which the Adjutant-General is Chairman.   *Individual memorials.*

3.   This Committee found that many very distinguished units would thus never be commemorated owing to lack of funds, from which other units, with strong financial and territorial associations, do not suffer.   *Many units uncommemorated.*

4.   Further, the Government of the Dominions have already arranged to spend very considerable sums of money on memorials to their troops in France and Flanders. Australia has already erected memorials at Polygon Wood and on the Hindenburg Line, and proposes to spend a further £100,000 as a general Australian memorial at Villers-Bretonneux. Canada has voted a million dollars, and a Special Commission under a Brigadier-General is now engaged upon the work of erecting five memorials to Canadians in France and Flanders. South Africa has bought Delville Wood, and New Zealand and Newfoundland are engaged upon memorials on various battlefields. India has also decided to spend some £10,000 on memorials to Indian troops in various parts of the world.   *Action by the Dominions and India.*

5.   The attention of the Cabinet was drawn to the above facts and it was represented to them that it would only be consistent with the dignity of the British Government that it should not fall behind the Dominions and India in paying homage to the Army and its exploits on the field of battle, and a scheme for rebuilding the Menin Gate at a cost of approximately £300,000 was submitted to the Cabinet as a suitable form which the National Memorial should take.   *Facts placed before the Cabinet.*

The selection of Ypres as the site for the main memorial was made for the following reasons:-   *Choice of Ypres for the major memorial.*

(i)   Practically every division on the Western Front passed through Ypres at one time or another.

(ii)   In its immediate neighbourhood there was continuous fighting from the beginning to the end; it was the scene of three desperate battles in 1914, 1915 and 1917, and was the starting point of the great advance in the north in October, 1918.

(iii)   Its defence stands to the British Army as that of Verdun is to the French: Ypres and Verdun are the only two towns that His Majesty had decorated with the Military Cross.

(iv)   Many thousand of men lost their lives in the salient.

6.   The Adjutant-General's Committee referred to in paragraph 2 had made some preliminary investigations regarding the possibility of Ypres as a site for a National Memorial, and an agreement had been reached with the Belgian Government in 1919 that the Menin Gate and the Ramparts were to be left in their ruined state pending the decision of the British Government as to a scheme for their reconstruction as a National Memorial. This Committee had also considered the possibility of the Grande Place at Ypres as a site and some reconstruction of the Cathedral or Cloth Hall, but the two latter alternatives have been abandoned, as they are less significant for the Army than the Menin Gate, and moreover the cost of rebuilding the Cloth Hall and the Cathedral should more appropriately be paid by those who destroyed them, viz., the Germans.   *Selection of the Menin Gate.*

7.   The Government accordingly at the end of 1919 decided in principle that public money should be devoted to this purpose, and appointed the present Committee to make   *Proposals approved in*

recommendations.  
                  principle by the Gov't.

8.     The Committee were faced at the outset with four main problems:

        (i)     The precise object which was to be commemorated.

        (ii)    The amount of money that should be spent.

        (ii)    The number of memorials to be erected.

        (iv)   The sites upon which they should be erected.

9.     (i) *Objects*. – The principal object was to commemorate fighting on battlefields, but as the Dominions had already made extensive preparations to commemorate their own exploits, the question arose as to whether the memorials to be erected should include or exclude them. The sense of the Committee was that while individual Dominions and units naturally would wish to commemorate in their own way the exploits of their troops, consideration of sentiment and history were strongly in favour of at least one general memorial at some outstanding locality which would serve to commemorate in an adequate manner the actions of the troops of the whole Empire, and that the memorials erected elsewhere should commemorate the troops of the United Kingdom. There would thus be a single Imperial monument commemorating the unity of the Empire, together with individual memorials representing the individual countries.     Objects to be commemorated.

10:    (ii) *The amount of money that should be spent.* – The Committee feel that it was a matter of difficulty to fix a sum that would provide for memorials adequate to the dignity of the Empire and yet would appear extravagant at a time when economy was so urgent.     Financial question.

        The figure of £300,000 originally suggested for the rebuilding of the Menin Gate at Ypres appeared very high when to was remembered that only £10,000 was spent on what after all will prove to be the most visible and accessible memorial of the war, namely, the Cenotaph, in Whitehall. At the same time for the British Army Ypres stands alone as a scene of action, and the memory of its action should be worthily commemorated in stone. The Committee have as one of their members Sir Aston Webb, P.R.A., and they had the advantage of the opinion of the President as the Royal Institute of British Architects and Mr. R. J. Allison, one of the chief architects of the Office of Works, and as advised by them the Committee were of opinion that an adequate memorial could be erected at Ypres at a cost of £150,000 and the Committee recommend that this amount should be spent on a general Imperial memorial at Ypres. For other battlefields the Committee suggest that a total of not exceeding £150,000 should be spent; they are bound to point out that this figure is somewhat tentative, but it balances that £150,000 which they recommend for Ypres.

11.    As the Committee could not proceed to decide upon the actual number and sites of memorials without knowing if His Majesty's Government were prepared to find the necessary money, reference was made to the Cabinet who decided in August last that:-     Authority for expenditure obtained from the Cabinet.

        (a) (i)    It is desirable to erect an Imperial memorial at Ypres, in the form of a gateway, at the Menin Gate, at a cost not exceeding £150,000 and that the Dominions should be given an opportunity of associating themselves with the scheme should they so wish.

        (ii)    Suitable memorials, such as a cross, an obelisk, a cenotaph or a sea mark, should be erected, at a total cost not exceeding £150,000 by the United Kingdom on the most memorable battlefields in France, and at Gallipoli and Salonika; the questions of Palestine, Mesopotamia and East Africa being reserved for further consideration, if necessary.

        (b) (i)    That the Secretary of State for India should be authorized to invite a contribution from the Government of India towards the Imperial memorial at Ypres.

12. The Governments of India and of the Dominions have now been asked whether they desire to associate themselves in the "Menin Gate" scheme, which the representatives of the Dominions here have assured us is likely to be favourably considered, but their replies have not yet been received. The Committee have suggested that, should they so desire, the Dominions and India might see their way to contributing one-third of the cost of the Menin Gate scheme (£50,000.) the remainder falling on the British Exchequer. This would release £50,000 which could, if required, be added to the £150,000 suggested for memorials elsewhere and still leave the total to be spent by the United Kingdom unchanged at £300,000.

<sub>Reference to India and other Dominions.</sub>

13. Having obtained the agreement of the Cabinet in principle to the expenditure of not exceeding £300,000. the Committee appointed a sub-committee to go into details as regards –

<sub>Problems consequent on the Gov't decision.</sub>

        (i)    Sites of memorials.

        (ii)    Number of memorials.

        (iii)   Form of memorials.

        (iv)   Selection of designs.

14. (i) *Sites*.- Before entering upon this question of sites the Chairman addressed letters to Viscount French, Earl Haig, Lord Rawlinson, Lord Horne and Lord Byng asking for their recommendations as to the most suitable battlefields to be commemorated, while in order to judge between the sites so recommended, bearing in mind the views that artistic opinion and accessibility to the public must be weighed, it was found necessary that a sub-committee should visit the sites in company with experts.

<sub>Sites Consultation of Military Commanders.</sub>

15. The Sub-Committee accordingly, with the exception of Sir Aston Webb, who was unable to leave England, spent four days from 5th November to 9th November in the most careful examination of the principal battlefields.

<sub>Visit to sites.</sub>

Owing to the absence of Sir Aston Webb, the Sub-Committee invited Mr J. W. Simpson, President of the Royal Institute of British Architects, to take part in the visit as technical adviser, and they had the further advantage of the advice of Mr. R.J. Allison, Principal Architect of His Majesty's Office of Works, who also attended at the request of the First Commissioner, as the latter is likely to be the Minister charged with the actual work of erecting any National Memorials.

The task of the Sub-Committee divided itself into two parts:-

(i) To explore the possibilities of the Menin Gate at Ypres as a memorial to the fighting in Belgium upon which the Cabinet have already in principle agreed to spend a sum not exceeding £150,000.

(ii) To report as to what memorials should be erected in France.

16. The Sub-Committee made a most careful examination of the gateway and were impressed with the artistic possibilities of the situation as well as by its military significance for the Divisions of the British Army. They were of opinion that a gateway or archway at the Menin Gate would be the most appropriate memorial. It was pointed out to the Committee that the town of Ypres is growing up on both sides of the ramparts, and the history of towns shows that owing to their growth and the exigencies of traffic, gateways are generally removed (like Temple Bar) or the traffic is diverted round them (like the Marble Arch); that the track of a tramway runs through the gateway already, and that the ramparts on either side of the Menin Gate may, at some future time, be removed and the moat filled in.

<sub>Objection to a gateway.</sub>

But having considered these objection, the Sub-Committee remain of opinion that an archway or gateway is the most significant form which the memorial contemplated could take. The Committee recommend that in drawing up the conditions for the architectural competition, a chief point should be that any design must include a striking and easily legible inscription; with this proviso the treatment of the Menin Gate should be left to the competing architects, the scheme of an archway or gateway being placed before them as a first of possible alternatives.

<sub>Advantages of an archway and necessity for an inscription.</sub>

17. In view of the rapid reconstruction now taking place in Ypres, the Belgian Government

has been asked without delay to re-affirm the agreement made with the Battle Exploit Memorials Committee in July, 1919, at Ypres, by which the Belgian authorities undertook to leave the ramparts in their ruined state pending the formulation of a scheme of memorial reconstruction by the British Government. (Probably not more than 100 metres of the ramparts on either side of the Gate would be required for the memorial). This opinion was conveyed, unofficially, to the British Military Attache who met the Sub-Committee at Ypres.

II FRANCE

18.   The case of France is much more difficult than that of Belgium. Small memorials are being erected on the various battlefields by individual units; larger memorials are contemplated by the Dominions, and it is understood that the Americans propose to put up memorials on a considerable scale. It is clear, therefore, that any National Memorial erected to commemorate the actions of the British Armies in France must be adequate to the dignity of the Empire.

*France. Difficulty of selecting sites.*

19.   The Committee, after careful consideration, are convinced that the character of any memorial in France must be such as to commemorate –

      (i)      Victory over the enemy.

      (ii)     Phases of the fighting.

*Principles of selection.*

There are considerations which would lead to the choice of the Marne as a suitable site for a memorial. It was there that the Germans suffered their first and, perhaps, decisive defeat. The number of British troops engaged, though they represented the flower of the old Army, was small compared with the troops that fought on the Somme or the Hindenburg Line. To some extent the Somme stands for France, much as Ypres stands for Belgium in the eyes of the British soldier, and it would, therefore, seem impossible not to include the Somme in any scheme for commemorating the fighting in France.

There are, moreover, the Arras region and Vimy Ridge. In these areas the site would obviously be the summit of Vimy Ridge, but arrangements are being made by the Canadian Government to erect a Battle Memorial there.

Finally, the successful arrest of the German attack in 1918, and the British victories later in the year point to the erection of a memorial at Villers-Bretonneux or on the Hindenburg Line.

From a military point of view, probably the best monument to a battle is at the culminating point of the battle itself; but the most famous battlefields (e.g. The Hindenburg Line and the Somme are remote from the ordinary routes of travellers, and a memorial which can only be reached by a long motor car journey will rarely be visited by the ordinary man, and if it is seen only by very few French peasants, it will fail to commemorate the sentiment of alliance of which such memorials should be perpetual reminder.

An alternative would be to place some striking monument in a large town which could be viewed by thousands of passers by every day; but the only town which would be really central for such a memorial is Paris itself, which was not a battlefield.

20.   The Committee were thus forced to the conclusion that a single monument in France would be inadequate and that to fulfil the double function of commemorating the victory and the battles that made the victory possible, more than one memorial is desirable.

*More than one memorial desirable.*

21.   After earnest consideration it appeared that the best method of arriving at the number of memorials would be to divide the war into its various broad phases and to commemorate these.

*Phases of the war.*

These phases may be roughly grouped under the following four heads:-

(i)   The actions of 1914, beginning with the retreat from Mons and ending with the battle of the Aisne.

(ii)   The fighting at Ypres (continuous throughout the war).

(iii) The immense sacrifices of 1916 and 1917 on the Somme and about Arras.

(iv) The retreat and advance of 1918.

22. The recommendations of the military commanders referred to in paragraph 14, were as follows:-

Views of the Military Commanders

| — | 1914 | 1914 -15 | 1916 - 17 | 1918 |
|---|---|---|---|---|
| F.-M. Lord French ... | La Ferté-sous-Jouarre (on the Marne). | ... | ... | ... |
| F.-M. Lord Haig ... ... | Troyon | Ypres | Pozières. Monchy-le-Preux Thièpval. | Troyon Villers-Bretonneux Bony Bellicourt |
| General Lord Rawlinson ... | ... | Polygon Wood | Pozières | Epéhy |
| General Lord Horne ... | Messines Givenchy | ... | Messines Albert Butte de Warlencourt Point Du Jour Vimy | Messines Givenchy |

The Sub-Committee visited practically all these sites and, assuming that the memorials are to be erected on the actual battlefields, had no difficulty in selecting the most suitable sites for the first and last phases of the war.

(ii) *The Fighting and Victory of the Marne, 1914.*

First Phase.

23. The Sub-Committee unanimously concurred in the recommendation of Lord French that the early operations of 1914 could best be commemorated at La Ferté-sous-Jouarre at the point where the 3$^{rd}$ Corps crossed the River Marne, giving invaluable assistance to General Maunoury in his operations on the enemy's flank at the crossing of the Ourcq. There is an admirable site on the hills above the town, south of the Marne, but the Sub-Committee felt that some memorial in the vicinity of the bridge, or on the bridge itself, which is also famous for the Crossing of the Marne by Napoleon in 1814 – exactly 100 years before – is the best means of commemorating the turning point of the war. It may be observed that the town has already renamed the boulevards along the river "Boulevards des Anglais".

(ii) *The Last Phase, 1918.*

24. The Sub-Committee were unanimous in the choice of Villers-Bretonneux as the most suitable spot to commemorate the actions of 1918. It was here that the 4$^{th}$ Army under General Rawlinson checked the German Advance in April, 1918, within 8 miles of Amiens and subsequently drove them out on 8$^{th}$ August, 1918, a day specially marked by Ludendorff in the German Military Calendar. There is an admirable site in the centre of the town at the junction of the Corbie-Villers-Bretonneux and Villers-Bretonneux – Amiens road.

Last Phase

These two sites (La Ferté-sous-Jouarre and Villers-Bretonneux) are also the choice of the two Commanders-in-Chief concerned, and are comparatively easy of access, the one from Paris, and the other from Amiens.

(iii) *The Intermediate Phase.*

25. The problem of commemorating the stupendous battles on the Somme and in the neighbourhood of Arras presents great difficulties, there being no central spot connected with both, though the Sub-Committee carefully considered the Vimy Ridge, Albert, Pozières and the

Intermediate

Butte de Warlencourt.

26. The Committee consequently recommend that to commemorate the whole of the fighting in France subsequent to the battle of the Marne there should be erected a monument at Amiens, as the most central point for the whole fighting, and that to commemorate the fighting on the Marne in 1914 a memorial should be erected at La Ferté-sous-Jouarre. They were also disposed to accept the recommendation of Villers-Bretonneux, but they were informed that the Australian Government propose to spend as much as £100,000 on a memorial there.

*phase.*

*Selection by Committee.*

*Amiens.*

*The Marne.*

27. The Sub-Committee also felt that commemorative tablets might well be erected in some of the cathedrals with which the British Army were connected, such as Amiens, Arras, Beauvais, Boulogne, Cambrai, Laon, Lille, Meaux, Noyon, Paris (Notre Dame), Rheims, Rouen, St. Omer, St. Quentin, Soissons.

*Tablets in Cathedrals.*

This recommendation the Committee endorse.

28. There remains for consideration the question of Gallipoli and the theatres of war other than Flanders and France.

*Other theatres.*

With regard to Mesopotamia, the Committee are informed that arrangements have been made locally for the erection of a memorial to the troops that fought with Sir Stanley Maude. In the case of Palestine, Lord Allenby has prepared a scheme for the erection, near Jerusalem, of a memorial, for which £11,000 has been subscribed. At Salonika, the troops under the command of General Milne have subscribed some £5,000 and arrangements are being made locally for the erection of a memorial near Salonika.

*Mesopotamia.*

*Palestine.*

*Salonika.*

The Indian troops are closely identified with the first two theatres, and in view of what has already been done and the necessity for ascertaining more precisely the intentions of the Indian Government, the Committee have not delayed their report till the problems of Mesopotamia, Palestine and Salonika are cleared up. The Committee desire to be instructed whether the Government contemplate erecting memorials in Salonika, Palestine and Mesopotamia in addition to those already provided for.

*Indian troops.*

29. As regards Gallipoli, a Committee of representatives of the three services has been investigating the possibility of erecting a joint memorial to all British troops that fought there (other than troops from the Dominions, &c.)

*Gallipoli.*

General Hunter-Weston, who is a member of this Committee, gave evidence before the Committee, and explained that an investigation of sites is now being carried out as to the actual sites. The Australian and New Zealand Governments already contemplated erecting memorials at Anzac, and with this proposal the Committee would not, of course, interfere.

General Hunter-Weston is proceeding shortly to Gallipoli, and the Committee gladly availed themselves of his offer to report in particular and detail upon the possibility of Kourgi-Baba and other sites in the neighbourhood.

30. The Committee would accordingly prefer not to make definite recommendations regarding Gallipoli until they had received General Hunter-Weston's report.

31. As regards the selection of artists and designs for the memorial, the Committee recommend that designs for all the sites should be thrown open to competition, and that competitors, in the first instance, should submit sketches. A suitable assessor of assessors should be selected, who should choose the best six sketches; the designers of these sketches should receive 200 guineas, and then proceed to a further competition, in which finished designs could be asked for. The actual terms under which the public competition should be held should be drawn by proper architectural authorities, such as the President of the Royal Institute of British Architects, in conjunction with the authorities of His Majesty's Office of Works, who would probably be charged with the duties of supervising the expenditure in connection with the erection of the memorials. The Committee would not be bound to accept any design, and the final freedom of the Cabinet to select is, of course, to be understood. The consent of the Belgian and French Governments to the designs selected should be obtained diplomatically.

*Design.*

*Open Competition.*

*Freedom of Committee and Cabinet to select or reject.*

32. As regards the machinery for the execution of the design, the Committee recommend that when the actual sum of money and the designs have been decided upon, His Majesty's Office of Works should enter into the necessary contracts for the proper execution of the work and should supervise and account for authorized expenditure.  
*Administrative machinery.*

33. The Committee are informed by the Admiralty representative that the Admiralty contemplate the erection of some general memorial to the Navy. Such a scheme has obviously much to commend it but the Committee consider that it should be left for separate consideration by His Majesty's Government.

34. The recommendations of the Committee may be summarized as follows:-  
*Summary.*

(i) That, as outlined in paragraph 16, the Menin Gate at Ypres be adopted as the memorial in Flanders at a cost not exceeding £150,000 – to which contributions of, say, £50,000 in all will be invited from India and Dominions.

(ii) That a central memorial in France be erected at Amiens, and a memorial be also erected at La Ferté-sous-Jouarre.

(iii) That tablets be placed in some of the Cathedrals in the area in which British troops operated, and possibly a somewhat more conspicuous memorial in the Cathedral at Arras.

(iv) That open competition be adopted in all cases, and that the terms of competition should be drawn up by an assessor or assessors in consultation with the Office of Works and submitted to the, Committee, and that the Treasury should arrange for the preliminary expenses.

(v) That the Office of Works be instructed to prepare the necessary surveys of the sites at the Menin Gate and at La Ferté-sous-Jouarre, and ascertain what site is available at Amiens.

(vi) That an announcement to Parliament should be made by His Majesty's Government.

35. The Committee desire to express their high appreciation of the services of their Secretary, Mr Kenneth Lyon.

MIDLETON, *Chairman.*
J. ALLEN
RUDOLF W. BENTINCK.
R.A. BLANKENBERG.
LIONEL EARLE.
D.S. MacCOLL.
G. M. W. MACDONOGH.
GEORGE H. PERLEY.
MALCOLM G. RAMSAY.
RIDDELL.
J.E.B. SEELY.

KENNETH LYON, Secretary.

REMARK BY LIEUT.- COLONEL T. NANGLE.

I am in agreement with the above Report with the exception of paragraph 34, Clause (ii), which I would amend as follows:-

"That a central memorial in France be erected on the actual battle-ground of the Somme, preferably in the vicinity of Albert-Pozières, and a memorial be also erected at La Ferté-sous-Jouarre."
T. NANGLE.

# JOURNAL OF THE ROYAL SOCIETY OF ARTS

No. 4676          FRIDAY, OCTOBER 13th, 1944          Vol. xcII

OPENING OF THE 191st SESSION, 1944-45.

The first meeting of the new Session will be held at 1.45 p.m., on Wednesday, November 1st, when the Inaugural Address, on "Chemistry in the Service of Man," will be delivered by Dr. E. F. Armstrong, F.R.S., President of the Society and Chairman of the Council.

After delivering his Address, the President will present the Swiney Prize for 1944, R.D.I. Diplomas and the Silver Medals awarded to lecturers for papers read during the Session 1943-44.

### FORMATION OF WAR MEMORIALS ADVISORY COUNCIL

At the Inaugural Meeting of the War Memorials Advisory Council which was held at the Society's House on Monday, September 18th, Admiral of the Fleet, the Rt. Hon. Lord Chatfield, G.C.B., O.M., K.C.M.G., C.V.O., was unanimously elected President; Dr. E. F. Armstrong, F.R.S., Chairman of the Executive Committee and Mr. A. R. N. Roberts, Honorary Secretary.

The following is the text of a printed survey which was approved at this meeting for circulation to the Press and to official bodies throughout the country

## WAR MEMORIALS

### A SURVEY MADE BY A COMMITTEE OF THE ROYAL SOCIETY OF ARTS AND PUBLISHED BY THE WAR MEMORIALS ADVISORY COUNCIL.

*"And having each one given his body to the Commonwealth they receive in stead thereof a most remarkable sepulchre, not that wherein they are buried so much as that other wherein their glory is laid up on all occasions, both of word and deed, to be remembered for evermore."*

*Pericles*

For the second time in a generation Britain and the cause of freedom have been saved by the willing sacrifice of life itself by thousands of our fellow countrymen and women. For a second time there will be a nation-wide desire that such self-sacrifice shall be worthily commemorated. Every town and village that erected a memorial to those who died in the 1914-1918 struggle will be concerned to hold in no less honour the fallen of the present "total war" – combatants and civilians alike. This fact compels a re-examination of the question of memorials lest ill-considered duplication of those of the last war should result. Furthermore, there will be a general wish that on this occasion a higher standard of war memorials may be reached. This aim is unlikely of achievement unless in good time some preliminary thought is given to the subject.

The present statement is issued to assist the many committees that will be charged with the institution of memorials – whether described as war memorials or peace or victory memorials. Whilst very properly retaining full freedom to express the sentiments of the community or organisation for whom they act such committees may yet welcome suggestions from a representative central body as to the principles which should underlie commemorative action with some examples of their application.

CONSTITUTION OF WAR MEMORIALS ADVISORY COUNCIL

Before advancing these suggestions the War Memorials Advisory Council submits a brief statement of their origin.

In April, 1944, the Royal Society of Arts convened a conference to stress the need for a high standard of artistic merit and social and cultural value in the memorials of the present war. The conference was opened by Admiral of the Fleet Lord Chatfield, and addressed by representatives of several bodies concerned with the arts and with social welfare. In response to the unanimous resolution of the conference the Royal Society of Arts set up a War Memorials Sub-Committee, co-opting representatives of other interested societies, to consider the subject further and to make recommendations.

In September, 1944, these recommendations were submitted to the inaugural meeting of the War Memorials Advisory Council, a body comprising representatives of a larger number of societies and men and women of individual distinction in public affairs and in the arts. By this Council – which will remain in being as a clearing house of general information for the guidance of local committees – they were adopted and are hereby published. The names of the associated national societies are given on the enclosed leaflet [see p. 589 of this issue], each of those marked with a * having kindly agreed to assist the Council – which cannot itself undertake consultative work – by advising local committees upon individual War Memorial projects hat fall within that society's sphere.

A RECORD OF NAMES

The Council's primary recommendation is that a worthy record of the names of all the fallen shall be kept by each community – in a location accessible to all. Throughout the centuries the art of the sculptor has provided such records, and few things are more satisfactory than a well-designed and well-cut inscription. Adequately spaced and in the right medium it provides a dignified and permanent record. In view, however, of the fact that on many memorials of the last year, where these considerations have been in-sufficiently regarded, names can now be read only with difficulty, the Council calls attention to an acceptable alternative.

A Book of Remembrance – of good vellum pages, of good binding and good script, would provide a beautiful and durable record, giving space for the details of service career and achievements.

## THE PURPOSE OF OUR MEMORIALS

In most communities a much larger sum is likely to be raised than will be required to achieve this primary task of providing a record of names, and further memorials will thus be possible. As to the purpose which should underlie these wider projects the Council calls attention to a passage from Lord Chatfield's opening speech at the War Memorials Conference: -

"We should commemorate in our war memorials the spirit in which we went to war, the unity of purpose and action which the war has brought about, and the spirit in which we have fought and our sons and daughters have given their lives. If that thought is to govern national feeling and action after the war that which is spiritual in a war memorial must not be lost. There is a feeling with which I sympathise that in honouring the dead we can perhaps do something for those for whom they died, but we must also take care that the other object is achieved.

As a consequence of Act of Parliament, much will be done after this war in improving social facilities ........ We must be careful therefore to see that the war memorial is not indistinguishable from that which is not a war memorial. Only thus will it fulfil its educational and spiritual purpose ..... as a guide and a light to future generations which can never be removed."

What follows from the above? First, that where the memorials take the form of monuments they must not be (as to often after the last war) mere standardised products of commerce. They must be the creation of individual artists well acquainted with or prepared to study the sentiments of the community that commissions them and the location chosen for the memorial. Secondly, where the memorials take the form of socially valuable projects they must meet permanent rather than temporary needs. Further, they should not consist in the provision of facilities which government, national or local, will in any case provide. Finally, they must be obviously and unmistakably war memorials. To achieve the last of these aims the Council recommends:-

(a) That each Record of Names should contain a reference to any other form that the local memorial takes.

(b) To make clear its memorial purpose any land or building dedicated as a war memorial should contain a group of sculpture or a relief panel in stone or metal or inscribed doors or gates.

(c) That on the site of the memorial suitable occasion be taken at least annually for a public act or recognition of the sacrifice the memorial commemorates.

## PROJECTS OF SOCIAL SERVICE

In submitting as suitable war memorials certain projects of social service – all of a tangible nature – the Council makes no suggestion that others of equal or greater merit cannot be devised, whether of the same general character or otherwise. It is however, the Council's hope that the following may be included amongst those projects from which committees make their choice.

The key-word of the larger memorials should be re-creation. For the whole population the smooth current of peace-time life, and the contentment of a quiet mind are shattered by the hideous calamity of war. Nature herself can best restore the balance which man's misguided mechanical ingenuity has so cruelly disturbed. In the restfulness and beauty of land developed as a memorial many districts may find the answer to their problem – an answer which will constitute a permanent enrichment of the neighbourhood. The following ways in which land may be used for memorial purposes are submitted for further examination by individual committees:-

(1)   The laying out (perhaps in the immediate neighbourhood of the memorial of the last war, the site of which would thereby be enhanced) of Gardens of Memory, places of rest and meditation. In such gardens generous use might well be made of flowering trees and the more fragrant shrubs and flowers. In war-damaged towns bombed sites could, by collaboration with the local planning authorities, be converted into beautiful oases in otherwise characterless deserts of brick and mortar. Disused churchyards and the gardens of city squares which are often neglected might be made things of beauty again. The ruins of certain bombed churches, preserved in a garden setting with the minimum of repairs necessary to ensure public safety, would be a permanent reminder of the suffering and loss which war inflicts.

(2)   The creation of parks and open spaces, including the improvement of riverside banks with public access thereto; on such land the individual dead could be commemorated by the gift from relatives or friends of an artistically-designed seat, or some other feature adding to its amenities.

(3)   The planning in suitable areas adjacent to towns and villages of groups of memorial trees in which individuals could be commemorated by their own trees. The improvement of the approaches to towns by avenues of suitable trees might be considered.

(4)   The acquisition of hill tops or view points. A hill to which in the course of one's daily round one can lift one's eyes in memory of the fallen, a hill which one can climb, away from the world's distractions for periods of reflection, may well be in rural areas where such land can be secured one of the most fitting of memorials. The acquisition of heaths and commons, and of nature reserves, planned under expert guidance, would also be a source of permanent inspiration and delight.

(5)   Playing fields and children's play-grounds are more utilitarian than any of the foregoing, but in the opinion of the Council suitable as war memorials for two reasons. Firstly, in honouring the dead we must not forget their wish that their children should enjoy a fuller life. Amongst the fallen those who have shown gifts of leadership on the battlefield would doubtless have become leaders also on the playing field, helping their juniors to acquire that team spirit which should increasingly be manifest in our civic life. Secondly, we should remember the surviving men and women of the Services for whom during the war exceptional facilities for recreation have been provided, facilities which, on any adequate scale, they may lack on their return to civilian life. For them, as for the rising generation, well equipped sports centres are urgently required.

(6)   The acquisition and preservation of buildings of historic interest or architectural importance would be a happy tribute to those who have themselves so notably enriched their country's history. The restoration of such buildings – including those which have suffered damage – may also arise.

Where a memorial is to take the form of land dedicated to public use its maintenance will, as a general rule, be best assured by appointing as trustees the appropriate local authority or a national organisation not subject to the changes caused by the death or resignation of individual trustees. The local authority, a body permanently representative of the community, possesses the power, which private trustees do not enjoy, of enforcing bye-laws for the prevention of nuisances and the preservation of order. Moreover, if the deeds be properly drawn, liability for rates and taxes can be avoided. Where the trusteeship of the local authority is not practicable, the National Trust might be invited to become guardians of sites of historic interest or especial natural beauty, and the National Playing Fields Association of recreation grounds.

## COMMUNITY CENTRES AND VILLAGE HALLS

The thoughts of our men on foreign service have turned back may times to the town or village that to them is home. They have longed that it might be kept safe, and that they might return to make it something better for those who follow them. The physical amenities of the homeland will be enhanced by the projects mentioned earlier. There are means of strengthening its mental and spiritual life which provide other acceptable forms of war memorials. For instance, the spirit of comradeship in public service which our Civil Defence Services have engendered would find a new outlet in the creation and maintenance in active being of the Community Centres and Village Halls, the lack of which in many areas has long been deplored. Here talks and discussions, displays of pictures and sculpture, performances of music, plays and films, with other recreational activities, would make happier and better citizens.

The much needed expert guidance in the design and lay-out of buildings for these purposes is obtainable with illustrative models and plans from two of the Council's associated societies.

## HOSPITALS AND OTHER HEALTH ORGANISATIONS

In the proposed national medical service the voluntary hospitals, to which thousands of Servicemen owe their restoration to health and happiness, will continue to have an honoured place. No memorial could in principle be more appropriate than the development of hospitals, convalescent homes, rest centres and child welfare clinics, for human suffering cruelly increased by war is, by such institutions, nobly lessened.

## AFTER-CARE OF THE WOUNDED

The claims of the Servicemen with long-term impairment of physical or mental health demand the most careful thought. Government, it may be confidently hoped, will make an ampler provision for them than in the past, but there may be need for the provision of small institutions, where the initial capital outlay having been met from war memorial funds, their pensions would secure for invalid Servicemen a higher standard of comfort and of readily available medical attention then in their scattered individual homes.

## DESIGN

The Council would stress the supreme importance of design in whatever enterprise of a tangible nature may be undertaken. The value of any sum of money raised will be enhanced, and the dignity, simplicity and suitability of the memorial assured if the best professional advice is secured. The architect, the sculptor, the painter and the landscape architect by natural gifts, by professional training and practice can place at the service of those who commission them a wealth of faculty and experience that will obviate the errors which hastily applied rule-of-thumb knowledge has in the past so-often entailed.

Inscriptions need the greatest care to ensure felicity of wording.

## MAINTENANCE

The Council wishes again to stress the importance of providing for the proper maintenance of war memorials. The condition of many memorials of the last war does honour neither to those whom they commemorate nor to the donors whose generosity permitted their provision. The better care of them might well have a place in the plans for memorials of the present war; and this time more forethought must be shown.

## CONSULTATION

To ensure co-ordination of effort it is recommended that committees be representative of all important local interests, and include branch members of national bodies whose headquarters may be issuing War Memorial appeals. Close contact should be maintained with the district's civic head and with the local authority. Early consultation with its Planning Officer (and through him, where necessary, with the Regional Planning Officer of the Ministry of Town and Country Planning) in the case of projects involving the use of land will facilitate the local authority's acceptance of the trusts above described. Committees are advised to register the name and address of their secretary with the War Memorials Advisory Council, so that they may receive further general statements as issued; and before finally deciding upon their memorial to consult the appropriate society amongst those offering advice, of which a list is enclosed.

## A NATIONAL WAR MEMORIAL

This statement is primarily directed to those committees who will be acting for towns and villages, for schools and other institutions, for Service units and commercial undertakings. The Council therefore submits no detailed recommendations for a National War Memorial, but supports in principle a suggestion of Lord Chatfield's at the War Memorials Conference:-

"London, to which come the imperial pilgrims who visit the mother country, should surely have a special memorial of its own ...... a shrine that will include in itself memorials to the dead of the fighting Services, the Civil Defence Services and all those who have taken part in this war and deserve to be remembered."

The creation of such a memorial at the heart of the Empire would crown the work of all the committees to whom this report is cordially, but with deference, addressed.

Among those who have already agreed to serve on the Council, which will consist of the representatives of fifty Societies and a like number of distinguished individuals, are the following:-

*President:* Admiral of the Fleet, The Rt. Hon. Lord CHATFIELD, P.C., G.C.B., O.M., K.C.M.G., C.V.O.
*Chairman:* Dr. E. G. ARMSTRONG, F.R.S. (President of the Royal Society of Arts).
*Honorary Secretary:* A. R. N. ROBERTS, Esq.

### ASSOCIATED SOCIETIES.

*(Those marked with a \* have kindly agreed to act in an advisory capacity on matters within their own sphere referred to them by the War Memorials Advisory Council. Names of the Societies' representatives on the Council are given in brackets.)*

| | |
|---|---|
| *British Hospitals Association, The | (J. P. Wetenhall, Esq.). |
| *Central Institute of Art and Design | |
| *Commons, Open Spaces and Footpaths Preservation Society.. | (Sir Lawrence Chubb). |
| *Council for the Encouragement of Music and the Arts | (Philip James, Esq.). |
| *Council for the Preservation of Rural England | (H. G. Griffin, Esq., C.B.E.). |
| *Institute of Park Administration (Inc.).. | (W. H. Johns, Esq.). |
| *London Society, The | |
| *Men of the Trees, The | (R. St. Barbe Baker, Esq.). |
| *Metropolitan Public Gardens Association, The | (Sir Patrick Gower). |
| *National Council of Social Service, The | (G. E. Haynes, Esq.). |
| *National Playing Fields Association, The | (Sir Lawrence Chubb). |
| *National Trust, The | (D. M. Matheson, Esq.; W. A. Forsyth, Esq., F.R.I.B.A.). |
| *Roads Beautifying Association, The | (Wilfred Fox, Esq.). |
| *Rotary International | (F. C. Hickson, Esq.). |
| *Royal Academy of Arts, The.. | (Gilbert Ledward, Esq., R.A.; E. Vincent, Harris, Esq., R.A.). |
| *Royal Designers for Industry, Faculty of | (Percy Smith, Esq., R.D.I.). |
| *Royal Institute of British Architects | (Edward Maufe, Esq., A.R.A. ; O.P. Milne, Esq., F.R.I.B.A.). |
| *Royal Society of Arts | |
| *Royal Society of British Sculptors | (Charles Wheeler, Esq., R.A.). |
| *Society for the Promotion of Nature Reserves | (Dr. F. G. Herbert Smith, M.A.). |
| *Society for the Protection of Ancient Buildings | (Rt. Hon. the Viscount Esher). |
| *Society of Scribes and Illuminators | (Miss Claire Evans). |
| *Sports Development Advisory Council | (P.W. Howard, Esq.). |

---

| | |
|---|---|
| British Council, The | (Major A. A. Longden). |
| Civil Service National Whitley Council (Staff Side) | (P. L. M. Hoey, Esq.). |
| Ecclesiological Society, The | (J. Dudley Daymond, Esq.). |
| Free Church Federal Council | ..(The Rev. S. W. Hughes, .DD.). |
| Headmasters' Conference, The | |
| Incorporated Association of Headmasters, The | |
| Institute of Journalists, The | |
| Institute of Landscape Architects, The | ..(G. A. Jellicoe, Esq.). |
| National Council of Women of Great Britain | ..(Mrs. Patrick Ness). |
| National Federation of Women's Institutes | ..(Freda, Countess of Listowel). |
| Royal Horticultural Society | ..(F. R. Durham, Esq.). |
| Sir Oswald Stoll Foundation, The .. | ..(W. J Roberts, Esq.). |
| Women's Group on Public Welfare | . (Miss M. L. Harford). |

## INDIVIDUAL MEMBERS.

The Rt. Hon. Lord Aberconway, C.B.E. [2]
Lady Allen of Hurtwood
The Rt. Hon Viscount Bennett, P.C.
Field-Marshal the Rt. Hon. Lord Birdwood G.C.B.
The Rt. Hon. Margaret Bondfield, P.C. [5]
Alfred C. Bossom, Esq., M.P. [7]
Sir Frank Brown, C.I.E.
Sir Richard Cooper, Bt. [9]
Sir Edward Crowe, K.C.M.G.
Sir Noel Curtis-Bennett, K.C.V.O. [10]
Sir Henry Dale, F.R.S. [11]
The Rt Hon. Viscountess Davidson, M.P.
Arthur J. Davis, Esq., R.A.
H.S. Goodhart-Rendel, Esq., R.I.B.A. [13]
Group Captain Sir Louis Greig, K.B.E.
Sir Robert Greig, M.C.

Dr. Somerville Hastings (Chairman, London County Council).
The Rt. Hon. Lord Horder, G.C.V.O. [3]
Major Walter L Irvine.
Commander Stephen King-Hall, M.P. [4]
A. B. Knapp-Fisher, Esq., F.R.I.B.A. [6]
Miss Megan Lloyd George, M.P. [8]
Dr. J. J. Mallon, C.H.
John A. Milne, Esq., C.B.E.
R. W. Moore, Esq. (Head Master of Harrow)
The Hon. Harold Nicolson, M.P.
Major Louis Osman, A.R.I.B.A. [12]
Professor Sir Charles Reilly, O.B.E.
Major-General Sir Fabian Ware, K.C.V.O.
The Warden of All Souls, Oxford.
The Rt. Hon. Lord Wigram. P.C. [14]

---

[2] Henry Duncan McLaren, 2nd Baron Aberconway of Bodnant (1879-1953). Industrialist. Educated Eton and Balliol College, Oxford. Called to the Bar by Lincoln's Inn 1903. Director of London Assurance; director of Bolckow and Vaughan & Company; director of Palmers Shipbuilding and Iron; director of National Provincial Bank; Chairman of Yorkshire Amalgamated Collieries; Chairman of English Clays Loverin Pochin & Company; Chairman of John Brown Ltd; Chairman of Tredegar Iron and Coal. Parliamentary Private Undersecretary to the President of the Board of Trade 1906-1908. Chancellor of the Exchequer 1908-1910. Inherited baronetcy 1934.

[3] Mervyn Horder, later 2nd Baron of Ashford (1910-1998). Educated Winchester College. physician and composer. War service with RAFVR at HQ Fighter Command, Air HQ India, SEAC, and after 1945 in Tokyo.

[4] William Stephen Richard King-Hall, later Baron King-Hall (1893-1966), Sailor, writer and broadcaster. Son of distinguished naval family and veteran of Jutland. In 1929 he resigned from the Royal Navy to take up research post at the Royal Institute of International Affairs. 1939 elected MP. Founded the Hansard Society in 1944.

[5] Margaret Bondfield (1873-1953). Trade unionist and highly effective campaigner on a wide range of women's issues. Secretary of the Women's Labour League 1908. Also active in the Women's Co-operative Guild. Strongly opposed Great War and advocated a negotiated peace with Germany. In 1923 became one of the first women to enter the House of Commons when she was elected as Labour MP for Northampton. When Ramsay McDonald became Prime Minister in 1924 he appointed her as Parliamentary Secretary to the Minister of Labour. 1929 appointed Minister of Labour. She lost her seat in the 1931 General Election. The Labour Party never forgave her decision to support Ramsay McDonald's National Government and she found it impossible to return to the House of Commons. Chairperson of the Women's Group on Public Welfare 1939-45.

[6] Arthur Bedford Knapp-Fisher, MVO, FRIBA, FSA, Hon. ARCA, FRSA (1888-1965). Influential architect prominent in the reconstruction of the City of London after the Blitz.

[7] Alfred Charles Bossom MP (1881-1965). Politician, later 1st Baron Bossom. Churchill said of him: 'Bossom? What sort of a name is that? It's neither one thing nor the other.'

[8] Lady Megan Lloyd George (1902-66). Daughter of David Lloyd George. Assiduous recoverer of Cabinet notes from the waste paper bins of 10 Downing Street. First female Member of Parliament for a Welsh constituency. Liberal MP 1922-1951. Vociferous campaigner on Welsh issues. Labour MP 1957-66.

[9] Sir Richard Ashmole Cooper Bt (1874-1946). Chairman, Cooper, McDougall & Robertson, chemical manufacturers 1913-46. Independent Unionist MP for Walsall 1910-1922.

[10] Francis Noel Curtis-Bennett (1882-1950). Author and senior civil servant. Inspector Ministry of Health 1912-1929. Chairman, Civil Service Sports Council 1923. Member International Olympic Committee 1933-50.

[11] Sir Henry Hallett Dale (1875-1968). Educated Tollington Park College, the Leys School, Cambridge and Trinity College, Cambridge. Physiologist. 1914 Fellow of the Royal Society. Knighted 1932. Winner of the 1936 Nobel Prize in Medicine. Chairman of the Scientific Advisory Committee to the War Cabinet 1942. KBE 1943. President of the British Council 1950-55.

[12] Major Louis Osman (1914-96). Architect, artist, goldsmith, ecclesiastical designer, medallist and craftsman. Designed the crown for the Prince of Wales' investiture at Caernarfon in 1969.

[13] Harry Stuart Goodhart-Rendell (1887-1959). Architect and influential author on architecture.

[14] Lieutenant Colonel Sir Clive Wigram (1873-1960). Courtier. Assistant Private Secretary to King George V 1911-33. Private Secretary to King George V 1933-36. 1st Baron Wigram. His lasting fame in the annals of British history was assured by his insistence that the King's last words spoke not of Bognor, but of the Empire.

# War Memorials (Local Authorities' Powers) Act 1923

## Chapter 18

A.D. 1923

An Act to enable local authorities under certain circumstances to maintain, repair and protect War Memorials vested in them
(18<sup>th</sup> July 1923)

Be it enacted by the King's most Excellent Majesty, by and with the advice and consent of the Lords Spiritual and Temporal, and Commons, in this present Parliament assembled, and by the authority of the same, as follows:-

1. A local authority may incur reasonable expenditure in the maintenance, repair and protection of any war memorial within their district which may be vested in them. — *Expenditure in maintenance, &c., of war memorials*

2. Any expenditure to be incurred under this Act by a local authority shall -

   (a) in the case of a parish council or parish meeting, be limited to an amount which will not involve a rate exceeding a penny in the pound for any financial year, and be subject to the approval of the county council; — *Approval of county council or Minister of Health.*

   (b) in the case of any other local authority, be limited to an amount from time to time approved by the Minister of Health.

3. The provisions of this Act shall not apply to a war memorial provided or maintained by a local authority in the exercise of any other statutory power. — *Application*

4. In this Act the expression "local authority" means the council of a county, county borough, metropolitan borough or other borough, or of an urban district or parish, and the parish meeting of a rural parish with no parish council. — **A.D. 1923** — *Definition*

5. This Act may be cited as the War Memorials (Local Authorities' Powers) Act, 1923. — **Short title**

Local Government Act 1948

Chapter 26

Clause 133

War Memorials 13 & 14 Geo 5.

1. In section one of the War Memorials (Local Authorities' Powers) Act, 1923 (which enables local authorities, as defined in that Act, to incur reasonable expenditure in the maintenance, repair and protection of war memorials in their district which are vested in them) for the words "which may be vested in them," there shall be substituted the words "whether vested in them or not."

2. The matters on which expenditure may be incurred under the said section one shall include the alteration of any memorial to which that section applies so as to make it serve as a memorial in connection with any war subsequent to that in connection with which it was erected and the correction of any error or omission in the inscription on any such memorial.

3. The War Memorials (Local Authorities' Powers) Act, 1923, as amended by the foregoing provisions of this section shall extend to Scotland subject to the following modifications –

    (i) sections two and four shall not apply; and
    (ii) the expression "local authority" means a county, town, or district council.

5 & 6 ELIZ.2.

Parish Councils Act, 1957

Chapter 42
Part II

Extension and Adaption of Other Powers

Clause 8   1. Every parish council shall be a local authority for the purposes of the Open Spaces Act, 1906, whether or not invested with the powers of that Act by the council of the county within which the parish is situate.   Powers to be exercisable without reference to county council.

2. The approval or consent of the county council shall no longer be required for any of the following matters –

    (a) for the incurring by a parish council or parish meeting of any expenditure under the War Memorials (Local Authorities' Powers) Act, 1923.

CH. 26.

Local Government
Act, 1948

PART VII
......cont.

 (iii) no cinematograph film other than a film illustrative of questions relating to health or disease shall be shown ; and

 (iv) no scenery, theatrical costumes or scenic or theatrical accessories shall be used.

(10) In the application of this section to Scotland –

(a) no money shall be borrowed for the purposes authorised under this section except with the consent of the Secretary of State;

(b) for any reference to the Minister there shall be substituted a reference to the Secretary of State;

(c) the expression "local authority" means a county, town or district council;

(d) for any reference to a rate of sixpence in the pound there shall be substituted a reference to a rate of four and four-fifths pence in the pound;

(e) expenditure incurred by a district council under this section shall not be taken into account in calculating the limit imposed on the district rate by section two hundred and twenty-six of the Local Government (Scotland) Act, 1947.

(11) No certificate shall be granted under the Licensing (Scotland) Acts, 1903 to 1934 for the sale of exciseable liquor in any premises provided under this section in Scotland, but nothing in this subsection shall render it unlawful to grant under section forty of the Licensing (Scotland) Act, 1903, a special permission for an entertainment in any such premises.

3 Edw.7. c. 25.

War Memorials
13 & 14 Geo.5. c.18.

133. - (1) In section one of the War Memorials (Local Authorities' Powers) Act, 1923 (which enables local authorities, as defined in that Act, to incur reasonable expenditure in the maintenance, repair and protection of war memorials in their district which are vested in them) for the words "which may be vested in them," there shall be substituted the words "whether vested in them or not."

(2) The matters on which expenditure may be incurred under the said section one shall include the alteration of any memorial to which that section applies so as to make it serve as a memorial in connection with any war subsequent to that in connection with which it was erected and the correction of any error or omission in the inscription on any such memorial.

(3) The War Memorials (Local Authorities' Powers) Act, 1923, as amended by the foregoing provisions of this section shall extend to Scotland subject to the following modifications-

(i) sections two and four shall not apply; and
(ii) the expression "local authority" means a county, town or district council.

## Parish Councils Act, 1957

### PART II
### EXTENSION AND ADAPTATION OF OTHER POWERS

8.- (1) Every parish council shall be a local authority for the purposes of the Open Spaces Act, 1906, whether or not invested with the powers of that Act by the council of the country within which the parish is situated.

*Powers to be exercisable without reference to county council.*

(2) The approval or consent of the county council shall no longer be required for any of the following matters -

(a) for the incurring by a parish council or parish meeting of any expenditure under the War Memorials (Local Authorities' Powers) Act, 1923;

(b) by reason that it will involve a loan, for the incurring by a parish council of any other expense or liability; or

(c) for the borrowing by a parish council of such sums as may be required for any of the purposes mentioned in section one hundred and ninety-five of the Local Government Act, 1933.

9. In the application to England and Wales of section one hundred and thirty of the Local Government Act, 1948 (which empowers certain local authorities to insure against accidents to their members), the expression "local authority" shall include a parish council.

*Power of parish councils to insure against accidents to members.*

10. A parish council may contribute towards the expenses incurred by any other person in maintaining any place of interment in which the remains of inhabitants of the parish are or may be interred.

*Power to contribute towards expenses of burial grounds.*

11. - (1) The trustees or administrators of every parochial charity, other than an ecclesiastical charity, shall deliver a copy of the annual accounts which are required to be prepared by section forty-four of the Charitable Trusts Amendment Act, 1855-

*Power of parish council to receive charity accounts.*

(a) to the parish council of any parish with which the objects of the charity are identified, or

(b) to the chairman of the parish meeting of any such parish, where there is no parish council.

who shall present the accounts at the next parish meeting; and the said section forty-four (which, as amended by subsection (6) of section fourteen of the Local Government Act, 1894, requires a copy of such accounts as aforesaid to be delivered to the chairman of the parish meeting in all cases) shall have effect accordingly.

(2) In this section "parochial charity" and "ecclesiastical charity" have the meanings respectively assigned to them by section seventy-five of the Local Government Act, 1894.

[13 & 14 GEO. 5.] [CH. 18.]

## War Memorials (Local Authorities' Powers) Act, 1923

### CHAPTER 18.

An Act to enable local authorities under certain circumstances to maintain, repair and protect war memorials vested in them. [18th July 1923]

A.D. 1923

Be it enacted by the King's most Excellent Majesty, by and with the advice and consent of the Lords Spiritual and Temporal, and Commons, in this present Parliament assembled, and by the authority of the same, as follows:-

1. A local authority may incur reasonable expenditure in the maintenance, repair and protection of any war memorial within their district which may be vested in them.

*Expenditure in maintenance, &c., of war memorials.*

2. Any expenditure to be incurred under this Act by a local authority shall-

*Approval of county council or Minister of Health*

(a) in the case of a parish council or parish meeting, be limited to an amount which will not involve a rate exceeding a penny in the pound for any financial year, and be subject to the approval of the county council;

(b) in the case of any other local authority, be limited to an amount from time to time approved by the Minister of Health.

3. The provisions of this Act shall not apply to a war memorial provided or maintained by a local authority in the exercise of any other statutory power.

*Application.*

A.D. 1923

*Definition*

4. In this Act the expression "local authority means the council of a county, county borough, metropolitan borough or other borough, or of an urban district or parish, and the parish meeting of a rural parish with no parish council.

*Short title.*

5. This Act may be cited as the War Memorial (Local Authorities' Powers) Act, 1923.

## INDEX

Page numbers in *italics* refer to illustrations.

Aaron, Flight Sergeant Arthur Lewis, VC DFM RAFVR  287
Abbots Langley, St Lawrence Parish Church  69
Aberconway, Lord  96
Aberdeen
    Gordon's College  27
    Trinity Cemetery, Annie Morrison's grave  *347*
    War Memorial  89, *89*, 105
    Wellington Bridge  11
*Aberdeen Daily Journal*  89
Aberdeen University, King's College Chapel  52
Abey, Lance Corporal Charles  98
Ablett, Sergeant Alfred, VC  287
Abu Klea, Battle of  26
Achnacarry, Commando Basic Training Centre  258
Ackroyd, Captain Harold, VC  287
Adair, Robert, Lord Waveney  17
Adams, Mr A R  47
Adams, George Canon  210
Adams, Lew  298
ADDER, HM Tug  77
Addiscombe, Surrey  20
Addison, Joseph  163, 206
Admiralty  *see also* Royal Navy
  and memorial that never was  224, 225, 226
    Naval Memorials Committee  221, 232
  and RNVR Club  250
    Room 40 code-breakers  290
Admiralty Church, St Martin's in the Fields  213
Admiralty Civilians Memorial  216, *217*
Afghanistan  31
    Dundas Bridge  194
Afghanistan Memorial, Royal Artillery  25, *25*
Agar-Robartes, the Hon Captain Thomas Charles Reginald  49
Aguiari, Eleonora  30

Air Forces Memorial  *see also* Commonwealth Air Forces Memorial; Flying Services Memorial; Royal Air Force Memorial, Victoria Embankment
    Plymouth Hoe  282
    Runnymede  264, 272-273, *272*, *273*
Air Ministry  188
*Air Vice Marshal Sir Keith Park* (Battle of Britain Class locomotive)  265
*Air Vice Marshal Sir Trafford Leigh-Mallory* (Battle of Britain Class locomotive)  265
aircraft
    Avro Lancaster ME576  264
    Consolidated Liberator 42-95191  277, *277*
    Faith, Hope and Charity  148
    Handley Page Halifax V9977  278
    Hawker Hurricane  266
    Supermarine Spitfire  266
    Vickers VC10  295
    Vickers Wellington  11
airship, German Navy Schutte-Lanz SL11  45, 289  *see also* Zeppelins
Aitken, Alex  XII
Alanbrooke, Field Marshal the Rt Hon Alan Francis Brooke, Field Marshal 1st Viscount Alanbrooke KG GCB OM GCVO DSO  196
Alban-Jones, Reverend Tim  298
Albert, Prince  286
Albert, Somme  51, 130
    Cathedral  130
Albert I, King of the Belgians  81
Albertini, Lieutenant W Reynolds, RNVR  250
Albury, New South Wales, Captain Borella VC commemorated  287
Alderson, Thomas, GC  296
Alexander, Rt Hon A V  226, 250
Alexander of Tunis, Field Marshal 1st Earl of, KG PC GCB OM GCMG GCVO CSI DSO MC KJStJ CD  158

Alexander-Sinclair, Rear Admiral Edwyn Sinclair  256
Alexandra, Princess  80
Alexandra, Queen  30, 76, 77, 78, 79, 80, 96
Alfred the Great, King  274
Alice, Princess, Duchess of Gloucester  100, 119
Allan, Pipe Major Rod  193
Allen, Colonel the Hon Sir James, KCB  109, 371, 379
Allen, Marjory, Baroness Allen of Hurtwood  136-137
Allingham, Henry  283
Allward, Walter S  122
Alton, Hants, St Lawrence Church  33
Ambrus, Jan  279
American Battle Monuments Commission  277
American Cemetery, Madingley, Cambridge  277
Amery, Rt Hon Leopold Charles Maurice Stennett, PC MP  225, 226, 232
Amiens  370
Amiens, Battle of  127
Amiens Cathedral, Australian Memorial Tablet  127, *127*
Amiens Cathedral, IWGC Memorial Tablet  110
amputees, Great War  190
Anderson, Private Eric, VC  287
Andrew, Brigadier Leslie W, VC  287
Andrew, Prince  162
Anglo-Zulu War  22-23
Angmering War Memorial  341
Angria, Conagree  204
Angus, Sergeant William, VC  287
Animals In War Memorial  181, *181*
Anne, Queen  206
*Anne Frank: The Diary of a Young Girl*  166
Anne Frank Trust (UK)  166
Anson, Lieutenant Colonel the Hon Augustus, VC  287
Anstruther Harbour, May Island Memorial Cairn  254, *255*
Anton, Gunther  280
Antwerp, Notre Dame Cathedral  249
ANZAC Day  172

ANZAC Memorial, Battersea Park  172, *172*
ANZAC Square, Brisbane  128, *128*
Apeldoorn, Holland, Historical Museum, Battle of Britain Lace Panel  267
Arbuthnot, Rear-Admiral Sir Robert Keith Bt  292
Archer, Colonel Stuart, GC OBE ERD  299
architects  46
architects of memorials after Great War  114
*Architectural Review*  137
*Architecture and Personalities*  46
Arctic Convoy memorials  218
Arenas, Mañuel  4
Arkwright, Sir John Stanhope  45
Armed Forces Memorial  192
*Armed Science* statue  17, *17*
Armistice, first anniversary  IX
Armistice announced  X
Armstrong, Dr E F, FRS  136, 380, 386
Armstrong, Sir Walter  313
Army, British
   Airborne Division, 6th  150
   Army, 2nd  113
   Army, 3rd  157
   Army, 4th  126
   Army, 14th  152, 169, 187
   Army Nursing Service  195
   Army Ordnance Corps  33
   Army School of Transport  100
   Bradford Pals  45
   Buffs, The (Royal West Kent Regiment)  77
   Cameron Highlanders  153, 193
   Carabiniers (6th Dragoons)  *39*
   Chindits  143
   City of London Regiment, 6th Battalion  68, *68*
   City of London Yeomanry  33
   Civil Service Rifles (London Regiment, 15th Battalion)  55
   Coldstream Guards  6, 15, *15*, 77
   Commonwealth Brigade, 27: 161
   County of London Imperial Yeomanry  213
   Devonshire Regiment  68, *68*

Division, 2 (British) 153
Division, 29th 121
Duke of Wellington's Regiment 52
Essex Regiment, 2nd Battalion 176
Finsbury Rifles (London Regiment, 11th Battalion) 51
Gordon Highlanders 89
Grenadier Guards 15, *15*
   2nd Battalion 158
Guards, 1st 11
Guards Brigade 6
Guards regiments 125
Gurkhas 170
(Highland) Division, 51st 121, 193
Highland Light Infantry (Glasgow Highlanders), 9th Battalion XII
Honourable Artillery Company 33
Household Brigade, 3rd Regiment of Cavalry 26
Household Cavalry Mounted Regiment 84
Household Division 60, 158
Hussars, 14th and 20th 14
Imperial Camel Corps 65, *65*
Imperial Yeomanry 40
Indian Corps 115
Infantry Division, 24th 66, *67*
Inniskilling Dragoons, 6th 11
Irish Guards 193
King's Liverpool Regiment, 'Pals' battalions 50
King's Own Yorkshire Light Infantry 52
King's Regiment, Waterloo Band 98
Lancashire Fusiliers 45
Light Brigade (later Light Division) 4, 84
London Regiment, 11th Battalion (Finsbury Rifles) 51
London Regiment, 15th Battalion (Civil Service Rifles) 55
London Rifle Brigade 52, 68, *68*
Machine Gun Corps 64, 66, *67*
Manchester Regiment 47
Monmouthshire Regiment 125
Newfoundland Regiment (later Royal Newfoundland Regiment) 120, 121
Normandy Band 176

Northumberland Fusiliers (later Royal Northumberland Fusiliers) 87, 112, 263
Oxford Light Infantry, 52nd 40
Oxfordshire and Buckinghamshire Light Infantry, D Company 150
Post Office Rifles 68, *68*, 69, *69*
Queen Alexandra's Imperial Military Nursing Service 195
Queen's Own Royal West Kent Regiment 153
Queen's Royal Irish Hussars 158
Regiment of Foot, 24th (later the South Wales Borderers) 14
   2nd Battalion, B Company 23
Rifle Brigade 62
Royal Anglian Regiment 176
Royal Army Medical Corps 125
Royal Army Service Corps, 67th Divisional Train 77
Royal Corps of Signals 68, *68*
Royal Engineers, Corps of 151, 175, 178, 194, 205, 262
   8th Railway Company 100
   Bomb Disposal 178
Royal Highlanders, 42nd 11
Royal Horse Artillery 36, 84
   King's Troop 9, 84, 158, 173
Royal Irish Regiment 180
Royal Logistics Corps, EOD Squadron 164
Royal Military Police 84
Royal Naval Division, 63rd 53, 231, 241 *see also* Royal Naval Division
Royal Norfolk Regiment (IX Foot) 77, 142
Royal Pioneer Corps 174
Royal Regiment of Artillery 16, *16*, 24, 36, *36*, 61, 134
Royal Regiment of Fusiliers 63, *63*, 160, 263
Royal Scots, The (The Royal Regiment) 48
   1/7th (Leith Territorial) Battalion 96
Royal Scots Fusiliers, 1st Battalion 91
Royal Sussex Regiment, 9th Battalion 66, *67*

Royal Tank Regiment 171
Royal Welch Fusiliers, 2nd 66, *67*
Royal Welch Fusiliers, 23rd 11
Royal Wiltshire Yeomanry 68, *68*
Scots Fusilier Guards 15, *15*
Scots Greys 84
Scots Guards 193
Sherwood Foresters 83
Staffordshire Regiment *191*
(Ulster) Division, 36th 44, 119, 130
Wagoners Reserve 82
(Welch) Division, 38th 118
Welch Regiment, The 160
(West Riding) Division, 49th *191*
Wiltshire Regiment 68, *68*
Worcestershire Regiment 112
Army Ordnance Corps Memorial 33
Arnold, Major General Benedict 369
Arras, Fauborg d'Amiens Cemetery, Flying Services Memorial 263, *263*
Arras Memorial 263, *263*
Art Bronze Foundry 157, 275, 282
Arthur, Max 241
Ashdon church, Essex 277
Ashfield, Lord 101
Asquith, Brigadier General Arthur Melland DSO** 231, 232, 233, 235
Asquith, Rt Hon Herbert, MP 99
ASSOCIATION 206
Association of Ammunition Technicians 177
Astor, Lieutenant William Waldorf Astor MP RNVR (later 3rd Viscount Astor) 250
Atatürk, Kemal 172
ATHENIA, SS 218
Atholl, 8th Duke, (Lieutenant Colonel Sir John George Stewart-Murray) 58
Atkinson, Dr Robert d'Escourt 271
Atlantic, Battle of the 218
Attlee, Rt Hon Clement, MP (later 1st Earl Attlee of Walthamstow, Viscount Prestwood) 140, 158
Auchinleck, Field Marshal Sir Claude John Eyre, GCB GCIE CSI DSO OBE 196
Aumonier (W) & Son 216
AUSTRALIA, HMS 254
Australian Commonwealth Military Forces 68, *68*

Australian Division, 2nd, Memorial 141
Australian Federation Guard 173
Australian Memorial Tablet, Amiens Cathedral 127, *127*
Australian National Memorial, Villers-Bretonneux 126, *126*, 373
Australian Tunnelling Company, 1st 113, *113*
Australian War Memorial, Hyde Park 173, *173*
Ava Fort, Battle of 193
Avenue of Remembrance, Sittingbourne 51
Avon, Earl of (Anthony Eden) 158
Aylesbury, Bucks, Cross of Sacrifice 103

background to memorials 53-54
Backhouse, David 181
Bacon, John, the Younger 4, 302
Badaire, Jean-Bernard 147
Badajoz, Spain 6
Baddeley, Sir John James, Bt 63
Baddeley, Sir Vincent Wilberforce KCB 216, 233
Baden-Powell, Lieutenant-General Lord GCMG GCVO KCB 314
Badges, Fovant 68, *68*
Baghdad, Iraq, *Victory Arch* 197
Bagnall, Air Chief Marshal Sir Anthony, KCB OBE FRAeS RAF 300
bagpipes, (Muz and Molly Pipes) 193
Baillie-Grohman, Admiral Harold Tom, CB DSO OBE 247
Baily, Edward Hodges, RA 9, 211, 216, 307
Baird, John Logie 369
Baker, Sir Herbert, RA 46, 114, 115, 124, 136, 209, 333
  biography 326
Balaclava, Battle of XIII
Balaclava, British Hotel 19
Baldwin, Rt Hon Stanley, PC MP 55
Ball, Captain Albert, VC DSO MC 287
Ball, George 292
*Ballad of Jack Cornwell* 293
Ballieu, 1st Baron 276

Ballymena Castle, County Antrim 17
Baltic Sea, Royal Navy service (1918-1920) 256-257
Band, Sergeant Harry 335
Banks, Sir Joseph, PRS 215
Barnes, Rt Hon George Nichol, MP 109, 371
Barclay, Brigadier F P 142
Bardsley, Dr Cuthbert 135
Barker, Roland 238
Barrett, Air Chief Marshal Sir Arthur Sheridan, KCB CB CMG MC DL 264
Barrett and Sons, Messrs 70
Barrington, Michael (later Sir Michael) 100
Barron, T R 174
Barry, Sir Charles 209, 210
Barstow, G L 233
Barstow, Sir George 225
Barter, Captain Frederick, VC 287
Basra, Iraq, War Memorial 53
Bastiaan, Dr Ross J 172
Bates, Corporal Sidney, VC 287
Bates, Harry, RA 31, 75
Bath, raids on 133
Bathia, Colonel 186
Bathurst, Sir Benjamin, MP 259
*Battle of Britain, The* 284
Battle of Britain Class locomotives 265
Battle of Britain Commemorative Lace Panels 267
Battle of Britain Historical Society 284
Battle of Britain Memorial, Capel le Ferne 270, *270*
Battle of Britain Monument 284
Battle of Britain Sunday 270
Baucq, Philippe 76
Bayerlein, Generalleutnant Fritz 148
Bayes, Gilbert, RA 247
Bayeux, Essex Regiment memorial 176, *176*
Bayeux, Rue Fabian Ware 151
Bayeux Memorial 151, *151*
*Bayeux Tapestry* 176
Bayeux War Cemetery 151
Bayonne 6
BBC, first radio broadcast of National Ceremony at Cenotaph 45

*BBC Radio Norwich* 178
Beard, J Stanley, FSA 70
Bearsden War Memorial 91, *91*
Beasley, Harper and Williams, Messrs 268
Beatty, Rear-Admiral David, KCB MVO DSO 210, 226, 254, 290, 291
Beaucourt, Royal Naval Division Memorial 235, 241, *241*
Beaumont Hamel, Battle of 120, 121
Beaumont Hamel, National Memorial Park of Remembrance 120, 121, *121*
Beauvais Cathedral, memorial tablet 110, *110*
Beck, Hermann 98
Beckenham, Elmers End bus garage 133
Bedale, Father Stephen 343
Bedford, St Peter's Church 26
Bedford Hotel, Bloomsbury 47
Bégué, Georges, MC 147
Beharry, Private Johnson Gideon, VC 300
Behnes, William 210
  statues 210, 309
Behrend, Louis and Mary 72
Belfast, raids on 133
Belgian Army 81
Belgian memorial tablets 111
Belgian War Memorial 81, *81*
Belgium 81
Bell, John XIII, 11, 15, 16, 17, 311
Belsky, Franta 351, 210
BENJAMIN GIMBERT GC (Class 47 No. 47577 and Class 66 No. 66077 locomotives) 298
Bennett, Air Vice Marshal Don 'Pathfinder' 282
Bénouville Bridge, Normandy 150
Bentinck, Rear Admiral Sir Rudolf W, KCMG 109, 371
Bentley Priory *see* Royal Air Force, Bentley Priory
Beresford, Admiral Lord 293
Bergen-Belsen Concentration Camp 166
Berlin 135
Berlin, Brandenburg Gate 8
Berlin Airlift Memorial 189, *189*
Berry-Pkory, Aladar 279

Beshell, Sir John, MP  292
Bethnal Green Underground station  146, *146*
Beverley Minster, alms dish  287
Biggin Hill, St George's RAF Chapel of Remembrance  268, *268*, 269, *269*
Bill, Sir William  197
Bingham, Honourable Sir Francis  95
Binney, Captain Douglas, CBE RN, and Binney Memorial Medal  247
Binning, Lieutenant Lord  26
Binyon, Robert Laurence  102
Birmingham
    Longbridge, Austin Motor Works  47
    Nelson memorial  208
    Northfield  47
    St Philip's Cathedral  26
    Selly Park, St Stephen and St Wulfstan churchyard  47
    'twinned' with Albert  51
    University of, fallen alumni  105
Birmingham Railway Museum, Tyseley  97
BISMARCK  260
Bladon, Oxon  158
Blake, William  369
Blake, Vice Admiral Sir Godfrey, KCB DSO  250
Blakeney, Robert  6
Blankenberg, Sir R A, KBE  109, 379
BLESMA (British Limbless Ex-Servicemen's Association)  190, *190*
Blitz, the  133, 136, 154
Blomfield, Sir Reginald, RA  114, 224, 232
    biography  321
    works  60, 81, 103, 114, 117, 125, 262, 321
Blore, Edward  9
Blumlein, Alan Dower  278
Blunden, Edmund  244
Blythin, Charles Frederick  245
Blyton, Enid  369
Board of Trade War Memorial  55
Boehm, Sir Joseph Edgar, RA  11, 30, 313
Boer War  31, 33, 69, 157
    Carabiniers (6th Dragoons) Memorial  *39*
    Guy's Hospital Memorial  37, *37*
    Norfolk Memorial  38, *38*
    Oxfordshire Light Infantry memorial  40
    Royal Artillery Memorial  36, *36*
    St Helens Memorial Plaque  195
    women in  195
Bois d'Ellvile, near Arras  124
Bolam, Morpeth, Northumberland, St Andrew's Church  280
Bolus, Lieutenant Commander  243
bomb disposal personnel, memorial to  177, *177*
*Bombed Churches as War Memorials*  136
Bonaparte, Napoleon Eugène Louis John Joseph, Prince Imperial  24
Bond Street Association  159
Bordeaux, France  2
Borella, Captain Albert Chalmers VC  287
Borg, Dr Alan  XV, 29, 47, 72, 201
Bosnia, Durrant Bridge  194
Botha, Mrs Annie  124
boulder memorials  XV, 172, *172*, 253, *253*
Bounds Green Underground station  146
Bowden and Abbot, Messrs  119
Bower, Dykes  142
Bowker, Richard, CBE  298
Bowring, Sir Edgar  120
Boxgrove Abbey  276
*Boy Stood on the Burning Deck, The*  293
Boyce, Admiral Sir Michael, GCB OBE ADC DL (later Lord)  257, 259
Boyes, Midshipman Duncan G, VC  287
Bradford War Memorial  45
Bradley, Very Reverend Peter  97, 98
Bradshaw, H Chalton  60, 345
BRAEMAR CASTLE  242
Bramall, Field Marshal the Rt Hon Edwin Noel Westby, 1st Baron, KG GCB OBE MC KStJ  170
Branson, Sir Richard  135
Braun, Werner von  133
Bredgar, Kent, Church of St John the Baptist  22

Bridgeman, William  213
Bridges, Lord  158
Briggs, A E  260
Brighton, Indian wounded at, and memorial to  85, *85*
Brill, Fred  356
Brisbane, Australia, ANZAC Square  46, 128, *128*
Bristol, Bishop of  136-137
Bristol, King Edward VII commemorated in  336
Bristol, raids on  133
Britain, Battle of  178, 266, 270
   Capel le Ferne Memorial  270, *270*
   Commemorative Lace Panels  267
   first American killed  276
   Monument  284
BRITANNIA, HMS  228
BRITANNIC  242
British Aerospace  171
British Expeditionary Force (1914)  81
British Expeditionary Force (1940)  178
British Korean Veterans Association  160
   memorial garden  161
British Legion *see* Royal British Legion
British Limbless Ex-Servicemen's Association (BLESMA)  190, *190*
British Maritime Foundation, Memorial Book  218
British Museum  XII, 305, 322
British Railways  174
British Women's Hospital Committee  80
Brock, Sir Thomas, RA  20, 60, 215, 315
Brock (Office of Works)  236
Bromhead, Lieutenant Gonville, VC  23
Bromley, Kent
   Civic Centre, Battle of Britain Commemorative Lace Panel  267
   St Peter and St Paul Church War Memorial  129
   War Memorial  129
BRONNINGTON, HMS  185
bronze casting  XII
Brooke, Captain James A O, VC  89

Brooke, Rupert Chawner  49, 233, 234
Brookwood Memorial  147
Brookwood Russian Memorial  165, *165*
Brown, Major Cecil  65
Brown, Henry  152
Browne, Lord Arthur  221
Bruce, Captain, William A M, VC  95
Brussels, Municipality of  28
   Edith Cavell hospital  77
   Everè Cemetery, Waterloo Memorial  198
   Everè suburb  28
   St Gilles prison  76
BRUSSELS, SS  99
Bryant, Hugh Arnold  37
BUCENTAURE  212
Buchanan, Flight Sergeant Ian Archibald, RAFVR  26
Buchanan, Mrs Margaret Chisholm  26
Buchanan, James  163
Buchman, Dr Frank  144
Buckinghamshire Railway Centre, Quainton Road  97
Bugbrooke, Northants, St Michael and All Angels Church  104, *104*
Bulford Camp, Wilts, Kiwi chalk figure  68
Bulleid, Oliver Vaughan Snell  265
Buller, General Sir Redvers, VC  31, 36, 287
BULWARK, HMS  228
Burgess, J  236
Burghclere, Hants, Sandham Memorial Chapel  72-73, *73*
Burma Campaign  152-153, 186, 187, 193
Burma Star Association  187
   Memorial Grove  186-187, *186*
Burn, William  119
Burnaby, Colonel Frederick Gustavus  26, 27
Burnet, Sir John James  84
   biography  322
Burnett, T S  27
Burridge, Air Chief Marshal Sir Brian, KCB CBE ADC RAF  283
Burton, Decimus  8
Burton, Edward  237, 238

Burton Foundry, A B  59, 61, 65, 81, 84
Bury War Memorial  45
bus shelters  XV
Bushey, Herts, St James Parish Church  136
business and war memorials  50
Butler, A S G  106
Butler, James, RA  259, 287, 352
Byron, Lord  5
Cabinet (1919/21)  108
Cadbury, Major Egbert, RFC  47
Cadbury, Dame Elizabeth  47
Cadw  48
CAESAR, HMS  228
Café Gondrée, Ranville  150, *150*
Cairn of Remembrance, Fort William-Dudley (Worcs)  199
cairns  XII, 199
Cairns, Sergeant Hugh, VC  287
Cairo, Shepheard's Hotel  128
Calcutta  31
Caledonian Club, London  49
Caligula, Emperor  XIII
Callideau, J P  147
Camberley, Princess Royal Barracks  33
Cambrai, Battle of  157
Cambridge, Duke of  23, 26, 28
Cambridge American Cemetery, Madingley  277
Camden Place, Chislehurst  24
Cammell Laird, Birkenhead  243
Campbell, Field Marshal Sir Colin, (later 1st Baron) GCB KSI  20
Canada, Jasper National Park  194
   Mount Edith Cavell  77
   Mount McBeath  287
Canadian Air Council, Battle of Britain Commemorative Lace Panels  267
Canadian Army  122, 123
Canadian Battlefield Memorials Commission  122
Canadian Corps  122
Canadian Division, 1st  122
Canadian National War Memorial, Ottawa  129, *129*
Canberra, Australia
   Australian War Memorial  126
   Captain Borella, VC commemorated  287
   Parliament Square, King George V statue  339
Canning, Earl  20
Canterbury, Archbishop of  299
Canterbury, Howe Barracks  VIII
Canterbury Cathedral  VIII
Canterbury University, New Zealand  104
Canterbury war memorials  54
Caplin, Ivor, MP  186, 187, 300
Cardiff, Cathays Park, Welsh National War Memorial  59, *59*
Cardiff, City Hall  336
Cardiff, Llandaff Cathedral  160
Cardot, Jean  159
Carew, I E  211
Carey, Lieutenant  24
caribou memorials  120-121, *121*, 331
Carless, Able Seaman John Henry, VC  97
Carlisle, Earl of  257
Carlisle Cathedral, Rev Theodore Bayley Hardy, VC commemorated  288, *288*
Carluke, Lanarkshire, Sergeant William Angus, VC commemorated  287
Carmarthen, obelisk  XIII
CARNARVON, HMS  228
Carnoustie, Jarvis Place  287
Carpmael, R  100
*Carve Her Name With Pride*  147
Carver, Field Marshal the Rt Hon Michael Power, 1st Baron, GCB CBE DSO MC  196
Casabianca, Giacomo Jocante  208, 293
*Case of the Vanishing War Memorial, The*  145
Cashford, Noel, MBE  178
Cassels, Field Marshal Sir Archibald James Halkett, GCB, KBE, DSO  196
Castillon, France  2
Castle Drogo, Devon  49
Castro, Rosalia de  5
Causley, Charles  293
Cavalry Memorial, Hyde Park  84, *84*

Cavell, Edith Louisa 76-79, *78*, *79*, 142, 369
Cavell Memorial Home, Norwich 76
Cawnpore Memorial Church of All Souls 20
Cecil, Lord David 136-137
cemeteries, military
   Bayeux 151
   Brandhoek, Belgium 286
   Cannock Chase, Deutscher Soldatenfriedhof (German Military Cemetery) 289
   Cappucini Naval, Malta 242
   Cross of Sacrifice 114
   Fauborg d'Amiens, Arras 263
   Great War Stone 114
   Hawthorne Ridge No 2, Beaumont Hamel 121
   Hunter's, Beaumont Hamel 121
   Kohima 153, *153*
   Maltese 148, *149*
   Mikra, Salonika 242
   Ovillers 112
   Poelcappelle 180
   St Sever, Extension, Rouen 288
   Y-Ravine, Beaumont Hamel 121
Cenotaph, Whitehall 56-57, *56*, 198, 202
   ANZAC Day ceremony 172
   dates carried by 53
   National Ceremony of Remembrance VIII, IX, 45, 50, 57, 177
   and Second World War commemoration 139
   temporary structure 56
Central British Fund for World Jewish Relief 167
ceremonies at war memorials 45
Cetswayo, King 22
Chacksfield, Air Vice Marshal Sir Bernard, KBE CB FRAeS 143
Chalfont St Giles, Vache Park 215
Challen, Albert Charles 19
Chamberlain, Venerable F Noel 244
CHAMPION, HMS 256
Channel Islands, Admiral Saumarez Memorial 141 *see also* Jersey *entries*
Chantrey, Sir Francis 9, 210, 306
Chapman, Lieutenant C M S 256

Chard, Lieutenant John RM, VC 23
Charles I, King 3, 32
Charles II, King 3
Charles V, Holy Roman Emperor 148
Charles VII, King of France 2
Charles Edward Stuart, Prince ('Bonnie Prince Charlie') 156, *156*
Charles Edward Stuart Society 156

CHARLES UPHAM, HMNZS
Chatfield, Admiral of the Fleet Rt Hon Lord, GCB OM KCMG CVO 132, 138, 139, 380, 386
Chatham, Naval Memorial Register 244
Chatham, Royal Engineers Officers Mess 27
Chatham Royal Naval Memorial 223
   extension 244-245
Chatteris, Cambs, Clare Street 287
Chavasse, Captain Noel, VC and bar 286, 287
Chavasse, Dr Christopher, Bishop of Rochester 244
Chelmsford, General Lord 22, 23, 24, 233
Cheltenham College, scholarship 287
Cheshire, Group Captain Lord Leonard, VC OM DSO** DFC 182
CHESTER, HMS 290, 291, 292, 293
Chester Cathedral, Jack Cornwell, VC commemorated 293
Chettle, Mr 236-237
children evacuated from Nazi occupied territories, memorial 167, *167*
Childs, Commander (Rtd) David 182, 183, *184*
Chillianwallah, Battle of, and Memorial 14
Chindit Forces Memorial 143, *143*
Chinese Government 27
Chislehurst, St Mary's Roman Catholic Church 24
Chislehurst War Memorial, Kent 103, *103*
CHITRAL, HMS 248
Chotek, Lady Sophie 53
*Christ in Glory in the Tetramorph* 135
Christian Victor, HSH Prince, of Schleswig-Holstein 33

Christina, Princess of Sweden  168
Church Building Act (1818)  XII
church furnishings as war memorials  52
Church of England  199
churches, bombed out, as war memorials  136-137
churches as sites commemorating great commanders  XI
CHURCHILL, HMS  159
Churchill, Winston (later Sir Winston)  32, 178, 188, 195, 258, 270, 282, 345
    Balaclava visit  XIII
    and Battle of Britain  267, 268
    as First Lord of the Admiralty  290, 291
    and Gallipoli  86
    and Great War demobilisation  44
    and Great War memorials  108
    memorialisation of  159, *159*, 350
    passing of  158
    and Post Office Rifles  69
    and Royal Naval Division  231, 234-235, 237
    and St Paul's cathedral  154
    and the tank  171
Churchill, Winston, MP (grandson)  240
Churchill College, Cambridge University  159
Civil Service Rifles War Memorial  55
Civil War, English  3
Clandeboye, County Down, Helen's Tower  119
Clare, Private George William Burdett, VC  287
Clarendon, Lord  250
Clark, Sir Kenneth (later 1st Baron Clark of Saltwood)  136-137
Clark, Philip Lindsay  105
Clarke, Mary  13
Clatt War Memorial, Aberdeenshire  53
Clayton, Commodore Christopher  259
Clayton, Reverend 'Tubby'  52
Clayton and Bell  125
Cleethorpes, cemetery and Baptist Chapel  47
Cleveland Bridge Company  54

clock memorial, astronomical, York Minster  271, *271*
Clowes, Brigadier F W  142
Clyde, Baron  20
Coalbrookdale Company  17, 37
Cochius, Rudolph  120
Cockerell, Professor Charles  14
    biography  308
Cockerill Company, Liège  7
Cockett, Olivia  238
Cockin, Reverend F A  136-137
Colenso, Battle of  31
Colleville Montgomery, Normandy  194, 355
Colne, Lancs, War Memorial  88, *88*
Colquhoun of Luss, Sir Iain  91
Colton, Professor Robert  33, 36
Combe, Lieutenant Roger Grierson, VC  89, 287
Commando Memorial, Spean Bridge  66, 258, *258*
Commando Memorial, Westminster Abbey  258
commerce and war memorials  50
committees, war memorial, Great War  43
Commonwealth Air Forces Memorial  281, *281* see also Air Forces Memorial; Royal Air Force Memorial, Victoria Embankment
Commonwealth personnel, memorial gates for  169, *169*
Commonwealth (formerly Imperial) War Graves Commission  X, 140
    architects after Great War  114
    and Commonwealth Air Forces Memorial  281
    and Cross of Sacrifice  103
    and dates of Great War  53
    *Debt of Honour* website  X, 147
    and disused churches  199
    Maidenhead Head Office  110
    Maltese cemeteries  148, *149*
    Merchant Navy Memorial  219
    nations' contributions to maintenance of graves  X
    and naval memorials  221, 222
    Rangoon Memorial  152, *152*
    and repatriation of bodies  248
    and USSR  165

and utilitarianism 48
and VC holders' graves 286
and Waterloo Memorial 28
community and war memorials 51
Comper, Sir John Ninian 59
   biography 330
Comrades of the Great War Association 44
Condon, Private John 180
Connaught, Prince Arthur, Duke of 60, 61, 64
Connolly, Mr 225
CONQUEROR, HMS 228
Cook, Captain James 215, *215*
Cooke, Chris 9
Coombs, Henry 50
Cooper, Sir Edwin 80
Cooper, Jilly 181
Copenhagen, Battle of 207
Copnall, Bainbridge 335
Cornish, Marcus 300
CORNWALLIS, HMS 228
Cornwell, Alice 292, 293
Cornwell, Eli 290, 292, 293
Cornwell, Boy 1st Class John Travers, VC 290, *290*, 291, 292-293
Corunna, Battle of 4, 5
Corunna, San Carlos Gardens 4, 5
Coulport and Jackfield, Shropshire, War Memorial footbridge 54
Cousins, Air Chief Marshal (Rtd) Sir David 279
Coventry, Bishop of 135
Coventry, Earl of 51
Coventry, raids on 133, 135
Coventry, reconciliation 135
Coventry, St Michael's Cathedral 135
   Home Front Memorial 195
Coventry City Council 135
Cowan, Rear Admiral Sir Walter Henry, Bt KCB DSO MVO 256
*Cowan's War* 256
Cowin, Father Malcolm 152
Cowley, Lieutenant General Sir John Guise, GC KBE CB 174
Cradock, Admiral Sir Christopher 290
Crannage, Herbert Somerset 142
Crawford, Robert 201
Crawford and Balcarres, 27th Earl of
Crawford and 10th Earl of Balcarres (David Alexander Edward Lindsay) 114, 224
Crepon, Normandy, CSM Stan Hollis, VC statue 287
Crich Stand 83, *83*
Crimea, Balaclava obelisk XIII
Crimean and Indian Mutiny Memorial, Westminster School 21, *21*
Crimean War XII, 16, 17, 18, 19, 84
Crimean War Memorial, Guards 15, *15*, 194
Crimean War Memorial, Royal Artillery 16, *16*, 17
Crisp, Skipper Thomas, VC 287
Crispin Wride Architectural Design Studio 162
Croad, Stephen 201
Cromwell, Oliver, 32, *32*
Cronje, General Piet 193
Cross, Harry 267
Cross of Sacrifice 103, *103*, 114
   Kohima 153, *153*
Crouch, Lieutenant Commander Cecil 243
*Croydon* (Battle of Britain Class locomotive) 265
Croydon Museum, Battle of Britain Commemorative Lace Panel 267
Crull, Jodocus 206
Crundale, Richard of 3
Crundale, Roger of 3
Cuffley, Herts
   Plough Inn 289
   St Andrew's Church 45
   The Ridgeway, Captain Leefe Robinson, VC commemorated 289
Culloden Moor, Battle of 156
Cumberland, Duke of 156
CUMBERLAND, HMS 312
Cunningham, Admiral 1st Baron 210
Cunningham, Patrick 180
CURACA, SS 230, *230*
Curtis, Air Marshal Sir John 189, 282
Curtis-Bennett, Sir Noel, KCVO 138
Curzon, Lord 56
Czechoslovak Army and Air Force Memorial 279, *279*

D-Day Museum, Portsmouth 176
Dabulamanzi kaMpande, Prince 23

Daedalus 259
Dahl, Michael 206
*Daily Herald* 341
*Daily Standard* (Brisbane) 128
*Daily Telegraph* 22, 145, 163, 181, 264
Dalou, Aimeé-Jules XIV, 316, 320
Darwin, Charles 369
Dalton, Hugh Rt Hon, PC MP 139, 145, 147
Daniel, Colonel Henry 19
dates carried by memorials 53
Dauderin, Charles 197
David Bell Restoration Ltd 78
Davidson, Ian XV, 200
Davidson, Jo 125
Davies, General Sir Francis 51
Davies, Major General Peter 181
Davies, Meredith 135
Davis, H L 236
Davis, Warrant Officer James (Jim) 282
Dawn Service 128, 172
Day, Paul 284
De Gaulle, General Charles 369
de Labilliere, Very Rev Dr Paul 138
de Lafontaine, Lieutenant Colonel Cart 110
   biography 342
de Normann, Sir Eric 236, 237, 238
*De Telegraaf* 76
Dearing, Captain W 256
Dedman, Joyce 298
DEFENCE, HMS 292
Defford, RAF Memorial 278
*Defiant* ('Castle' class locomotive No. 5080) 97
Delane, John Thadeus XII
Delhi 20
Delville Wood and Commemorative Museum 124, *124*
Demarne, C T, OBE 154
Deolali, Nasik Road Camp 31
Depage, Dr Antoine 76, 77
Department for Media, Culture and Sport 202
Deptford Borough Council 44
Derby 156
   Midland Railway Memorial 33
   Rolls Royce works, stained glass windows 269
   'twinned' with Fonquevillers 51
*Descent from the Cross, The* 249
Destailleur, Gabriel 24
destruction of war memorials 141
Devizes, Wilts, Women's Land Army memorial 195
Dick, Sir William Reid 114, 117, 225, 262, 263, 339
Dickie, Reverend Mr 91
Dieppe, Belleville-sur-mer, Avenue Captain Portéus 194
Diksmude, Belgium, Vladslo German Cemetery 54
Disabled Society IX
Disraeli, Rt Hon Benjamin, MP 22
Dixon, Professor Norman, MBE 157
Dlhopolcek, Frantisek 279
Dobson and Browne Ltd 267
Dodd, Francis 338
Dodd, Rev Dr William 144
Dolores de Leon, Juana Maria de los 6
DOLPHIN, HMS 227
Donald Install Associates 168, 284
Donaldson, Pipe Major Brian 193
Donegal Pass, Northern Ireland 130
'Doodlebug' (V1) 97, 133, 134, 136
Doubleday, John 342
Dover Marine Station 77
Dover Patrol Monument 109
Dowding, Air Marshal Sir Hugh Caswell Tremenheere, (later Air Chief Marshal 1st Baron) 266, 268, 274
Dower, Reverend William 278
Drake, Sir Francis 223
Drew, Adrian 49
Drew, Julius 49
Drury, Alfred, RA 51, 320
Du Plat Taylor, Major J L 69
Du Puis, Dr George Bonello 299
Dublin, Nelson's Pillar 208
Dublin, Wellington Testimonial 11
Dublin Civic Museum, Nelson's stone head 208
Dudley, Worcs, Vicar Street Bible Class 199
Dufferin, Helen, Baroness 119
Dufferin, Lord 119
Dundas, Captain James, VC 194

Dundee, remembrance ceremony (1921) 44
Dungannon, Northern Ireland, Royal School 20
Dunkirk 178
Dunn, Reginald 99
Dunning, Richard 112
Durham, Colonel 222
Durnford, Colonel Anthony W 22
Durrant, Sergeant Frank, VC 194
Dye, Air Commodore 283

Earle, Colonel 70
Earle, Sir Lionel, KCB KCVO CMG 109, 225, 232, 235, 379
East Chinnock, Somerset, church of the Blessed Virgin Mary 280
East London Cemetery Company 50
Eastney, Hants, Royal Marines Museum 228, 287
Easton, Hugh 268, 269, 279
Eastwood, H (Assistant Secretary, Admiralty Naval Law Branch) 221, 224, 225, 232
Edderton, Dornoch Firth, Scotland 161
Eden, Sir Anthony 219
Edinburgh
   Castle, benches commemorating pipers 193
   Princes Gardens, boulder XV
   Princes Street, Scottish American War Memorial 193
   Royal Scots Club 48
   Scottish National War Memorial 58, *58*, 193
Edinburgh, Duke of 143, 173, 187, 214, 219, 244, 245, 251
Edward VII, King 34, 286
Edward VIII, King 122 *see also* Wales, Prince of
effigies, tradition of XI
Egypt 69
Egyptians XI
Eilean Donan Castle, Loch Duich XI
Eisenhower, General (later President) Dwight 276
El Teb, first and second Battles of 26
Eleanor of Castile, Queen of England 3

Elgin, Lord XII
Eliot, T S 136-137
Elizabeth II, Queen 160, 162, 168, 169, 170, 171, 173, *184*, 195, 274, 299
   and Air Forces Memorial 272, 273
   inaugurates first overseas Second World War memorial 148, 281
   opens Union Jack Club 34
   Patron of Royal Star and Garter Home 80
   Royal Seals of the Realm 345
   and Sir Winston Churchill 158, 159
   unveiling of Merchant Navy Memorial 219
Elizabeth, Queen, the Queen Mother 142, 147, 154, 169, 244, 258, 270, 296, 299
Elvas, Portugal 6
Elviña, Spain 4
Elwell, Frederick W, RA 293
English Heritage 68, 75
   Blue Plaque scheme 369
   Grants for War Memorials Scheme 200
environment, memorialisation in 194
Epstein, Sir Jacob 135, 157, 340
Esher, Viscount 75
Essex Regiment Memorial, Normandy 176, *176*
Estonia 256-257
Eton College, MacNaghten Library 48
Eugénie of France, Empress 24
Evans, Nursing Sister Clara 195
Evans, Ellis Humphrey (Hedd Wyn) 49
Evans, Mary 49
*Evening Standard* 30, 46, 238
'Ever Victorious Army' (Chinese) 27
Everard, Bertha 54
Everitt, Betty 277
Evesham War Memorial, Worcs 336
Ewers, Ray 172
EXCELLENT, HMS 158
Explosive Ordnance Disposal Memorial, Kineton 177, *177*

Fairbrother, William 230
Fairhaven Stonemasons, Cambridge 223

Falkland Islands Memorial Chapel 162, *162*
Falklands Conflict 162, 295
   St Paul's Cathedral memorial 162, *164*, 198
      Tumbledown Mountain 193
Far East Prisoner of War Memorial Church 152
Far East Prisoners of War Memorial 213
Faringdon, Lord 136
Farington, Joseph 10
Farmer & Brindley 99
Farnborough, St Michael's Abbey 24
Fay, John 98
Fay, Sir Sam 98
Fayolle, Maréchal Marie Emile 120
FEARLESS, HMS 254
Felix Memorial Garden, Lisburn, Northern Ireland 164, *164*
Fergusson, General Sir Charles, Bt, GCMG KCB DSO MVO 97
Festing, General (later Field Marshal) Sir Francis Wogan, GCB KBE DSO 152
Festubert, France, Post Office Rifles Cemetery 69
field marshals 196
Fielding, Sir Bernard 142
Fielding, Major George XIV
*Fighter Command* (Battle of Britain Class locomotive) 265
*Fighting Newfoundlander, The* 120
*Figure of Justice* 197
finance of war memorials 44
Finney, Trooper Christopher, GC 296
Firefighters Memorial Trust 154
Firefighters National Memorial, United Kingdom 154, *154*
First World War *see* Great War
Fisher, Rt Hon Andrew 109, 371
Fisher, Admiral Sir John Arbuthnot, GCB OM GCVO LLD 254
Fisher, Sir Norman Warren 225
Fisher, Dr, Archbishop of Canterbury 219
Fiske III, Pilot Officer William Meade Lindsley 276
Fitch, Reverend E A 100
FITTLETON, HMS 213, 260, *260*
Fittleton, Wilts, village church 260
Fitz-Hugh, Richard Truman 37
Fitzmaurice, Sir Maurice 114
Fitzpatrick, Sir James Percy IX
Flather, Baroness 169
Flaxman, Professor John 9, 210, 304
Fleet Air Arm Memorial, Lee-on-the-Solent 246, *246*
Fleet Air Arm Memorial, Victoria Embankment 259, *259*
Fleet Air Arm Memorial Chapel 245
Fleet Air Arm Roll of Honour 105
Flers-Courcelette, Battle of 171
Flixton Hall, Suffolk 17
Florence, Cathedral of Santa Maria del Fiore (Duomo) 2
'Flying Bomb' (V1) 97, 133, 134, 136
*Flying Scotsman* locomotive, No 1472 (later 4472) 145
Flying Services Memorial 263, *263*
Foch, Maréchal Ferdinand, GCB OM 56, 74, *74*, 75, 81
Folkestone, Capel le Ferne, Battle of Britain Memorial 270, *270*
Folkestone, Shorncliffe, Sir John Moore Barracks 4
Fonquevillers, France 51
footbridge, memorial 54
*For the Fallen* 102
Ford, Onslow 210
Forgan, Liz 284
*Forgotten Voices* 241
Forster, Frank 143
Fort George, benches commemorating pipers 193
Fort William-Dudley, Worcs, Cairn of Remembrance 199
Foster, Rachel 300
Foster and Partners 209
Fovant, Wilts, badges 68, *68*
Fovant Badges Society 68
Fox, Edward, OBE 284
FOYLEBANK, HMS 246
Frai, Commander Peter, RNVR 250
Frampton, Sir George 50, 78, 324
Franco Prussian War 24
Frank, Anne, Memorial Tree 166, *166*
Franz Ferdinand, Archduke 53
Fraser, Lieutenant Ian, VC DSC RD 299

Fraser, Admiral Lord 238
Fraserburgh, Jarvis Street 287
French, Field Marshal the Rt Hon John Denton Pinkstone, 1st Earl of Ypres, PC KP GCB OM GCVO KCMG 125
French memorial tablets 110, *110*, 378
French teachers of sculpture XIV
Frere, Sir Henry Bartle Edward (later 1st Baron) 22
Frères Pinton 135
Freud, (Sir) Clement Raphael, MP 298
Freyberg, Colonel (later Lieutenant General 1st Baron), VC, 231, 241, 287
Freyberg, Valerian, 3rd Baron 172
Fricourt, France 51
Friends of War Memorials XV, 200
see also War Memorials Trust
*Friends of War Memorials Newsletter* 202
Frink, Dame Elizabeth 135
Frome Art Metal Works 197
Frome War Memorial Theatre, Somerset 144
Fryatt, Captain Charles Algernon 99
Fuentes de Oñoro, Battle of 84
Fulham, Bishop of 125
*Für das Kind* 167
Furness, Reverend Peter 189

Gahan, Reverend Stirling 76, 77
GALATEA, HMS 291
Galbraith Bros 238
Gall, J H 90
Gallipoli 45, 86, 172, 228, 371
   Chunuk Bair 172
   Helles Memorial 322
Gallipoli Association 172
Gallipoli Memorial 86, *86*, 108
Gamtofte, Denmark 264
Gardens of Memory 132, 161, 164, *164*, 190, *190*
Gascons 2
Gaspar, Dr Pedro 200
gates, memorial 169, *169*
Gaviard, Lieutenant General Jean Patrick 283
Geerling (architect) 28
Geographical Society of Alberta 194
George, Prince 223
George III, King 205, 215, 302
George IV, King 9, 210, 303
George V, King 32, 50, 57, 80, 89, 144, 218, 286, 288
George VI, King 57, 129, 135, 148
   and George Cross 296, 299
George Cross 296
German army 127
   Afrika Korps 148
   Panzer Division, 21st 150
German destruction of war memorials 141
German Embassy, London 82
German Legion, King's 7, *7*
German Navy, 2nd Scouting Group 291
Germans, memorials to 54
Germany, memorials in 54
Gibbons, Grinling 206, 210, 274
Gibbs, James 213
Gibraltar, capture of 206
Gilbert, Sir Alfred, RA 30, 313, 320
Gilbert, William 114
Gilbert Scott, Sir Giles, RA 21, 135
Giles, Canon Alan S 281
Giles, John 368
Gill, A A 181
Gill, Eric 341
Gillick, Ernest 114
Gillon, Piper 193
Gimbert, Benjamin, GC 297, 298
Gladstone, William Ewart 26, 27
Glasgow, Bearsden, War Memorial 91, *91*
Glasgow, Park Terrace, Earl Roberts' statue 31
Gleichen, Major General Count (later Lord) Edward 66, 312
Gleichen, Countess (later Lady) Feodora 66, 312, 356
Gleichen, HSH Count Victor 312
   sculpture 25, 312
GLORY, HMS 228
Gloucester, Duke of 151, 219
GNEISENAU (Great War) 290
Goatham, Private Ashley 22
Goddard and Gibbs 269
Godson, E Probyn 205
Goetze, Sigismund 53
Golberdinge, J H van 99
Goldsmiths' Company 247

Gommecourt, France 51
Gonzi, Monsignor Michael 281
*Goodbye to All That* 118
Goode, Reverend Tim 190
Goodhart-Rendel, H S 136-137
Goodrich Castle, Memorial Window 278
Gordon, General Charles George 7, 26, 27, *27*, 210, 224
Gordon, Hannah Taylor 166
Gore, Major H G N 30
Gort, Field Marshal Lord, VC 287
Gosse, Edmund XIV, 316, 320, 323
Gotto, Captain Basil 120, 316
  biography 331
  sculpture 120, 121,
Gough, Brigadier-General, VC 287
Gough, General Lord 14
Gough, William D 59
GRAF SPEE 272
Graham, J A 174
Graham, Lieutenant General Sir Peter 193
Grahame, Mrs Didy, MVO 300
Grant, General Sir James 20
Grant, Sir John 20
Grant, Field Marshal Sir Patrick 20
Grant, Lieutenant General Sir Scott 175
Grant, Warrant Officer 291
Grantham, Lincs, St Wulfram's Church 64
Granville, Walter 20
Graspan Hill action 214
Graspan Parade 214
Graves, Robert von Ranke 66, *67*, 118
Great Central Railway 97
Great Central Railway Memorial, Sheffield 98
Great Central Railway Society 98
Great Clacton, Essex, St John's Church 104
Great Eastern Railway Staff War Memorial, Liverpool Street Station 99, *99*
Great War VIII
  air war over Britain 47
  losses 42
  war memorial committees 43
Great Western Railway 97

Great Yarmouth, landmine fatalities 178
Great Yarmouth, Nelson memorial 208
Greatstone-on-Sea, Kent, USAAF memorial 277, *277*
Greeks, Ancient XI
Green, Fireman 50
Greenwich
  and Royal Naval Division Memorial site 236-238
  Royal Navy College Chapel, Arctic Convoy Memorial 218
  Royal Observatory 271
  St Alphage under the Hill church 106
  War Memorial 45
Greenwich Park 106, *106*
  General Wolfe statue 196
Gregg, Company Sergeant Major William, VC 287
Griffiths, Rear Admiral Guy AO DSC DSO RAN 173
*Grimsby Evening Telegraph* 292
Grimshaw, Lieutenant Colonel John Elisha, VC 287
Grofcik, Nikulas 279
GUARDIAN, THE 204
Guards Crimean War Memorial 15, *15*, 194
Guards Memorial 60, *60*
Gujrat, Battle of 14
Gulf War, First VIII
Gulf War, Second 193
Gurkha Brigade Association 170
Gurkha Soldier Memorial 170, *170*
Guthrie, Sergeant Stewart, GC 296
Guy's Hospital Boer War Memorial 37, *37*
Guyenne, France 2

Haidar Pasha Cemetery and Scutari Monument, Turkey 18, *18*
Haig, General (later Field Marshal the Rt Hon 1st Earl Haig, KT GCB OM GCVO KCIE 48, 50, 56, 75, *75*, 98, 112, 120, 121, 124
Halifax, Nova Scotia
  Fairview Cemetery 230, *230*
  Harbour 230

Hall, Viscount 237
Halliday, Lieutenant General Sir Lewis, VC 287
Halling, Medway, Harris House 287
Hallowes, Odette, GC 147
Hallward, Reginald 110
Hamilton, Lord Claud 99
Hamilton, Lord George 196
Hammond, Peter 330
HAMPSHIRE, HMS 223
Handel, Georg Friederich 369
Handley, J G 174
Hankey, Colonel Sir Maurice Pascal Alers (later 1st Baron) 171, 225
Harcourt, Admiral Sir Cecil Halliday Jephson 245
Hardiman, Alfred F 75
Hardy, Reverend Theodore Bayley, VC MC DSO 288, *288*
Harman, General Jack 145
Harpur, Anne 180
Harris, Air Chief Marshal Sir Arthur Travers, Bt 274
Harris, Sergeant, Thomas J, VC 287
Harrison, Barbara, GC 296
Harrison, Elizabeth Lucas MBE 147
Harrison, General Sir Richard 37
Harrow School Chapel 26
Harrow Weald
   All Saints' churchyard extension 289
   *The Leefe Robinson VC* (restaurant) 289, *289*
Hartlepool, naval bombardment 47
Hartley, Mike 97
Hartley, T H 88
Hartnett, W A 216
Hartwell, Charles Leonard, RA 53, 99
Harvey, Major Francis, VC RMLI 287, 291
Hastings, Warren 20
Havelock, Major General Sir Henry Bt 20, 209, 210
Hawaii, Cook Memorial 215
Hawke, Admiral Sir Edward 204
Hawker, Major Lance, VC 263
Hawkwood, John 2
Hayes, Gerald 237
Hayton, Cumberland, War Memorial 51

Head, Rt Hon Anthony, MP 219, 245
Heanor, Derbys, CSM William Gregg, VC commemorated 287
Heard, Sir Isaac 208
Heasman, Mr 233, 235, 236
Heath, Rt Hon Edward, PC MP 350
Heathrow Airport, BOAC jet fire 296
Heber, Harry 167
HECLA, HMS 286
Hedd Wyn (Ellis Humphrey Evans) 49
Hedley, Ronald 247
Henderson, Rt Reverend G D 219
Henderson, Rear Admiral Iain 259
Hendrix, Jimi 369
Henrietta Maria, Princess XII
Henriques, E C 85
Hepworth, Dame Barbara 197
Hepworth, Philip 151
Herbert, Alan Patrick (later Sir A P) 231, 237
Herbert, Sidney 15
Hereford, Dean of 175
Heritage Lottery Fund 284
HERMIONE, HMS 228
Herod, W Mr 267
Herodes, Mr Priit R 257
Hesketh, Air Vice-Marshal Ron 283
Hewitt, Patricia, PC MP, 55
Hewlett, Barry 298
Hicks, Colonel William 26
Highley, Shropshire, National War Memorial to British Railwaymen 175
Highton, Cecil Denny 170, 171
Hill, Brigadier Stanley James Ledger, DSO MC 355
Hill, Lieutenant Colonel M V D, DSO MC 66
Hill, Vernon 273
Hill 60 Memorial 113, *113*
hillside chalk figures 68, *68*
Hirohito, Emperor of Japan 196
Hiroshima, Japan, Peace Garden 135
Hitch, Private Frederick Brook, VC 23, 227, 287
Hitler, Adolf 148, 178
Hobart, Tasmania, War Memorial 53
Hockaday, Sir Arthur, KCB, CMG 145
Hogg, Commodore Tony 259

Holbourne, Mary Ann Barbara  6
Holden, Charles  46  338
Holland, Hannen and Cubitts Ltd  57
Hollard, Michel, DSO  97
Hollis, Company Sergeant Major Stanley, VC  287
Hollybrook Memorial, Southampton  223
Holocaust Memorial, Toronto  197
Holofcener, Lawrence  159
Holyhead, Maeshyfryd Cemetery, HMS THETIS memorial  243, *243*
Home Front Memorial, Coventry Cathedral  195
Hone, William  309
Honourable East India Company  20, 204
HOOD, HMS  260
Hook, Reverend Norman  142
Hoon, Geoff, PC MP  183, 192, 300
hops  94
Hornchurch, Essex, Cornwell Cottages  *293*
Horner, Brigadier F Bassett  142
Horrobin, James  158
*Horses of Helios, The*  197
Houdon, Jean Antoine  210
Hough, Richard  256
Hough, Dr William Woodcock, Bishop of Woolwich  45
House of Commons  139, 178, 188, 192, 196
   Expenditure Committee  145
   Members' Lobby, Sir Winston Churchill statue  159
   Public Accounts Committee  145
House of Lords  138, 139, 141
Howard, Major John, DSO  150
Howard, Peter  144
Howe, Commodore Earl, RNVR  251
Howson, Major George, MC  IX
Huaut, F  95
Hughes, Emrys  140
Hughes, Lawson Jervis  37
Humphreys, Rob  223
Hunt, William Holman, OM  133
Hunter, Kelvin  164
Hunter Weston, Lieutenant-General Sir Aylmer, KCB  370

*Hurricane* (Battle of Britain Class locomotive)  265
Husar, Rudolf  279
Hutton, John  135, 273
Huxley, Julian  136-137

Ieper *see* Ypres
IMO (merchantman)  230
Imperial Camel Corps Memorial, Victoria Embankment  65, *65*
Imperial War Graves Commission *see* Commonwealth War Graves Commission
Imperial War Museum  167, 293 *see also* United Kingdom National Inventory of War Memorials
Imphal, Burma  153
*In Flanders' Fields*  IX
inaugurations of war memorials  45
INDEFATIGABLE, HMS  228
India, North Western Frontier  40
Indian Mutiny  20
Indian Mutiny (and Crimean) Memorial, Westminster School  21, *21*
Indian National Memorial, La Bombe  115, *115*
Indian troops, Great War  85
Industrial and Commercial Finance Corporation  34
INFLEXIBLE, HMS  228
Inglis, Major General Sir John  20
Inglis, Dr Elsie Maud  195
Ingram, Lieutenant George M, VC  287
Initiatives of Change UK  144
Innocent VI, Pope  2
International Centre for Reconciliation  135
Inverness, 5 Perceval Road  193
INVINCIBLE, HMS (Great War)  228, 291
IOLAIRE, HMY  220
Ipswich, 'twinned' with Fricourt  51
Ireland, Oliver Cromwell in  32
Irish Republican Army/Brotherhood  208
Irishmen, contribution of, in Great War  180
IRON DUKE, HMS  11
Irvine, Major Walter  132

Isaacs, Captain Michael, MC 236
Isandhlwana, Battle of 22, 23
Ismay, General Hastings Lionel 1st Baron, GCB, CH, DSO 158
Italian foundrymen XIV
ITHURIEL, HMS 254
Ivanic, Ludovit 279
IVERNIA 242

*Jack Tar March* 34
Jacko (the monkey) 47
Jackson, Philip 168, 170, 197, 354
Jackson, Sir Thomas Graham 214
Jackson, W R 267
Jagger, Charles Sargeant III, 46, 114, 132, 225, 232, 324, 343
James, Clive 172
James, Robert Rhodes, MP 172
James, Commodore Sir William 204
James, Lady 204, 205
James II, King 210
JAMES NIGHTALL GC (Class 47 No. 47579 and Class 66 No. 66079 locomotives) 298
Japanese 15th Army 153
Japanese 31st Division 153
Japanese Naval Memorial, Malta 242, *242*
Jarvis, Lance Corporal Charles A, VC 287
JEAN D'ACRE, HMS 312
Jekyll, Gertrude 333
Jellicoe, Admiral 210, 290, 292
Jenkins, Thomas James 247
Jenner, Edward 210
Jersey, Victoria College War Memorial 95
*Jersey Liberation Sculpture* 354
Jews
   in Boer War, death of 33
   memorial to XV *see also* Holocaust Memorial, Toronto names erased from memorials by Nazi Party 141
   Nazi treatment of 166, 167, 168
Joass, J J 92
Joffre, Maréchal 124
John, Sir William Goscombe 87, 129, 132, 323
John Condon Memorial Committee 180

*John H Carless VC* (Class 31 locomotive No. 31107) 97
Johns, J P 278
Johns, M C B 174
Johnson, Warrant Officer Barry, GC 296
Jolly, Major General A 174
Jones, Captain Adrian 8, *39*, 84, 214, 314
Jones, Inigo 3
Jones, Reverend Ray 125
Jones, Thomas 37
*Journal of Remembrance, The* 57
*Journal of the Royal Society of Arts* 380
Joyce, James 369
Jupp, R 204
Jutland, Battle of 216, 290-292

K-class submarines 254
Kaliber Engineering, Derby 178
Kandahar, Relief of 31
Kansas City, Missouri, The Plaza, Sir Winston and Lady Churchill statue 159
Kapyong, Battle of, and British Commonwealth Memorial 161, *161*
Kassassin, Battle of 69
Keating, Paul 126
Keats, John 369
Keighley, J E, JP 88
Kelly, Lieutenant Commander Frederick Septimus, RNVR 240
Kemal, Mustafa (later Kemal Atatürk) 172
Kempenfelt, Admiral Richard 211
Kempster, Tim 259
Kennington, Eric 66, 346
Kenny, Yvonne 173
Kent, Duchess of 182, 246
Kent, Flor 167
Kent, William 194
Kenyon, Colonel Sir Frederic 132, 221
   biography and works 329
Keynes, Lord 136-137
Khan, Princess Noor Inayat, GC 147
Khartoum 26, 27
Khyber Pass, Pakistan, carved badges 68

Kidderminster station, railwaymen's Roll of Honour  175
Killen-Strait tractor  171
Kindersley, Richard  300
Kindertransport Memorial  167, *167*
Kineton, Warks, Marlborough Barracks, Explosive Ordnance Disposal Memorial  177, *177*
King, Captain H Douglas, RN MP  224
King, J, JP  88
King Alfred Club  250-251
Kingsley, Sir Ben  166
Kipling, John  60
Kipling, Rudyard  60, 220, 222
Kirman, Private Charles,  53
Kirkpatrick, Messrs Wm  88
Kitchener, Field Marshal the Rt Hon Horatio Herbert, 1st Earl Kitchener of Khartoum, KG, PC, KP, GCB, OM, GCSI, GCMG, GCIE, KJStJ  43, 86, 118, 223, 369
Knee, Ron  249
Knight, Sergeant A J, VC  69
Knights Hospitaller of the Order of St John  148
Knutsford, Cheshire, St John the Baptist Church  52
Kohima, Burma, and Battle  142, 143, 153, *153*
Kollwitz, Käthe and Peter  54
Korea (South), Seoul, Anglican Cathedral  160
Korean War Memorial, St Paul's Cathedral  160, *160*
Korean war memorials  160-161
Kortgé, Colonel Hasso  189
Kõuts, Rear Admiral Tarmo  257
Krithia, Second Battle of  231

L55 submarine  256
L'ORIENT  208, 293
La Ferté-sous-Jouarre  370, 377
La Perriere, Amiral Brac de  280
Lace Panels, Commemorative, Battle of Britain  267
Laidlaw, Piper Jock  193
Laidoner, General Johan  256
Laing Construction  135
Lalaing, Comte Jacques de  28
Lamb, Air Vice Marshal G C  189

Lamont, Donald  162
Lancaster, Osbert  75
land mines, laying of  178
Landowski, Paul  74, 141
Landseer, Sir Edwin  21, 211
Lang, Lieutenant W  228
Langley, Brigadier  100
Lanhydrock, near Bodmin  49
Lantéri, Professor Édouard  XIV
    biography and sculpture  11, 316
Lapenotiere, Lieutenant John, RN  208
Lascelles, Lord  144
Laurence, Janet  173
Laurence, Philip  247
Laurie, Pipe Major  193
Lawrence, A K  326
Lawrence, General Sir Herbert  101
Lawrence, T E (Lawrence of Arabia)  34, 65, 326, 329
Lawson, Captain Robert N, RN  291, 292
Le Quesne, C J  95
Le Sueur, Hubert  XII, 3
Lebrun, Albert  116
Leconfield, St Martin's Church  100
Ledward, Professor Gilbert  136, 225
    biography  345
    sculpture  60, 114, 258, 345
Lee, Lord Arthur  225, 226
Lee-on-the-Solent, Fleet Air Arm Memorial  246, *246*
Leeds, Street Lane Gardens Synagogue, boulder  XV
Legros, Alphonse  XIV
Leicester, De Montfort University, Mary Seacole Research Centre  19
Leicester, Earl of  76
Leighton, Lord, PRA  209
Leith, Rosebank Cemetery  96
Lennox-Boyd, Lieutenant, RNVR  250
Lenton, Notts, Albert Ball, VC DSO MC Memorial Homes  287
Lettow-Vorbeck, General Paul Erich von  157
Lever, William Hesketh 1st Viscount, Baron Leverhulme  90
Lewes, Battle of, Memorial  XV
Lewis, Western Isles, War Memorial  90, *90*
Liberty & Co store, London  133

*Light of the World, The* 133
Lincoln Cathedral, stained glass window 269
Lincolnshire, Marquess of 93
LION, HMS 228, 291, 292
Lisburn, Northern Ireland, Thiepval Barracks 164, *164*
Lisle, Lord de 2
Little (Australian clerk) 128
Little Walden, Essex 277
Little Wigborough, Essex, St Nicholas Church 52
Littlejohns, Captain, RAN 222
Liverpool
   Captain Noel Chavasse VC commemorated 287
   Cotton Exchange Buildings 50
   Merchant Navy Memorial 245
   St Luke's Church 136
Liverpool Cotton Association 50
Livingstone, Ken 209
Llandudno, 'twinned' with Mametz 118
*Lloyd George* (locomotive) 97
Lloyd George, David (Later Earl Lloyd George of Dwyfor) X, 112, 118, 120, 157, 171
Lochnagar Crater Memorial 112
*Lockheed Hudson* ('Castle' class locomotive No. 5081) 97
locomotive 48773 (Stanier 8F Class goods) 175, *175*
locomotives as memorials 97, 174-175, 265, 298
London *see also* Cenotaph, Whitehall; Greenwich *entries*; St Paul's Cathedral; Trafalgar Square; Westminster Abbey
   Aldersgate, St Botolph's Church, Post Office Rifles Book of Remembrance 69
   All Hallows by the Tower Church 218
   Baker Street Station, memorial 96
   Battersea Park, 24th Infantry Division Memorial 66, *67*
   Battersea Park, ANZAC Memorial 172, *172*
   Bethnal Green, war memorial committee 43

   Bethnal Green Underground Station 146, *146*
   Birchin Lane, 23: 247
   Bishopsgate, St Botolph's Church 33
   Black Friar Public House 336
   Bloomsbury, Bedford Hotel 47
   Borough, St Saviour's Church and War Memorial 105
   Borough High Street, London Hop Trade Memorial 94, *94*
   Bounds Green Underground Station 146
   Bow, Grove Road 133
   Buckingham Palace 9
   Caledonian Club 49
   Change Court, UK Firefighters National Memorial 154, *154*
   Charing Cross 3
   Chelsea Embankment, Carabiniers Boer War Memorial *39*
   Chiswick, Private Frederick Hitch VC commemorated 287
   Chiswick, Staveley Road 133
   churches, bombed out 136
   Circus Place, obelisk XIII
   Constitution Hill, Commonwealth Gates 169, *169*
   Covent Garden, St Paul's Church 3
   Cumberland Place, Wallenberg Monument 168, *168*
   Cyprus Street War Memorial 102, *102*
   Dolphin Tavern 50
   Duke of York's Column 13
   Eaton Square, Church of St Peter 136
   Finsbury War Memorial 51
   Grosvenor Gardens, Rifle Brigade Memorial 62, *62*
   Guildhall, Duke of Wellington statue 11
   Guy's Hospital Memorial Arch 54
   High Holborn, Royal Fusiliers Memorial 63, *63*
   Hill Street, 38, Naval Club 251, *252*
   Horse Guards Approach Road, Guards Memorial 60, *60*
   Horse Guards Parade Ground 194

Earl Roberts' statue 31, *31*, 75, *75*
Royal Naval Division Memorial 45, 233-235, 239-240, *240*
Hyde Park
  Achilles statue 10, *10*
  Australian War Memorial 173, *173*
  Cavalry Memorial 84, *84*
  Duke of Wellington statue 11, *11*
  Royal Norwegian Navy and Merchant Marine Memorial 253, *253*
Hyde Park Corner, Machine Gun Corps Memorial 64, *64*
Hyde Park Corner, Royal Artillery War Memorial *III*, 46, 61, *61*
Hyde Park Gate, 28: 159
Inns of Court & City Yeomanry, Officers Mess 33
Kennington, Royal Surrey Gardens 19
Kennington, St Mark's Church 101
Kensal Green, St Mary's Roman Catholic Cemetery 19
Kensington, Middle Row Garage 50
Kensington Gore 30, *30*
Lewisham Market 133
Liverpool Street Station
  Great Eastern Railway Staff War Memorial 99, *99*
  Kindertransport Memorial 167, *167*
Lower Grosvenor Gardens, Maréchal Foch statue 74, *74*, 75
Maida Vale 194
THE HERO OF THE ALMA public house 194
The Mall, Captain James Cook statue 215, *215*
The Mall, Royal Marines Memorial *39*, 214, *214*
Manor Park, Jack Cornwell VC commemorated 293, *293*
Manor Park Cemetery 194, 292, 293
  Vigiland Memorial 248, *248*, 249, *249*
Marble Arch 9, *9*
memorialisation in 194

National Liberal Club War Memorial 93, *93*
The Naval Club, Hill Street 105
New Bond Street, Roosevelt and Churchill statues 159
New Row, WC2, Roundhouse public house 166, *166*
Newham Town Hall 45
Old Bailey 197
Paddington, St Mary's Hospital 33
Pall Mall, King Alfred Club 250-251
Park Lane, Brook Gate, Animals In War Memorial 181, *181*
Parliament, Palace Yard, Oliver Cromwell statue 32, *32*
Parliament Square, Field Marshal Jan Christiaan Smuts statue 157, *157*
Parliament Square, Sir Winston Churchill statue 159, *159*
Petty France, Transport for London 101, *101*
Poplar, Upper North Street School 47
Poplar Recreation Ground, Air Raid Memorial 47
Putney Vale Cemetery 194
raids on 133
The Ridings, Alan Blumlein's house 278
Roman finds in XI
Royal Hospital, Chelsea
  Chillianwallah Memorial 14, *14*
  Gordon House 236
  Wellington Hall 11
St Clement Danes Church 264, 274, *274*
  American Airmen Roll of Honour 276
  RAF Escaping Society Memorial 147, 275, *275*
St James's Park 36
  Chinese Pagoda XII
St Katharine's Dock, HMS PRESIDENT 260, *260*
St Mary-Le-Bone, St George and the Dragon statue 53
Shooters Hill, Severndroog Castle 204-205, *205*

Somerset House, Civil Service Rifles Memorial 55
Stockwell, 18 Burnley Road 147
Tothill Street, Caxton House 55
Tower Hill, Merchant Navy Memorial 218-219, *219*
Tyburn Convent 9
Victoria Embankment
   Battle of Britain Memorial 284
   Belgian War Memorial 81
   Chindit Forces Memorial 143, *143*
   Cleopatra's Needle XIII
   Fleet Air Arm Memorial 259, *259*
   Gordon monument 27, 210
   National Submariners Memorial 224, 227, *227*
   Royal Air Force Memorial 262
   Viscount Portal statue 196
Victoria Embankment Gardens, Imperial Camel Corps Memorial 65, *65*
Victoria Street, DTI headquarters 55
Waterloo, St John the Evangelist church XII
Waterloo Place, Guards Crimean War Memorial 15, *15*, 194
Waterloo Road, Union Jack Club 34, *35*
Waterloo Station 34, 194
   Victory Arch 96
Wellington Arch 8, *8*
Wellington Barracks 11
   Guards Chapel 136
Wellington Road 11
Westminster Cathedral, rolls of honour 105
Westminster Hall 158
Whitehall
   Admiralty Building (Ripley Block) 216, *217*
   Earl Haig statue 75, *75*
   Ministry of Defence *see* Ministry of Defence
   Palace of, Banqueting Hall 3, 94
   Queen Victoria statue 57
   Raleigh Green 196
   Whitehall Court, Gurkha Soldier memorial 170, *170*
   Whitehall Court, Tank Crews Memorial 171, *171*
Willesden Cemetery 33
Woolwich War Memorial 105
Zeppelin raids 47, 50
London, Bishop of 101
London, Museum of 167
London, HM Tower of, Chapel Royal of St Peter ad Vincula 160
London, Treaty of 81
London and North Western Railway 97
London, Brighton and South Coast Railway Company 97
London County Council 205, 224
London Fire Brigade Headquarters, Lambeth 154
*London Gazette* 296
London General Omnibus Company 50
London Hop Trade War Memorial 94, *94*
London, Midland and Scottish Railway 97
London Transport, Bethnal Green and Bounds Green Underground stations 146
London Transport Museum 133
London Transport Veterans Association 50
London Underground War Memorial 101, *101*
London Zoo War Memorial 92, *92*
Longmore, Air Chief Marshal Sir Arthur Murray, CB DSO 264
Longparish, Hants 263
Longueval, France, New Zealand National Memorial 114
Longueval, France, Pipers Memorial 193
Loos, Battle of 49
Lorimer, Sir Robert 58, 221, 222
Loring, Captain, RN 221
Lowestoft, Royal Naval Patrol Service Memorial 246
Lowestoft, St Margaret's Church, 'VC Bell' 287
Lucas, Mate Charles, VC 286

Lucas, E V 333
Lucas, W 126
Lucas-Harrison, Elizabeth, MBE 275
Ludendorff, General Erich 126, 127
Ludovicy, Mlle 82
Luftwaffe 133
Lukin, Major General Sir Henry Timson 124
Lumsden, Brigadier-General Frederick W, VC CB DSO*** 89
Lutyens, Sir Edwin, OM, PRA 45, 55, 103, 105, 114, 116, 126, 139
   biography 333
   Castle Drogo 49
   the Cenotaph 56, 57
   Flying Services Memorial 263
   Merchant Navy Memorial 218
   Royal Naval Division Memorial 232, 233, 234, 238
   Second World War memorials 132
   Trafalgar Square 209
LÜTZOW 291
lych gate, war memorial 70, *71*
Lyon, K, OBE 109, 379
Lyttleton, Lieutenant General N G 33

Machine Gun Corps Memorial 64, *64*
Madonna, fallen 130
Magnoni, Carlo 82
Mahdi, the 26, 27
Mahratta Rajah 204
Maida, Battle of 194
Maidstone, All Saints' Church, Ramnugger Memorial 14
maintenance of war memorials 202
Major, Rt Hon John 182
Making, Brigadier, MP 84
Malan, Wing Commander Adolphe Gysbert, DFC DSO** CdG 268
Malissard, François Georges 74, 75
Mallett, Edward 278
Mallock, Vivien 355
   sculpture 171, 355
Malone, Lance Corporal Ian 193
Malta 148, *149*
   Cappucini, Japanese Naval Memorial 242, *242*
   Floriana, Commonwealth Air Forces Memorial 281, *281*
   Ta'Braxia Cemetery 148, *149*

Malta, National Trust for (Din l-Art Helwa) 148
Mametz, 'twinned' with Llandudno 118
Mametz Wood memorial 118, *118*
Manchester Grammar School, Roll of Honour 54
Manenti, M 94
Mannock, Major Edward, VC 263
Mansfield, Vice Admiral J M 243
Mantle, Leading Seaman Jack Foreman, VC 246
March, Vernon 129
March family 129
Margaret, Princess 159
Margate, Kent, War Memorial 47
Marlborough Club 250
Marochetti, Baron Carlo, RA 310
   sculpture 18, 20, 211,
MARQUETTE 242
*Married Love* 159
Marsh, Sir Edward Howard 49, 231
Marshall, William Calder 210
Marston Brewery 156
Martyn (H H) & Co 258
Mary, Queen 80, 218
Mary Louise, Princess 6
Mary Seacole Centre for Nursing Practice and Nursing Leadership Award 19
Mary Seacole Research Centre 19
Mason, Herbert 154
Mathy, Kapitänleutnant Heinrich 50
Maufe, Sir Edward, RA 219, 244, 264, 273
Mawson, Thomas 48
Maxwell, Professor 298
'May Island, Battle of' 254, *255*
McBeath, Lance Corporal Robert, VC 287
McCarthy, Councillor Billy 180
McCaul, Ethel, RRC 34
MacColl, Dugald Sutherland, MA LLD 109, 331, 371, 379
McCrae, Lieutenant Colonel John IX
MacDonald, Pipe Major John 193
MacDonogh, Lieutenant General Sir G M W, KCB KCMG 108, 109, 371, 379
McFall, David 159

MacGregor, Neil 73
Mackennal, Sir Bertram *198*, 327
Mackenzie, A G R 89
Mackenzie, Dr A Marshall 89
MacKenzie, Dr R Tait 106, 193, 196
McLean, Pipe Major 193
McLellan, Captain D R 193
McLellan, Captain John 193
McLeod, Pipe Major Donald 193
Macmillan, Harold 158
McMillan, William, RA 344
   sculpture 89, 196, 209, 210, 244
MacNamara, Colonel R J R, MP 188
Macnamara, Dr, MP 292
McNeill, Charles 258
McQueen, Captain (Rtd) Bob, RN 190
MacRae Clan XI
McReady-Diarmid, Captain, VC 95
Meade, Lieutenant Richard 95
Mearns, David 260
Medal, Binney Memorial 247
MEDITERRANEAN, SS 281
Medland, Mr Herbert M, MP 140
Memorial Gates Trust 169
memorialisation, forms of 43
memorialisation of notable individuals 49
MENDI, SS 223
Menin Gate, Ypres 108, 114, 117, *117*, 371, 373
Mentmore Towers 145
Menzies, Sir Robert 158
Merchant Navy Memorial, Liverpool 245
Merchant Navy Memorial, Tower Hill 218-219, *218*
Méric, André 147
MERMAID, HMS 260
Mesopotamia 370, 371
Metcalfe, Percy 296
Metropolitan Railway 44, 96
Michael, Moina IX
Michael of Kent, Prince 240
*Michel Hollard* (Eurostar train) 97
Michelham, Lord 8
Midland Railway Memorial, Derby 33
Midleton, Earl of 108, 109, 370
Millennium Commission 182
Miller, Glenn 277
Millington (Australian clerk) 128
Millington-Drake, Sir Eugen and Lady Effie 272
Mills, John (BBC) 178
Mills, John W 154, 353
Millward, Corporal Malcolm James 196
Milne, J A 49
Milne, Captain John Theobald, MC RFC 49
Milner, Lord 86
Milner-White, Dr Eric 271
miners 53
Ministry of Defence 198, 213
   Victoria Cross and George Cross Memorial 300, *300*
Ministry of Labour Memorial 55
Ministry of Works 236, 238, 239
Mitchell, Sir Philip Euen 248
Molotov-Ribbentrop Pact 165
MONARCH, HMS 228
Monchy-le-Preux, 37th Division Memorial 66
Mond, Sir Alfred 56, 108
Mond, Captain Francis, RAF 324
MONMOUTH, HMS 228
MONT BLANC 230
Mont St Quentin, 2nd Australian Division Memorial 141
Montcalm de Saint-Véran, Marquis Louis Joseph de 106
Montefiore, Right Reverend Hugh 186
Montfort, Simon de XV
Montgomery, Field Marshal (later Viscount) 174, 196
Montreal, Notre Dame Cathedral 197
Montreuil-sur-Mer, Earl Haig statue 141
*Monument to Raoul Wallenberg* 197
Moore, General Sir John 4-5
Moore-Brabazon, Lieutenant Colonel J T C (later Lord Brabazon of Tara) 276
Moral Re-armament (MRA) 144
Moriarty, Dr Catherine 201, 345
Morison, Stanley 341
Morning Post 69, 334
Morrell, Dr, Squadron Leader, OBE RAF 277
Morris, William 55
Morris, Lieutenant Commander 220
Morris Art Bronze Foundry 60, 197

Morris Singer Foundry  171, 197, 227, 284, 339, 345 *see also* Singer, Morris
Morrison, Herbert, MP  139, 140
Morrison, Robert Warrack  347
Morrison, W S  157
Moscow, Lubyanka Prison  168
Mozart, Wolfgang Amadeus  354, 369
Mount Edith Cavell, Jasper National Park, Canada  77
Mountbatten, Admiral Lord Louis, 1st Earl, KG  158, 187, 258
Mountbatten of Burma, Countess  186
Mulraj, Governor of Multan  14
Mundesley-on-Sea, Norfolk Landmines Clearance Memorial  XV, 178, *179*
Munns, Richard  298
murals  130
Murdoch, Keith  172
Murdoch, Rupert  172
Murphy, Lieutenant Colonel Reginald  264
Murray, Lord George  156
Murray, Sir O A R  225
musical instruments as memorials  193, 228, 229
Mustafa Kemal (Kemal Atatürk)  172
Mutaguchi, General Renya  153
Muzvuru, Piper Christopher  193

Nairac, Captain Robert, GC  296
Nangle, Major (later Lieutenant Colonel) the Reverend Thomas  109, 120, 121, 331, 371, 379
Napier, General Sir Charles  209, 210
Napier, Captain William  4
Napier, Field Marshal Lord, of Magdala GCB GCSI CIE  30, *30*
Napoleon, Emperor  6
Napoleon III, Emperor  24
Narborough, Admiral Sir John  206
Naseby  XIII
Nash, John  9, 209
  biography  303
Nasiriyah, Iraq, War Memorial  53
NATAL, HMS  228
Nathan, Lord  141
National Army Museum, Chelsea  160
National Battlefield Memorial Committee  108-109, 110, 372

National Curriculum  X
National Gallery  209
National Heritage Memorial Fund  145
National Land Fund  139, 145
National Liberal Club War Memorial  93, *93*
National Lottery  169
National Memorial Arboretum, Alrewas, Staffs  161, 182-183, *182*, *183*, *184*
  Armed Forces Memorial  192
  Berlin Airlift Memorial  189, *189*
  BLESMA Memorial Garden  190
  Burma Star Memorial Grove  186-187
  49th (West Riding) Division, Polar Bear Memorial  *191*
  General Post Office Memorial  69
  Mediterranean Plot  XI
  Millennium Chapel  182, 190, 192
  RAF Regiment Memorial  188, *188*
  Staffordshire Regiment Memorial  *191*
  Ton Class Memorial  185, *185*, 260
National Merchant Navy Day  218
National Records Office, Kew  230
National Submariners Memorial  227, *227*
Naval Club, Hill Street, London  251, *252*
Naval Memorial Register, Chatham  244
naval memorials, principal  221-223
  after Second World War  244-245
  inscription and design  222
naval memorials, recent  260, *260*
naval memorials, Second World War, other  246
Naval War Memorial, (that never was)  224-226
Naylor, Janet and Andrew, Sculpture and Conservancy Consultancy  28
Nazi Party  141
Neill, Very Reverend Ivan  98
Nelson, Admiral Horatio Viscount  148, 207-208, 212, 369
Nemon, Oscar  159, 196, 351
Nesbitt, Lieutenant R, RNVR  250
Neuendorff, Dr Bernhard  54
Neuve Chapelle, Battle of  122

Neuve Chapelle, Indian National Memorial 115, *115*
New Kilpatrick Pipe Band 91
New York and Pacific Steamship Company 230
New Zealand
   Canterbury University 104
   Levin, Horowhenua College, 'the Les Andrew, VC Scholarship' 287
   National Memorials 114
New Zealand Railways 97
Newcastle upon Tyne, Barras Bridge, St Thomas the Martyr Church 87, *87*
Newcastle upon Tyne, raids on 133
*Newfoundland National War Memorial* 121
Newfoundland Royal Naval Reserve 222
Newfoundlanders 120-121
*Newry Telegraph* 5
Newtownards Green, Northern Ireland, snow memorial 44
Nicholls, Brigadier C R 174
Nicholson, Sir Charles 142
Nicholson, Harold 333
Nicholson, Brigadier General John 20
Nicolle, E T 95
Niemeyer, Commandant 289
Nightall, Fireman James, GC 297, 298
Nightingale, Florence 15, 18, 369
Nile, Battle of the 207, 208, 293
Nine Elms Stone Masons 233, 236
*No 46 Squadron/No 141 Squadron/No 219 Squadron/No 222 Squadron/No 229 Squadron/No 249 Squadron/No 253 Squadron/No 264 Squadron* (Battle of Britain Class locomotives) 265
*No 501 (County of Gloucester) Squadron Royal Auxiliary Air Force* (Battle of Britain Class locomotive) 265
*No 602 (City of Glasgow) Squadron, Royal Auxiliary Air Force* (Battle of Britain Class locomotive) 265
*No 603 (City of Edinburgh) Squadron* (Battle of Britain Class locomotive) 265

*No 615 (County of Surrey) Squadron Royal Auxiliary Air Force* (Battle of Britain Class locomotive) 265
Noble, Lieutenant Colonel Eric 143
Norfolk, Duke of 158
Norfolk Landmines Clearance Memorial XV, 178, *179*
Norman & Beard Ltd 52
Normanbrook, Lord 158
Normandy 150-151, 176, 280
Northampton, Sixfields Stadium, Walter Tull Memorial and Garden of Rest XV
Northampton General Hospital 140
Northern Counties Housing Association 48
NORTHERN HORIZON 260
Northern Ireland 177
   bomb disposal operations 164
Norway, King of 287
Norwegian Army XV
Norwich, Bishop of 142, 99
Norwich, Corporal Bates VC commemorated 287
Norwich, Edith Cavell memorial 76, 77, 79, *79*
Norwich Boer War Memorial 38, *38*
Norwich Cathedral
   Anglian Regiment Chapel 142
   Edith Cavell, service and interment of 77, *79*
   Edith Cavell grave 142
Norwich Cemetery, Soldiers Memorial 17
Norwich Roll of Honour 105, *105*
Nottingham, Museum of Costume and Textiles, Battle of Britain Lace Panel 267
Nottinghamshire ESCAPE Group of pensioners 300
Nu, U 152
Nugent, Private George James 112

*O Valiant Hearts* 45
obelisks XIII, 12
O'Brien, Tim 283
O'Connor, Liam, RIBA 169, 192, 300
Officers Roll of Honour 43
OHIO 148
Okri, Ben 169

Old Contemptibles Chapel, St Martin's in the Fields 213
Old Contemptibles Memorial, The, Westminster Abbey 163, *163*
Old Victorians Association 95
Oliver, Lieutenant Colonel James 6
Omdurman, Battle of 84
*101 Squadron* (RAF) (electrically hauled control trailer No. 821010) 97
Onraet, Lieutenant Hugh Bernard 37
*Operation Dynamo* 178
*Operation Gardening* 264
*Operation Hope Not* 158
*Operation Longcloth* 143
*Operation Moonlight Sonata* 135
*Operation Pedestal* 148
*Operation Sealion* 178
*Operation Thursday* 143
*Operation Vittles* 189
Orange, Prince of 7
Orkney, 1st Earl of 196
ORONTES, HMS 24
O'Sullivan, Joseph 99
Oswestry School 26
Ottawa, Canadian National War Memorial 129, *129*
Outram, Lieutenant General Sir James, Bt 20
*Overlord Embroidery, The* 176
overseas memorials, Great War, the task 114
Oxford
   Bonn Square, Tirah Memorial 40
   Captain Noel Chavasse VC commemorated 287
     Christ Church Cathedral 40, 54
     Colleges, memorialisation in 54
     Magdalen College 40
     Magdalen College Chapel 33
     Merton College, Great War Memorial Arch 54
   New College, memorial to German alumni 54
     Wellington Square 11
Oxford Group 144

Paardeburg, Battle of 193
Page, Captain Chris, RN (Rtd) 231-232
Page, Wing Commander Geoffrey 270

Paget, General Lord George 19
Paignton War Memorial 69
Palestine 370, 371
Palliser, Hugh (later Sir Hugh) 215
Pallister, L K 246
Pangbourne College, Berks, Falkland Islands Memorial Chapel 162, *162*
Paraffin, Private 223
Paris, Champs Elysée, Sir Winston Churchill statue 159
Paris, Les Invalides 24, 74
Paris, Major General Sir Archibald 231, 234
Paris memorial 108
Parker, Admiral Hyde 207
Parker, Samuel 9
Parker Bowles, Brigadier Andrew 181
Parlanti, Alessandro 336, 337
Parlanti (E J) foundry 227
*Passchendaele* (Pacific 4-6-2 'Ab' locomotive No. 608) 97
Pateley Bridge, snow memorial 44
Paterson, Reverend Mr 91
*Patriot* (Claughton class 4-6-0 locomotive No. 1914) 97
Paulin, George Henry, ARSA RBS RI 171
Payne, Joseph 83
Peace Celebrations Committee (Great War) 56
*Peace Triumphant Descending on the Chariot of War* 8, *8*
Pearl Assurance 50
Pearson, Lionel III, 72
Peel, Sir Robert 9, 210
Pegasus Bridge 150, *150*
Pegram, Henry Alfred, RA 328
   sculpture 59, 76, 79, 328
Pelly, Captain J N, CBE RN 250
Penarth War Memorial 45
Penicuik, Scotland 48
Peninsular War 4, 6, 62
Penrose, Francis Cranmer 29
Perley, Hon Sir George, KCMG 109, 371, 379
Pershing, General John 56
Pershore, Worcs, war memorials 51
Perth, North Inch, 51st Highland Division Memorial 193

422

Perth Museum, Australia, Battle of Britain Commemorative Lace Panel 267
Peterborough, Lynchwood, St George and the Dragon sculpture 50
Peterborough, Northants, Edith Cavell hospital 77
Philip, John Birnie 21
Pick, Frank 338
PICKLE 208
Picton, General Sir Thomas XIII, 6
Pilckem Ridge 49
Piobaireachd Society 193
pioneers 174
Piper, David 157
Piper, John 135
pipers and memorialisation 193
Pipers Memorial, Longueval 193
Pir, Very Reverend Gustav Peeter 257
pirates, Malabar Coast 204
Pistrucci, Benedetto 296
Pitt, E G 197
Pitt, William, the Elder 302
Pittman, Corporal Thomas, DCM MM 120
Plaistow War Memorial 50
Plath, Sylvia 369
Plazzotta, Enzo XV
Plumer, Field Marshal the Rt Hon Herbert Charles Onslow, 1st Viscount Plumer of Messines, GCB GCMG GCVO GBE KJStJ 66, 117, 125
Plunket, David Robert Rt Hon, MP (later 1st Baron Rathmore) 27
Plymouth
   Air Forces Memorial 282
   raids on 133
   Royal Naval Memorial *222*, 223
     extension 244
   ruined church as war memorial 137
Plymouth City Council 282
Poelcappelle Cemetery 180
Polish Navy, Free 147
Pollock, Dr Bertram 77, 142
Polygon Wood, Belgium, New Zealand National Memorial 114
Pomeroy, Frederick William RA 197
Pompadour, Madame de 176
Pontypridd, and Memorial Park 48

Poole, Dorset, Flight Sergeant Aaron, VC commemorated 287
Poole, Henry 336
   sculpture 221, 222, 336
Poperinghe, Belgium, Talbot House 52
poppies and Poppy Appeal IX
Port Stanley, Falkland Isles, Memorial Plaque 162
Portal of Hungerford, Marshal of the Royal Air Force Viscount 158, 196
Portland, Jerome Weston, 2nd Earl of 3
Portland, Richard Weston, 1st Earl of 3
Portsmouth *see also* VICTORY, HMS
   D-Day Museum 176
   Eastney, Royal Marines Museum 228, 287
     HMS DOLPHIN 227
   memorialisation in 194
   Royal Naval Memorial 223, *223*
     extension 244
Post Office Rifles 69, *69*
Powell, Rt Hon J Enoch, MP 145
POWERFUL, HMS 312
PRESIDENT, HMS 260
Prestatyn, Comrades of the Great War Association branch 44
Price, D 143
Price, Eluned 181
PRINCESS MARGARET 257
PRINCESS ROYAL, HMS 228, 291
Princip, Gavrillo 53
*Private Eye* 284
Procter, W A 236, 237
PROTECTOR 204
Proudfoot, Alexander, ARSA 91
Prudential Assurance Company 63, *63*
Prvonic, Warrant Officer Antonin, RAFVR 279
Prynne, Brigadier Harold Gordon Lusby 174
Pulleine, Colonel Henry 22
*Punch* 19
Purdon, Major General Corran 193
Purves, Reverend Mr 91
Pusan, South Korea, British Commonwealth Memorial 161, *161*

*Quadriga* 8
Quebec, Heights of Abraham 106
QUEEN MARY, HMS 216, 228
Queensland National ANZAC Memorial, Brisbane 128, *128*
Quintinshill rail crash 96

*RAF News* 284
Raglan, General 1st Baron (Rt Hon Fitzroy James Henry Somerset) (later Field Marshal) 36, 369
Railton, William 211
railway explosion at Soham 297-298
Railwaymen, British, National War Memorial to 175
railways and war memorials 96-100
*see also* locomotives as memorials
Raleigh, Sir Walter 196
Ramnagar, Battle of 14
Ramsay, Sir M G, KCB 109, 371, 379
Ramsay, Captain Norman, RHA 84
Ramsden, Jesse 205
Ramsden, Omar 94
Rangoon Memorial, Taukkyan War Cemetery, Myanmar (Burma) 152, *152*
Rank-Broadley, Ian 192
Ranville, Normandy 150
   Avenue du Major Howard 150, 194
Rappaport, Helen 19
Ratcliffe, J 174
Ratee and Kett, Messrs 271
Ravensbrück Concentration Camp 147
Rawlinson, General Sir Henry 126
*Red Arrows, The* (High Speed Train power car No. 43155) 97
Red Cross unit, British X
*Red Flag, The* 44
REDOUTABLE 212
Regent, Prince (later King George IV) 303
Reich, Erich 167
Reid, Sir William XIII
religious connection to war memorials 52
*Remembrance* (Class L express 4-6-4T locomotive No. 333) 97
Remembrance, Commonwealth Service of 161

Remembrance, National Ceremony of VIII
remembrance and the National Memorial Arboretum 183
remembrance in Britain VIII-IX
Remembrance Sunday VIII
   Cenotaph ceremony and march past VIII, IX, 50, 57, 177
   tradition of 45
Remembrance Travel 183
Renwick, Sir George and Lady 87
Response Memorial, Barras Bridge Newcastle upon Tyne 87, *87*, 129
Reyntiens, Patrick 135
Rhodes, Cecil John 326, 332
Rhondda Cynon Taff Borough Council 48
Rhynie and Kearn War Memorial, Aberdeenshire *42*, 347
Richard Ormond Shuttleworth Remembrance Trust 264
Richardson, A E 136
Richmond, Surrey
   obelisk in churchyard XIII
   Royal Star and Garter Home 48, 80
      Jack Cornwell Ward 293
*Richmond Times* 80
Riddell, Pipe Major James 193
Riddell, Rt Hon the Lord 109, 371
Rifle Brigade Memorial 62, *62*
Rimmington, Sidney 98
Rivett, John 3
RK Conservation and Design 249
RNVR Club 250-251
Roberts, A R N 380, 386
Roberts, Lieutenant the Hon Frederick Hugh Sherston VC 31
Roberts, Field Marshal Frederick Sleigh, VC OM (later 1st Earl Roberts of Kandahar, Pretoria and Waterford) 20, 31, *31*, 75, *75*, 287
Roberts-Jones, Ivor 159, 196, 350
Robertson, Field Marshal Sir William Robert, 1st Bt, GCB GCMG GCVO DSO 101
Robinson, Colonel and Mrs Abbot 52
Robinson, Captain Leefe, VC 45, 289, *289*
Rochester, Bishop of 244, 268
Rochester, Corn Exchange 206

Rodin, François-Auguste-René XIV, 316, 323, 327, 331, 332, 340, 352, 354
Rokeby, Lord 19
Rolls of Honour 54, 105, *105*, 175, 192
   for American airmen 276
   Civilian 146
   Officers 43
   Royal Marine Band Ranks 228
   Soldiers 43
Rolls Royce, Derby works, stained glass window 269
Romans XI
Rome, St Peter's Square, obelisk XIII
Romford, Essex Road 133
Romford, St John's Church 133
Rommel, General (later Field Marshal) Erwin Johannes Eugen 196
Rorke's Drift 22, 23, *23*
Rosebery, 5th Earl 32
Ross, Lieutenant General Sir Robin, KCB OBE 239
Ross, Pipe Major William 193
Rothenstein, Sir William 326, 346
Rothermere, Lord, and Rothermere Foundation 239
Rothley, Leicestershire, St Mary's Church 52
Rousseau, Victor 81
Rovezzano, Benedetto da 208
Rowell, Right Reverend Geoffrey 125
ROWENA, HMS 77
Rowson, Reverend G P H 174
Roy, Major General William 205
Royal, Princess 154, 181
Royal Academy, War Memorial Exhibition 103
Royal Air Force 147, 188, 262, 263, 272 see also Royal Flying Corps
   Arthur Barrett Memorial Prize 264
   Battle of Britain Memorial Flight 186
   Bentley Priory 266
      Officers Mess 265, 266, *266*, 267
   Biggin Hill 268, *268*
   Fighter Command HQ 266
   foreign connections 280
   and Second World War memorialisation 264
   squadrons
      10: 295
      27: 186
      31: 186
      54: 173
      71: 276
      101: 295
      121: 276
      133: 276
      576: 264
   Telecommunications Flying Unit 278
   Vickers VC10 295
*Royal Air Force, The* (4-6-0 express locomotive No. 6159) 97
Royal Air Force Association 281
   Sheltered Housing Project, Dumfriesshire, Battle of Britain Lace Panel 267
Royal Air Force Escaping Society Memorial 147, 275, *275*
Royal Air Force Memorial, Victoria Embankment 262, *262 see also* Air Forces Memorial; Commonwealth Air Forces Memorial; Flying Services Memorial
Royal Air Force Museum, Hendon 265
   Battle of Britain Commemorative Lace Panel 267
Royal Air Force Regiment Memorial 188, *188*
Royal Army Ordnance Corps Trust 177
Royal Artillery Afghan/Zulu War Memorial 25, *25*
Royal Artillery Boer War Memorial 36, *36*
Royal Artillery Crimean War Memorial 16, *16*, 17
Royal Artillery Memorial, Hyde Park Corner *III*, 46, 61, *61*
Royal Artillery Memorial Committee 25
Royal Artillery Museum, *Firepower* exhibition 16
Royal British Legion, The IX, X
   and the National Memorial Arboretum 183
   Poppy Appeal and Poppy Factory IX

standard bearers *184, 191*
Thiepval service, annual  116
Royal Commission on the Historical Monuments of England, National Monuments Record  201
Royal Fine Art Commission  238
Royal Flying Corps  262, 283 *see also* Royal Air Force
Royal Fusiliers Memorial  63, *63*
ROYAL GEORGE  211
Royal Logistics Corps Trust  177
Royal Marine Commandos  66, 258, *258*
Royal Marines Band Service, drums and fanfare trumpets of  228, 229
Royal Marines Memorial  *39*, 214, *214*
Royal Marines Museum, Eastney  228, 287
Royal Military Academy, Sandhurst  196
    Anson Memorial Prize  287
    Memorial to Other Ranks  66
Royal Military Academy, Woolwich  24, 294, *294*
Royal Naval Air Service, Armoured Car Experiments  171
Royal Naval Cemetery, Haslar  256
Royal Naval College, Greenwich,
Royal Naval Division Memorial, Horse Guards  237, 238, 239
Royal Naval Division  53, 231, 241
    Drake Battalion  228, 236
Royal Naval Division Association  235, 238, 239
Royal Naval Division Memorial, Beaucourt  235, 241, *241*
Royal Naval Division Memorial, Horse Guards Parade  45, 231-240, *240*
Royal Naval Memorial, Chatham  223
    extension  244-245
Royal Naval Memorial, Plymouth  *222*, 223
    extension  244
Royal Naval Memorial, Portsmouth  223, *223*
    extension  244
Royal Naval Patrol Service Memorial, Lowestoft  246
Royal Naval School of Music  228, 229

Royal Naval Volunteer Reserve, and Club  250-251
Royal Naval Volunteer Reserve Officers' Association  251
Royal Naval Volunteer Reserve Roll of Honour  105
Royal Navy  *see also* Admiralty *entries*
    Baltic Battle Squadron  53, 256-257
    Battle Cruiser Squadron, 5th  291
    and Bismarck statue  141
    Grand Fleet  290-291
    and HMS VICTORY  212
    Jack Mantle VC Naval Gunnery Trophy  246
    K-class submarines  254
    Submarine Service  148
    Submarine Service Memorial  224, 227, *227*
    Ton Class minesweepers  185, 213, 260, *260*
Royal New Zealand Air Force Museum, Christchurch, Battle of Britain Lace Panel  267
Royal New Zealand Navy, Charles Upham VC and bar commemorated  287
Royal Norfolk's Regimental Chapel  142
Royal Norwegian Navy and Merchant Marine Memorial  253, *253*
*Royal Observer Corps* (Battle of Britain Class locomotive)  265
*Royal Pioneer Corps* (Patriot Class locomotive No. 45506)  174
*Royal Pioneer Corps, The* (diesel locomotive D54)  174
Royal Scots Club, Edinburgh  48
Royal Society of Arts  138
Royal Star and Garter Home, Richmond  *see* Richmond, Surrey, Royal Star and Garter Home
Royal Stuart Society  3
Royal United Services Institute for Defence and Security Studies  31
    Duke of Wellington Hall  11
Royston, Herts, Captain Ackroyd, VC commemorated  287
Rubens, Sir Peter Paul  249
Rudge, Thomas  51

Rugby School Chapel  49
Runnymede, Air Forces Memorial
264, 272-273, *272*, *273*
Russell, Captain Frederick Murray  37
Russell, Sir William Howard  XII, 19
Russian Civil War  53
Russian Memorial, Brookwood  165, *165*
Rye, East Sussex, Old Town War Memorial  VIII
Ryle, Herbert  77

St Albans street memorials  102
St Clement Danes Church  264, 274, *274*
   American Airmen Roll of Honour  276
   RAF Escaping Society Memorial  147, 275, *275*
St George and the Dragon  50, 53, 84, 134, *134*
*St George and the Dragon*  197
St Helens, Lancs, Boer War Memorial Plaque  195
St John's, Halifax, King's Beach, Newfoundland National War Memorial  121
St John's, Halifax, Newfoundland, Bowring Park  120, 121
St Margaret's Bay, Kent, Dover Patrol Monument  109
*St Michael and the Devil*  135
St Omer Memorial  283, *283*
St Paul's Cathedral, London
   American Memorial Chapel  276
   ANZAC Day ceremony  172
   Arctic Convoy memorial  218
   Boer War plaque  33
   crypt cafeteria  XI
   Duke of Wellington Memorial  29, *29*
   Duke of Wellington's tomb  208
   Earl Roberts' tomb  31
   Falklands Conflict memorial plaque  162, *164*, 198
   Field Marshal Sir Henry Wilson, burial of  99
   Kitchener Memorial Chapel  52
   Korean War Memorial  160, *160*
   Major A B Thruston monument  40

   Nelson's tomb  *207*, 208
   Sir John Moore's burial, depiction  4
   and Sir Winston Churchill  158
   VC holders commemorated  287
   women who fell, memorial commemorating  195
Salisbury, E J  136-137
Salonika  370
Salonika, Mikra British Cemetery  242
Saltoun, Lord  141
*Salvo News*  202
SALVO organisation  202
SAMA 82 (South Atlantic Medal Association 1982)  162
Sandham, Lieutenant Henry Willoughby  72, 73
Sandham Memorial Chapel  72-73, *73*
Sandhurst *see* Royal Military Academy, Sandhurst
Sandle, Professor Michael  148, 197
SAPPHIRE  206
Sarajevo, assassination of Archduke Franz Ferdinand  53
Sargent, John Singer, RA  109
Saskatchewan, Canada, Hugh Cairns VC Elementary School  287
Satchell, Fusilier Stephen  VIII
Sato, Vice-Admiral Kozo  242
Sauberzweig, Generalmajor Traugott von  76
Saumarez, Admiral Lord de  212
Saunders, Admiral Charles  106
Saunders, Charlotte  45
Savory, Michael  201
Scarborough, naval bombardment  47
Schadow, Gottfried  8
Schell, Sherril  49
Schludecker, Willy  280
Schwarz, Ivan  279
Scilly Isles  206
Scott, Sir Giles Gilbert, RA  21, 135
Scott, James Robb  96
Scottish American War Memorial, Edinburgh  193
Scottish National War Memorial, Edinburgh  58, *58*, 193
Scottish Veterans Garden City Association  48
Scottish Women's Hospitals for Foreign Service  195

Scout Movement, Cornwell VC badge 293
Scutari Monument 18, *18*
Seacole, Mary Jane 19
Secker, Sergeant Major, RM 208
Second World War, memorials 132
Seely, Major General the Rt Hon J E B, CB CMG DSO MP 109, 371
Selborne, Earl of 147
Sells, Charles Bernard 37
Serre, France 51
Service Casualty Branches X
Sevastopol 286
   British Hotel 19
Severn Valley Railway 175
Severndroog Castle, Shooters Hill, London 204-205, *205*
Severndroog Island 204
Sewell, Brian 46
Sewell, Harry Bolton 45
Sharpshooters Memorial 213
Sheen, John 112
Sheerness, Kent, War Memorial 47
Sheffield, Great Central Railway Memorial 98
Sheffield, 'twinned' with Serre 51
Shepherd, Keith 178
Sheppey Leisure Complex, Battle of Britain Commemorative Lace Panel 267
ships, Ton Class minesweepers 185, 213
Shovel, Admiral Sir Cloudesley 206
Shrewsbury, John Talbot, 1st Earl of 2
Shurrock, Francis 316
Shute, General 231
Shuttleworth, Pilot Officer Richard Ormond RAFVR, and Shuttleworth Collection 264
Sidmouth, 4th Viscount 32
Sikh Army 14
Sikh War, Second 14
Simmons, Boatman James T 328
Simpson, Ward 97
Sinclair, Sir Archibald 276
Singer, John Webb 197
Singer, Morris 55, 75, 148, 197, 344, 345, 355 *see also* Morris Singer Foundry
Singer & Co 30

*Sir John Moore* (Britannia Class locomotive) 4
Sir William Legatt Museum, Villers-Bretonneux 126
*Sir Winston Churchill* 350
Sittingbourne, Kent, Avenue of Remembrance 51
Slade, Sir Thomas 212
Sleaford, Lincs, war memorial committee 43
Sledmere, Yorks, Wagoners Memorial 82, *82*
Sleigh, W H 278
Slicer, H 55
Slim, General William (later Field Marshal 1st Viscount) 152, 153, 158, 187, 196
Slim, 2nd Viscount 169, 186, 187
Slough, Berks, Speakman Street 194
Smik, Otto, Sqn Ldr, DFC 279
Smirke, Sir Robert 209, 308, 322
Smith, Captain Archibald, VC 89
Smith, Private A 171
Smith, Corporal C H 216
Smith, George Herbert Tyson 245
Smith, Graham 298
Smith, Major Harry (later Lieutenant General Sir Harry) 6
Smith, J C 246
Smith, Lewis 284
Smith, Stanley Harold 245
Smuts, Lieutenant General (later Field Marshal) Jan Christiaan PC, OM, CH, DTD, ED, KC 157, *157*, 262
Smyth, Brigadier the Rt Hon Sir John George Bt, VC MC 299
snow memorials 44
Snowdon, Lieutenant J B 174
Society of Nautical Research 212
Soham, explosion at 297-298
Soissons Memorial to the Missing 346
*Soldier, The* 49
Somerby church, Leicestershire 26
Somme Heritage Centre, Northern Ireland 44
Somme Offensive 45, 112, 130
   High Wood cairn XII
   Lochnagar Crater Memorial 112
   Ulster Memorial Tower 119, *119*
   Welsh memorial 118, *118*

Soomre, Linda, MBE  165
Soukop, Willi, RA  349, 356
Soult, Maréchal Nicolas Jean-de-Dieu, Duc de Dalmatie  4, 6
Sousa, John Philip  34
South African Brigade  124
South African High Commission, London  54
South African National War Memorial, Delville Wood  124, *124*
South African War  *see* Boer War
South Atlantic Medal Association 1982 (SAMA 82)  162
South East Asia Command  186
South Western Railway Company  96
Southampton
   Hollybrook Memorial  223
   Indian soldiers' hospital  85
   raids on  133
   St Mary's Church, Battle of Britain Commemorative Lace Panel  267
Southern Railway  265
Southey, Robert  208
Southwell Minster, Battle of Britain Commemorative Lace Panel  267
Spalding, Major Henry  23
Speakman, Sergeant William, VC  194
Spean Bridge, Commando Memorial  66, 258, *258*
Special Operations Executive (SOE)  147
*Spectator, The*  163, 206
Spee, Admiral Count Maximilian von  290
Spence, Sir Basil Urwin  135
Spencer, Lavinia, Lady  10
Spencer, Sir Stanley  348
   works  72, 73, *73*, 348
Spooner, Dr William Archibald  54
Squire, Air Chief Marshal Sir Peter GCB DFC AFC DSc  189
Stabler, Phoebe  101
Staffordshire Regiment Memorial, National Memorial Arboretum  *191*
stained glass  104, *104*
   RAF commemorative  269
Stalin, Josef  XIII, 189
Stamfordham, 1st Baron  233
Stammers, Harry  269
Stamp, Gavin  46, 338

Stanier 8F Locomotive Society  175
Stannus, Hugh  29
statuary, casting  XI, XII
Steer, Brigadier Frank, MBE  22
Steggles, Dr Mary Ann  319
Stephens, Assistant Constructor A K  216
Stephenson, Dr  292
Stevens, Alfred  29, 325, 332
Stevenson, Eric  142
Stevenson, J A  329
Steward, Norman  298
Stewart, General Sir Herbert  26
Stoddart, Alexander  284
Stones, Anthony  156, 351
Stonewest Ltd  170
Storey, Herbert  48
Stormont  135
Stornoway, HMY IOLAIRE disaster  220
*Stornoway Gazette*  90
Stowe, obelisk  XIII
Strachan, Douglas  58
street memorials  102, *102*
Stuart, General Sir John  194
Sturdee, Admiral Sir Frederick Charles Doveton (later 1st Baron)  290
submarine L55, HM  256
submarines, K-class  254
Such, Reverend Howard  98
Sudan  26, 27
Sueter, Rear Admiral Sir Murray Fraser CB  171
Suleiman the Magnificent  148
*Sun*  162
*Sunday Express*  335
*Sunday Times*  181
Sutherland, Graham  135
Sutherland, Scott  258
Swansea, The Mumbles  43
Swardeston, Norfolk, parish church  76, 77
Swarkeston, Derbyshire, Crewe and Harpur Arms  156
Sykes, Lieutenant Colonel Sir Mark  82
Szabo, Violette Reine Elizabeth, GC CdG  147
Szlumper, Major General Gilbert Savil, CBE  100

Taiping Rebellion 27
Talbot, John, 1st Earl of Shrewsbury 2
Tallinn, Estonia, Garrison Cemetery 165
Tallinn, Estonia, Pulavaimu Church, naval memorial 257, *257*
Tanga, German East Africa, Prince Otto von Bismarck statue 141
tank, development of 171
tank, first use of the 112
Tank Crews Memorial 171, *171*
Tankard, Mr 99
Taplow Court, Berks, Apollo sculpture *198*
Taunton Deane Borough Council 12
Taylor, George Ledwell 209
Taylor, Pam 282
Tebbit, Lord 284
television, development of 278
Templer, Field Marshal Sir Gerald Walter Robert, KG GCB GCMG KBE DSO KStJ 145, 158
Tenniel, Sir John 18
Tennison, A Heron Ryan, FRIBA 227
Tennyson, Alfred Lord 95
Ternouth, J 211
Thames Ditton Statue Foundry 8
Thames Valley University, Mary Seacole Centre for Nursing Practice 19
theatres, war memorial 144
Theodore II, Emperor of Ethiopia 210
THETIS, HMS 243, *243*
Thetis Families Association 243
Thiepval, Ulster Memorial Tower 119, *119*
Thiepval Memorial to the Missing 116, *116*
Thomas, Ivor, MP 140
Thomas, James Havard 49
Thomas, Trooper Morris Clifford 66, 67
Thorney Island, church engraved window 269
Thornycroft, Sir (William) Hamo 27, 32, 210, 318, 328, 331, 332
Thourout, Belgium, Artillery Wood Cemetery 49
Thouvenot, General Pierre 6
Thruston, Major A B 40

THUNDERBOLT, HMS 243
Tilney, John, MP 350
*Times, The* XII, 19, 25, 43, 101, 123, 136-137, 138, 201, 219, 244, 245, 276, 284
Tirah Campaign and Memorial 40
Tobin, Sergeant Major Richard, RND 241
Toc H 52
Tocher, Peter 89
Toft, Albert 63, 325
'Tommy', bronze 132
Ton Class Association 185
Ton Class Memorial 185, *185*, 260
Ton Class minesweepers 260, *260*
*Ton Talk* 185
Tonkin Zulaikha Greer Pty Ltd 173
Toronto, Holocaust Memorial 197
Toronto, Sir Winston Churchill statue 159
Törring zu Jettenbach, Count Hans von 81
Toulon, Blockade of 207
Toulouse, Battle of 6
Townsend, Brigadier Ian 183
Trafalgar, Battle of 207, 212
Trafalgar Square 194, 209-210
  Admiralty Arch 209, 225
  Canada House 209
  Christmas tree 209
  Edith Cavell Memorial 78, *78*
  fountains 197
  General Gordon statue 224
  King Charles I statue 3
  King's Mews site 3
  lions 197, 211
  naval memorial, proposed 224, 225, 226
  Nelson's Column 209, 211, *211*, 216
  St Martin's in the Fields Church 213
  South Africa House 209
  South African High Commission 54
  statuary 210
Travers, Martin, ARCA 100
Trawsfynydd, Moriah Chapel 49
Treasury, HM 145, 188, 226

Trenchard, Major General Sir Hugh (later Air Marshal 1st Viscount), GCB OM GCVO DSO  188, 262, 263, 283
Trimingham, Norfolk  178
Truman, Harry S  351
TRURO  256
Tull, Second Lieutenant Walter D J  XV
Tunmore, Sergeant Major Jesse  77
Turkey, Haidar Pasha Cemetery, and Scutari Monument  18, *18*
Turner, Alfred, RA  95, 124, 337
Turner, Colonel Sir Ralph Lilley, MC  170
Turner & Sons, Messrs E  59
Tweed, John  332
   sculpture  29, 62, 332
Tweedsmuir, Lord  346
24th Infantry Division Memorial  66, *67*
'twinning' of communities  51
two minutes' silence  VIII, IX

U-30  218
U-33  99
Uccello, Paolo  2
Uckfield village church  69
Ulster Memorial Tower, Thiepval  119, *119*
Ulundi, South Africa  22
Underground stations, Bethnal Green and Bounds Green  146
Union Jack Club  34, *35*, 286
United Kingdom Firefighters National Memorial, Change Court  154, *154*
United Kingdom National Inventory of War Memorials  X, XV, 52, 140, 201, 202, 287
United States  276
United States Army Air Force  269, 277
Unknown Soldier, Australian  126
Unknown Soldier, Canadian  *129*
Unknown Warrior, tomb of  VIII
Upham, Captain Charles H, VC and bar  287
utilitarianism  48

V1 (Vergeltungswaffe 1 FZG-76)  97, 133, 134, 136
V2 rocket  133
Valençay, SOE F Section Memorial  147
Valletta, Malta, Memorial Siege Bell  148, *149*
Valletta, Malta, Sir Winston Churchill statue  159
*Valour* (Class 66 No. 66715 and Class 9P 4-6-0 No. 1165 locomotives)  97
Vandenbraambusche, Superintendent  117
Vandervell, Commander Harry, RNVR  250, 251
VANGUARD, HMS  228
Vanko, Sergeant Antonin, RAFVR  279
Vasconcellos, Josefina de  135
Venturi, Robert  209
Versailles, Treaty of  X, 53, 74
Vetch, Major Quinten Reid  37
Vickers  171 *see also* aircraft: Vickers VC10, Vickers Wellington
Victoria, Queen  18, 24, 27, 32, 286
Victoria Cross  286
   aircraft commemorating holders  295
   casting  16
   holders, commemoration of  194, 287
   and memorialisation  287, 294, *294*
Victoria Cross and George Cross Association  34, 286, 294, 299
Victoria Cross and George Cross Memorial, Ministry of Defence  300, *300*
Victoria Cross and George Cross Memorial, Westminster Abbey  299, *299*
Victoria Cross Memorial, Royal Military Academy Woolwich  134, *134*
VICTORY, HMS  207, 208, 212
Vigiland, Able Seaman David John, RN  248
Vigiland Memorial  *248*, 249, *249*
Village, War Memorial  48
'Villages, Thankful'  53
Villeneuve, Amiral Pierre Charles de  207
Villers-Bretonneux, Australian National Memorial  126, *126*

Villiers, Lieutenant Colonel George 24
Vimy Ridge 122, 123
   Canadian Memorial 122-123, *122, 123*
Vincent, Captain Paddy 186, 187
Vindolanda Roman Fort 201
Vittoria, Battle of 6
Volksbund Deutsche Kriegsgräberfürsorge 298

Wade, Fairfax 38
Wade, George 38, 319
Wade, General George 156
Wagoners Memorial, Sledmere 98, 8*2*
Waite, Air Commodore Rex 189
Wales, National Eisteddfod (1917) 49, (1983) 350
Wales, Charles, Prince of 150, 185, 259, 355
Wales, Prince of (later Duke of Windsor) 58, 59, 74, 85, 87, 116, 122, 223, 231
Wales, Prince of (later King George V) 30, 34
Walker, Major Charles Pope 37
Walker, General Sir Michael GCB CMG CBE ADC 176
Wallenberg, Raoul, and Wallenberg Monument 168, *168*
Wallwork, Sergeant Jim 150
Walmer Castle 11
Walter Tull Memorial and Garden of Rest, Sixfields Stadium XV
Wand, Dr John William Charles 276
Wantage, Oxon, King Alfred's School, War Memorial Lych Gate 70, *71*
War Cabinet IX, 56, 178
War Department list of fallen 132
war memorial, definition of XI
war memorial, the case of the vanishing 145
war memorial that never was 224-226
*War Memorials* 47
war memorials, British government policy on 198
war memorials, recent 164, *164*
War Memorials Advisory Council 57, 136, 138-140, 380
*War Memorials Handbook, The* 201

War Memorials (Local Authorities' Powers) Act (1923) 202, 393
War Memorials Trust X, 200, 202
War Office 43, 69, 85, 86, 286
Ward, Frederick Townsend 27
Wardle, Colonel Gwyllym Lloyd 13
Ware, Major General Sir Fabian X, 57, 138, 139, 151, 218, 221, 321
   biography 334
Washington, George (later President) 210
Washington, Captain, RN 221, 222
Washington DC, British Embassy, Sir Winston Churchill statue 159
Washington DC, National Cathedral 159
Waterford City Council 180
Waterloo, Battle of 7, 28, 62, 84
Waterloo, Hanoverian Memorial 7, *7*
Waterloo Memorial, Everè Cemetery, Brussels 28, *28*, 198
Watson, Fred 347
Watson, M L 211
Watson, Vice-Admiral Charles 204
WAVE Heritage Trust 251
Waveney, Colonel Robert Adair, Lord 17
Weare, Reverend T 21
Weatherill, Lord 169
Webb, Sir Aston, KCVO CB PRA 36, 51, 109, 224, 225, 371, 374, 375
   biography 317
   works 209, 317
Webber, John 215
Webster, Alf 267
Wellesley, Sir Arthur 4 *see also* Wellington, Duke of
Wellford, Surgeon-Captain Francis 37
Wellington, Duke of 4, 6, 7, 10, 11, *11*, 12, 36, 62, 196
   funeral 29
   St Paul's Cathedral Memorial 29, *29*
   statue 8
   tomb 208
Wellington, New Zealand
   National Art Gallery 215
   Royal New Zealand Air Force Museum, Battle of Britain Lace Panel 267

Wellington, Somerset 12
Wellington College, Berkshire 11
Wellington Monument 12, *12*
Welsh National War Memorial, Cardiff 59, *59*
Welshmen, memorial to fallen 118
Wembley Park, Forty Lane, Remembrance Hall 96
West, Admiral Sir Alan, GCB DSC ADC 257, *257*
West, J G 216
West Riding Division, 49th, National Memorial Arboretum Polar Bear Memorial *191*
Western Front Association X, 118, 368
*Western Mail* 59
Westfield Memorial Village 48
Westmacott, Professor Sir Richard 9, 10, 13, 14, 305
Westminster, Dean of 138, 139
Westminster Abbey
    Armed Forces memorial plaque 192
    Civilian War Dead Roll of Honour 146
    Commando Memorial 258
    Czechoslovak Army and Air Force Memorial 279, *279*
    Edith Cavell's memorial service 77
    Gallipoli Memorial 86, *86*
    Nurses Memorial Chapel 269
    The Old Contemptibles Memorial 163, *163*
    Royal Air Force Chapel, Battle of Britain Memorial Window 269
    Sir Cloudesley Shovel's monument 206
    Victoria Cross and George Cross Memorial 299, *299*
    war memorials 163
    William Pitt the Elder monument 302
Westminster School, Crimean and Indian Mutiny Memorial 21, *21*
Westminster Theatre 144
Weybread, Suffolk, Ablett Close 287
Wheeler, Sir Charles, RA 114, 209, 210, 244, 281, 326, 349
Wheeler, Frederick, FRIBA 37
Whicher, Stanley 37
Whiffen, Charles 96
Whitby, naval bombardment 47
Whitton, Reverend John 300
Wigan, Brigadier-General J T 94
Wigram, Colonel Sir Clive (later 1st Baron) 139, 380
Wilhelm II, Kaiser 127, 196
Wilkins, William 209
Willcocks, Lieutenant General Sir James 115
Willem I, King of the Netherlands 7
Willett, Reverend Eric 298
William Hill and Son 52
William Morris & Co (Westminster) Ltd 55
Williams, Morris and Alice Meredith 58
Wilsey, General Sir John, GCB CBE DL 273
Wilson, Sir Albert, RA 271
Wilson, General Sir Charles 27
Wilson, Rt Hon Harold PC MP 158
Wilson, Field Marshal Sir Henry Hughes, 1st Bt, GCB, DSO MP 99, 119
Wilson, Venerable J Hewitt 189
Wilson, Colonel Sir Leslie 238
Winchester, Sir John Moore Barracks 4
Winchester Cathedral, VC holders commemorated 287
windows, memorial 196
windows, stained glass XIV
Windsor, Holy Trinity Church 26
Windsor, St George's Chapel 24
Wingate, Major General Orde Charles, DSO 143
Winnington-Ingram, Dr A F 63
Winnipeg, Manitoba
    Billy Bishop Building, Battle of Britain Commemorative Lace Panel 267
    Valour Road 194
*Winston Churchill* (Battle of Britain Class locomotive) 158
Winston Churchill Memorial Forest, Israel 159
Winston Churchill Memorial Trust 159
Winter, Faith 274, 356

Winton, Sir Nicholas, MBE 167
Woking, Gordon's School 27, 210
Wolfe, Reverend Charles 5
Wolfe, General James 106, *106*, 196
Wolseley, General Sir Garnet (later Field Marshal 1st Viscount), PC KP GCB OM GCMG VD 26, 69
Wolverhampton, 'twinned' with Gommecourt 51
women and war memorials 195
Women's Land Army Memorial, Devizes 195
*Wonderful Adventures of Mrs Seacole in Many Lands* 19
Wood, Field Marshal Sir Henry Evelyn, VC GCB GCMG 287
Wood, Professor Francis Derwent 225
   biography 335
   sculpture 50, 64, 132, 335
Woodford Green, Essex, Sir Winston Churchill statue 159
Woodington, W F 211
Woods, Sergeant J 66, *67*
Woods, Lieutenant 243
Woolwich
   Prince Imperial Road 24
   Repository Road 25, *25*
   Royal Artillery Barracks
     Crimean War Memorial 16, *16*, 17
     Officers Mess 14, 17, *17*
     Parade Ground, obelisk XIII
     Royal Garrison Church of St George 134, *134*, 136
   Royal Military Academy 24, 294, *294*
Worcester Cathedral, Boer War Memorial 33, *33*
Worshipful Company of Gold and Silver Wyre Drawers 177, 342
Worth, Jack, MBE 185
Worthington, Sir Hubert 148, 281
Wrexham, Hightown, Captain Frederick Barter, VC commemorated 287
Wright, Stephen 4
Wurst Farm Ridge, Battle of 69
Wyatt, Benjamin 13
Wyatt, Matthew Coates and James 8
Wyatt, Thomas Henry 134

Wymondham, Norfolk, Catholic Church of Our Lady and St Thomas of Canterbury 152
Wynne, Lieutenant-General Sir A S, KCB 38
Yeovilton, Somerset, St Bartholomew's Church 105, 245
YEOVILTON, RNAS 245
*Yomper, The* 197
York, Prince Andrew, Duke of 259
York, Duke of (1924) 223
York, Frederick Augustus, Duke of 13
York, National Railway Museum 4, 97
York, Strensall Barracks, Hollis Crescent 287
York Minster
   Astronomical Clock Memorial 271, *271*
   memorial chapels 52
   memorial commemorating women who fell 195
Young, Leon 228, 229
Young, Sergeant Thomas George 98
Younger, Alan 196
Ypres 81, 117
   Menin Gate 108, 114, 117, *117*, 372
   St George's Memorial Church 125, *125*
Ypres League 125
Ypres Salient 117, 180
   Caterpillar 113
   Hill 60: 113, *113*
Ypres, Second Battle of 122, 180
*Yr Arwr* 49
Yule, Henry 20

Zeebrugge Memorial 141
Zeppelins *see also* airship, German Navy Schutte-Lanz SL11
   L13 50
   L21 47
   L22 47
   L33 52
   L41 47
   L70 47
Zoological Society of London 92
Zulu army 22, 23, 24
Zulu/Afghan War Memorial, Royal Artillery 25, *25*

Printed in the USA
CPSIA information can be obtained
at www.ICGtesting.com
LVHW070902251123
764796LV00015B/1546